'This is a smart, accessible, au[thoritative...] the most dynamic figures in E[urope...] writes with clarity and discern[ment...] between the reader and her grimly fascinating subject; she earns the reformer, situating him psychically as well as geographically in a Germany she describes as vividly as if we lived there... She creates a context for a man who arouses both admiration and horror in the modern reader. Here he stands: never more vocal, more controversial, more compelling'
Hilary Mantel

'A fine achievement, deeply researched and fluently written, and it brings its difficult and cantankerous subject to life as no other biography has... A magnificent study of one of history's most compelling and divisive figures'
Richard J. Evans

'Lyndal Roper provides a fine scholarly narrative of Luther's extraordinary life... She paints the picture of a "difficult hero", with full attention to both light and shadow. A compellingly readable and richly documented study'
Rowan Williams

'Lyndal Roper's new book is a compelling and provocative attempt to restore some flesh and blood to this static icon...the work of one of the most imaginative and pioneering historians of our generation'
Alexandra Walsham, *Guardian*

'Beautifully written... Among the most interesting, provocative and original biographies of Luther to appear in recent years... This unfailingly inventive and compelling account is a welcome gust of fresh air... Anyone seriously interested in one of the most influential figures of the last half-millennium will need to make time to read this one'
Peter Marshall, *Literary Review*

'Roper's immaculate scholarship...gives a complex account of his inner life, without ever straying beyond what the evidence will allow'
*Guardian*, Books of the Year

'An impressive and fascinating read'
*Spectator*, Books of the Year

'This is the book about Luther we've missed among all the holy books and the case studies: the whole engrossing story of a soul and a mind and the man who broke the old world and its old ways for ever. Lyndal Roper brings alive the struggle for ideas, adds a subtle sense of how human beings work, and distils a lifetime of scholarship to conjure Luther's own world with its princes, demons, scandals and sheer brave defiance of a whole old order'
Michael Pye, author of *The Edge of the World*

'Magnificent and surely definitive – a work of immense scholarship, acute psychological insight and gloriously fluent prose. Lyndal Roper has got under the skin of her subject and the result is thrilling'
Jessie Childs, author of *Henry VIII's Last Victim* and *God's Traitors*

'Roper writes with the virtuosity of an unsurpassed archival researcher, the grace of an elegant stylist, and the compassion of a seasoned student of human nature. Her nuanced and insightful portrait brilliantly evokes the inner and outer worlds of the man Luther. The book is a complete triumph'
Joel F. Harrington, author of *The Faithful Executioner*

'It deploys its considerable learning with the lightest of touches: a seductive, shimmering and significant retelling'
Thomas Penn, author of *Winter King*

# LYNDAL ROPER

Lyndal Roper is Regius Professor of History at Oxford and one of the most respected historians at work in Britain today. An expert on early modern Germany, her previous books include a study of witchcraft, *Witch Craze: Terror and Fantasy in Baroque Germany*. In 2016 she received the prestigious Gerda Henkel Foundation Prize, which recognises outstanding scholarly achievement.

LYNDAL ROPER

# Martin Luther

Renegade and Prophet

**VINTAGE**

1 3 5 7 9 10 8 6 4 2

Vintage
20 Vauxhall Bridge Road,
London SW1V 2SA

Vintage is part of the Penguin Random House group of companies whose
addresses can be found at global.penguinrandomhouse.com

Penguin
Random House
UK

First published by Vintage in 2017
First published by The Bodley Head in 2016

penguin.co.uk/vintage

A CIP catalogue record for this book is available from the British Library

ISBN 9781784703448

Printed and bound by Clays Ltd, St Ives plc

Penguin Random House is committed to a sustainable future for
our business, our readers and our planet. This book is made
from Forest Stewardship Council® certified paper.

For my father
Stan Roper
21 June 1926 to 22 May 2016

# Contents

# List of Illustrations

# Colour plates

Lucas Cranach the Elder, Hans and Anna Luder, 1527 (*Bridgeman Art Library*).

View of Wittenberg, 1536, drawing from the travel diary of Count Ottheinrich of the Palatinate (*Universitätsbibliothek Würzburg*).

Lucas Cranach, *The Conversion of Saul*, 1547 (*Bridgeman Art Library*).

Johann von Staupitz, 1522 (*Imagno/Getty Images*).

Lucas Cranach the Elder, *Georg Spalatin*, 1509 (*Museum der bildenden Künste Leipzig*).

*Pilgrimage of Friedrich the Wise to Jerusalem* (*Stiftung Schloss Friedenstein Gotha*).

Lucas Cranach, *Martin Luther and Katharina von Bora*, c.1529 (*Bridgeman Art Library*).

Lucas Cranach the Elder, *Martin Luther and Philipp Melanchthon*, 1546 (*Bridgeman Art Library*).

Detail of epitaph of Michael Meienberg, after Lucas Cranach the Younger, copy of original, 1558 (*Bridgeman Art Library*).

Albrecht Dürer, All Saints altarpiece, 1511 (*Bridgeman Art Library*).

# Introduction

For Protestants it is almost an article of faith that the Reformation began when Martin Luther, the shy monk, nailed his Ninety-Five Theses to the door of the Castle Church in Wittenberg on 31 October 1517, the eve of All Saints' Day, and set in motion a religious revolution that shattered Western Christendom. For Luther's closest collaborator Philipp Melanchthon, to whom we owe the trenchant description of the event, the posting of the theses advanced the restoration of the 'light of the gospel'. Luther himself liked to celebrate the moment as the beginning of the Reformation, and drank a toast to it with friends later in life.[1]

A little historical debunking, especially with events of such significance, is always salutary. As the Catholic historian Erwin Iserloh pointed out in 1962, Luther himself never mentioned the event, but said only that he sent letters to Archbishop Albrecht of Mainz and the bishop of Brandenburg, Hieronymus Scultetus, in which he condemned the abuses of selling papal indulgences in forthright tones, and enclosed his theses.[2] The story that he posted them on the door of the Castle Church has come down to us through Melanchthon and Luther's secretary, Georg Rörer, but neither of them was in Wittenberg at the time to witness the event.[3] Others have suggested that, far less dramatically, the theses might have been stuck to the door, rather than nailed to it.[4]

Whether Luther used a nail or a pot of glue will probably never be known for sure, but it is certain that he sent the theses to Archbishop Albrecht, the most important churchman in all Germany, on 31 October. The accompanying letter had a tone of remarkable self-confidence, even of arrogance. After an obsequious opening, it roundly condemned the archbishop's lack of care for his flock and threatened that if Albrecht did not take action, then 'someone may rise and, by means of publications, silence those preachers' who were selling indulgences which promised the buyers time off Purgatory.[5] Luther wrote a similar letter to his immediate superior, the bishop of Brandenburg, and, more than the posting of the theses in a backwater like Wittenberg, these letters were the provocation which ensured a response. One of Luther's talents, evident even then, was his ability to stage an event, to do something spectacular that would get him noticed.

Luther's Reformation sundered the unity of the Catholic Church for ever, and can even be credited with starting the process of secularisation in the West, as Catholicism lost its monopoly in large parts of Europe. Yet it all began in a most unlikely place. The tiny new University of Wittenberg was struggling to make its name; the town itself was a building site of 'muddy houses, unclean lanes, every path, step and street full of mud'. It was situated at the end of the earth, as southern humanists scoffed, far away from grand imperial cities like Strasbourg, Nuremberg or Augsburg with their connections to fashionable Italy. Even Luther remarked that it was so distant from civilisation that 'a little further, and it would be in barbarian country'.[6] And the man himself was an unlikely revolutionary. Just short of his thirty-fourth birthday, Luther had been a monk for twelve years, working his way up through the Augustinian order and becoming a trusted administrator and university professor. He had published almost nothing, and his experience of public writing was restricted largely to theses for disputation, works of exegesis and ghostwriting sermons for lazy colleagues. Although the Church was slow to respond, the Ninety-Five Theses took Germany by storm. There was a huge readership for them, lay as well as clerical. In just two months they were known all over Germany, and soon beyond it.

Whatever really happened on 31 October 1517, there is no doubting the significance of the theses themselves: the Reformation truly was sparked by a single text. Theses were sets of numbered propositions designed for an academic debate, although in this case that debate never occurred and Luther probably never intended it to. They were not composed in continuous prose, nor were they statements of truth; rather they set out hypothetical claims to be tested through subsequent argument, and were terse to the point of being difficult to understand. Few copies of Luther's text survive, and there are none from Wittenberg itself.[7] Printed single-sided on a large sheet of paper, they were meant to be posted on a wall – which suggests there may be some truth in the story of the church door – even though the size of the typeface would make them difficult to read. At the top, in a larger font, is an invitation in Luther's name that these theses should be debated at Wittenberg.[8]

The first begins with the words 'When our Lord and Saviour Jesus Christ said "do penance" he willed the whole life of a believer to be one of repentance.' The Latin puts the emphasis on the main verb – *voluit* – on what Christ *willed* the believer's life to be. Luther goes straight on to say that this cannot be interpreted to mean simply performing the devotional penalties that a priest might impose, such as saying prayers, or indeed, buying indulgences. The statement is deceptive in its simplicity; in fact, it implied a root-and-branch critique of the whole edifice of the late medieval Church.[9]

How could such a simple message have such implications and cause such uproar? Luther was not even the first or the only person to criticise indulgences; Luther's confessor, the Augustinian Johann von Staupitz, for example, had done so in sermons in 1516. At one level, Luther was simply articulating a long-standing position on the nature of grace that went back to St Augustine: the idea that our own good deeds can never ensure salvation, and that we must rely on God's mercy. Luther, however, alleged that the sacrament of confession was being perverted from a spiritual exercise into a monetary transaction. What sparked his anger, so he later reminisced, was the preaching of a Dominican friar, Johannes Tetzel, in the nearby town of Jüterbog, who went so far as to claim that his indulgences were so efficacious that even if a person had raped the Virgin Mary they would be assured complete remission from Purgatory. Still, the issue of indulgences was a lively subject of theological and political debate, and initially, some saw the indulgences controversy as little more than one of the frequent spats between the monastic orders, part of the old rivalry between Dominicans and Luther's Augustinians.

But it was much more. By arguing that Christians could not earn their way out of Purgatory through good works, viewing relics or acquiring indulgences, Luther was assaulting the medieval Church's claim to be able to grant forgiveness and facilitate salvation through the dispensation of the sacraments. For him, such practices showed a fundamental misunderstanding of the nature of sin, repentance and salvation. The Protestant chronicler Friedrich Myconius later recorded that some of Luther's parishioners had complained that he 'would not absolve them, because they showed no true penitence nor reform' and had appeared with letters of indulgence from Tetzel as they 'did not want to desist from adultery, whoredom, usury, unjust goods and such sins and evil'.[10]

By attacking the understanding of penance, Luther was implicitly striking at the heart of the papal Church, and its entire financial and social edifice, which worked on a system of collective salvation that allowed people to pray for others and so reduce their time in Purgatory. It financed a whole clerical proletariat of priests paid to recite anniversary Masses for the souls of the deceased. It paid for pious laywomen in poorhouses who said prayers for the souls of the dead, to ease their path through Purgatory. It paid for brotherhoods that prayed for their members, said Masses, undertook processions and financed special altars. In short, the system structured the religious and social lives of most medieval Christians. At its centre was the Pope who was the steward of a treasury of 'merits' – grace which could be disbursed to others. Attacking indulgences, therefore, would sooner or later lead to a questioning of papal power.

No one compelled people to buy indulgences, but there was a huge market for them. When the indulgence-sellers arrived at a town:

> the papal bull [the charter approving the indulgence, with the Pope's lead seal affixed] would be carried about on a satin or golden cloth, and all the priests, monks, town council, schoolmaster, schoolboys, men, women, maidens and children all met it singing in procession with flags and candles. All the bells were rung, all the organs were played . . . [the indulgence-seller] was led into the churches and a red cross was erected in the middle of the church where the papal banner would be hung.[11]

So efficiently organised was the system that the indulgences were even printed locally on parchment which could be filled in with the name of the person on whose behalf they were purchased.

Part of the explosiveness of Luther's Ninety-Five Theses lay in the timing of their appearance. On the feast day of All Saints, the magnificent collection of relics belonging to the Elector Friedrich, ruler of Saxony and Luther's sovereign, were displayed in Wittenberg's Castle Church to pilgrims from miles around and indulgences granted to all who viewed them. The theses were probably posted on or just before this celebration. True, illiterate pilgrims could not have read them; and even literate townsfolk would have been hard pressed to understand them. But the recipients of Luther's letter would have fully grasped the significance of the date, as would his fellow theologians at Wittenberg. For the latter, the theses touched on their own livelihoods, as the university depended on funding from the All Saints foundation, derived from the saying of Masses for the dead and from the pilgrims who came to see the relics in order to gain time off Purgatory.

What Luther did not know at the time was that the particular 'indulgence scandal' he attacked involved much more than the crude preaching of Johannes Tetzel, whose advertising jingle allegedly ran 'As soon as the coin in the coffer rings, the soul from Purgatory springs'. Rather, Tetzel's activities fed into a series of fundamental practices which financed the Church. The money raised by the preacher was supposed to go to Rome, to pay for the rebuilding of St Peter's. In fact, half of it was going directly to the Fugger banking family in Augsburg, the richest merchant capitalists of the day, to whom Albrecht of Mainz owed money. The younger son of a powerful princely family, Albrecht had become archbishop of Magdeburg at the age of twenty-three. But then there had been an unexpected vacancy in the archbishopric of Mainz, the richest of the German sees. This was not a chance to miss, but the papacy was trying to stop bishops amassing multiple offices and, after Albrecht's succession to Magdeburg, had also ordered that henceforth bishops would have to be at least thirty years old.[12]

The conflict was resolved in Albrecht's favour when he agreed to pay a contribution of 21,000 ducats to support the building of St Peter's, money he did not have. So he borrowed from the Fuggers, even though their involvement in monopoly capitalism was regarded as usury by the Church. He then moved to divert money, such as that collected by Tetzel, into paying the debt. Luther's theses, in other words, not only attacked papal power, but also, unbeknown to him, one of the most powerful people in Germany and the richest financial house in Europe.

In the short run, not much happened in response to the Ninety-Five Theses. No disputation took place. The bishop of Brandenburg does not seem to have answered Luther's letter. Instead, when Luther sent him his fuller explanations and defence of the theses, the bishop recommended a delay in publication which Luther appears to have – mistakenly – believed showed sympathy for his ideas. Albrecht of Mainz was away in Aschaffenburg when the theses arrived, but did not reply either when he eventually received them. Instead, he sent the document to the University of Magdeburg for theological judgement, and then on to Rome. This step ensured that the theses would become a serious matter by triggering a papal investigation for heresy. Albrecht's bureaucratic act meant that the matter was no longer an issue affecting a small part of Germany: it had become an event concerning the universal Church.

*

Luther's life and habits were very parochial. He was born in Eisleben in Saxony, and by strange chance, he died there too. He was brought up in the mining town of Mansfeld, seven miles to the north, went to university in Erfurt, forty-five miles to the south-west, and spent most of the rest of his life in Wittenberg, fifty miles to the north-east. He only once ventured outside the boundaries of the Holy Roman Empire when he visited Rome, and this merely provided a fount of anti-papal anecdotes and nourished his intolerance of everything that was not German. He travelled widely within Saxony, but when he was placed under imperial ban he was unable to venture further afield where he would not have the protection of the Saxon ruler. By the end of his life, he was further confined by poor health, reliant on a little cart even to get to church to preach. However, he developed a network of correspondents and pastors, whose appointments he had arranged and whose careers he furthered, which spanned the empire and beyond. And the effects of his Reformation spread from Germany to Italy, England, France, the Scandinavian lands and Eastern Europe.

The outlines of his biography are simply told. His childhood was unremarkable, except in one respect: he came from a mining area. The economy of mining was very different from the world of craft workshops and small enterprises that characterised most sixteenth-century towns, the environment that formed so many humanists and scholars. Luther's family invested in their son's education and destined him for the law, a profession that would have helped protect the family's mining enterprise. But in 1505, to his father's dismay, the young man gave up his legal studies and entered the Augustinian monastery at Erfurt. There he came under the influence of Johann von Staupitz, a leading Augustinian instrumental in establishing the new University of Wittenberg, who persuaded the young monk to move to higher studies in theology and obtain a doctorate. Progressing steadily up the rungs of the order, Luther eventually succeeded to Staupitz's university position and became active in reforming the university. Then, in 1517, the Ninety-Five Theses burst upon the world.

The theses did not contain a full theological programme; rather, Luther was radicalised by the opposition he encountered, and the arguments and attacks of others made him develop his theology and pursue his ideas further. The Reformation emerged through a series of disputations and arguments with his antagonists at Heidelberg, Augsburg and Leipzig. Luther knew that the penalty for heresy would be burning at the stake, and that if he was imprisoned and tried by the Church he was likely to lose his life. This meant that his theology was formed under the double pressure of increasingly aggressive argument from his opponents and the threat of martyrdom.

In 1521 Luther, now known throughout Germany, was called upon to answer to the emperor at the Diet of Worms in front of the assembled estates of the entire empire. Many thought he would not take the risk of attending, but as he said, nothing would stop him, even if he had known that there were 'as many devils as . . . tiles on the roofs'. The courage he showed at Worms was breathtaking. For a commoner to stand up to the emperor and the most powerful princes in the empire, and to resist the might of the Church, was as extraordinary as it was unforgettable. A defining event, it probably did more to win people over to the Reformation, and shape their hopes and expectations, than did his theology. Like any revolutionary movement, Luther's ideas were magnified and refracted through what people heard in the street or in sermons, or through news of what he did.

The Diet concluded with the emperor's emphatic condemnation. On the way back from Worms, Luther, now in mortal danger, was kidnapped on the instructions of his ruler and protector Friedrich the Wise, and taken for his safety to the Wartburg Castle, where he spent the next ten months in isolation, writing furiously and translating the New Testament. In the meantime, the Reformation at Wittenberg proceeded apace without him and, under the guidance of Andreas Karlstadt, became increasingly radical, addressing issues of poor relief and morality. When Luther returned to Wittenberg in March 1522, he immediately called for the reforms to be reversed because they had happened too fast. He also broke decisively with Karlstadt, who had begun to take a different line on the Lord's Supper, arguing that Christ was not actually present in the bread and wine, a view Luther passionately rejected.

This split presaged the future, for people applied his theology, as they perceived it, to their own experience – a process Luther might oppose, but which was beyond his control. As the Reformation spread it also began to fragment, as many people in south Germany, the Swiss towns, Silesia, and even within Saxony, were persuaded by those who denied that the body of Christ was truly present in Communion. In towns and villages throughout the empire, people began to demand gospel freedom, to insist on appointing evangelical preachers, and to overturn established authorities. Just as Luther's antagonists had predicted from the very start, his message brought revolution. In 1524, the Peasants' War broke out, the greatest uprising yet seen in German lands and unequalled in Europe until the French Revolution. Luther at first seemed to rebuke both sides even-handedly, castigating the peasants while, like an Old Testament prophet, also criticising the rulers, but he eventually gave his support to the princes. With this stance, the social conservatism of Luther's Reformation became apparent.

While the Peasants' War was at its height, Luther determined to marry, 'to spite the Devil', as he explained – surely one of the strangest justifications a new bridegroom ever gave.[13] The marriage was indeed shocking, but its audacity was as much a challenge to the Church as it was to the Devil. He was a priest and a monk, while his bride, Katharina von Bora, was a nun: they had both taken vows of celibacy. No longer the sallow, ascetic monk, Luther entered a new phase of life, and soon became a father. He did not have to leave the now deserted monastery, however: the Saxon rulers simply conferred the buildings on him and his heirs. There his household, with its assortment of visitors, students and colleagues, became the template of the evangelical parsonage on a grand scale.

The new Church still needed to be established, and in 1530, Emperor Charles V held another Diet on German soil, this time at Augsburg. It was now clear that there could be no accommodation between Lutherans and the Catholics; but the Reformation itself was by this time also split over Communion, and Luther's opponents were not given a voice at the Diet. The final years of Luther's life were dominated by attempts to reach some sort of agreement with the 'sacramentarians'. A precarious accord was finally reached, but it left Luther convinced that he had been right all along – a psychological dynamic that stored up future trouble for the movement. At the same time, his anti-papal rhetoric became increasingly bitter. His denunciation of the Pope as the Antichrist hardened to a fundamental axiom of his theology, and his declining years were further marked by violent disputes with erstwhile followers and furious diatribes against the Jews. After Luther's death, splits emerged between different wings of his own movement, leading to a legacy of division within Lutheranism where each side passionately claimed his authority.

*

These are the external facts, but they do not convey Luther's inner development, which is the abiding focus of this book. How did he have the inner strength to resist the emperor and estates at Worms? What drove him to this point? Why did he break with Andreas Karlstadt, his close supporter in the early years of the Reformation? Why did Luther, time after time, fall out with those with whom he had worked most closely, creating searing enmities and leaving his followers terrified that they might also incur his wrath? How did the man who had been convinced that 'they won't wish a wife on me' become the model of the married pastor? This book charts the emotional transformations wrought by the religious changes Luther set in motion. For Luther's personality had huge historical effects – for good and ill. It was his remarkable courage and sense of purpose that created the Reformation; and it was his stubbornness and capacity to demonise his opponents that nearly destroyed it.

Psycho-history has long had a bad press due to its tendency to explain complex personalities and historical processes in terms of basic patterns set in early childhood. Luther's life has inspired some of the most famous psycho-biographies, including Erik Erikson's *Young Man Luther* and Erich Fromm's chapter on the reformer in his *The Fear of Freedom*. Both men were psychoanalysts.[14] Erikson was also a developmental psychologist who worked with adolescents, and his lively book, published in post-war America, remains a classic; but one of the most important features of Luther's Reformation is that it was not that of a *young man*. As this book will argue, although Luther's relationship to his father was fundamental to his personality and his religiosity, and although his understanding of paternal relations pervades his theology, father figures were only part of what shaped him.

It may seem foolhardy to attempt a psychoanalytically influenced biography of the very man whose biography has become a byword for the worst kinds of reductionist history.[15] Such an approach, it could be contended, risks overestimating the role of individual agency in much the same way that sixteenth-century Lutheran hagiography did, making it impossible to understand why Luther's ideas might have appealed to so many and how they created a social movement. It could be further argued that it also cheapens theology, reducing major ideas to the outcomes of unconscious wishes or conflicts, and making it impossible for us to grasp why ideas about the presence of God in the sacrament or the nature of repentance should have become so urgent.

However, the wealth of material that has survived on Luther is so great that we probably know more about his inner life than about that of any other sixteenth-century individual, allowing us to trace his relationships with his friends and colleagues through his correspondence and even to examine his dreams. His collected works, the famous Weimar Edition, extend to 120 volumes, including eleven volumes of letters and six volumes of his dinner-table conversations. Where many historians have used this abundance of material to trace his theological development in detail, and to date specific events with greater accuracy, I want to understand Luther himself. I want to know how a sixteenth-century individual perceived the world around him, and why he viewed it in this way. I want to explore his inner landscapes so as to better understand his ideas about flesh and spirit, formed in a time before our modern separation of mind and body. In particular, I am interested in Luther's contradictions. Here was a man who made some of the most misogynistic remarks of any thinker, yet who was in favour not only of sex within marriage but crucially that it should also give bodily pleasure to both women and men. Trying to understand this apparent paradox is a challenge I have not been able to resist.

A man of immense charisma, Luther's passionate friendships were matched by equally unrelenting rejections of those he believed to be wrong or disloyal. His theology sprang from his character, a connection that Melanchthon, one of the first of his biographers and his closest co-worker, insisted upon: 'His character was, almost, so to speak, the greatest proof' of his doctrine.[16] Luther's theology becomes more alive as we connect it to his psychological conflicts, expressed in his letters, sermons, treatises, conversations and biblical exegesis. Such a rereading of the original sources, which sets aside the accretions of denominational scholarship, will show us why seemingly remote and abstruse theological questions mattered so deeply to him and his contemporaries, and in what ways they may still be important to us today. Drawing on the insights of psychoanalysis thus yields a richer understanding not only of Luther the man but also of the revolutionary religious principles to which he dedicated his life, the legacies of which are still so powerful.

This book is not a general history of the Reformation, or even of the Reformation in Wittenberg; still less can it provide an overall interpretation of what became Lutheranism. It does argue, however, that our understanding of the Reformation in German lands has been distorted by the preoccupation of western post-war scholarship with the cities of the south. This is a legacy of the Cold War, when historians of the West found it hard to use archives in the East, while their colleagues in the German Democratic Republic were interested at first more in social movements and in the legacy of the religious radical and revolutionary Thomas Müntzer than in Luther. As a result, the social history of Lutheranism is still underdeveloped, and we lack the kind of rich, nuanced account of the progress of the movement which we have for the major cities of the south. Because West German historians after the war were so eager to identify a democratic lineage in their own past, they idealised the free independent cities with their

elected councils. They wished to escape the deadening equation of
the Reformation with political conformism and obedience, by pointing
to the variety of local, popular Reformations, with ideas about the
sacrament, images and social reform very different to those of Luther.
But the result has been that our account of the Reformation has been
skewed. We lack a proper assessment of Lutheranism in its home
social and cultural context, which was so unlike that of the southern
cities: its political values and its economic structures were not those
of the south. Nor do we understand how Lutheranism developed in
dialogue with what became reformed religion, the precursor of
Calvinism, through bitter enmities and tragic broken friendships. This
is an absence this book cannot repair, but I hope to suggest a new
and unexpected approach to Luther's theology by placing him in the
social and cultural context that formed him.

*

Luther has been part of my life for longer than I care to admit. He
was a feature of my childhood, because my father was for a few years
a Presbyterian minister. I was only briefly a daughter of the manse,
but I saw the toll that living a family life in public took on both my
parents. The strange black cassock and gown seemed to transform
my father into another being. He had a study lined from floor to
ceiling with works of theology, but the congregation hankered after
his predecessor, who had been less intellectual. All this confronted me
with issues of authority – the authority the congregation invested in
my father; the seriousness conferred by the pulpit and the heavy black
robes, so unsuited to the Australian climate; and the strain this role
put on him. We were set apart, and yet we were humiliatingly
dependent – nothing could be repaired in the manse and no furnish-
ings could be chosen except with the agreement of the congregation,
one of whom opined, 'You don't need carpets to do the work of God.'

By a quirk of historical accident, the Melbourne Presbyterian
Church at that time was more influenced by Luther than it was by
its ostensible founder John Calvin, because several Australian university theologians had studied in Tübingen with Lutheran professors.
Some years later, when my father had left the Church and I was
beginning doctoral research, I studied in Tübingen myself with

Professor Heiko Oberman, a Dutch scholar who had established the Institute for Late Middle Ages and Reformation and whose work was transforming our understanding of late medieval theology. In my first semester I attended the lectures that would become his study of Luther, a classic that is still to my mind the best biography of the man. And it was while I was at Tübingen that Hans Küng, a Catholic professor at the university, lost his licence to teach Catholic theology because he had questioned papal infallibility. It seemed that the questions of authority, freedom, and obedience, which Luther had raised centuries ago, were very much alive. These were burning issues that kept Lutheran theology at the centre of my intellectual and personal concerns.

Most biographies of Luther are written by church historians. The great exception is the magnificent recent biography by the historian Heinz Schilling, the first to put Luther in a more rounded historical context and to give equal weight to his opponent Charles V.[17] I am not a church historian but I am a historian of religion, shaped by the social and cultural history of the last decades, and by the feminist movement in particular. I do not wish to idolise Luther or to denigrate him; nor do I wish to make him consistent. I want to understand him and make sense of the convulsions that he and Protestantism unleashed, not just in relation to authority and obedience, but also in regard to the relations between the sexes and how men and women perceived their physical existence.

When I began graduate study, there were very few studies by Western scholars of the Lutheran regions of the Reformation in eastern Germany, owing to the division of the country at the time. One of the few exceptions was the late Bob Scribner who wrote his PhD on the Reformation in Erfurt and who would become my doctoral supervisor. Most local studies of the Reformation were of towns in southern Germany that were influenced by the theology of reformers such as Huldrych Zwingli or Martin Bucer, not of Lutheran regions.[18] For its part, East German scholarship focused on the Peasants' War and on the figure of Luther's antagonist Thomas Müntzer as a revolutionary leader. The social history of Wittenberg, meanwhile, remained largely untouched. As a result the history of the Reformation was profoundly distorted. Biographies were largely written with no sense of the social and cultural world of Saxony or of Wittenberg, and thus tended to reinforce the view of Luther as a lone theological hero, who stands above time and space. Even so, there have been some subversive moments. By a fine irony, the best scholarly study of Wittenberg, unmatched since, testifies to the legacy of the early women's movement: the 1927 work by the economic and social historian Edith Eschenhagen in which she analysed Wittenberg's tax records.[19]

All these works had a strong influence on me when I began work on this book in 2006, and reinforced my view that a sense of place was essential to understanding Luther's reformation. I spent as much time as I could in the archives at Wittenberg, which are housed in Friedrich the Wise's castle. During the lunch hour I wandered around the town. I visited all the places where Luther had lived before going to Wittenberg, and I often read in the archives, not so much to find out about Luther as to get a sense of the local economy and power structure. I read accounts of Luther by his contemporaries, foes as well as friends – and I discovered that his antagonists often proved surprisingly shrewd about his psychology and motivations. But it was reading his letters that gave me the greatest pleasure and the richest encounter with the man. I read them not to corroborate or date Reformation events, but as literary sources that conveyed his emotions and illuminated his relationships with others. Luther's letters were designed to make things happen. His mistakes, slips, self-justifications and fondness for particular words reveal much about what moved him. In the early years of the Reformation, for example, he talked constantly of *invidia*, or envy, attributing it to his opponents – although it is hardly likely that they would have envied a penniless, powerless monk, whilst he, on the other hand, had every reason to be preoccupied with those he envied. I began to reflect that many of his theological concerns were closely related to the strong conflicts that shaped his psychology.

Luther's letter-writing habits offered perhaps the most intriguing insights. Although he had had secretaries since his days as a monk, he wrote his letters himself, except when severe illness prevented him. His hand – small, neat, and well-shaped – moves confidently across the page, and Luther almost always knew what size paper he would need, suggesting a remarkable ability to judge in advance how much he was going to write. Over the years his handwriting remained largely unchanged except for a tendency to become slightly smaller and more angular, the hand muscles evidently becoming more tense. Extraordinarily, in an age when letters were routinely passed from person to person, were forged or intercepted, and when every chancellery filed drafts, Luther kept no copies. This gave his correspondents huge power, because they alone had records of what he had written, but Luther was relaxed about this, joking that he could always deny his own 'hand', a remark which reveals his remarkable confidence.

This breezy indifference to formalities is one of Luther's most appealing characteristics. A brilliant, engaging personal correspondent, he had a sure sense of what would make his recipient laugh. He enquired about illness with genuine interest, but he also knew exactly how to cut to the chase, confronting a correspondent's anguish with directness. More than anything else, the letters give us a sense of the charisma he must have radiated, and the sheer delight his correspondents must have experienced in being his friends. It was Luther's vivid friendships and enmities which convinced me that he had to be understood through his relationships, and not as the lone hero of Reformation myth. Luther's theology was formed in dialogue and debate with others – and it is no accident that the disputation, the form in which he proposed the Ninety-Five Theses, remained an intellectual tool he cherished right up to his death.

This book also presents an unfamiliar picture of Luther's theology. We are used to regarding him as the advocate of 'salvation by grace alone', the man who insisted on *sola scriptura*, the principle that the Bible is sole authority on matters of doctrine. But just as important to Luther himself was his insistence on the Real Presence of Christ in the Eucharist. This is probably the issue many modern Protestants, suspicious of ritual and of the idea that the divine can be manifest in objects, find most alien. Yet the question dominated Luther's later years and mobilised his deepest energies; it also split the Reformation. It was here that Luther was at his most original as a thinker, refusing to make the easy distinction between sign and signified, and insisting that Christ really *was* present in the Eucharist, which truly *was* the body and blood of Christ. Though he was an intellectual, Luther mistrusted 'reason, the whore', as he called it.[20] His position on the Eucharist was at one with his striking ease with physicality, a trait which modern biographies find it hard to come to terms with. A deeply anti-ascetic thinker, Luther constantly undermined and subverted the distinction between flesh and spirit, and this aspect of his thought is among his most compelling legacies. This is also why his theology has to be understood in relation to Luther the man.

Luther's Reformation unleashed passionate emotions, anger, fear and hatred as well as joy and excitement. Luther himself was a deeply emotional individual, yet much of the history of the Reformation edits those emotions out, as unbecoming or irrelevant to the development of his theology. It is hard for historians and theologians to tackle what now seems so alien, his disturbing obsession with the Devil, virulent anti-Semitism and crude polemic. Exploring his inner world, however, and the context into which his ideas and passions flooded, opens up a new vision of the Reformation.

# I

# Mansfeld and Mining

'I am the son of a peasant,' Luther averred, 'my great-grandfather, grandfather and my father were all true peasants.'[1] This was only half the truth. If he came from peasant stock, Luther grew up in a mining town, and his upbringing was to have a profound influence on him. Martin's childhood was spent in Mansfeld, a small mining town in the territory of the same name, where wagonloads of charcoal would file along the muddy roads, and where the smell of the fires of the smelters hung on the air. He would remain loyal to Mansfeld throughout his life, referring to himself as 'from Mansfeld', enrolling at the University of Erfurt as 'Martinus ludher ex mansfelt', and corresponding with the counts of Mansfeld until he died.[2] In 1546, he set out, ill, on what was to be his final journey to Eisleben, trying to settle yet another dispute between the counts. He knew that the trip could cost him his life, and it did: he died still trying to put matters right in Mansfeld. Yet this deep connection has been almost completely obliterated in the image of Luther we have today.[3] Most biographies have little to say about Luther's childhood. Unlike his birthplace Eisleben, and unlike Wittenberg, where he spent most of his life, Mansfeld never became a site of Lutheran pilgrimage. But to make sense of Luther, one has to understand the world from which he came.

There had been mining in the Mansfeld area since about 1200 but in the mid-fifteenth century a new process of refining allowed silver and pure copper to be separated after the initial process of smelting.[4] Highly capital-intensive, this technological innovation led to the involvement of the big financiers of Leipzig and Nuremberg, and it brought an economic boom to the area. Mansfeld was soon amongst the biggest European producers of silver and it produced a quarter of the continent's copper.[5] Copper was used in combination with tin

1. Eisleben, where Luther was born.

or zinc, as bronze or brass, in the hundreds of household items produced in towns like Nuremberg, and it played a large part in the lifestyle revolution in this period, as people began to acquire not only glass and crockery but also metal dishes, pans and other implements for use at home. Luther's father, Hans Luder, probably through connections of his mother's family, heard of the new mining leases that were up for sale in the 1480s, and moved first to Eisleben, where Luther was born in 1483, and then to Mansfeld.

Luther himself later described his father as 'a metal worker, a miner'; but the story told by his early biographers of Hans Luder's rise from rags to riches is not true.[6] Although his family were clearly not educated people, Hans was certainly never one of those hooded, squat men who toiled lying down in the low mine tunnels with their pickaxes.[7] The Luder family had been peasants, yet even though he was the eldest son, Hans did not inherit: according to local custom at Möhra, where his parents lived, it was the youngest son who took over the farm. The value of the property was probably equally divided between the children, and this may have given the oldest son some capital. Recent research also suggests that the Luder family may have owned a rudimentary copper-smelting works near Möhra, where Hans might have gained some experience.[8] He must have had serious prospects, however, for it is otherwise hard to explain why the Lindemanns, an established urban family in Eisenach – whose members included

Anthonius Lindemann, the highest-ranking official in the county of Mansfeld and himself a smelter-master – should in 1479 have betrothed their daughter to a young man without a trade and with no promise of an inheritance.[9] It turned out to be a wise decision. Within a short period of time Luder was not only running mines, but by 1491 at the latest had become one of the *Vierer*, an adjunct to the town council representing the four quarters of Mansfeld, and would eventually become a mining inspector (*Schauherr*), which made him one of the five most senior mining officials in the area.[10] By the early sixteenth century, he was operating seven smelters in joint ventures with others, placing him amongst the bigger operators in Mansfeld.

In 1500 the town had a population of around 2,000–3,000 people, with five 'hospitals' to care for the poor and houses for the sick; more unusually, it also boasted a Latin school for boys. Mansfeld nestled in a valley, with four gates and two portals allowing entry. Its 'quarters' had mushroomed out from a much smaller initial settlement.[11] One of its two main streets wound steeply up the hill to the church on the main square, and it was on this street that the smelter-masters and the officials of the counts had their houses. The church, dedicated to St George, the patron saint of Mansfeld, had been erected in the thirteenth century but burned down when Luther was in his early teens (thanks to an absent-minded organist who forgot to put out the fire that heated the bellows). It was rebuilt between 1497 and 1502, with a choir finally finished in 1518–20.[12] The sword-wielding knight St George was locally believed to have been a count of Mansfeld, who had fought the dragon on the nearby Lindberg hill. The counts certainly made capital out of this fictional connection, and the saint was depicted on their coins, fountains and above doors; there were even St George weathercocks.[13]

Hans Luder's house was located opposite the Golden Ring tavern, one of two hostelries where travellers might stop. The town lay on the trade route from Hamburg to Nuremberg via Erfurt, but there were few reasons why travellers would have broken their journey in Mansfeld, unless they were going to visit the counts or were involved in mining.[14] Luder's house still stands, and it is now believed to have been twice as big as previously thought. (We do not know for certain when Hans Luder acquired the house; he certainly owned it in 1507.[15]) There is a wide entrance through which a horse and cart could pass, and a big barn and stables for horses.[16] From the house the effects of mining would have been visible everywhere: slag heaps pockmarked the landscape and the large pond below the town was polluted with the slagwater from the two smelters outside the town walls. Further up the street, towards the square in front of the Church of St George, stood the large house of Luther's best friend, Hans Reinicke, whose father was also a mine owner and one of the most prosperous men in Mansfeld. Next door, between Luther's house and the school, lived another friend, Nickel Öhmler, who would later become related by marriage.

Above the town loomed the castles of the Mansfeld counts. It is hard to imagine a set-up more likely to impress on a young lad like Luther the power of the town's rulers. There was no primogeniture among the counts. Instead, all sons inherited, and when Luther was a boy there were three lines of Mansfeld counts; in 1501, when a formal pact was made dividing the territory, the ruling collective consisted of no fewer than five counts.[17] Not surprisingly, they did not always get along, and one of the points of tension between them was the castle. In Luther's childhood, two castles stood on the site along with two other dwellings, two bakeries, two breweries, stables and a dividing wall with a shared path. It must have been an impressive set of structures, for in 1474 the counts had been able to host the king of Denmark and 150 of his knights for three nights.[18] In 1501, when Count Albrecht decided to build a third castle on the site, he met with opposition from the other counts. The dispute was eventually settled, and Albrecht was allowed to realise his ambitions. With the wealth from the mines, three pocket-handkerchief-sized Renaissance castles – one painted red, one yellow and one blue, with shared access to the chapel – were now rebuilt and restructured to form one of the best-fortified castle complexes in Germany. It was popularly believed that when one of the counts commissioned an altarpiece for the chapel depicting the Crucifixion, he had the thief on Christ's right painted as his most hated co-ruler. True or not, the thief has the individualised features of a portrait and is unusually not naked but sports the outfit of an executioner, with garish parti-coloured hose. Since executioners were shunned as dishonourable, this would have been a delicious insult.[19]

The Luder family lived well.[20] They particularly relished the tender meat of suckling pigs, a comparatively expensive food at a time when beef imported from central Europe was starting to become more

2. The altarpiece at Mansfeld Castle.

common. They also ate songbirds which they trapped. At least one member of the family was a passionate bird-catcher, because several of the goose-bone whistles used to attract birds have survived in the midden outside the house. There was a well-stocked kitchen, amply furnished with simple green and yellow plates and crockery; there were drinking glasses too, still a luxury in this period.[21] This was certainly a family who liked their food, enjoyed the pleasures of life, and did not have to watch the pennies.

In most sixteenth-century urban households, the master's wife shared in the business of the workshop, bustling over the apprentices

3., 4. and 5. In the illustrations to Georg Agricola's treatise on mining, *De re metallica* (1556), two buxom women pound the ore on the long tables, a method that would still be in use in the nineteenth century. Two other women sieve charcoal, while in the background of a view of the gigantic bellows, a short-skirted maid can be glimpsed going about her work.[24]

and journeymen, sometimes even doing the bookkeeping. But amongst the mine-owning class the realms of husband and wife were sharply distinct. The miners lived in their own cottages with their families and the smelter-master's wife was not responsible for their food or upkeep. Hans Luder himself went out to work each day beyond the town walls, where he was immersed in that strange world of smoke, shafts and tunnels, while Luther's mother stayed at home with the servants and children. This was a separation of spheres much more like that of the nineteenth-century bourgeoisie, and very different from what was then the norm in early-modern German towns and farmsteads where women raised the poultry, grew the herbs, undertook the dairy work, and trekked to market. Here women had to be able to take over the farm or business should they become widows. The strict demarcation between the sexes in the Luder household was therefore rather unusual, and it may help explain why Luther's later ideas about gender roles exaggerate the differences between the sexes: 'Men have broad shoulders and narrow hips, and accordingly they possess intelligence. Women have narrow shoulders and broad hips. Women ought to stay at home; the way they were created indicates this, for they have broad hips and a wide fundament to sit upon.'[22]

Women were not entirely absent from mining lower down the social scale. In account books from the early sixteenth century, the miners' wives are listed as well as their menfolk with the amounts they earned per week, testimony to their importance in the industry.[23] Alongside the men, they turned the winding handles to haul weights in and out of the shafts, and with their children, they helped break up the ore according to quality. They did the backbreaking work of sieving the charcoal, to make the fine powder for the lime needed to line the smelters; they washed the miners' clothes, heavy with dust; and they used the slag the men brought home as heating.

Luther's father was one of the *Hüttenmeister*, the smelter-masters who oversaw the highly skilled operation of the copper-smelting process and who effectively ran the mines. Each shaft was allocated to a smelter or 'fire', and the *Hütten* (huts) were situated near streams, because water power drove the bellows that fanned the flames of the smelters. One hut might have several ovens, and in 1508 there were some ninety-five 'fires' in Mansfeld, which were run by about forty smelter-masters.[25] These contracted with gang masters who provided the miners, and who worked alongside them underground. Labour relations were therefore mediated, and when the miners rose up in protest against their conditions, as they did in 1507, they put their complaints to the counts in writing. The counts, for their part, knew not to try the patience of the miners too far: while they might have executed rebellious peasants, on this occasion they imposed whopping fines of a hundred guilders on the dozen or so ringleaders, but allowed them to pay by instalment.[26] The authorities had to exert their power, but the highly skilled labour force was too precious to waste. Proud men who were aware of their skills, the miners did not give up and in 1511 they formed a brotherhood to advance their interests.[27]

Court books from the period give some rare insight into what life was like in the world of mining. There were constant thefts of wood, ladders and equipment from the shafts, and violence was never far away.[28] A man killed a prostitute in a brothel in nearby Hettstedt and was executed for it. Another slew a man and threw the body down a mineshaft – he too paid with his life – while a third attacked his own father, damaging his fist so seriously that he was unable to work.[29] Criminal law at the time mixed Roman law with older traditions that placed the emphasis on mediation. Thus murder could still be settled by paying the victim's family compensation, though even so, between 1507 and 1509, at least three criminals were executed for murder.[30]

There were constant quarrels between different groups of miners. The *Haspeler*, who wound the winches, hated the *Sinker*, who sank the shafts. The *Sinker* were mostly from Silesia and, scorning marriage, lived with girlfriends in houses near the mines where they also kept chickens and other livestock.[31] Mining was dangerous work. The tunnels which led off from the shafts were narrow, and miners had to work lying down on their bellies. There was little light. If the weather turned bad, the lamps would suddenly go out as sulphur gas accumulated in the mineshaft, poisoning any miners still below. It was believed that the gas was a product of the evil airs drawn from the brimstone and metals, rising in the tunnels and chilling men to death.[32]

Mining was thirsty work, and as water was not drinkable, brewing was the town's other major industry. Alcohol fuelled quarrels, and since just about all men carried knives, fights tended to become bloody. Most brawls took place in taverns or drinking shops.[33] Luther's own unclc, 'Little Hans', a wastrel who went from one pub brawl to another, would meet his death in a fracas at a drinking-house in 1536.[34] People used whatever was to hand, grabbing the tavern lamps to bash an opponent, or hoisting the beer jugs to buffet an opponent about the head. Representing comradeship, these jugs also had symbolic significance: one man would insult another as not worthy to share a jug with a respectable man.[35] Drinking was surrounded with bonding rituals and there were competitive drinking games where a man had to stand his ground. One favourite required the use of the 'pass glass', ridged with bands separated by different widths, from which the drinker had to down his tipple exactly to the next ridge; the Luder family owned at least one of these.

In such a pugilistic culture, insults were routine. One man might taunt another: 'If you were born of a pious [i.e. chaste] woman, come out and fight, but if you were born of a rogue, stay indoors.' There was little chivalry in the taverns. A man would tell a woman to go hang out with the priests and monks in Hettstedt 'as she had doubtless done before'. 'There are no more than two or three pious women in the whole of Mansfeld,' another man announced angrily. He stayed pointedly silent when his companion asked him whether he included his wife in that number.[36] Work disputes could rapidly descend into arguments about an individual's sexual, moral and social behaviour because honour, the central social category, was both sexual and economic.

During Luther's childhood, Hans Luder would have been a force to be reckoned with. He was a physically powerful man, and once, when a pub fight broke out in his presence, he poured beer over the two combatants to separate them, clouting both on the head for good measure with a jug until the blood ran.[37] He was also not a man to be crossed lightly. We find him complaining about the high charges of the winch-winders, and about another mine operator who, he claimed, was stealing his ore (the accused countered that Luder was taking his charcoal).[38] The court books are littered with disputes between the mine operators – small wonder, with 194 shafts at the industry's peak in the early sixteenth century in the Mansfeld and Eisleben areas, where it could be hard to know where one mine's territory began and another ended. Time and again, the mine inspector would be called to check the location of boundary stones. Tunnels honeycombed the hills. The longest was a remarkable 13.5 km long, and it was rumoured that a man could reach Eisleben from the castle in Mansfeld through the tunnels.

It was also a world of dizzyingly complex financial arrangements. Much of the mining structures had to be maintained collectively, and the records afford a glimpse of the maze of loans, counter-loans and securities as money circulated amongst the small group of mine operators, or was advanced by the capitalists of Nuremberg, and as mines were relinquished and redistributed.[39] Hans Luder would have been caught between several competing forces: the counts, who leased the mines and constantly sought to extract more money by altering the legal terms; the other mine managers, who were only too quick to seize an advantage; the miners, whose labour actually produced the wealth from the ground, and who were beginning to organise collectively; and the capitalists in faraway Nuremberg and Leipzig, who drove hard bargains and to whom it was only too easy to become irrevocably indebted.

These economic relations were new, and they were complicated. The large-scale mining leases given to new mine owners and the silver refining introduced in the fifteenth century brought in the capitalists from outside. These developments created deeply uncertain relationships, legally, economically and socially. The new leases issued by the counts were no longer permanent but temporary, and created a two-tier legal arrangement amongst the small elite of mine owners. There was no guarantee of success, however. Some entrepreneurs earned vast amounts of money – families like the Heidelbergs and the Drachstedts made fabled fortunes – while others were sinking deeper and deeper into debt.

Mansfeld mine owners frequently had to join forces in order to secure the necessary capital and machinery. But instead of forming exclusive and permanent joint ventures, they relied on contracts, just as merchants did, agreeing to work together for a stated period of time.[40] Hans Luder worked his way up to a substantial position in Mansfeld, taking on seven 'fires' and probably 200 workers in the second decade of the sixteenth century.[41] He also knew that he needed someone who understood legal contracts and who could protect his interests from the merchant capitalists and the counts, and this probably played its part in his decision that his son should study law. Luder's partnership with Dr Drachstedt, who had a doctorate in law and would become the richest mine owner in the district in the second half of the 1520s, may also have inspired Hans's plans for his son.[42]

Where contracts did not protect, blood might. Like all the members of this tiny mining elite of twenty to thirty families, Hans Luder used marriage alliances to cement his position. With three or four sons – we do not know for sure – and four daughters, Hans Luder could dream of a dynasty, but two of his sons would die of plague in 1506 or 1507, and a daughter in 1520.[43] Three daughters married into the local elite. Dorothea into the Mackenrodt clan, who had been in the area for at least a century and were amongst the privileged group of those who enjoyed secure titles. Margarethe, named after her mother, married Heinz Kaufmann, who between 1508 and 1512 ran only one 'fire', but would later go into partnership with his father-in-law, as would Martin's younger brother Jacob (whose name his family

pronounced 'Jacuff'). The third sister married Claus Polner who, like
Luder, belonged to the group of mine owners without secure leases.[44]

Yet all Hans Luder's careful calculations and long-term strategies
would eventually come to nought. The Mansfeld mines were collectively administered by the five counts, with the exercise of jurisdiction
alternating amongst them. It seems to have been a fair system, but
the mining income also had to produce enough funds to support the
Renaissance palaces looming over the town. It was long after Luther
had left home, in the 1520s, that this balance became increasingly
difficult to maintain. While the counts continued to squeeze money
out of the leaseholders, income from the mines began to decline – the
seams were deeper and therefore harder to reach, water had to be
pumped out, and they required more machinery. The numbers of
smelter-masters shrank and the silver-refining companies (*Saigergesell-
schaften*) which had been financing the mine operators now began to
gain possession of the mines as the smelter-masters became indebted
to them.[45] A proud, independent man, by the 1520s Hans Luder himself
was unable to pay off his debts and was forced to work for the hated
capitalists, in his case the *Saigerhandelsgesellschaft* at Schwarza, on a
salary of fifty guilders a year with, humiliatingly, a supervisor at his
side.[46] When he died in 1530 there were no mines for his son in Mansfeld to inherit, only the family property – worth a not insubstantial
sum – to be shared equally amongst the children.[47] While in 1508 there
had been forty-two smelter-masters in Mansfeld, by 1536 their number
had halved.[48] In the 1560s, by which time the counts were running the
Mansfeld mines themselves, the entire mining enterprise went bankrupt.[49] By the end of the century, the seams were exhausted and
German silver production had given way to competition from the
silver of the New World.

Hans Luder and his contemporaries tried to make sense of economic
relationships which no one could understand or control, and which
were eventually to destroy them. They had no economic theory and
little understanding of how wealth was created: no one knew why
the capitalists in Nuremberg and Leipzig profited while the mine
owners suddenly became impoverished. Economic thought was
based on the assumption that wealth was limited. If one person had
wealth, another could not get it. Metals, it was believed, resulted from
the mixing of quicksilver and brimstone and were shaped by the

6. In the folklore of mining, each ore had its respective planet, Venus in the case of copper. In Ulrich Rühlein von Calw's mining book from 1527, copper is depicted as the large-breasted naked goddess of love gazing into a mirror, her curly tresses falling luxuriantly down her back, while a pair of scales, emblems of justice, are held in her right hand.

influences of the planets. Mining was a matter of luck. There were diviners, and there were printed advice books, but no one knew where the rich seams might lie. Small wonder that the figure of Fate should have been so ubiquitous in the Mansfelders' lives.

There was a rich mining folklore which left its mark on Luther. With water essential to the process of smelting, he grew up with the belief in 'nixes' or water sprites, mischievous creatures who played tricks on humans. The fossils found in the mines were said to be drawings made by the spirits of the earth and of the air; and strange uncanny lights were believed to point to the rich seams. The adult Luther thought the lights were Satan's work. Satan was the arch deceiver and, Luther wrote, 'in the mines the Devil vexes and deceives people, puts spirits before their eyes so that they believe they see a huge pile of ore and silver, where there is nothing'. And although Luther ostensibly rejected much superstition about mining, he held on to ideas about luck. Some people, he admitted, were lucky to find the rich ores. 'I have no luck in mining', Luther wrote, 'because the Devil won't permit me this gift of God's.'[50] As so often, Luther provided a theological explanation that overlay older beliefs about fortune – and, only half in jest, attributed power to the Devil instead.

The mine owners' bitter experiences shaped Luther's economic thought. His periodic outbursts later in life against the 'little tricks' of the 'thieves', 'robbers' and 'interest squires' expressed a populist hatred of major capitalists like the Fuggers, who engaged in the sinful practices of usury, and who tried to gain a monopoly on sources of wealth such as trading minerals.[51] Luther reached for the moral language of sin to explain economic behaviour, castigating their avarice, one of the seven deadly sins, but this ethical approach left him unable to deal with the mechanisms of the new capitalism. He rejected many commercial practices as unchristian and maintained all his life that usury was a sin, although he was willing to countenance a basic rate of return on lending. Offered shares in the mines of the Saxon dukes later in life that would have returned him a much-needed 300 guilders a year, Luther refused, declaring 'I am the Pope's louse, I torment him, and he keeps me, and I live off his goods.' Luther did not want to be a capitalist. For him, shares were *Spielgeld*, toy money.[52]

It is hardly surprising that when Johannes Tetzel, the preacher who would eventually spark Luther's Ninety-Five Theses, began to sell indulgences in 1508, he headed straight for the new mining region of St Annaberg, named after the miner's saint, the mother of the Virgin Mary: miners needed all the protection they could muster. As Myconius, the town's Lutheran preacher, would put it later, they hoped that 'if they just put in the money and bought grace and indulgences, all the mountains around St Annaberg would become the purest silver; and as soon as the coins clinked in the bowl, the soul for whom they had put it in would fly straight to heaven with their dying breath'.[53]

It may have been that omnipresence of uncertainty, danger and risk in the mining world which settled in Luther's soul and gave him a deep conviction of the complete omnipotence of God: a sense that human beings are utterly exposed in their dealings with Him, and that there are no mediators or strategies that could protect them. Magic would not work, insurance did not exist, law offered only flimsy protection. The miner could call on the saints, especially St Anna. But in the end, he faced God alone.

*

Around 1527 Lucas Cranach the Elder painted portraits of Luther's parents, when they visited their son in Wittenberg. The painting of Hans shows a man with a powerful physical presence, and chunky features. A man of action, he looks almost uncomfortable sitting still, his hands awkwardly folded. He is dressed in black, the colour favoured by men of substance, and wears the obligatory fur collar. The resemblance to Martin is unmistakable. He has the same deep-set eyes and the heavy jowls that Luther inherited. His mother Margarethe's white coiffe and shirt complement the dark colours of her husband's portrait. With her simple, conventional attire, and wearing no jewellery, she is presented as a model wife, although her chin juts forward, suggesting a less conventional character. There is also a surviving sketch of Hans Luder in pencil and watercolour by Cranach, probably a study for the portrait. Focused only on the face, it is more revealing: Hans's eyes are wrinkled against the light and his face is weathered, as befits a man used to working out of doors. The mouth is firm, the nose emphatic. This is a man used to speaking his mind, but the clouded gaze also suggests someone whose power is now spent, a patriarch grown old. When the portraits were produced, the glory days of mining were already over.

It is difficult to know what kind of a father Hans Luder made. Conventionally pious, he practised the devotion common to his generation. A member of the brotherhoods of St Anna and of St George, he also helped found the local Marian brotherhood, and a fragment of a horn from Aachen, found in the house, shows that someone in the family may have undertaken this famous seven-yearly pilgrimage: the horns were blown when the relics were displayed.[54] But it is doubtful that Luther's intense spirituality came from his father: Hans Luder was a man used to relying on his own ability to get things done, who had chosen not to work for others, but to assume responsibility himself. We know that Luther was surprised to find out about his extensive kinsfolk on his father's side when he visited them in Möhra after the Diet of Worms in 1521, so Hans had evidently not kept in

7. Lucas Cranach the
Elder, Hans Luder, 1527.

touch with his wider family once he had struck out on his own.[55] He
had acquired his skills and talents himself, and not through inheritance. Yet even if his family background gave him some basic knowledge of mining, this could not have taught him how to run a
substantial mining enterprise, manage large amounts of capital, or
discipline a difficult workforce. This irascible, competitive man, who
knew how to make his way in a rough man's world, would have made
an exacting father. It seems that he was unable to accept that his son
wanted to pursue a path in life different from his own. The bitterness
of the conflict between father and son that ensued when Martin
entered the monastery suggests how closely Hans had identified with
him, and how deeply he was hurt by Martin's rejection of the life he
had planned for him.

Luther, who inherited his father's determination to succeed, might
seem like a classic eldest son, although he may have had an elder
brother who died.[56] The Luder household was full of children. Luther's
younger brother Jacob seems to have been a close companion, and
their mother is reported as saying that 'There was always such mutual

good feeling between the two brothers so that neither of them preferred any companion to the other brother, nor took any delight in any food or any game without the other.'[57] Perhaps, like many eldest children, Martin felt the arrival of the new siblings keenly, envying how they monopolised his mother's attention – infants were normally suckled for a couple of years. In 1532, watching his own pregnant wife Katharina von Bora feed their young son Martin, Luther remarked, 'It is hard to feed two guests, one in the house, the other at the door.'[58] When their fifth child Paul was born in 1533, Luther held him in his arms and mused 'how much Adam must have loved his firstborn son Cain, and yet he became his brother's killer'. At one level, this was a conventional recognition that fathers love their children no matter what they do, but the off-kilter remark may also reveal that he knew how envious a displaced firstborn can feel.[59] Whether or not Luther ever had an older brother, it was his education in which his father chose to invest, and this special treatment would have made him proud and confident of his ability to succeed like his father.

But it may also have made him feel guilty towards his siblings, and worried about their envy. Luther knew the price of his university education: two years of smelting had to pay for his studies at Erfurt, something his father doubtless made sure he never forgot.[60] He also knew that this was money not spent on his brothers and sisters. Seven or possibly eight children, five of whom survived into adulthood, had to be trained or found dowries – all to be funded from Hans Luder's mining operations. The structure of the family economy, where the children were meant to make their way from the income of the Mansfeld ores, was likely to have fostered a sense of common purpose, and the family seems to have remained close-knit throughout Luther's life.[61] When his parents died there was some bad feeling over the inheritance, which was to be equally divided, an irritation which may perhaps have reawoken conflicts from the past. Luther, as the eldest, acted as peacemaker and drew up the contract of division, insisting that now all 'dislike and unwillingness' be set aside.[62] But Martin's privileged position may have left occasional envy and bitterness as well. Luther's almost allergic reaction whenever he thought others envied him would become a settled feature of his character.

Whereas most of Luther's generation of scholars came from the craft towns, and many were familiar with the large imperial towns and their elegant fashions and civic pride, Luther's character was forged in a very different and much rougher world. His upbringing in Mansfeld would have given him a toughness and a readiness to put himself physically on the line, qualities that would be tested to the limit in the years ahead. From his father and the other mine owners he would have learned the importance of creating networks, a skill that would make the Reformation possible. He would have learned how to be a leader – and to expect not deference but assaults, arguments and brickbats. Mansfeld nurtured in him a sense of politics that was grounded in authority and class division, and rested on a clear distinction between the counts who ruled from the hill and the 'black miners', as Luther termed them, who worked below.[63] Socially, it taught him the importance of friendship and kin. Through marriage he would become related to most of his Mansfeld friends and he would replicate the same patterns years later, as Lutheran clergy intermarried, creating a new professional caste, bound by ties of kinship.[64] Theologically, his childhood may have inclined him towards a powerful sense of the unbridgeable distance between God and man, and of the unpredictability of God's providence. Nothing stood between the miner and disaster; and for every miner who struck a lucky seam there were more who lost everything. But those who did not trust Lady Luck, or grasped at superstition, might be left with a shrewd realism about the operations of the world, and a cynical distrust of the stars.

# 2

## The Scholar

When young Martin left Mansfeld in 1497 to go to school in Magdeburg, he was in his fourteenth year and his father's future as a substantial smelter-master still looked rosy. He went with Hans Reinicke, the mining inspector's son; ambitious as ever, his father wanted the same education for Martin as that enjoyed by the son of the most prominent man in town. Young Martin lodged with the archbishop's official, Dr Paul Moshauer, who also came from a mining family.[1]

The careers of the two bright young lads offer a telling contrast. Martin went on to university at Erfurt, becoming a monk, while Reinicke followed in the family business, and married in 1511, aged around twenty-eight. By 1512, Luther had risen to become sub-prior and director of study for the monastery, while Reinicke ran his first two smelters.[2] In 1519, when Martin was a famous but penniless monk, Hans inherited the family house in Mansfeld, and by 1522 he had become one of the wealthiest mine owners in the town.[3] Luther meanwhile had made his famous appearance at the Diet of Worms, and in 1522 he was hiding in the Wartburg Castle. Throughout the 1520s and 1530s, alone of all the mine owners of his generation, Hans Reinicke made a success of it, joining the capitalists of the Steinacher *Saigerhandelsgesellschaft*, dominating the silver production of Mansfeld, and acting as spokesperson for the mine owners; in the same decades, Luther became world famous.[4]

Reinicke's was the life that Luther could have led and had chosen not to. The two men remained friends and kept in contact, the friendship a powerful anchor in both their lives. Reinicke visited Luther during the Diet of Augsburg in 1530, while the reformer was suffering from loneliness in Coburg Castle. It was Reinicke who broke the news of Hans Luder's death: when a letter arrived from his friend shortly afterwards, Luther took one look and said 'Now I know that my father is dead.' As Melanchthon put it: 'There was exceptional mutual kindness between these two, Luther and Reinecke, whether by some concord of nature or whether rising from that companionship of boyhood studies.' When Reinicke died in 1538, Luther lay ill, and the news of the loss of 'my best friend' was kept from him for some months, because those around him knew how serious a blow it would be.[5] Their experiences together as boys had bound the two men throughout their lives.

The bond may have had as much to do with shared misery as with shared boyhood pleasures, and Luther was scathing about the teaching his generation had received: 'Everywhere we were obliged to put up with teachers and masters who knew nothing themselves, and were incapable of teaching anything good or worthwhile. In fact, they did not even know how to study or teach.'[6] He wrote this in 1524, and some of the bitterness that lay behind his words may be related to another reminiscence: that at school he 'was once beaten fifteen times one after another in one morning'. One must beat and punish children, Luther conceded, 'but at the same time one should love them'.[7] It was surprising that Mansfeld, a small mining town, should have had its own Latin school and it suggests the cultural aspirations nursed by its elite. Whatever its deficiencies, the school must have at least succeeded in imprinting Latin in the young boy's consciousness, since his later ability to play with the language, to use Latin to express a whole gamut of emotions, and to form ideas with precision, can only have developed through a very long familiarity with it.

Latin was the language of scholarly debate and intellectual discussion across Europe, and learning it was the first step into an exclusive world; girls mostly did not learn it. But for those who had the language, there was the whole of classical literature to encounter, a world of heroes, soldiers, goddesses and fables. The further Luther proceeded down this path, the more he moved out of his father's orbit: he had a language the older man could not understand, and access to knowledge and intellectual analysis that Hans Luder could not guess at. And yet in one sense this was exactly what his father wanted for him.

When the two lads set out for Magdeburg, they appeared to be on a path that would lead to a starry future together. But barely a year later, in 1498, Martin was moved from Magdeburg to school at

Eisenach, a town that would play an important role again later in his life. On the face of it, the move was strange, for the Eisenach establishment was neither particularly famous nor large, and the town with its 3,000–4,000 inhabitants could not rival Magdeburg in wealth or prestige. At the turn of the fourteenth century Eisenach had backed the wrong side in the Wettin wars, hoping to gain independence from its Saxon rulers. As a result, it lost its status as the preferred residence for the Wettin dukes, who began to favour Gotha and Weimar instead. The plague also hit the town repeatedly in the fourteenth century, and there were pogroms against the Jews, who were expelled. Conflicts amongst the ruling elite, the creation of a new high court for Saxony at Leipzig which undermined Eisenach as a legal centre, declining wealth and increased taxes, all contributed to the town becoming a backwater.[8]

However, Luther's mother's family came from Eisenach, where they were respected citizens, and it is likely that Luther changed school at her instigation.[9] She was clearly a powerful influence on her clever son, but we have much less evidence about her and scant information about their relationship. We do know that she came from a background very different from that of her husband. What young Martin gained from her may have been one of the reasons why he eventually decided not to follow the path his father had laid out for him.

Luther later reminisced that his mother 'carried all her firewood on her back'. We can sense, from her slightly bowed back in Lucas Cranach's portrait, that this woman was not an elegant burgher's wife who left to the servants the work of fetching water or carrying weights. And yet she had learned relatives, and was the bridge to the more refined world of Eisenach.[10] Tellingly, Luther gave her a copy of *On the Love of God*, written by his mentor and confessor Johann von Staupitz, dedicating it in his own hand to 'my dear mother'.[11]

One of Luther's first biographers, Johannes Mathesius, tells a revealing story of how Luther first discovered a Latin Bible, which contained so many more 'texts, letters and gospels' than he had ever imagined. He excitedly leafed through it, coming to the story of Samuel and his mother Hannah, which he read with 'heartfelt pleasure and joy'.[12] Hannah – or 'Anne', as Mathesius calls her – had been barren, and her son, conceived in answer to her prayers, was named 'God has heard'. She presented him to the priest Eli, intending that he should pursue the religious life. As Mathesius's readers would also have remembered, as a youth, Samuel was called by God three times, finally replying 'Speak Lord, for thy servant heareth.'[13] He then became not a priest, as his mother had intended, but a prophet. Three of Luther's companions – Mathesius, Johann Aurifaber and Anton Lauterbach – all provided versions of Luther's first encounter with a Bible in their notes of Luther's table talk, from 1531, 1538 and 1540, so it was evidently a story that Luther liked to tell. Its emotional significance suggests how central his mother – also known as 'Hannah' – may have been to his sense of religious vocation; Luther too would later style himself a prophet, having also ended up on a different path from what his mother might have envisaged.[14]

Luther's mother later became a target for Catholic polemicists who wanted to show that the reformer was the scion of the Devil. Johannes Nas, for one, a Catholic controversialist of the second half of the sixteenth century, alleged that Luther's mother had been working as a bath maid – a dishonourable profession and a byword for loose morals. She had been seduced by a stranger dressed in luxurious red, who promised her that she would never suffer want and would catch a rich husband if only she would give herself to him. Thus Luther was the outcome of a liaison with what must have been the Devil himself. This was a throwback to sexual slurs which the Catholic Johannes Cochlaeus, a contemporary originally sympathetic to Luther's ideas and then his determined antagonist, had cast as early as 1533: that Luther was 'a lousy runaway monk and rascally nuns' fanny who had neither land nor people, an ignoble changeling who was born of a bath maid as they say'.[15] Luther laughed off these attacks: either, he quipped, he was a bath maid's son or else he was a changeling, he could not be both. But although he affected not to care, he remembered the insult and quoted it several times.[16]

*

However much in decline from its glory days, Eisenach was very different to his home town. While Mansfeld was a town of slag heaps and taverns, Eisenach boasted churches, monasteries and books. Many of Luther's relatives on his mother's side were university graduates who had made careers as doctors, academics, administrators and lawyers. This was the background that would have prompted him to think of university, and to become active in public life. Significantly, when he angrily refuted suggestions in 1520 that his parents were from Bohemia – intended to taint him with connections to Hussite heretics – he referred to Eisenach and his relatives there: 'Nearly all my kinfolk are at Eisenach, and I am known there and recognised by them even today . . . and there is no other town in which I am better known.'[17] It was his mother's side of the family, not his father's, that exercised a powerful influence on his scholarly and religious identity.

Like Mansfeld, Eisenach nestled in the shadow of a castle, the Wartburg. The townspeople's relationship to the surrounding nobility was, however, turbulent. In the thirteenth century Sophie of Brabant had constructed a fortress in the town which the locals called the *Klemme*, or clamp, for it was designed to control them – and they destroyed it with glee at the first opportunity.[18] There were repeated conflicts, and in 1304 the Eisenachers even demolished the towers of Our Lady's Church, so as to strengthen their defences, an act of sacrilege which resulted in the whole town being put under the ban. In 1306–8 the townsfolk tried to gain independence, even storming the Wartburg itself, and when they failed, were besieged themselves. All this history gave the Eisenachers a powerful sense of their own identity, and a stroppy antagonism towards the lords on the hill.[19]

The town had few industries but it did specialise in religious services. As a seventeenth-century chronicler put it, Eisenach was 'a true religious emporium of a town', crammed with ecclesiastical institutions: he counted one foundation, three parish churches, seven monasteries and nine chapels. St Mary's had twenty-three altars and St George eighteen, all of which had to be staffed with clergy. Civic pride may have got the better of the chronicler, however, for some of these 'monasteries' were hardly major institutions.[20]

While Eisenach was another town that, like Mansfeld, venerated St George, here the martial spirit of the dragon-slayer was counterbalanced by its own woman saint: St Elisabeth of Hungary, who had married Ludwig IV of Thuringia in 1221 and had lived in the Wartburg. The Franciscans arrived in Eisenach at about this time, and Elisabeth was devoted to them. A wonderfully subversive figure, she rejected the power and ostentation of the counts, coming down from the castle to spend her time in the town below with the down-and-outs, tending the sick and promoting the building of hospitals. There were many legends surrounding her. One time, when her husband was away, she let a leper sleep in his bed. Understandably annoyed when he heard about it on his return, he pulled back the cover only to discover that an image of the Cross was imprinted on the sheets. When Ludwig died on crusade, however, his brother Heinrich von Raspe stepped in as regent, and banished Elisabeth from the castle; she was forced to seek shelter with the Franciscans, who hid her.[21]

In fact, there is no historical evidence for Heinrich's cruelty, and Elisabeth later seems to have moved to Marburg of her own volition where she practised ascetic works. Indeed, she proved a huge asset to the dynasty, and Heinrich himself founded a church in her memory. Elisabeth would remain important in Luther's life. Years later, he could still rattle off her biography, giving her date of birth and age at death.[22] He never spoke disrespectfully of her, even when other saints became the target of his invective; he also named his first daughter Elisabeth.

Eisenach's reputation as a spiritual town was enhanced, too, through tales of extravagant penances and of powerful figures humbled by sudden spiritual conversion. Hermann, Baron Dreffurt, who had led a life of robbery, whoring and violence, headed to Eisenach to become a Franciscan monk when he saw the error of his ways in 1329. Before he died nearly twenty years later he insisted on being buried at the place 'where the schoolboys had their toilet'.[23] But there was a downside to this febrile spirituality: both Luther and Melanchthon recalled seeing in Eisenach the worst example of a moving statue.[24] These were statues of saints made with adjustable parts that were intended to fool the credulous into believing that they moved miraculously, inclining their eyes or interacting with the believer. They were part of the devotional culture designed to inculcate powerful emotions in the worshipper, but they also offered a ready target for the sceptical.

When Luther arrived, he had to beg for his supper. The young lad had a good voice, and sang in the choir, a gift that could be put to use in begging; it would later flourish in his abilities as a preacher and in the hymns that he composed. Begging was common – for Franciscan monks, forbidden to own property, it was godly work to ask for alms – and it was usual for schoolboys to do the same to pay for their upkeep. But the vehemence with which Luther would later speak out against mendicancy may suggest how uncomfortable he found it. Around

1520 he wrote to a friend that he would rather learn a trade than support himself by begging. Condemning monasticism around the same time he complained that the monks' 'running about the country has never done any good and never will do any good. My advice is to join together ten of these [monastic] houses or as many as need be, and make them a single institution for which adequate provision is made so that begging will not be necessary.'[25]

For four years, Luther lived in his mother's world, staying in the house of the Schalbe family. Well-respected relatives of his mother, Heinrich Schalbe was a town councillor and served as mayor in 1495 and 1499.[26] The family lived a Franciscan life of modesty and good works, and were devoted to a small monastery run by the Minorites, which had originally formed part of an institution founded by St Elisabeth herself.[27] This piety deeply influenced Luther, and the family remained so important to him that when he came to celebrate his first Mass in 1507, he wanted to invite them to come to the celebration; he was deterred only by the costs he knew it would impose on them.

Little is known about Luther's schooling in Eisenach. The school buildings were probably not very impressive, for they were demolished in 1507.[28] One story, reported by Luther's doctor and early biographer Matthäus Ratzeberger and perhaps apocryphal, conveys the atmosphere of respect for students and learning: the rector used to doff his cap to his pupils and made all the teachers do the same, telling them that they might well be addressing a future mayor, chancellor, learned doctor or regent.[29] This story of respect is far removed from the beatings Luther recalled from his early years, and it may be that the school allowed the young lad to blossom intellectually. Having mastered the elements of Latin in Mansfeld, he now turned his attention to literature, and his immersion in the classics hugely affected his writing style. He began to love poetry and as he later reminisced, the contemporary poet Baptista Mantuanus was the first he read. Probably at this time, if not earlier, he also read Ovid's *Metamorphoses* and Aesop's fables.[30]

Luther constructed a lasting relationship with one of his teachers, Wigand Guldenäpf, and sent him a copy of one of his sermons fifteen years after he had left the school. Another older man, Johannes Braun, vicar at St Mary's, became a significant friend as well. Braun, who had matriculated at the University of Erfurt in 1470, had close connections with St George's school and regularly invited students to his home, lending them books. He cultivated an atmosphere of scholarship, rather like the humanist circles of schoolteachers and their former pupils that would become such a feature of the educational landscape in the second half of the sixteenth century. Like the Schalbes, Luther later wanted him also to witness his first Mass.[31] The relationship between the younger and the older man continued long beyond Luther's schooldays in Eisenach, into his first years at university and after his decision to become a monk. It seems to have faded, however, after Luther's departure to Wittenberg, and Luther wrote to reassure his friend that although he thought 'a cold and proud north wind had extinguished all warmth of love', in fact his silence was simply because he had no 'time or leisure' to write, an explanation that may not have set the old man's mind at rest.[32]

His days at Eisenach certainly made a lasting impression, and it was through the Schalbes that Luther heard about another figure who would later become significant to him: a renegade Franciscan monk named Johann Hilten.[33] In the 1470s Hilten had started making apocalyptic prophecies, warning of Turkish power and criticising monasticism openly. He ended up imprisoned in a cell in Eisenach, where, according to later Lutheran propagandists, he died of starvation around the turn of the century – a victim of the cruelty of the monks. Decades later, in 1529, the story came up again when Luther was visiting his friend Friedrich Myconius. By now the parallels between Luther and Hilten were striking: both were graduates of Erfurt who had become monks and rebelled against the Church. Moreover, the Turks had just laid siege to Vienna, making Hilten's warnings suddenly prescient. When he got home, Luther wrote excitedly to Myconius, wanting to find out everything he could about the monk, and begging his friend to leave nothing out.[34]

Why was Luther so excited? Hilten had apparently prophesied that soon someone would arise and attack the papacy. In the story Luther first heard from Myconius, the event had been predicted for 1514, but there were other versions which more helpfully foretold the prophet's arrival in 1516. Later biographers saw this as proof of Luther's divine mission, even if it was out by a year. Luther himself cited the prophecy approvingly with the date of 1516, believing that it referred to himself.

When Melanchthon, Luther's most important collaborator, wrote the *Apology* for the Augsburg confession of 1530, the founding articles of the Lutheran faith, he began the section on monastic vows with the life story of Hilten and his maltreatment by the 'pharisaic bitterness and envy' of the monks. Melanchthon added that, in an echo of John the Baptist, Hilten had predicted before he died that 'Another man will come . . . who will destroy you monks . . . him you will not be able to resist.'[35]

The figure of Hilten then made its way into Luther hagiography, and his prophecies were republished in the late sixteenth century and again in the seventeenth. For later Lutherans, Hilten was a prophet and proof that Luther was a man of God. Yet he was also an awkward hero, who reputedly had written letters in blood to a beloved, and whose truculent apocalypticism hinted at mental instability. It may be telling that the Lutheran chronicler Ludwig Rabus, who had lived for a time in Luther's household, referred to the prophecy but did not include Hilten in his compendium of Lutheran martyrs and the 'elect of God'.

Luther's conception of the role of childhood in forming an individual was very different from ours. He paid attention to Hilten not because the monk-seer was imprisoned in the monastery near where he went to school, and therefore formed part of his childhood. Rather, he felt that Hilten verified his own prophetic role and his crusade against the monks. It was not the individual, but the divine scheme which mattered. Yet at the same time, Luther's interest allows his own emotional landscape to emerge with greater clarity. When he read Melanchthon's *Apology* in 1531, he marked Hilten's name in red, and wrote in the margin how he remembered hearing about the monk when he was a boy 'aged fourteen or fifteen' at Eisenach with the Schalbes. The prophecy placed Luther's battle against ascetic monasticism at the very heart of his theology, something which his friend understood. Melanchthon therefore recorded in this important document of Lutheran theology an intimate truth about the movement's founder.[36]

He also indirectly acknowledged the importance of Eisenach and Luther's mother's world to the development of Luther's spirituality. Certainly the Schalbes and the group around Johannes Braun appear to have shaped Luther's devotional attitudes.[37] That piety may have incorporated a strong feminine side: St Anna and Mary became important figures in Luther's devotional universe, and the myths and stories surrounding his time in Eisenach hint at a motherless lad far from home and in search of tenderness. One tradition has it that the widow Ursula Cotta took him in because she liked his singing and sympathised with his reluctance to beg; another story tells of how he was left alone suffering with fever while the rest of the household was in church, and had to crawl to the kitchen on hands and knees to get the water he needed.[38] Apocryphal though the stories may be, perhaps they reflect the psychological reality that Luther both needed and found a connection to his mother in Eisenach.

*

From Eisenach, Luther moved on to university at Erfurt in 1501, the institution that his revered older friend Johannes Braun had attended. Although further away from home than the rival University of Leipzig, it was closer to Eisenach and his maternal family. Luther may have lodged at the student house of St George – choosing another institution named for the patron saint of Mansfeld – or he may have joined the Amplonian College near St Michael's Church, Heaven's Gate, the biggest of the student bursas or residential colleges. These institutions followed a strict quasi-monastic regimen: students had to be in bed at 8 p.m., rose at 4 a.m., and Luther would have shared a room. Many students seem to have found their way around the rules, however, for as Luther acidly remembered, 'Erfurt is a whorehouse and beerhouse; these two lessons are what students got from that gymnasium.'[39]

Founded in 1392, the university was the oldest German institution to have a charter, and in the early sixteenth century it boasted an outstanding collection of humanists, interested in the revival of ancient learning and in returning to the sources. Yet although he was influenced by these intellectual trends, Luther apparently developed no contacts to leading humanists at Erfurt, such as Eobanus Hessus and Conrad Mutian, in contrast to two of his later friends, Georg Spalatin and Johannes Lang, who were both part of Mutian's circle. And although the humanist Crotus Rubeanus later described Luther as his good friend and remembered how he and Luther were united by an enthusiasm for study, there is perhaps something extravagant about his claims to friendship as he avers that 'my soul has always remained yours'.[40] After all, he was writing in 1519 after Luther had become famous.

Luther started out as a rather average student, coming thirtieth in his cohort of fifty-seven baccalaureates.[41] We do not know what it was that opened his scholarly imagination at university, but it seems likely that it was philosophy – even though he complained about being forced to study the subject.[42] Erfurt University was a hotbed of the *via moderna* and nominalism, a direction in philosophy that reached back to William of Ockham in the fourteenth century. Luther's teachers included cutting-edge nominalists who wrote textbooks that would become standard teaching tools. The *via moderna* distinguished itself from the *via antiqua*, of Thomas Aquinas and Duns Scotus. With its roots in the philosophy of Aristotle, the *via antiqua* had started from the position that things are what they are because they are a particular instance of a universal. Nominalists, however, argued that universals were not real entities, but simply labels for lots of particular objects. As Luther put it, describing twenty years later what must have seemed rather rarefied disputes to the next generation:

The dispute and squabble amongst them was: whether the word *human-itas*, Humanity, and words of this kind, meant a general humanity, which was to be found in all humans, as Thomas and the others hold, 'Yes' say the Ockhamists and 'terminists', this common 'humanity' is nothing, it means all humans in particular, just as a painted image of humanity means all human beings.[43]

It was the techniques of the *via moderna* that were formative for Luther, not so much the programme of the emerging humanism. And critical as he would later become of philosophy, he was shaped by its style of argument.[44] He made it clear later that he had been on the side of the Ockhamists who encouraged critical thinking and stressed the importance of empirical evidence. True to the humanist principle of returning to the sources, his teachers, Bartholomäus Arnoldi of Usingen and Jodokus Trutfetter, used Aristotle's original texts, not just medieval commentaries on them, and it must have been dizzying to tackle the works themselves rather than view them through a haze of inherited comment and glosses.

At this point, nothing indicated the course his thinking would later take. Apart from steeping himself in the philosophy of Aristotle, Luther probably continued his studies of Cicero, Livy and Virgil. Around 1505 he gained his MA and something of the sense of achievement is captured in his later remarks about the celebrations: 'My, it was such a great majesty and splendour when Masters of Arts graduated, and torches were carried before them and they were honoured; I think that no temporal, worldly joy can equal it.'[45] On becoming a 'master', the student received a special master's ring and a biretta, and he had to give a speech. Out of respect, his father now addressed him not in the informal 'du', but with the polite 'Ihr'[46] and almost certainly at his father's instigation, he then determined to study law. Everything looked set for him to return to Mansfeld in a couple of years, perhaps to marry into the local elite of mine owners as his brother and sisters would eventually do, and use his legal knowledge to advance his family's interests.

*

It was not to be. Luther's life was about to change for ever. Three incidents from his time in Erfurt stand out, hinting at some of the anguish that this young man, apparently destined for a successful career, was suffering. First a fellow student and friend fell ill and died; his death affected Luther deeply and appears to have plunged him into melancholy. Then while travelling home to Mansfeld, about half a mile out of Erfurt he somehow managed to injure himself with his sword, severing an artery at the top of his leg. He pressed his finger on the wound to stop the bleeding but the leg began to swell up massively. Luther could easily have bled to death. Seized with terror, he prayed: 'O Mary, help!' A doctor was summoned who treated the wound, but that evening, while he was lying in bed, the wound burst and again Luther called on Mary to save him. It looked as if his prayers were answered, for the wound healed. When he told it years later at table he neatly inverted the story, so that the true miracle was not that Mary saved his life, but that God preserved him from dying trusting in Mary, and not putting faith in Christ as the Christian should.[47]

A similar incident happened not long after, but with far more serious consequences. Again, Luther was on the road, this time returning to

Erfurt from Mansfeld on a summer's day. He was near Stotternheim when a terrible thunderstorm broke. Terrified, Luther called on St Anna – the patron saint of miners – vowing to enter a monastery if she saved him. His response might seem extreme, but storms were believed to be caused by the Devil or by witches, and church bells were rung during tempests to ward them off. As before, Luther called not to Jesus but to a woman saint. When he told the story in 1539, he again gave it a twist: God had kindly taken the word 'Anna' to be the Hebrew word for 'grace', rather than the name of the saint. This tongue-in-cheek interpretation allowed him to maintain that the vow in the storm had indeed been another divine intervention, but once more without female intercession.[48]

When the thunderstorm passed Luther kept his vow: he joined the Augustinian order in Erfurt on 17 July 1505. This was a momentous step. At a stroke, it destroyed his father's plans. Hans Luder's investment in his son's education had been for nothing. Luther sent his academic gown and ring home to Mansfeld, telling his parents that he had drawn a line under this part of his life. He sold some of the fine legal textbooks his father had bought him and donated others to the monastery.[49] Then he invited all his student comrades to a lavish meal, with music and entertainment. At the height of the party, he told his shocked companions of his decision to become a monk, announcing melodramatically, 'Today you see me and never again!'[50] He then left for the monastery, accompanied by his sobbing companions. Luther had staged his departure in the form of a Last Supper, a dramatic enactment of his separation from the world of the flesh.[51]

Luther's entry into the monastery was a major act of disobedience, a repudiation both of his father's plans and of the values of Mansfeld society. Once inside, he remained in seclusion for the first month, which made it impossible for his irate father to intervene, or for his friends to try and change his mind. Moreover, he did not return home to explain his decision in person, but rather told his family of the decision by letter. Enraged, his father wrote back bitterly, returning to the informal '*du*' address. He at first withheld permission for his son to enter the monastery and, as Luther noted, eventually only gave way 'unwillingly'. One version of the story has it that he gave way only after he lost two of his children to the plague in 1506.

What the rebellion must have cost Luther is evident in a story about his first Mass as a priest in 1507 at which his father was present. When he arrived at the moment of consecration where the wafer becomes the body of Christ, he experienced such panic that he would have fled had the prior not prevented him from doing so.[52] As Luther told the story in 1537, it was the words *tibi aeterno Deo et vero* (to you, eternal and true God) which plunged him into terror. The incident concerned the miracle of the Mass, where the bread, now the body of Christ, is displayed or is administered by the priest to the believer.

At the ensuing feast to celebrate his first Mass, for which Luther's father, always the man for the grand gesture, had given the sum of twenty guilders, the breach was still evident. Luther asked whether his father now accepted his decision, and in front of everyone at table, Hans Luder replied: 'Remember the fourth commandment, to obey father and mother'; 'What if it was an evil spirit' behind the events in the storm, he asked? It was a very serious charge, made at the point where Luther had just acted as Christ's representative on earth for the first time. As everyone at the table knew, Satan could easily trick the believer into thinking an apparition was divine when it was in reality demonic. There could hardly have been any comment more calculated to rattle a young man's sense of spiritual vocation and certainty, and Luther's shock was still evident in the way he told the story years later, stressing that the comment was made in front of the other guests at the table.[53] Luther recalled in a letter to Melanchthon in 1521 that it 'took such deep root in my heart that I have never heard anything from his mouth which I remembered more persistently'.[54] Luther's antagonists too, first Cochlaeus and later Johannes Nas, would see the importance of trying to query the role of the storm. The thunder, Nas mocked, was not divine sanction. It was proof of God's anger.[55]

The Luther biographer and psychologist Erik Erikson was no doubt right when he argued that Luther's difficult relationship with his father was reflected in his theology: God became Luther's father, far more powerful than Hans Luder could ever be.[56] But there was more to it than this. Luther's understanding of God grasped the distance that separates humans from Him, stressing the essential unknowability of God, and his hiddenness in suffering on the Cross. He emphasised the whole gamut of the fatherly aspects of God's nature; not for him the cosy evangelical view of Jesus as one's friend. Luther's notions of manhood and fathers were forged by the rough world of Mansfeld as well as in his relationship with his father. Nor was Luder the only person to shape his son: his mother was profoundly important, as were his siblings. Nonetheless, Luther's revolt would inevitably bring him up against authorities, including the Pope and the emperor, which at the time were understood as forms of paternal authority. His ability to speak out against such figures had to come from within, and the first step was the rebellion against his father.

# 3

# *The Monastery*

When Luther became a novice, he had to kneel before the high altar, by the tomb of Andreas Zacharias, the Erfurt monastery's most famous son. Doing so would have given the supplicant a sense both of physical abasement and of spiritual connection as his body felt the cold of the stone. A theologian of some renown, Zacharias had made a name for himself at the Council of Constance (1414–18) where he attacked the theology of the Bohemian reformer Jan Hus: he was credited – perhaps unfairly – with causing Hus to be burned as a heretic in 1415. Hus had called for Communion in both kinds, bread and wine, for laypeople. It is ironic that Luther himself came to hold many of the same views as Hus, who became a hero of the Reformation.[1]

The monastery at Erfurt played an important part in turning the young Luther into the reformer he later became. Why did he choose the Augustinians? The town had many substantial monasteries: there was another Augustinian monastery and the Carthusians, Servites, Dominicans and Franciscans all had houses there; with Luther's connection to the Franciscans at Eisenach, that monastic order might have been particularly attractive. However, the 'Black Monastery', as the observant Augustinian house was known, would have been the intellectual's choice. Many members of the house were also teachers at the university, and the monastery had a good library. It was expanding, with new buildings under construction while Luther was there, and it had a strong reputation amongst the citizenry. It housed a substantial community of some forty-five to sixty monks, and was supported by a generous and growing endowment, owning substantial properties in and around the town.[2]

It was also caught up in a major conflict within the order: the struggle between the observants, who wanted strict obedience to the original rules, and the so-called conventuals, who were less rigid. Monastic orders tended to undergo cycles of renewal, as successive generations found that obedience to the rules had become lax. The latest Augustinian reform movement had begun in the 1480s and continued well into the early sixteenth century, and the Erfurt monastery was one of the major houses in Thuringia leading the observant side. The nature of their concerns can be glimpsed in the questions the reformer Andreas Proles had asked in 1489. Do the brothers 'eat together in the refectory at a long table, as is customary in reformed monasteries? Do they eat in silence? Do any of them get food or drink for themselves alone at times other than common meal times?'[3] In observant institutions the monks were ordered to turn up punctually for matins, and attend a general confession every Friday. The hours were to be strictly observed, and all property, even clothing, was held in common.[4] Obedience, poverty and chastity were the foundation of the religious life and they were to be strictly adhered to.

Thus Luther chose an institution with a strong academic mission, close ties to the university where he had been a student, and a strong commitment to the Augustinian rule. Moreover, by remaining in Erfurt, he chose a different environment from the small town where he had been raised. A large and bustling urban community with 24,000 inhabitants, Erfurt was far bigger than Eisenach or Mansfeld, and something of the impression it made on Luther can be gauged in his gross overestimation of its size – he believed that it had '18,000 hearths', which would have made it at least three times bigger than it really was.[5] Erfurt possessed grand ecclesiastical buildings. The cathedral still dominates the town, rising out of the vast arena of the town square and perched atop a grand series of steps like an Italian basilica. No urban structure could possibly rival it.

This was a prosperous town – Luther guessed its income at a fabulous 80,000 guilders a year.[6] As he would put it later, 'Erfurt is in the best place, it's a gold mine, a city simply would have to be there, even if it burned down.'[7] The city's powerful merchant elite had become prosperous on the profits of the woad trade, the dye that was used to colour cloth blue and the fashionable black favoured by richer townsfolk. With a large rural hinterland, it had impressive stores of grain, enough to tide its citizenry through difficult times.[8]

Even so, Erfurt was not what it had once been. The city had never gained the civic freedoms it longed for. It wanted to be an imperial free city, like the fabled cities in the south – Nuremberg, Ulm, Augsburg, Strasbourg – that were subject to no lord but the emperor and were able to make their own laws. But it was caught between two rival powers, Saxony and the archbishopric of Mainz, both of which wanted to exploit its wealth. When the two were at loggerheads, the city could play them off against each other but unfortunately for Erfurt, the election of Adalbert of Saxony to the archbishopric in 1482, and the absorption of the Thuringian lands into the patrimony of electoral Saxony, meant that the two now often acted in concert. Forced to pay a crippling indemnity and annual 'protection money' to Saxony in 1483, its citizens were left burdened with taxes for a generation; by 1509 its civic debt had swelled to half a million guilders. To make things worse, a fire had destroyed large parts of the city in 1472, adding to the financial strain.[9] In such circumstances, it was easy for the clergy, who were exempt from taxation, to become the scapegoats for the town's woes. Just how deep Erfurt's anticlericalism ran would be revealed in the early years of the Reformation, when the town saw some of the earliest and most destructive anticlerical riots.

It was also a town with turbulent internal politics. In 1509 there was a citizen revolt, as Erfurt became split between the patrician elite, who mainly supported Saxony and wanted its protection, and the populace, who inclined to Archbishop Uriel of Mainz. The archbishop had his agents in the town who successfully fomented unrest amongst the citizenry, alienated by the high taxes and the city's financial woes. Ruled over by a tiny oligarchy of patricians, neither the economically important woad merchants nor the guilds folk wielded real political power. When the populace realised the extent of the financial misery of the town, the mayor tried to ride the storm, insisting that 'we are all one community', pointing at himself. This was a major blunder – it looked as if the 'common good' meant his self-interest – and he soon met his end, strung up on the gallows outside the city.[10] Refused an honourable burial, he was left to swing in the wind in his fox fur coat – a final humiliation, for fox was the cheapest fur.

In the following years, the agents of Saxony and of Mainz continued to fight for dominance, each manipulating the urban factions. For

their part, the Saxons tried to get the town put under imperial ban.[11] The archbishop of Mainz, on the other hand, supported a new constitution that excluded the patricians, and in 1514 a much more radical council was able to secure the fall of a group of leading politicians.[12] The clergy and monastic institutions in the town were sucked into the turmoil, partly because they were major creditors and stood to lose financially if the town defaulted. During this unrelenting sequence of bloody infighting, most of the monasteries joined the town's elite in supporting the Saxon interest, as these years revealed the archbishop of Mainz at his most vicious. All this would have done little to enthuse

8. Erfurt in Hartmann Schedel's *Weltchronik* of 1493. The cathedral is the large building on the far left, with the steps leading up to it also visible; opposite is the Church of St Severus.

Luther about the civic unity and urban freedoms on which Germany's imperial cities prided themselves.[13]

Ultimately, Mainz lost in the Erfurt power struggle: by 1516, the old elite was back in power, with Saxon support. Even though Luther probably had little detailed knowledge of politics and, as far as we can tell, had no relationships with citizens outside the monastery walls, he cannot have been ignorant of what was taking place, or of the role of Mainz in fomenting disturbance.[14] In 1514, Albrecht, a Hohenzollern opposed to the Wettin Saxons, succeeded as archbishop, and it may be that the memory of the see's behaviour was one reason why Luther addressed the Ninety-Five Theses directly to him. Certainly, in the affair that ensued, some contemporaries traced Friedrich the Wise's support for Luther back to the quarrel over Erfurt.[15]

\*

Early biographies of Luther described his life as a monk as a period of drudgery. Johannes Mathesius, whose biography published in 1566 was one of the first full-length works, wrote of how he was forced to do menial tasks, even cleaning the latrines, and Luther himself remembered that he had to beg and clean the privies when he was already a master of theology.[16] These are of course partisan accounts, written to show his sufferings at the hands of the envious and cruel monks, and to account for his later hatred of monasticism. Even so, they may contain some truth. Like all novices, Luther had to undergo a period of transition into the new life and this involved doing domestic labour. This experience must have been a shock for a mine owner's favoured son, sent off to school and university from a home where servants and the mistress of the house would probably have done most of the domestic chores. Only after he had begun to lecture on the Psalms was he relieved of these duties, but the order's concern with the sin of pride suggests that making a former law student clean the latrines was designed to teach him humility. By the time he had been in the monastery for several years, however, others seem to have provided for his basic needs, while on the orders of his mentor Johann von Staupitz, a fellow monk even acted as secretary.[17]

The new life Luther had chosen involved strict discipline. The physical sign of his entry into the monastery was the tonsure, the removal of a circle of hair from the top of his head. It immediately set the monk apart from other men, even from other clergy. Luther had now vowed chastity, poverty and obedience, the opposite of the male conduct with which he had grown up in Mansfeld, where men were quick to avenge with their fists any insult to their honour, where the most powerful were those who amassed the most wealth, where independence of mind secured respect, and where having many children cemented family success. In the first year, the novice did not wear the full habit, but once fully professed, he was dressed in a cassock and cowl, tied with a cord. Whereas men of Luther's age and station would have worn a figure-hugging doublet and hose in gorgeous colours and soft fabrics, graduating to a looser outer garment or cloak in sober black as they aged, the monk's shapeless clothing hid the body. He had chosen strict observance and, as he later reminisced, this meant physical chastisement and wearing coarse wool which chafed the skin. He had to endure the bitter cold during services in winter, wearing the same thin cassock all year round, and undertake a taxing regimen of fasting. More than fifteen years of observance would leave a deep mark, and he believed it had damaged his health: 'if I hadn't done it, I would be healthier and stronger'.[18] As he also noted in later life, he found it difficult at first to dare to eat meat on Fridays, even though he firmly believed that fasting was bad for the health.[19]

Luther deliberately chose a life of extreme mental and bodily mortification, and he undertook it with great seriousness. The monastery day was divided into regular sections with prayers to be said throughout. Sleep was broken in the middle of the night when the monks woke to say matins; there were further 'hours' at six, nine, and midday, followed by nones, vespers and finally compline after the evening meal.[20] Mass was said daily. There was some flexibility, however: if a monk fell behind in his prayers, he could catch up with them later. Some even paid other monks to pray for them, but it was a practice Luther did not countenance. Instead, he began to save up the week's hours until Saturday, going without eating or sleeping and praying through the day and night to get them done. This schedule was not easy to reconcile with the concentration needed for academic work, something which Staupitz recognised later by freeing him from having to attend matins when he began to lecture in Wittenberg in 1508. Nonetheless, the severe asceticism took its toll: Luther was pushing his body to its absolute limits, losing weight and suffering periods of depression, so much so that he assumed he did not have long to live.

Why did his religiosity take such an ascetic form? A naturally spontaneous, impulsive person throughout his life, it seems that he deliberately chose a monastic environment to subordinate himself, and control his wishes and desires. By entering the monastery he had rebelled against his father and rejected the male identity and patriarchal power that was his to inherit. Instead he chose a religious life of learning but also of obedience that centred on physical mortification.

He referred to his own punctiliousness and his competitive streak – it seems that he wanted to win in the holiness stakes. There was also a sense of overwhelming guilt, but it is difficult to guess where this came from. It may have had something to do with being the favoured son, but this hardly accounts for the force of these feelings, and their all-consuming nature. Luther seems almost to have luxuriated in feelings of guilt, as if, by driving them to their extreme, he could experience a heightened devotional state of self-hatred that would bring him as close as possible to God.

There was a pervasive silence in the monastery, with no talking after the evening meal. Strict Augustinianism was an extreme version of late medieval piety that focused on repetition and control of external behaviour such as fasting. It sanctified pain and sensory deprivation, and the interrupted sleep could send the individual into a trance-like devotional state. Later, Luther was to speak with anger about the kind of seeming holiness that focused on externals, leaving consciences burdened, because it was impossible for the monks to fulfil every duty. All the monks, he recalled, thought 'that we were utterly holy, from head to toe', but in their hearts 'we were full of hatred, full of fear and full of unbelief'.[21] He remembered a proverb from his youth that ran 'If you like to remain alone, then your heart will remain pure', and he later recalled a hermit in Einsiedeln in Switzerland who would speak to nobody, for 'whoever has dealings with men, to him the angels cannot come'.[22] To the older Luther, this kind of aloofness was unnatural and dangerous, as those suffering from melancholy (as he did himself) should be encouraged to eat, drink, and above all socialise with others.

The later Luther is not necessarily the best interpreter of his younger self, especially since he rejected monasticism so vehemently. It is worth noting, however, that as he looked back on his life as a monk his views always focused on the same triad: in monasticism, he argued, consciences were burdened by endless religious duties; Christ was perceived as a judge; and Mary became an intercessor with Christ. Replacing Christ with Mary, in particular, distorted the true message of Christianity. As monks, Luther preached in 1523, 'We believed that Christ sat in heaven in judgement, not caring about us on earth, but that he would only give us life after death (even if we had done good deeds) if the Mother had reconciled him with us . . . Therefore I wish that the Ave Maria would be completely rooted out because of this abuse.'[23] Moreover the pictures of God sitting in judgement that decorated medieval churches 'painted how the Son fell before the Father and showed him his wounds, and St John and Mary prayed to Christ for us at the Last Judgement, and Mary pointed Jesus to her breasts, at which he had sucked'. Such images should be removed, 'because they made people imagine that they should fear our dear Saviour, as if he wanted to drive us away from him and as if he would punish our sin'.[24] His later anti-asceticism was closely linked with this passionate rejection of both Marianism and his own monkishness. 'When I was a papist, I was ashamed to utter Christ's name', he recalled; 'I thought: Jesus is a womanish name.'[25] To the later Luther, his youthful revolt against his father had been a retreat from manhood, into a matriarchal world populated with female religious figures and a false, perverted religiosity.

*

During his time as a monk, Luther was subject to what he termed *Anfechtungen*, which we might translate as temptations, or spiritual attacks like those Christ experienced in the wilderness, and which became a source of great fear and anxiety. As he later put it, 'Then I was the most miserable person on earth, day and night was pure howling and despair, that no one could steer.'[26] When he realised his confessor's incomprehension of his torment, he understood that he was undergoing something out of the ordinary, and became, as he put it, 'like a dead corpse'.[27] The anxiety expressed itself physically: he perspired copiously, and as he later remarked, the monks' false path to heaven was like a 'sweat, yes anxiety bath', in which he 'had bathed full well'. During a procession at Corpus Christi at Eisleben in 1515, he was suddenly struck with terror of the Eucharist and broke out in a sweat, thinking he would perish.[28] On this occasion it was Christ's presence in the monstrance which frightened him, just as the divine presence had caused a similar panic attack during his first Mass. Both events seem to be related to his father, who had attended that first Mass, while Eisleben, where Luther was born, would have reminded him of his upbringing and the mining world of his father.

It is difficult to know exactly what role the conflict with his father might have played in these struggles, but it does seem that his spiritual troubles stemmed from the relationship he was forging with a paternal God. All the crises cluster around the terror of being confronted directly with God the Father, who is also God the judge, without any intermediary; whereas the whole purpose of the monastic life as Luther experienced it was to create a security net where the intercessions of Mary, prayers said on one's behalf, and exercises to subdue the flesh all cushioned him against God's transcendent power. So if Luther's entry into the monastery was a retreat into a matriarchal world, that retreat was raising spiritual problems of its own.

Luther's *Anfechtungen* were physically overwhelming. They were not to do with sexual desire but concerned what Luther called 'the real knots' – his struggles with faith. So apparently untroubled was he by his sexuality that he unabashedly mentioned experiencing nocturnal emissions, which he simply dismissed as physical phenomena. For him, true 'concupiscence of the flesh' was not primarily lust but concerned bad feelings towards a brother, such as envy, anger or hate.[29] Luther worried at this time about his relations with others: living in a monastic community, where he had to get on with the same small group of people all the time, could not have been easy. It may well have reawakened in him feelings of jealousy and anxieties about the envy of others that sprang from childhood relations with his siblings. Whatever the reasons, it was not lusts of the flesh, but Luther's troubled relationship with God the Father that lay at the heart of his distress.

These temptations or tribulations would continue all his life and they are fundamental to understanding Luther's religiosity. For the first year in the monastery, he recalled, they did not trouble him; later he had a rest from them when he got married and had 'a good time', before they returned once more. During his time as a monk, the *Anfechtungen* seem to have chiefly concerned the idea that if he was a sinner, and if God was a judge, then God must hate him. The *Anfechtungen* were the corollary of his growing sense that there were no intermediaries, that nothing stood between the believer and God, and that nothing could be done to make the sinner acceptable. Looking back on these experiences in 1531 he concluded that the *Anfechtungen* were also necessary, for they set him on his path that would lead to the Reformation. He added a wry reminiscence about his superior Staupitz, who had remarked that he himself had never experienced temptations of this kind, 'but, as I see, they are more necessary to you than eating and drinking'.[30]

By the time Luther had left the monastery and broken with the Church of Rome, the *Anfechtungen* were more clearly centred on his battle with the Devil, though they still took physical form. He suffered from fits of ringing in the ears, sure that they were a diabolic attack. As he grew older, he confided to trusted companions about his temptations. Complaining in 1529 to a friend in Breslau that he had suffered headaches, nausea and a dull noise in his ears for eight days, he wondered 'whether it was exhaustion or a temptation of Satan'.[31] In 1530 he wrote to Melanchthon about a weakness in his head that stopped him from working: like Paul's suffering, the angel of Satan was 'beating him with his fists'.[32] At the same time he suggested that those suffering from melancholia should not only eat and drink more, but also joke and play games so as to spite the Devil.[33] We do not know how far the early *Anfechtungen* were the same as the attacks of depression and sadness he experienced later, nor whether at this early stage he thought that the Devil was involved; but it is clear that they concerned his relationship with God – and to that extent, Staupitz was quite right that they were essential to Luther's form of devotion.

\*

Every monastery is a living as well as a devotional community, involving practical organisation and labour within a clear system of hierarchy. Despite his apparent difficulties with paternal authority, this was an environment in which Luther thrived, rapidly moving up the monastic ladder. He quickly became a sub-deacon, and then a deacon; and in 1508–9 he was sent briefly to the University of Wittenberg, where he taught philosophy and continued studies in theology. Erfurt was a prosperous monastery, and it had many properties to administer. Luther learned how to ensure that debts were paid, annual dues delivered and the monastery provisioned. Listing his various duties in 1516 (by which time he had left Erfurt and was back in Wittenberg), he wrote, 'I am a preacher at the monastery, I am a reader during mealtimes, I am asked daily to preach in the city church, I have to supervise the study [of novices and friars], I am vicar (and that means I am eleven times prior), I am caretaker of the fish [pond] at Lietzkau, I represent the people of Herzberg at the court in Torgau, I lecture on Paul, and I am assembling [material for] a commentary on the Psalms.' But mostly, he complained, 'my time is filled with the job of letter writing' – so many that he often forgot what he had already written, asking his friend and fellow Augustinian Johannes Lang to tell him if he was repeating himself. All that – and then, he went on, 'there are my own struggles with the flesh, the world, and the Devil. See what a lazy man I am!'[34] Luther might gripe about the administrative burdens, but he clearly relished the intellectual work; and he was evidently good at managing people and organising, skills he may have picked up from his father. He could be firm, too. He admonished Lang to send a disobedient monk for punishment to the monastery at Sangerhausen and he ordered the prior in Mainz to send back a runaway.[35] All this administrative experience, especially his judgement of people, would stand him in good stead when he began to build his own church.

His talents began to be recognised from his early years within the Erfurt monastery and more widely in the order. In an attempt to end the long-running struggle over the future direction of the order, Staupitz tried to unite the Augustinians, but seven monasteries, including Erfurt, suspected that his attempts would dilute the values of the observants and therefore tried to secure an exemption. Despite Luther's close relationship with Staupitz, Erfurt chose Luther and his former teacher Johannes Nathin to put their case, first to the bishop of Magdeburg. The mission was unsuccessful, and so that same year the monastery decided to send a delegation, which included Luther, to appeal to the Pope.[36]

The visit to Rome was by far the longest journey he ever undertook, and his only trip outside German-speaking lands. It seems to have confirmed his sense that he was a 'German'. Throughout his later work, he unfailingly talks about Italians in negative terms, writing of the papal emissary Karl von Miltitz, for example, that as an 'Italian' he was fond of flowery prose, while deceiving him with his warmth and friendliness. The one place where he seems to have felt at home in Rome was the German church of Santa Maria delle Anime, where he thought that religious devotion was being properly carried out. In

1540 he gave a damning verdict: 'By miraculous advice I came to Rome, so that I saw the head of all wickedness and the seat of the Devil.'[37]

His initial excitement can be sensed from his recollection of arriving in the Eternal City: Luther flung himself on the ground, hailing the city hallowed by the blood of martyrs.[38] Rome in 1510 would have been a strange place, much of it a ghost town, with building having barely commenced on what would become the largest church in Christendom, St Peter's. Even the existing church, Luther later judged, was too big to preach in.[39] Rome's medieval population was only a fraction of what it would have been in Roman times. Luther mentioned the catacombs and the hills but, for someone formed by the classics, he made surprisingly little reference to the classical heritage. He would have seen, however, just what ancient Rome had accomplished – and how far the sixteenth century was from equalling it. Buildings like the Colosseum and other antique ruins lay unused, their stone being carted off for St Peter's. Years later Luther still remembered that the Colosseum could accommodate 200,000 spectators, but only its foundations and some of its crumbling walls had been visible.[40] He recalled the oppressive Italian nights and the resulting nightmares. Desperately thirsty, and knowing that the water was polluted, the monks were advised to eat pomegranates to cure their headaches, and by this fruit 'God saved our lives'.[41]

For the young Luther, a papal loyalist, Rome was a treasure trove of religious benefits. 'We ran to Rome . . .' he wrote in 1535, 'and the Pope gave indulgence for it, this is all forgotten now, but those who were stuck in it will not forget it.'[42] His month-long visit to the 'seat of the Devil' became the source for many later anecdotes over dinner. Two in particular stand out. Luther was astonished how fast the priests would say Mass, reciting six or seven Masses for payment before he had even got to the end of his first. One cleric shoved him out of the way, telling him to hurry up and 'send her son back home to Our Lady' – that is, to clear things up ready for the next Mass. To Luther, who worried endlessly about whether he had said the words with true feeling, the insouciance was profoundly shocking. They even joked about it over their supper, boasting how at the elevation they had said 'Bread you are and bread you will remain.' Luther later recalled their ridicule when the Real Presence of Christ in the sacrament became the keystone of his theology, important enough to split with the

followers of the leading Swiss theologian Huldrych Zwingli, who
denied the Real Presence. As he used the episode to illustrate the
abuses of the papal Mass, his listeners would have been aware of the
parallel.[43]

Luther's other memory concerned a visit to the Scala Sancta in
St John Lateran, the 'Pilate stairs' that Christ had mounted on his way
to his trial and which supposedly had been brought by St Helen from
Jerusalem. Here the pious believer had to climb the steps on his knees,
reciting an 'Our Father' on each step to gain remission from Purgatory.

9. and 10. Something of what Luther was trying to convey in the 1530s to a generation
that had grown up with the Reformation can be grasped from a pamphlet printed in
Nuremberg in 1515. It provided a handy tourist guide to the indulgences the devout
could obtain in the Eternal City, listed through the year with the precise numbers of
days' remission. The calculations are dizzying. A special symbol marks the days when
the pious pilgrim could get significant fractions of remittance from Purgatory, with 'p'
indicating full indulgence. For convenience, the guide supplies a list of all seven
pilgrimage churches and the remissions on offer, with a brief description of the highlights, such as the Jerusalem Chapel which women could enter only on one day every
year. The pamphlet also provides a haunting woodcut of Christ's face on the Veronica
cloth for meditation, and a final image of Christ on the Cross surrounded by a ring of
Hosts. Focused on salvation, it would have reflected the devotional state of mind of
Luther and many others as they approached Rome.

Luther, who wanted to save the soul of his paternal grandfather Heine Luder, mounted the steps but, overcome with tiredness, began to wonder whether the prayers would work. This was a story he repeated later in life in sermons as well as at table, its interpretation shifting with time. When his eleven-year-old son Paul heard it in 1544, it had become part of the story of how Luther had broken with Rome. As he now recalled, when he climbed the steps he suddenly remembered the phrase of the Old Testament prophet Habakkuk, repeated in Paul's Letter to the Romans, that 'the just shall live by faith alone', importing into the episode his later theological understanding.[44]

It is impossible to tell what Luther really thought at the time. He certainly did not see the city through the eyes of a reformer, but through those of a pious Augustinian monk. His determination to secure indulgences for his paternal grandfather suggests how much these meant to him. He even remembered wishing that his parents were already dead so that he could exploit this lifetime opportunity to gain indulgences for them. The rather pat theological message of his later reminiscences suggests that hindsight had blotted out everything he might then have found compelling.[45] Despite his critical memories, however, his Rome visit must have been deeply significant to him. He would not otherwise have linked it so closely to his key theological discoveries, or to his lifelong identity as being a 'German', hostile to all things Italian.

There are some things Luther does not mention. We do not know the identity of the man who went with him, nor do we hear about their companionship on the way. The negotiations with the papacy, the entire point of the journey, are also completely missing from the story. As a junior member of the order, Luther would not have been the chief negotiator – he knew nothing of how the Curia functioned, and such a serious mission would not have been entrusted to someone so inexperienced. It is possible, as Johannes Cochlaeus later stated, that the monk who Luther accompanied to Rome was Anton Kress, a patrician from Nuremberg, although it is more likely to have again been his former teacher Johannes Nathin. Nathin was highly experienced, having saved the Augustinian monastery at Tübingen in 1493 by reforming it in accordance with the wishes of the duke of Württemberg. He was a senior academic, a proven negotiator, and he would have had a sure grasp of how the Curia worked.

We do know, however, that the negotiations in Rome were a comprehensive failure. The two monks did not secure an exemption for the
Erfurt monastery which would have permitted them to continue their
observant practices, and they were instead ordered to obey the policy
of the vicar of the order, Staupitz. It seems likely that Luther soon
embraced Staupitz's view of the matter, rejecting Nathin's and the
Erfurt monastery's attempt to safeguard the traditions of the observants. All this must have put him in an uncomfortable position: he
had to represent a line which was designed to wreck his confessor's
long-standing plan for the order, a matter very close to Staupitz's
heart.

On the way back, the two Augustinians stopped at Augsburg, where,
Luther recalled, he was taken to meet the holy Anna 'Laminit', or
'leave me not'. The daughter of simple craftspeople, she was believed
to live miraculously without eating. This kind of religiosity – or what
modern writers have termed 'holy anorexia' – was a powerful streak
in late medieval devotion, encouraged by an extreme asceticism that
regarded bodily appetites as inimical to religious perfection. Female
saints in particular might fast to extremes and undergo mystical
experiences. In a church which was deeply distrustful of women,

11. Anna Laminit by Hans
Holbein, 1511. On the left,
the sketch is labelled
'lamanätly'; on the right,
in another sixteenth-
century hand, dz nit ist,
'who is not' – in other
words, who is a fraud.

asceticism offered them an avenue of expression and authority. Laminit reported visions of St Anna, her name saint and the saint to whom we know Luther himself was attached. Not only did she go without food, she was famed as passing neither water nor stools. She had drawn people since 1498, and her following included rich Augsburg patricians.

Luther shrewdly asked her whether she wanted to die, a question to which it would have been difficult to give a correct answer. As he remembered it, she replied, 'No! There I don't know how things work; here I do.' She was unmasked soon after by the duchess of Bavaria, who discovered her secret stash of luxury food, such as pepper-cakes and pears; it turned out that she emptied her stools out of the window. It was also rumoured that she had a child by a leading patrician and merchant. Laminit was consequently drummed out of town. For the later Luther, Laminit was a fraud, a 'whore' and schemer, but whether he saw through her or not at the time we cannot know. It may be that he, like others, was already beginning to have doubts about this extreme and exhibitionistic mortification of the flesh, a scepticism that would colour his later theology and that was fostered by his relationship with his confessor, Johann von Staupitz.[46]

*

At least fifteen years older than Luther, Staupitz was utterly different in background, well travelled, and at home amongst the nobility and at court.[47] A patrician who had grown up with Friedrich the Wise of Saxony, he was initially vicar general of the observant wing of the order, but would also become head of the conventuals in Saxony, those Augustinians who took a laxer line.[48] He and Luther probably met in April 1506 when Staupitz was in Erfurt; it would have been Staupitz who gave Luther formal permission to become a priest – monks were not automatically priests – deciding too that he should study theology.

Being Luther's confessor was a most demanding task. The young monk's relentless pursuit of perfection meant that he once confessed for six hours at a time, and Staupitz must have been at his wits' end. Staupitz had a relaxed attitude to sin – he once joked that he had given up making vows, for he was simply unable to keep them – but what worried Luther were not the usual sins but the 'real knots': his lack of love of God and his fear of judgement. On one occasion when confronted with Luther's over-scrupulous confessing, Staupitz told him: 'I don't understand you' – which, as Luther later remarked, was hardly comforting. Staupitz believed that temptations were good because they taught one theology. For his part, Luther believed Staupitz thought he was largely battling against the sin of pride, but his own later view was that the opposite was true: the *Anfechtungen* were the Devil's 'thorn in the flesh'; they were not warnings against arrogance. Like a good father, Staupitz consistently tried to calm Luther's fears, reminding the young monk that God loved him. He toned down his perfectionist streak and countered his vehemence and anger with a mild self-deprecation and a little teasing. He was probably just the kind of steady interlocutor Luther needed, but both men realised that Staupitz did not truly grasp his passionate religiosity.

Staupitz was also different from Luther in that he enjoyed the good things in life. His idea of the 'proper Christian man', described to friends at Nuremberg, was close to a self-portrait: 'he suits his mood and being each time with that which the circumstances of the time, place and people demand, for in the church he is pious, in counsel brave and wise, at table and with honourable people he is pleasant and happy'.[49] At home in courts and civic circles as well as in the world of the Augustinian order, Staupitz was constantly travelling, trying to sort out one problem or another. He knew all about patronage, and Luther and his other friends, like Wenzeslaus Linck, benefited enormously from this knowledge. Both owed their careers within the order to Staupitz who, like a cunning chess player, systematically placed 'his men' in key posts. He trained Luther up to replace him as professor at Wittenberg and Linck became vicar general of the order. But his protégés were not always grateful. Staupitz later said ruefully that 'when I raised somebody up to the highest they shat through their hands onto my head'.[50]

Staupitz made Luther study theology but, as an admirer of the late thirteenth-century philosopher Duns Scotus, it was probably he who made sure that the young monk also studied philosophy. Almost certainly at his behest as well, Luther spent a year at the new University of Wittenberg in 1508–9, which the older man had been instrumental in founding in 1502 and where he was a professor. As he was constantly on the road in the service of the order, however, Staupitz had little time to give lectures himself. Wanting Luther to become his successor at Wittenberg, he suggested that he study for a doctorate in theology. Decades later Luther recalled the conversation, describing to his own students how he and Staupitz sat under the pear tree in the courtyard of the monastery at Wittenberg (the tree was still there when he told the story). Luther said he did not want to become a doctor, as he believed that he would not live very long – a gloomy reference to his relentless mortification of the flesh. Staupitz, however, knew just how to puncture Luther's morbid grandiosity: God had need of clever people, whether on earth or in heaven, he replied.

Luther obeyed, and finished his doctoral studies in 1512, throwing a celebration to which he invited the entire monastery at Erfurt as well as guests from Wittenberg. Doctoral celebrations were major events with processions through the town followed by a banquet – one fabled celebration involved a hundred guests and thirty-five guilders spent on the food alone, with drinking and dancing afterwards attended by 'honourable' women. Luther's celebration would not have been in the same league, but the invitation to the Erfurt monks begins with the usual pieties, although it also opens with an unconventional excusing of his failure to make the customary statements about his unworthiness since this 'would make him seem to be taking pride in or seeking praise for his humility'. He continues that 'God knows, and my conscience also knows, how worthy and how suitable I am for this display of fame and honour', by which he meant that God and his conscience knew how *unworthy* and *unsuitable* he truly was. Of course the remark can also be read literally to express his pride in what he himself described as his occasion of 'pomp'.[51]

Staupitz had joked that getting a doctorate would give Luther work to do – a comment that was wonderfully ambiguous in German between 'will give you a real job to do' and 'will really cause you bother' – and he turned out to be right.[52] The 'real bother' was that several Erfurt Augustinians had been offended that he had pursued his studies at Wittenberg, and not Erfurt, where he had first matriculated. They tried to get the doctorate declared void and have him fined, on the grounds that he had broken the oath taken when he became a student at Erfurt that he would follow no other university. Luther replied that he had not actually sworn such an oath – it had been overlooked – but the damage had been done. What should have been a joyous occasion was marred by the envious attacks of men who had once been his teachers. Luther was particularly irritated by the fact that the assault was headed by Johannes Nathin, the man who had probably been his companion to Rome; this bitter betrayal may be another reason why his memories of Rome became so dark. Two years after the doctoral celebration, he was still complaining about his treatment, and objected in a letter to the Erfurt monastery to a new missive from Nathin, composed 'as if in the name of you all', that accused him of being a shameful perjurer. Luther insisted that he was neither a perjurer nor oath-breaker, and had good reason to be angry at the attack. But just as he had received undeserved blessings from the Lord, so now he wanted to set aside the bitterness his opponents deserved and accord them cordiality.[53]

The incident was deeply wounding, but may have had more to do with the politics of the order than the location of Luther's studies. He had undertaken the doctorate because of Staupitz, whose more conciliatory line within the Augustinians Nathin had opposed. He may have seen Luther as a turncoat, which would explain the depths of resentment and the refusal to come to the celebration.[54] Luther had been caught up in a fight over different visions of the order's future.

Luther would have spent time with his confessor both in Erfurt and Wittenberg; they would also have met on their travels across the region. Luther claimed 'I got everything from Staupitz'[55] and, after his death, he recalled his former mentor as a good and comforting presence. In 1518, in the letter he sent with his explanations of the Ninety-Five Theses to Staupitz, he reminded him of a conversation about 'true repentance' which had pierced him like an arrow, in which the older man had said that it must begin 'with the love of God and righteousness'. Indeed, in a letter to Elector Johann Friedrich in 1545, he wrote of his debt to his confessor, saying that he must praise him 'if I don't want to be a damned, ungrateful papist ass', because he was 'my father in this teaching who gave birth to me in Christ'.[56] Yet rather like his relationship with Johannes Braun in Eisenach which also grew cold, Luther seems often to have projected qualities onto Staupitz that were not actually there, and while he later recalled Staupitz's sayings in his table talk and writings, he often repeated the same remarks, as if his image of Staupitz had become ossified.

Like Braun before him, Staupitz was another paternal figure whom Luther outgrew. In both theology and temperaments the two men were fundamentally different. Luther came to insist on the primacy of Scripture as the source of all authority. Although Staupitz draws, like Luther, on Paul, he did not make such a radical claim and repeatedly cited St Augustine and other Church Fathers.[57] Like Luther, he emphasised the sinful nature of human beings and argued that our works can never earn us salvation; he too criticised indulgences. But he did not have much to say about faith as a gift from God: his emphasis is more on the sinfulness of human beings than it is on God's gift of grace or on the Bible. He focused on the emotional disposition of the believer, who has to be encouraged to leave attachments to this world behind. Luther, although highly attuned to his own religious emotions, did not believe that attaining a particular emotional state was spiritually important.

Staupitz liked to talk about the 'sweetness' of God, the 'sweet Saviour', the 'sweet bliss-maker', the 'sweet word' and the 'continuous sweetness' of the mystical union of the soul with Christ.[58] This had its darker side. A brilliant preacher, his sermons were also laced with the anti-Semitism which was common currency at the time, and which Luther could also share, exploiting feeling against the Jews as persecutors to intensify emotional identification with Christ and Mary. So Staupitz describes Jews as 'dogs', who 'spat at him [Christ] with all the filth that they could muster', and believed that 'the Jews sinned much more seriously than Pilate' in killing Jesus because they did it out of 'envy'.[59] 'All the world testifies to the envy of the Jews', Staupitz wrote. 'O you evil Jew! Pilate shows you that your nature is harsher than a pig, for it has mercy with its own kind.'[60]

Staupitz's German writing, different in literary quality from Luther's, draws on a long medieval tradition of devotional works written for laypeople by Meister Eckhart, Johannes Tauler and the so-called 'German Theology'. It often uses repetition to inculcate a state of meditative calm, and visual metaphors in order to grasp a spiritual truth. In Staupitz's hands language is less an intellectual vehicle than a form of meditation, a means to mystical contemplation and dissolution of individuality. Luther never wrote in this manner. Once he had finally rejected the obligation to pray his 'hours', he also opposed what he described as 'mummery' – the simple and repeated mouthing of prayers.

The differences between the two men are most pronounced in their attitude to the flesh.[61] Following preachers such as St Augustine, St Bernard of Clairvaux and the German mystics Johannes Tauler, Meister Eckhart and Heinrich Suso, Staupitz used the metaphor of sexual union to convey the idea of the mystical union of the believer with Christ. These writers aimed at the dissolution of the self within the divine, and at a powerful inward-looking style of devotion; such mysticism was taken up by monks and nuns across German lands as well as by laypeople. Staupitz could therefore write in an explicit manner of the revelation of Christ, the eternal bridegroom, 'now with kisses, now with embraces, now with advancing of the naked to the naked' – but all chastely revealed.[62] He wrote of different 'stages' of union of the soul, the first being that of 'young maids in faith', the second that of the 'concubine', the third, the 'queens': 'They are naked and copulate with the naked one. They taste that outside Christ there is nothing sweet and they enjoy [his] continuous sweetness. For the naked Christ cannot deny himself to these naked', whilst in the fourth stage, which Mary alone experienced, Jesus 'sleeps naked with her naked and he shows other signs of such love'. Highly sensual language is also applied to Christ's suffering – the naked Christ is the suffering Christ, and Staupitz had referred in his earlier sermons at Salzburg to Christ's 'little bed of enjoyment' (lustpetel), by which he meant the Cross.[63]

These Salzburg sermons, preached to the townspeople, were transcribed by the Benedictine nuns of St Peter's convent next door to the church, and one wonders what they made of this fairly explicit eroticism. Staupitz defended himself against the objection that human love cannot be a model for divine love because it springs from concupiscence, by arguing (in line with tradition) that what matters is not 'the contact of bodies but . . . the perversion of the [natural] order, that is when temporal enjoyment is given preference to eternal ones'.[64] But this hardly obliterated the powerful sexual charge of his language. Erotic mysticism was not unusual in the late Middle Ages, dwelling on sweetness, pleasure, melting and union, but in Staupitz's hands it has a saccharine literalness that exploited its potential for eroticising suffering.[65]

Eroticism of this variety, characterised by displaced desire, can readily be twinned with suspicion of the other sex. Some of Staupitz's most evocative and yet harshest writing is about the love of women, which is inborn in us through the love of our mothers, and through the fact that Eve is made from Adam's rib. 'We suck it from our mothers, yes we draw it from the maternal hearts hidden in the body', Staupitz wrote. At the same time he warns that for the sake of women 'we leave honour, body and good virtue and reason, and are captured in their love, becoming stupid and losing reason'.[66] His 1504 preface to the revised statutes for the united Augustinian order states that:

> Even if your eyes fall on some woman, let them rest on none . . . For women's desire . . . seeks . . . not with silent feelings alone, but with feelings and glances too. And do not say that you are keeping your minds chaste if you have unchaste eyes: the unchaste eye is the messenger of an unchaste heart. And when unchaste hearts announce themselves in turn with mutual glances, even if the tongue is silent, and if, following desire, the flesh of each is delighted by ardour, even if the bodies are untouched by unclean violation, chastity herself flees from their morals.[67]

The monks should only go to the baths in groups of two or three; they should only wash their clothes when the provost thought fit, 'lest excessive appetite for clean clothing should bring with it internal squalor of the mind'. An almost allergic reaction towards women – although he dedicated both his German treatises to female followers[68] – accompanies Staupitz's passionate love of the Virgin, who pleads our case with God. Luther, in contrast, came to reject both attitudes, scorning adulation for Mary on the grounds that there can be no mediator between God and man, and also rejecting the idea that sexual renunciation was necessary for holiness.

*

In this context, Luther's sermon in May 1515 to the Augustinian chapter meeting at Gotha is illustrative not only of some of the emotional underpinnings of his later theological development, but also of both his dependence on, and difference from, his father-confessor. The sermon was organised by Staupitz, and again had more than a little to do with the complex internal politics of the order; as a result of it, Luther won the position of district vicar overseeing monasteries in the region, the most senior position he had held in the order up to that time.[69]

The sermon dwelt on envy, and was delivered at a time when Staupitz was experiencing some of his greatest difficulties in trying to unite the order; indeed he shortly afterwards gave up the attempt altogether. It may therefore have reflected particular tensions within the Augustinians and direct attacks on the vicar general. In addition, the debacle over Luther's doctoral celebrations – and Nathin's role in this episode – would have given Luther good reason to think about the subject as well.

Yet while its origins had a practical purpose, the sermon hardly reads like a response to a particular incident, still less a tactical sally in a dispute within the order.[70] It shows Luther backing up his superior, but also signals how the two men differed. It employs a style which is almost a mirror version of Staupitz's own devotional approach, for, like Staupitz he uses sensually overwhelming allegories in quick succession, but whereas the older man deploys this technique to create a sense of meditative reflection on God's love, Luther exploits it to propel his hearer into an unbearable world of existential disgust and abandonment. The sermon takes us closer than any other testimony to the religious despair and overwhelming sinfulness that Luther felt as a monk.

To make his point about envy, Luther compares the backbiter to a murderer and to a debaucher, using language that goes far beyond the biblical text to make the hearer experience revulsion. Just as the Word of God is holy seed, which conceives in the spirit purely and without violation, so by contrast the word of the backbiter is the adulterous and spurious seed of the Devil, corrupting the listener's soul; indeed, the very name of the Devil is backbiter.[71] Backbiters are 'poisoners' and 'witches', Luther says, who 'bewitch' and 'subvert' the ears of their listeners.[72] Just as witches can impede the sexual act and prevent conception, so the backbiter can destroy a community by poisoning relations between individuals, and he who was once loved and 'embraced' is rejected. To be in good odour is to have a good reputation, which is born from without; to be in bad odour is to have a bad name, which comes from the ordure within. The backbiter does not allow the ordure of others to remain hidden but loves 'to roll in it' like a pig. He is like the bird who hops about in muck so that people say, 'Look how he has shit himself', to which the best response is: 'eat it yourself'.[73] In the most lurid of all the comparisons, Luther describes how backbiters are like hyenas or dogs who dig up stinking human corpses, pullulating with decay and full of worms, and bite into them – 'Ugh, what a dreadful monster the backbiter is!'[74]

We are all sinners, Luther argues, and should be preoccupied with our own excrement. Those who rejoice in the sins of others are avoiding their own sin, and they destroy not only the person of whom they speak ill but also those who are polluted by their poison. 'If we do not consider our sin,' Luther warned, 'but see only the cover and veil of our external dealings, hiding our true inward self from others, then we become dirty with the excrement of others.'[75] Hatred, envy and speaking ill of others clearly troubled Luther deeply – for they are among the 'real knots'. It was not accidental that he drew on the language of demonology here, for the ultimate envier was the witch, who whips up storms, blasts the crops, destroys fertility, digs up dead and rotting bodies, and destroys prosperity and life.

But the emotional pitch suggests that Luther too struggled with backbiting: quick to impute envy to others, Luther wrestled with his own feelings of envy, hate and aggression which he could all too readily turn against others, and which he therefore saw as the greatest obstacle to recognising God. It may be that this led to the sensations of utter unworthiness and anxiety that characterised his religiosity. It was Luther's own internal 'shit' – his sinful nature – that created the barrier between himself and God.

Although Luther does not say so here, the remedy for sin is confession, as our failings are named and confessed before God. In this respect, this highly emotive sermon is a testament to the relationship with his own father-confessor, Staupitz. The sermon is also a psychological document at a more profound level. By stopping just short of the point where the listener might have been comforted by the idea of confession, Luther leaves his audience, as it were, 'in the shit', having evoked in his hearers the kind of unbearable revulsion that was his own spiritual staple. It is almost the exact opposite of Staupitz's devotional style. The Gotha sermon takes us closer than any other testimony to the religious despair and overwhelming sinfulness that Luther felt as a monk. And it was at this point that he had begun to study Paul's Letter to the Romans, an intellectual and devotional exercise that would transform his spirituality.

# 4

# *Wittenberg*

In 1511, probably under Staupitz's orders, Luther had returned to the small town of Wittenberg in Saxony where he had spent a year of study in 1508–9, this time for good. Wittenberg would become the stage for Luther's Reformation, which in turn transformed the town's economy and social structure. An obscure university in an unknown corner of the empire became an institution of international renown to which students flocked in droves; and an insignificant town became a leading publishing centre. But it was the university's provincialism that created the kind of small community in which a man like Luther could flourish, where he could develop his ideas unhindered, outside the restrictions of an older, more established institution.

When Luther arrived in Wittenberg, the town was a building site. The castle and church were being extended and remodelled, the new university buildings were under construction, and ambitious plans for a town hall had been set in motion – a monster five-storey Renaissance edifice that would not be completed until 1535.[1] It was not just civic buildings that were rising out of the Wittenberg plain. The scholars and officials whom the Saxon ruler attracted to Wittenberg needed to be housed, not to mention the craftspeople who provided for them and the associated trades that a university required, such as printers and bookbinders. Town regulations used a mixture of stick and carrot to encourage construction, ordering that anyone who bought a plot of land had to build on it within a year, but giving them full tax relief for the time in which construction took place. The new houses, although they could not rival the palaces of patrician merchants in Augsburg or Nuremberg, were aspirational: they sported sandstone window frames, elegant doorways, and Renaissance motifs, and their imposing frontages along the street hid elegant courtyards within.[2]

12. Map of Wittenberg, 1623. The Elector's castle is at the bottom left of the triangle;
the Augustinian monastery at the right, at the other end of the street, by the wall.
The city was surrounded by a moat, and the fortifications had been extended since
Luther's day; he had complained about the works to improve the wall.

Like most Saxon towns, Wittenberg was built around the intersec-
tion of two major streets. Luther's friend Friedrich Myconius, who
arrived in the 1520s from the silver-mining town of Annaberg, mocked
the low wooden houses that looked more like village huts than town
residences.[3] One end of the town was dominated by the Elector's
castle, the opposite end by the Augustinian monastery and the university. There were no more than nine streets in all, and once you stepped
off the two main thoroughfares, the houses were far less imposing
and the streets narrow. There were three main gates, leading out onto
the main trade routes and the river port, with the River Elbe the major
artery for transporting heavy building materials.[4]

Wittenberg was also a fortress town. Through the sixteenth century,
the rulers of Saxony constantly extended and improved its fortifications, adding to them substantially in the 1540s – much to Luther's
annoyance when the defensive structures encroached on the former

monastery in which he lived with his family. Like other Saxon towns of this period, Wittenberg had been a colonial foundation, founded in Slavic territory as Germans migrated eastwards to seek new land in the late tenth century: the town had been designed to suppress the area's indigenous population. German splendour and cultivation masked the town's brutal past, and the new building work covered over any remaining traces of earlier habitation. The Wends, a Slavic people, were only allowed to live in the suburbs and could not become citizens; only those who spoke German and had four German grand-parents were given citizenship.[5] There were still Wends villages not far from Wittenberg, and Slavic influences lived on in the names of settlements. Luther thought the Slavs to be 'the worst nation of all', their towns and villages full of devils. He shared the colonisers' fear of those they had dispossessed. If it had not been for the pious Elec-tors, he said in 1540, 'the university couldn't have lasted a year thanks to the Wends; they would starve us out'.[6]

The other minority which had been expunged from Wittenberg were the Jews. Myths of the 'blood libel' were still current at the time, especially in southern Germany, where Jewish communities were regularly accused of kidnapping Christian children and killing them for their blood to use in religious ceremonies. In Wittenberg, anti-Semitism had a different colouring. The main parish church was situ-ated just behind the town hall, and it was here that the town's prominent citizens were buried. High up on the outside of the building, there is a stone sculpture of a 'Jewish sow' dating probably from the 1280s. It shows a large sow with dangling teats, which are suckled by two Jews, recognisable in their distinctive hats and with the yellow circles on their garments which they, like prostitutes, were forced to wear. Another grips a piglet by the ears and tries to ride it, while a fourth large Jew has his head close to the sow's backside. The sculp-ture suggests that the Jews are not only pigs themselves but that they look into the pig's anus. The statue is supposed to ward them off, placing the Jews like demons and gargoyles on the church's external face.[7]

The Jews had been expelled from Wittenberg in 1304, but the exist-ence of a 'Jews street' in the centre of the town – as in so many other German towns – testifies to their former presence.[8] Indeed, one of the four quarters into which the town was divided for military and

13. The Jewish sow on the outside of the Wittenberg parish church.

taxation purposes was still called the 'Jews' quarter' in Luther's time. Jews populated many of the villages in the surrounding countryside. When Luther travelled the route to Eisleben from Wittenberg in the last months of his life, he was terrified by passing through villages with 'scores' of Jewish inhabitants, writing to his wife that he feared their breath had made him ill.[9] Like many other towns where pogroms had taken place in the fourteenth and fifteenth centuries, the expulsion of the Jews was linked to a powerful revival in devotion to Mary, whom Christians believed Jews dishonoured: the parish church at Wittenberg was dedicated to her.[10]

The wealth of the silver mines in the Erzgebirge, part of Friedrich's territory, made all this new building in Wittenberg possible. Friedrich was an Elector, one of the seven princes of the empire who were entitled to choose the emperor, and therefore an important player in imperial politics. Compared to the rich merchant cities of southern Germany like Nuremberg or Ulm, which benefited from trade with Italy, electoral Saxony was backward: it had mining wealth but it lacked fashion and taste. Friedrich was determined to acquire these attributes, and moreover was in competition with his cousin Georg who had inherited the other half of Saxony, including Leipzig with its university. A shrewd ruler, Friedrich knew how to exploit his assets. He founded the university in Wittenberg on the cheap, cleverly transforming the town's Augustinian monastery into an arm of the new institution, using its staff as core lecturers, while also adding the talent from the Franciscan monastery. Everybody and everything did double duty. The new Castle Church also functioned as the university meeting hall; the main university building, the 'Leucorea', or white mountain – a literal Greek translation of the town's name – was constructed close to the Augustinian monastery.[11] The whole enterprise was funded out of the foundation of All Saints, which had grown rich on the money made from pilgrims who came to view Friedrich's astonishing collection of relics. These funds were topped up with money from the Elector's own treasury, yet the university's finances were still stretched and Wittenberg found it difficult to compete with the academic salaries offered by Tübingen, Leipzig or Cologne. Periodically, rival universities would attempt to poach the leading professors: more than once Luther would have to wring more money or better conditions out of the Elector to help keep Melanchthon, the new professor of Greek, who became Luther's right-hand man.

It is a strange irony that Luther's academic work was initially made possible by the trade in relics. He was acutely aware of this tension. Because viewing each relic gave the pilgrim a certain number of days off Purgatory, Friedrich's collection offered straightforward competition to papal indulgences. Its highlights were a monstrance containing a thorn from Christ's crown and the entire corpse of one of the Holy Innocents, the young male children executed by Herod.[12] With 117 reliquaries and 19,013 fragments of saints' bones, by 1520 Friedrich's relics collection rivalled that of Albrecht of Mainz.[13] Friedrich refused to permit indulgences to be sold in his territory partly because he feared that the Wittenberg pilgrimage trade might be endangered if indulgences were preached in other churches in Saxony.

The money the pilgrims brought was not the only reason why Friedrich was so keen to acquire ever more relics, however.[14] Piling them up was a way of making Saxony a holy place, so that its people did not have to travel to Rome but could gain grace on home soil. Relics thus inculcated local patriotism, and the more, the better: this kind of religiosity had its own in-built expansionist dynamic.[15] Popular piety could also be put to good use for the dynasty. Those who knelt before the reliquary shrine containing the holy thorn and prayed for the souls of Friedrich, his brother Duke Johann and their ancestors – as

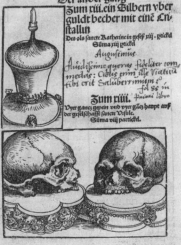

14., 15. and 16. Illustrations by Lucas Cranach from a book advertising Wittenberg castle church and its treasures. The etching shows Elector Friedrich and his brother, Duke Johann; the woodcut depicts the castle church. Each relic was illustrated and the lower picture shows St Catherine's oil and two whole heads of St Ursula's Virgins.

well as those who contributed to the rebuilding of Friedrich's church or remembered it in their wills – gained a hundred days of indulgence.[16] It was good business. In 1490, Friedrich and Johann had even secured a papal 'butter letter', which allowed Saxons to eat dairy products in Lent if they paid an annual sum to their rulers; the money was then used to pay for building a new stone bridge over the Elbe.[17]

Relics were also designed to overwhelm the viewer with the beauty and ingenuity of the reliquary that housed them. These were made of the most costly metals, gold and silver, and studded with gleaming jewels. They were intimidating statements of a ruler's access to treasure – and grace – and unlike the later collections of princely precious objects, they were periodically displayed for all the prince's subjects, not kept in a private curiosity cabinet. Friedrich ordered his court artist Lucas Cranach the Elder to produce a printed and fully illustrated catalogue of his treasures, a work of art in itself, which appeared in 1509. Albrecht of Mainz copied it two years later, going one better by having the title page graced with a portrait of himself by Germany's premier artist, Albrecht Dürer.[18]

The relics were shown in the Castle Church, and Friedrich commissioned leading artists to provide its altarpieces. Unlike patrons of later periods, he used mainly German artists, not Italian or Dutch painters, which added to the sense that this was a distinctively local, patriotic style, with its own heartfelt devotional simplicity, unlike the rich and beautiful Italian religious art of the period. With its nine works by Dürer, Cranach, and Matthias Grünewald, the church's collection of altars rivalled any other of the time for artistic quality. Just half a century later, when electoral Saxony was defeated, the collection would be broken up, so it is impossible now for the visitor to the church, remodelled extensively in the nineteenth century, to get a sense of what it looked like in Luther's day. As a devotional space it must have been electrifying. But it was also the final flowering of a style of painting that would be destroyed by the Reformation itself, its spiritual function lost.

The magnificence of the church was all the more remarkable because it dominated a town with just 2,000–2,500 inhabitants.[19] Politically, Wittenberg was a settlement of new men, which lacked a patriciate and had fairly rudimentary systems of government. All contracts – whether deeds of sale, property divisions, wills, testaments or marriage licences – were registered before the civic court, the judge's record serving as the repository for all legal deeds. This system made notaries dispensable, but it could work only as long as there was not enough business to overwhelm the court. For the most part, the old-town elite lacked university degrees or legal training, while the incomers were literate in Latin and skilled in the new learning. Printers like Johann Rhau-Grunenberg soon set up shop right by the monastery and near the new Leucorea. Next door to the university building a perfume shop opened, testifying to the refined tastes of the town's growing population.[20]

The town council itself was unlike the proud gatherings of citizens in the imperial cities of southern Germany. These cities, subject directly to the emperor, could make their own laws. They could judge their citizens, condemn them to death and execute them without appeal; and their councillors, dressed in their elegant black, could attend Imperial Diets, participate in imperial politics and even devise their own foreign policies. *Stadtluft macht frei* – city air makes you free – ran the adage. Even though they were in practice often ruled by small oligarchies of patricians and merchants, the myth of civic participation remained powerful. Their city councils comprised several hundred citizens, and each year a mutual oath-swearing would be held, as the council pledged to uphold the good of the citizenry. In Wittenberg, by contrast, even though the town had sovereignty in its application of criminal justice, almost nothing could happen without the Elector's agreement. The council minutes from the early sixteenth century make depressing reading. Discussions would be held and suggestions made to the Elector, who would then either agree or disagree; in each case, his word was final. Ultimate power was vested in the princely ruler, and closeness to the Elector, not membership of the council, was what gave an individual political influence.

Luther would have been familiar with this arrangement, for it was what he had grown up with in Mansfeld. He naturally expected power to descend from above, not legitimacy to be conferred from below. This helps explain why his Reformation would be so different from that which would emerge in the south, and why his theology of power appears so reactionary. He simply had no experience of the more democratic values of southern German communes – and in Erfurt he had witnessed political chaos, as the warring factions of the citizenry tore each other apart: there could hardly have been a better demonstration of the damage factionalism could do. As conservative as Luther's politics might have been, they were also in tune with the newly emerging political realities of the time; for it was the large territories of the princes that became the mainstays of the Reformation, while the civic communes of southern Germany were entering the twilight of their power.

*

Lucas Cranach the Elder was one of the incomers to Wittenberg. He arrived in 1505, shortly before Luther, and, as painter to the Elector, established a studio in the castle. His portraits of Luther – at first young, thin and intense, and later, large, four-square and authoritative – would shape the reformer's public image, and the partnership between the two men would be immensely important for the Reformation. In 1512 Cranach purchased two adjacent houses on the market square which he rebuilt to include a studio big enough to create large panels, transforming the number, size and ambition of works he could produce. Then, in 1518, he acquired the Cranachhof, a complex of buildings which included a four-storey house and six outbuildings to create an inner courtyard, and with plenty of windows. His residence on the main square was one of the grandest houses in town, a massive building with an elegant Renaissance facade and room for stores and workshops, capable of hosting important visitors such as the exiled king of Denmark or the ruler of Brandenburg.

Cranach, known as 'the fast painter', had an eye for business. Since there was no other painter in town, and no one who could supply the pigments, bristles, oils and panels he needed and which would have been so easy to obtain in Nuremberg or Augsburg, he had to import everything. He made a virtue of necessity. Since his cargoes left plentiful room on the wagons, he set up a business importing fine wines and pharmaceutical goods. Cranach even acquired a monopoly on the import and sale of such items – a concession the town council later had cause to regret, for they complained that the painter, who by 1528 had become the richest man in town, was exploiting his stranglehold on medicaments to palm off poor-quality drugs on the townsfolk.[21]

Cranach's move into commerce not only speaks volumes about his business sense but also tells us what kind of place Wittenberg was at the time. It reveals how meagre the town's business elite was up to then, and how little appetite there had been for the systematic import of luxury items. Cranach's warehouses would become treasure troves, containing cloth and all kinds of materials; Luther rummaged amongst them to see what goods had arrived from the Leipzig fairs, and he no doubt would have sampled the fine Rhine wines which Cranach also imported.

Luther's new life barely resembled his previous time in Erfurt. Apparently uncomfortable until he had acquired position and authority, the doctorate he was awarded in October 1512 gave the twenty-eight-year-old a public persona. Whereas in Erfurt he seems to have known virtually none of the citizens, in Wittenberg he quickly became acquainted with the small circle of intellectuals, printers and artists in this town rising from the mud. His friendship with Cranach, who was one of the first 'new men' to penetrate the council in Wittenberg, brought him into contact with the town's old elite, such as the mayor Hans Krapp, who died in 1515 and whose daughter Melanchthon later married. The goldsmith Christian Döring, who worked with Cranach, became another friend.[22]

Luther now also enjoyed a more senior place within the Augustinian order. As district vicar, a post to which he was elected for three years after the Gotha sermon in 1515, he was in charge of eleven monasteries. He proved a determined manager. It seems that Luther had inherited his father's head for business, and he was tenacious in defending the Wittenberg monastery's income, insisting on scrupulous financial record-keeping. Much of his work, however, concerned personnel matters, promoting people within the order and transferring them from one monastery to another. He unceremoniously sacked the prior at Neustadt an der Orla, telling the monastery that 'the whole or prime cause of [the monastery's] disturbance is the discord with your head and prior, and this is more harmful than when a single brother is in discord with another. Therefore, I command . . . you Brother Michael Dressel to resign the office and its seal.'[23] He certainly did not forget his friends. One of his first acts after he became district vicar in 1515 was to appoint his old companion and fellow monk Johannes Lang to be prior at Erfurt.[24] A humanist and close friend of Luther, Lang had followed him from Erfurt to Wittenberg in 1511. Sending him back not only helped a friend, it also stamped Luther's authority on his former community, a mere two years after the bitter correspondence about the doctorate. Lang was about Luther's age, and his appointment at barely thirty marked the arrival of the new generation of 'Staupitz's boys'. Luther was aware that Lang's task would not be easy – he knew there would be 'grumblings amongst the brothers' – and he advised him to keep a budget, noting down all income and expenditure, so that he could work out 'whether the convent is more of a monastery than a tavern or inn' – a strategy not likely to smooth his friend's path.[25] Meanwhile Wenzeslaus Linck, another of Staupitz's protégés, had been made prior of the monastery at Wittenberg: he would become one of Luther's lifelong friends.

A new circle of friends beyond as well as inside the Augustinian order solidified around him. Georg Spalatin – secretary, librarian and later confessor to Friedrich the Wise – was one of the most important, as he made the Reformation possible by securing the Saxon ruler's protection. In the years up to 1525 he became Luther's most frequent correspondent, and the interlocutor to whom he revealed his daily preoccupations and deepest anxieties. Their friendship began by the circuitous route common amongst humanist circles: Spalatin knew Johannes Lang, and had him secure an introduction to Luther. As the Elector's librarian, Spalatin was responsible for the university library and also advised on university policy, so the two men had to work together.[26]

Spalatin had unlimited access to the Elector and all correspondence ran through him: he had Latin, whereas the Elector was truly comfortable only in German.[27] This was an era in which individuals were much more important than the formal offices they held and in which politics was intensely personal, so those who had access to a ruler wielded enormous power themselves. Not only did Spalatin give Luther an opening to Friedrich and his court, he also introduced him to a circle of Nuremberg humanists, which provided essential support in the early years of the Reformation. Although Staupitz had long had a group of admirers in Nuremberg, it was Spalatin who introduced Luther to Christoph Scheurl, the powerful civic secretary of the city and a brilliant legal mind, who had also spent time at Wittenberg's

law faculty. This connection to the wealthy south of Germany took
Luther for the first time out of the narrow horizons of a world
bounded by Erfurt, Mansfeld and Wittenberg. He later acknowledged
how much he owed his cultured Nuremberg friends, who became
some of his most important supporters.

★

There was much to be accomplished at the new University of
Wittenberg. The buildings still had to be completed, its courses of
study firmly established, staff hired and students attracted.[28] And
although it was a new foundation, Wittenberg swiftly invented its own
traditions, which Luther would come to cherish. Shortly after it was
established, the university found its own publicist, Andreas Meinhardi,
whose Latin dialogue in its praise was published in 1508. Though this
work did not win him the academic post he craved, it secured him a

17. Portrait of Christoph Scheurl by Lucas Cranach the Elder.

position as civic secretary to the town council, a post he held until his death. Meinhardi described the rituals through which new students were admitted, and they were probably not unlike initiation rituals elsewhere in Germany. The initiate would be surrounded by a troupe of old hands, his face would be blacked with soot and dirt, his beard (if he had one) would be tugged, pig's bristles would be wiped across his face, he would be anointed with 'what people leave behind hedges', and he would be 'baptised' with wine. The so-called 'Beanus' would have to host a celebratory meal for the professors while bound with chains and ritually humiliated. His hair would be washed with 'horse eggs', horns would be placed on his head and his teeth filed; his learning would be mocked, and he would be teased first about girls and then quizzed about the quality and extent of his anus. It is hard to imagine a more complete humiliation, or a more searing introduction to academic hierarchy, as those who had experienced it would later inflict it on someone else.[29]

The university was to be part of the new learning, but although several famous humanists and scholars visited and gave lectures, in the first few years none stayed long. In fact, the university was scholastic in orientation and its first rector, Martin Pollich von Mellerstadt, was an old conservative who adhered to the *via antiqua* and resisted any departure from the teachings of Aristotle and Duns Scotus. Against Mellerstadt's influence, Staupitz and others strove to introduce the *via moderna*, but the humanist ideas that were exciting so many in Europe at this time were not on their agenda. Theology held pride of place in the university, and many of its professors – including Mellerstadt himself – had moved from other disciplines into what was regarded as the queen of the sciences to make it the university's intellectual powerhouse. Within the theological faculty, Andreas Karlstadt was a follower of Thomas Aquinas. Johannes Lang lectured on moral philosophy. Lang had mixed in humanist circles at Erfurt and learned Greek and Hebrew so he could read the Bible in the original languages; Luther had studied Hebrew with him. An immensely productive friendship, Luther may well have picked up humanist ideas through Lang, and together they brought the new biblical humanism, critical of scholasticism and determined to return to the original texts, to university teaching.[30] Yet this was not a friendship of equals. Although Luther was probably only four years older, the younger man's admiration for

18., 19. and 20. Three woodcuts from
1578 illustrate the rituals involved at
Wittenberg, showing the blackened
faces and horned fools' caps of the
initiates. The ceremonial tools – gilded
saw, pliers, axe, brush, bell and the
like – have survived from the University
of Leipzig. The rituals, which also
involved a mock confession, are clearly
parodies of religious ceremonies, yet
Luther supported their retention. Just
as Staupitz joked that Luther needed
the Devil, so Luther never frowned
upon a ritual which captured
something of the state of utter sinfulness of the Christian – and in this case,
the university initiate.

him was evident from the beginning, and Luther did not mince his
words when, in 1517, sending him the Ninety-Five Theses, he felt Lang
did not understand his new theological direction.[31]

Luther's position at the university, which he had inherited from
Staupitz and would hold until his death, was professor of the Bible,
and it required him to lecture on Scripture, hold disputations and
preach to students and members of the university.[32] He undertook the
task with gusto, lecturing first on the Psalms. Using the new technology

of printing when he lectured on Romans in 1515–16, he had the university printer Johann Rhau-Grunenberg set the Vulgate text in double-
spaced format, with generous margins on all sides. In his lectures
Luther then read out his glosses and emendations to the text, based
on the more up-to-date editions of Faber Stapulensis and Erasmus's
edition of Lorenzo Valla's text which the students would insert into
their individual copies. Luther would expound the meaning of the
text, working from notes he had prepared but sometimes speaking
extempore.[33] Johann Oldecop, later an opponent of the Reformation,
recalled how well Luther explained biblical passages, not using Latin
but German.[34] This style of lecturing, which engaged closely with the
text, would have given the students an almost tactile experience of
encountering Scripture and working with it themselves.

It was also transforming Luther. As he looked back on his life the
year before he died, and wrote a brief autobiography as the preface
to his collected Latin works, Luther remembered how important his
encounter with the text of Romans had been. 'Up till then it was not
the cold blood about the heart', he wrote, referring to his emotional
state of melancholy, 'but a single word in chapter 1[:17], "In it the
righteousness of God is revealed", that had stood in my way. For I
hated that word "righteousness of God", which . . . I had been taught
to understand philosophically regarding the formal or active righteousness, as they called it, with which God is righteous and punishes the
unrighteous sinner.' Luther had tried to be a perfect monk, yet 'I felt
that I was a sinner before God with an extremely disturbed conscience . . . I did not love, yes, I hated the righteous God who punishes
sinners.'[35]

Yet the manuscript commentary on this passage in his lectures from
1515–16 cited Augustine and stated much more soberly that 'the righteousness of God is the cause of salvation . . . the righteousness by
which we are made righteous by God. This happens through faith in
the Gospel.' It would probably not have been obvious at the time, not
even to Luther, that this was anything other than orthodox Augustinianism.[36] The implications of this intellectual breakthrough did not
become evident at once, but gradually emerged over the next years,
as Luther lectured on the Psalms, Hebrews and Galatians, and engaged
closely with the biblical text; indeed, as we shall see, he dated it much
later, to 1519.[37]

Intellectual work clearly suited him. Alongside studying theology he had taught from the outset, and now the experience of lecturing, together with his doctorate, may have conferred a sense of authority. His first proper work, however, a translation into German and exposition of the seven Penitential Psalms, did not appear until 1517.[38] As Luther explained, his translation drew on the old Latin Vulgate of Jerome but he corrected it by referring to the Hebrew edition of the humanist Johannes Reuchlin, the leading Hebraist of the time. The proud author wrote to Lang that, even if it pleased no one else, it did please him. This work was not, so he wrote to Scheurl in Nuremberg, intended for an academic audience: it was not even aimed at highly educated Nurembergers but at 'rough Saxons'. Luther was certainly wrong about this, for the price of the book, and its polished literacy, might have made it just about accessible to the Wittenberg elite, but hardly to most Saxons.[39]

On the face of it, it was surprising that Luther so rapidly became a central figure in the new university. He was neither senior in age, nor of higher social class, and before 1517 he had published virtually nothing. One of the reasons may lie in the fact that when he arrived in 1511, there was a group of academics all about the same age, creating more of a level playing field. In addition to Lang, there was Andreas Karlstadt, three years younger, but his academic senior and the man who conferred his doctorate on him. The professor of law, Hieronymus Schurff, was just two years older; Wenzeslaus Linck, prior of the Wittenberg monastery from 1511 to 1515, gained his doctorate in 1511, a year before Luther. Nikolaus von Amsdorf, Staupitz's nephew and a highly competent dialectician, was just a few months younger; he taught in the philosophy faculty but soon switched to theology. Although they all taught different subjects they formed a cohesive peer group; many of them shared a similar formation and several were Augustinians living together in the Wittenberg monastery which housed about forty monks.[40]

Another reason for Luther's rise may have been the effect of his forceful personality in what was still a minor institution. Even in 1536, there were only twenty-two faculty posts at Wittenberg: four each in theology and law, three in medicine and eleven in the arts.[41] Karlstadt, for one, was profoundly influenced by his erstwhile junior colleague and new friend, and rapidly absorbed his ideas. In 1516 Luther's student

Bartholomäus Bernhardi gave a disputation, part of the customary academic training, and advanced some of Luther's ideas on grace developed in the lectures on Romans; in its course, Luther publicly stated that he did not believe St Augustine was the author of the treatise attributed to him, *De vera et falsa poenitentia*. Karlstadt vigorously disagreed and immediately procured his own copy from Leipzig. But on rereading the text he decided that Luther was correct, and began to be influenced by Luther's understanding of Augustine.[42] Both radical and passionate, Karlstadt easily got lost in the thread of his own thought and needed direction: Luther's intensity seems to have unleashed his creativity, sparking him to rethink all his intellectual and spiritual positions. Schurff, more cautious by nature, was also captivated, perhaps because Luther was able to articulate the desperation and sense of sinfulness he too had felt. Luther clearly had an intellectual drive that drew others to him, in part because they recognised their own ideas in what he argued. He was intellectually independent and decisive, and could communicate complex opinions with passion. His energy and conviction rather than intellectual superiority may explain why he became the leading figure at Wittenberg so quickly.

\*

These were exciting times as a generation of intellectuals felt that they witnessed the dawn of a new era. It seemed that scholasticism, with its tortured deference to Aristotle, was finished. The university syllabus at Wittenberg had been a careful compromise between *via moderna* and *via antiqua*, but by 1516 Johannes Lang was enthusing that students were 'eagerly hearing lectures on the Bible and the Church Fathers, while the so-called scholastic doctors have hardly two or three listeners'.[43] In 1517–18 Luther lectured on Hebrews, Karlstadt on Augustine, the humanist Aesticampianus on Jerome – this was a whole programme of study invigorated by a humanist-style return to the sources.

There were also causes to be passionate about. Humanists united to defend the Hebrew scholar Johannes Reuchlin when he was persecuted by the Dominicans of Cologne, who wanted to destroy all Hebrew texts. Spalatin sought Luther's view of the affair in 1514 and received a forthright reply, defending the man whose grammar Luther himself had used when he learnt Hebrew with Lang in Erfurt. Jewish blasphemy, Luther argued, could not be purged as the Dominicans demanded, because the prophets of the Old Testament foretold that the Jews would insult and blaspheme against Christ, so destroying it would delete the evidence and turn God and the prophets into liars. This insight clearly gripped him, 'more than language can say', and he insisted that those who did not understand this paradox understood nothing of theology. He showed no sympathy with Jewish writings for their own sake, however: he would maintain throughout his life that these were indeed blasphemous.[44]

Two of Luther's most significant writings from this time were theses of disputation composed for his students, like the one he had composed for Bernhardi. The custom was for the pupil to expound theses that reflected the master's views as part of their progression through the degrees. Ritualised debates, they depended on skill in argument and rhetoric, and provided a kind of licensed intellectual aggression. With the position set out as a series of related sequential claims, it was easier to accept or reject particular points of the argument, and to inspect the links between one proposition and another. It permitted intellectual adventurousness and freedom, because ideas could be tried out, without claiming that they were established truths. Such tests and intellectual combat greatly appealed to Luther, and the Reformation would develop the technique into a high art.

In 1517, Luther's student Franz Günter defended a set of theses written by Luther against scholasticism, which are in many ways more radical and shocking than the Ninety-Five Theses. They proclaimed that Aristotle was not only unnecessary for the study of theology, but positively harmful. In a university where Aristotle formed a major part of the syllabus, this position was a slap in the face for those like Nikolaus von Amsdorf, who lectured on Aristotle's Ethics. But Luther's student won, the faculty collectively awarding him victory. Luther then sent the theses to Erfurt, although not under his name, as he knew that they would meet with opposition. He joked that although the Wittenbergers considered them acceptable and 'orthodox', the Erfurters would judge them 'cacodoxa' – shit doctrine.[45] He was right. His former colleagues and teachers at the monastery were outraged.[46]

The theses are an extraordinarily confident set of propositions, which are ordered as though they follow one from another, but their sequence is emotional as much as logical. Briskly, Luther labels one after another of his statements as 'contrary to common opinion', or 'in opposition to the scholastics'.[47] They capture his rejection of the whole tradition of medieval theology in all its passionate fury as he concludes: 'No one can become a theologian unless he becomes one without Aristotle.'[48] They begin with an aggressive defence of St Augustine, and culminate in the radical statement: 'The truth therefore is that man, made from a bad tree, can do nothing but want and do evil.' As Luther memorably puts it, 'Man is by nature unable to want God to be God. Indeed, he himself wants to be God, and does not want God to be God.'[49] In passing, Luther rejects the argument of Duns Scotus that the brave man can love the public good more than himself. It is a throwaway remark that hints at Luther's later political theory: its denial that men could ever put the common weal above self-interest and its lack of comprehension of any form of government other than authoritarian princely power.[50] 'Outside the grace of God it is indeed impossible not to become angry or lustful', Luther argues, and he insists that 'there is no moral virtue without either pride or sorrow, that is, without sin'. These are not the first sins that would come to mind as likely to trouble a monk, but they reveal his state at this time as he worried about melancholy, the *Anfechtungen* and his own anger and pride.[51] Ironically, the entire set of theses, while rejecting philosophy as inimical to theology, employs philosophical argument. Luther may have complained to Braun years before about his reluctance to study the discipline, but he had evidently mastered its methods. As his biographer Melchior Adam put it, 'he fell upon the crabbed and thorny *Logick* of that age', and the skills he acquired gave him a confidence in debate that came from knowing its techniques inside out.[52]

\*

Then, on 31 October 1517, Luther posted his Ninety-Five Theses. If they were seriously intended to bring about a disputation, their formal function was soon an irrelevance: nobody ever took up the challenge. Written in the style of his theses against scholasticism, they have a cumulative rhetorical force that is far removed from dispassionate academic writing. The opening insistence on the importance of penance and repentance postulated a whole new religious outlook, not an academic debate, mounting to a crescendo indicting the entire system of devotion based on the calculus of indulgences.

The placard print of the theses, its closely printed type covering a whole nearly A3-size sheet, is a powerful document.[53] And yet it is something of a puzzle that the Ninety-Five Theses were known as such: of the two surviving placards, one numbered the theses in batches of twenty-five, and the other presented 'Eighty-Seven' theses, because the printer made several mistakes in numbering them. There must have been other printings now lost. Luther insisted later, in a letter to his Nuremberg humanist friend Christoph Scheurl, that he never intended them to be published or read more widely beyond a small circle; and some scholars have taken this as evidence that he did not arrange for them to be printed. But Luther was also explaining why he had omitted to send Scheurl a copy, as he should have done, so his statement is hardly conclusive evidence.[54] When he sent the theses to Johannes Lang in Erfurt, he did not ask his friend to restrict circulation to a small circle. It is difficult to escape the conclusion that Luther, even though he later insisted that 'the Word did it all', may have helped things along a little. Certainly it strains credulity that he should have arranged for the theses to be copied out laboriously by hand so many times to send them to his various friends.[55] His letter to Lang, dated with some significance as St Martin's Day, 11 November, seethes with emotion, announcing that he is sure the theses would not please 'your theologians' and defending himself against any accusations of pride and temerity.[56]

Penned by an unknown German professor in an intellectual backwater, the most amazing part of the story is how the Ninety-Five Theses spread so fast. It was indeed, as Luther wrote to Lang, 'unprecedented'. In just two months they were known all over Germany, and were already being met with refutations. In Augsburg the cathedral preacher Urbanus Rhegius remarked that Luther's 'disputation note' was available everywhere. In Hamburg, Albert Kranz had received them by early December; in Alsace, Conrad Pellican remembered getting them in early 1518; Erasmus sent them to Thomas More on 5 March 1518. In Eichstätt in late 1517, Bishop Gabriel von Eyb was discussing a copy with Johannes Eck, a friend of Luther. Luther himself recalled, exaggerating perhaps a little, 'they ran through the whole of Germany in just a fortnight'.[57]

When writing to the bishop of Brandenburg a few months later, he denied that the theses were theological truth and insisted that they were no more than propositions designed to be debated, but he was soon engaged in defending them vigorously.[58] Within six months, he had published his *Sermon on Indulgences and Grace*, which went through twenty-five printings between 1518 and 1520. Whether the Ninety-Five Theses were intended for a wider audience or not, this sermon, written in German, was clearly designed to spread his ideas beyond the boundaries of Wittenberg and throughout the whole empire.

How could Luther have had the courage to mount such an assault on both the papacy and on the fundamental values of the Church? He later said that at this time he was like a 'blinded horse', forced to wear blinkers to keep in a straight line. He prayed that 'if God wants to start such a prank using me, he should do it by himself, and not mix me (that is, my wisdom) up in it'.[59] He described a state of mind in which he was not fully in control of his actions but had handed over responsibility to a higher power. Later he often used the word *Spil*, game or play, a word which in German can have connotations of frivolity, to describe the events surrounding the publication – as if God had been using him to cause mischief, and he were not fully in charge of what he was doing. A game is also an activity where the outcome is unknown.

Certainly Luther's letters from around this time communicate a sense of exalted determination to make his views public: here is someone who is looking to neither right nor left. While the earlier Theses had stopped just short of questioning the power of the Pope, Luther now wrote that 'the Pope does very well when he grants remission to the souls in Purgatory, not by the power of the keys, which he does not have'. He later recalled that Hieronymus Schurff had asked incredulously, 'You want to write against the Pope? What do you want to do? They [the Church] won't stand for it.'[60] Luther was well aware that he was setting out on a path which could end in martyrdom.

The response to the theses did not consist merely of plaudits, and one of the first refutations came as a bitter blow. Johannes Eck, a humanist and an admired acquaintance, recommended to Luther by none other than his Nuremberg friend Christoph Scheurl, penned a demolition of the arguments. Luther was deeply hurt by what he saw as a personal betrayal and retaliated with anger. On the other hand, the passionate support he received in Nuremberg contributed to the rapid spread of the theses amongst Germany's educated elite. Although Nuremberg had no university itself, it was a centre of trade, learning and political power, located on the trade routes from Italy to northern Germany. When Johannes Cochlaeus penned his *Brief Description of Germany* in 1512, he put Nuremberg literally at the centre, connecting all the different regions of the country. Luther's Nuremberg connections – humanists, patricians and politicians – now made his cause their own. There was even a coterie of 'Augustinian diners', including some of most powerful men in town: 'Almost the whole talk over the table was about the one Martin: they celebrate him, adore him, defend him, are prepared to endure everything for him; they recite his work . . . they kiss his pamphlets . . . eagerly they read every word of them.'[61] Originally these men had been devoted to pursuing the spirituality of Luther's mentor and confessor Staupitz; now they gave his brilliant protégé shrewd advice and support, and created an audience for him in southern Germany. Scheurl acted as the conduit, and he and others translated the theses into German. When Luther had begun corresponding with the lawyer in January 1517, his slightly florid and obsequious tone revealed how important the relationship was to him: 'I do not want you to become my friend, because this friendship will not redound to your fame, but to your harm, if the proverb be true: "Friends have everything in common." If then through this friendship everything of mine becomes yours, then you will become richer in nothing but sins, folly and disgrace.'[62]

People were not just reading the theses, but acting on them. By March 1518, Luther was already writing pre-emptively to Lang in Erfurt in case rumours reached him that Tetzel's *Positiones* (his defence of indulgences) had been publicly burned by students in Wittenberg's market square. He himself, Luther claimed, had nothing to do with this, and he deeply regretted the offence caused to the poor salesman, whose works had in part been bought, in part simply seized and then thrown on the flames. All of which would have been more persuasive had not Luther enclosed with the letter a copy of Tetzel's work, 'seized from the flames', so that Lang could see how the papists were raging against him.[63] The first book burnings, which were to become such a feature of the Reformation, were thus instigated not by the Roman

Church but by Luther's supporters, and it was clear where they might lead. Tetzel was already threatening that Luther himself would be burned and that he 'would go to heaven in his bath shirt' within two weeks.

\*

It is not difficult to understand why the Ninety-Five Theses caused such uproar. The indulgences question was linked with the assault on scholasticism and was part of a general impatience with old ways of doing things. Humanists could see in them an attack on the established authorities, who clung to their philosophy instead of returning to the sources and reading texts anew and critically. The theses also reflected a lay devotional piety that sought true repentance and aimed at mystical union with Christ: indulgences were anathema to this spiritual sensibility. Indeed, that questioning was probably more important than anything else. So far as Luther himself was concerned, the theses marked a profound shift in his own understanding of himself, for around the time of their posting, he changed his name. He no longer signed himself 'Luder', his father's name, but took on the new Greek name 'Eleutherius' – the freed one – which he continued to use for several months. 'Luder' was a somewhat unfortunate name to inherit because in German it has associations with looseness and immorality. Even when he stopped signing himself as Eleutherius, he kept the kernel of the name and from then on called himself 'Luther'.[64]

How did Luther become 'the freed one', reaching his theological conviction that human beings are justified by faith alone? More ink has probably been spilled on when, where and exactly what Luther's 'breakthrough' consisted of than on any other issue surrounding the Reformation. Theologians interested in Luther's early development usually place it at the so-called 'tower experience', when Luther suddenly understood the nature of grace, long before the formulation of the Ninety-Five Theses. Yet it is not clear that it was a single experience, although part of the process certainly happened in 1517 when he changed his name. Later on, he sometimes felt it was important to identify a 'Pauline moment', a point at which he truly understood that man could be saved through faith alone because, as an emotional transformation that changed everything, it had to be located in a single event.

In 1532, he told the story of his Reformation discovery to his table companions. Describing how burdened he had been by the thought of the punishing justice of God, the idea that the righteous shall live by faith alone had struck him 'like a thunderbolt', in the monastery's privy tower where his study was situated. As he put it, 'This art the Holy Spirit gave me on the cloaca.' It was clear that Luther wanted his audience to be struck by the contrast between the importance of the revelation and the lowly place where it occurred.[65] Unlike other reformers, Luther rarely claimed divine inspiration for his ideas. It is interesting too that he uses the word '*Kunst*' – art – for it suggests that the insight, like the skill of a craftsman or artist, opened up a whole new ability to accomplish things in a different way.

However, the most famous account of his Reformation discovery came in 1545, the year before he died, in his Preface to the first edition of his collected Latin works when he described his reading of the Psalms in 1519 and his renewed encounter with Paul's Letter to the Romans:

At last, by the mercy of God, meditating day and night, I gave heed to the context of the words, namely, 'In it the righteousness of God is revealed, as it is written, "He who through faith is righteous shall live."' There I began to understand that the righteousness of God is that by which the righteous lives by a gift of God, namely by faith. And this is the meaning: the righteousness of God is revealed by the gospel, namely, the passive righteousness with which the merciful God justifies us by faith, as it is written, 'He who through faith is righteous shall live.' Here I felt that I was altogether born again and had entered paradise itself through open gates. There a totally other face of the entire Scripture showed itself to me. Thereupon I ran through the Scriptures from memory. I also found in other terms an analogy, as, the work of God, that is, what God does in us, the power of God, with which he makes us strong, the wisdom of God, with which he makes us wise, the strength of God, the salvation of God, the glory of God.

And I extolled my sweetest word with a love as great as the hatred with which I had before hated the word "righteousness of God". Thus that place in Paul was for me truly the gate to paradise.[66]

Significantly, Luther dated the transformation not to 1515, the year when he lectured on Romans, nor even to 1517, the year of the Ninety-Five Theses, but to 1519.[67] Scholars have treated this chronology with scepticism, however, and insisted that Luther's understanding of faith must have been arrived at well before the Ninety-Five Theses were formulated. In reality it seems more likely that Luther was still forming his ideas then, and continued to do so for quite some while afterwards.[68] Nor was it entirely clear in which direction his theology might develop, for some of the ideas and themes present before 1520 were subsequently dropped.

Just how fluid early evangelical thought was can be seen in Luther's enthusiasm for mystical ideas, especially those of Johannes Tauler and of the so-called *Theologia deutsch*. The latter was a fourteenth-century text in the vernacular, which Luther published in part in December 1516 with a brief preface, and then again in full, with a more detailed introduction, in 1518.[69] There he described it as the book from which, after the Bible and the writings of St Augustine, he had learnt most.

Yet the booklet makes disconcerting reading for any adherent of Luther's theology. Calvin later dismissed it as 'twaddle' that confuses the Christian, and as 'poison' for the Church. It demands that the Christian should surrender his or her will utterly, letting in the Divine will and becoming possessed by the spirit of God. The individual whose will has become merged with that of God thus becomes divine – he or she is *vergöttlicht*. The emphasis on overcoming the individual will can be seen as pointing towards Luther's theology of grace, yet it is based on a belief in the perfectibility of human beings which is completely alien to his later thought.

The experience of giving up one's will is a process of renunciation, of letting go – the relaxation of all that is individual. Although the *Theologia deutsch* does not use the word, what the text described is reminiscent of *Gelassenheit*, a key term in Staupitz's sermons at about this time. For Staupitz, *Gelassenheit* is a kind of meditative absorption in God's love where the individual ceases to strive and opens up to God's love. The *Theologia deutsch* is ambivalent, however, about what the believer can do to secure this divine status (*Vergött-lichung*). For while it is emphatic that external works will not please God, the text does not make clear whether the individual should

21. *Eyn deutsch Theologia: das ist Eyn edles Buchleyn*, Wittenberg, 1518. The cover features
a woodcut showing the risen Christ, with the flag of salvation and the wounds of the
Crucifixion, and a simple box-like tomb, plain but for the faintest hint of a Renaissance
border. In the foreground lies Adam, a snake issuing from his mouth, while angels
armed with agricultural implements plough him back into the soil. The work speaks
of the death of the 'old Adam' and the resurrection of Christ in the believer.

adopt an attitude of renunciation, or whether it will come as a gift
from God.

*Gelassenheit* later became the watchword of the radical wing of the
Reformation, and the *Theologia deutsch* was enormously attractive to

those who aimed to spiritualise religion and wanted no truck with an established Church. The idea of the inner and outer man would again be promoted by thinkers like Andreas Karlstadt in Wittenberg and Claus Frey in Strasbourg. If the individual will were united with the Divine will, then God himself dwelled in the believer, providing an inner source of authority. Yet the *Theologia* also warned against the 'false freedom' that could result when people thought they had become *vergöttlicht* – and indeed, Luther later argued that Thomas Müntzer, Karlstadt and other radicals were guilty of false freedom arising from spiritual pride. But whatever his later position, at this point Luther's ideas seem to have contained a powerful streak of meditative mysticism. He read the *Theologia deutsch* in the crucial years up to 1516, and again between 1516 and 1518 as he began to work through the implications of the Ninety-Five Theses.[70] At this time, his theology was capacious enough to encompass a spiritualising, inward-looking mysticism as well as the rational argument of the Ninety-Five Theses. It took him until Karlstadt's complete appropriation of *Gelassenheit* in the years after 1524 to reject this possibility forever.

The view of human nature that characterises the *Theologia deutsch* is also very unlike that of the later Luther who does not habitually distinguish between the inner and outer man; nor does he locate the spirit of God, still less the spirit of the Devil, within the individual. Equally, the mature Luther lacked the denigration of the flesh that was so central to other mystical thinkers, paradoxically, because his estimation of humankind was so low; indeed, man was so sinful that a union with God was not possible.

As Luther moved away from the piety of the *Theologia deutsch*, both *Gelassenheit* and rejection of the world were lost. Lutheranism separated from the meditative dimension that was such a powerful part of late medieval devotion. Luther's increasing inclination towards a more intellectual engagement with the Bible may have been part of the change of direction in his thought. What he lost was the emotional dimension of faith, the potential for radical critique of institutions, and the meditative dimension of religion that we are more familiar with in Hindu or Buddhist devotional practices. Instead, the side of Luther which was more concerned with action, scriptural exegesis and authority, won out. This would shape the character of Lutheranism and of Protestantism itself for centuries to come.

# 5

# Journeys and Disputations

In early April 1518, Luther set out for Heidelberg, a journey of nearly 250 miles as the crow flies. Staupitz had called a meeting of the Augustinian order for 25 April, at which one of Luther's students, Leonhard Beyer, was to defend forty theses composed by his teacher. Many had advised Luther not to travel: he wrote to Lang that he had been warned that preachers were condemning him from their pulpits and 'the people' would try to burn him, but he nonetheless insisted on walking all the way with Beyer and with Urban, the monastery's messenger. It seems that, at this juncture, he did not anticipate much popular support for his cause.

But he was in high spirits. Writing to Spalatin on 15 April, six days into the journey, he reported that they had reached Coburg, one of the Elector's castles. Ever resourceful, and travelling as a mendicant without money, Luther had managed to get the Elector's man Degenhart Pfeffinger – who had unwisely joined them at an inn – to pay for all the brothers' meals: as Luther quipped to Spalatin, he always enjoyed separating a rich man from his cash.[1] He hoped to get the castellan to pay for their stay at Coburg as well. But the footsore monk had also realised the error of his ways, and resorted to travelling by wagon: he had sinned, he joked, 'since I determined to go on foot' and had failed, but as he had repented, he had no need to purchase an indulgence.[2] It would be a good year for wine, he added, as he passed through the premium vineyards of southern Germany. At Würzburg, Lang joined the travellers for the leg to Heidelberg.[3]

The Heidelberg Debate offered Luther a chance to make his theology more widely known within the Augustinians. But Staupitz was playing a dangerous game. By this time he was under pressure from the provincial of the whole order to persuade Luther to recant;

indeed, Luther had promised to send the Pope an explanation of the theses.[4] It was therefore playing with fire to publicise the new theology by airing it at the meeting of the German province, and in a university town to boot where other academics were likely to attend.

In their content the Heidelberg theses are reminiscent of those against scholasticism, with their radical denial both of man's free will and of the usefulness of philosophy to theology.[5] Yet they are far more accomplished than the earlier work, and reflect Luther's more developed theology. Just as no one can employ the evil of sexual desire properly unless they are married, he argues, so no one can philosophise well unless he is a fool – that is, a Christian. He means that pagan philosophy cannot be the lens through which to interpret Scripture. Luther here draws an interesting parallel, suggesting that sexual desire is no worse than any other human activity, while comparing the practice of philosophy with sensual indulgence: philosophy must be tamed by a healthy Christian disrespect for reason. Indeed, Luther would repeatedly refer to reason as 'the whore'.[6] Most significantly, he further develops his theology of the Cross, which he had begun to set out in his Ninety-Five Theses the previous autumn. 'A theologian of glory calls evil good and good evil', he writes. 'A theologian of the Cross calls the thing what it actually is.' The theologian of glory, that is, celebrates God's majesty and power, and loves 'works and the glory of works', while the true theologian proclaims that 'God can be found only in suffering and the Cross' – a difficult truth which humans prefer not to hear. Thus suffering must also be part of the Christian life: 'It is impossible for a person not to be puffed up by his good works unless he has first been deflated and destroyed by suffering and evil until he knows that he is worthless and that his works are not his but God's.' Luther elaborates the idea of the 'hidden God' (Deus absconditus), God hidden in suffering, which would become a powerful theme of his theology in his debate with Erasmus: the God who is not inside us, and who can never be fully known by humans. Surprisingly, the theses make no mention of indulgences and they once again expound a theology rather than deducing an argument from propositions. The themes of Luther's thought were moving well beyond what he had set out in the Ninety-Five Theses; and the full implications of his attack on 'philosophy' were becoming evident.[7]

At the meeting in Heidelberg on 25 April 1518 Luther's theses were presented in front of Bernhard von Usingen and Jodokus Trutfetter, his former teachers in philosophy. Trutfetter was one of the leading logicians of his day, whose *Summulae* had synthesised all the latest thinking about modal logic – that is, logic which considers not only what is actually the case, but also what is possible. Trutfetter's textbook, printed at Wittenberg, presented sequences of binding syllogisms, or logically valid arguments, in visual, tabular form, making them a powerful tool with which not only to understand thought itself but also to overwhelm an opponent in debate.

Luther reported to Spalatin that everyone had been persuaded by his disputation – except one newly minted doctor, who had exclaimed, much to the hilarity of the audience that, 'if the peasants heard this, they would stone you to death'. And except for Usingen and Trutfetter. As Luther noted later, his former teachers were revolted 'to death' by his views. In fact, when he left Heidelberg after the meeting, Usingen had joined him in his wagon, and during their journey to Erfurt, Luther had tried to persuade him round. But there was no budging either of them, and now, he told Spalatin on 18 May, he was going to leave them behind, just as Christ had left behind the Jews – a mean-spirited equation.[8] Luther had already confronted his former teachers with his views about scholasticism in February 1517,[9] and it could hardly have been pleasant for a senior member of the order to have their travelling companion harangue them about the emptiness of philosophy.

Breaking his journey back to Wittenberg at Erfurt, Luther then turned up at Trutfetter's door on 8 May, determined to reply in person to a critical letter his old teacher had sent.[10] When his servant refused to allow him in, claiming his master was too ill, Luther wrote instead. He began by assuring his former teacher that he would never shame him with 'biting and insulting letters' as 'you fear I might'. But he went on to explain that 'I simply believe that it is impossible to reform the Church if we do not root out the canons, the decretals, scholastic philosophy, logic as we have it now', and replace them with study of the Bible and the Church Fathers. He rejected the allegation, as he had previously done to Lang, that he had been responsible for burning copies of Tetzel's pamphlets, a dangerous insinuation which made him look like a violent rabble-rouser who did not respect other scholars.[11] He also denied that he had defended the Zwickau preacher Johannes Egranus against the Leipzig professors, who had been attacking saints' legends from the pulpit, including those about St Anna, the patron saint of miners. Luther observed to Spalatin that people only honoured her because they believed she would make them rich, but all he had done was write Egranus a letter of support. Still, this was hardly as innocuous as he made it sound, as the letter had been published with Egranus's pamphlet on the subject.[12]

Luther was quite unapologetic to Trutfetter, however, about presenting his own theology in vernacular sermons addressed to the German people, even though he knew full well that it 'displeases you'; it seems he was already intent on moving the debate out of the university and into the marketplace. He concluded by telling him that he had the right to attack the scholastics, and that 'neither your authority (which is certainly most serious with me), far less that of others, would deter me from this view', and urged him to 'vomit up' any objections he may have to Luther's views.[13] The letter betrays little sympathy for the old man's serious illness, about which he does not enquire, or of how it might feel to be told that his life's work had become an irrelevance. Small wonder that Trutfetter's manservant judged his master would not be able to stand a visit by the rebellious monk.[14] This was the darker side of Luther's personality which arose from his sense of mission, his growing preoccupation with martyrdom, and his new-found relationship with God. While the lean monk with the deep-set eyes was able to inspire and lead others, he was also fostering a certainty that could be ruthless in its dismissal of those who disagreed with him – those 'Jews' who belonged to the false church, the 'synagogue'.

*

Luther returned home from Heidelberg in excellent health, writing to Spalatin that despite the long journey he had put on weight, and that the food had suited him very well; the Wittenberg monastery's dreadful meals were something for which he regularly apologised to visitors.[15] More importantly, he must have felt also that he had strong support, being surrounded by the young ready to sweep away the old. At his side he had Karlstadt, whom even Luther's opponent Johannes Cochlaeus would later describe admiringly as a man who had 'cultivated his rough intellect, which was like a hard crag'.[16] The fact that the man who had conferred Luther's doctoral degree on him now enthusiastically joined his junior colleague signalled a profound change in Luther's position within the university and the order. 'You know the brilliance of those who support us', he wrote to Trutfetter; the whole university, he averred, was on his side.[17]

The battle lines were now being drawn. The debate at Heidelberg was a turning point because it showed that Luther's emerging theology was going beyond the criticism of indulgences. It had brought new followers, in particular Martin Bucer and Wolfgang Capito, who would promote his ideas beyond the Nuremberg network to the humanists of southern Germany. As a Dominican, Bucer was a particularly surprising convert. A student at the University of Heidelberg and a passionate follower of Erasmus, he took careful notes on the disputation and would eventually leave his order – deeply moved by what he had witnessed, he wrote to his friend the humanist Beatus Rhenanus, 'as if in a dream'.[18] He became one of the most important theologians of the Reformation, and a powerful advocate of unity and compromise amongst the evangelicals. Capito, a Benedictine, was cathedral preacher and university professor at Basle, another important intellectual centre; he was also a friend of Albrecht of Mainz. Other members of the audience at Heidelberg were Theobald Billican, Martin Frecht and Johannes Brenz, who would all become future leaders of the Reformation in southern Germany.[19] The disputation made a huge impression on each of them, changing their lives forever, even if they would not agree with all of Luther's later teachings.

But once back in Wittenberg, the optimism of the spring quickly dissipated. Trutfetter had written, repeating what he had said at Erfurt, but his tone was now much more bitter, Luther told Lang, 'than what you heard at the meeting of the chapter'.[20] Worse, Johannes Eck, one of Germany's leading humanists and theologians, and a man whom Luther had counted a friend, had penned a refutation of the Ninety-Five Theses. Luther had read Eck's text, titled the 'Obelisks', and circulating in manuscript, before his journey to Heidelberg. He had composed a reply he wittily named the 'Asterisks', but had put the matter aside to deal with until after his return.* Luther had evidently

---

* 'Obelisks' were printers' markers for errors; 'asterisks' for things to be added. The titles were in-jokes by humanists who knew all about the new technology of print.

assumed that Eck was 'one of us', and he felt stabbed in the back, complaining that Eck should have followed the gospel and admonished his brother 'in private'.[21] His letter to Eck, written in May when his temper had cooled somewhat, was a controlled expression of anger and hurt. Insisting that he would not return evil with evil, Luther left it to Eck to decide whether to respond to the 'Asterisks' in private, or in print – and in the latter case Luther would do likewise, and in force. Only towards the end did the mask slip, as he accused Eck of acting like an irritated prostitute, who 'vomits up exactly the kind of curses and oaths that you have inflicted on me'.[22]

But while Luther was in Heidelberg, Karlstadt had obtained a copy of Eck's 'Obelisks', and composed and printed a reply, consisting of 406 theses. Thus the matter had already been made public and Luther's insistence that he had kept it private was disingenuous. It would have been surprising, too, if he had not discussed the affair with other members of the order at Heidelberg. In June he also wrote to Scheurl, who, aghast at the rift that had developed between Luther and Eck, was attempting to mediate. Luther was willing to compromise by not going public, and wrote ingratiatingly of his admiration for Eck's learning. It would have been foolish indeed to risk alienating Scheurl and his humanist network in Nuremberg, so far the only real support outside the order and Wittenberg. Luther insisted, however, that Eck should not be too bitter in his response to Karlstadt, a proviso which would have infuriated Karlstadt had he known of it, as he was only too eager to take Eck on.[23] It was a wise precaution, however, for Eck would soon be trying to get the matter of Luther's assertions heard at Rome rather than on German soil; had he succeeded, Karlstadt might have been in danger too.

*

Matters had rumbled on slowly in the Curia. Albrecht of Mainz had sent the Ninety-Five Theses to the University of Mainz for judgement, before passing them on to Rome in December 1517. There, the Dominican Sylvester Prierias produced a refutation on behalf of the Pope, and published his *Dialogue Against the Arrogant Theses of Martin Luther Concerning the Power of the Pope* the following summer. Luther considered it so bad that he simply had it reprinted, and then produced a withering retort. Other responses also began to appear. In January 1518, the indulgence-seller Tetzel, a Dominican who was also Inquisitor for Saxony and thus charged with fighting heresy, defended a set of 106 theses attacking Luther composed by the theology professor Conrad Wimpina; he also published a refutation of Luther's *Sermon on Indulgences and Grace*.[24] Luther soon had to deal with what became a long line of attacks on his work, many intemperate, and some malicious. And then Rome finally concluded that the Ninety-Five Theses were heretical: on 7 August 1518, a summons to Rome reached Luther in Wittenberg. This was the first step towards a trial which might end at the stake.

The papal legate Tommaso de Vio, known as Cajetan, had arrived at the Imperial Diet, the meeting of the estates of the empire, in Augsburg in the spring of 1518. Recently made a cardinal, Cajetan was a serious churchman who led a simple, exemplary life. He was also a scholar who for many years had been writing a modern commentary on the *Summa Theologica* of Thomas Aquinas. Yet he was open to humanist ideas too and had advised his fellow Dominicans that wars of subjection should not be fought against native peoples in the New World. The mission to Augsburg was his first diplomatic posting and it was a difficult one, for he was trying to secure German support for Pope Leo X's crusade against the Ottomans. The German estates proved recalcitrant, unwilling to raise the taxes required, and insisting that the Pope and Emperor Maximilian accept their complaints about the exactions of the papacy as a condition of any further subsidy.[25]

Luther's ruler Friedrich the Wise was in a powerful political position at Augsburg. Not only was his support crucial for getting the estates to pay up, Maximilian's key aim at the Diet was to secure the election of his son Charles to the imperial title. As one of the Electors, Friedrich's vote mattered, and so Cajetan, disappointed and furious at the short-sightedness and self-interest of the estates, had to tread carefully when the question of the Elector's professor at Wittenberg was raised. Both Friedrich and Spalatin were impressed by Cajetan's apparent good faith and open-mindedness: indeed, the cardinal stated that he was willing to avoid a trial in Rome by meeting with Luther on German soil, at Augsburg. He seemed to be a man with whom they could deal; Spalatin wrote to Luther calming his fears and assuring him that the cardinal was well inclined towards him.

By the summer of 1518, however, it was clear that matters were serious. There were further reports of plots against his life, and Count Albrecht of Mansfeld was warning him not to leave Wittenberg.[26] On 28 August Luther wrote to Spalatin in Augsburg, weighing up what to do: 'In all this I fear nothing, as you know, my Spalatin. Even if their flattery and power should succeed in making me hated by all people, enough remains of my heart and conscience to know and confess that all for which I stand and which they attack, I have from God, to whom I gladly and of my own accord entrust and offer all of this. If he takes it away, it is taken away; if he preserves it, it is preserved. Hallowed and praised be his name forever. Amen.'[27] But while he seemed to be putting his life in God's hands, he was at the same time working out how far he should go before putting himself in mortal danger. Luther had no reason to trust Cajetan, who was an Italian and a member of the papal court; rumours were circulating that the cardinal had been instructed by the Pope to get emperor and princes to unite against him. Not for the last time, therefore, Luther came up with a cunning ruse: he would avoid going to Augsburg by requesting safe conduct from the Elector, which he knew Spalatin would get Friedrich to refuse, thereby giving him an excuse not to travel. But it turned out to be a miscalculation. Spalatin rejected the suggestion out of hand, for both he and the Elector trusted Cajetan and were anxious for the meeting to take place.[28]

Again Luther set out on a journey on foot, walking another 300 miles to Augsburg, accompanied once more by his fellow brother and student Leonhard Beyer. It was Luther's choice to walk when he could have travelled by wagon – as he had eventually done on the journey to Heidelberg – but he was determined to travel as a humble mendicant. Even at an average rate of about twenty miles a day, though, the journey would have taken longer than a fortnight, so he may have taken the odd ride on a passing cart. Years later, Luther began his account of the meeting in the preface to his collected Latin works with the words, 'So I came to Augsburg, afoot and poor.' He had been given a mere twenty guilders by the Elector to cover his expenses, and his early biographer Johannes Mathesius reported that along the way he had to borrow a cassock from his old friend Wenzeslaus Linck. When they passed through Weimar, the provisor at the Augustinian monastery warned him: 'Dear Mr Doctor! Those Italians are learned folk, by God. I'm worried that you won't be able to beat them. And they'll burn you for it.' Luther, making light of it, retorted that nettles he could bear, but fire would be too hot, a jibe at the 'nettling' of the scholastics who were attacking his work.[29]

Luther was an observant traveller who loved nature, and he would have passed through one distinctive landscape after another, such as the forests, gravel and sandy soil around Nuremberg. His route was punctuated by the imperial towns, with their big half-timbered houses, imposing town halls, guild houses and workshops where craftsmen produced outstanding metalware, fabrics and scientific instruments.[30] The journey that allowed Luther to get to know the country's rich south probably also strengthened his profound sense of being 'German', first imprinted on him during his trip to Rome in 1511. The two travellers reached Nuremberg on 3 or 4 October, and they finally arrived at their destination on 7 October. The pig-headed Luther was forced to change to a wagon about three miles out of Augsburg, because a stomach complaint had made him so weak that he could walk no further. But he quickly recovered, ready to meet with the papal legate four days after arriving in the city.[31]

Augsburg was one of the largest cities of the empire, and would soon surpass Nuremberg as the leading centre of culture and wealth. It was home to the Fugger family, the richest merchants of the day, whose interests stretched from Europe to the New World. The Fugger-häuser, their palace located in the centre of town, were an opulent set of buildings that took up a whole block, rather like the palaces of the Italian nobles with whom they traded. Yet, around the same time as their own residence, the Fuggers also constructed the first modern social housing. The 'Fuggerei', an equally impressive set of housing for the poor built in the St Jakob's suburb, was a gated estate of tiny one-up, one-down dwellings, each with their own doorway; it had its own chapel and over the entrance the Fuggers inscribed their motto: 'Don't waste time'. The Fuggerhäuser, by contrast, consisted of three interlinked courtyards, their design featuring distinctive Renaissance circle motifs and garlands; they were decorated with frescoes by leading artists, including scenes from the *Triumph of the Emperor Maximilian*, proclaiming the close links between the ruler and the Fugger family. Befitting his standing as papal emissary, Cajetan lodged in the luxury of the palace, and it was here that the discussions were held.[32]

Since, unusually, there was no Augustinian monastery in town, Luther was housed in a simple cell on the first floor of the Carmelite monastery of St Anna where the prior, Johannes Frosch, was a friend from student days in Erfurt.[33] Humble though the cell was, he was staying in a remarkable place. The Church of St Anna, attached to the monastery and dominating the view from Luther's cell, was popular among Augsburg's leading patricians and merchants and contained the Fugger chapel, separated from the rest of the church by a grille. A masterpiece begun in 1508 and consecrated in January 1518, neither Erfurt nor Wittenberg had anything to rival it. Famed as the first work of the Renaissance on German soil, the chapel breathed an entirely different aesthetic from the Elector's Castle Church. Costing 15,000 guilders to build, it deliberately eschewed the Gothic; rather, its design contains the same circles and arches that can also be found in the Fuggerhäuser courtyards, picked out in red marble, in Italianate Renaissance style. Light floods in from a circular window above the organ. There is no ostentatious display of relics and nor are there altars to saints. At its centre, the Corpus Christi altar, one of the most remarkable sculptures of the sixteenth century, shows the crucified Christ with Mary and John and an angel. The line of their entwined arms gives the statue movement and weightlessness but also ambiguity: the viewer cannot tell whether Mary and the angel carry Christ or whether it is he who carries them. Appealing to the worshipper's emotions, the sculpture presents Christ's suffering and resurrection as the sole focus of devotion – it is the kind of Christocentric piety that Staupitz would have endorsed.[34]

In his Augsburg cell right by the chapel Luther composed his response to Cajetan and formulated more clearly his view that the authority of Scripture overrode both papal decree and the Church Fathers: it was a principle that would from now on determine his thinking. It was also at Augsburg that he first appealed to 'conscience', a concept that would become forever associated with him. Gradually, as he debated with his opponents, the elements of his mature theology were coming together.

*

Augsburg marked another turning point in the course of the Reformation. Until then, Luther's cause had been primarily a matter for the Augustinians and for Rome; now it was a matter of secular politics as well. In Augsburg, Luther met a new group of lay supporters, who were some of the leading politicians and intellectuals of the day. Conrad Peutinger, civic secretary of Augsburg and not only an eminent imperial politician but also a noted humanist, dined with him. Christoph Langenmantel belonged to an important patrician family in Augsburg and his support would prove vital in protecting the movement. Luther also met the Benedictine Veit Bild, and Bernhard and Conrad Adelmann von Adelmannsfelden, cathedral canons at Augsburg, who were associated with Peutinger's humanist circle.[35] The Imperial Diet held in the town had just finished, and men like these, conversant with power at the heart of the empire, were interested in containing the power of the Pope, reducing German financial contributions to the Church, and reforming political relations between the emperor and the estates. Luther's ideas excited them intellectually, and connected with the political issues that were on their agenda.

Yet in planning his encounter with Cajetan, Luther was on his own. There was no Spalatin to help him, for the Elector had left on 22 September. Scheurl, whom the Elector had wanted to assist Luther, had somehow failed to meet him at Nuremberg – perhaps because Spalatin's request had been too vaguely formulated, perhaps because Luther did not want his assistance, or perhaps because Scheurl himself wanted to avoid too close an involvement. Staupitz, who had promised to attend the discussions, did not arrive until the day after the first meeting with Cajetan. Thus, to start with, Luther had to decide on tactics without any advice.

Before the first formal encounter, Serralonga, the Italian churchman appointed as mediator, advised Luther to appear before the cardinal and admit his errors. When Luther objected, the Italian repeatedly asked: 'Do you want to stage a tournament?'[36] Cajetan, however, had carefully planned the meetings to avoid an undignified verbal slanging match; he intended to speak to Luther in a 'fatherly' way, admonish him for his errors, set him on the right path, and avoid a trial in Rome. Yet Luther was fresh from trouncing his former teachers Trutfetter and Usingen at Heidelberg and the paternal approach was bound to enrage him, not least because he had arrived at his own sense of identity by falling out with his father. Indeed, time and again when writing about the meeting, Luther expressed his annoyance with the cardinal who kept calling him his 'dear son'. Moreover, Cajetan, a Dominican so enthusiastic a follower of Aquinas that he had adopted his first name, Thomas, symbolised the scholasticism which Luther now detested. Consequently, while the cardinal tried to avoid debate by setting out clearly where Luther's theses departed from Church doctrine, Luther refused to be instructed unless he could be shown where he was wrong – a somewhat different thing. Not surprisingly, the first meeting failed. Despite his well-meaning intentions, Cajetan ended up shouting Luther down and laughing with his Italian supporters at the German monk's arguments.

What Luther did next is extraordinary. He appeared at the second meeting the next day not on his own but accompanied by four imperial counsellors, the newly arrived Staupitz, and a group of witnesses. He also brought a notary. Luther opened the interview by reading out a document stating that he would submit to the 'judgement and the lawful conclusion of the Holy Church and of all who are better informed than I', but denying that he had said anything contrary to Holy Scripture, the Church Fathers or papal decrees. He then refused to say anything more but instead 'promised to answer in writing'. Then, at the third meeting the following day, he produced a long written document setting out his position on the issues discussed together with supporting citations from Scripture, concluding, 'As long as these Scripture passages stand, I cannot do otherwise, for I know that one must obey God rather than men . . . I do not want to be compelled to affirm something contrary to my conscience.' Luther had thus turned what Cajetan had intended to be a private admonition into a public, ritualised battle, where positions were formally set out in writing rather than evolving through discussion. He had done exactly what Serralonga had warned him against: he was staging a tournament.

Luther's discussions with Cajetan centred on two issues in particular: the nature of the 'treasury of merits', which underpinned the practice of indulgences, and the role of faith in the sacrament. On the first point, Cajetan accused Luther of denying that the merits of Christ were the treasury of the Church, from which indulgences could be issued to deliver sinners from Purgatory; and that this was counter to the papal bull *Unigenitus*. This bull was not always included in collections of canon law, and Luther suspected Cajetan of appealing to it because he thought his opponent might not know it.[37] But he did, and called the cardinal's bluff, countering that the text of the bull in fact said that the merits of Christ 'acquired' the treasury of Christ – and if this was the case, then merits and treasury could not be identical. Tempers became short. The cardinal kept shouting 'Recant! Acknowledge your error, this is what the Pope wants!' and Luther, hardly able to get a word in edgewise, started to shout as well: 'If it can be shown that *Extravagante* teaches that Christ's merits are the treasury of indulgences, then I will recant, as you wish.' The cardinal then seized the book of canon law, riffling through to find the page, only to discover that the text said that Christ *by* his merits *acquired* the treasury of indulgences. Luther triumphantly replied: 'If Christ has acquired the treasury *by* his merits, then the *merits* are not the treasury; rather the treasury is that which the merits earned, namely the keys of the church; therefore my thesis is correct.'[38] Luther, who wrote an account of all this in a masterly letter to Spalatin, could not resist pointing out to his friend that the German monk had proved a better Latinist than Cajetan expected.

This may look like semantics; the underlying issue, however, was the relationship between Church and sinner, and the nature of forgiveness. If the merits of Christ – and those of the saints, that is, their virtuous works – constituted a treasure stewarded by the Pope, then the Church was just a gigantic bank. On this view, because the treasure which had been built up by Christ and the saints exceeded what was needed to 'pay' for their own salvation, the 'excess' could be sold off as indulgences to the repentant sinner. But if the merits of Christ were not the same as the treasury, then the way was open to rethink the theology of repentance, and to relate Christ's sacrifice on the Cross to the believer through the concept of grace, as Luther was beginning to do. Interestingly, Luther passed over this particular exchange in his protocol of the discussion at Augsburg, although he exploited Cajetan's mistake to the hilt in his correspondence with Spalatin and in his report to the Elector. In any case, since Luther was now arguing for the primacy of Scripture over papal decrees, the exact wording of *Unigenitus* was becoming a sideshow.

For Luther, Christ's merits did not constitute any kind of credit system. Rather his merits gave the church its 'keys', that is, the power to admit or reject individuals from the sacrament and the fellowship of Christians. Moreover, because every human action was tainted with sin, there could be no satisfactory payment for sin, no good deeds to be set in the balance, no way for the individual to make him or herself acceptable to God by purchasing indulgences or any other means; the banking-system model of 'merits' had to be rejected altogether. The flipside of the argument is that whereas the practice of indulgences permitted people to pray for one another, and fostered the creation of a whole series of co-operative prayers, sayings of Mass, chantries and collective efforts towards salvation, for Luther the Christian stood alone before God, devoid of any assistance. On the face of it, this is a bleak and individualistic concept of salvation, where the emphasis is squarely placed on the believer's encounter with the living God. It must also have accorded with Luther's own experience – and perhaps his sense of isolation, as he stood alone to defend himself.

The other topic of debate concerned the role of faith in the efficacy of the sacraments. Luther argued that the sacraments were ineffective without faith, while Cajetan insisted that they were valid in and of themselves; indeed, as the cardinal argued, since one could never be entirely sure of one's faith, it was vitally important that the sacraments did not depend on it. Yet Cajetan eventually proved willing to compromise on this issue, insisting that Luther recant only on the other point, that the Pope had the power of the keys. The underlying intellectual issue at Augsburg concerned authority. When Luther presented his scriptural passages in support of his position on indulgences and repentance, it seems that Cajetan hardly bothered to read them. One person's interpretation of the Bible, Cajetan believed, could not possibly be as weighty as papal decree. The proceedings thus exposed what Luther felt to be the authoritarianism of the Church and the Pope.

At the end of the third and last meeting on 14 October, Cajetan finally lost patience. He sent Luther away, telling him not to return unless he was willing to recant. He then demanded that Staupitz intervene as Luther's superior; Staupitz replied that he would do what he could but Luther's knowledge of Scripture exceeded his own. In the meantime, Cajetan declared, he would report to Rome and await further instructions; but later that day, Staupitz heard rumours that Gabriele della Volta, the head of the Augustinian order, had requested that Cajetan seize Luther and send him to Rome. In response, Staupitz released him from his Augustinian vows – which included obedience towards those set over him in the order. Staupitz was effectively refusing to control or discipline his former protégé.[39]

The meeting at Augsburg thus ended with Luther losing Staupitz as his superior. Not for the first or last time, Luther reached an intellectual breakthrough by attacking authority, but his victory unleashed enormous creativity as well as sadness and fear. The righteous anger and aggression he displayed seemed to give him the energy to develop his own identity – and may have helped smother the feelings of melancholy, 'tristitia', which so often plagued him and blocked his way. The rejection of the cardinal's authority, however, was one thing; the separation from Staupitz quite another. His other close friend and fellow Augustinian, Wenzeslaus Linck, too, also left Augsburg. Years later, Luther recalled feeling very alone at this time. Staupitz 'left me alone at Augsburg', he recalled in 1531, and 'when I departed from Augsburg, I was afraid because I was alone'.[40] Luther had been a monk for years, an institutional man who knew how to manage those in his care and to owe obedience to superiors. Now without authority and institutional support, he was left alone in his relationship with God – the singularity that he both craved and feared.

Four days passed without any summons from Cajetan or reply to the written defence. On 18 October, Luther composed a formal letter to the Pope protesting against his treatment, and had it certified by two notaries. He also wrote again to the cardinal: an extraordinarily rude letter that boasted of his 'flawless obedience': 'You, Most Reverend Father, have seen – and I emphasise this – and become sufficiently acquainted with my obedience. This obedience made me undertake such a long journey and endure so many dangers – weak in body and with extremely limited means – in order to appear before you and make myself available to you.' This was hardly likely to cut much ice with Cajetan, who, after all, had been forced to delay his own return to Rome on Luther's account for several months. Luther continued that he did not 'want to spend time here in vain', pointing out that 'you . . . have ordered me, *with a loud voice* [my italics], not to return to your sight unless I wish to recant' – impudently presenting his imminent departure from Augsburg as an act of 'obedience' to Cajetan's ill-tempered order. He signed off as 'your dedicated son'.[41]

Like the letter to the archbishop of Mainz which accompanied the Ninety-Five Theses in October 1517, Luther's tone was utterly lacking in contrition, his protestations of 'obedience' deeply ironic. Cutting through the relations of authority, he put himself on an equal footing with the letter's recipient. Nor could he resist another little joke, when he wrote of appealing to 'a pope ill-informed who should be better informed'.[42] Although his Appellation to the Pope, written in formal legal language, was ostensibly more polite, Luther made it clear that he had no confidence in the judgement of the Church.

By this point, Luther's new Augsburg friends, fearing that Rome was going to put him on trial, urged him to leave town, and on the night of 20/21 October, he apparently climbed over the city wall. The next day, his Appellation to the Pope was posted on the door of Augsburg Cathedral: an event almost certainly arranged by Luther to give his appeal legal force and make it public. It also ensured that Cajetan now had no choice but to pass on his appeal to Leo; it was no longer a matter that could be dealt with through private reconciliation. An incomplete version of the appeal also somehow reached Johann Froben in Basle, one of the leading printers of the day, and before long it flew all over Europe.[43] Once again, Luther had proved master of the dramatic act. He was also emphatically burning his bridges.

*

The 'tournament' at Augsburg had a long afterlife, both in personal letters and in print. In the intervals between his meetings with Cajetan, Luther wrote a series of letters to Spalatin, Karlstadt and the Elector, explaining and justifying his behaviour but also setting out the events as a drama. He chose Karlstadt as his confidant, asking him to circulate the letters to Melanchthon, Nikolaus von Amsdorf, Luther's colleague Otto Beckmann and 'our theologians'.[44] The letters, with their detailed narrative and quotation, were designed to be read aloud, to entertain, to keep the Elector on side and, crucially, to contradict Cajetan's version of the encounter.[45] A month after the meeting, when the cardinal presented his own account of events to Friedrich, Luther had already given his side of the story. He then set out to rebut Cajetan's version point for point. And whereas the cardinal's letter consisted of ten neat paragraphs and a postscript, composed in precise, classic Latin, Luther's response, five times as long, was written in verbose, emotional prose.[46]

Luther had another important card to play. He, and not his opponent, had the discussions at Augsburg recorded by a notary. This, he knew, was a time bomb. On 31 October 1518 – exactly one year after the posting of his Ninety-Five Theses – he arrived back in Wittenberg and soon after sent this record to the printer, where it was printed as the *Acta Augustana*. When the Elector tried to stop publication, Luther explained to Spalatin that, since the first sheets had already been sold, it hardly seemed sensible to stop the remainder. The Elector relented but insisted that the first paragraph of Luther's 'Reflections', which insinuated that the papal breve condemning his work was a forgery, was blacked out. This was not the first time that Luther had acted quickly, before the authorities could intervene. Just a few months earlier, when the bishop of Brandenburg had stepped in to stop the publication of Luther's *Sermon on Indulgences and Grace*, his first work in German for a wide popular audience, Luther ensured that it was already on sale; by 1520 there would be twenty-five printings in all major cities in Germany.[47] Now he disingenuously explained to Spalatin that he had arranged for the *Appellation* to Leo to be printed, but had then agreed with the printer to buy up all the stock so as to stop publication, but that when he turned up with the money the copies had all been sold.[48]

With his every action, therefore, Luther was driving the conflict with Rome forwards. His use of print was tactically brilliant: he knew exactly how to forestall censorship and protect his ideas by spreading them as widely as possible, each new work marking yet another radical advance delivered to an audience that was hungry for more. The logic of the market and its craving for novelty was part of what propelled Luther's cause. Publishing largely in Latin, his writings were still mainly directed at a clerical, intellectual elite, but they were now also being translated. No one had previously used print to such devastating effect.

But there were deeper reasons for Luther's refusal to compromise. His letters at this time, especially those to Spalatin, convey a sense of exaltation and exhilaration as he came to accept that he was likely to die a martyr. The letters written before Augsburg are marked by a sense of urgency: 'This affair has to be handled in a great hurry. They have given me only a short time', or 'Fast action is necessary here. The days fly by and the appointed day draws near.'[49] All this increased the singular importance of the meeting. In May 1518, when he dedicated his explanations of the Ninety-Five Theses to Staupitz, he had written that 'only one thing is left, my poor, weak little bit of body, worn out by constant abuse . . . if they want to take that away by force or intrigue, they will only make me poorer of my life by one or two hours'.[50] With his health weakened by excessive asceticism, he had never expected to live long, and this belief had stamped his religiosity. The prospect of martyrdom now intensified that streak in his spirituality, and increased his conviction of election that had marked him ever since St Anna had saved him from the storm.

From Augsburg on 11 October, he had written to Melanchthon who, to his delight, had just been made professor of Greek at Wittenberg, telling him that there was no news 'except that the whole town is full of rumours of my name and everyone desires to see the man of such fires of Herostratus'. In classical mythology, Herostratus burned the temple of Artemis to the ground, but it seems that Luther was using the reference in a double sense, suggesting that he, like Herostratus, was not only destroying the 'temple' of the papacy, but that he himself was also likely to be burned. 'I will be burned for you and them, if it pleases God', Luther continued. 'I would prefer to perish, and which upsets me most gravely, I would prefer to lose your most sweet conversation in all eternity than that I should revoke.'[51] It is almost as if he were admonishing Melanchthon not to join him in martyrdom, while he 'burned for you and them', sacrificed himself for their sake. Indeed, Luther was not just thinking about himself. As he wrote to Spalatin from Augsburg soon after 14 October, if he were to be oppressed by force, then Karlstadt and the whole Wittenberg faculty, which had been supporting Luther's theological position, would find itself under threat. The survival of the university, so recently founded, would be imperilled.[52]

Convinced he was destined for martyrdom, Luther increasingly began to compare himself to Christ. In a letter from Nuremberg to his Wittenberg friends as he journeyed to Augsburg, he wrote, 'May God's will be done . . . May Christ live, may Martin and every sinner die (Psalm 17, v. 47), as it is written, praise be to God for my salvation.'[53] In the *Acta Augustana*, he was even more explicit: 'my writings are in the house of Caiaphas, where they seek false testimony against me and have not yet found it', so that the papists are 'seiz[ing] Christ first, and then look[ing] for a charge against him'. Like Christ, he had kept silent when Cajetan told him where he had erred; like Christ, he would be put to death.[54]

But he did not actively seek martyrdom. His correspondence veered between elevated spirituality and hard-nosed practicality, as he tried to manoeuvre the Elector into protecting him. Writing to Spalatin in September, he insisted that he did not want Friedrich to suffer as a result: 'I am ready and willing to be exposed to all who want to act or write against me. I hope the Sovereign will not get involved in my affairs, unless he could, without inconvenience, keep force from being used against me.' Yet he went on to proclaim that 'Even if he cannot do this, I still want to carry the whole danger alone. In spite of all the opinions of the Thomists, I hope I can well defend what I have undertaken to defend, so that I may glory in Christ's leadership. Even if it [then] will be necessary to yield to violence, at least truth will not be hurt.' He was reminding his friend with every word, however, of the danger he was facing, and of how desperately he needed the Elector's support.[55]

The prospect of martyrdom brought Luther ever closer to God, creating a spiritual intensity which acted as an emotional ratchet, driving him on to new iconoclastic insights. Each new argument left him at once more isolated and more elated. Every new step he took theologically was freighted with intense feeling, for it genuinely was a matter of life and death as he followed Christ's progress to martyrdom. There was no room for tawdry compromise in this elevated state. As he wrote to Spalatin, 'In all this I fear nothing, as you know.'[56]

Meanwhile imperial politics intervened. In January 1519 the emperor Maximilian died, and for the next six months two rival candidates – Francis I of France, and Charles of Spain – competed over the imperial succession. Pope Leo determined to support neither, fearing that either, as overmighty princes, would bring difficulties for the Medici papacy. For a while the Pope contemplated supporting Friedrich the Wise as an alternative candidate, and even presented him with the coveted Golden Rose, a rare symbol of papal favour. These intricacies of imperial politics helped keep Luther safe from persecution through the first half of 1519.

In the meantime yet another emissary was sent, this time Karl von Miltitz, a courtier and a man of considerably less intelligence than Cajetan, who now tried to cajole Luther into recanting. While the aftermath of the Augsburg meeting was played out in correspondence between Luther, Cajetan, Spalatin and Friedrich, the conflict with the papacy was now replayed as farce. Luther was acid about the 'Italian', whom he easily bested in argument. Nor did he trust his false protestations of friendship, wincing as Miltitz kissed him, a kiss 'of Judas', as he wrote to a friend.[57] With Cajetan comprehensively defeated, or so it appeared to Luther, and with the Elector on his side, Luther seemed to be immune from attack, at least for the moment.

# 6

# The Leipzig Debate

The long-awaited debate with Johannes Eck, which had been brewing since the spring of 1518, was finally arranged for June 1519 at Leipzig, in the territory of Georg of Saxony. The meeting was another of the dramatic intellectual set pieces which pushed the Reformation forward, and was a decisive step in the movement reaching a wider public beyond an academic audience. But while it saw the emergence of a pro-Luther party, it also gave rise to the beginnings of a coalition against him. Moreover it marked yet a further radicalisation of Luther's theology; indeed, the older Luther would date his Reformation 'break-through' to around this time. For Luther, there was no going back after Leipzig.

If the battle with Cajetan had been a tussle with father figures, the disputation with Eck was a battle of brothers. Unlike the hated Italians at Augsburg, Eck was no papal courtier. Born in Egg near Memmingen in Swabia, he was the son of a peasant and had been raised by his uncle, a priest in Rottenburg am Neckar, who taught him classics and sent him to the University of Heidelberg. Eck's intellectual formation was not unlike that of Luther's: he had read Ockham, Aristotle and Augustine before becoming interested in mystical theology and humanism. He could not be dismissed out of hand as

22. (*Overleaf*) Lucas Cranach the Elder, *Karlstadt's Wagon*. Divided horizontally into two halves, the woodcut shows a wagon driven by an old man in a beard, the true Christian, leading to the Cross. Behind it stands the 'hidden God', Christ in suffering, an idea Luther had been developing in the Ninety-Five Theses and in the Heidelberg Debate. Below, a wagon driven by Eck leads to hell. Only faith in Christ, the cartoon argues, can lead the believer to truth. In the lower part of the picture, devils nuzzle up to Eck and cluster around the corners of the image as the wagon descends inexorably towards the fires of hell, while Eck and his Thomist allies repeat the old formulae of scholastic theology.

...er. yeglicher wol ermessen mag. was yedem Christglaubigen zu wissen. not ist. Dan an zweyfel. welche diese wagen...

...lich. vnd widderumb. wortlin des vndersten. vndienlich vnd schedlich. eynen außgezogen. Das ich alles durch hey...

...hem schwerd das ist gottis wort. sonst mugt ich auch schelden. vnnutzet wie wol mir der weg widder vñ nicht helen.

Fleisch streit geist zu dē mich reist. st mit mir .2c.

Got i vns schaft. Alles dz er gut acht er pflātzt gutē wille mit fruchtē vñ wurtzeln.

durch dei Creutz mich mich selig.

Auß mer furent mich So ich mich ansehe aschrecklich. Wie gent wer ich mir frem Wā mich recht erkēt Aug. Bern:

Dein wil geschech.

Christus ist vnser selickeit

Zwang zu Christo

Gots schrifft ist gut vñ heilig. Vnd macht die sund krefftig. Dindt vbertrettig. zorn vñ tot. Bschlust all meschen in not. Gemert begerüg. furet yn schand. Dz Christ einiger heyla werd brāt Paul. et Aug.

Mei gerechtigkeit acht ich mist. dz mich got entheb arger list.

Vnguttig natren. so i freudheit harrē. gebe got ei tail. gutter werck hayl.

Du hast mei gewissen bwegtvñ i hart bdrieg geleget . bē biß gnedig. Den du gemacht hast rewhig.

Got sei folck nit vacht. weil gerechtickeit im vteryl vacht. ps 93

...isti zyhe vnß wol. vbergeuß deyn gnad vol. spruch ...nd grossem danck 2c. Andreas Carolostadius.

...nser wil mit gutte werckē außsticht. vñ sie durch sich selb...gesteet. das vnser wil fürgeet. der sal vor vnser schrifft. so...gege ie swr sindtzen. vñ sich mit Crebere wol petzen.

...hreyt. Szo keret gott zu euch alletzeyt. David Geent zu dē...werckē in gewisse beruff ig fleucht. Paulus sagt. lauffent...Got zuter macht vñ erleucht. aber wir kunne diftig wirē...nihil potestis facere. das ist volkulich. ma ich oatie lassā mi fare.

Las faren boser helde. vvir habē dz hymel erwelt. reichen lon . aus eigen krefften vvol gethon. Vmb

Der hat ein sichern muth. der so vil thut. als er selbst kā wircke. dā got muß hulf gebe

Regir dich nach deinehoch stē.so kupstu zu beste.

Der todt sund. kan an wüd. wol wircke vñan spot. zitlich en lon erlāgen von got.

Do ich lebet noch mir. vil ich i dz dir

Noch got soldten wir leben. vnd ym allein ere gebe.

Wil gie vnße compann nicht weßen. So muthe gie desse twe wagen met fliethe leeßen.

an old-fashioned scholastic or a Thomist like Cajetan. Fluent not only in Latin and Greek but also, unusually, in Hebrew, he was numbered amongst the 'humanist theologians' by the Augsburg civic secretary and fellow humanist Conrad Peutinger.[1] Eck had become pro-chancellor at the University of Ingolstadt in 1512, where he introduced a number of reforms. His students included men like Urbanus Rhegius, who later became an influential cathedral preacher in Augsburg, and who praised his teacher as someone whose sheer intellectual brilliance incited the envy of others, and blinded 'the horde of those suited to evil darkness'.[2] Not only did Eck defend Johannes Reuchlin against the Dominicans but he also invited him to Ingolstadt, where he stayed from late 1519 to the spring of 1521; Eck regarded the lectures Reuchlin gave there as amongst his major intellectual influences.[3]

The Leipzig Debate had originated in Karlstadt's reply to Eck's refutation of the Ninety-Five Theses, the 'Obelisks', in late spring 1518. Eck had tried to prevent a debate on the grounds that his 'Obelisks' were intended for private discussion only, but by then Karlstadt's 406 theses had already been printed. The Elector issued Karlstadt with a safe conduct to engage Eck in disputation. In the meantime, insults had begun to fly – Luther predicted that Karlstadt would leave Eck 'a dead lion' – and the temperature of the discussion became unusually heated.[4] In January 1519, Karlstadt teamed up with Lucas Cranach to produce a giant satirical cartoon which soon became known as *Karlstadt's Wagon*, depicting Eck driving a wagon all the way into the fires of hell.

The cartoon was published first in Latin, and then, in a sign of the times, in German. As visual propaganda, it was not exactly a success. So many words litter the drawing that the viewer can hardly discern the image: even the figure of God the Father is hidden by text. Indeed, even Karlstadt's supporters told him that they could not understand its message. In response, the intellectual Karlstadt produced more words, writing a fifty-five-page treatise of explanation.[5] Still, the cartoon had some impact: it was one of Eck's major complaints to the Elector. The humanist theologian was particularly insulted by the fact that his likeness had been labelled 'own will', mocking his belief in the role of the individual in reaching salvation as though he were just determined to have his own way.

Eck, however, wanted to tangle with the master himself, and had suggested such a possibility when he met Luther in Augsburg.[6] Luther

too was eager to debate with Eck in public and had no wish to leave
it to Karlstadt. Like a pair of boxers, the two sides then went through
tortuous semi-public arguments over judges, safe conducts, and where
the debate should take place.[7] Leipzig was ruled by the Elector's cousin
Duke Georg of Saxony, known to be critical of indulgences and eager
to stage the debate, although his attitude to Luther's theology was as
yet unclear. The nearest large town to Wittenberg, it was on a major
trade route, and it was some distance away from Eck's home ground
of Ingolstadt. Wittenberg University's connections with Leipzig dated
back to its foundation, and many of its early staff were drawn from
the older institution. Hence, from Luther's point of view it seemed
a good option, but he soon realised that he had chosen a particularly
hostile environment.

Eck's ambition and aggression equalled Luther's own. Like Luther,
Eck was sensitive to the envy of others, as his student Urbanus Rhegius
had noticed. And as Luther would later be, Eck was already doubtful
about Erasmus, northern Europe's leading humanist; early in 1518, he
had written to Erasmus criticising him for placing St Jerome's authority
above that of St Augustine.[8] Erasmus was by then at the height of his
fame and his many followers did not take kindly to attacks on the
Renaissance superstar. The young Justus Jonas – an Erfurt law graduate
and later a prominent humanist and reformer – was one of those who
made the pilgrimage to Antwerp to meet his idol, and wrote excitedly:
'I was with my father in Christ Erasmus of Rotterdam, say it as much
as you like, I was, I was, I was with Erasmus!'[9] Writing critically to
Erasmus was a calculated act, for Eck would have known that his
letter would be passed around. Like Luther, therefore, he was deliberately using irreverence to make a name for himself.[10] Luther's private
correspondence from this period was also peppered with deprecating
remarks about Erasmus, and he would later write that Eck was more
to his taste because at least he attacked the enemy openly, whereas
Erasmus moved by stealth.[11] Like Eck, Luther had little use for petty
politeness.

Unlike the monk from Wittenberg, however, Eck had experience
in politics. He had been chosen to participate in the disputation about
usury which took place in Augsburg in 1514–15. This was an issue of
immense importance to the rich merchant families of southern
Germany, as Church doctrine continued to prohibit the taking of

interest on risk-free money loans altogether. Money was different
from other commodities, Thomas Aquinas had argued, because it
was not consumed when it was used. Charging interest was therefore
sinful because it was fraudulent: if the borrower had the use of the
capital and then repaid it, he would be being charged twice if he had
to pay interest. Such arguments had led to moneylending being
concentrated amongst the Jews and associated with evil. But the new
complex money economy that developed in the sixteenth century
linked money to securities, which meant that it was no longer simply
'used'; moreover, Church restrictions created difficulties for big
merchants like the Fugger family in Augsburg, whose long-distance
trade required the movement of money. Eck was entrusted by Conrad
Peutinger, who had himself married into a prominent merchant
house, with the task of finding a way forward. Eck championed an
interest rate of 5 per cent, which he regarded as reasonable, and
developed a theological argument that took account of the new
environment in which risk could be minimised and finance made
available globally. It was an important intellectual departure that broke
free of the economic thinking that had been dominated by the ethics
of usury. Eck also defended monopolies, as firms tried to gain
complete control of particular commodities. Copper was one such
commodity, and the Nuremberg merchants attempted to command
its price by dominating the output of the mines in Mansfeld and
elsewhere.[12] Eck's work ensured him the patronage of the Fuggers,
and placed him squarely on the side of the merchants and capitalists
of the day. A man with wide interests, fascinated by the world beyond
Europe, he toyed with writing a book about the customs of the
recently discovered West Indians and in 1518 he translated a work on
the Sarmatians, an Iranian nomadic people, which he dedicated to
Jakob Fugger.[13] Luther, on the other hand, with his mining background, was deeply opposed to the ethics of capitalism and the new
kinds of economic practice, which the poor in particular blamed for
their misery. He would have been familiar with Eck's views, and the
fact that he had seen the Fuggerhäuser with his own eyes when he
debated there with Cajetan would have done little to endear Germany's
new economic masters to him.

Last but not least, unlike Cajetan, Eck understood the importance
of the printing press. From the very beginning of the debate with

Luther, he exploited print to get his views across, and he knew how to keep the dispute alive by publishing new challenges. In late December 1518, after his first reply to Luther, he had a set of twelve theses printed in placard form in Augsburg. Unlike Karlstadt, he also grasped the importance of brevity. Ostensibly the theses were addressed to Karlstadt, but all of them aimed at key points of Luther's theology.[14] Luther rose to the bait and replied to them himself.

In any other man, the combination of aggression, ambition and intellectual gifts would have ensured preferment to high church office, a bishopric or perhaps even a cardinal's hat; and it may be that this was what Eck hoped for by taking on Luther. Indeed, he considered the key issue underlying the dispute to be obedience to the Pope. He would be awarded the title of 'papal legate' in 1520, but the bishopric, if hoped for, never materialised, and Eck spent the rest of his life as a pastor and professor in Ingolstadt on a modest salary. He later wrote that all he had ever wanted in life was to 'remain a schoolmaster'. But he preached assiduously in his parish; again like Luther, he was determined that his preaching should reach the common man, and he published five volumes of sermons in the vernacular because he thought priests were being driven to use Lutheran sermons for lack of anything serviceable from their own side. Eck's parishioners found his sermons tough going, however: intellectually challenging, they made no concessions. Like Luther, Eck translated the Bible, publishing in 1537 a German New Testament based on Hieronymus Emser's text, translating the Old Testament himself.[15]

*

Just what a mistake Luther had made in agreeing to meet in Leipzig was evident from the start. Held at the height of summer when, as Luther's friend and chronicler Friedrich Myconius put it, the weather was good for hiking, the debate attracted large crowds from all around. Eck got there first, timing his arrival for the day before Corpus Christi, and was entertained by the mayor, with whom he lodged. He was therefore able to take part in the town's Corpus Christi procession alongside the town dignitaries. As the festival, during which the boundaries of the parishes are reaffirmed, was an important celebration of local identity, this was a shrewd move.[16]

Luther arrived on the Friday after Corpus Christi, 24 June, having travelled to Leipzig with Karlstadt and Melanchthon, this time not on foot but by open wagon. On this occasion, there was no need to demonstrate his humility in contrast to papal pomp. Karlstadt had insisted on bringing a whole reference library with him but his books were so heavy that his wagon got stuck in the mud, breaking the axle, just as it was about to enter the city gate. This was hardly a good omen for the man who had tried to ridicule his opponent with his 'wagon cartoon'; it seemed that it was Karlstadt's cart rather than Eck's which was bound for disaster.[17] The Wittenberg delegation stopped off not at a monastery but, perhaps tellingly, at the house of the printer Melchior Lotter.[18] Despite the cheerful summer mood, there was an underlying menace in the Wittenbergers' behaviour, however. Luther's and Karlstadt's wagons were escorted by ranks of students, armed with spears and halberds. Armed men were posted to prevent fights breaking out in the lodgings where the students stayed, while seventy-six guards stood watch daily at the castle where the debates took place.[19]

The disputation lasted nearly three weeks, beginning on 27 June and concluding on 15 July 1519. It was held in the parlour of the castle, where a room had been especially decorated for the event. Two pulpits stood facing each other, one decorated with a tapestry featuring St George in honour of the Saxon duke, the other, St Martin. After a festive Mass in the Church of St Thomas – a new twelve-part Mass had been specially composed for the occasion – the audience adjourned to the castle where Petrus Mosellanus, the university's professor of Greek, gave a ceremonial speech, admonishing both sides to stick to the substance of the matter and to avoid harshness in their exchanges.[20] The contest was not confined to the debate, however: when Luther was invited to preach by the duke of Pomerania, he attracted such large crowds that the event had to be moved from the ducal chapel to the disputation chamber. Eck felt compelled to preach three sermons in response to the attention his rival was attracting.[21]

Appearances mattered, too. Eck, a strong, tall and vigorous man, was described by some of the humanist onlookers who wrote about the debate as a 'soldier' and a 'butcher', a 'lion' and a Hercules whose comportment conveyed self-confidence and ease.[22] He presented himself as a man of the people, a 'peasant priest' who loved nothing better than to ride across the fields. He would spend the time outside the debate – discussions were held from 7 a.m. to 9 a.m., and from 2 p.m. to 5 p.m. – in his beloved woods, whilst his opponents sat indoors poring over the last session's transcripts. Luther, by contrast, was painfully thin after years of mortifying the flesh. Johannes Rubius – who had been a student at Wittenberg but was a supporter of Eck, and who wrote an account of the debate – described him as 'pale of face'; while Petrus Mosellanus wrote of Luther's 'thin body, so exhausted by cares and study that if you look closely you can almost count all his bones'. Karlstadt, he said, was the least prepossessing of the three contestants: 'He is shorter, his face dark and burned, his voice thick and unpleasant, his memory weaker and his anger more prompt'; another observer remarked on his 'repulsive, unbearded face'. Karlstadt had trouble making himself heard and he complained that Eck's voice was loud, 'like an ox'. Luther's voice, though clear, could often sound an unattractive mocking note, some commentators noted.[23]

After all the build-up, the disputation itself was a rather wearisome event. Writing his chronicle some years later, Myconius could hardly be bothered to rehearse the issues, directing his readers to look elsewhere to find out what exactly was discussed. Eck's supporters, so the Lutheran minister Sebastian Fröschel acidly recalled, slept peacefully through most of the afternoon debates, and had to be woken for their evening meals. Much of the initial sessions were taken up with arguments over formalities. Karlstadt wanted to refer to his books, but Eck insisted that he rely on memory and not 'childishly spout what others had written' – a provision that greatly benefited Eck, whose memory was prodigious and who also excelled at extempore speaking. But the Wittenbergers did win one battle: they insisted that the debate should be minuted by the notaries, a procedure that slowed matters down, making the proceedings far less interesting for the audience who had to wait for the scribes to keep up.[24]

To Luther's surprise the debate did not focus on indulgences: it turned out that Eck shared much of Luther's critique. Instead the proceedings began with a discussion between Karlstadt and Eck about the role of free will, and what part human agency might play in saving one's soul. It went on tediously for a week. Eck sometimes insisted that there was a part of the will that could co-operate with grace, while at others he admitted that good works were wholly dependent on grace. Karlstadt stuck to his line that the human will was wholly evil, but he was unable to catch Eck out on his inconsistencies. It looked like a technicality, but the topic was a central plank of the new theology: human beings do not have free will, the evangelicals argued, because they are unable to choose the good and have to rely on God's grace. The matter would come under much more powerful scrutiny in the following years, when Erasmus picked this as the issue on which to attack Luther.

The exchange with Karlstadt concluded for the moment, Eck then turned to face his real opponent. The debate with Luther moved on to other issues, in particular the nature and authority of the papacy. Luther interpreted 'rock' in the biblical phrase 'on this rock I shall build my church' as referring to Christ, not to Peter. Since this text was adduced to legitimate the papal succession from St Peter, whose authority derived from Christ's statement, this was a major assault on the papacy; and he twinned this with a rather abstruse account of Church history designed to prove that not all the Christian Churches, the Greek Church in particular, had originally been subject to the authority of the Pope. Hence, Luther concluded, papal power was a historical accretion, not biblically sanctioned. None of this argument had featured in the original Ninety-Five Theses: Luther had worked it out piece by piece in correspondence with Spalatin over the preceding months. Yet paradoxically it made Eck look like the one who stuck to the clarity of Scripture, while Luther drew on a range of little-known authorities, such as the papal historian and humanist Barto-lomeo Platina.[25]

Eck knew how to tempt an opponent into ever more radical positions. And Luther was easy game, for this was how he character-istically formed his own thought, working outwards from one position to the next. Eck lured him into agreeing that the Bohemian heretic Jan Hus had been right on several key issues, although here Luther had not exactly fallen into a trap: he had already speculated in May that some of Hus's claims may have been right. Nonetheless, it did not play well with his audience, especially not with Duke Georg, whose family had won both the duchy and the electoral title from the emperor for fighting the Hussites. The University of Leipzig had also provided a refuge for many of the German professors who had left Prague during the Bohemian conflict. Moreover, the statement also implied that Luther was questioning the authority of the Council of Constance, which had condemned Hus in 1415. In so doing, his critique of the Pope also began to part company with the conciliarists, who over the last hundred years had attempted to limit papal power by arguing that councils were superior to the Pope.[26]

Melanchthon realised the dangerous consequences of this admission. Writing at the time, he believed Luther had not intended to deny the authority of councils, but merely meant that they could not introduce new matters of doctrine. All he had said was that the Council of Constance had not condemned all the beliefs of the Bohemians.[27] But the damage was done. Sebastian Fröschel remembered how Luther had casually said to Eck, in the presence of Duke Georg, that there were some 'pious and Christian articles' amongst those condemned at Constance. Georg was deeply shocked: he shook his head, placed his hands on his hips and shouted 'A plague on it.'[28] However one interpreted Luther's remarks, though, it was clear that he was beginning to build on the ideas developed at Augsburg: that Scripture was superior to the authority of popes, councils and Church Fathers. Eck considered other things Luther said to be 'senseless' and 'offensive' as well, such as his insistence that the existence of Purgatory could not be proved from Scripture. And if the Pope were head of the Church solely according to human law, then who, Eck asked, had given Luther his monastic habit, his power to preach or to hear confession? Luther retorted that he wished that there were no mendicant orders. Criticism of the mendicants was not unusual at the time, but coming from an Augustinian monk, it was hardly likely to commend him to his brethren.[29]

The debate concluded with a series of exchanges between Eck and Karlstadt, with the latter insisting again that all human action is sinful. Even the saints do evil, Karlstadt proclaimed, that is, 'they feel evil desires in nature', and these will not cease so long as we are clothed in mortality; only when death is swallowed in victory will it be possible to have a pure, good will without evil desire. Good works, he went so far as to say, were utterly 'impure', like the 'filth' that pours out of women's bodies – menstrual blood being the most shocking and revolting comparison he could think of. Eck retorted that if all good works were evil, confession itself would be pointless and humans would not need to do anything to ensure their own salvation – they could eat, drink and be merry, leaving it all to God. This was a crude travesty of Karlstadt's position. But it revealed how uncomfortable the new ideas could be, and how difficult it was to accommodate them to familiar views of human nature.[30]

The idea of the sinfulness of all human action had by now become central to early Reformation thinking. It is a difficult concept to grasp, but it is evidently an idea that a man like Karlstadt found liberating. It could lead to a very negative conception of humanity, and to hostility to the flesh, as it did in Karlstadt's case. Not so in Luther's, for whom it led to a surprisingly positive attitude towards physicality. Behind it lies the idea, familiar too from psychoanalytic thinking now, that all our actions, even the ones we think stem from the most laudable of motives and of which we feel most proud, are tainted with sin – or as we might put it today, can involve quite murky psychic drives, such as anger, pride or envy. Therefore, far from being something which might be piled up to make the sinner acceptable to God and help reach salvation, good works can do nothing to make us other than what we are – imperfect people. But while Karlstadt and Luther denied that human beings had free will, Eck argued that this would lead to antinomianism – a state of affairs where people reject all laws and commit all sorts of sin. This matter would soon become a major fissure within Reformation thought.

Leipzig was a defeat for Luther, as he bitterly recognised when he told Lang that Eck was boasting of victory.[31] His supporters tried to put a positive gloss on the affair; Mosellanus proclaimed that 'Eck triumphed with all who either follow like donkeys and understood nothing of the whole matter . . . or who wished the Wittenbergers ill for some other reason', while Amsdorf wrote to a friend that comparing Eck with Luther would be likening 'stone or rather dung' with 'the most beautiful and finest gold'. But even Amsdorf had to admit that Eck 'screamed' better than Luther; and that to every one of Luther's arguments, Eck had responded with eight or nine of his own, making sure always to have the last word.[32] Popular opinion also gave Eck the laurels. He had taken on two opponents all by himself, producing 'Herculean and Samsonite arguments' that were delivered in a voice 'like thunder and lightning'. Luther and Karlstadt had been accompanied by a whole posse of assistants: Lang, Melanchthon, three jurists and a host of graduates who all pored over the protocol of the debate by night and who helped Luther during the day.[33] Yet all their scholarly learning combined had not managed to get the better of the bluff Eck.

Luther was particularly irked by the fact that the Leipzigers had presented Eck with a robe and a beautiful chamois coat.[34] No such honour had been shown the Wittenbergers, who also had been given only an obligatory welcome drink on their arrival, whilst Eck was feted all over town. Luther thought that Eck was motivated solely by self-glory and envy, an allegation which became a leitmotif of every account of the debate he gave for the rest of his life, most strongly in his brief autobiographical reflections that prefaced the collected edition of his Latin works in 1545.[35] Eck's supporters accused Luther of the same self-interest.

The recriminations, the insults and the obsession with 'envy' on both sides suggest that the debate raised disturbing emotions in all the participants. Reflecting on the events in 1538 shortly before he died, Eck wondered why it had all been so unpleasant: his later debates with the Swiss and south German evangelicals had been nowhere near as hostile.[36] Johannes Cochlaeus, writing about the disputation years later, repeatedly drew attention to Luther's anger. When he did not get his way over who was to judge the disputation, Luther's face was 'wrathful', and he was 'overcome by anger'; and when Eck accused him of being a supporter of Hus, Luther 'exclaimed angrily, in German, that this was a lie'.[37] To slip into German during an academic debate was bad form. Even Mosellanus remarked on Luther's tendency to refute his opponent 'a little too uncaringly and more bitingly' than was appropriate for a theologian, probably because he had come to learning late in life – a comment which may betray how much of an intellectual outsider Luther still was, and how unformed his public persona. He did not know how to look the part: Johannes Rubius described seeing him in the main square at Leipzig, clutching a posy of flowers, as if he were awaiting a lover or clutching a victory wreath.[38]

When the debate finally ended in mid-July, Luther and Karlstadt quietly slipped out of town while Eck stayed on to relish his triumph, before leisurely returning to Ingolstadt. His only error of judgement had been to pen a letter commenting on Leipzig's 'women of pleasure' which, once it had been passed from hand to hand, suggested to his enemies that his acquaintance with the ladies of Leipzig was not platonic.

The universities of Paris and Erfurt were meant to judge the outcome of the debate, and all publication on the proceedings was banned until they reached their decision. Unsurprisingly, both universities dragged their feet, Erfurt finally declining to give a decision at all. Paris did not reach a judgement until April 1521, when it commented not on the debate itself but on the heretical nature of all of Luther's writings.[39] By then it was an irrelevance. Both Eck and Luther had long since resorted to print to get their side of the story across. Luther republished his positions as he had set them out before the debate, prefacing them with his account of the proceedings. He published the sermon he had preached at the castle during it on Matthew 16: 13–19, which included the verse 'on this rock I will build my church'; the preface again insinuated that Eck was motivated by envy: 'Envy can attack the truth but will never again be victorious.'[40] In August, he published a commentary on his Leipzig theses, prefaced with a long letter to Spalatin in which he summarised the debate: it sold out by early September. Finally in December an unofficial protocol of the debate was published in Erfurt by Luther's supporters, and quickly reprinted.[41] Humanists from Leipzig and Wittenberg – the Hebrew scholar Johannes Cellarius, Johannes Hessius Montanus, and Rubius – all wrote rival accounts, attacking each other and their respective universities. The tone of the exchanges became yet more shrill as the post-debate squabbling continued, and began to move from a humanist spat towards a much wider discussion of religious truth, with Cellarius finally proclaiming 'that Martin loves the gospel truth more than do all his adversaries together'.[42]

Eck for his part published a string of pamphlets, accusing Luther of bad faith and of having broken the conditions both sides had agreed on for the debate. His final salvo was a collection of documents, including letters from Luther written during the negotiations which, so Eck claimed, proved that Luther had acted perfidiously. He translated them all into German; but Eck had to publish the collection with a member of his family, for by now he was finding it difficult to get his writings printed. Across the empire, printers were eager to publish the new, evangelical message for a hungry audience: works by conservative propagandists could no longer command a market.[43]

If the Leipzig Debate had been a personal disaster, Luther's recovery from the debacle was extraordinary. The proceedings had revealed him as a poor performer, liable to resort to personalised abuse, and unable to shine in oral, extempore debate. He had been 'harsh', as he himself admitted in the preface to the republished Leipzig articles, and he had not comported himself in the measured, peaceable manner urged by Mosellanus. Politically he had shown himself naive at best, arriving with an armed gang of Wittenberg students, which was unlikely to win him support in the rival university town of Leipzig. Where Eck had schmoozed with the elite, Luther had barricaded himself in with his companions, failing even to exploit the audience he was granted with the duke. If Duke Georg had been open to the new theology before the debate, he certainly was not afterwards, for the disputation had revealed clearly that Luther's theology was a radical break with the traditional Church. This was a serious blow for the evangelical movement. The fact that the Elector's cousin, and ruler of the other half of Saxony, was opposed to the Reformation would be a continuous problem for Luther until the duke died in 1539.

And yet within a few months, Luther had again seized the initiative. This was partly because Germany's humanist elite did not care for Eck, whose earlier attack on Erasmus had cost him their support. Men like Justus Jonas and Petrus Mosellanus mocked Eck as an ambitious show-off, engaging in gladiatorial combat with Luther for his own glory. The aggression and tricks of argument that pleased the crowd in Leipzig did not resonate well with them. Then, in the summer of 1520, Eck's reputation took a sharp knock from which it never recovered, when a brilliant anonymous satire was published, full of puns, anagrams and humanist wit. A fantastic flight of fancy that would have done Aristophanes proud, *Eccius dedolatus* was one of the best satires of the period – if Luther had described the Leipzig Debate as both a 'comedy' and a 'tragedy', now it had become pure farce. In the satire, Eck has his own witch, Candida, run his errands for him. Ill from the effects of drink, he sends her to Leipzig to get Rubius's advice and to fetch him a doctor, where the gatekeeper tells her 'you'll find the fellow keeping house in the nearest synagogue', insinuating that Luther's opponents are Jews. The highlight is their return to Ingolstadt by flying goat, which will only ascend when the names of Hoogstraaten and Pfefferkorn are uttered backwards. As they fly over

Nuremberg, Augsburg and on to Ingolstadt, Rubius, Eck's close supporter, defecates all over the goat: he is, the author implies, a truly 'shitty' poet.[44]

The second half of the satire is lifted from students' initiation rituals, as the surgeon 'planes off Eck's corners', a play on his name which meant 'corner'.[45] The scene climaxes with Eck's gelding – Eck's dalliances with the ladies of Leipzig was now common knowledge – as the surgeon proclaims that he will remove 'the carnality from this little grandson of Venus and hang it from his neck like a rattle on a child'. Witches, defecation, castration: the satire's deadly effect was to ally Eck with the old guard of Hoogstraaten, Pfefferkorn, and the other anti-humanists who had been so wittily trounced in *Letters of Obscure Men*, a text that had appeared during the persecution of the Hebrew scholar Johannes Reuchlin by the Dominicans. Luther, the satire suggests, is another Reuchlin, whose cause any humanist ought to support. Ironically, Eck had once been one of Reuchlin's staunchest supporters, but *Eccius dedolatus* destroyed Eck's reputation and excluded him for ever from the Nuremberg humanist circles to which he had so proudly belonged. (It was rumoured that the Nuremberg lawyer Willibald Pirckheimer was the author. Eck certainly believed so, vengefully making sure that Pirckheimer was included in the bull of 1520 that condemned Luther, even though the satire contained nothing heretical. Pirckheimer was formally excommunicated and was further humiliated by having to seek absolution from Eck himself, which he gained in late 1520.)[46]

But humanist support was not the only reason why Luther overcame the setback of Leipzig: in the end, Eck's victory did not matter because it was not interesting. Writing over a decade later, Luther's opponent Johannes Cochlaeus described how Luther moved with startling rapidity from one heresy to the next. No sooner had one been refuted than Luther had come up with another, and more extreme, claim. And people were keen to know what he would say next, and where he would next attack. Forward momentum meant that they wanted to read, discuss and argue in order to grasp where he was heading.

And indeed, Luther soon delivered. In December 1519, picking up on Eck's taunt that he was a Hussite, Luther argued in a sermon published in German that a Church council ought to consider whether the laity should receive the sacrament in both kinds.[47]

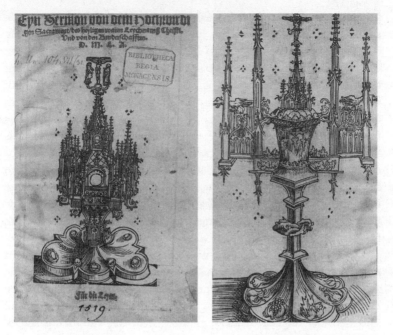

23. and 24. Martin Luther, *Eyn Sermon von dem Hochwirdigen Sacrament*, Wittenberg, 1519. The demand of the cup for the laity was clearly signalled in the illustrations too. The very first page showed a ciborium, the container in which the Host was kept and displayed to the people. When the page was turned, the reader saw the cup containing the wine, and facing it, Luther's provocative statement: 'For my part, however, I would consider it a good thing if the Church should again decree in a general council that all persons be given both kinds, like the priests.'[48]

The sacrament, Luther argued, was instituted by Christ and it consisted of two elements, bread and wine, and so laypeople, not just the clergy, must receive both. By calling for this publicly, and in German, Luther had made a demand that could be easily grasped by laypeople. Duke Georg immediately alerted the Elector to Luther's latest pronouncement, writing also to the bishops of Merseburg and Meissen.[49] This was Bohemian poison: the cup for the laity was exactly what Jan Hus had advocated. Demanding the sacrament in both kinds was more radical, and heretical, than anything Luther had said in Leipzig. And unlike the insistence on the sinfulness of human works, or the attack on indulgences, this was not a theological argument but a simple demand for practical reform that could be taken up by ordinary people and would lead to far-reaching changes in every parish. Although Luther was careful to concede that those who were given only the bread still received the whole sacrament, the genie could not be put back in the bottle.[50] It was the call for Communion in both kinds that popularised the early Reformation as parish after parish demanded to be given the wine as well as the bread. It was also a frontal attack on the status of the clergy as a separate, priestly estate, who therefore merited receiving the whole sacrament and not just the bread. It would only be a matter of time before Luther launched his attack on the nature of the priesthood itself. His criticisms of indulgences had attacked papal authority and the Church hierarchy; now, he was questioning something basic to every parishioner's experience.

Not only that, but he went on to attack brotherhoods, the most important of lay religious organisations, which underpinned the whole system of indulgences with the practice of Christians praying for each other to ensure salvation. These brotherhoods, Luther wrote, were nothing more than excuses for 'gluttony, drunkenness, useless squandering of money, howling, yelling, chattering, dancing, and wasting of time . . . If a sow were made the patron saint of such a brotherhood she would not consent.'[51] Luther was beginning to develop a distinctive German prose style – vivid, energetic, bursting with repeated verbs, and as earthy as Bruegel's pictures.

There was a growing market for such writing. In the months after the Leipzig Debate, printing suddenly exploded. Between 1518 and 1525, publications by Luther in German exceeded those of the seventeen next most prolific authors put together. Indeed, Luther alone was responsible for 20 per cent of all the works published in German presses between 1500 and 1530.[52] As a result of his efforts, printing became one of Wittenberg's new industries, and it would eclipse Leipzig altogether: when Duke Georg decided against the Reformation, and banned the printing of works by Luther, numbers of titles published there annually plummeted from an average of 140 to forty-three, to the consternation of Leipzig's printers. Catholic works simply would not sell.[53]

It was not only theologians who were turning to print. Now laypeople were weighing in on Luther's side as well, and their work

25. On the title page of the printed Leipzig sermon Luther's 'rose', the monogram he
had chosen to represent himself and which would soon become famous, is displayed
below in a shield and he is shown gesturing, as if preaching. He wears his doctor's cap
and monk's garb, and is clearly identified as an Augustinian, and as a Wittenberger,
although the artist ran out of room to write the full name of Luther's university.

was finding keen readers. A sign of what was to come was the 1519
publication (in German) of *Apology and Christian Reply of an Honourable
Lover of the Divine Truth of Holy Writ*, by the layman and Nuremberg
civic secretary Lazarus Spengler; it was the very pamphlet that the
author of *Eccius dedolatus* claimed Eck wanted to burn.[54] Spengler's
broadside was published in Nuremberg, Basle, Leipzig, Wittenberg
and Augsburg, and went into a second edition. 'Whether Luther's
teaching is in accord with Christian ordinance and reason I leave to
every rational pious person's judgement', Spengler wrote. 'But this I
know for certain, that although I don't consider myself to be particularly skilled or intellectually educated in these matters, I have never
known any teaching or sermon pierce my mind so strongly, my whole
life long.' Those who were attacking Luther's teaching as 'sour beer'
were not worthy 'to do up his shoelaces'. In particular, Spengler
attacked those who argued that Luther's teaching was suitable only
for universities and educated folk: 'If [his teaching] is just and godly,
then it ought to be shouted and proclaimed publicly, and not just

taught in the universities, or to speak more truly, in the Jewish syna-gogues.'[55] Lutheran rhetoric increasingly equated scholastics and university conservatives with Jews, a mobilisation of anti-Semitism that would create a difficult legacy for the movement.

Luther's teaching, as Spengler understood it, attacked the abuses of the Catholic Church and was based on Scripture. As far as his posi-tive theology was concerned, however, Spengler was less clear: Luther, he said, relieves the conscience which has been burdened with error and false scruples, through which Christians have been made anxious rather than comforted, driven to despair rather than recovery, even though the way to salvation is 'utterly sweet and healing'.[56] In other words, Luther seemed to be repeating pretty much what Staupitz had preached. It seems that at this stage Spengler – a linchpin of Staupitz's Nuremberg sodality – could see no real difference between Luther and his former confessor. But all seemed united against the rapacious indulgence-sellers.

Before the debate, Luther had been an unknown. Now, in the wake of the debate, the very first image of him appeared on the title page of his printed Leipzig sermon. It showed him as a thin, diffident monk, his anonymous features dwarfed by his giant cowl and beret. A circular border labels him as 'Dr Martinus Lvtter. Avgvstiner. Wittenb.', the artist clearly struggling with how to make the letters legible. Barely a year later, after Cranach had produced what would become the most famous etching of the reformer, so familiar would Luther's features become that there would be no need even to name him: by then, everyone knew what Luther looked like.

# The Freedom of a Christian

The year that followed the Leipzig Debate was the most intellectually creative period in Luther's life. The development of his views during this short time was extraordinary. The debate may have looked to contemporaries like a spat between two rival universities, a tussle between men with notoriously big egos, and of interest only to the educated; but by 1520, the 'Lutheran matter' was on everyone's lips, and it concerned not just the Church but politics, and the relationship between the empire and the papacy. That transformation is encapsulated in Luther's three major works of 1520: *To the Christian Nobility of the German Nation*, *On the Babylonian Captivity of the Church*, and *On the Freedom of a Christian*. These made the breach with Rome irreparable, and established the foundations of what would eventually become a new Church, splitting western Christendom forever.

What led to this burst of intellectual creativity? To earlier historians, Luther's story was one of unfolding inevitability: after his 'religious awakening' in the tower – an experience they dated to sometime well before 1517 – the Reformation followed on straightforwardly as its logical consequence. But as we have seen, Staupitz and many others shared Luther's views on God's mercy and justice, and were also inclined towards the mystical religiosity that characterised his devotion at this time, yet they would not join his attack on the Church. Furthermore Luther only arrived at his mature theology step by step, as he argued with his antagonists.

As we have seen, Luther later dated his spiritual transformation to the period after the Leipzig Debate; and his confident assurance that he now understood the righteousness of God – if he was correct about the date – may explain this release of energy, even if an outsider might think he had reached that intellectual position in 1515 when he lectured on Romans. Whatever the truth about this, something fundamental and new was certainly emerging in Luther as he entered this period of profound creativity, and it involved his devotional practice, his theological orientation, and his closest relationships.

First of all, in the wake of the Leipzig Debate, Luther's attitude to his monastic vocation began to alter. From his early years as a monk, he had been obliged to attend services and perform the 'hours', the repetition of prayers which took a prominent place in a monk's daily routine and consumed much of his time.[1] Even after the Augsburg discussions, when Staupitz had released Luther from his vows, he still found it hard to give up this duty, as if it were a burden he could not put down. At some point in 1520, however, he stopped altogether. He recalled in 1531, 'Our Lord God pulled me by force away from the canonical hours in 1520, when I was already writing a great deal, and I often saved up my hours for a whole week, and then on Saturday I would do them one after another so that I neither ate nor drank anything for the whole day, and I was so weakened that I couldn't sleep, so that I had to be given Dr Esch's sleeping draught, the effects of which I still feel in my head.'[2] In the end, a 'whole quarter-year' of hours had mounted up: 'This was too much for me, and I dropped it altogether.'[3] The resulting liberation – and the amount of time it freed up – may have played a great part in the burst of creativity he experienced in 1520: now he could devote himself to writing and thinking without interruption or guilt.

All this was the more intense as, the more radical his positions became, the more likely was a summons to Rome and a trial for heresy. As all those around him knew, such a trial would end with him being burned. With every theological departure he became bolder, because there was less and less to lose – and this made him think through all the logical consequences of the theological positions he had adopted. On 24 June 1520 the bull condemning Luther's doctrine was published, and he was given sixty days from the date he received it to recant or be banned as a 'notorious heretic'. The language is chilling and it is crammed with animal and hunting metaphors – the 'foxes have arisen, trying to destroy the vineyards', a wild pig is trying to attack Peter, the sheep need protecting – which may owe something to the fact that Leo approved the bull on 2 May 1520 when he was watching a sow hunt at his castle in Magliana, south-west of Rome.[4]

Luther had rejected the compromise attempts of Cajetan and of the papal envoy Karl von Miltitz, so there was no going back in his fight with the Curia. Rumours of attempts on Luther's life also persisted; it was reported, for example, that a doctor of medicine who could make himself invisible 'by magical arts' had been ordered to kill him.[5]

All this coincided with a major change in Luther's thought, and in the character of his religiosity. Up to this point, he had been deeply influenced by the *Theologia deutsch*; in the months leading up to the Leipzig Debate, Luther vigorously defended the mystical text against Eck, who insisted that the *Theologia deutsch* and other works by authors such as Johannes Tauler did not have the authority of the Church Fathers and should not be cited in debate. Luther accused Eck of denigrating these texts simply because they were written in German rather than Latin, and felt that their devotional style was the best guide for any Christian. While the book shared with Luther and Augustinianism a negative attitude towards human works, however, it also taught that through dedicated devotional piety, the individual can bring their will into conformity with God. This focus on the perfectibility of human nature was increasingly at odds with Luther's emphasis on the lack of free will, but he continued to praise the book, even when his own religious practice began to diverge from it as he spent less time in contemplation.[6]

Prayer, however, would remain hugely important to Luther. From a short work he wrote in 1535, we know that he prayed either kneeling or standing up, with his hands folded, and looking towards heaven with his eyes open. As he described it, prayer is a process: its purpose is to 'warm the heart'. Luther advised the believer to contemplate each line of the 'Our Father' and elaborate it in his prayer, before going through the Ten Commandments, each of which should be considered 'as a book of doctrine, a song book, a confessional manual and a prayer book'. 'If you have time left over', he suggested adding a creed. His advice clearly contains traces of the methodical system of the hours, although he also insisted that 'a good prayer should not be long and should not be drawn out, but should be frequent and fiery'.[7]

As Luther now moved away from the kind of spirituality he had explored with Staupitz, his relationship with his former patron and confessor also began to change. Although throughout his life he would consistently credit Staupitz with having been his sole teacher and having 'begun the matter', there are indications in his letters that his attitude towards him was much more ambivalent. In 1516, when Luther heard that the Elector wanted to have Staupitz made bishop of Chiemsee, a plum posting, Luther had written to Spalatin refusing to have any part in the scheme. To be a bishop, he averred, means 'to practise Greek ways, to sodomise and to live in a Roman manner', and to amass personal property, 'that is, the insatiable hell of avarice'. Although Luther was careful to point out that Staupitz was of course far removed from such vices, he asked Spalatin straight out: 'do you want to be guarantor that when the opportunity is there . . . or when he is driven to it by necessity, this man will not be sucked into the maelstrom and raging storms of the courts of bishops?'[8] It seems that by this point Luther thought that Staupitz's love of luxury – or perhaps his sexual inclinations (the verbs *pergraecari*, *sodomari*, *romanari* hint at homosexuality or pederasty) – outweighed his zeal for the Christian life.

Now, in a letter of 3 October 1519 Luther castigated Staupitz for being too busy to write to him – usually it was the other way around, as Luther endlessly apologised to his correspondents for his failure to write. In one chatty letter sent to the older man in February of that year, packed with gossip about friends, he cheerfully said that the bishop of Brandenburg had taken to remarking, as he put logs on the fire, that he would not be able to have a good night's sleep until Luther was thrown into the flames as well. Then in the October letter Luther lamented that his confessor was 'deserting him too much', making him feel, in the words of Psalm 131, 'like a child weaned from its mother'. Luther continued: 'I am empty of faith, full of other gifts, Christ knows how little I desire these, if I cannot serve him' – an appeal to his confessor who like no one else understood his *Anfechtungen*. Then in the letter's final paragraph, he described a dream: 'This night I had a dream about you, as if you wanted to retreat from me, but I wept bitterly and suffered; but you waved to me and said I should be calm, and that you would return to me. This certainly has come true this very day.'[9]

Having not heard from Staupitz for some time, Luther was clearly suffering from what he felt to be his increasing coldness. Indeed, it would not be long before the rift between the two men became irreparable as Staupitz refused to follow Luther in rejecting the Pope and leaving the Church; he finally deserted his former protégé when Luther was excommunicated in early 1521. The instruction Staupitz gives Luther in his dream – to be calm – is exactly what he found difficult. Indeed, in a previous letter to Staupitz on 20 February Luther had opened dramatically, saying he wanted to be 'still', but was seized and driven by God, and 'thrown into the noise'.[10] The entire October letter is full of noise: news about disputations, envy and argument. So what does the dream mean? Is Staupitz's moving hand reaching out to Luther or waving him goodbye? Is his confessor's return dependent upon Luther becoming 'calm' or 'still' (*quietus*'), or indeed, on his keeping 'quiet', as the Latin word may also imply – that is, halting his struggle against the Pope?

It was psychologically prescient. Staupitz almost certainly sent back the copies of the commentary on Galatians that Luther had enclosed with his October letter, refusing his protégé's gift: he could hardly have made it clearer that he would have no truck with the new theology.[11] In January 1521, Luther reminded him of the words he had spoken at Augsburg: 'Remember, Friar, you began this in the name of our Lord Jesus Christ', warning him that now matters were becoming serious.[12] By the time the final bull of excommunication was published on 3 January 1521, Luther could no longer be sure of Staupitz's loyalty. In February he was complaining that his confessor had already betrayed him by writing to the Pope, accepting him as judge in the matter, for Leo would certainly force him to deny Luther's teaching. Luther underlined the extent of Staupitz's capitulation: if God loved him, he would force him to revoke his acceptance, for in the bull the Pope had condemned all that Staupitz had himself taught and believed until now. 'But this is not a time to fear, but to shout', Luther expostulated, adding that 'As much as you exhort me to humility, so I exhort you to be proud.' He concluded: 'You have too much humility, just as I have too much pride.' Luther contrasted what he termed Staupitz's 'submission' with the Elector's prudence, wisdom, and – in a dig at his confessor's pusillanimity – constancy; and he described how others, like the humanist and knight Ulrich von Hutten, were standing by him. 'Your submission has saddened me, and has shown me another Staupitz than the earlier Staupitz, the proclaimer of grace and of the Cross', Luther wrote. 'If you had done this before finding out about the bull and the insult to Christ, you would not have saddened me so greatly.'[13]

It seems that Luther did not write to Staupitz again for over a year. For his part, Staupitz wrote sadly to Wenzeslaus Linck in October 1521 that he was now his only friend, 'destitute of the other, oh sorrow, whose voice I never once hear nor whose face do I see'.[14] Luther's disenchantment was complete when in 1522, Staupitz suddenly became a Benedictine abbot and retired to his beloved Salzburg, to which he had earlier invited Luther. 'It is my wish, that you should leave Wittenberg for a time and come to me, so that we may live and die together', Staupitz had written, probably in December 1518.[15] Yet although Luther felt this as a betrayal, it is hard not to see this decision as utterly in character for a man who loved a good and ordered life, whose friend Ursula Pfeffinger, abbess of the Frauenchiemsee convent, secured the best fish for him, and whose other friend Christoph Scheurl sent him oranges.[16]

For Luther, the betrayal would have been multiple. Church law only permitted a monk to transfer to a stricter order, not to one which was more lax. The principle naturally led to much argument over which order was the most demanding but it could hardly be contended that the Benedictines were stricter than the observant Augustinians. The move also marked Staupitz's retreat from the dramatic changes that had been taking place in the Augustinian order, at just the moment when, as Luther saw it, the transformations for which Staupitz had fought seemed to be coming to fruition. Last but not least, even if Staupitz shared some of the fundamentals of the Augustinian theology Luther espoused, Luther was not wrong to believe that his confessor's retreat to Salzburg – where he would be near the implacable opponent of the Reformation, Cardinal Matthaeus Lang – was a withdrawal of affection. The favourite pupil, protégé and confessional son, had (in Staupitz's words) 'shat through his hands on his head'.[17] Each man had idealised the other; now both were bitterly disappointed.

In June 1522, after sixteen months of silence, Luther wrote to Staupitz, incredulous at his decision to leave the order, but determined not to judge. The tone was now distant, telling him what 'we' – he, Linck and others – were doing to 'publicise the pure Word among the people'. He remonstrated with Staupitz for writing that Luther's works were 'praised by those who patronise brothels, and that my recent writings have given great offence'. 'My Father', he continued, 'I must destroy that kingdom of abomination and perdition which belongs to the Pope, together with all his hangers-on.'[18]

Over a year later on 17 September 1523, with the Augustinian order unravelling as monk after monk left the monastic life, he wrote to Staupitz for the last time, interceding for a brother who had left Staupitz's monastery in Salzburg, 'now a free man in Christ', and who needed financial support from 'the great wealth of your monastery'. Once again, Luther began by upbraiding Staupitz for his silence, assuring him that 'even if I have lost your favour and good will, it would not be right for me to forget you or to be ungrateful to you, for it was through you that the light of the gospel first began to shine out of the darkness into my heart'. He was disappointed that Staupitz had aligned himself with the 'infamous monster' that is Cardinal Lang. Alternating with praise and imprecation, Luther pleads with Staupitz: 'I shall certainly not cease wishing and praying that you will be turned away from your cardinal and the papacy as I am, and as certainly you yourself once were.' He signed the letter 'your son'.[19] But there was to be no reconciliation. Staupitz died on 28 December 1524, and in January Luther wrote to Amsdorf, Staupitz's nephew: 'Staupitz has departed this life, having enjoyed only a little time in his position of power' – another dig at his becoming abbot.[20] Linck, Staupitz's grateful protégé, decided to publish his last sermons posthumously but Luther took no part in it. His judgement about his former confessor's preaching was acid: 'it's rather cold, just as he always was, and not vehement enough'. He added faint praise: 'It's not unworthy of seeing the light of day, since so many monstrosities are produced and sold these days.'[21]

Luther had outgrown yet another father figure. There would be no new ones; instead, Luther himself would now act as a father to his many acolytes at Wittenberg. This can be seen in the way he endlessly fussed over Melanchthon, recently appointed to the chair of Greek at Wittenberg, worrying about his health and chivvying him to marry. Luther acknowledged that Melanchthon was the better Greek scholar and he was delighted to have won him for the university. It would not be long before Melanchthon's lectures attracted a larger audience than Luther's. However, Luther never saw him as a rival but treated the younger, physically more slight and frail man as someone who needed to be looked after.

As he reminisced later in life, Luther cast his former confessor in a purely positive light. 'I got everything from Staupitz', he would say; 'Staupitz gave me the *occasionem*'– an ambivalent word which can mean chance, opportunity, or reason.[22] He seems to have both recognised that Staupitz's patronage had given him a public platform, and acknowledged his intellectual and emotional debt to him. By that time Luther himself had become a father, and his own father had died. Perhaps the greatest – albeit indirect – tribute Luther paid to Staupitz was that although he rejected all sacraments except baptism and Communion as lacking biblical foundation, he remained hesitant about what place to accord confession and penance in Christian life, which was, after all, the issue over which the Reformation had begun. Moreover, Luther continued to make use of private confession, retaining his colleague Johannes Bugenhagen as his confessor. Regarding it as a powerful spiritual solace, Luther received public absolution from the pastor at Eisleben shortly before he died.[23]

*

In the months following the Leipzig Debate, the tone of polemic became increasingly strident. It was not just the litany of hatred and bile which Luther now poured out against Eck, accusing him of vainglory and envy at every opportunity. The Catholic party began to become more organised. Alongside Eck there were attacks on Luther by the Italian Dominicans Sylvester Prierias and Ambrosius Catharinus, and the theologian and secretary to Duke Georg, Hieronymus Emser.[24] Responding now became part of Luther's daily routine, and his letters constantly discussed which to dignify with a personal response and where a reply could be delegated. But Luther found it difficult to let anything go: having decided that he could let his '*famulus*', or servant-cum-secretary, Johann Lonicer reply to Augustin von Alveld, a Franciscan from Leipzig, he could not resist penning one in German when Alveld had his polemic published in the vernacular.[25] The attacks became ever more extreme and personal. Alveld sent a virtual letter of feud, refusing to dignify Luther with his title of doctor and accusing him of acting out of vanity 'in a womanly manner'.[26] Luther's opponents attacked his parentage, and Luther quipped that they would soon be saying that he had a wife and children in Bohemia – the birthplace of the Hussite heresy – only to find himself soon put on the defensive, insisting in a letter to Spalatin that his relations in Eisenach would hardly have claimed him as their 'nephew', 'uncle', or 'cousin', 'had they known that my father and my mother were Bohemians or other such people, rather than those born in their midst'.[27]

Luther began to discover a talent for mocking polemic. When the bishop of Meissen banned his *Sermon on the Sacrament of the Body of Christ*, he at once sat down and dashed off a reply in German. When the papal nuncio Karl von Miltitz read it, hot off the press and in the company of the bishop, he could not stop laughing – although the bishop did not join in. The author of the notice, Luther wrote, surely could not be the bishop of Meissen: someone in his chancellery at Stolpen must have misused his seal. Playing on the word '*tolpisch*', or 'stupid', he joked that the note will be viewed as more '*tolpisch*' than '*stolpisch*' (that is, from Stolpen), and advised the author to write in the 'sober morning' and not when he's 'lost his brain up the Ketzberg mountain [vineyards]' – when he was drunk. The whole matter had been sparked by 'Mr Envy', and what a shame it would have been had the 'note' appeared at any time but carnival. But for all the jesting, Luther was serious: for the bishop himself must admit 'that the whole sacrament consists in both kinds'. Catholic theology, Luther allowed, maintained that he who received only the bread 'receives the whole Christ'. But, even so, Luther triumphantly concluded, he 'receives only one part of the whole sacrament, that is, only one form of the two'.[28]

Once again Luther had pulled a fast one. He had not informed Spalatin before printing the sermon in 1519, although he was perfectly aware of the dynamite it contained. When he cheerily sent a copy to Spalatin, Luther knew it was too late for the courtier to ban it. Now, as he responded publicly to the bishop of Meissen, he did not bother to check with Spalatin either, who was furious when he read it. Luther reacted with splenetic indignation to Spalatin's rebuke.

> I have written to you before, that you should not think this matter was conceived or done according to your or my understanding or indeed that of any man; for if it is of God, it will be accomplished far beyond, against, outside, above and below your and my comprehension . . .

26. This title-page woodcut of a book by Johannes Agricola, a supporter of Luther's, from 1522 features caricatures of six Roman Catholics: Johannes Eck (with fool's cap), Jerome Aleander (as lion), Augustin von Alveld (as donkey), Dam (as pig), Thomas Murner (as cat) and Hieronymus Emser (as goat).

I beg you, if you understand the gospel rightly, don't think that the matter can be done without revolt, offence and unrest. You can't turn the sword into a feather, or make peace out of war: the Word of God is a sword.

Moreover, he added in a postscript, Spalatin's advice reached him late, when the booklet was 'almost printed' – the 'almost' clearly a slip, for if the book were indeed only almost printed, it could certainly have been withdrawn on Luther's instructions.[29]

Luther playfully invented nicknames for his enemies. There was the plodding Hieronymus Düngersheim von Ochsenfahrt, who became 'the ox'; Emser was dubbed the goat, Eck the fool, Alveld the donkey, Pope Leo 'that wolf', and the theologians became the 'asses' of

27. Title page of *The Great Lutheran Fool* by Thomas Murner, 1522. Here Murner tried to turn Luther's epithet to his advantage, showing Luther as a large fool around whom demons flutter, while Murner is represented as the doughty cat defending Catholic truth.

Louvain and Cologne.[30] He punned with the name of his adversary, Thomas Murner, christening him the 'cat fool' (*Mur* means 'tomcat' in German, and *Narr* means 'fool'). It made excellent cartoon material, and soon their grotesque portraits decorated the cheap pamphlets. Turning one's opponents into animals denies them the status of worthy intellectual antagonists, and laughter removed some constraints on aggression – on both sides.

Luther's immersion in this kind of polemic took place at the same time as his personal devotion was changing from contemplation to engagement. It was as if his rational authorial manner had suddenly matured from a thin 'head voice' into a rich bass coming from the belly, mobilising the playful, non-rational aspects of his personality; and with it, the emotional engagements that were needed to

accomplish a spiritual revolution of this order, capable of transforming
people at the most personal level.

*

By 1520, therefore, after the rupture with Staupitz and the routines of
monasticism, and with martyrdom becoming ever more likely, something profound in Luther's religiosity was beginning to shift. He now
published three treatises which together mounted a coherent assault
on the entire edifice of the Catholic Church, articulating the positions
he would elaborate for the rest of his life. They are by any measure
an extraordinary achievement.

Just how far he had come in the year since Leipzig is apparent if
we look at his position on papal power. In 1519, Luther had stated in
passing that, in the face of death and necessity, every priest is a bishop
and pope.[31] He had not yet reached the point of articulating the priesthood of all believers. But in 1520, in *On the Freedom of a Christian* he
writes with breathtaking simplicity: 'Hence all of us who believe in
Christ are priests and kings in Christ, as I Pet. 2[:9] says: "You are a
chosen race, God's own people, a royal priesthood, a priestly kingdom,
that you may declare the wonderful deeds of him who called you out
of darkness into his marvellous light."'[32]

The writings of 1520 reflect a new, relaxed style, in spite of the
pressure he was under. They radiate confidence and certainty. Up to
this point Luther had specialised in writing theses – compact, pointed
and well-defended sets of propositions – lectures and sermons. Now
he developed a form of writing which could breathe and engage the
reader. Partly he achieved these effects by employing techniques he
took from preaching, such as numbering his different points, using
memorable similes and deploying humour. But above all he addressed
the readers directly, pulling them into the argument and leading them
through the steps by which he had reached his own position.
Condemning papal pomp in *To the Christian Nobility of the German
Nation*, for example, he expostulated 'Dear readers, how does such
satanic pride compare with Christ, who went on foot, as did all his
disciples?' Or, examining the clergy's immunity from secular courts,
he wrote: 'consider for a moment how Christian is the decree which
says that the temporal power is not above the "spiritual estate" and

has no right to punish it. That is as much as to say that the hand shall not help the eye when it suffers pain. Is it not unnatural, not to mention unchristian, that one member does not help another and prevent its destruction?' He concluded that if temporal power were to be prevented from doing its job, 'then the tailors, cobblers, stonemasons, carpenters, cooks, innkeepers, farmers, and all the temporal craftsmen should be prevented from providing pope, bishops, priests, and monks with shoes, clothes, house, meat and drink, as well as from paying them any tribute'.[33]

The fact that many of these tracts were often illustrated with pictures of Luther on the front not only made the man and his message

28. Lucas Cranach the Elder's etching of Luther that was sold at the diet and became hugely influential. An earlier verison had shown a more confrontational Luther.

inseparable, but helped readers to establish a relationship with their author. In the first woodcut image of Luther produced in Leipzig, his face had been indistinct. Now one of the most important partnerships of the Reformation came into its own: that between Luther and his long-standing friend, Lucas Cranach the Elder. Cranach loved new technology and, with the goldsmith Christian Döring, he had even bought a printing press. In early 1520, he depicted Luther as a monk in front of a niche, holding a Bible and gesturing as he preached. The etching was not circulated as a woodcut or used in printed books, but its effect was immense.[34] A similar image of Luther soon graced the cover of the Latin edition of *On the Babylonian Captivity of the Church* printed in Basle, and cruder versions by local artists were used for covers printed across Germany. Some, including a high-quality portrait by the Strasbourg artist Hans Baldung Grien, showed Luther as inspired by the Dove of the Holy Spirit (though in one poor version from Lübeck, the dove looks more like a pigeon). The wide circulation of

29. and 30. Other portraits of Luther clearly owe a debt to Cranach's etching. The image above appeared on a pamphlet in low German on the reasons why Luther burned the books of the Pope, published in 1520. This has the initials that were to become famous: D.M.L., the doctor title forming part of the name. Luther's famously deep-set eyes are powerfully presented. Versions of the portrait opposite were used on editions of many different works, including *On the Babylonian Captivity of the Church* and *On Secular Authority*.

these pictures meant that Luther's likeness was recognisable well before his appearance at the Diet of Worms made him famous. And the readers who embarked on Luther's writings encountered his theology equipped with a sense of the character and personal history of the author.

The first of Luther's three great Reformation writings, *To the Christian Nobility of the German Nation*, published in August 1520, was audacious in its very conception. On the instructions of his superior in the Augustinian order, Staupitz had advised him not to publish anything for a while, but by the time Luther received the letter, 4,000 copies of the tract were rolling off the press.[35] It sold out in a fortnight and its effect was electrifying: Luther's friend Johannes Lang thought that it was 'frightful and wild'.[36] Written in German, it was addressed to laypeople not clerics. Luther argued that since the Church seemed unable to reform itself, lay authorities must step in. In a single stroke, Luther swept away the obstacles that had prevented lay authorities from dealing with abuses in the Church, because they did not have ecclesiastical authority or imperial backing. Papal power, Luther argued, was buttressed by 'three walls': that the Church had its own spiritual law; that the papacy alone had the right to interpret Scripture; and that only the Pope could call a Council of the Church. He made short work of each of these defences: spiritual law was merely an invention of the papacy, designed to frustrate laypeople from reforming the Church; the authority of Scripture must come before that of the Pope; anyone can call a council when the need arises, and those most suitable to do so are the temporal authorities. Luther's rhetoric brilliantly exploited the opposition between the Curia and the emperor and the German princes, as he drew out the political consequences of granting the German secular authorities power to act. Rome is a centre of business, sucking Germany dry of money, Luther argued as he listed the Church's financial abuses, from the pallium fee incoming bishops had to pay to charging money for matrimonial dispensations. 'If that is not a brothel above all imaginable brothels, then I do not know what brothels are', he concluded.[37]

These complaints were not new. They had been part of the 'Gravamina' literature, German grievances presented to the Imperial Diets which had circulated since the mid-fifteenth century; at the Diet of Worms in 1521 too, the German princes would ask the emperor to reform the Church.[38] We know that the electoral court had briefed Luther on these long-standing complaints, but what made Luther's argument so effective was that he presented the abuses he attacked as examples of avarice – one of the seven deadly sins.

The whole papacy, Luther argued, was organised around its lust for money, making it a monstrosity. He described the complicated financial vehicles of the papacy as *Wucher*, or usury, a brilliant polemical move that aligned the financial practices of the Church with the complex manipulations of the big merchant houses – the hated 'big Jacks' – and the Jews. This is the rhetoric of the mine owner's son, who had witnessed how the big capitalists' control of money manipulated the world of his father in Mansfeld. But the genius of the tract was to combine the economic grievances about the Church's financial affairs with the religious issue of the authority of Scripture. While it has been argued that the work shows Luther at his least theological, and betrays the influence of his new friends versed in law and imperial

31. Avarice lurks on the reverse of Dürer's *Portrait of a Young Man*, 1507: an old woman with a wrinkled, exposed breast, reaching with her other hand into a fat sack of gold.

politics, it is the theological radicalism which makes the old calls for reform far more potent.

The rest of the polemic draws out the consequences for Church and society. Luther makes a bonfire of all the collective practices of the penitential Church: the cult of saints should be stopped, pilgrimages should be ended, religious orders should not beg, monastic vows should not be binding, yearly Masses in memory of the dead should be abolished, even brothels (considered a necessary evil by the Church) should be closed down – the sheer extent of the practices Luther calls into question is breathtaking. His yardstick is the Bible. Clerical celibacy, for instance, is not commanded in Scripture, and Luther writes movingly of the 'pious priest against whom nobody has anything to say except that he is weak and has come to shame with a woman. From the bottom of their hearts both are of a mind to live together in lawful wedded love, if only they could do it with a clear conscience.'[39]

For Luther, the book of Genesis explains how men and women were created. Putting them together and forbidding them to have sex is like 'like putting straw and fire together and forbidding them to smoke or burn'. Sex is natural, and 'the Pope has as little power to command this [chastity] as he has to forbid eating, drinking, the natural movement of the bowels, or growing fat'.[40] This is a forthright attitude towards sex, and part of his acceptance of physicality, which is also reflected in his scatological and animal humour when discussing the body. The remarkable tolerance of corporeality struck a new note in theological thinking.

Significantly, the tract identified the German princes as the only authorities who could undertake reform: not the emperor, not the Pope, not the bishops, not the local towns and municipalities. Given the failure of the Church to reform itself, the princes must function as 'emergency bishops', Luther argued. They were not mere vassals of the emperor, but divinely instituted rulers with their own authority.[41] This would give carte blanche to the princes to organise what would eventually become the new, reformed church, and to set up church governments under their rule right across Germany and it provided the intellectual foundation for what would become a territorial church. In the years that followed, towns and territories would appoint evangelical preachers, and institute the reforms Luther had proposed: establishing schools, abolishing begging, reorganising poor relief, closing brothels and dissolving monasteries. As a result, the responsibilities of both secular and religious authorities would be redefined. In the process, Protestant secular rulers would also seize the chance to gain control of some of the vast wealth of the Church.[42]

Some of the rhetoric of *To the Christian Nobility of the German Nation* may echo what Luther might have heard at Mansfeld or at Eisenach as his parents' generation grumbled about hard times in the mining industry. Some sections – on brothels, finance and the law – reveal a man who looks over the monastery walls; who wants to intervene and change the secular world. This wider perspective may well have been won through the long journeys by foot he had made through central Germany on his way to Augsburg and Heidelberg; or through the men of influence he had met over the previous few years. It may also have been shaped by his discussions with Spalatin, well abreast of imperial as well as local politics. Luther now began to see it as his duty to take a stand on political matters: lay society was no longer the world 'outside', which those who entered the monastery left behind once and for all.[43] It was part of the parish for which Luther now had responsibility.

★

Then, just a few months after *To the Christian Nobility of the German Nation*, Luther published an even more radical treatise in October 1520, this time in Latin: *De captivitate babylonica ecclesiae praeludium, On the Babylonian Captivity of the Church*.[44] That month, he finally received his own official copy of the papal bull threatening excommunicaton and giving him sixty days to recant. The clock started ticking. The striking title of the treatise suggested that the Church was so corrupt that, like the Jews in Babylon after the destruction of Jerusalem and the temple, Christians were now in exile. When the emperor's confessor read it, he was so shocked that he felt as if someone had 'split him with a rod from head to toe'. He refused to believe that Luther had written it because it lacked his former 'skill'.[45] But if he were the author, he mused, perhaps it had simply been written in a fit of rage in reaction to the bull. Had Luther simply fallen prey to anger, one of the seven deadly sins? His opponent Thomas Murner decided to translate the tract into German, because he was convinced that as soon as people read it, they would be appalled. He could hardly have made a bigger mistake. The translation appeared with what had now become the standard image of Luther – based on Cranach's depiction of him as the pious monk – and, printed in Augsburg, it simply served to spread Luther's teaching yet more widely.

The treatise opens with Luther jesting that booksellers and readers should burn his earlier work on indulgences, for it was simply not radical enough. Indeed, Luther now denounces the Pope as Nimrod, the 'mighty hunter', the biblical king and tyrant who set himself up against God. The papacy is the 'GRAND HUNTING OF THE BISHOP OF ROME', that is, Rome is Babylon and the Pope is the Antichrist. Luther had already depicted the Pope as the Antichrist in *To the Christian Nobility of the German Nation*, but there it had been hidden in the final sections of the tract; here it is emblazoned in block capitals at the start.[46] Luther claimed that he owed this new insight to the attacks of Eck, Emser and their ilk, because their lame defence of existing theology revealed just how corrupt it had become. His opponents' works are dismissed as the 'the filth of this vile-smelling cloaca'. They are 'wicked men', one of them even described as 'driven by a messenger of Satan'.[47]

Whereas Luther had tentatively suggested in 1519 that a Council of the Church might consider whether laypeople should receive the sacrament in both kinds, here he attacked the entire sacramental system of the Church and its significance for accompanying the individual through the different stages of life. Of the seven sacraments – baptism, confirmation, Communion, confession, marriage, ordination, last rites – only baptism and Communion were definitely sanctioned by Scripture. The others were just accretions of the Church, and should not be considered sacraments at all.

Sacraments, Luther argued, are not works performed to please God. They are signs of God's promise of future salvation and they require faith. Faith is what justifies the sinner, Luther proclaimed; 'the sacraments . . . are not fulfilled when they are taking place, but when they are being believed'. Baptism is a sign that one belongs to the saved, and it is not just allegorical: it signifies 'actual death and resurrection'. Once you are baptised, Luther argued, the sacrament remains valid forever: you lose its promise only if, out of despair, you turn your back on salvation.[48] But the Pope had introduced endless numbers of works and ceremonies that destroyed the true meaning of baptism. Monastic and clerical vows, for instance, should be abolished, Luther argued, because in the baptismal vow we have already pledged enough. Monastic vows and works needlessly snare our conscience and we lose the freedom baptism has given us.

To some degree, Luther's assault on the sacraments grew out of his anti-Aristotelianism. In the years leading up to 1520, he had been attacking the dominance of the philosopher in the university curriculum, and engaged in reforming the Wittenberg syllabus. He rejected the notion that one could explain the miracle of the Mass – that the bread and wine become the body and blood of Christ – by using Aristotle's distinction between essences and accidents. This had been the philosophical solution to the conundrum of how Christ could be present in the bread and wine. Aristotle had argued that everything has qualities which can be perceived with our senses – taste, smell, sight and so forth – the so-called 'accidents'. But these are not the essence of the object itself, which exists independently of our perception. Theologians used this to argue that at the moment of transubstantiation, the external 'accidents' of the bread and wine – their colour, taste and smell – remained the same, but their 'essence' was miraculously transformed into the body and blood of Christ.

It made sense that having rejected Aristotelianism, Luther should also reject the Aristotelian account of the Mass. But there was more to it than that. One of the most revealing passages in *On the Babylonian Captivity of the Church* is where Luther imagined how an Aristotelian theologian would explain the Virgin birth. He would say, he guffawed, that 'the flesh of the Virgin was meanwhile annihilated, or as they would more aptly say, transubstantiated, so that Christ, after being enfolded in its accidents, finally came forth through the accidents!'[49] Luther reacted vehemently against the abstractions of Aristotelianism: he demolished the attempt to escape from *physical* reality by focusing *literally* on how Christ emerged from the Virgin. The Aristotelians' lofty distance from the body, their refuge in abstraction, provoked his mockery. Whether human reason could grasp it or not, Christ's physicality in all its dimensions was not something that could be explained away by insisting that it is only a matter of 'accidents' and external appearances. Christ *really* was made man, and his being could not be split into two parts. To explain what he meant, Luther looked at the iron on the blacksmith's anvil: the red-hot iron is simultaneously both iron *and* fire – an interesting choice of analogy which would have drawn on Luther's childhood memories of the mining world.[50]

This is one of Luther's most creative insights. His positive attitude towards the body represented a major rupture from the asceticism of late medieval Christianity, which had marked him deeply. As he looked back twenty years later, and talked with his friends at table, being a monk was all about controlling one's diet and sleep, castigating the flesh, and fighting sexual urges. Luther's original insight had been into the nature of sin and penance: human beings could not make themselves perfect and win acceptance with God because of their good deeds – they had to accept their sinfulness, and recognise that God in his justice accepts sinners. Thus they were at one and the same time sinners and saved.

Luther's radical Augustinianism had enabled him to come to terms with his own sinfulness. But it now also made him accept human physicality, along with emotional constitutions (which in humoral thought were allied), and here Luther went well beyond Augustine and perhaps also beyond Staupitz's good-humoured acceptance of human imperfection. It was one of the gigantic leaps that Luther made between 1519 and 1520, and it was as much a personal transformation as it was intellectual.

Calvin's later solution to the dilemma of the Eucharist would be to say that Jesus was speaking symbolically, and so language did not refer to the actual thing. Such an interpretation was anathema to Luther, for whom it was vitally important that the miracle of the Mass was exactly that – a miracle. It did not need to make logical sense. This was why Luther liked to cast himself as a 'fool', whose foolishness was God's wisdom – a conventional trope but one whose appeal was very deep. In theology, Luther believed, philosophy was just a distraction from the meaning of Scripture, and one must give up on attempting to find God through 'the whore' of reason, for the point of faith is that it exceeds rationality and reveals the distance between God and man.[51]

\*

The most beautiful writing from this period is Luther's *On the Freedom of a Christian*, which appeared in November 1520. Written in German, it is barely thirty pages long. With delicious irony, Luther wrote it at the same time as a letter of 'apology' to Pope Leo, and presented the essay as a gift to the Pope along with the letter. Although the treatise is divided into thirty points – the numerals are usually omitted from modern editions in English – it is not so much a sermon as a comforting devotional tract.[52] There is no polemic or aggression. Deeply musical, one can almost hear Luther's voice conversing with the reader. He begins by stating a paradox: 'A Christian is a perfectly free lord of all, subject to none. A Christian is a perfectly dutiful servant of all, subject to all.'[53]

How can this be? Luther argues that we have a spiritual and a physical nature, but he does not make this distinction in order to denigrate the flesh. Rather, he argues that the inner man should have

32. Martin Luther, *Von der freyheyt eynes Christenmenschen*, 1520.

faith in God, and we cannot arrive at faith through works of the outer man. What clothes we wear, what regulations we observe – none of it matters and it cannot make us acceptable to God. We are free from doing works. Faith concerns the inner man and – using the simile he had employed to explain the Real Presence – just as the iron becomes red hot, uniting with the flame, so our inner self becomes united with faith and with God.

As he continues to describe faith, Luther makes a uniquely sixteenth-century comparison. To believe someone is to consider them to be a pious, truthful person, whose word will always be pious and truthful, 'which is the greatest honour which one man can do another'. In the kind of honour society in which Luther lived, and in which one's word was binding and contracts depended on trust, honour was a fundamental value, an economic as well as a moral quality. The biblical law teaches the outer man just how sinful he is, and this recognition is essential before we can arrive at faith. Nothing, no human act, can be free of what Luther calls sin; we cannot, for example, avoid 'evil desires'. This is why good deeds cannot make us pleasing to God. As externals, they cannot enter into the realm of 'faith'. Luther's gloomy assessment of human nature actually leads to an uplifting conclusion:

if everything we do is tainted with sin, then it also doesn't matter: that is just how we are, and we cannot make ourselves godly by trying to pile up good deeds.[54]

Throughout the tract Luther uses seemingly simple but powerful words – freedom, faith, honour. The directness of the language allows them to resonate, but they could be understood in a variety of different ways. His use of the word 'freedom', alongside the idea that the Christian is both lord and servant, was dynamite. By addressing all Christians as equals, be they princes or commoners, and by insisting on their freedom, he broke with social deference. Addressing his reader repeatedly with the informal '*du*', he speaks to '*alle*' ('all') and '*yderman*' ('everyone'). Moreover, he argues that 'everyone' is entitled to make up their own minds on spiritual matters: 'From what has been said, everyone can pass a safe judgement on all works and laws and make a trustworthy distinction between them and know who are the blind and ignorant pastors and who are the good and true.'[55] This gave ordinary Christians the ability to decide who was preaching true Christian doctrine, rather than blindly accepting the word of the priest set over them. Scripture was clear, Luther argued, and its meaning apparent to all.

*

On 10 December 1520, the sixty days Luther had been given to recant by the bull *Exsurge Domine* ran out. When he had finished the morning lecture at the university, he went out through the Elster Gate to the Chapel of Holy Cross, near the hospital, accompanied by his students. Here, probably at the place where the hospital rags were burned, one of the masters of theology lit a fire, and Luther cast the papal decretals, the canon law, and the bull onto the flames, proclaiming in Latin: 'Because you saddened the holiness of the Lord, so may the eternal fire destroy you.' Then he returned to the university.

It was a carefully staged act.[56] Melanchthon had composed a formal announcement of what was to happen, and had nailed it up on the door of the parish church, inviting all those who 'were lovers of evangelical truth' to convene at the allocated place at 9 a.m. Spalatin knew what was afoot a week earlier: he had warned the Elector that Luther intended to burn the bull as soon as he knew for certain that his books had been burnt at Leipzig.[57] Luther had chosen the time and place to make the boldest statement possible. He was condemning the books and the bull to death, giving them a mock execution. The meaning was clear to those who had gathered to witness the spectacle: he was breaking not only with the authority of the Pope, but also with the entire tradition of canon law, built up over centuries to cover all kinds of religious issues. Once again, Luther had staged a 'happening', a public act that conveyed his theological convictions irrevocably and memorably. He proudly wrote about it to Staupitz, telling the old man just how final his break with Rome was: 'I have burned the books of the Pope and the bull, at first with trembling and praying; but now I am more pleased with this than with any other action of my life for [these books] are worse than I had thought.'[58]

The spectacle was followed by a student festival of anti-papal activity. With Karlstadt, Melanchthon and Luther having left, the students staged a play based on their initiation ritual, the Beanus rite. A trumpeter in tow, several hundred students mocked the bull, cut it up and turned it into flags, stuck one on a sword and processed around with it, then stuffed others into a giant barrel which they drove about on a wagon. To great laughter they read aloud from the works of Eck and Hieronymus Düngersheim von Ochsenfahrt as well as from the bull, and then they too built a fire, on which they burnt bull, books and barrel. They picked up the ashes like trophies, and in the afternoon they wandered about the town with their trumpets and sang funeral Masses for the bull.

This was a definite escalation of the morning's spectacle. No longer were events being safely performed outside the city walls: the students were attempting to involve the townsfolk and seize the public space of Wittenberg as a theatre for their protest. Once again, Luther claimed he had nothing to do with it; by the time the festival took place he had returned to the monastery. But their rowdy support provided the muscle that transformed a university event into something that involved the entire town.[59] So delighted were the students with their impromptu carnival that they put on a similar performance at New Year, with a mock Pope and ecclesiastical procession around the town, celebrating the event with a printed poem.[60] Just as he had allowed the gang of armed Wittenberg students to accompany him to Leipzig, Luther tacitly exploited student power to help his cause.

Above all, he knew the value of laughter. A year later, he was still poking fun at the bull. As a New Year's prank for 1522, he published a mock version complete with glosses of the bull *In coena Domini*, issued regularly by the Pope at Easter to condemn heresy. Luther, of course, condemned the 'bull-sellers, cardinals, legates, commissaries, under-commissaries, archbishops, bishops, abbots, provosts, deacons, cathedral clergy, priors . . . and who can list the gang of all these rascals, which the Rhine would hardly be big enough to drown?'[61] Although his adversaries wrongly accused him of having fomented

33. A woodcut by Hans Holbein the Younger, depicting Luther as the German Hercules, with a cudgel, *c*.1519. Reuchlin's opponent Hoogstraaten is being strangled with Luther's left hand, and Aristotle, Aquinas, Ockham and Peter Lombard have already been slain: at this point, Luther's main antagonists were thought to be the scholastic philosophers and opponents of humanism.[62]

sedition and falsely alleged that he had taught that there was no need to obey secular authority, they were not wrong to scent the potential for social disturbance in Luther's message.

The tempo of events now quickened. Each day brought news of fresh attacks by Ambrosius Catharinus, the papal nuncio Jerome Aleander, and Hieronymus Emser; as Luther put it, he felt like Hercules battling the many-headed Hydra.[63] Keeping up with the Catholic responses was taking up all his time. Armed with the bull, Eck had returned from Rome to Germany. Just how far opinion had moved within German lands was evident when he and Aleander had set out to publish it in the autumn of 1520. In Meissen, Merseburg and Brandenburg, he managed to have it posted, with great fanfare and with an accompaniment of armed men. But as soon as his escorts left, 'pious children' put up counter-notices, to such effect that Eck had to flee to a monastery. Songs were sung mocking him, letters of feud were sent threatening his life and goods, and a gang of fifty students arrived from Wittenberg who began to hound him.[64]

On 3 January 1521, Luther was finally excommunicated by the bull *Decet Romanum Pontificem*. Luther noted what was happening with fascination, following the progress of the original bull and gathering the accounts through the spring of 1521 of its fate.[65] In Leipzig, to his surprise, the bull was ripped and dung was thrown at it; in Döblin the crowds did the same, erecting a notice saying 'The nest is here, the birds have flown!' In Magdeburg, Emser's book was put up on the pillory.[66] It seemed that Germany was thumbing its nose at the power of the Pope.

Book burnings were also in the air. In 1518 it had been the students at Wittenberg who had burnt the work of the indulgence-seller Tetzel. In Louvain in 1520, Aleander managed to have over eighty Lutheran books publicly burnt by the executioner in the market square, partly by getting the councillors to seize the books from the booksellers. In Mainz late that year, however, the ritual went badly wrong. The hangman asked the assembled crowd whether the author had been legitimately condemned; they roared back that he had not been – and so he refused to light the fire, much to the audience's delight.[67] Luther mocked Aleander for having spent hundreds of ducats buying his books to burn. But burning heretical texts prefigured burning the heretic himself: Luther knew what fate awaited him if he were to be seized by the Pope's forces.

# 8

## *The Diet of Worms*

All the resources of the Saxon electoral court now turned to having Luther's case heard by the emperor rather than the matter being referred to Rome. The emperor Charles V had in fact offered to hold a hearing in November 1520, before the end of the sixty-day deadline that was stipulated by the bull, but countermanded his order the following month when the papal representative objected.[1] In their correspondence with the imperial court, Friedrich and his advisors argued that Luther should not be condemned 'unless he were heard first . . . so that the truth . . . could be brought to light'. If he were shown to err 'by Holy Scripture', Luther would 'humbly allow himself to be instructed', they assured Charles. As their formula of complaint put it, Luther was 'unheard and undefeated by Holy Scripture' – and it made brilliant propaganda.[2] The Elector's men were successful in securing a hearing: on 6 March the emperor instructed Luther to appear before him at Worms and gave him a safe conduct.[3]

Luther thanked the Elector for his efforts, but he was well aware that he owed his protection largely to Spalatin and others in the Saxon court; it was his friendship with Spalatin that probably saved him. As well as being the Elector's chaplain and librarian, Spalatin had at first acted as tutor to Friedrich's nephew, the future Elector Johann Friedrich, and he travelled incessantly with Friedrich from one Saxon castle to another, from Altenburg, to Torgau, to Wittenberg.[4] As Friedrich's advisor, Spalatin was in an extraordinarily powerful position, summarising theological arguments for the Elector and suggesting what action to take. Moreover, his influence over the education of the future Elector and the progeny of other princely lines probably helped ensure that they would in time become not only personal supporters of Luther but firm advocates of the Reformation.[5] Indeed, from about

1520, the young Duke Johann Friedrich asked Luther for advice on spiritual matters while Luther, for his part, dedicated some of his most important writings to him.[6]

However, Spalatin also tried to rein Luther in, commenting time and again that his printed pamphlets were too aggressive, and trying to prevent him from publishing them or at least to modify his tone. For his part, Luther teased Spalatin by calling him 'the courtier', and sent one of his trusted students, Franz Günter, to be educated by him in the affairs of the court.[7] On the face of it, the two men were unlikely friends. An early portrait of 1509 shows Spalatin with delectable curls, dressed in a simple grey gown with a black lining which combines academic reserve with courtly display. A woodcut from 1515 depicts a serious young man in sober garb, meditating on the Cross. But Spalatin was not a courtier by birth. His father was a tanner, and he came from Spalt near Nuremberg. One of the 'new men', he had risen through education. He joined the court but knew that, as a commoner, he was not an aristocrat's equal; there was also speculation that he may have been illegitimate. While he was a trusted servant and important advisor – and on occasion intimate enough to be present when the Elector did his toilette before dinner – he was not invited to join the table afterwards.[8]

Spalatin seems to have had a sure touch for negotiation and manoeuvre, a grasp of the possible and a sense of realism which Luther lacked. Like Luther he was educated in Greek as well as Latin, and he became part of the humanist circles around Conrad Mutian and Nikolaus Marschalk at the University of Erfurt. He did not possess Luther's abrasive self-confidence, and was a poor speaker. But the two men formed a hugely creative partnership. Spalatin bought books for the university library and supported university reforms that brought in biblical studies and those of the Church Fathers. Together they made a series of brilliant appointments, of whom Melanchthon was the star. Repeatedly Luther would recommend people to Spalatin, asking for small favours, pensions from Friedrich or seeking posts for them. Spalatin worked tirelessly in the service of the Elector, often late into the night; he nevertheless found time to translate Luther's Latin works into German, and did so with a fine musical sense.[9]

We have just Luther's side of the friendship, because it is only his letters that have survived – carefully catalogued and reverentially

34. Lucas Cranach the Elder, *Georg Spalatin Honouring the Cross*, 1515.

annotated, often in Greek, by Spalatin.[10] As the sheer number of Luther's letter indicates – over 400 – this was perhaps *the* central relationship in his life in between 1518 and 1525: he wrote more letters to Spalatin than to anyone else, even though they saw each other regularly. To start with, their correspondence opened with the elaborate formulae of affection and regard that were the staple of humanist epistolary rhetoric, but increasingly Luther's letters became less carefully written and dispensed with flattery, coming straight to the point. Spalatin became the sounding board for some of Luther's most radical ideas; it was Spalatin and then Johannes Lang whom he first told, in 1519, about his growing conviction that the Pope was the Antichrist, 'or at least his apostle'.[11] Perhaps he preferred to try out his new theological insights with Spalatin because he was not a theologian; his letters to Lang and Wenzeslaus Linck, his brothers in the order, were often more defensive and less exploratory. He also knew when to circumvent him. As we have seen, at Leipzig he refrained from consulting Spalatin, pretending that he had not known where to find him; and at Augsburg, too, he had avoided asking his advice, even though it was Spalatin who had set up the meeting with Cajetan in the hope of reaching a compromise. In the months leading up to Worms, however, Luther wrote to Spalatin several times a week, sometimes even daily.

By mid-January 1521 Spalatin and the Elector had arrived in Worms, as the Diet began its formal meeting. Luther and Spalatin could therefore consult only by letter. The Lutheran matter soon took centre stage. On 13 February, Ash Wednesday, the papal nuncio Jerome Aleander gave a three-hour speech in Latin, in which he set out Luther's heresies and insisted that he be condemned.[12] The choice of date was highly significant, for Ash Wednesday is the day of repentance before Easter, and penance was closely linked with the need to proceed against heretics. Aleander compiled a list, which he sent to Spalatin, setting out the propositions which he demanded Luther recant, most of them taken from *On the Babylonian Captivity of the Church*. There was still room for compromise: the papal emissary Miltitz was hopeful.

But Luther was determined not to compromise. As he wrote to Spalatin, if the emperor was going to summon him to Worms just to recant, he would not go; but if he were to be summoned to be condemned as an outlaw and killed, 'I would offer myself to go' – the carefully chosen grammatical form (*offeram me venturum*) styling himself as a martyr.[13] In another letter, to an unknown correspondent, he wrote that he had no care for himself, but that the great adversary of Christ, 'the universal author and teacher of murders', was doing everything to destroy him, adding that 'my Christ will give me the spirit so that living I shall defy those ministers of Satan and dying I shall be victorious'.

In the next breath he returned to more mundane matters, reminding his correspondent that he had not yet sent the money he owed to 'your brother Peter, as he told me: make sure you do'.[14] In the midst of it all Luther also found time to answer a query from the seventeen-year-old Duke Johann Friedrich about whether Christ normally slept. The Gospels did not relate absolutely everything that Christ did, Luther explained, but Christ was a natural man and 'He certainly prayed, fasted, went to the toilet, preached and did miracles more times than is mentioned in the gospel.' These natural actions pleased the Father just as much as the greatest miracles, he told the young duke: Christ's humanity was fully physical, encompassing even defecation.[15]

Finally on 26 March, in Easter Week, the summons arrived in Wittenberg, ordering Luther to appear at Worms to give 'information about the doctrines and the books . . . produced by you'.[16] It did not specify that he had to recant.[17] Luther, who was not a hoarder, chose to keep this document and it would pass down through the family. He knew that this was a historic moment.[18]

*

Luther undertook the journey to Worms setting out on 2 April with a group of friends and supporters. There was the fellow Augustinian every brother was required to take with them (Johannes Petzensteiner was chosen); Peter Suave, a young Pomeranian nobleman; probably Thomas Blaurer, an enthusiastic follower of Luther who was studying at Wittenberg; Luther's old friend Nikolaus von Amsdorf; and Caspar Sturm, the imperial herald, who had travelled to Wittenberg to summon Luther to Worms – he later became a major supporter of the Reformation. This time Luther did not attempt to walk but travelled in an open carriage, provided by the Wittenberg goldsmith Christian Döring. The Wittenberg town council contributed twenty guilders to Luther's expenses and his old friend Johannes Lang stumped up a guilder too, although by the time the travellers reached Gotha, the funds had mostly been spent, as Luther confided to Melanchthon.[19]

The little Saxon party must have been conspicuous on the road. Sturm and his servant rode out in front, the herald sporting the imperial eagle on his sleeve, followed by the open wagon with its famous occupant and his companions. Luther was now a celebrity. Crowds thronged to meet him and see the 'miracle-man who was so brave as to oppose the Pope and all the world, who held the Pope to be a God against Christ'. Disconcertingly, Myconius tells us, many of those who came to see the monk also assured him that he would be burned as a heretic.[20] Luther received a rapturous reception by the University of Erfurt where sixty horsemen and the rector rode out to meet him. This must have given Luther immense personal satisfaction, particularly after the bitter conflicts over his doctorate. Even at Leipzig, where his passing stirred less interest, the council at least honoured him with a drink of wine.[21] The journey, which lasted ten days, was the opposite of the ignominious progress of the papal bull: it was a triumphal procession.

It also created its own mythology. In Erfurt, the church where Luther preached was so full that the gallery creaked ominously and people were about to jump out of the windows into the churchyard. As a witness recalled, Luther calmed them by saying that 'they should stand quietly, the Devil might do his tricks, they should just stand quietly and nothing bad would happen', and 'indeed no accident occurred'. The sermon, recorded by someone in the congregation, was immediately printed.[22] After Luther preached another sermon in the Augustinian monastery at Gotha, 'the Devil ripped some stones off the church tower . . . they had lain there firmly for two hundred years', and Myconius, the chronicler who told the story in 1541, added 'until today it has not been rebuilt'. For Myconius, this was proof that the Devil was fighting Luther with all his might.[23]

Even before they reached Gotha, though, Luther heard from a bookseller travelling in the other direction that messengers had already set out to affix the imperial mandates demanding sequestration and burnings of his books.[24] Anxiety over the looming trial took its toll. At Eisenach, Luther was taken so seriously ill that his friends despaired of his life; he recovered only after being bled and given some spirits. He was convinced that the Devil was trying to stop him reaching Worms.[25] As he described it later, many said that 'Dr Martin and his books had already been condemned at Worms.' The twenty-one-day safe conduct issued him by the emperor was running out, and by the time the party reached Oppenheim, there were only three days left. At this point, so Luther later recalled, the archbishop of Mainz tried to trick him into a detour from his route, using Martin Bucer as an intermediary to arrange a private meeting. If Luther had attended it, he would have lost time and been guilty of disobeying an imperial summons; he mistrusted Bucer for ever after, which would have wide-ranging consequences.

In the meantime, at the Diet itself there was speculation about whether Luther would appear. As one Dominican asked excitedly, 'But where is he? He isn't coming, he won't show up, he won't come.'[26] Indeed, Spalatin warned him not to enter the city, because condemnation looked the likely outcome,[27] but Luther insisted, writing that 'we shall enter Worms in spite of the gates of hell and the powers of darkness'. Reminiscing a year later in a letter to the Elector, he wrote that even if there had been as many devils as tiles on the roofs at

Worms, he would still have gone. It was this punchier phrase that Luther liked to repeat at table and which Spalatin recorded in his history of the Reformation.[28] As he looked back, Luther relished that strength of purpose. Myconius recalled that Luther had proclaimed that even if the fires against him should reach from Wittenberg and Rome to Heaven, he would answer the summons 'and kick the Behemoth in the mouth between his big teeth'.[29]

The expectant mood of the time is reflected in a mock Ash Wednesday pamphlet *Litany of the Germans*, which gave voice to people's anxious identification with Luther. It begged Christ, Mary, all the holy bishops ('of whom there are few') and all the saints to pray 'for the Germans' and to protect them not only from such things such as lightning and storms, but also 'the Pope's tyranny', and 'the terrible threats, bulls and fulminations' of the popes. 'May Martin,' the author continued, 'the pillar of Christian faith who cannot be overturned, be protected from all Venetian poison, when he soon arrives in Worms', a reference to rumours of assassination plots.[30] His travelling companion Peter Suave likened their entry to Erfurt to Palm Sunday, and Luther wondered to Melanchthon whether this was Satan tempting him with pomp, or whether it was a sign he would be martyred; in any case, he enclosed Suave's description. Clearly Luther was entertaining the parallel with Christ.[31] Talking to his companions at table years later, he remembered his own emotional state with some surprise: he had felt, he said, 'unshocked', and recalled that 'I was not frightened', commenting, 'God can make you that crazy – I don't know if I would be so crazy now.'[32]

When he arrived at Worms on 16 April, 2,000 people thronged the streets trying to get a look at him. The papal nuncio Aleander noted that as Luther climbed down from the wagon, a monk stepped forward to embrace him and then touched his cassock three times as if he were a saint.[33] He was lodged in a house of the Knights of the Order of St John where Ulrich von Pappenheim, the imperial marshal, and the knights Friedrich von Thun and Philipp von Feilitzsch were also staying.[34] Accommodation worthy of nobles, it was situated close by the hall where the Diet was meeting. It was a reversal of the situation at Augsburg: now it was the papal nuncio Aleander who had to make do with a tiny room without heating, so unpopular was his cause.[35]

When the time came for Luther to appear at the Diet in the late afternoon of 17 April, the press of people was so great that he had to be taken through a garden and then into the meeting room through a side entrance. 'Many climbed to the rooftops in their eagerness to see', one observer reported in a conscious echo of the crowds who greeted Christ on Palm Sunday.[36] Luther walked past the ranks of German princes, some of whom shouted encouragement. The very splendour of the event must have been intimidating for the monk in his simple black cassock. The princes and nobles crowded into the room were all dressed in their finery, sumptuous cloaks, golden chains, jewellery, and dazzling headwear; and then there was the emperor himself in his magnificent robes. Luther, by contrast, wore a simple black belted cassock. As one delegate described it, 'a man was let in whom they said was Martin Luther, about forty years old or there-abouts, coarsely built and with a coarse face with not especially good eyes, his countenance restive, which he carelessly changed. He wore a cassock of the Augustinian order with its leather belt, his tonsure large and freshly shorn, his hair badly clipped.'[37]

Luther had received only the barest briefing from the imperial marshal, who told him what he would be asked and instructed him simply to answer the questions. They were read aloud first in Latin and then in German, for the proceedings had to be understood by both the scholars and the German princes and nobility. In front of Luther, on a bench, was a pile of the Basle editions of his books, bound specially for the occasion. The secretary of the bishop of Trier asked Luther whether the books were his, and whether he would recant. At this, Hieronymus Schurff, the professor of law at Wittenberg acting for Luther shouted, 'Let the titles of the books be read.' The extraordinary list of titles, which together constituted such a printing sensation, were then read aloud to the estates of the German nation and the emperor, reminding those assembled of the issues at stake. It demonstrated as nothing else could the depth and range of Luther's attack on the papacy and the established Church.[38]

Luther was expected to answer the questions with a simple yes or no, and the procedure was not designed to allow him to make a speech. He took his time to reply, and his voice, so onlookers said, was barely audible in the large room. Yes, the books were indeed his and he would never deny them, but he could not say immediately whether he would defend them or recant, 'because this is a question of faith and the salvation of souls, and because it concerns the divine Word, which we are all bound to reverence, for there is nothing greater in heaven or on earth'. He went on that it would therefore 'be rash and at the same time dangerous for me to put forth anything without proper consideration', and so he requested an adjournment.[39]

This must have been a huge anticlimax for those gathered in the crowded hall. It was also an inspired tactic, because it defused the tension and slowed matters down, giving Luther a second opportunity to speak. Luther never reacted well to being silenced.[40] His fury at being muzzled was still evident afterwards, when he wrote to Cranach (slightly twisting the truth) that he had expected a proper hearing and at least one, perhaps fifty doctors of theology, all ready to refute his views. But instead all that was said was: 'Are these your books? Yes. Do you want to renounce them or not? No. Then go away!'[41]

Luther got his adjournment and was ordered to return the next day. According to the account of events written by his supporters, they admonished him to 'act manfully, and not to fear those who can kill the body but cannot kill the soul'. One reminded him, 'When you shall stand before kings, do not think about what you are saying, for it will be given to you in that hour', and a bystander shouted, 'Blessed is the womb that bore you' – all quotations from the Gospels which once more likened Luther's appearance at Worms to Christ's Passion.[42] Luther's strategy was to insist that the arguments be heard, and he succeeded in subverting the imperial side's attempts to force him either to retract or be silent. In summoning him before the Diet, they had given Luther the best possible stage to voice his ideas. The papal nuncio himself, Aleander, had warned of this danger from the outset.[43]

The Diet was occupied with other business too, and Luther was not called until the late afternoon of 18 April, and then had to wait another two hours before he was heard. This time he was conducted to a yet larger hall that was still so overcrowded that even some of the princes had to stand. Luther remembered the scene as dark, lit only by burning torches. The imperial orator repeated the questions he had asked the day before. Again, Luther replied in a modest voice, first in Latin, then in German, styling himself as 'a man accustomed not to courts but to the cells of monks'. Formally addressing the emperor and the Electors, he begged pardon if he accorded anyone

a less honourable title than they merited – a rhetorical breach of
protocol which allowed him to try to create a more level playing field.
He acknowledged that he had written the books but they were not
all of the same kind. In some he had preached God's Word simply
and clearly. In others he had attacked the false teachings of the Roman
Church. In a third kind of book he had written against some private
'and (as they say) distinguished individuals' – a jibe Luther could not
resist – who had wanted to protect papal tyranny.[44]

He could not revoke the books that discussed 'religious faith and
morals simply and evangelically, so that even my enemies themselves
are compelled to admit that these are useful, harmless, and clearly
worthy to be read by Christians'. Nor could he contradict what he
wrote against the Pope's idolatry and tyranny, for he did not wish to
'add . . . strength to this tyranny and I should have opened not only
windows but doors to such great godlessness', continuing pointedly:
'especially if it should be reported that this evil deed had been done
by me by virtue of the authority of your most serene majesty and of
the whole Roman Empire'. The third kind of book he also could not
revoke, for there he attacked the advocates and protectors of the
papacy, and although in these works he was 'more biting' than his
religion and profession demanded, 'I do not set myself up as a saint.'[45]

Therefore he was ready to be 'taught', as soon as anyone was able
to 'expose my errors, overthrowing them by the writings of the prophets
and the evangelists' – the line that Friedrich's negotiators had taken all
along. If this could be done – and of course Luther was confident it
could not – he would be the first to throw his books onto the flames.
With regard to the 'excitement and dissensions aroused in the world
as a result of my teachings', he echoed the passage in the Ninety-Five
Theses where he had written 'Away then with all those prophets who
say to the people of Christ, "Peace, peace," and there is no peace!',
adding: 'To see excitement and dissension arise because of the Word
of God is to me clearly the most joyful aspect of all in these matters.
For this is the way, the opportunity, and the result of the Word of God,
just as he [Christ] said, "I have not come to bring peace, but a sword."'[46]

In a society which ranked concord, peace and brotherhood amongst
its highest values, this was a most disconcerting statement, and one
listener at least, Johannes Cochlaeus, was alert to its discordant note:
he later blamed Luther for raising the spirit of revolt and causing the

Peasants' War.[47] Still, the speech was an intellectual masterpiece, deflating the claims of the other side, without arguing from his own authority.[48]

The imperial orator responded somewhat tetchily that Luther 'had not answered the question'. What was required, Luther recalled, was 'not a horned response, but a simple one: whether or not I wished to retract'.[49] This was a dig at Luther's intellectualism, for scholastics liked to evade arguments by using devices like the 'horns' of a dilemma. Luther's reply now was 'neither horned nor toothed': 'Unless I am convinced by the testimony of the Scriptures or by clear reason (for I do not trust either in the Pope or in councils alone, since it is well known that they have often erred and contradicted themselves), I am bound by the Scriptures I have quoted and my conscience is captive to the Word of God. I cannot and will not retract anything, since it is neither safe nor right to go against conscience.' In contrast to the previous speech, this was directness itself. According to the official transcript of the proceedings, this was all he said; according to the account his supporters published at Wittenberg, Luther concluded with the words 'I cannot do otherwise, here I stand, may God help me. Amen.' If he did not say these words, this was the phrase that soon became famous. It certainly encapsulated the spirit of his appearance.[50]

After Luther's speech, discussions continued, but by now darkness had fallen, and the Diet soon broke up. As the report from Luther's circle put it in another self-conscious reference to Christ's Passion, when Luther departed, 'a large group of Spaniards followed Luther, the man of God, with jeers, derisive gestures, and much loud noise'. They were heard to shout 'Burn him! Burn him!'[51]

\*

What had Luther meant by this appeal to 'conscience'? It has a modern resonance, suggestive of freedom of thought and of the right of all individuals to decide for themselves. But this was not what Luther meant. The German term he often used, *Gewissen*, is closely connected to words like 'knowing' and 'certainty'; in Latin, the root of *conscientia* – another word he used regularly – means 'with-knowing'. Luther was of course writing long before Freud formulated his three-part model of the mind, where conscience is identified with the superego, the part of the mind which imposes external norms and moral prohibitions. Nor did he mean an inner voice containing the authentic individual. For Luther, the Word of God is absolutely clear and plain in its meaning, and 'conscience' is the individual's internal knowledge of that objective meaning of God's Word. This is what he meant by his insistence that his conscience was 'captive to the Word of God'.[52] Moreover, for Luther the conscience is not just an intellectual faculty but is also strongly linked to a complex palette of emotions. A conscience can be sad, burdened, clouded, joyous, happy or peaceful. It can be weak or strong, or even courageous. It may be paired with the heart, another seat of emotions, and with faith. And it has a special relationship to God, with whom it communicates directly.

'Conscience' had a long history with Luther. During his years as an unhappy monk he had felt burdened in his conscience, which led him to confess with extreme frequency. This was the unhappiness from which Staupitz had freed him, by showing him that God accepts us not because of our good works, but as sinners. Staupitz's own writings showed a profound awareness of the danger of imposing on an individual's conscience: he advised that it should only be burdened if one had committed a mortal sin. But if, he says, you find yourself burdened over sins that are not infringements of the Commandments, and if you can perceive that they are not, then you should simply jettison your 'errant' conscience; or if that is not possible, you should turn to your confessor so as to attain relief – advice that must have been honed in dealing with oversensitive consciences like Luther's.[53] But even though Staupitz was such an effective minister to Luther's conscience, his understanding of the word differed from Luther's. Whereas for Staupitz a conscience could be mistaken, and could be troubled with matters that were unimportant, for Luther it was the seat of certainty and could never be wrong. When Luther said his conscience was 'captive to the Word of God' he meant that it could not be moved or altered; he 'knew' with his whole being – mind and emotion – what God's Word was, and could not deny it.

*

Nothing Luther had written or done previously had such an effect as his dramatic defiance of the emperor and the entire assembled estates of the Reich. As Spalatin recalled, Luther returned to his quarters comforted and happy in the Lord, saying that 'if he had a thousand heads, he would rather they were all chopped off than that he should recant'. As he passed through the crowds he noticed the humanist Conrad Peutinger from Augsburg. 'Dr Peutinger, are you here too?' he said, and enquired after his family. Peutinger was evidently astonished by Luther's cheerful calm in such a situation. Back in his quarters, Friedrich the Wise told Spalatin: 'The father, Dr Martinus, spoke well . . . But he is too bold for me.'[54]

Even for those who were not interested in the intricacies of his theology, Luther's resistance at Worms was inspiring because it showed that it was possible for a simple monk to argue with the greatest powers of the day. By refusing to debate with him openly, the Catholic side had handed him a huge moral and intellectual victory, a fact which Luther was not slow to underline.[55] It was a deeply shocking lesson for a deferential society. It truly seemed as if the Word would sweep all before it, overturning the old order.

Soon there would be more than enough of the 'excitement and dissension' Luther had welcomed in his speech at the Diet. Ulrich von Hutten, the German knight and humanist, identified so closely with the event that he wrote two letters to his *amico sancto*, exhorting Luther to stand firm but warning of the 'dogs', his opponents, and talking of the need for swords, bows and arrows. Both letters were soon printed, joining a flood of pamphlets Hutten had authored which bemoaned the burning of Luther's books and called for 'manly' resistance against the 'effeminate' bishops.[56] Luther also had the enthusiastic support of the knight Franz von Sickingen, who made his living as a mercenary and by levying 'protection' money from the rich towns along the Rhine. Opportunistic attacks on merchants by armed knights and bandits were a frequent occurrence – in fact, one such raid had occurred not far from Worms itself earlier on during the Diet.[57] By a fine irony Sickingen had undertaken a feud against the city of Worms almost a decade before.

Hutten had convinced Sickingen of the rightness of Luther's cause, and Sickingen now offered the monk sanctuary at Ebernburg, one of his castles. Luther, however, was careful to keep his distance. These knights not only offered armed protection but were willing to take up arms in support of the gospel. In the autumn of 1522, they would take on the archbishop of Trier, who had been prominent in attempts to reach a negotiated settlement with Luther in the wake of the Diet, expecting the peasants to flock to their support. But the peasants did not rise up, and within a week Sickingen ran out of gunpowder. The knight was forced to retreat, first to Ebernburg and then to his castle at Landstuhl where in May 1523 he was besieged by Philip of Hesse and the Palatine Elector. He counted on being able to hold out for four months in his newly reinforced castle, but modern artillery blew it to bits in short order, and Sickingen perished from a wound soon afterwards. Hutten too died that year. Their revolt was not quite the last hurrah of the power of the knights, a group that found itself becoming marginalised as the wealth and political reach of the princes increased, and as the cities grew richer and stronger: such feuds were to continue throughout Luther's lifetime. Their defeat in 1523, however, did mark the end of the ideal of the united 'Christian nobility' of which Luther had dreamed three years before, when he wrote *To the Christian Nobility of the German Nation*.

*

On the evening of 18 April 1521 in Worms, Emperor Charles himself composed a reply to Luther in his own hand.[58] He was careful not to pretend to have theological knowledge of the issues Luther had raised, stating simply that 'Our ancestors, who were also Christian princes, were nevertheless obedient to the Roman Church which Dr Martin now attacks.'[59] Moreover, it hardly seemed likely that one monk could be right and centuries of learned theologians could be wrong. He concluded that Luther and his adherents must therefore be excommunicated and 'eradicated'. It was a clear decision for the Church and for tradition.

For the imperial side, the issue at stake was who had the authority to interpret Scripture. As the imperial orator cautioned, Luther should not claim that 'you are the one and only man who has knowledge of the Bible'.[60] The chancellor of Baden, Dr Vehus, took this line in discussions with Luther after the Diet too, but also addressed his appeal to conscience. Luther's conscience, like that of every Christian, he argued, should have taught him three things. First, not to rely on his own understanding, for 'if he went into his own conscience he could easily judge for himself, whether it would be better for him to follow the understanding of others out of humility in matters which are not against the command of God'. Scholars should keep humility and obedience always in front of their eyes so that they will not be seduced by their self-willed understanding and pride. Second, conscience should warn him to flee scandal and offence. And third, his conscience should tell him that he had written many good works, and brought many abuses to light; yet if he did not recant, he would imperil all the good things he had done. Vehus was a jurist and a politician, not a theologian, and his admonition gives a rare view of how others understood conscience. For Vehus it was an inner faculty that policed behaviour, and it had to be the same for every Christian. The nub of the matter was that Luther, trusting in his own intelligence, was guilty of the sin of pride.[61]

None of this would have convinced Luther or his supporters. Luther could not show humility in matters which, as he saw it, were against the command of God: conscience did not permit him to do so. Like many of Luther's opponents, Vehus refused to engage with Luther's actual arguments, insisting that it was unlikely that Luther could be right and the Church Fathers wrong. Conscience should be about obedience, not about one man's interpretation of Scripture. In fact, constantly urging Luther to show 'humility' was only likely to inflame the situation. By moving the debate into the realm of moral theology and targeting his character, it only served to increase the focus on Luther the man.

For the humanist Johannes Cochlaeus it was not so much the question of conscience as the authority to interpret Scripture that was key. His remarkable memoir gives us a sense of the hectic atmosphere of Luther's camp: people coming and going, arguments, and a not very effective watch on the door.[62] Cochlaeus managed to wheedle his way into Luther's lodgings and even to insinuate himself into a meal, where he found himself seated between the man himself and a noble whom he took to be none other than the Saxon Elector. Over the meal, the two began to argue about transubstantiation. Cochlaeus challenged Luther to give up his safe conduct, which did not allow him to preach or write, and debate with him man to man in public. It was a dangerous challenge, for had Luther done so, the Catholic side could have taken him captive. Luther was almost ready to agree, and had to be restrained by his supporters: he may have continued to believe that a public debate could settle the matter, and part of him was inclined to risk martyrdom as a result.

Cochlaeus did not let go and followed Luther up to his private sleeping quarters. He wanted to continue the argument with Luther alone, and threw back his cloak to prove that he was unarmed. There was an extraordinarily reckless bravery, or perhaps naivety, in Luther, who was willing to discuss matters with anyone, anywhere, any time. Cochlaeus later described himself as the one who almost persuaded Luther to recant. For him the question Luther had to answer was: how can you know that your interpretation of Scripture is right? Interpretation can never be clear, and this is why we have to trust the tradition of the Church, he argued. Cochlaeus reported that tears streamed from Luther's eyes as the humanist exhorted him not to close the door on the Church, and not to corrupt the young Melanchthon.

On this issue, as on many others, Cochlaeus was not entirely wrong. Luther himself knew that he suffered from the sins of anger and pride. But for Luther, authority of interpretation was not an issue, because Scripture was unambiguous. It was a position he had first developed in his debate with Cajetan. Scripture must be invoked against the papists and decisions of the Church councils, and Scripture clearly showed that the Pope was the Antichrist. This did not mean that it did not require people learned in Hebrew and Greek to understand it; that was why the education of the clergy was so important. But then, Luther believed, after immersion in the Scripture and careful reflection, the meaning of God's Word would be plain. It would not be long, however, before people on his own side began to read the self-evident truths of Scripture differently from the reformer. And it would be easy for his opponents to conclude that what Luther proclaimed to be the clear Word of God was just his interpretation. By denying that he had any authority, and attributing everything to the Word, Luther seemed to put his own authoritarianism beyond debate.

Luther's supporters were furious at Cochlaeus for attempting to trick Luther into giving up his safe conduct. Cochlaeus, who by his own account had begun as a Luther sympathiser, was excoriated by the 'enraged' Lutherans who, he complained (writing in the third person), 'published songs, or to speak more truly, accusations and slanders, which they sent out into other cities so quickly that these songs arrived in Nuremberg and Wittenberg before Cochlaeus had returned to Frankfurt'. His name had become a byword for treachery.[63] Mocked as a 'snail's brood', he was expelled for ever from the learned circles to which he had once so proudly belonged, and forced to make his peace with the hated Eck. His passionate admiration rapidly turning to vituperation, Cochlaeus became obsessed with Luther and spent the rest of his life attacking the reformer's writings.[64] Luther soon decided not to respond, because 'this way he will get much angrier, for if I were to answer him, he would only get proud'.[65]

But Cochlaeus's relentless observations of Luther were not devoid of insight. Luther's inner certainty depended on identifying his cause with Christ's: if you did not share Luther's views, there was no higher authority to which you could appeal. And after Worms, Luther was everywhere, hero-worshipped on medals and engravings. We know that the electoral court took care to ensure that Cranach made their man look like a pious humble monk, toning down the first, more dramatic etching. Cranach's image then became the inspiration for many others, including artists less constrained by the Saxon court. They created an image of the pious monk which became instantly recognisable, and which depicted him as a holy prodigy. As Aleander bitterly complained, woodcuts were on sale in the city showing Luther with a dove, as if he were inspired by the Holy Spirit, or with a nimbus as if he were a saint.[66]

As the lines between the evangelical and conservative humanists were being drawn, the defenders of the Catholic Church were beginning to form alliances.[67] In Augsburg, Bernhard Adelmann von Adelmannsfelden, who had been threatened with excommunication in the bull *Exsurge Domine*, sought absolution from Eck. Conrad Peutinger, the powerful civic secretary of Augsburg, who had appeared to support Luther in 1518, was careful to rebuild his bridges: he took a leading part in negotiations at Worms, and shrewdly used the opportunities for back-room dealing that the Diet afforded to secure benefices for his underage grandson; it was clear now which side he was on. But the Catholic party had not achieved very much. Aleander might remark waspishly that by the time Luther appeared in public at Worms, people already knew he was a drunkard and a scoundrel, his 'many oversteppings in looks, attitude and comportment, in word and deed' having

35. This portrait of Luther faces the title page of an account of his actions at Worms, *Acta et res gestae, D. Martini Lvtheri* and it was printed in Strasbourg in May or June 1520. This image may well have been the one that annoyed Aleander so much. It is clearly based on Cranach's original (see p. 157), but the artist, Hans Baldung Grien, has added a halo to make Luther appear as a saint, and a dove to indicate that he is inspired by the Holy Spirit.

robbed him of all respect. And although he described how Luther had gorged himself on food offered him by various princes and dignitaries before leaving, and had washed this down with a good deal of malmsey wine, this kind of gossip was hardly likely to dent Luther's image as a man of the people.[68] The Catholics had, however, secured the support of the emperor, which they had been unable to take for granted: Aleander's account of what transpired at the Diet betrays his relief that Charles had not been fooled by Luther.

But what should be done with Luther himself? Some at the Diet had insisted that the monk, as a heretic, did not merit a safe conduct. On these same grounds, Jan Hus's imperial safe conduct had been breached and he had been executed in 1415 at the Council of Constance. Fortunately for Luther, this was not the line Charles V took. The emperor kept his promise and granted Luther a safe conduct back home.[69]

The simple friar who proclaimed the Word of God had become a hero. A pamphlet that appeared not long after the Diet depicted the events as a replay of Christ's Passion:

In 1521 Luther crossed the Rhine at Frankfurt to continue on to Worms. He and his disciples assembled for the evening meal where they broke bread together. Luther warned them that one of their number would betray him, and they all denied that they would. But the very next day, Saxo,[70] who had been firmest in his protestations, denied him three times. The Romanists howled for Luther's blood, worst amongst them, the bishops of Mainz and Merseburg. Luther, in the house of Caiaphas, remained calm. The bishop of Trier considered what to do: Luther was a pious Christian and he could see no reason to condemn him. But the priests yelled 'Burn him!' So they took Luther's writings and put them on a pyre with the image of his face on top of the books. To the left of him they put Hutten's writings and to the right, Karlstadt's. Yet although the fires burnt the books to ashes, the portrait of Luther refused to burn.

Entitled *The Passion of the Blessed Martin Luther, or his sufferings*, the author was the humanist Hermann Busche, who named himself Marcellus after the man who had buried the martyred St Peter.[71]

The equation of Christ and Luther seems blasphemous. Yet the pamphlet, which enjoyed huge success, was in line with much of Luther's own understanding of Worms: Luther himself saw it as a passion, and believed he was imitating Christ. In his account of events at Augsburg in 1518, he had compared himself to Christ in the house of Caiaphas, and he had been prepared to see his arrival at Erfurt on the way to Rome as his 'Palm Sunday'. There was a long tradition of profound devotional identification with Christ reaching back through mystics and saints, which encompassed pious laypeople

36. Hermann von dem Busche's, *Passion D Martins Luthers, oder seyn lydung*, printed in Strasbourg in 1521. The work is prefaced with an unusual woodcut of Luther, which found no contemporary imitators, and owes nothing to Cranach. Luther stands full height, a monumental hero clutching a giant Bible, tonsured and in monastic habit, gazing out at the reader.[72]

as well as clerics. Paintings of the Crucifixion or of the Holy Family routinely showed the onlookers, aside from Christ himself, dressed in the sumptuous silks and velvets of the day, with slashed trousers and sleeves with extravagant patterns. This was not because the artists did not know what people wore in biblical times: rather, their devotional images imported the present into the biblical past, allowing viewers to overcome historical time as they entered into devotional time and participated in the stories of Christ's Passion. In 1500, Albrecht Dürer had painted himself, facing the viewer, with long, curling hair and with his hand raised in blessing in the style of Christ – a self-portrait that was anything but a proclamation of the divine status of the artist. For Dürer this would have been a devotional act, attempting to model himself as closely on Christ as possible as he reached his twenty-ninth year, about the age it was believed that Christ had begun his ministry. Luther's description of his sufferings as a 'passion' was not the only way he understood what was taking place – he had too great a sense of irony ever to credit it completely. But he habitually applied biblical drama to present his experience. On the journey to Worms he interpreted the book of Joshua for those travelling with him in the wagon. It was an interesting choice, for the biblical Joshua was the leader of the Israelites after the death of Moses; he had fought the battle of Jericho, and led the Israelites during their exile in the desert, just as Luther was now leading the members of the true church against the forces of Rome.

When Luther later insisted that 'the Word did everything', it was true in the sense that he made himself into Christ's vessel and tried to resign his own agency, thus greatly strengthening his ability to act and face danger.[73] But his appearance at Worms was even more a devotional act, a sacred drama, where he stood on Christ's side whilst his enemies attempted to try him. Identifying his cause with that of Christ gave Luther immense certainty and courage. It enabled him to accept the possibility of martyrdom, without embracing it as a destiny. But he also initiated an understanding of events that would brook no argument. At Worms, God's Word had been at work, an authority that trumped all emperors and princes.

Luther had appealed to the emperor against the Pope, and though he had escaped martyrdom, he had lost; now both imperial and papal power were ranged against him. On 26 May, the day after the conclusion of the Diet, and when Luther had long ago left town, the emperor signed the Edict of Worms that declared Luther an outlaw, forbade anyone to house him or eat with him, and banned the sale, reading, possession or printing of his works. Luther had known what was coming, but he was in exhilarated mood. Comparing his travails at Worms with Christ's Passion and Resurrection, he had written to Cranach on 28 April, two days after leaving Worms: 'For a little while we must suffer and be silent. A little time, and you will not see me again; a little more time and you will see me.'[74]

# 9

## In the Wartburg

No one was to know Luther's whereabouts. After the excitement of Worms, where the great princes of the empire had queued up to meet him, where he had been surrounded by supporters and friends from dawn till dusk, and where his every word had been noted and its significance weighed, Luther was now alone. On 4 May, having visited his relatives in Möhra on his way back from the Diet, Luther had been kidnapped near Burg Altenstein and brought by a circuitous route to Wartburg Castle, towering high up above Eisenach, hidden in the woods. The castle walls are hewn into the rock of the hills with views on three sides; to Luther it felt as if he was in the kingdom of the birds. The monk who was now famous throughout the empire had returned to where, as a schoolboy, he had stolen strawberries in the woods, and where his mother's family still lived.[1]

The kidnapping had been staged by the Elector, who feared the emperor's wrath for harbouring a man the Edict of Worms had now declared a 'stubborn schismatic and public heretic'.[2] So he was kept in the Wartburg in disguise. Dressed in the clothes of a knight, Luther let his tonsure grow out, and was no longer clean-shaven. The figure-hugging attire, with hose designed to show off well-turned legs, fine linen shirt, doublet and showy codpiece, must have been a shock for a monk used to wearing a shapeless woollen cassock belted at the waist. When he secretly returned to Wittenberg in December six months later, his friends did not at first recognise him: in his riding coat he looked like a nobleman with 'a thick beard over his whole mouth and cheeks'.[3]

Luther did not make much of a knight, however. He had not found the ride from Altenstein to the Wartburg easy – he was used to trav-elling in wagons, not to riding and the muscular control it required.

IMAGO D MARTINI LVTHERI, EO HABITV
EXPRESSA, QVO REVERSVS EST EX PATHMO WI-
TEBERGAM, ANNO M. D. XXII.

Quæsitus toties, toties tibi Roma petitus,     Vita mihi ipse est, quo non fraudabor, IESVS,
Ea ego per Christum viuo Lutherus adhuc.     Hunc mihi dum teneam, perfida Roma vale.
ANNVS CONFESSIONIS          ANNVS PATHMI,          ANNVS REDITVS EX
     PFumane 1521.                     1521.                     Patmi, 1522.

WITEBERGAE Iohannes Schwertel excudebat, Anno 1

37. Lucas Cranach the Elder, *Luther as Junker Jörg*, 1522.

Noble life was not much to his taste either. He tried hunting, but his instincts were all wrong: he wanted to protect the quarry. On one outing, he scooped up the hare and wrapped the injured animal in his sleeve to protect it from the dogs, but they bit right through his cloak, broke the hare's leg and choked it to death. Luther, ever the preacher, turned the incident into a theological metaphor. The hare was the Christian soul, attacked by the Pope and Satan. In heaven, the tables would be turned, and the noble hunters who so loved eating game would become Christ's prey. Stuck in the castle, where he would remain for ten months, Luther evidently did not relish being a victim, incapable of fighting back. For all his distaste for hunting, he would rather be a hunter than a hare.[4]

Hans von Berlepsch, the castellan, treated him well, but it was difficult to keep the secret about the mysterious guest. The wife of one of the Elector's notaries had let Luther's location slip, and since this rumour originated at court, it was credible. Moreover, Berlepsch was convinced that Luther's whereabouts were already general knowledge. Not for the first time, therefore, Luther determined on a ruse to fool his enemies – and like many of his other cunning plans, this one was a little too clever. He wrote to Spalatin in mid-July 1521 enclosing another letter in his own hand, that purported to have been sent from 'my quarters' in Bohemia. He asked Spalatin to 'lose' it 'with studied carelessness': 'I hear a rumour is being spread, my Spalatin, that Luther is living in the Wartburg near Eisenach . . . Strange that nobody now thinks of Bohemia', he wrote. He 'would love the "hog of Dresden"' (that is, Duke Georg) to find the letter, Luther wrote in his accompanying note. It was obvious that the letter has no point apart from where it was supposedly sent. It would have fooled nobody. Worse, for many, it would have confirmed that he was indeed in the Wartburg, the letter too eager to deny the rumour in the first line.[5]

The letter also revealed how much Luther blamed Duke Georg, the Elector's cousin, under whose patronage the Leipzig Debate had been held, for the problems he and his supporters now faced within the empire. Straight after his appearance at the Diet, in the exhilaration of having got out of Worms alive, Luther had written to Cranach of how he would 'have preferred to suffer death at the hands of the tyrants, especially those of the furious Duke Georg of Saxony', but had listened to the advice of others.[6] This enmity would last until Georg died in 1539, and it would elicit some of the most bitter and baroque of Luther's invective. As so often, Luther was reducing a complex pattern of political opposition to his movement within Germany as a whole to a simple fight against 'the hog of Dresden', whom he could hate with gusto.

The danger of discovery meant that Luther became utterly dependent on Spalatin, who was now his chief means of communication with the outside world. The solitude soon irked Luther, and he wrote to his friends complaining of his enforced 'leisure', that made him heavy-headed and inclined to drunkenness.[7] In the castle, he rigged up the small chamber he was assigned as a study, and asked Spalatin for books. But this 'leisure' also gave him time for reflection, and his letters from this period are amongst his fullest and most revealing. Not only do they tell us much about the nature of his friendships, but they show Luther beginning to reassess his own life and especially his relationship with his father as he gradually came to terms with the public figure he had become.

Sitting high up in his eyrie, Luther had no way of controlling what was happening in the world below. He had to wait for news from Wittenberg. The pattern of his correspondence betrays the shrinking compass of his world. There are letters to his friend Nikolaus Gerbel in Strasbourg, but remarkably, none that survive to Nuremberg, Augsburg or Basle, and therefore nothing to suggest that he was increasing his influence in the prosperous south.[8] We do not know whether this was because of the difficulty of sending messengers to southern Germany without betraying his hiding place, or because the Nurembergers, once such enthusiastic members of the Staupitz sodality and so keen to spread the word about Luther, now wanted to distance themselves from him. Two of them, the lawyer Willibald Pirckheimer and civic secretary Lazarus Spengler, had been named in the bull of excommunication alongside Luther, but Pirckheimer had humiliatingly sought and received absolution from Eck. Luther's correspondence network contracted, concentrating on Wittenberg, Saxony and the mining areas of Mansfeld, and so did his political reach. Beyond it, other reformers emerged who would take his Reformation in different directions.

In the Wartburg, Luther began to suffer from severe constipation, which had first affected him at Worms. As he wrote to Spalatin, 'the Lord strikes me in my posterior with serious pain'. The pains were his own special 'relic of the Cross', he quipped.[9] He went for four, sometimes even six days without a bowel movement and the excrement was so hard that it caused bleeding. 'Now I sit in pain like a woman in childbirth, ripped up, bloody and I will have little rest tonight', he wrote.[10] Just as he was in isolation from the outside world, so his body also seemed sealed off, unable to 'flow' – the process humoral medicine considered fundamental to physical health. The condition lasted until the autumn and must have added to Luther's sense of physical discomfort, with a different diet, a sedentary lifestyle and clothing that constantly constricted the body. But perhaps, after the fevered rush of the period leading up to the Diet of Worms, the constipation may have reflected his own turning inwards, entering a period of inactivity as essential as it was difficult, before he could become creative again.[11]

He also experienced attacks of the Devil. The story which was to become famous, of Luther throwing an inkpot at the Devil – the stain still visible today on the wall of his castle room – almost certainly rests on a misreading of Luther's remark that he would fight the Devil with ink: that is, the printed word. But there was a new urgency about the Devil's attacks, partly because without his friends and colleagues to talk to, his inner world loomed larger. 'In this leisurely solitude' he was 'exposed to a thousand devils', he wrote. In one sense he was a monk because he was alone, he told Spalatin, and yet 'I am not actually a monk [i.e. a hermit, alone], because I have many evil and astute demons with me; they "amuse" me, as one says, but in a disturbing way.'[12] What were these attacks of the Devil about?

During his time in the Wartburg, Luther had to come to terms with his body in new ways. 'I sit here like a fool and hardened in leisure, pray little, do not sigh for the church of God, yet burn in a big fire of my untamed body. In short I should be ardent in spirit, but I am ardent in the flesh, in lust, laziness, leisure and sleepiness.'[13] It was not just constipation that made him painfully aware of the flesh; nor was Luther describing sexual lust alone. As the monastery in Wittenberg gradually emptied, he knew that he had to change and give up the life of a monk. Gone was all the discipline, the importance of keeping time, the collective eating, the disruption of sleep patterns for services in the night, the structure of daily life. The transformation of Luther was as much physical and emotional as it was theological.

Meanwhile, matters were moving fast in Wittenberg. While Melanchthon became Luther's main collaborator and instrument in the town, the relationship between the two men was not without its difficulties. Melanchthon had embarked on the *Loci communes* (*Common-places*), his great work of systematisation of Reformation theology, which would create a doctrinal corpus for the new movement. Luther's

respect for the younger man grew, and as he read Melanchthon's drafts
in the Wartburg he would repeatedly state that Melanchthon was the
better scholar. Yet his colleague was not easy to keep on the straight
and narrow. Far from taking on Luther's mantle in his absence from
Wittenberg, he seems to have found inspiration in the sermons of a
monk, Gabriel Zwilling, who had moved into the Augustinian cloister
from Zwickau, and who preached radical reform. A contemporary
reported that Melanchthon never missed one of his sermons.[14] Luther's
irritation showed through. 'As is your way, you are just too gentle',
he told the younger man, grumbling to Spalatin that Melanchthon
'gives in too easily to his moods, and bears the Cross more impatiently
than is fitting for a student, let alone such a great teacher of teachers'.[15]
Chivvying him to be a leader, Luther toyed with the idea that Melanchthon should preach or at least (since he was not ordained, though
Luther no longer thought this an obstacle) he should give public
lectures, so that all could hear his exegesis of the Bible.[16]

For his part, Karlstadt, Luther's co-debater at Leipzig, was producing
a flood of treatises. First he attacked monastic vows, then he began
to ponder sexuality and marriage, before condemning religious images
and finally, moving towards a reinterpretation of the Mass and
Communion. His new theological views had ramifications for his ideas
about society, too; and he began to question hierarchies of all kinds.
Luther read much of his work and, as he was prone, arrived at many
of his own views in response to Karlstadt's arguments. Alone in his
'Patmos' – as he called his study in the Wartburg, likening it to the
island where John wrote the biblical book of Revelation – his intellectual development at the time paralleled in many ways that of
Karlstadt. But whereas Karlstadt was dealing with new situations
arising in Wittenberg and was forced to make policy in reaction to a
host of different pressures – from the Elector, the populace, the university, the radical Augustinians – Luther was alone with the Devil.

In *To the Christian Nobility of the German Nation*, Luther had argued
that priests who lived with concubines ought to be allowed to marry,
and in the spring of 1521 the Wittenberg graduate and university rector
Bartholomäus Bernhardi had been the first to do just that, in public.[17]
However, in 1520 Luther had not included monks like himself in his
musings about marriage because they had made special vows of chastity
of their own free will. Now, in Wittenberg, matters were moving apace

as Karlstadt attacked monastic vows, first in a set of theses for debate, then in longer writings in both Latin and German. Luther not only read these tracts, but discussed them in letters to Melanchthon.[18] Then in early September 1521, he penned a first short set of theses for discussion within Wittenberg. He soon added others which were published in early October, but Luther did not complete his own full tract on vows until November.[19] If earlier in the Reformation it had been Karlstadt learning from Luther, now Karlstadt was forcing the pace.

For a work advocating marriage, Karlstadt's tract is strangely anti-erotic, even anti-sexual. He does not mince his words in the Latin text, however: monks only manage celibacy, he argues, by committing the sin of Moloch – that is, masturbation – shedding seed on the ground, or on their robes, and that is worse than fornication or adultery. Karlstadt's pamphlet evokes the horror of frustrated lust, making the reader feel revolted by the sexual perversions to which it gives rise. He names some of these 'beastly sins' – 'I say that there are some young nuns and monks who commit sins (I lay them upon their conscience and into their hearts and shall keep silent on account of my shame) which are weightier than bestiality' – but in its German version the tract stops short there, leaving the reader to imagine the worst.[20] Karlstadt is fascinated by the flows that come out of the body, with women's menses and with men's – and women's – 'seed': at the time, it was believed that both men and women had to release seed for conception to take place. Regarding marriage as a 'medicine' for the ills of sexual lust, he concludes that the bishops should drive all priests to marry, because this is the remedy for concupiscence designed by God. The only thing stopping them from marrying, he claims, is avarice – one of the seven deadly sins, and one to which sixteenth-century society was particularly sensitive. But the financial costs of having a married clergy would indeed turn out to be a major issue for the new Church.

It is not surprising that Karlstadt's treatise would be listed in the Catholic *Index of Forbidden Books*.[21] When he issued it in German, and toned down much of the invective, Karlstadt included passages on the appropriate behaviour of wives, which emphasise their duty to obey: 'For this reason God made women (who are normally soft and gentle) especially tough. He hardened them so that they may serve their husbands.'[22] While Karlstadt advocated marriage, his revulsion towards sexuality and the flesh ironically owed a great deal to the Christian monastic ascetic tradition from which he was trying to escape.

It was strong stuff. When Luther read it, he admired the learning but was taken aback by Karlstadt's narrow and literalist understanding of the passage about Moloch, fearing it would lead to ridicule from their opponents. He worried that by exciting 'such a big crowd of unmarried people to matrimony' through what seemed to Luther to be a biblical passage referring not to masturbation but to something as harmless as nocturnal emissions, they might create even greater burdens for their consciences. It was easier for Karlstadt, a secular priest, to be more radical than Luther, who still agonised over whether priests and monks were in the same position in relation to celibacy. Pondering it all, Luther joked to Spalatin that he certainly would not be driven to take a wife himself.[23] Some of his unease sprang from the fact that Karlstadt understood 'flesh' more literally and narrowly than Luther, for whom it was a much more capacious term, including sins like envy, anger, or even reliance on other people's physical presence.

A letter of 9 September 1521, one of the most revealing letters Luther wrote from the Wartburg, shows him almost thinking aloud, as he considered the draft passages on monastic vows in Melanchthon's *Loci communes*, which its author had sent him and which were also influenced by Karlstadt's treatise. Luther's thoughts suggest that he was grappling with his own sexuality. He opens by wishing that he and Melanchthon could engage in a face-to-face disputation, for then it would be possible to see where the real disagreements lay. Underneath the ostensible subject of debate – vows and their validity – it seems that what is actually disturbing Luther is the idea of the 'burning flesh', to which he comes at the end of the letter: what, Luther wondered, did Paul mean by 'burning', which both Karlstadt and now Melanchthon interpreted to mean sexual desire? And how serious a sin was it?[24]

Uncharacteristically indecisive, Luther first set out what he saw as the flaws in Melanchthon's argument. If, as Melanchthon argued, vows had to be broken because of the severity of the sins that would otherwise be committed, then the same could be said of marriage vows. And then people could just dissolve marriages at will. Does it not make a difference, Luther asked, that the vows were entered into by free Christians? Trying another tack, he suggested that just about everyone entered into monastic vows in the belief that they would ensure salvation – they were a good work that would make them pleasing to God. This alone would be enough to render them invalid, because they were entered into for the wrong reasons. Luther added that monastic vows included poverty and obedience as well. These were 'for boys', Luther wrote, the kind of thing designed to keep youths in check. A man, on the other hand, should not aim to lead this kind of life: not only were monks vowing to obey someone else, they were resorting to begging instead of earning a living.[25] Luther was evidently beginning to reject the monastic life as an estate of perpetual childhood.

Luther adopted a much more personal tone as he talked about his own vows. Recalling the promise he made in the storm, he wrote, 'I was practically seized by God, rather than drawn' into the monastery.[26] Yet in the very same sentence he admits he fears that 'I, too, may have taken my vow in an impious and sacrilegious way'. Revealingly, he recalled his father's reaction: 'Let's hope that this was not a delusion from Satan', the words which, Luther told Melanchthon, at the time 'took such deep root in my heart that I have never heard anything from his mouth which I remembered more persistently. It seemed to me as if God had spoken to me from afar, through my father's mouth.' Now his father's words struck him in a different way. Instead of concluding that his father had been right, and that the visitation had been diabolic, Luther feared that perhaps there had been nothing miraculous about his vocation at all. So, if it had not been a calling, he concluded, 'Am I myself already free and no longer a monk?'[27]

Then dropping the confessional tone and returning to marriage, Luther's mood suddenly changed. Perhaps, he teased Melanchthon, you are just trying to pay me back, by wishing a wife on me 'in order to get even with me for having given you a wife'. Indeed, it was Luther, fearing for the small and sickly-looking Melanchthon, who had found him a wife. 'Philipp is marrying Catharina Krapp,' he had written to Johannes Lang in August 1520, 'which they say I was the author of. I do for men whatever is best if there are means.' He added insouciantly that he was 'not at all bothered by the universal clamour'.[28] Catharina brought only a small dowry and was not especially good-looking. It seems that the first years of the union were not happy, with Melanchthon describing marriage as a 'servitude'.[29] Yet for all his bluster that sexuality was not a problem for him, and his insistence that 'flesh' was a broad term, one senses that Luther was confronting his own 'flesh'. It is surely significant that here he chose the married man Melanchthon as his confidant, and not the bachelor Spalatin (to whom, by contrast, he had been remarkably frank about his constipation). Moreover, Luther was beginning to discuss his sexual identity by way of examining the relationship with his father.

*

These musings would find their way into the treatise *De votis monasticis* (*On Monastic Vows*), which Luther finished in November 1521. Its preface took the form of a 'letter' to his father, in which Luther developed the ideas he had explored in the letter to Melanchthon, sometimes in the very same words. It was a letter only in a fictional sense: as it was written in Latin, his father could not have read it, nor could he have read the treatise itself which was dedicated to him. It is a remarkably compact, emotional and dramatic piece of writing. Luther now offered his father an apology. I disobeyed your wishes, he confessed, and I know that you had other plans for me: 'you were determined, therefore, to tie me down with an honourable and wealthy marriage'. He told the story of his first Mass, and he recalled that even after they had made their peace with one another, his father had again exploded: 'Have you not also heard . . . that parents are to be obeyed?' Yet at the time, Luther wrote, 'I hardened my heart as much as I could against you and your word' – a revealing terminology that would have reminded the reader of Christ and the true Word. Now, Luther wrote, he realised that the apparition in the storm could not have been from God, because his decision to enter the monastery was against his father's will. Conceding that the vision was indeed diabolic, he still placed it within a wider divine plan: it was one of the Devil's attacks on Luther that proved that he was one of the elect. Satan, he wrote, 'has raged against me with incredible contrivings to destroy or hinder me, so that I have often wondered whether I was the only man in the whole world whom he was seeking'.

All this, he realised, was part of God's purpose that he should get to know monasticism and the universities from the inside, so he could write against them with real knowledge. This was why he became a monk, and still was a monk. 'What do you think now?' he asked his father. 'Will you still take me out of the monastery?'[30]

But his father could not boast that he freed his son from monasticism. That was God's doing, and God's rights over him were greater than those of any earthly father, just as his Word was greater than any human wisdom: 'God, who has taken me out of the monastery, has an authority over me that is greater than yours. You see that he has placed me now not in a pretended monastic service but in the true service of God.' Luther insisted that the real miracle was not his rescue from the storm but his deliverance from monasticism through Christ. Far from confirming his obedience to his father, therefore, the letter marks his full independence. 'Therefore – so I am now absolutely persuaded – I could not have refused to obey you without endangering my conscience unless [Christ] had added the ministry of the Word to my monastic profession', Luther concluded. This was what gave him 'liberty', a word ambiguous between Christian freedom and the 'liberty' from paternal power which is realised when one comes of age. He concluded by reminding his father of the danger in which his son now found himself. While the Devil might try to wring his neck, it was the Pope who might truly burn or strangle him, should God consider him worthy of martyrdom.[31]

Luther was frank about the rage and anger on both sides – his own 'hardened heart' that will not permit the 'flow' so important to the body; his father 'implacable', full of 'wrath' and 'indignation against me'. His father had planned to tie him down in marriage but Luther managed to evade this destiny by becoming a monk. But now his conscience was freed, and 'Therefore I am still a monk and yet not a monk.' Now that he is a 'free' monk, however, he is also free *not* to marry. Luther concludes his 'letter' not by asking for a paternal blessing but by blessing his father himself. It seems that he had won the Oedipal struggle and achieved manhood, whilst simultaneously managing to refuse to become a married man and father himself. He had also secured the last word. This was a letter to which his father could literally not respond.[32]

The preface to *On Monastic Vows*, which had grown out of his letter to Melanchthon, may also reflect Luther's changing relationships with his closest friends, in particular Melanchthon and Karlstadt. His friendship with the latter had by now clearly cooled; it is significant that

Karlstadt had not been among those whom Luther took with him to Worms. So far as we know Luther did not write a single letter from the Wartburg to the man who had stood shoulder to shoulder with him in Leipzig, and he never asked to pass on his greetings in any of the letters he wrote to the other Wittenbergers.[33]

The relationship between Luther and Karlstadt had always been one between equals; Luther's friendship with Melanchthon, by contrast, was founded on the older man's patronage of the scholar he had worked so hard to lure to Wittenberg. Indeed, in finding Melanchthon a wife who would further tie him to Wittenberg, Luther had bound the younger man every bit as much as Luther's own father had tried to trap him. Although there is warmth and engagement in his letters to Melanchthon, Luther also maintained a certain distance. As he tried to force Melanchthon to take charge of the Reformation in Wittenberg, he cajoled and bullied him, by turns flattering his intellectual gifts, fretting about his delicate constitution, and castigating him for giving in 'too much to your emotions', when he ought to be building up the 'walls and towers' of Jerusalem.[34] This was a very different kind of friendship from that with Karlstadt, who could not be bullied. By publishing this extraordinary Preface, however, which established the narrative of his divine election, Luther strengthened his charismatic authority as the leader of the movement.

According to Freud, Oedipal struggles are universal because the path to sexual identity lies through experiencing murderous hatred and passionate love for our own parental figures. Whether one agrees with him or not, it is remarkable how Luther put his struggles – of which he was unusually aware – to the service of his theology. His relentless sense of the drama of his relations with his own father led him to the most profound understanding of God. In his theology, Luther contrasts God's absolute power with human beings' childlike inability to do anything to earn salvation – as well as the believer's frustration at his or her childlike helplessness. Luther's theology made God's paternal relationship to the Christian the pattern of theological truth. If he is less able to transmit a sense of God's fatherly care for the believer, he certainly conveys the awesome distance that lies between God and human beings. It is the distance, rather than the personal closeness, of God, that lies at the centre of Luther's theology.

Luther would not boast of a direct line to Jesus. Ever mistrustful of
those who claimed that God talked to them, he spoke instead of his
conversations with the Devil.

The very intensity of his struggle with his father no doubt
prepared Luther to attack the Pope with such enormous energy. It
also enabled him to write so compellingly about the 'freedom' of
the Christian – after all, his own independence had been fought for
very bitterly and at huge emotional cost. It perhaps explains why
he was able to arrive at such a contradictory position in relation to
freedom and authority. Luther managed to hold in tension both a
conviction of the freedom of the Christian – and, correspondingly,
of the ephemeral nature of externals, ceremonies and rules – and
a belief that humans are not free to act at all. Every human action
is tainted with sin, and, as he would later argue in his battle with
Erasmus, human beings' wills are in bondage. We are both free and
not free.

*

By October, as the days grew shorter, and as it became clear that
Luther would not be returning to Wittenberg any time soon, he
determined on a new project: translating the New Testament into
German. This soon absorbed all his energies and from this point on,
he did not appear to suffer from his earlier insecurities or boredom;
even his constipation had apparently passed, perhaps because of the
resolution he had achieved in his relationship with his father. In under
eleven weeks, he translated the entire New Testament from the original Greek, not from the Vulgate, the Latin translation that had dominated the Church hitherto. It was a work of genius. Luther's New
Testament reshaped the German language itself, as Luther's German
became dominant, unifying what had been a wide range of local
dialects. He was not the first to translate the Bible into German – there
were many fifteenth-century German Bibles and other sixteenth-
century reformers and traditionalists would also produce their own –
but what sets Luther's translation apart is his sense of the music of
language. His style is direct and unadorned, using alliteration and the
rhythms of everyday speech. He writes in a populist German, not in
Latinate prose. This makes his translation very unlike, for instance,

the English King James version, which is deliberately literary in style. Luther's version is earthier, and his sentences shorter. This is a Bible designed to be read aloud and to be heard by ordinary people.

It was not without its tendentious features. Luther built his own theological understandings into his translation, rendering Romans 1:17, for example, as 'Since therein is revealed the justice which is valid before God, which comes from faith in faith, as it is written, The just person will live of his faith' – a translation which elaborates on the process of justification before God. This was the passage that had been central to Luther while he was caught in the deepest of his *Anfechtungen* over his hatred of the 'justice of God'. Reflecting on his life in 1545, he wrote about these words: 'Here I felt that I was altogether born again and had entered paradise itself through open gates.' The King James Bible would not add Luther's emphasis, but translates the passage as: 'For therein is the righteousness of God revealed from faith to faith: as it is written, The just shall live by faith.'[35] When it came to translating Romans 3:28, Luther wrote, 'So we now maintain, that man becomes justified without the work of the Law, through faith alone.' Luther added the word 'alone' which is not in the original text, and which places emphasis on the exclusivity of faith – indeed, Luther argued that the '*allein*', which is idiomatic in German, conveyed the sense of the passage. Because Luther himself never went in for biblical literalism, he tried to get to the heart of what the text was saying, and was not afraid to bring out what he thought were its emphases. By contrast, the King James Bible has 'Therefore we conclude that a man is justified by faith without the deeds of the law.' He also included a short didactic preface to the Gospels and to each of the Epistles, so that the reader encountered the text through Luther's eyes. Introducing Romans, he wrote 'This Epistle is the true main piece of the New Testament . . . which every Christian should not only know word for word by heart, but should treat as a daily bread for the soul', making his own encounter with Scripture the touchstone for all Christians.[36] The literary style and typeface were indistinguishable from the rest of the text, so that Luther's exegetical prefaces exuded almost scriptural authority.

For Luther, the intellectual process of meditating on Scripture and its essential meaning was fundamental to his faith, and he would practise it throughout his life. This was how he had arrived at his Reformation insight, and it was how he would approach both his office

38. Melanchthon and Cranach's *Passional Christi vnd Antichristi*, 1521. On the left, Cranach depicts Christ driving the moneylenders out of the temple, whilst the illustration on the right, captioned 'Antichrist', shows the Pope surrounded by fat cardinals and bishops, signing letters of indulgence and granting dispensations affixed with seals, for which he has received the pile of coins placed on the table below.

as a professor of Holy Scripture at the university, and his task as translator. The period of isolation in the Wartburg, without his library and largely without the advice of his friends, enabled him to encounter the New Testament with a rare directness and intimacy. The result was a deeply personal translation that seems to have been written in a single breath.

*

In the meantime in Wittenberg, the excitement caused by the events at Worms could not be put on hold. Luther had braved the threat of martyrdom, and now others wanted to put the idea of the restoration of the pure Christian Church into practice. Luther's own increasingly apocalyptic rhetoric added urgency to reform. In May 1521, Melanchthon and Cranach published their *Passional Christi und Antichristi*, a set of thirteen paired illustrations by Cranach that contrasted the pomp and grandeur of the Pope with Christ's humility. A co-operative venture, the texts were compiled by Melanchthon with the quotations from canon law put together by the Wittenberg jurist Johannes Schwertfeger. First a Latin and then German versions appeared, appealing as much to the unlettered as to the educated. Once seen, the visual contrasts, and the proclamation that the Pope was the Antichrist, could not be forgotten. The pamphlet concluded with a brief tongue-in-cheek explanation that the booklet was not defamatory because everything in it was in canon law. It was being published for the benefit of Christian folk, to give a handy summary of the basis of 'spiritual fleshly law'. Its legacy for Lutheran art was to be long-lasting. 'Antithetical' treatments of the church of Luther and the church of the Pope would be painted on the walls of the Torgau chapel, and in the castle chapel in Schmalkalden.[37] Propaganda based on denigration of the Catholic Church, it added further urgency to reform with its message that the Day of Judgement was nearing.

Now Gabriel Zwilling began to push for radical changes in Wittenberg. In his attack on the celebration of private Masses he was supported by Nikolaus von Amsdorf and Justus Jonas, both members of the foundation of All Saints and Luther's powerful allies. Luther, it seemed, also approved of this move, and in November he wrote *De abroganda missa privata* (*On the Abrogation of the Private Mass*), which rejected the idea that the Mass was a sacrifice. The Mass, Luther argued, was not a work that we undertake to please God; rather, it is a sacrament in which we receive God's grace. This might seem a fine distinction but its effects were shattering. If Masses were not something that needed to be said perpetually to please God, there would be no need for the vast clerical proletariat of Mass-sayers at the many altars, paid to perform that duty for the souls of the departed in order to reduce their time in Purgatory.[38]

At the same time, clergy in Wittenberg were starting to live out the consequences of Luther's ideas. Zwilling began to encourage his Augustinian brothers to give up their vows and leave the monastery. By the end of October, twelve monks had left and by November another three had gone. They grew their hair, disguising their former tonsures, and they wore everyday clothes. They took up ordinary trades: one became a baker, another a cobbler; another, perhaps from a richer family, became a salt trader. It seems that the town council supported their decisions, conferring citizenship on one former brother

Paſſional Chꝛiſti und  Antichꝛiſti.

39. The final pages of the *Passional* juxtaposed Christ's Ascension with the descent of the Pope, accompanied by a crew of devils with fantastical snouts, beaks and claws, into the flames of hell where a rotund, tonsured cleric is already roasting.

who had become a carpenter. Staupitz's dream of a unified, reformed Augustinian order was beginning to evaporate: under the impact of Luther's ideas, monasticism was gradually collapsing from within. A movement which had characterised Western Christianity almost from its beginnings, and which had developed powerful institutions throughout Europe, was losing credibility.

Zwilling now began to push for a fully reformed Mass, which offered the wine as well as the bread to the laity. Consequently, on 29 September, in a private ceremony, Melanchthon received Communion in both kinds with his students.[39] Zwilling must have been a powerful personality and preacher – one contemporary describes him as a 'second prophet' sent by God, 'another Martin' who perhaps even exceeded the first. A sense of his preaching style emanates from hostile reports about his later sermons at Eilenburg, shortly after he had left Wittenberg around New Year 1522. Not only did he speak the words of consecration in German and give Communion in two kinds, but he dressed in lay clothes. Indeed, he seems to have designed his own preaching 'look', which would later be adopted by Luther and others. In place of a monkish cassock he wore a black student gown (Luther and the other

preachers would wear an academic talar), a shirt with black braiding
and a hat of beaver fur. He had no tonsure but his hair had been
combed forward: to one shocked observer he looked 'like a devil'. But
it was the hat that probably outraged contemporaries the most: to
cover one's head showed disrespect for the sacrament.[40] Beaver fur was
a fashion item; and the colour of his clothing – black, an expensive dye
in this period – connoted status, so Zwilling may have been attempting
to make himself look like a man of standing. His preaching style seems
to have been simple and forthright, offering a rather cut-down version
of Luther's theology. There were two paths, he was said to have told
his congregation: one led to hell, and that was the broad path of doing
good works, the other was narrow and led to heaven.[41]

Zwilling's preaching first and foremost addressed his fellow Augustinians, but theirs was a public church, and people flocked to hear
him. He allegedly proclaimed that 'no one could get to heaven in a
cowl' and that saying Mass was a 'diabolical thing'. These reports of
his preaching were partisan, but he appears to have exploited the
widespread anticlerical feeling at the time. In his services Zwilling also
began to remove everything that smacked of the idea that the Mass
was a sacrifice, and he abolished the elevation and adoration of the
sacrament. The Augustinians themselves were divided over Zwilling,
with the prior Conrad Helt opposed to these changes; he subsequently
complained that, because he had forbidden Communion to be celebrated in two kinds, he could not go safely about the streets for fear
of the 'loose mob'.[42] Meanwhile a committee of university members
and members of the collegiate church chapter was set up to develop
a policy that would steer a course between the Augustinians, intent
on reform, and the Elector, whose approval would be needed for any
change. The hand-picked committee consisted mainly of supporters
of the Reformation, including Melanchthon and Karlstadt and the
jurist Hieronymus Schurff, who had accompanied Luther at Worms.
Its recommendations backed reform: private Masses should be abolished and Communion should be held in both kinds. It tried to put
the brakes on a little, however, pressuring Zwilling to explain that he
had never rejected the adoration of the sacrament.[43] But the nascent
movement soon found itself facing more serious opposition from the
clerics of the foundation of All Saints, who began to lobby the Elector
direct. Moreover, despite its largely evangelical membership, the

committee was not united, and when it went so far as to advocate abolishing private Masses and offering Communion in both kinds, one of its members, Johann Dölsch, put in a separate memorial, arguing that since the sacrament was spiritual, one kind was sufficient.[44]

Zwilling was not acting alone. Students and townspeople themselves began to take direct action to bring about religious change; and their targets reveal what they understood by Luther's Reformation. These were not what one might expect. Top of their agenda was the rejection of begging, which was itself an expression of their anticlericalism. During the summer there were sporadic attacks on priests' houses, and in October, when 'St Anthony's messenger' would traditionally walk around town ringing a bell and requesting alms, the hapless man was mocked and students pelted him with dung, some of it mixed with stones. 'How well you ring that bell,' the students taunted him, 'but you'd have to ring a long time before I'd give you so much as a penny.'[45] Again, these attacks seem to have had much in common with the students' own rituals, which they had used to such effect with the burning of the bull. They were picking up on the idea, however, expressed very early by Luther, that begging was wrong and should be stopped; 'Nobody ought to go begging among Christians', he had written in To the Christian Nobility of the German Nation; 'every city should support its own poor'. Mendicant monks who asked for alms were not performing pious works but diverting money away from those who truly needed it.[46] Luther, writing to Spalatin, did not exactly approve of the students' behaviour, but then, he asked, 'who can hold everyone in check everywhere and at all times?'[47]

The next targets of the Wittenberg reformers were Marianism – veneration of the Virgin – and the Mass. On 3 and 4 December, a group of evangelicals prevented priests in the parish church from saying the Marian office. Invading the parish church, they drove the priests from the altars, took their Mass books and threw stones at them.[48] The town council's report to the Elector claimed that they carried knives and weapons, concluding that several citizens had been about to stage a riot. In the Franciscan monastery, students smashed a wooden altar and posted threatening letters on the monastery door. Some suggested that next Maundy Thursday they should get the 'bath maids' – that is, prostitutes – to wash down the idolatrous altars with strong lye. It would be better, they had allegedly said, to turn the altar stones into gallows and execution blocks, where they would do more for *Gerechtigkeit*, the word meaning both salvation and justice: 'the hangman's office was not as dangerous to souls as the idolatrous monks'.[49] These were strong words, with hangmen being the lowest caste in sixteenth-century society. This was verbal iconoclasm, the students besmirching the holy altars with the foulest connotations they could imagine – and there was more than a hint of sexual humiliation in their reference to the prostitutes, too. The Council was careful to play the incident down in its report to the Elector, insisting that only fourteen students had been involved, with some outsiders; and that they had all been punished. Something like a popular Reformation was brewing, but its extent is clear only from the outraged comments of its opponents, who had every reason to paint it as violent and subversive.[50] A week later, on the night of 10 December, it was reported that about forty well-armed 'students and nobles' were roaming the streets with pipes and drums, threatening to storm the monasteries and kill all the monks.[51] The council managed to quieten things down, however, placing a guard around the Franciscan monastery.

Wittenberg was not the only place where the new evangelical ideas were being put into practice. Shortly after the Diet of Worms, in the summer, there had been attacks on the houses of priests in Erfurt. Luther was appalled by these disturbances, and still more by the fact that the town council apparently approved the action, refusing to punish the culprits. Johannes Lang, now the prior of the Erfurt monastery, was keeping mysteriously silent about the matter.[52] Marooned up in the Wartburg, Luther was desperate for news, asking his correspondents about the latest from Erfurt. Luther had experience of politics in Erfurt in the days when the town had been so factionalised that it had hanged its own mayor; he would have been suspicious of anything that smacked of popular Reformation under the leadership of a town council.

By late 1521 it was being alleged that Erfurt students were arriving at Wittenberg and had joined in the organised riot or *'Pfaffenstürm'* on 3–4 December. Immediately after these events, Luther made a secret snap visit to Wittenberg, where he discovered that Spalatin had prevented the printing of his three most recent works – *De abroganda missa privata*, his broadside against the 'idol of Mainz', and his treatise on monastic vows. Furious, he wrote the most angry letter of his entire correspondence with Spalatin. He reported his satisfaction with the changes in Wittenberg that he had just seen for himself –

'everything pleases me very much', he wrote – here, in contrast to Spalatin, true Christians were at work. Yes, he had heard rumours of disruption caused by some of 'ours' and promised to write against them.[53] But he did not mention any specific disturbances. It seems unlikely that he did not know about the events of the days before; he may have considered them nothing more than the kind of disruption and popular festival that regularly accompanied momentous events.

On his return from his secret visit to Wittenberg, Luther wrote *A Sincere Admonition by Martin Luther to All Christians to Guard Against Insurrection*, which was printed in early January 1522.[54] But although Luther represented disturbance as the work of the Devil, he did not condemn the forceful removal of images, which was so often the trigger for unrest. He also rejoiced that in recent events, 'the ignorance of the papists has been revealed. Their hypocrisy has been revealed. The pernicious lies contained in their laws and monastic orders have been revealed. Their wicked and tyrannical use of the ban has been revealed. In short, everything with which they have hitherto bewitched, terrorised, and deceived the world has been exposed.' This did not look like back-pedalling, but full-throated advocacy for change.[55]

In the meantime, the targets of the evangelicals in Wittenberg began to widen. By 10 December, matters became more clearly political. A group of citizens including members of the so-called 'forty' – representatives of the four quarters into which the town was divided – disrupted a council meeting and demanded that those involved in the disturbances of 3 and 4 December should be set free. They formulated a set of six articles aimed at bringing about reform.[56]

Popular agitation continued. On Christmas Eve, a group of laypeople invaded the parish church, and threatened to throw 'lead pellets' at the altar. They smashed a few Mass lights as well, and sang scurrilous songs including 'O beer of Brunswick', and 'A maid has lost a shoe' – girls who lost their virginity were paid with a ritual gift of a shoe, so the point of the song was plain. Then they moved on to the Castle Church, where they howled 'like dogs and wolves' so as to disrupt the service, and went up into the church balcony, where they 'wished the priests plague and the flames of hell'. Although this might have frightened the clerics, it was all comparatively good-humoured, and it was direct action concentrated solely against the saying of private Masses. Nevertheless it was a clear provocation to the Elector, whose own church the protestors had invaded.[57] Meanwhile, in late

December, three radicals who became known as the Zwickau prophets arrived and began preaching, one of them staying in Melanchthon's house, and the atmosphere of religious fervour increased yet further.[58]

Now attention returned to begging with the establishment of a system of poor relief. At some point in 1521, the Wittenberg council had instituted a Begging Ordinance, the first council in Germany to do so.[59] This followed naturally from the abolition of the Mass, because if there was no point in saying Masses for the dead, there was no sense in the brotherhoods or in the benefices that paid for the priests. Brotherhoods, as Luther had argued, were useful only for getting drunk and eating too much. Instead, the money should go into a common chest, and be given to support the poor. This was a whole new approach to poverty. Instead of mendicancy being a sign of monastic virtue, begging could be conceived as an issue of social justice. The Wittenberg council ordered that the funds be kept in a chest with three locks – two for the four overseers and their three advisors, and one for the mayor. The four overseers should note down which people were needy, especially those who were too ashamed to beg. In line with Luther's strictures in *To the Christian Nobility of the German Nation*, the money should be spent on supporting Wittenberg's own poor, not on outsiders, and certainly not on mendicant monks.

It seemed as if the Reformation, under the guidance of the Augustinians and the town council, was about to be perfected in Wittenberg. The Augustinian prior of Eisleben, Caspar Güttel, who attended the chapter meeting in Wittenberg in January 1522, wrote to a friend about his conviction that he was living in exceptional times: 'It looks to me as if God intends to offer us all great grace and high seriousness.' That sense of excitement is also evident in a newsletter report from early January: 'The prince can no longer stop matters, let other princes do what they will, they won't be able to prevent or suppress it; it is from or by God, we will yet see miracles; all around in all little towns strange events and happenings are taking place, may God grant His grace, Amen.'[60] The author went on to report how a merchant had arrived in Wittenberg, asking for the Augustinian monastery. When locals pointed it out, he tied up his horse, went inside and found only one monk left. Stretching out his arms in the shape of the Cross, he gave God praise and thanks, and wept from his heart, rejoicing that he could tread the ground of 'the holy city'.[61]

# Karlstadt and the Christian City of Wittenberg

Luther's friendship with Andreas Karlstadt is airbrushed out of most biographies of the reformer, starting with those by Mathesius and Spangenberg in the late sixteenth century.[1] Karlstadt had originally idolised Luther, acted as his right-hand man and his co-debater at Leipzig, and led the way on several key theological issues. Yet the debt Luther owed him is often forgotten.[2] Luther followed in his wake in his theses against scholasticism, and it was Karlstadt who first saw the propaganda potential of images and articulated the argument for breaking monastic vows. The story of their tortured relationship explains not only some key psychological and emotional patterns in Luther's life; it also illuminates why Luther's theology, and with it the Reformation as a whole, took the path that it did.

During Luther's time in the Wartburg, Karlstadt played a major part in introducing the Reformation in Wittenberg. To start with, however, he had been far from radical. Until the end of 1521, he had consistently urged caution against Melanchthon's enthusiasm and distanced himself from any signs of disorder. In October that year, during a disputation on the Mass, he had been careful to ensure that all points of view were represented, and held the position that private Masses should not simply be abolished. With his training in law and his experience, he was probably more clear-sighted than others about the huge legal and financial consequences, arguing that the consent of the whole community should be sought before changes were carried out. Melanchthon, by contrast, wanted private Masses dispensed with right away.[3]

40. Andreas Karlstadt, c.1541/2.

In November 1521 Karlstadt published *Regarding the Worship and Homage of the Signs of the New Testament* which he dedicated to Albrecht Dürer in Nuremberg, designed to indicate to the Nurembergers and the public at large that events in Wittenberg were proceeding in a measured and orderly fashion.[4] In this treatise he elaborated the reasons why one should pay reverence to the sacrament, insisting that Christ really was present in the bread and wine. At this point, he seemed to be agreeing with Luther and taking a firm stand against Zwilling, who preached against the elevation of the Host and the adoration of the sacrament. But even at this early date, Karlstadt's pamphlet had an importantly different emphasis, arguing that we should honour the sacrament because it contains, in addition to the bread, the spiritual presence of Christ. By splitting the significance of the sacrament, and distinguishing its spiritual and physical parts, Karlstadt introduced a demarcation which would eventually lead him to take the view that the sacrament was a memorial act only, valuing the spiritual over the physical.

Shortly before Christmas Day 1521, Karlstadt – who as archdeacon of the foundation of All Saints was Wittenberg's main preacher – announced that he would celebrate Communion in both kinds at New Year. This was a serious step to take, because the Elector had made it perfectly plain that he was opposed to it. It meant open disobedience and set the Reformation on a path of opposition to secular authority, whilst also pitting the power of Wittenberg's town council against that of Saxony's ruler.

Why did a man who had been so cautious take such a dangerous step? In fact, this was not the first time that Karlstadt had tested Friedrich's power. In 1515, he had become involved in a dispute over rent he owed and had made a counterclaim for hay owed to him; the difference between the two sides was a paltry half-guilder but Karlstadt threatened to appeal to the Pope himself, to the Elector's annoyance. Then in early 1517, he had unilaterally nominated and confirmed a priest to the benefice at Orlamünde, a parish directly subject to the foundation of All Saints. Friedrich had taken umbrage because Karlstadt had not asked his permission; the Elector even threatened that if he did not back down, he would appoint someone else and pay him from Karlstadt's income. Relations were strained for some time thereafter.[5]

And they were strained within the foundation of All Saints too. Although Karlstadt's position as archdeacon was well paid, it involved spending a good deal of time saying Masses and officiating at church services, which he found difficult to combine with his academic pursuits. He had therefore long nursed the ambition to gain one of the highest-paid benefices, such as the office of provost of the foundation. He secured the doctorate in law that was necessary for the provostship, spending the years of 1515 and 1516 in Rome and Siena. Alienating the Elector yet again, Karlstadt's Italian sojourn had lasted far longer than the agreed four months, he failed to provide a replacement at All Saints during his absence, and returned only when the provost threatened to imprison him. Money troubles apparently dogged him, and he had a ghoulish habit of lobbying for the benefices of recently deceased clerics.[6] He also had a weakness for fine clothes. Luther remembered that when Karlstadt returned from Italy, he sported strikingly beautiful outfits, and when in mid-1521 he was to be sent on a mission to Denmark, he asked for the chapter to provide him with a 'damask gown trimmed with a good lining' and even a gown in black or purple – the most expensive colours – so that he would be worthy to appear before the Danish king.[7] Karlstadt was therefore in the unenviable position of being financially dependent upon the Elector, yet finding himself caught in positions where he had to assert himself against his ruler's authority.

The relationship with Luther was also complicated. Karlstadt, three years younger than Luther, had arrived at Wittenberg in 1507, and his first tract, *De intentionibus*, published in the same year, was also the first major book to be published by a member of the Wittenberg faculty. Christoph Scheurl lauded it in an oration at All Saints: 'If we had a lot of Karlstadts, I think we could easily . . . be a match for the Parisians.' A convinced Thomist at the time, Karlstadt was the new star of the university, and with the patronage of the rector, Martin Pollich von Mellerstadt, soon became archdeacon of All Saints. The archdeaconry also involved university duties, and Karlstadt speedily rose to the position of dean of theology. In this role he had taken Luther's doctoral oath in 1512, presiding at his doctoral disputation. He was an aspirational humanist too, with one humanist visitor to Wittenberg praising him as a 'very famous philosopher, orator, poet and theologian'. Between 1517 and 1521, however, Luther's reputation eclipsed Karlstadt's almost completely.[8]

The friendship between the two men began when Karlstadt rushed to Leipzig in the middle of winter, on 13 January 1517, to buy a copy of Augustine so that he could refute Luther's claims, only to discover that Luther was right to reject scholasticism. It seems originally to have unleashed intellectual energy and creativity on both sides. Karlstadt now attacked scholasticism with vigour in a set of theses in April 1517, setting out a theology based on Augustine and criticising the use of Aristotle's metaphysics.[9] Luther, for his part, wrote his theses against scholasticism under Karlstadt's influence, and his first ringing declaration, 'To say that Augustine exaggerates in speaking against heretics is to say that Augustine tells lies almost everywhere', is a clear adaptation of one of Karlstadt's theses.[10] In turn, Karlstadt's support for his ideas evidently emboldened Luther, especially since his fellow Augustinian friends Linck and Lang were decidedly more cautious about his emerging theology. Indeed, from mid-1517 on Luther began to talk of 'our theology', and soon would speak of 'us Wittenberg theologians'.[11]

Karlstadt did not at first share Luther's opposition to indulgences – perhaps, as some have suggested, because he could see that their abolition would lead eventually to the collapse of the All Saints foundation and his own income. On the other hand, he took a firm line against the veneration of saints far earlier than Luther did, daring to make his views public despite the important role that the Elector's collection of relics played in the town, not least in bringing pilgrims whose money was vital to the financial health of the foundation.[12] Moreover, study in Rome had left him with a powerful anti-Roman animus. He had, for example, been quick to advise the Elector that new arrangements for benefices at All Saints must build in independence from the papacy or else Friedrich might find that Rome and its 'courtesans' would seize control. His extreme anti-Romanism may have rubbed off on Luther, whose own negative experience of Rome had been neither as extensive nor as disillusioning.

The first strains in their friendship emerged at Leipzig in 1519. Although Karlstadt had been Eck's original target, the final theses for debate scarcely hid the fact that Luther was the real antagonist. During the negotiations about where and how the debate was to be held, Luther corresponded directly with Eck, making no bones about the fact that he and Eck were the ones who counted. Moreover, all observers agreed that Karlstadt had the worst of the debate. Where Luther's and Karlstadt's theology converged was in their admiration for the *Theologia deutsch* and the mystic Johannes Tauler.[13] Indeed, as we have seen, in the preliminary skirmishes before the Leipzig Debate, one of the major points at issue between Luther and Eck had been that the latter would not accept the authority of the *Theologia deutsch* because it was not a work by one of the Church Fathers and was written in German, not Latin. In October 1520, two weeks after he had received news of Eck's bull – which to Karlstadt's shock named him alongside Luther and five others[14] – Karlstadt wrote a treatise on *Gelassenheit*, the meditative 'letting go' of human attachments in order to allow God to enter, which reveals the extent of his debt to medieval mysticism. It was personal, written in the form of a letter to his 'dear mother and all my friends'.[15] Just as Luther did at times, Karlstadt likened his situation to Christ's: 'I stand in hellish anguish, in pain of death, in hellish trials, with hands and feet I am nailed to your cross.' He saw himself as standing at a junction: on the right, there was death which threatened to kill his spirit, and 'On the left, stands the death to my flesh.'[16]

By contrast, Luther did not draw on the theology of *Gelassenheit* when preparing himself for martyrdom. While he regularly considered the possibility of his own death in his letters, he was also concerned about protecting others. As he worked out his strategy with Spalatin before Worms, one of the arguments he deployed was that if he were not given a hearing, then *everyone* in Wittenberg would be imperilled. From quite early on, therefore, he tried to stop Karlstadt attacking Eck because he thought it would endanger his colleague. And he ensured through his negotiations via Spalatin that he alone was summoned to Worms.

For Karlstadt, on the other hand, *Gelassenheit* gave him strength for his own martyrdom. The concept was locked into his emotional experience of being saved; it was part of the cycle of dark anxiety, and feelings of worthlessness, to which the answer was to develop a 'tough, serious and rigorous hatred and envy against myself'. From this sprang detachment, or leaving behind all things and all human bonds. Karlstadt returned to the theme in 1523, publishing a far longer meditation on the meanings of *Gelassenheit*. Here it was clearly linked with asceticism. 'All pleasure is sin', he wrote. 'It would be better for us were we to sprinkle food and drink with ashes than to have our food praised in song.' The believer must develop 'a holy dread of myself' and 'become wholly ashamed of my thoughts, desires, and works as of a horrible vice which I would avoid as one avoids a yellow, pus-filled boil'. Karlstadt took the reader through different kinds of detachment, including 'yieldedness of intellect' and finally even 'letting go of Scripture' itself: understanding its spirit was more important than the letter of the Word of God. The term he used for this process of detachment was to have a 'circumcised heart', as if true believers must be set apart in tribal fashion.[17]

For Luther, it was the conviction that all our works are sinful and that we are saved by God's grace alone that led to a sense of freedom. If everything we do is tainted with sin, then asceticism has no point; instead we should enjoy God's creation. His position was both different from medieval Catholicism, which valued renouncing the flesh, or from what would become Calvinism, which was obsessed with disciplining pleasure. For Karlstadt, on the other hand, the aim of

*Gelassenheit* was to arrive at a complete surrender of the self and a merging with God so that the believer becomes 'immersed in God's will'. It is a state of mystical receptivity and openness where the boundaries between oneself and God disappear – as if one were to return to the womb where there is no separation between mother and child. Thus Karlstadt's striving for *Gelassenheit* – his tract outlining the different stages for its achievement – came pretty close to the kind of willed state of perfection which Luther rejected. Indeed, Luther would later charge Karlstadt with setting up, just like the monks, 'a new kind of mortification, that is, a self-chosen putting to death of the flesh'.[18]

*

This was the man who, just before Christmas 1521, openly defied the Elector and announced that he would administer Communion in both kinds at New Year in the Castle Church. Cautious and even punctilious by nature, and slow to change, once convinced, he had all the passion of the convert. He believed he was witnessing the triumph of the gospel, and he committed himself utterly to what he termed 'the Christian City of Wittenberg'. The academic was becoming a bold popular leader. Whereas earlier he had avoided preaching, now Karlstadt preached frequently and with passion. People remarked that he had become a new man, 'such exquisite things did he now preach'.[19] When it became clear that the Elector would be hostile to any 'innovations', Karlstadt ignored him and, on Christmas Day, he invited those present who wished to take Communion to do so, whether or not they had made confession. A thousand people are reported to have attended. To the horror of the canons of All Saints, many of those who took Communion had not kept the obligatory fast but had eaten and drunk beforehand; some were even said to have consumed brandy. Dressed in lay clothing, Karlstadt officiated at Mass in the parish church, and when the wafers were twice dropped – one falling on a man's coat, another onto the floor – he simply told the parishioners to pick them up. Yet touching the Host was too great a taboo even for convinced evangelicals, and Karlstadt had to do it himself. At New Year he celebrated Communion in both kinds again, and this time too a thousand people participated. Wittenberg was undergoing an evangelical revival.[20]

Just six months after he had written his tract against vows,[21] Karlstadt
acted upon his beliefs. A newsletter, which he may not have written
himself, included not only the resolutions of the Augustinian order who
met in Wittenberg in January, and a Latin prayer in praise of Luther –
'We should rather believe one truthful Martin than the whole mob of
the papists. We know that Christ was truly reborn through Martin; you,
O God, do guard him for us'[22] – but also the announcement that Karlstadt was going to marry. On 26 December 1521, Justus Jonas and
Melanchthon, along with two wagons filled with 'educated, valiant
people' from Wittenberg, travelled to the village of Segrehna where
they witnessed Karlstadt's engagement to Anna von Mochau.[23] Although
it squared with his tract on vows, Karlstadt's decision sat oddly with
his admonitions to *Gelassenheit*, to leaving all human attachments behind.

Anna von Mochau was on the face of it an extraordinary choice as
bride. Aged fifteen, she was the daughter of a poor nobleman, chosen
neither for her looks – she was 'not very pretty' according to one
contemporary – nor her wealth.[24] Interestingly, Luther later made a
similar choice, marrying outside the Wittenberg elite, and choosing
a former nun who was also from a minor noble family. Status clearly
mattered to Karlstadt: his own family claimed nobility, and he used
their coat of arms as his 'brand'. By marrying such a young woman,
he was also following noble conventions. While townswomen were
usually ten years older at marriage, young brides were more common
in noble circles. Even so, the difference in age was striking: Karlstadt
was aged thirty-five, almost a generation older than the bride. It is
unclear how they met but she probably had connections to Wittenberg,
because Luther said that he 'knew the girl', when he welcomed the
news of the engagement from the Wartburg.[25] It was a bold choice
on her part too, for although Karlstadt was not a monk, he was a
cleric. The very idea of a priest's wife was radically new; those who
lived with priests had previously been denounced as priests' whores,
excluded from honourable society, and their children considered
bastards. Indeed, not everyone hailed the wedding. A pamphlet of a
mock 'wedding Mass' was published, which called Karlstadt a 'fisherman of wives' when he should have been, like the disciples of Jesus,
a fisher of men.[26]

A man who liked to give splendid parties, Karlstadt spent fifty
guilders on the wedding feast held on 19 January, even travelling to

Leipzig for special spices: he clearly intended the banquet to be a public statement. There was a large guest list, including the whole town council and the university, while his invitation to the Elector was even printed. Spiteful stories about the wedding soon circulated among the Reformation's opponents. Cochlaeus told the tale of Karlstadt's neighbour who was asked to procure the prized game for the wedding feast, and killed 'the miller's donkey' instead. The guests only discovered what they were eating when they came across its cloven hooves.[27]

*

The pace of reform in Wittenberg further accelerated. On 6 January 1522, the Augustinian order met in the town. From the sidelines, Luther had written to Linck and Lang, admonishing them to follow the gospel and support reform. The meeting was not very well attended but it reached radical conclusions: the chapter decided that any who wished to leave the order might do so, and that begging and Masses for the dead should be abolished. The prior of the Wittenberg house, his authority undermined by the charismatic preaching of Zwilling, received no support from the order, which refused to punish those monks who had left. Then, on 10 January, the remaining Wittenberg Augustinians went even further and, probably under Zwilling's leadership, 'made a fire in the cloister square, went into the church, broke the wooden altars, and took them with all the paintings and statues, crucifixes, flags, candles, chandeliers, etc. to the fire, threw them in and burnt them, and cut off the heads of the stone statues of Christ, Mary and other saints, and destroyed all the images in the church'.[28]

Karlstadt too now turned his attention to images, writing a treatise on begging and the removal of images – not a chance combination. At one level, the tract, published in late January in Wittenberg, rejected images on biblical grounds: the first Commandment condemned the worship of idols. But it also made a clear distinction between flesh and spirit, the inner and the outer, a theme which could already be discerned in his earlier writing on the adoration of the sacrament. Images, Karlstadt now argued, 'point to nothing other than to mere flesh which is of no benefit'. The Word of God, however, 'is spiritual'; 'Christ says that his flesh is of no avail but that the spirit is of much

value and gives life.' Consequently, 'you will have to admit that one
learns mere carnal living and much suffering from [images] and that
they cannot lead beyond the flesh'.[29]

It was the indeterminacy of images, and their ability to move the
emotions, that had earlier both fascinated and irritated him. Karlstadt
had been the first, after all, to employ visual polemic in the service
of the Reformation when he published his 'wagon cartoon' to ridicule
Eck. Now he wrote passionately about what was wrong with images,
in language suffused with sexual rhetoric: 'Our eyes make love to
[images] and court them. The truth is that all who honour images,
seek their help, and worship them, are whores and adulterers.' He
admitted that he had been seduced himself: 'my heart has been trained
since my youth to give honour and respect to images and such a
dreadful fear has been instilled in me of which I would gladly rid
myself, but cannot. Thus I am afraid to burn a single idol.' What
emerges again from these lines is a very different approach to the
body and to the physical world from that of Luther, a deep mistrust
of the senses that could be readily allied to sexual puritanism. Indeed,
such condemnation of images would become a powerful current
within Calvinist Protestantism, leading to the destruction of centuries
of Christian art in churches across Europe.[30]

The same treatise also included a passage on begging, with Karlstadt
explaining why there should be no beggars among Christians. Just as
images moved the pious to emotional identification with the sufferings
of saints, and thereby distorted devotion, so beggars moved people
to pity. The result was that they gave money not to those who needed
it most, but to those whose plight most seized the senses. Karlstadt
clearly realised the implications of abolishing begging for the university in Wittenberg; after all, it was customary for students to beg for
their food and expenses. His conclusions were radical. If abolition of
begging meant that students would no longer be able to study, did it
matter? Children of pious parents would be better off being 'sent back
to their parents' and taught a useful trade, Karlstadt wrote: 'How
much better by far, that they learn the trade of their parents instead
of begging for bread which makes them good for nothing other than
to become papistical, uncouth, and untruthful priests.' These were
strong words in a town so heavily dependent on the university. Karlstadt evidently meant them.[31]

But Wittenberg and the university also faced other problems. Luther's renown had attracted hordes of students and the university had seen a strong growth in numbers up to 1521, so much so that Luther had fretted about how to house them all. Melanchthon's lectures were also famed, and students had thronged the halls to hear them. But the Reformation's attack on scholasticism was also a general assault on intellectual training itself, and it offered little to replace it. With theology the most important intellectual discipline of the day, a crisis in theology heralded a crisis of intellectual life. After hearing Karlstadt preach, the student Philipp Eberbach, who had come to Wittenberg to study the Roman rhetorician Quintilian, no longer saw the point: 'I said farewell to the Muses.'[32] With begging, the major source of student funding, gone, and with intellectual endeavour put into question, student numbers dropped precipitously. Many were reported to be leaving town; even Melanchthon was rumoured to be planning to leave Wittenberg by Easter.[33] The fall in enrolments greatly worried the Elector and Spalatin, but the problem did not concern just Wittenberg. Right across the empire student numbers collapsed throughout the rest of the 1520s: the University of Greifswald even had to close its doors for a generation.

The clergy too was transformed by the evangelical message. The immediate effect of the attack on private Masses was to destroy at a stroke the whole ecclesiastical career structure. And who would now want their sons to enter the Church? Whatever else the Reformation meant, it would entail a massive reduction in the numbers of clergy, culling both the clerical proletariat of priests saying private Masses and the upper clerical ranks with their substantial benefices.

Neither priests nor university men had a monopoly on religious truth any longer. Anyone, even the unlettered, could understand the Bible for themselves. In late December 1521, a group of three prophets arrived in Wittenberg from nearby Zwickau, claiming that God spoke to them directly. Nikolaus Storch and Thomas Drechsel were journeyman cloth-makers; the third, Markus Thomas or Stübner, had attended university in Wittenberg, but he was the son of a bathkeeper whose name 'Stübner' betrayed his origins. Because of their close contact with the body, bathkeepers were regarded as dishonourable, their status so low that marriage to a bathkeeper's child meant social death. Storch had already caused considerable excitement in his home town where he set up conventicles and stressed the importance of direct revelation. Stübner, who knew Melanchthon well, argued that infant baptism could not be found in Scripture. The Zwickau prophets represented a new kind of evangelical movement that owed little or nothing to universities. God's spirit, it seemed, was being poured out onto laypeople to preach and prophesy, bypassing traditional authority.[34] The sense that these were exceptional times was further heightened by the arrival of the plague in Wittenberg. Confronted with the reality of death, many worried about the state of their souls.

Melanchthon, Luther's representative in the town during his prolonged absence, was thrown into a flurry of indecision. He was unsure what to make of the prophets' claims that God spoke to them directly, and defended them against the students. At the same time he tried to persuade Spalatin and Friedrich to permit Luther to return: only Luther, he urged, could judge these spirits. He sent the request to the Elector via Spalatin, leaving the letter unsealed so that Spalatin could read it.[35] Luther for his part was breezily unworried about the prophets, writing to Spalatin: 'I do not come to Wittenberg, nor do I change my quarters, because of the "Zwickau prophets", for they don't disturb me.'[36] It was easy for Luther to discern spirits, far away in the Wartburg; however, those involved in the frenetic pace of politics and religious reform in Wittenberg found it much more difficult to work out what path to take.

*

Luther always regarded political authority as resting in the hands of the ruler, a perception strengthened by his stay in the Wartburg where his main contact was the Elector's right-hand man, Spalatin. Karlstadt, by contrast, seems to have believed that the town council should be empowered to introduce the Reformation, and placed his faith in 'the Christian city of Wittenberg', as he termed it in his pamphlets. This was a line he had been taking since the disputation on the Mass in October 1521, when he advocated that the whole community should decide what evangelical reforms to introduce. Karlstadt's marriage, the departure of Zwilling – who had been a leading figure advocating change, and who now left the Augustinian order altogether to preach in Eilenburg – and the arrival of the charismatic Zwickau prophets may all have played their part in radicalising Karlstadt.[37] Or perhaps it was just that, although it always took a long time to persuade Karlstadt of anything, once convinced, he became a zealot.

Another factor in Karlstadt's enthusiasm for civic ideals may have been his experience of working closely with laypeople, and his conviction that a Christian community truly was being established in the town. He now signed his pamphlets as 'A New Layman'. The council's mandate of 24 January 1522 introducing the Reformation in Wittenberg and reorganising poor relief in line with its earlier ordinance reflected some of Karlstadt's views, and may even have been written in part by him, but it was also the result of close co-operation between evangelical preachers and the town's elite: a group of around thirty people had been meeting daily to draw it up. In addition to supporting the poor, the monies were also to be used to provide cheap loans for newly-weds and deserving craftspeople – a significant extension of the group who stood to benefit from the common chest. Old themes of civic morality joined with new Reformation ideas, as the ordinance thundered against those living 'in unmarriage', insisting that anyone who housed such people should be punished as well. The town brothel, essential in a university town, was to be closed.[38] 'Masses', it stated simply, 'should not be held otherwise than as Christ instituted them at the Last Supper': that is, laypeople should receive bread and wine, and the communicant should be allowed to 'take the consecrated host in their hand and put it in their mouth themselves'.[39] Finally, three altars were to suffice for the main parish church and all images should be removed – although no date was set for this to take place. The ordinance was issued by 'the princely city of Wittenberg'.[40]

It would not have been possible to draw up such an ordinance without the involvement of Wittenberg's leading local politicians, both the present and the incoming mayor, Christian Beyer. Its indebtedness to long-established ideas of civic moralism, such as exiling prostitutes and those living in sin, bear the imprint of council values and expertise, and reveal a powerful faction within the council of craftspeople, middling folk and the town's elites backing the changes. They must have known that their plans would hardly find favour with the Elector, and yet they were willing to risk his displeasure by submitting them to him in printed form.[41]

In late January and early February 1522 meetings were held at Eilenburg not far from Torgau between the Elector's representative, Hugo von Einsiedeln, and Christian Beyer.[42] Something of the nature of this tiny social elite can be gauged from the fact that Beyer, who entered his mayoral term of office in February, had been acting on the Elector's behalf; now he found himself defending the actions of the council he had earlier been seeking to rein in. Meanwhile Christian Döring and Lucas Cranach, members of the council since 1519 and very close to the Elector's court – the Elector was Cranach's main patron – were likely to see things the Elector's way. Eventually a meeting of representatives of the university, the foundation of All Saints, the mayor and the Elector's advisors managed to reach an agreement on the reforms to be introduced in Wittenberg. It stipulated that the words of consecration of the sacrament would be said in German; part of the canon of the Mass would be omitted; the elevation would be reintroduced as a sign, but it would be explained that the Mass was not a sacrifice; the priest should give the sacrament to the communicant 'according to their wish'; and the poor-law provisions would remain in place. There was no mention of whether Communion should be given in one kind or two; and the images that had been destroyed were not ordered to be replaced.[43] Karlstadt volunteered to stop preaching so as to broker a compromise, safeguarding the provisions of the ordinance. It looked as if the Reformation in Wittenberg would be secure.[44]

However, the Catholic side had not been idle either. Duke Georg, alarmed at what was happening in electoral Saxony, successfully campaigned for strong action at the Imperial Council, which was sitting at Nuremberg. On 20 January 1522 an imperial mandate was issued giving the conservative Catholic bishops with jurisdiction in Saxon areas – those of Mainz, Naumburg and Merseburg – authority to carry out 'Visitations' and punish all those guilty of innovations. The Elector was deeply alarmed and now unilaterally rejected the Eilenburg compromise as he knew that if he were to disobey the mandate, he would find his rule imperilled.[45] It would be easy for his dukedom and electoral honours to be transferred to his cousin Duke Georg – and indeed, this is exactly what happened after the Schmalkaldic War of 1546–7.[46]

Surprisingly, Luther now backtracked from his previous support for the Reformation in Wittenberg and came to the Elector's aid. On or around 22 February, having heard about what was afoot in town, he wrote an extraordinary letter to the Elector, congratulating him on his new 'relic' – 'a whole cross, together with nails, spears, and scourges', which he had secured 'without cost or effort'. He was refer-ring to the religious changes in Wittenberg: 'Satan' had come 'amongst the children of God'. 'Stretch out your arms confidently and let the nails go deep', he wrote. 'Be glad and thankful, for thus it must and will be with those who desire God's Word.' Luther teased the Elector for his fondness for relics but while making light of the unrest, he assured him that 'my pen has had to gallop' because he had no time: he was already setting out for Wittenberg.[47] It is not clear what role Spalatin played in the course of events but much of Luther's political advice, when he was in the Wartburg, must have come from the Elec-tor's right-hand man. The letter made clear which side Luther was on: the Elector would have known that he could count on his support to reverse the 'innovations' which the Nuremberg mandate condemned.

Immediately, the Elector dictated a lengthy letter to his official at Eisenach, ordering him to meet with Luther and instructing him what to say. It was a tortuous missive, in which the Elector first forbade Luther to return, but then, taking Luther's quip about his relic, 'a whole cross', seriously, gave him authority to return if this was the cross the Elector had to bear. Quite how all this was conveyed to Luther we do not know; but the length of the letter reveals just how much weight the Elector attached to the meeting. Time was of the essence, which is why Friedrich resorted to instructing his official on the spot rather than sending for Luther or ordering Spalatin to see him.[48]

Luther knew what was afoot politically. He assured the Elector that he would enter Wittenberg, just as he would enter Leipzig, 'even if (Your Electoral Grace will excuse my foolish words) it rained Duke Georgs for nine days and every duke were nine times as furious as this one'. He was aware that Duke Georg was behind the imperial mandate, and that electoral Saxony's interests were directly at risk. He warned the Elector not to protect him: 'I am going to Wittenberg under a far higher protection than the Elec-tor's. I have no intention of asking Your Electoral Grace for protec-tion. Indeed I think I shall protect Your Electoral Grace more than you are able to protect me. And if I thought that Your Electoral

Grace could and would protect me, I should not go. And since I have the impression that Your Electoral Grace is still quite weak in faith, I can by no means regard Your Electoral Grace as the man to protect and save me.'[49] In a postscript he offered to write any letter the Elector would like, to make it clear that it was his wish alone to return to Wittenberg.

Luther later remarked that this was the harshest letter he had written to any prince. And yet it marked a complete capitulation to the Elector's point of view. Up to mid-January 1522 Luther appeared to have been very satisfied with how the Reformation was proceeding in Wittenberg. 'Everything else that I see and hear pleases me very much. May the Lord strengthen the spirit of those who want to do right', he had written to Spalatin in early December, even though he knew that there had been disturbances in the city church the day before he reached Wittenberg. As late as 13 January, he had congratulated Karlstadt on his forthcoming wedding.[50] He had not condemned the removal of images, the abolition of private Masses, the institution of Communion in both kinds, or even the rejection of the adoration of the sacrament. Yet now he returned to Wittenberg, supporting the Elector and Spalatin in their wish to reverse all innovations in line with the imperial mandate.

It is hard to avoid the conclusion that the 'disturbances' in Wittenberg, such as they were, formed a useful pretext for a joint campaign by Luther and the electoral court to bow to the provisions of the imperial mandate. This meant permitting the Catholic bishops to move against evangelical clergy, driving those who had married away from their parishes, imprisoning them and even threatening them with martyrdom. However, it was important for the Elector not to be seen to support Luther, still less to permit him to return. To this end, Luther did as he promised and wrote another letter, drafted by Spalatin, saying that he was returning against the Elector's will. Edited by the jurist Hieronymus Schurff, it took at least two and possibly three drafts before they had a serviceable text. It was immediately sent to the Elector's brother Johann, who was asked to make copies. Again, speed was paramount: copies were soon sent to influential people at Nuremberg – and one conveniently fell into the hands of Duke Georg. It had the desired effect: Friedrich was exonerated from the suspicion of having allowed Luther to return.[51]

When he arrived in Wittenberg on 6 March, Luther set about turning the clock back.[52] Meeting with Amsdorf, Jonas and Melanchthon, he did little else for the first two days but take counsel. With the faction sympathetic to the Elector now dominant in the council, the councillors soon also fell into line, and with unintentional irony, the council made the returning Luther a present of cloth for a new cowl: the knight was to be clothed as a monk once more.

On 9 March, Luther began to preach a series of eight sermons, which became known as the 'Invocavit Sermons', in the parish church – 'his' pulpit and the one from which Karlstadt had been banned. There was a new certainty and confidence in his style. Didactically clear, Luther's sermons mixed humour, insult and biblical exegesis. There was no hiding his scorn for the preachers – 'Dr Karlstadt, Gabriel and Michael' – who had convinced the Wittenbergers of their own godliness. Anyone can teach people the right phrases, Luther stated, even an ass can do that; but the true works of faith are deeds, not words. He insisted on the power of Scripture: the Word did everything, he said, 'while I drank Wittenberg beer with my Philipp [Melanchthon] and Amsdorf'.[53]

From the outset, Luther reminded his parishioners that he was the first reformer: 'therefore, dear brothers, follow me . . . I was the first whom God placed on this arena. It was also me to whom God first revealed to preach these his words.' He concluded the first sermon imagining 'how would it be, if I had brought my people to the "Plan" [that is, field of combat] and I (I who was the first to persuade them to come) wanted to flee death and not wait joyfully: how the poor flock would have been led astray!' Those who make radical changes in religion, he argued, forget that you have to raise children first with milk, then pap, then eggs and soft food. The radicals are like brothers who, when they have sucked their fill, 'cut off the teat', when they should let their brother 'suck, as you have sucked'.[54]

Luther rested his claim for leadership on a paradox. Because he fought with the Devil, and because those whom 'Death and the Devil constantly attack' have the strongest faith, his election was proven. Here Luther developed an insight originally taken from Staupitz, but now the intensity of his inner battles with the Devil had become the overwhelming proof of his own rightness. 'You don't yet know what it costs to fight with the Devil and overcome him', Luther proclaimed. 'I know it well, because I have eaten a piece of salt or two with him;

I know him well, and he knows me well too.'[55] Other preachers might insult their opponents as creatures of Satan, or denigrate the Catholic Mass as 'devilish', but this was not the same as telling the congregation about one's own encounters with the Devil. It was a risky undertaking: those who met with the Devil were regarded as possessed or witches. Indeed, Cochlaeus, who had become one of Luther's fiercest antagonists after their meeting at Worms, thought his encounters with Satan were the surest proof that he was a heretic. None of the other reformers made such a claim – indeed, the Wittenberg prophets had claimed the opposite, namely that they spoke with God.

The events in Wittenberg reveal what became a pattern in Luther's life: time and again, though he might rail against them and insult them with surprising impudence, Luther would in the end always align himself with the authorities. The account first propagated by the Catholic side – that Zwilling and Karlstadt had engaged in subversive preaching, which had caused armed sedition in the town – Luther now adopted as the official narrative of what had happened in Wittenberg. It was a convenient fiction for all sides, because it minimised the extent to which the council, leading reformers and others had been actively involved in introducing the Reformation. In fact, until January, Melanchthon had taken a far more radical line than Karlstadt, but once the imperial mandate made the Elector reject the Eilenburg deal, someone had to be blamed.

As we have seen, for some time Luther had been uncomfortable with Karlstadt. He pointedly did not correspond with him from the Wartburg and he wanted Melanchthon to become the leader of the movement in Wittenberg, a snub to the older and more experienced man. In fact, Melanchthon turned out to be less clear-thinking, more mercurial and less constant.[56] Yet there is no sign that Luther blamed Karlstadt for what had happened in Wittenberg until after his return from the Wartburg. Then, he rapidly personalised developments: it had all been the fault of Zwilling and Karlstadt. Their headstrong preaching had caused the populace to riot and had undermined civic order. This was of course the line that the forces of reaction – the conservative canons of All Saints – had been pushing for some time, presenting minor disruptions of church services as serious breaches of public order. As Luther set about restoring this 'order', his indebtedness to them became clear. He repeated their slur about people taking the sacrament after drinking brandy, although he had them drinking *after* they had taken Communion; and he told the story about the hosts that dropped on the floor, exclaiming that the sacrament was treated with such disrespect 'that it is a surprise that thunder and lightning didn't strike you into the ground'. Taking the wafer in your hands, Luther reckoned, does not make one a good Christian – at that rate, a sow would be the perfect Christian because it could pick it up with its snout.[57]

Zwilling rapidly fell into line. He apologised and recanted so fully that Luther recommended him to Altenburg for a post as pastor, getting him safely out of the way but putting him under the Elector's supervision in a town dominated by one of Friedrich's castles. That left Karlstadt alone with his head in the noose, as he later put it.[58] The ban on preaching, to which Karlstadt had already agreed, was reinforced and when he tried to publish, he found the university censor would not permit him to have his work printed.[59]

It is hard to resist the conclusion that Karlstadt was a convenient scapegoat. While Luther forgave Zwilling with remarkable speed, he did not readily forgive Karlstadt, to whom he had been much closer. In Luther's narrative the events in Wittenberg were transformed into the story of a broken friendship, and a personal betrayal by Karlstadt. He was the first in what would become a long line of former acolytes who were seen to have betrayed their leader. There is something chilling about the no-holds-barred nature of Luther's hatred. In the Invocavit Sermons, he had refrained from criticising Karlstadt directly, but there is no mistaking the note of sarcasm as he called his former colleague 'Dr Karlstadt'. Very soon, however, Luther was linking him with the Devil: it was Satan who, in the shape of Karlstadt, turned against Luther to shatter the Reformation. Karlstadt was an 'angel' who had become an 'angel of light' – that is, he was of the Devil.[60]

Luther had originally approved many of the changes that Karlstadt had introduced – Communion in two kinds, a service in German – but in 1523, when he introduced a new liturgy, it was in Latin, and until 1523, Communion for the laity was to be bread only. The distinctive features of the Wittenberg Mass, with priests wearing secular clothing, and the congregation permitted to touch the bread and wine themselves rather than receiving them from the priest, were abolished. In other respects, however, Luther's later German liturgy of 1526 was little different from Karlstadt's. Indeed, although Luther later rewrote the story of the dispute as a doctrinal breach, Karlstadt had been no sacramentarian at this point: to all intents and purposes he held the same position on the Eucharist as Luther. It would be tempting to conclude that the real breach was over the leadership of the nascent Reformation movement.

And yet this would be only half the truth. At a deeper level Luther grasped a key difference between himself and Karlstadt. Although they were shaped by the same spiritual tradition, the *Theologia deutsch*, and both were influenced by Staupitz, they were taking different paths and this led them, in time, to take different attitudes to the sacrament. Two years later, Karlstadt would argue that Communion was a memorial act only – the presence of Christ in the Eucharist was his spiritual presence, not his actual existence in the bread. Luther had already sensed Karlstadt's hostility to the flesh when he read his treatise on vows. Soon the two men's theologies would become irreconcilable.

With Luther back, Zwilling brought into line, Karlstadt muzzled, and the council's radical ordinances overturned, it seemed that the Wittenberg Reformation had been comprehensively defeated. And yet not every trace was obliterated. The begging ordinance and the Common Chest remained in force. The monks could not be brought back, and the smashed images could not be restored. In the end, most of Karlstadt's reforms would be reintroduced – although Luther pointedly waited until he died in 1541 before abolishing the elevation of the sacrament in Wittenberg. Still, the council had resigned from its religious role, and thereafter the Wittenberg Reformation was a princely Reformation, not one driven by a popular civic movement. It was Luther who decided when weak consciences were strong enough to graduate from pap. The visionary excitement of the Wittenberg movement, the sense of the great things that could be done with the funds liberated from Masses and monasteries, the feeling of evangelical power as thousands of citizens took Communion in both kinds – all this was lost as Luther insisted on his leadership, not collective action.

It is unlikely that a communal Reformation would ever have had much chance in Wittenberg. The town was simply too small to support it, and its reliance on the Elector, with so many in the town's political elite close to the court, meant that it had no tradition of independence. The tinder of economic and political grievance amongst large numbers of artisans was also missing. The other great institution in the town, the university, was not likely to risk alienating its founder;

and the students, who did have a tradition of activism, had little loyalty to Wittenberg, especially since many of them were beginning to question the point of academic studies altogether. Once Duke Georg had secured the imperial mandate that enabled Catholic bishops to roll back the Reformation, the Elector had no choice but to knuckle under – or risk losing his power and title. Had Luther, ever the realist, not reversed the changes of December and January, as the mandate required, the Reformation in Wittenberg is unlikely to have survived.

But the idea of a communal Reformation made by the people was not dead. In town after town – Zwickau, Augsburg, Nördlingen, Nuremberg and Strasbourg – popular movements would bring in the Reformation, as crowds attacked clergy and petitioned their town councils, and evangelical preachers gave their listeners a glimpse of what a reformed commune could mean. All the actions that had galvanised the Wittenberg populace were repeated across the empire, with evangelicals interrupting sermons, destroying altarpieces, tearing up Mass books, urinating in chalices or mocking the clergy – and they drew on the same repertoire of carnivalesque ritual and comedy that the Wittenberg students had developed.[61] Nor was Karlstadt forgotten. In Riga and Livonia it was his ideas, not Luther's, that were picked up and put into practice by local reform movements; in Oldersum and other parts of East Frisia, his views about the sacrament were taken up, whilst Luther's seemed superstitious; the town of Magdeburg adopted features of the Wittenberg reform movement; and as late as 1524, a pamphlet published in Speyer could depict Luther and Karlstadt leading the Reformation together.[62]

By setting his face against a communal Reformation, and siding with the authorities, Luther had also cut himself off from what was going on in the rest of the empire. During his time in the Wartburg, he had lost his networks beyond Saxony and Mansfeld. He would have difficulty in gaining any lasting foothold in major towns like Augsburg or Strasbourg; and even Nuremberg, nominally Lutheran, did not seek his advice on a regular basis, relying instead on their own local preachers. The issues that animated the Reformation in towns throughout the empire – the tyranny of confession, the opposition to images, the demand for immediate liturgical change – all these Luther had taken off the agenda at Wittenberg. He did not understand communal values or communal politics, and ideals of 'brotherhood'

and compromise were alien to him. There was no compromising with the Devil, and, as he reiterated in his Invocavit Sermons, each one of us must face death and the Devil alone. He returned from the Wartburg a more forthright preacher, secure in his role as pastor of his flock. What had given him this increased confidence was both his appearance at Worms and his isolation in the Wartburg. But that had been won at the cost of dangerously narrowing his vision. While he had begun the Reformation for his 'dear Germans', and had faced down all the princes of the empire, the world he now seemed to care about most was the small backwater where he lived.

41. This woodcut shows Karlstadt and Luther on either side of a wagon in which Christ sits, driving towards salvation, while Ulrich von Hutten in armour leads the chained clergy of the old church, Murner visible as a cat. Luther and Karlstadt both hold palms of salvation, but Karlstadt is almost more prominent than Luther. The woodcut is reminiscent of *Karlstadt's Wagon*, illustrated by Cranach, the first visual propaganda for the Reformation (see pp. 126–7). It folds out of a pamphlet by Hermann von dem Busche, *Trivphvs veritatis. Sick der warheyt*, a long poem in praise of the Reformation published in Speyer in 1524.

# 11

# The Black Bear Inn

At 7 a.m. on 22 August 1524, Luther preached in the main church of Jena. It was a memorable sermon, lasting an hour and a half. Luther was at his most pugilistic and roundly attacked those who questioned the Real Presence of Christ in the Eucharist. He also condemned the radicals who insisted on removing all images from churches. Such people, Luther said, were driven by the spirit of Satan, and though they were few in number, their presence as sectaries was a sign that the Devil was raging.[1]

Jena was not territory hospitable to Luther, who was on a Visitation of the Saxon churches. Karlstadt now had his own parish in the small nearby town of Orlamünde, where he had begun to introduce the kind of Reformation he had failed to establish in Wittenberg. His ally Martin Reinhard was the preacher at Jena, where the local printing press had also been publishing Karlstadt's work. In fact, Karlstadt himself was among the congregation at Jena that morning, disguised as a peasant under a felt hat. He was convinced that Luther's tirade against the 'crazies' was directed against him.

After the sermon, he dashed off a letter to Luther proposing a meeting. Luther replied that he had no objections. A few hours later, Karlstadt – accompanied by Reinhard and Karlstadt's brother-in-law and fellow preacher Dr Gerhard Westerburg – arrived at the Black Bear Inn where Luther was staying with his retinue of Saxon court officials.[2] When the visitors entered the parlour, Luther motioned Karlstadt to a chair opposite him, insisting that their exchange take place in public.

Karlstadt, facing the crowd of assembled dignitaries, began by objecting that Luther had attacked him in the same breath as the 'riotous murdering spirits' who were followers of Thomas Müntzer.

42. In this hostile pamphlet from 1524, Luther, identified by his initials above him on the wall, is shown in league with the Devil, who is handing him a booklet. The Devil's claw foot makes him instantly recognisable, and his felt hat is marked 'S' for Satan. The Devil is dressed in peasant garb and the image insinuates that Luther is part of an unholy alliance with peasants.

Müntzer, whom we will meet again later, had originally been inspired by Luther's ideas, but developed a radical theology that called for social as well as religious change; he was starting to worry the Saxon authorities and had recently been forced to leave the town of Allstedt. Luther's charge, Karlstadt insisted, was unjust, for although he held different views on the sacrament from Luther, he did not agree with Müntzer. 'He who wants to . . . put me in the same pot with such murdering spirits ascribes that to me without truth and not as an honest man', Karlstadt declared. This was a stinging rebuke, for in a society which depended on people giving their word, to insult someone as dishonest was to attack their manhood and respectability. Karlstadt also accused Luther of stopping him from preaching and publishing. In words that evoked Christ's flagellation, he said: 'Was I not bound and struck when you alone wrote, printed and preached against me and arranged that my books were taken from the press and that I was forbidden to write and preach?'[3]

The two men argued for a long time, sometimes falling silent. They knew each other well, and their jibes hit home. You 'go about in a grandiose fashion, boast grandly, and want only yourself to be exalted and noticed', Luther told Karlstadt. 'You must always speak in such a way that you maintain your reputation and stir up hatred for other people', Karlstadt replied. In the midst of these highly emotional exchanges, Karlstadt turned to the audience and declared: 'Dear brothers, I pray you, don't pay attention to my harsh speech. Such harsh speech is a matter of my complexion but my heart is not on that account wicked or angry.' With anger being a deadly sin, Karlstadt here drew on the theory of the humours to explain that he was a choleric individual, but his 'heart' was not therefore full of anger, nor was it wicked.[4]

Luther taunted Karlstadt with not daring to attack him in public; Karlstadt retorted that it was Luther who was preventing him from doing so. Then, taking a coin from his pocket, Luther announced: 'If you do, I will present you with a guilder for it.' Karlstadt accepted the challenge, took the coin, 'showed it to all bystanders' and declared: 'Dear brothers, this is a pledge, a sign, that I have authority to write against Dr Luther.' Karlstadt bent the guilder and put it in his purse. The two men shook hands and Luther drank a toast to Karlstadt. Then they parted.[5]

It was a momentous meeting. By bending the coin, Karlstadt took it out of circulation and marked it forever as a token. This was common sixteenth-century practice: binding marriages could be concluded by giving a coin as a token, while commercial contracts, agreed without paper records, were given force by rituals like the handshake and the drink. Yet the meaning of this ritual was not clear. Luther regarded it as a declaration of enmity, a formal initiation of feud; Karlstadt, as his right to publish. Martin Reinhard published a pamphlet describing the event, so for once Luther did not have control of the propaganda. Luther was furious when he read Reinhard's account, written 'to my infamy and Karlstadt's glory', even though the tone of the text was scrupulously neutral.[6] But no reader could miss Luther's contempt for Karlstadt during their meeting, capped by the gift of the valuable coin (gold, no less). And now there was no turning back: Luther's promise to Karlstadt allowing him to publish was on public record.[7] Luther made certain that the author of the pamphlet did not get away with it. Shortly afterwards, Reinhard was forced to leave his post in Jena, and when he moved to Nuremberg, he was driven from there too. Reinhard soon knuckled under, asking forgiveness, but Luther was unwilling to intervene on his behalf.[8]

★

How had the former allies come to this? The answer lies in the efflorescence of reforming ideas in the two years since Luther had returned from the Wartburg, as the movement began to go in different directions beyond his control. After the defeat of the Wittenberg movement in 1522 and his own silencing, Karlstadt, who retained his post of archdeacon, had at first resumed his university position and kept a low profile. But he was isolated and treated with disdain by Melanchthon and others. Increasingly radical, he began to take a grim view of university life, arguing that academic work and degrees generated nothing but dissension and boastfulness. 'What does one seek in the higher schools than to be honoured by others?' he asked. 'Therefore, one aspires to be a master, another a doctor and then a doctor of sacred Scripture.' University scholars 'seek doctoral honours with such avarice and greed that they envy and persecute all other equal teaching'. All this was wrong because we 'cannot . . . believe and trust God while we receive such honours'. This was an astonishing pronouncement by someone who had always relished disputations and the cut and thrust of debate. Now he castigated academic rituals: 'on account of academic glory we kneel down, give money and set up festivities and costly meals to gain some clout with and earn respect from people'. Karlstadt drew the consequences and repudiated his doctoral title – although Luther studiously referred to him throughout his life as 'Dr Karlstadt'. It was country life and rural labour that now began to attract the man who had once insisted on his noble lineage, and he increasingly spent time outside Wittenberg, purchasing his own farm in Wörlitz.[9]

In yearning to be a farmer, Karlstadt was in step with the times. Peasants, so often regarded with contempt as rural boors, began to be idealised for their honest toil and simple evangelical faith. The figure whose remarkable success best encapsulated this mood was Diepold Peringer, the so-called 'peasant of Wöhrd'. Peringer claimed that he could neither read nor write, but he preached inspirationally and published evangelical tracts. These were printed and circulated widely throughout Germany, often illustrated with a striking woodcut of a staunch peasant in stout boots, holding a flail and gesturing with his right hand like a preacher. These images were the more remarkable because they seemed to hark back to the revolutionary peasants of the *Bundschuh* organisation in the late fifteenth century, which had united the peasants in rebellion under the sign of the peasant boot.

Peasants, so the images seemed to suggest, were pious evangelicals – simple Christians who could preach better than the educated clergy. It seemed that in Peringer's sermons God's spirit was being poured out on ordinary folk. Even Spalatin, who heard him preach at Nuremberg, was impressed. But in 1524 Peringer was unmasked as an ex-cleric, who certainly knew how to read and write (and preach) – much to Luther's amusement, who teased Spalatin for being taken in. Yet if Peringer had not existed, he would have had to be invented. His imposture gave voice to a prevalent mood in Germany of admiration of simple folk, especially peasants, and suspicion of intellectuals.

Karlstadt, who shared in this mood, now began to toy with leaving the university for good and becoming a vintner – he had grown up in a wine-growing area – or living as an ordinary priest. He eventually opted for the latter and chose to move to Orlamünde, for which he was technically responsible as archdeacon. Karlstadt was careful to square this with the authorities, and in May 1523 the parish formally asked the Elector to appoint him as pastor. It was quite a comedown. It meant taking on a lowly paid job that he had previously employed someone else to do, in the days when he had aspired to the richest benefice in Wittenberg. Instead of the fine clothes he had worn after his return from Italy, the former university professor now took to wearing grey peasant attire, and donned the peasant felt hat in place of his doctor's cap.[10] As he later put it, 'I now have a grey coat (thank

43. and 44. Two illustrations from Diepold Peringer's tracts. In the first, the peasant holds a rosary and gestures like a preacher with the other hand; in the second the pious peasant, wearing peasant boots, holds a flail.

God) in place of the finery which at one time greatly delighted me and caused me to sin.' Luther mocked his 'felt hat and a grey garb, not wanting to be called doctor, but Brother Andrew and dear neighbour, as another peasant', but these were visible signs of Karlstadt's determination to relinquish social superiority.[11] The parsonage in Orlamünde was falling down and the fences were broken; the woods had not been properly tended and the previous incumbent, who had left under a cloud, had used the manure set aside for the priest's vines for his own fields. Yet this was the peasant life which Karlstadt had craved – although it is unclear how much labouring he did himself.[12]

Karlstadt's period of enforced silence in Wittenberg after 1522, difficult though it had been, had also been very creative as he used the time to develop further his mystical theology. He could still not publish in Wittenberg, but in late 1523, the printer Michael Buchfurer

moved from Erfurt to Jena and began printing his work, a move possibly facilitated by financial help from Karlstadt's brother-in-law Gerhard Westerburg, a prosperous patrician from Cologne. Now at Orlamünde, Karlstadt put his new theology into practice in a manner which had not been possible while in Wittenberg under Luther's watchful eye. He held his services in German and he translated Psalms from the Hebrew for the congregation to sing. The translations were dreadful and the singing lame, according to one hostile observer, but it was an attempt to involve the congregation through music and to stress spiritual closeness to God.[13] Increasingly he engaged with the Old Testament, and when a parishioner with a marital problem sought his advice, he recommended that he should, like the Old Testament prophets, take a second wife. They will be introducing circumcision next, quipped Luther, who was well informed about the developments.[14] Karlstadt also seems to have encouraged women to play a more active role in the congregation, and he held Bible study classes, giving his parishioners confidence in their own interpretation of Scripture; indeed, his key theological concept of *Gelassenheit*, he began to argue, was a Saxon peasant word.[15] All this was very different from Luther's Wittenberg, where, out of respect for the 'weak', most of the liturgical reforms had been reversed and where the service was now again held in Latin.[16]

Luther and the university did not stand idly by. Discovering that Karlstadt had managed to circumvent university censorship by having his writings printed at Jena, Luther wrote to the Saxon chancellor to get the printer subjected to censorship or closed down. In April 1524 the university summoned Karlstadt to Wittenberg, presenting him with the choice of either leaving his post at Orlamünde and remaining at the university, or losing his archdeaconry and associated university duties. It seems that Karlstadt chose to remain archdeacon, a decision which Luther derided: 'Had he then been certain that he had been called to be pastor, he should not have given it up, but rather have given up his life.'[17] In fact, Karlstadt tried to have it both ways. He petitioned to stay on at Orlamünde through the summer, explaining that he needed to recoup his investment in farming and the vineyard; and the parishioners at Orlamünde evidently remained attached to their preacher, petitioning the duke for him to be allowed to stay.[18]

This might look like a conflict between the right of a congregation to appoint its own pastor (something which Luther had supported) and the right of the legal patron (in this case the university) to select the incumbent, except that Karlstadt had throughout been careful to subject himself to the university's authority. Legally trained, he was not at this point questioning property rights within the Church, and it was his responsibility as archdeacon for Orlamünde which had brought him to the parish in the first place. The university for its part proceeded to replace him with the university's rector Caspar Glatz – a suspiciously senior figure for such a post. The new vicar poured out bile in letters to Luther informing him of what was going on, even alleging that Karlstadt employed a chaplain who pretended to be a poltergeist, frightening and fooling the people.[19]

Detached from university life – and the scrutiny of any censor – Karlstadt was departing ever further from Luther's theology. He

explored his new understanding of Communion as a spiritual sacrament, and argued that Christ was not actually present in the bread
and wine, which were fleshly things. As he put it, bread is what
you get in a baker's shop: it isn't Christ. Karlstadt became more
convinced that images were idolatrous and should be removed
entirely from churches. He also exchanged letters with Thomas
Müntzer.

*

Thomas Müntzer, who would become Luther's most hated opponent,
was born in Stolberg, not far from Eisleben, and probably came from
a family of goldsmiths or minters. He had studied in Frankfurt an der
Oder and had spent some months at Wittenberg in the autumn of
1517 to hear the lectures of the humanist Johannes Aesticampianus; it
was at that time that he also got to know Karlstadt. It was of course
a dramatic time to be in Wittenberg, although how much Müntzer
was influenced by Luther and how far he had arrived at his views
himself (as he claimed) is unclear.[20] After a series of poorly paid and
insecure positions, including acting as confessor at a nunnery, he moved
to Zwickau to a temporary post replacing the evangelical preacher
Johannes Egranus, where he began to develop a much more radical
conception of the Reformation.[21] Egranus had baited the Catholics
and had himself become the focus of attack; Müntzer, who had
discovered a talent for preaching, would go much further.

When Egranus returned, another parish was found for the bold
preacher in Zwickau, at St Catherine's, where his congregation
included many poor cloth-workers, with whom he quickly established
a rapport. Here he also got to know the later 'Zwickau prophets'.
Although their theologies may have been different – Nikolaus Storch
seems to have been a follower of the Free Spirit heresy – there were
also points of contact and influence. But all was not plain sailing in
Zwickau: Müntzer also became a target of hostility. The windows of
his lodgings were smashed and he received a broadsheet of threats
and abuse. Some of the reasons may emerge from a letter by Luther's
supporter Johann Agricola, in which he tried to get Müntzer to
moderate his tone in sermons: 'when you ought to be teaching what
is right you impugn others in an unjustified way and even mention

them by name', adding, in large letters 'YOU BREATHE OUT NOTHING BUT SLAUGHTER AND BLOOD'.[22] Müntzer also began preaching against Egranus, whose theology he found lacking in seriousness – Luther and Agricola would eventually agree – and Egranus replied in kind. As a result, the town council banished both preachers, appointing Nikolaus Hausmann, a close follower of Luther and a steadier head, in their place.

Müntzer decided to go to Prague in June 1521, and by this time he seems to have been convinced of the imminent end of the world and his own martyrdom. His apocalyptic mood is evident in his Prague Manifesto, a diatribe against the clergy and a statement of mystical theology; one version of it he wrote down on a piece of paper a metre square, as if he intended to publish his own colossal version of the Ninety-Five Theses.[23] Returning from Prague in December 1521, he again took a series of temporary posts until he finally managed to find a position as preacher at Allstedt in April 1523. Here, like Karlstadt, he set about introducing a thoroughgoing Reformation, and even established a printing press. Allstedt was a tiny market town some 50 kilometres north-east of Erfurt, in an enclave of electoral Saxony, controlled by Duke Johann, the Elector's brother, but surrounded by hostile Catholic territories. Enough was known about Müntzer's radical views by this time for the duke and Spalatin to take an interest in the new preacher, and in late 1523 they visited the town, staying in the castle. Yet at this juncture the Saxon authorities, always cautious and slow-moving, took no further action. It seems that Duke Johann was reluctant to take measures against Müntzer, well aware of his local support and not wishing to repress evangelical preaching.

Luther, however, soon became convinced that Müntzer was dangerous and his writings from the summer on are peppered with references to the 'spirit of Allstedt'. In late July 1524, worried that the authorities were not intervening, he published his *Letter to the Princes of Saxony Concerning the Rebellious Spirit*.[24] Luther reminded the worldly rulers that false sects have always attacked Christendom, linking Müntzer with violence and rebellion. He also proclaimed that all those who destroy images are driven not by the 'spirit', as they claim, but by the Devil – an argument that implicitly bracketed Karlstadt with Müntzer. Luther did not name either man, referring only to the 'spirit of Allstedt', but the term could be seen to include Karlstadt's theology.

After all, both men prized *Gelassenheit*, although Müntzer, who knew the insecure life of a clerical proletarian, placed far more emphasis on suffering as part of the process through which the believer found God. Both had created godly parishes, removed images and reformed the liturgy, and they had corresponded with each other. Karlstadt too had argued that the letter of Scripture was worthless without the spirit, and that academic theology was not the path to truth. As he had told Müntzer in 1522: 'I have said more about visions and dreams than any of the professors.'[25]

These people, Luther argued, claim to be so spiritually superior, but they had not fought the Pope as he had. To underline the point, he provided a brief autobiography, including his debate at Leipzig and his appearances at Augsburg and Worms,[26] presenting himself as the sole Reformation hero while obliterating Karlstadt altogether. The Allstedtian spirits were profiting from Luther's victories 'though they have done no battle for it and risked no bloodshed to attain it. But I have had to attain it for them and, until now, at the risk of my body and my life.'[27]

A rhetorical tour de force, Luther here made the touchstone of truth his own physical existence, his preparedness to put his 'body and life' on the line. He equated the evangelical movement with the narrative of his own deeds, even with his physical being. This had already been evident in the words attributed to him at Worms: 'Here I stand' – his body implacably the guarantee of his truth and commitment. Karlstadt's brush with danger, as Luther well knew, could hardly stand comparison with his own. Yet the 'martyr's crown' was important to both men. It had been the prospect of martyrdom which had impelled Karlstadt's heightened understanding of *Gelassenheit*, and with it, the unfolding of his mystical theology. However, by 'spirit' – so important to his understanding of how the Bible should be read – Karlstadt did not mean the spirit of violence, but the spirit of God with which the soul should seek union, through *Gelassenheit*, and in preparedness for martyrdom. No wonder Karlstadt was so angry by the time he met Luther at the Black Bear Inn.

*

While Karlstadt was establishing his church at Orlamünde, matters at Allstedt were proceeding apace. In March 1524 a nearby pilgrimage chapel was burnt to the ground – and if Müntzer had not been involved, he had also not disapproved, believing the pilgrimage to be godless idolatry that had to be brought to an end. In June, the atmosphere in Allstedt became tense when villagers from nearby Sangerhausen fled to the town after Catholic persecution, and as passions mounted over how the arsonists would be punished. Müntzer became convinced that the Last Days were imminent. In July, Duke Johann and his son passed through Allstedt, again staying in the castle, and Müntzer seized the chance to preach in front of them. He chose as his text the second chapter of the book of Daniel, which he interpreted to mean that secular princes must root out the ungodly. 'God is your shield,' he told the princes, 'and will train you for the battle against his enemies . . . But at the same time you will have to endure a heavy cross and a time of trial, so that the fear of God may be manifest in you. That cannot happen without suffering.' If they did not heed the call, he threatened, 'the sword will be taken from them'.[28] This was seditious. But Müntzer did not stop there, and had the sermon – with a long passage on dreams added – printed at Allstedt. Not surprisingly, he and several of his supporters were summoned to appear at Weimar to answer for their actions in late July.

On 24 July, in an increasingly fraught situation, Müntzer appealed to the people of Allstedt to form a league, urging them to swear a formal oath. Over 500 of his supporters did so, which included not only citizens of Allstedt but peasants from the surrounding countryside and miners from Luther's own Mansfeld as well. Council members and even the duke's official were impelled to join in a covenant with God that replaced earthly political allegiances. This was a revolutionary reconfiguration of politics, and it brought ducal officials, townsfolk, miners and peasants together in a shared sense of communal belonging that overcame class antagonism. But when Müntzer and the Allstedt authorities (many of them his allies) were interrogated at Weimar, his supporters caved in, blaming Müntzer alone for the disturbances. The local ducal official too switched sides and took action, shutting down the printer, ordering Müntzer to refrain from incendiary preaching, and disbanding the league. In early August, having been effectively silenced and feeling betrayed by his supporters who turned out to be 'Judases', Müntzer decided that the cause in Allstedt was lost and left in the middle of the night, leaving his wife and child behind. With one of his followers, he escaped to the small imperial town of Mühlhausen.

Despite the similarities in their apocalyptic outlook, Karlstadt parted company with Müntzer when it came to the use of violence: Müntzer believed that the divine kingdom should be ushered in by the use of the sword, while Karlstadt insisted on non-violence. Very careful to distance himself, Karlstadt had his reply to Müntzer's invitation to join his league printed, and ensured that a letter from his congregation of Orlamünde rejecting Müntzer's overtures was also printed at Wittenberg. By the time of their meeting at the Black Bear Inn, Luther may have thought that Karlstadt was changing his views, since the danger from Müntzer, now forced out of his stronghold at Allstedt, had apparently passed. If he did, this would prove to be a major miscalculation.

*

This was the immediate history preceding the events at the Black Bear Inn on 22 August 1524. And matters did not end there. The next day, Luther preached in the small town of Kahla, where the pastor was a supporter of Karlstadt. On mounting the pulpit, Luther found a smashed crucifix where he was to preach. When he then arrived in Orlamünde the following morning – he had decided that it was too dangerous to spend the night there – he found nobody in the village to greet him; it turned out that everybody was busy with the harvest. The impatient Luther was finally met by the mayor and other local dignitaries, but refused to doff his hat as they did to him, a gesture of studied contempt. When the mayor invited a discussion, Luther replied that he had to leave soon, but that they might talk indoors.[29] The Orlamünders may have wanted to engage with the reformer in debate out of doors: there was a long tradition of holding democratic meetings under the open sky.

Democratic debate, however, was the last thing Luther had in mind. First he chided the Orlamünders for a letter they had sent him on 16 August complaining that his letter to the Saxon princes had traduced Karlstadt as a heretic; he suggested contemptuously that it had been composed by Karlstadt misusing their seal.[30] The villagers, however, maintained that he had not written a single line of it. Then Luther's former collaborator appeared himself, but Luther would not permit him to remain, insisting 'you are my enemy, and I gave you a gold guilder on it'.[31] After Karlstadt left, Luther attacked the Orlamünders' theological ignorance, but instead of meek obedience, he was met with spirited argument. A cobbler stepped forward, addressing Luther with the informal 'you', a claim to social equality with the man who insisted on his title of 'Doctor'. 'If you will not follow Moses, you must nevertheless endure the gospel', the man told the reformer, accusing him: 'You have shoved the gospel under the bench.' When Luther expostulated that getting rid of images was as good as saying that one should kill all women and pour away all wine just because they could be misused, another villager replied that unlike images, women and wine had been created for human comfort and need. Then the cobbler adduced the text, 'the bride must take off her night-gown and be naked, if she is to sleep with the bridegroom', which he wrongly claimed was a saying by Jesus, concluding that 'Therefore one must break all the images, so that we are free and cleansed of what is created.'[32] It was easy for Luther to mock the Orlamünders' ignorance and he made endless capital of it in the polemic he published against them in late 1524, *Against the Heavenly Prophets*, laughing at the peasants who 'take the nightgown off the bride at Orlamünde and the trousers off the bridegroom at Naschhausen'.[33]

Karlstadt's ministry had given his parishioners confidence in their own ability to interpret Scripture and articulate their views.[34] The cobbler's choice of words and use of a biblical text shows how villagers made sense of Karlstadt's preaching, but may also hint at an uneasy ambiva-lence between sexual prurience and asceticism. 'God wants the souls of all creatures to be naked, that is, unclothed and free', another villager declared.[35] Luther's opposition to Karlstadt's stress on Mosaic law may have been driven by his deep-seated anti-Judaism – he termed Karlstadt's followers the 'Jewish saints'.[36] Not only did he mock Karlstadt's adher-ence to Old Testament law but in starting to insist that churches *ought* to have images – a rather different position from the ambivalent line he had originally taken – Luther ensured that his churches would have nothing in common with the undecorated walls of Jewish synagogues.

Tiring of the debate, Luther recommended that the villagers read his books. Then he and his supporters 'hurried to their wagon' – accompanied, Luther later said, by shouts of 'Go in a thousand devils' name, so you break your neck before you get out of town.'[37] Two or three days later, Karlstadt reportedly rang the church bells for over an hour to summon his parishioners from the surrounding area. Luther, he preached, had 'unfortunately kicked the gospel under the bench', the same accusation the cobbler had made. 'Oh dear brothers and sisters, men and women citizens of God! Do not be afraid, but endure until the end, and you will be saved. God has made him [Luther] twist the Scriptures according to what he thinks right.'[38]

*

Karlstadt was fighting for his right to publish, preach and be heard. Having, as he saw it, won that right after meeting Luther at the Black Bear Inn, he set about rallying support. He now signed his letters and tracts as Andreas Karlstadt, 'exiled on account of the truth without a hearing', or 'unheard and unvanquished'.[39] Luther commented wryly that 'I who ought to have become a martyr have reached the point where I am now making martyrs of others' – a comment which, despite its irony, betrays a recognition of how far things had moved.[40]

In September 1524, however, a few weeks after the events at Jena, the Elector summoned Karlstadt to Weimar to inform him that he was being banished. Forced to leave Saxony, he embarked on a long pilgrimage through southern Germany, which Luther tracked with bitter precision through the letters of his various informants. He headed for Rothenburg ob der Tauber, Basle and Strasbourg, while his colleague and brother-in-law Gerhard Westerburg, travelled to Zurich and then Basle, where he was instrumental in getting Karlstadt's work published.[41] Back in Orlamünde, Karlstadt's wife gave birth before being forced to leave as well, and she now joined her husband on his travels.

Karlstadt certainly made use of his permission to publish, printing seven tracts in Basle when beyond Luther's reach. Under Westerburg's reassuringly patrician patronage, Karlstadt's ideas gained a new readership; meanwhile his supporter Martin Reinhard had travelled to Cologne to spread his message there as well.[42] There were rumours that Karlstadt had got his views about the sacrament from Luther himself, in secret discussions, and that Luther, who did not yet dare to deny publicly that Christ was truly present in the bread and wine, would soon come out in support. In Strasbourg, Wolfgang Capito and the humanist Otto Brunfels read Karlstadt's works and agreed with his views on the sacrament; in Basle, the reformer and humanist Johannes Oecolampadius was taking Karlstadt's side; in Nuremberg too, Karlstadt was finding readers, and in Magdeburg, Königsberg and even the Netherlands, people were joining in what Luther and his followers would soon denounce as the 'spirit of Müntzer and Karlstadt'.[43] Luther's man in Strasbourg, Nikolaus Gerbel, warned that Karlstadt was distributing copies of his works printed in Basle and gaining supporters; apparently he was telling everyone that he had been banished by Luther because he could not overcome him with Scripture. The Strasbourg preachers wrote collectively to Luther, sending five of Karlstadt's writings and asking for his advice. The letter, brilliantly formulated so as to stress their loyalty, reveals that their position was in fact closer to Karlstadt's, since they too were purifying their churches of images and beginning to raise questions about the Real Presence in the sacrament. They bluntly informed Luther that in Zurich, Basle and even in Strasbourg, most biblically informed people shared Karlstadt's views.[44]

Indeed, it seems that many found Karlstadt's explanation of the sacrament and his belief in the spiritual presence of Christ to be the more persuasive. Karlstadt's maturing theology was clearly marked by his experiences at Wittenberg, where the communal reformation had fired his enthusiasm. This vision was popular elsewhere too, particularly in southern Germany, because it entailed social reform with a renewal of morals, reorganised poor relief, and popular lay involvement. It was very different from Luther's ideal of a top-down Reformation. Some also disliked Luther's attempt to impose his views on others by appealing to their personal loyalty. 'I am very upset by the dissension between Karlstadt and yourself,' Otto Brunfels wrote, 'for I favour you both, and I do not love you in such a way that I cannot also embrace Karlstadt most sincerely.'[45] The grammarian Valentin Ickelsamer complained of Luther's writings, 'what are these booklets against the spirit of Allstedt . . . but a cunning attempt to provoke the princes against good Karlstadt?'[46] Outside Wittenberg, the spectacle of the two reformers in discord was seen as disastrous for the Reformation's image, and while Karlstadt had been careful to hold back from attacking his former colleague, Luther had taken to publicly accusing Karlstadt of being possessed by the Devil.[47] Yet

Karlstadt never set himself up as a rival to Luther; had he done so, the story of the Reformation might well have been different.

Luther seemed well aware of just how much was at risk, and it is an indication of his concern that he replied to the letter of the Strasbourg preachers not with a manuscript missive, but with a printed public letter, which he duly dispatched via their messenger.[48] The delay in his response, caused by printing his letter, had far-reaching consequences. The Strasbourgers had written to Huldrych Zwingli in Zurich at the same time, who now also denied the Real Presence in the sacrament, and his handwritten letter arrived before Luther's printed reply. Martin Bucer, previously inclined to Luther, was persuaded by Zwingli's views 'with hand and foot', as a delighted Capito reported.[49] In his response, Luther mused unwisely, 'I confess, that if Dr Karlstadt or someone else had been able to instruct me five years ago, that there was nothing but bread and wine in the sacrament, he would have done me a great service. I suffered such great temptations at that time and twisted and struggled, because I saw well that this would have been the biggest coup against the papacy.' The letter may well have lent credence to the rumours that Karlstadt had got the idea from Luther himself.[50]

In a letter to Spalatin in October 1524, Luther referred to Karlstadt as his 'Absalom', the man who stole away the hearts of the Israelites. But the term also hinted at the depths of his feeling for Karlstadt: Absalom was David's handsome son, whose rebellion broke his father's heart, because he was forced to act against the child he loved so much.[51] Increasingly Luther linked Müntzer and Karlstadt; but his most hostile rhetoric was reserved for Karlstadt alone, as is evident in Luther's monumental *Against the Heavenly Prophets*, the first part of which was published in late 1524. The treatise articulated what Luther believed to be the indissoluble links between an emphasis on the spirit, denying the Real Presence of Christ in the sacrament, destroying images, and engaging in sedition. He was determined to put as much clear water as he could between his views and any form of rebellion or violence.

*

For the rest of his life, Luther's rhetoric about Karlstadt and Müntzer would become a fixed formula. They were *Schwärmer*, literally 'the

swarmers', as if they were a swarm of madly buzzing bees, 'enthusiasts' who claimed to be led by the spirit. 'He wants to be thought the
highest spirit, who has swallowed the Holy Spirit, feathers and all',
Luther famously satirised Müntzer's spiritualistic theology.[52] Time and
again, Luther punctured the heightened emotionality of the *Schwärmer*
by translating their high-flown claims into crude physical terms, using
earthy reality to deride abstraction.

For his part, Karlstadt became more and more adamant about the
distinction between flesh and spirit. In early 1525 he wrote of how
we must 'choke lusts and desires through affliction and persecution
which befall us and by living daily according to the will of God'.
Martyrdom, achieved through *Gelassenheit* and spiritual humility,
remained a key component of his thought. Where Luther talked of
spiting the Devil by getting married, Karlstadt wrote that 'We, too,
must overcome the Devil through suffering and through the truth
which we have come to know. Through suffering we must subdue,
break, and subordinate to the spirit our untamed flesh in order to
assist hope, strengthen faith, and firm up the word.' Replying to
Luther's attack on him for wearing peasant grey, Karlstadt mocked
the reformer's predilection for wearing 'scarlet, satin, brocade, angora
cloth, velvet, and gold tassels' – a well-chosen barb, for Karlstadt
knew how irritated Luther had been in 1519 at the Leipzig Debate
where the citizens had given Eck the fine angora cloth which Luther
had longed for.[53]

Karlstadt, the former provost of All Saints who had once driven a
hard bargain over how much his chaplain should pay him from the
income of the Orlamünde property, now wrote: 'Would to God that
I were a real peasant, field labourer, or craftsman, that I might eat my
bread in obedience to God, i.e., in the sweat of my brow. Instead, I
have eaten from the poor people's labours whom I have given nothing
in return. I had no right to this nor could I protect them in any way.
Nonetheless, I took their labours into my house. If I could, I should
like to return to them everything I took.'[54] In 1524 he was not only
idealising peasant life: he was now also reaping the consequences of
his theology for social relations, realising how as a priest he had been
complicit in the exploitation of the poor. For him, the Reformation
was becoming a movement of liberation of the common people. He
was not alone.

# 12

# The Peasants' War

In the autumn of 1524, the biggest social uprising in the German lands before the era of the French Revolution began. The Peasants' War started in south-west Germany as a series of local rebellions which gradually joined together, most areas adopting the 'Twelve Articles of the Peasants', drawn up by a furrier and a Lutheran preacher in Memmingen. Each demand, whether for the abolition of serfdom or the free hunting of game, was supported with biblical quotation, and the articles opened with the bold evangelical insistence that every community should be able to call its own pastor to preach the gospel. In the Twelve Articles, the key concepts of the Reformation – 'freedom', 'Christ alone', Scripture as the only authority – were applied to the peasants' situation, creating a forthright programme that found support all over Germany. Print played a powerful role: the articles were rapidly disseminated and they enabled the diverse peasant bands to unite, even though many areas formulated their own local grievances as well. It was not just expedience that caused the peasants to appeal to evangelical ideas: many monasteries and Church foundations owned land and were amongst the most rapacious landlords, whilst the massive monastic tithe barns that stood in so many towns were a visual reminder of their economic power in an agrarian society. Evangelical 'brotherhood' and the idea of the freedom of the Christian resonated with peasant insistence on the need for relations between lords and peasants to be regulated by Christian values, not property rights.[1]

As the Twelve Articles expressed it in the article on serfdom, 'It has hitherto been the custom for the lords to treat us as their serfs, which is pitiable since Christ has redeemed and bought us all by the shedding of his precious blood, the shepherd just as the highest, no one excepted.

Therefore it is demonstrated by Scripture that we are free and wish to be free.'² Many have claimed that the peasants misunderstood Luther's ideas, and that they conflated the spiritual elements of his message with their worldly concerns, but Luther's advocacy of Christian freedom, his robust tone towards rulers with whom he did not agree, and the model of resistance that his stance at Worms represented, were inspirational. Luther could not control how others interpreted his words and deeds. As the uprising unfolded, Luther, the grandson of a peasant, proved increasingly unable to comprehend the peasants' point of view, though for them, he was the vital point of reference, so much so that they even invited him to judge their case.

Luther's response to the articles of the Upper German peasants, *Admonition to Peace. A Reply to the Twelve Articles of the Peasants in Swabia* began with heavy-footed irony, praising the article in which the peasants offered to take instruction as by far the best. Although he opened by castigating the lords for their failure to introduce the gospel, describing the peasant uproar as God's judgement on them for their hard-heartedness, this rhetorical strategy hardly balanced out the rest of the tract, which unequivocally condemned the peasants. Luther set up a kind of moral equation: the peasants might object to the dues they are forced to pay, but that was only 'petty robbery', while the lords stood to be robbed of *everything*: their authority, their property and their rights over the peasants. This procedure of weighing wrongs reduced complex political arguments and protest into simple varieties of sin. And it depended on accepting that the existing order was right, including the ownership of individuals. Luther mocked the peasants' use of his theology to argue that because 'Christ has bought us all with his precious blood', no Christian should own another as in serfdom. He even went back on his own insistence that a congregation should have the right to call its own preacher, the first of the peasants' articles. Instead, he defended property rights in the tithe. If the community owned the tithe, well and good, Luther argued, but if it did not, then the lord or institution which owned the tithe and paid the preacher should have their property rights respected, and they could appoint a preacher of their choosing. If the congregation was unhappy with the arrangement, they could raise a tax of their own to support a vicar – a completely unrealistic plan, as he well knew.³

The late medieval church was a property church, in which many individuals and institutions had a financial stake, and the peasants' first article called this into question fundamentally. The issue of tithes was a litmus test. Paid by the peasants, they were used to support the clergy, but if, as was usually the case, the tithe was owned by an individual or an institution, these would take a cut out of whatever was collected. Karlstadt, for example, had paid a lowly priest out of the income he received as archdeacon, leaving the bulk of the revenues for himself. The tithe question was also to prove a major dividing line in the Reformation in Zurich, where those who would eventually move towards Anabaptism argued that the tithe should no longer be paid.

For Luther, respecting property rights in the tithe trumped even evangelical preaching. So completely did he misunderstand the ideas of the peasants that he argued that 'evil preachers' like Karlstadt and Müntzer were responsible for the 'disturbances'. In fact, Müntzer's role in the events that unfolded was unusual, and most of the peasant leaders were not pastors but laypeople. It was obvious that Luther was anxious because of the widespread taunt against him that his teachings would lead to disorder and the overthrow of authority, and he therefore argued firmly that 'This rebellion cannot be coming from me. Rather the murder-prophets, who hate me as they hate you, have come among these people and have gone about among them for more than three years, and no one has resisted and fought against them except me.'[4] By collapsing the whole story of the peasant rebellion into his own personal struggle with 'the murder-prophets', Luther made the matter an issue of his authority and of preaching – which were certainly not the issues that concerned the peasants. He devoted a mere paragraph to discussing eight of the peasants' articles, spending time on the ones that interested him. Meanwhile the forces of the peasants from the Bodensee and from Allgäu suffered heavy losses, and in April 1525 they concluded a peace treaty with the Swabian League in which they promised to dissolve their union and obey their lords. Luther at once published its text with an introduction and conclusion written by himself, and his tone was uncompromising: 'No one can deny that our peasantry has no just cause, but has burdened itself with serious, heavy sins and has called down God's dreadful and unendurable anger upon themselves by breaking their oaths and duties that they have sworn to the authorities.' Again, Luther insisted that Müntzer and Karlstadt were to blame: 'Woe and again woe to you damned false prophets that have led the poor simple people to such ruin of their souls and perhaps even loss of body and goods.'[5]

In fact, the reality was quite different. The revolts often began locally with an informal strike, as peasants simply refused to work. A meeting of the commune might be summoned by ringing the storm bell, and the heads of households would consult together, often under a tree – the kind of meeting that Luther had attended in Orlamünde. Matters might escalate as a rally was held, drawing peasants from a wider area, and eventually larger groups of armed bands formed that were bound together by oaths of brotherhood.[6] These peasant bands, armed largely with pikes and swords, had remarkable success. By the early summer of 1525, they were in control of vast swathes of south and central Germany, largely because there was no one to stop them: the imperial armies were fighting in Italy. Even after the emperor's victory at the battle of Pavia, many returning mercenaries refused to fight against people with whom they felt common cause and who might even be their kinsfolk. Shrewdly the peasants were building alliances with the poor in the towns, and began attacking convents and monasteries. In Memmingen they got the town council to swear allegiance to their cause and adopt their articles; the same happened in many other towns, including Erfurt. In the south-west, peasant bands spread throughout Swabia, the Allgäu and around Lake Constance, and by May 1525 they took Freiburg and Breisach, while in Württemberg peasant rebels supporting Duke Ulrich, who opposed the Habsburg administration, managed to occupy Stuttgart, the ducal seat. Large parts of Alsace were also now held by the peasants, and Strasbourg was trying to negotiate a peace, while Upper Austria and the Tyrol had also risen in revolt. In Franconia in particular, the rebellion spread rapidly; Albrecht of Mainz's representative had to cede the whole territory to the rebels in early May at Miltenberg. Würzburg, a regional centre and the seat of an archbishopric, was their next major prize: after a siege the rebels occupied it on 8 May 1525, although the peasants failed to take its fortress of Marienberg and by June, they had been defeated by the Swabian League. In Thuringia, town after town fell to the rebels; in Eisenach town leaders were canny enough to invite the peasant leaders into the town, but then arrested them.[7] So serious was the situation that on 4 May, the day before he died, Friedrich the Wise considered making a treaty with the peasants: he wrote to his brother Duke Johann hoping that someone 'who enjoyed their respect and in whom they had faith and trust' might act as intermediary, so that the matter might be settled amicably, 'and the people satisfied'.[8]

In Mühlhausen, meanwhile, Müntzer had created another Allstedt, this time in the bigger environment of a city of about 7,500 inhabitants. As an imperial city, Mühlhausen was directly subject to the emperor and could make its own laws. Banished from Mühlhausen in late 1524, Müntzer returned with popular support in February 1525, to a reformed city under the influence of the radical preacher Heinrich Pfeiffer. This was a world made anew, as people were fired by the ideals of godly law and Christian brotherhood. Together Pfeiffer and Müntzer created an Eternal Council, a group of committed followers who replaced what had been an elected oligarchy, and set about forming alliances with like-minded towns.

Müntzer prepared for the apocalypse. 'Don't let your sword get cold, don't let it hang down limply! Hammer away ding-dong on the anvils of Nimrod, cast down their tower to the ground!' he wrote to the people of Allstedt, urging them to join in the rebellion. 'Go to it, go to it, go to it', he urged repeatedly in this letter, and one can get an echo of what must have been electrifying preaching – a heady brew of visual metaphor, rhythmic repetition, and violent language.[9] Müntzer was particularly eager to attract the miners, and many of those from the Mansfeld region where Luther had grown up were drawn to his movement. By early May, the Mühlhausen–Thuringian peasant army was plundering convents and castles and forcing local nobles in the Eichsfeld to join by entering into a Christian covenant; only Count Ernst, Müntzer's long-standing foe since the Allstedt days, remained firm. But then the peasant army split. No more than a small contingent went to join the Frankenhausen band, which desperately needed reinforcements, whilst the rest headed back for Mühlhausen. Müntzer mustered only 300 men to accompany him to Frankenhausen. By the time they arrived on 12 May, the revolt there had lost momentum. Stuck in the town, the peasant army was unable to continue its advance.

Müntzer pushed for a confrontation with the region's rulers. He ended the overtures that had been made to Count Ernst and Count

Albrecht of Mansfeld and his correspondence became increasingly
driven by his hatred of Luther and the princes. As he wrote to Count
Ernst: 'Brother Ernst, just tell us, you miserable, wretched sack of
worms, who made you a prince over the people whom God redeemed
with his dear blood? You shall and will have to prove that you are a
Christian'; while to Count Albrecht of Mansfeld, Luther's supporter,
he wrote on the same day: 'Couldn't you find in your Lutheran pudding
and your Wittenberg soup what Ezekiel has prophesied in his thirty-
seventh chapter? You haven't even been able to detect the flavour,
because of that Martinian peasant filth of yours, of what the same
prophet goes on to say in the thirty-ninth chapter, that God instructs
all the birds of the heavens to consume the flesh of the princes; whilst
the brute beasts are to drink the blood of the bigwigs.'[10] Müntzer's
tribal vision of a new godly kingdom might seem far removed from
calls for peasant brotherhood, but thousands of people in Mühlhausen
and beyond were prepared to give their lives for it.

Müntzer's violent rhetoric now issued in real violence. When three
of Count Ernst's servants were found in the camp they were accused
of being spies and executed by popular 'divine justice', with his agreement.[11] According to the Mansfeld councillor Johann Rühel, who wrote
to Luther about what happened, Müntzer rode around the camp on
the day of the battle on 15 May 1525, shouting that the peasants should
trust in the power of God, that the very stones would give way to
them, and the shots would not harm them. But the peasants had been
surrounded and, mostly foot soldiers, they were no match for the
cavalry of Hesse and Brunswick, and the troops of Duke Georg of
Saxony. Perhaps as many as 6,000 were slaughtered; 600 were taken
captive. Most of the population of Frankenhausen died or were taken
prisoner, and as Rühel recounted, when the women petitioned for
their captured men, they were released on condition that they punished
two rebel priests who were still in the town. The women beat the
two priests with cudgels in the marketplace, so mercilessly that they
kept going for half an hour after the two men had died. 'Whoever
does not pity such a deed is truly not human', Rühel commented.[12]

Müntzer fled from the battlefield but was found hiding in a bed in
a room in Frankenhausen. The man who had once inspired thousands
with his bloodcurdling biblicism now cried: 'Ey, I am a sick poor man.'[13]
The contents of his bag, including a letter from Count Albrecht, gave

him away, and he was taken prisoner. What happened next, however, was astonishing and reveals just how comprehensively the Peasants' War had shaken established hierarchies. Brought to the princely commanders, Duke Georg himself sat down next to Müntzer on the bench, and asked what had driven him to execute Count Ernst's three servants. Müntzer replied, addressing the duke as 'Brother', that divine justice, not he, had done so. Soon he became embroiled in an argument with Duke Heinrich von Braunschweig and Count Albrecht of Mansfeld, with the count quoting the New Testament as Müntzer adduced the Old. For one last defiant time Müntzer sat down face to face with the lords, addressing them as equals, and engaging them in debate.[14]

On 27 May 1525 Thomas Müntzer and his fellow preacher Heinrich Pfeiffer were executed and their heads and bodies displayed on pike-staffs. Müntzer had recanted on 17 May, reconciling himself to the Catholic faith, probably as a result of torture. But his final letter to the people of Mühlhausen, written on the same day, does not revoke anything. Instead he told them that he awaited martyrdom and saw his death as a sign: 'Since it is God's good pleasure that I should depart hence with an authentic knowledge of the divine name, and in recompense for certain abuses which the people embraced, not understanding me properly – for they sought only their own interests and the divine truth was defeated as a result – I, too, am heartily content that God has ordained things in this way . . . Do not allow my death, therefore, to be a stumbling block to you, for it has come to pass for the benefit of the good and the uncomprehending.'[15] Luther refused to believe that Müntzer had recanted – he grumpily insisted that his interrogators had asked him the wrong questions. His confession, Luther said, was 'nothing other than a devilish, hardened obstinacy in his undertaking'.[16]

*

Crows and ravens were reported to have flown over the roofs of the Mansfeld castles, attacking each other and screaming. Many fell dead to the ground – a portent, it was later believed, of the coming Peasants' War.[17] Fear that the miners would rebel and down their tools drove the counts of Mansfeld to call on Luther for help. They were right to be worried. The miners of Heldrungen and Stolberg, where Müntzer had first preached, proved some of his most fervent supporters and in 1524 seem to have responded to the energy and violence of his apocalyptic language, though they did not join the peasants at Frankenhausen. So in mid-April and early May 1525, Luther undertook short preaching tours, at the invitation of Count Albrecht of Mansfeld. He and Melanchthon went to Eisleben via Bitterfeld and Seeburg, and Luther preached at Stolberg, Nordhausen and Wallhausen near Allstedt.[18] It was a courageous itinerary, with peasants and miners rebelling throughout the region, although it carefully avoided Mühlhausen.

Luther had written his first tract on the Peasants' War, the *Admonition to Peace*, published on 19 April 1525, in the idyllic surroundings of the garden of the Mansfeld chancellor Johann Dürr at Eisleben.[19] Now he encountered real hostility everywhere, travelling, as he put it, 'in danger of life and limb'.[20] He wrote an account of what he had seen in a letter to Johann Rühel, which formed the basis of what would become one of his most infamous tracts, *Against the Robbing Murdering Thieving Hordes of Peasants*.[21] In this highly intemperate work, which appeared in May, Luther likened the peasants to 'mad dogs' who did nothing but 'pure devil's work' and were all driven by 'that archdevil [*ertzteuffel*] who rules at Mühlhausen, and did nothing except stir up robbery, murder and bloodshed'. Because they had engaged in rebellion, every person was both their 'judge and executioner'; and Luther urged them to let 'everyone who can, smite, slay. And stab, secretly or openly, remembering that nothing can be more poisonous, hurtful, or devilish than a rebel. It is just as when one must kill a mad dog; if you do not strike him, he will strike you, and a whole land with you.' Its urgent rhythms and tripling of verbs and adjectives were not unlike Müntzer's incendiary rhetoric.[22]

By the time Luther's violent attack rolled off the press, the peasants had been defeated. Although it was printed together with his milder, previous *Admonition to Peace*, its bloodthirsty tone was tasteless after the deaths of many thousands, and was felt by many to be deeply offensive. Even Johann Rühel, who had written to Luther in such detail about Müntzer's last days, was taken aback. Nikolaus von Amsdorf wrote to Luther that the Magdeburg preachers were now calling him a 'flatterer of princes'; and Wenzeslaus Linck too felt compelled to tell him how it had shocked people.[23] Luther seems to have taken the response to heart, for he composed a letter of explanation to the Mansfeld chancellor Caspar Müller, which he also had printed. Yet the letter, while it began mildly enough, hardly modified the message and the tone soon reverted to harshness: 'So I still write: no one should have mercy on the stiff-necked, obstinate, deluded peasants, who won't listen to anything, but whoever can should hew, stab, strangle and lay about himself as if amongst mad dogs.'[24] It seems that Luther had burned his bridges. The grandson of a peasant who liked to make much of his rural roots, Luther had set his face against them.

Yet there was nothing surprising in his stand. It was already prefigured in his conflict with Karlstadt, from the moment that Luther decided to defeat the Wittenberg movement and support the Elector's attempt to make peace with the Diet by slowing the pace of evangelical reform. Luther had already rejected the communal Reformation, powered by popular pressure, which inspired Karlstadt. This was the Reformation that was also popular among the lower townsfolk in Allstedt, Mühlhausen and Frankenhausen, where Müntzer had his most loyal and zealous supporters.[25] But it could inspire rich and educated men too, such as Christoph Meinhard, an Eisleben citizen who was probably related to Johann Agricola, a close friend of Luther.[26] The bounded community of a congregation where people knew each other, and could count on the bonds of oaths and a collective morality, drove Müntzer's Reformation just as it had powered Karlstadt's. This was not what animated most of the peasant protest, however: Müntzer was repeatedly outraged by those who would not follow his biblicist vision, and at the end blamed the disaster of Frankenhausen on the fact 'that everyone was more concerned with his own self-interest than in bringing justice to the Christian people'.[27]

Müntzer remains a difficult character to assess.[28] Direct divine inspiration was very important to his theology, with biblical texts playing only a supporting role. Most of all, he was a radical mystic, who sought union with God, not primarily a social radical. His theology displays an underlying tension between his mysticism, rejecting everything to do with the flesh, and his revolutionary radicalism, which led him to engage with the material world. Some of these paradoxes are evident in his views of sexuality, for example. For Müntzer, like

Karlstadt, Christ's call to his disciples to leave behind wife and family was a key text, and there is a powerful streak of asceticism in his writings. When Melanchthon defended the marriage of monks, Müntzer castigated him: 'By your arguments you drag men to matrimony although the bond is not yet an immaculate one; but a Satanic brothel, which is as harmful to the church as the most accursed perfumes of the priests. Do not these passionate desires impede your sanctification?'[29] Yet although he commended virginity, he took a wife in June 1523, and like Karlstadt, he chose a noblewoman.[30] Müntzer seems to have nursed a strong sense of dispossession, and his conviction of being a persecuted outsider made him able to articulate a shared sense of social alienation, reaching out to others across class barriers. A powerful speaker, he knew how to inspire groups of peasants, townsfolk and villagers, women as well as men. Throughout his career, whether in Zwickau, Allstedt or Mühlhausen, he seems to have followed the same political strategy. Starting from his local community, he created a movement which he interpreted in apocalyptic terms, and he gave his followers a sense of imminent danger and excitement by identifying and denouncing their enemies. He then proceeded to build alliances and coalitions, at first locally and then further afield. His theology had the capacity to inspire large groups of people, drawing intense personal commitment from them, even to risk their lives. He enjoyed no network of large urban presses to print his work, there was no university behind him, and no territorial ruler to protect him. His success, albeit short-lived, suggests that what the Reformation meant to many ordinary people in Saxony and Thuringia could be very different from what it meant to Luther.

*

In the meantime Karlstadt, having been forced out of Orlamünde and a series of south German cities, had ended up more than 400 kilometres to the south-west in Rothenburg ob der Tauber, where he was living in hiding. The city was surrounded by a peasant army and one day, when he went on a stroll outside the city, he came upon a group of illiterate peasants, who ordered him at gunpoint: 'Are you a brother, then read the messenger's letters. If you are not a brother, we will have you give account of yourself.' In fear for his life, Karlstadt complied. Indeed, 'one of the peasants wanted very much to knife me; another would have liked to run me down', he later recalled.[31] He had then wandered from place to place for some weeks, although on which side of the peasant lines remained less clear. As it turned out, both the peasants and the lords rejected him: 'the spiritual lords chased me as if I were game, and the peasants imprisoned me and would have devoured me, had not God protected me'.[32]

In June, with the peasants defeated, Karlstadt took the humiliating step of writing to Luther for help. Addressing him as '*Gevatter*' he begged forgiveness for 'all I sinned against you, moved by the old Adam'.[33] Astonishingly, Luther took him in and housed him secretly in the monastery in Wittenberg for about eight weeks, together with his wife and child. Karlstadt meanwhile wrote an *Apology*, which was printed at Wittenberg, including a preface by Luther himself.[34] He told the story of his wanderings, and while he was certainly trying to minimise the extent of his involvement with the peasants, he was no doubt honest when he insisted that he was not a peasant leader. In the preface, Luther declared that 'In matters of doctrine, Dr Karlstadt is my greatest antagonist and we have clashed so fiercely in these matters that all hope for reconciliation or for further dealings has been dashed.'[35] But perhaps aware of the unfairness of his equation of Karlstadt and Müntzer back in Jena, Luther demanded that Karlstadt ought to be allowed to prove that his was not 'a rebellious spirit', and given a hearing. This intervention was probably enough to save Karlstadt's life. Had Luther not given him shelter or had he persisted in condemning him as a 'rebellious spirit', he might well have been executed, as many other priests were.

Luther still did not trust him, however. While he lived under Luther's roof, Karlstadt was compelled to write a full recantation of his views on the Last Supper, again printed at Wittenberg and once more prefaced by Luther.[36] Luther conceded that Karlstadt's treatises on the subject had been presented as theses, matters for discussion, not as statements of truth; but like others, Luther said, he had forgotten the form in which they had been issued and taken them to be statements of his real views. Turning Karlstadt's emphasis on the spirit against him, Luther insisted that it was clear that his views were not 'of the spirit', because the spirit made people certain and bold; Karlstadt and his ilk, on the other hand, spoke only out of craziness and human darkness, and therefore everyone should be warned against his views. This was humiliating enough, but in early September, Karlstadt was writing to Luther as Luther's 'slave', apologising for disturbing his 'sweet dream' and begging him to get the Elector to permit him to live in Saxony, preferably in Kemberg. He knew, he grovelled to 'your reverend lordship', that it lay in Luther's 'might, not to say, power' to have his exile lifted.[37] Luther duly wrote to the Elector but, possibly on Spalatin's advice, the Elector refused to permit Karlstadt to reside in Kemberg, because it was on the road to Leipzig and therefore 'suspicious' travellers might pass through and spread his message. He was to live only in 'villages and hamlets' within three miles of Wittenberg, securely marooned in the country and away from the town and the university, but still under the authorities' watchful eye.[38] The wellsprings of Karlstadt's intellectual life – colleagues and students, a printer and a pulpit – were all denied him. It seems that he was now condemned to work as a farmer.

It left Karlstadt a broken man. He kept his word, publishing virtually nothing once he returned to the Wittenberg area. He did manage to move to Kemberg, however, from where he journeyed to meet sympathetic figures like the noblemen Caspar Schwenckfeld and Valentin Crautwald in Silesia. A few years later, he moved to Basle, where he found a more congenial intellectual home, but he did not publish much. His theology continued to develop the idea of *Gelassenheit*, and when he died in 1541, he was in the process of composing a major synoptic work on theology in which *Gelassenheit* would have played a central role. It is puzzling that he failed utterly to capitalise on either the Peasants' War or on the support his ideas were gaining in the cities of southern Germany. The man who wanted to engage in honest toil like a peasant found himself attacked and hunted by peasants who saw him as a learned *grosser Hans*, just another 'big Jack'. And instead of moving south after the Peasants' War, to his supporters in Basle, Zurich and Strasbourg, he had returned like a moth flying around a candle to Saxony, and to the embrace of the relationship with Luther who had proved his nemesis. Perhaps at some psychological level he depended on Luther's approval and wanted fervently to persuade him. It is revealing that when he set out his theological views in one of his last pamphlets in early 1525, he did so in the form of a dialogue in which he ventriloquised the man who had refused to engage in a proper debate with him at Wittenberg.[39] In print at least, he could triumph over Luther and win the argument. For both sides the encounter at the Black Bear Inn had been the culmination of a personal battle, a struggle between two former friends and allies. Karlstadt as much as Luther had been mesmerised by that confrontation, and he remained trapped in his promise, sealed with the guilder, to attack Luther – and unable to see beyond him, to his own sources of support.

*

By June 1525 the peasants had been defeated, but things would not be the same again in Saxony. Friedrich the Wise, who had supported Luther through his appearance at the Diet of Worms and protected him afterwards, was dead. There had been portents: a rainbow that Melanchthon and Luther saw in the night that winter over Lochau, some twenty miles from Wittenberg, where there was a castle used by Friedrich; a child born at Wittenberg without a head, and another with bent feet.[40] The trusted Spalatin had been beginning to think of leaving the Elector's service, and wrote to Luther for advice on behalf of a 'friend', who was tempted by sexual thoughts. Luther got the message, and warned Spalatin to forget about marrying and to remain with the Elector, not leaving him while he was 'perhaps so close to the grave', for if he were to leave him now, he would be eternally sorry.[41]

And so it proved. At the height of the Peasants' War, in early May, Spalatin and other councillors were with the Elector at Lochau. As Spalatin described the scene later in his chronicle, the castle was completely deserted, with Duke Johann and all the men away fighting the peasants. Only the court marshal, the secretary and the doctor were present alongside Spalatin, and the Elector was on his deathbed. Spalatin had rushed to his bedside, having already sent written words of comfort in case he could not reach him in time. Friedrich, who had relied for so many years on Spalatin to read his correspondence, had reached for his glasses and read the letter himself. When Spalatin arrived, the Elector summoned him to read aloud, until Friedrich announced: 'I can't any more.' Spalatin waited a little, and then asked: 'My most gracious Lord, have you any trouble?', to which the Elector replied, 'Nothing but the pains.' He seems to have died in his sleep, while Spalatin read to him from Hebrews.[42] Messengers arrived from the princes on the battlefield, calling desperately for reinforcements against the peasants, but their shouts echoed through the empty halls. The man who had been such a powerful prince of the empire died on 5 May, not knowing whether the lords would prevail over the peasants. Yet as Spalatin noted, at the very moment Friedrich breathed his last, the first peasants were being slaughtered by Count Albrecht of Mansfeld.[43] Nothing better conveys the uncertainty and turmoil of the Peasants' War.

# 13

# Marriage and the Flesh

Both Müntzer and Luther interpreted the events of the Peasants' War as a sacred drama and drew upon apocalyptic rhetoric: the Devil was raging, presaging the Last Days. But whereas Müntzer believed that the Last Days were imminent and must be ushered in with the sword, Luther never predicted a specific date. His apocalyptic language was more of a rhetorical intensifier than a literal prediction. He imbued his own times with significance as he identified the Pope as the Antichrist, but such language paradoxically also helped make the present seem less important compared with the divine drama of the coming end of the world. It never, however, led Luther to retreat from engagement with the present, nor did it lead him to attempt to overthrow the existing order.[1]

Equally, while Müntzer, at least at first, seems to have believed that the seriousness of these exceptional times demanded sexual abstinence from the godly and complete dedication to the divine, Luther drew the opposite conclusion. He decided to annoy the Devil by committing a particularly large sin: he got married. Moreover, his choice of wife was the most provocative possible, which he knew would enrage the Devil – and the Catholics – most. He married a nun.

From 1523, groups of nuns, convinced by evangelical teachings against monasticism, had begun leaving their convents and arrived in Wittenberg, where it fell to Luther to find lodgings for them and even provide them with new clothes.[2] He was not entirely innocent in all this. That year, Leonhard Koppe, a businessman and a relation of his friend Amsdorf, smuggled a group of nuns out of the Nimbschen convent in Duke Georg's territory and over the border to Wittenberg, hiding them amongst barrels of herrings.[3] When Luther then published an open letter of congratulation to Koppe, he revealed that he had known all about the plan, which was an impudent snub to his old enemy Duke Georg. The women came from the upper nobility of his lands; but their families were unable to welcome them back for fear of offending their Catholic ruler – or so Luther argued. One of them was Staupitz's sister.[4]

Luther needed to settle the women in respectable marriages as soon as possible, so as to avoid malicious gossip, and thus found himself in the unexpected position of marriage broker. As a result, the situation forced him to think about female desire. In August 1524 he wrote to some nuns, candidly informing them that, although they might not like to think so, God had created them with powerful sexual urges, which they ignored at their peril: 'Though womenfolk are ashamed to admit to this, nevertheless Scripture and experience show that among many thousands there is not a one to whom God has given to remain in pure chastity. A woman has no control over herself.'[5] It may have been that the subject came to mind because he was beginning to be tempted himself.

The progress of this transformation can be charted through banter with his old friend Spalatin. While in the Wartburg, the subject of marriage had arisen more than once in their correspondence, but Luther insisted he had no sexual desires, and that marriage was not for him. Although Karlstadt, Jonas and Melanchthon all married, 'They won't force a wife on me', he had written in 1521.[6] When Luther first returned from the Wartburg he put on his old monastic habit again – the town council even presented him with a new one, specially made.[7] But there was no returning to the monastic life. Most of the monks had left under the impact of Zwilling's fiery sermons and only the prior and a couple of old monks remained. The monastery was no longer a going concern.

In mid-April 1525, having been busily arranging matches for the nuns, Luther could still joke to Spalatin:

I do not want you to wonder that a famous lover like me does not marry. It is rather strange that I, who so often write about matrimony and get mixed up with women, have not yet turned into a woman, to say nothing of not having married one. Yet if you want me to set an example, look, here you have the most powerful one, for I have had three wives simultaneously, and loved them so much that I have lost two who are taking other husbands; the third I can hardly keep with my left arm, and she, too, will probably soon be snatched away from me.

Luther was jesting here about the matches he was busy arranging for the former nuns in his care. The 'wife on his left arm' was, as Spalatin would have known, Katharina von Bora, for whom he was then arranging a marriage. He continued to tease Spalatin about his friend's reluctance to get married: 'But you are a sluggish lover who does not dare to become the husband of even one woman. Watch out that I, who have no thought of marriage at all, do not some day overtake you too eager suitors.'[8]

So it proved. On 13 June, Luther married Katharina, and on 27 June he held the wedding feast.[9] Just how much the confirmed bachelor had changed was apparent when, shortly before the wedding, Spalatin asked his advice about a couple who wanted to delay the public ceremony for a while, despite being sure of each other. It would have been obvious to Luther that Spalatin was talking about himself: the young courtier had fallen in love with a young woman but had been forced to delay marriage while he remained in the Elector's service. Luther responded by pouring out a veritable flood of quotations from Scripture, proverbs and history all designed to prove that weddings should never be delayed, concluding: 'when you're driving the piglet, you should hold the sack ready' – a rather disconcerting metaphor for marriage.[10]

But Luther's decision to marry also had a more sombre impetus. It was made at the moment he had become embroiled in the Peasants' War, which he saw as the triumph of the Devil. Writing to Johann Rühel in early May 1525, he toyed with the idea that the Devil had in fact caused the conflict simply to get rid of him: 'I would even believe and it almost seems that I was the Devil's cause, the reason why he made such a thing happen in the world, so that God should plague the world.'[11] Marrying 'my Käthe', he continued, was therefore the way to spite him: it was an affirmation of his 'courage and joy', his insistence on life in the midst of death.

Like Karlstadt and Müntzer, Luther chose a noblewoman, albeit poor. But as he presented it, the initiative to marry had come from her. Katharina had originally fallen in love with Hieronymus Baumgartner, a rich merchant patrician from Nuremberg, but his family

had better plans for him than marriage to a runaway nun. Luther had then suggested Caspar Glatz, the man who had supplanted Karlstadt at Orlamünde – hardly an enticing prospect, with his tumbledown house and farm. Indeed, the twenty-six-year-old Katharina rejected Glatz out of hand as an old 'miser', and told Luther's friend Nikolaus von Amsdorf that she would marry either him or Luther, nobody else.[12] However this account contrasts sharply with Luther's behaviour in all other areas of his life, where he always took the initiative. It seems that on this occasion, he was happy to be seduced, overruled by a strong woman. As he put it in a letter to Amsdorf: 'I feel neither passionate love nor burning for my spouse, but I cherish her.'[13] This narrative conveniently defended him against any accusations that he was acting out of lust.

45. Lucas Cranach the Elder, *Martin Luther and Katharina von Bora*, 1526. These double portraits, of which the Cranach workshop produced scores over the years, show Luther without tonsure, and with his familiar features: the piercing eyes, the kiss curl and the increasingly heavy jowls. He is depicted as a powerful personality, whose direct gaze addresses the viewer. By contrast, like all of Cranach's females, Katharina is an identikit woman, with an impossibly narrow waist. Her attire, with the tightly laced bodice, netted hair and simple ring, is that of a respectable woman, and she is shown sometimes with and sometimes without the wimple worn by married townswomen; she was, after all, a noblewoman and not a burgher. Only the breadth of her cheekbones, tapering to a pointed chin, and her slant, slightly cat-like eyes create anything approaching distinctive characteristics; but even then, the various versions the Cranach workshop produced are so different as to be barely depicting the same woman.

Luther claimed that he married in order to please his father and give him 'the hope of progeny'.[14] But his choice would hardly have fitted into Hans Luder's dynastic plans. Katharina did not come from the mining elite, and Luder had carefully married all his children into the small circle of mine owners and smelters at Mansfeld, hoping to buttress his position; indeed, his son's refusal to follow suit was one of the reasons why his monastic vocation had been so resented. Nor did Katharina come from an urban family packed with lawyers, which might at least have provided access to the legal expertise Hans Luder had sought when he destined his son for the law. Luther married up by choosing a poor noblewoman, but not in a way that would benefit his family. However, Katharina was, by all accounts, attractive, feisty and passionate.

Why did it take Luther so long, when so many of his associates had gone to the altar years before? Bartholomäus Bernhardi had married in August 1521. In Luther's immediate circle, Karlstadt followed later that year, and Justus Jonas in February 1522.[15] Johannes Bugenhagen, a more recent arrival in Wittenberg, married on 13 October 1522, Wenzeslaus Linck, the vicar general of the Augustinian order, on 15 April 1523,[16] whilst Johannes Lang had tied the knot by 1524. Just about all Luther's old comrades, apart from Spalatin and Amsdorf, were now married men. It seems that the end of the Peasants' War and the death of Friedrich the Wise marked a point of transition. Karlstadt and he had now moved into a settled enmity. And then there was the death, in late 1524, of his old confessor.

In his last letters, Johann von Staupitz had written of his love for his former protégé, 'surpassing that of women'.[17] As monks, nuns and priests broke their vows by marrying, he castigated Luther for letting fleshly lusts have their sway under the cover of the gospel – this was not what he had meant by *Gelassenheit*. Although he sent Luther a young monk to be instructed in the ways of the gospel – a sign of his trust – he clearly saw Luther as having chosen a different path. For his part, Luther was still raw from Staupitz's decision to leave the Augustinians for, of all things, a fat prebend as a Benedictine abbot. Indeed, when the news came of Staupitz's death, Luther commented waspishly that the old man had had little time to enjoy his plum posting. There is no doubt that Staupitz would have been appalled by Luther's marriage, and to a nun – a double violation of oaths of chastity. Perhaps it was only when Staupitz had died that Luther, freed from the man who had been his spiritual father, finally felt able to become a father.[18]

The delay was also connected with deep changes within Luther himself. It took several years for him to accept that he, too, had fleshly desires. He had always claimed that continence was not his problem as a monk – the 'real knots' were to do with salvation. Nor had he greeted the first marriages of priests with unalloyed joy, fretting that Bernhardi, the first evangelical priest to marry, would be expelled and then 'two stomachs' along with 'anything that came out of them' (Luther was referring darkly to children) would suffer want.[19] Indeed, Luther's conviction of the pervasiveness of sin had remarkably little to do with a sense of sexual frustration. Although he had advocated that priests should be allowed to marry by 1520, he did not at first think that monks were in the same situation, as they had taken vows of chastity of their own free will and could not therefore break them. When the first evangelical clergy married, it was Karlstadt, not Luther, who wrote a set of theses and then a pamphlet in their support, even proposing that only married men should become priests. And it was Karlstadt who then justified the marriage of monks because sexual continence was just another vain attempt to secure salvation through works. Luther originally objected to this line of reasoning, but he eventually approved it, using much the same arguments.

Certainly Melanchthon thought that something had changed in Luther by 1525, and he did not like it. The ascetic was becoming a sensualist. A month after Luther's wedding, Melanchthon wrote to a friend that 'the nuns used all their arts to draw him to them', so that perhaps 'the frequent commerce with the nuns had softened and inflamed him, despite all his noble nature and the greatness of his soul'.[20] But Luther's feelings were initially more mixed. On the eve of his wedding, in June 1525, he published a provocative letter to Albrecht of Mainz admonishing him to marry his concubine. If Albrecht should ask, he wrote to Rühel, why the man who was advocating marriage for everyone else had not got married yet himself, he should be told that 'I still feared, that I was not capable enough for it.' But now he was determined to marry before he died, even if it just be 'an engaged marriage of Joseph' – that is, an unconsummated engagement of an old man and a young woman.[21] Such words hardly sound like the sexual bravado that had begun to colour his letters to Spalatin, the 'sluggish lover who does not dare to become the husband of even one woman', perhaps because Spalatin was, like him, a bachelor, whilst

Rühel, to whom he wrote about Albrecht, was married. For Luther, now aged forty-one, sex may have been a daunting prospect, given that Katharina was fifteen years younger than him.

Sixteenth-century weddings were not for the faint-hearted. Wedding feasts were ribald occasions, and the couple would be bedded down together in front of the guests, with a cover placed over them; later, the revellers would 'sing them on' as they spent the night together. As was customary in Saxony, Luther and Katharina's marriage was consummated before the wedding, in the first half of June, and the celebrations – 'leading her home' – took place two or three weeks later. If the marriage was not or could not be consummated it could be annulled: according to late medieval understandings of the sacrament of marriage, it consisted in the free exchange of a marriage promise between the couple plus their physical union. Sexual intercourse made a promise of marriage fully binding, or to put it another way, what we would call an 'engagement' became a fully binding marriage if the couple had sex.

By mid-June, Luther's tone in his letters changed markedly, as he joked to none other than Leonhard Koppe that when he came to the wedding banquet, he should 'help my bride give good testimony, how I am a man'. In the same letter he wrote that 'I'm woven into my girl's plaits', a remarkable metaphor that had nothing of the usual masculine bravado about possessing a woman.[22] It was also a male joke about female sexual power. In other invitations, he referred to Katharina as 'my mistress'.[23] There was much innuendo at weddings about who would 'wear the trousers' in the marriage. As the proverb had it, at the ceremony a bride should hide 'mustard and dill' in her shoe, so that she could rule the household: 'I've got mustard and dill; man, when I speak, keep still!'[24] Indeed, Luther would join in this kind of jocularity for the rest of his life: in 1542 he recalled how, after Lucas Cranach had got married, the new husband wanted to be with his wife the whole time, but one of his friends had teased him: 'Listen, don't go on like this! Before six months are up, you will have had enough of her, and there won't be a maid in your house you wouldn't rather have than your wife.'[25]

Luther invited his parents, family and people from Mansfeld, as well as the Wittenberg theologians and several of his Augustinian friends. But so far as we know he did not invite people from further afield, from Nuremberg or Strasbourg, and he was uncertain whether to invite the Mansfeld counts. He fussed over the arrangements, inviting Spalatin no fewer than three times, and requesting game, the special wild meat for the feast that only the Elector could provide, more than once. There are remarkably few letters, wedding invitations apart, from these few weeks. In the midst of the Peasants' War, Luther seems truly to have been preoccupied by the new phase in his life.

Shortly afterwards, in late November 1525, Spalatin also finally married, possibly the young woman on whom he had had his eye since 1524.[26] The wedding was held in Altenburg in December, but Luther was unable to attend. He wrote explaining that his wife would not let him travel because of the danger of the journey: he had taken in yet more nuns and their furious parents would be out to attack him. For whatever reason, Luther did not seem especially inclined to attend: there seem to be too many explanations in this letter, as Luther described Katharina's tears and talked about how busy he was with his reply to Erasmus, an excuse which must have wounded Spalatin. The former courtier had just retired from the Elector's service and was finding his feet in a new post as preacher at Altenburg, where he was facing bitter opposition from Catholics. Instead, Luther said, he would think of his friend and 'love my Käthe through the same act as you' on the night that he calculated his friend would wed.[27] However, while Luther had no fear by now that he might be unable to 'love' his wife, Spalatin, forced to live in a household with his mother-in-law with whom he did not get on, proved unable to have children for the first six years of the marriage, a failure which made him the butt of Catholic jokes.[28]

*

What kind of relationship did Luther and Katharina von Bora have? There is something rather chilling in Luther's insistence that Katharina always address him as 'Mr Doctor' and that she use the polite 'you'. In the will he wrote in 1537, when he expected to die from an attack of stone, he wrote that 'She served me not just as a wife, but even as a servant'. But since *famulus* was the word Luther used for his academic secretaries, men who went on to important careers in the Church, he may have meant this as a term of respect.[29] Nonetheless, the apparent distance and obsession with hierarchy is symptomatic of the contradictory mixture of warmth, jokiness, and a certain condescension, even cruelty in his interactions with others.[30] He could also be wittily earthy. Writing to Wenzeslaus Linck in Nuremberg shortly after his marriage, Luther punned that 'I am bound and captured in chains [*Ketten*] / Käthe, and I lie on the Bora / bier [*Bahre*], as if dead to the world.'[31] But although he might have pretended to be a reluctant bridegroom, he evidently relished married life, remarking that 'Man has strange thoughts the first year of marriage. When sitting at table he thinks, "Before I was alone; now there are two." Or in bed, when he wakes up, he sees a pair of pigtails lying beside him which he hadn't seen there before.'[32] Katharina regularly became pregnant and gave birth every one to two years, suggesting that the couple enjoyed a full sexual life. Luther had none of the instinctive revulsion for the female body that characterised so many monks, perhaps because he had grown up with younger sisters. He would often joke about sex, even remarking that 'pious Christ himself' had committed adultery three times – once with Mary Magdalen and once with the woman at the well, and once with the adulteress whom he let off so lightly.[33] This remark was extraordinary: one cannot imagine Huldrych Zwingli or John Calvin saying such a thing. But Luther loved to tease, especially those who considered themselves righteous.

When it came to the proper roles of women and men, Luther was always inclined to turn to the Old Testament. He can often appear to be the ultimate spokesman of patriarchy, and it is easy to plunder his works for sexist aphorisms. His table talk was peppered with sexist banter, which was part of sociability at table where largely men were present, yet where Katharina was visible and perhaps within earshot. These were men who after all had been socialised in the all-male cultures of school, monastery and university. For most of the years when Luther's table talk was recorded, Katharina was pregnant or caring for small infants. 'Let them bear children to death' is often cited to suggest that Luther saw women as nothing but baby-machines. But he was insisting that the pains of childbirth were natural and pleasing to God, and he was arguing against a widespread belief that a woman giving birth was under the sway of the Devil, and that if she were to die before being churched, she could not be buried in the churchyard.

Luther lived in a society where women ran household workshops, looked after apprentices and journeymen, and even engaged in the production processes. Women could incur debts, invest and in some areas do business on their own account. Yet his comments assumed a sharp division of labour that simply did not accord with most people's lives in the sixteenth century. Instead they reflected academic life, where a radically gendered division of labour made it possible for a man like Luther to write and read undisturbed whilst Katharina provisioned the household, saw to the accounts, and organised the student lodgers, who were a major source of income.[34] Katharina and the servants thus provided the invisible labour that allowed Luther to devote himself to study. As part of her responsibilities Katharina purchased land at Zülsdorf near Wittenberg to grow produce, in addition to the garden the family owned just outside the town walls close to the pig market. She was famed for her beer brewing, a necessity in a period when water was not safe to drink.[35]

The marriage infuriated his opponents beyond measure. They soon turned their fire on Katharina herself, and in 1528 two young graduates from Leipzig wrote a couple of scurrilous pamphlets. Johann Hasenberg's letter-cum-dialogue, addressed to 'Martin Luther disturber of the peace and of piety', called on him repeatedly to 'convert, revert', and was twinned with an offering by Joachim von der Heyde. His pamphlet called on Katharina to leave her 'damned and shameful life', and insulted her as a nun who had donned lay clothes and tripped off to the university at Wittenberg like a 'dance girl'. Other nuns had been misled by her example, and gave up 'true freedom' of body and soul for the 'fleshly freedom' Luther advocated in his pestilential writings. They would end up, wrote the pamphleteer, not in their lovely convents with their good food but in 'dishonourable brothels' where they would be beaten, their clothes sold, and they themselves pawned like common whores.[36]

Luther responded with a virtuoso display of invective, *News from Leipzig*, that far outclassed the young scholars' feeble efforts. As was his wont, Luther used scatology to trump pornography. The letters, which he said were delivered in person to his house, had been taken to the toilet, where they had been 'illuminated' with dung, and used to wipe the bottoms of the household.[37] Hasenberg gamely made another attempt, this time a set of four dialogues, *Lvdvs lvdentem lvdervm*

46. Johann Hasenberg, *Lvdvs lvdentem lvdervm lvdens*, Leipzig, 1530.

*lvdens*, the first of which imagined the dialogue between Luther and Katharina, as Luther addresses his *'delicium'*, his Venus, his *'unica voluptas'* Katharina.[38] It even had an illustrated cover, but lost impact because it was in Latin and so its audience was limited; and the illustrations were oddly respectful: Luther is well dressed but there is no implication of luxury, there is no beer mug, and Katharina, though she looks harried and bossy, is dressed as a respectable wife. The Catholics, it seemed, had not yet grasped the art of the popular polemic.

Behind these two was the figure of Luther's old antagonist Cochlaeus, now ensconced at Leipzig as Duke Georg's chaplain. Taking the idea of mocking Luther's marriage in drama to a whole new level, he wrote a vicious satirical play about the marriages of evangelical reformers, in which their wives reminisce about the wonderful times they enjoyed while their menfolk were away at the Imperial Diet. Luther appears as the stud who all the other wives want to bed. Mrs 'Bishop of Altenburg', Spalatin's wife and a frightful snob, complains that no child will come of 'kissing and cuddling', and wants to borrow Luther for the night – in line with the reformer's own advice that a woman who cannot conceive a child with her husband should lie with another, as Cochlaeus is not slow to point out.[39] In the play's final scene, Katharina tries to get Luther to go to bed with her, insisting that as Paul says, she is the owner of his body and so he must be subject to her. Luther, impressed by her biblical knowledge, fears that she may have had recourse to another teacher – Cochlaeus insinuating that she had not been a virgin when she married Luther.

\*

Luther's remarkably uninhibited views about sexuality – and consequently marriage – were the result of his radical Augustinianism. If we can never do anything good, as all human acts are sinful, then sexual acts are no different or worse in kind than other types of sin. This gloomy anthropology paradoxically freed Luther to take a relaxed view of sexuality. Lust was part of human nature – it was how God had created mankind. Moreover, despite his decades of monastic observance, Luther believed that chastity could never be willed; indeed, we have no free will because we are always in bondage to the Devil. This was where Luther parted company with Karlstadt. Rooted in the tradition of the mythical theology of the *Theologia deutsch*, Karlstadt wanted his will to conform to that of the divine, leaving the flesh behind, escaping the body and ascending to a more spiritual plane of existence. Luther was moving away from any such ideas of self-perfection, and it was this rejection and his denial of a free will that led to his conflict with Erasmus.[40]

He had been spoiling for a fight with the great humanist for years. In 1522 he had written disparagingly about his views on predestination in a letter: 'Erasmus is not to be feared either in this or in almost any other really important subject that pertains to Christian doctrine . . . I know what is in this man just as I know the plots of Satan.'[41] The letter passed from hand to hand, as Luther knew it would, and soon

47. Portrait of Erasmus by Hans Holbein the Younger, 1523.

reached the man himself, wounding him greatly Finally, in late 1524, Erasmus rose to the bait and published *A Discussion or Discourse Concerning Free Will*, which he apparently dashed off in just five days. In the months after Luther's wedding, the struggle with Erasmus preoccupied Luther so intensely that, having attacked Karlstadt in *Against the Heavenly Prophets*, he neglected the controversy about the sacrament, much to the concern of his Strasbourg friend Nikolaus Gerbel, who complained that Luther should be concentrating his fire on the sacramentarians.[42]

The battle with Erasmus marked the final parting of the ways between the Reformation and humanism. Erasmus had been a great influence on Luther: his letters are dotted with aphorisms taken from Erasmus's *Adages*, which he must have known by heart. Now Erasmus the 'eel' became the 'viper'.[43]

Erasmus insisted – as Eck had done at the Leipzig Debate in 1519 – that there was a part of the will which could participate in doing good works, thus denying that humans were totally corrupt. He discussed a range of conflicting biblical passages, conveying the difficulty of knowing who had the 'spirit', that is, whose interpretation was correct. In his reply, *De servo arbitrio* (*On the Enslaved Will*), Luther argued with vehemence and passion, rejecting the need for the 'spirit' to inspire truth, insisting again on the sole authority of Scripture, which was 'a spiritual light far clearer than the sun', in spite of the 'pestilent claim of the sophists that Scripture is obscure and ambiguous'.[44] At the same time, he conveyed a powerful sense of the radical otherness of God and his 'inscrutable will' – the 'hidden God' whom human beings cannot understand, and who is beyond human rationality. Humans will always tend towards Satan, and there is no way in which they can ever truly 'choose'; and if we are not free, only God's grace can enable us to do anything good. Towards the end of the tract, he moved to a dramatic counterfactual testimony:

As for me, I firmly confess that if it were possible I would not wish to be given free will or to have anything left in my power by which I could endeavour to be saved, not only because, in the midst of so many adversities and dangers and also so many assaults by devils, I would not be able to stand firm and keep hold of it (since one devil is stronger than all men put together and no person would be saved), but also because even if there were no dangers, no adversities, no devils, I would still be forced to struggle continually towards an uncertainty and beat the air with my fists; for no matter how long I should live and do works, my conscience would never be certain and sure how much it had to do to satisfy God. For no matter how many works I did, there would always remain a scruple about whether it pleased God or whether he required something more, as is proved by the experience of all self-justifiers and as I learned over so many years, much to my own grief.[45]

'I would not wish to be given free will': to modern ears this is a remarkable statement. It is a rejection of everything we associate with the importance of the individual, the striving for human perfection, the role of human agency. Luther wanted none of it. His newfound relationship with God required there be no free will, because 'I am certain and safe, because he is trustworthy and will not lie to me, and also because he is so powerful and great that no devils, no adversities could break him or snatch me from him.'[46] Luther's psychological insight was acute. If Christians had even a small remnant of free will, they would be plunged into radical uncertainty about salvation because it would not be clear how much this remnant contributed to it. Luther had experienced this despondency, trying vainly to please God through works and unable to love him.

The personal tone places these intellectual struggles within the context of his early married life. He exulted to Katharina when Justus Jonas, a former acolyte of Erasmus, changed his view about the famous scholar after reading his reply to Luther. He told Jonas that when he read his wife parts of his letter, she had exclaimed 'Look what a toad the man [Erasmus] has become!'[47] He later liked to weave Katharina into his reminiscences of the battle with the famous humanist, even suggesting that it had been she who had persuaded him to write against Erasmus.[48]

Luther's forthright tone has repelled many since,[49] but aggressive rhetoric was part and parcel of academic debate. Erasmus's scholarly tone of ironic detachment was a provocation to Luther, whose most profound convictions were at stake here. As he later recalled, the *Anfechtungen* dissipated during the first years of marriage. To what might have been his surprise, Luther now experienced physical pleasure and yet also felt secure in his relationship with God; and this personal revelation shines through in his absolute conviction that the human will is always inclined to evil and enslaved to Satan. He had known intellectually that Augustine was right, but now he experienced in his own body that accepting the radical Augustinian denial of the freedom of the will and the utter corruption of all human action was essential for a right relationship with God.

Luther would later class his attack on Erasmus as amongst his very best works, and although the tract does not break new ground, it is a passionate treatise that works through the implications of his theological position with great emotional depth. Luther did not reject good works: they were vital to Christian life. But they were actions that flowed from being saved. And they could not earn salvation: that was a free gift of God.

The implications of the denial of free will for Luther's understanding of human psychology and motivation were immense, and it is a doctrine which many, then and now, have found hard to accept. Yet his view shares much with philosophical positions which see human action as determined by social, economic or unconscious forces, and regard our sense that we are 'choosing' to act in a certain way as an illusion. Perhaps the most helpful way to think about it is to consider its implications for practical theology. If all human actions are sinful in some respect, and if our motivation for anything we do is always mixed with egoism, then we do not need to focus on spiritual soul-searching but can concentrate rather on God's saving love.

Luther shrewdly got his attack on Erasmus to the printers shortly before the Frankfurt spring book fair of 1526, expecting that Erasmus would have to wait until the autumn fair before his reply could be on sale. But he underestimated the great humanist and his network. Erasmus wrote his reply in ten days, got his old friend Johann Froben in Basle to print it using six presses at once, and the response made it to Frankfurt in time.[50] Erasmus also complained to the Elector about the attack, which was guaranteed to annoy Luther, who wrote to Erasmus after publication, appearing to apologise for his 'passionate' tone. He had certainly not minced his words. 'You are confident you can lead the world wherever you want with your empty verbal bubbles', Luther had written in De servo arbitrio, mocking Erasmus as a 'Proteus' constantly shifting his ground.[51] But it was not so much the insults to 'my dear Erasmus', as he addressed him throughout, which caused the greatest offence, as the way Luther had managed to present the great scholar as an insincere quibbler, someone lacking in true faith, and who put shallow academic achievement above biblical truth.

Someone may laugh at me for explaining the obvious and offering great men such an elementary tidbit of syntax, as if I were teaching boys learning their alphabet. What am I to do when I see them seeking out darkness in full daylight and making a deliberate effort to be blind, reckoning up so many centuries, so many talents, so many saints, so many martyrs, so many doctors, and boasting with so much authority about this place in Moses, and still not deigning to look at the syllables and not curbing their thoughts so as to actually consider the place they are boasting about?[52]

Luther also wrote to the Elector in no uncertain terms telling him not to get mixed up in the matter, as the 'viper' demanded; if he must write, he should tell Erasmus that it was a matter for 'a far greater Judge than a secular prince'. Luther had no desire to heal the rift with Erasmus.[53]

*

At the same time, the bitter conflict with Karlstadt, now living in Luther's house, continued. While it had arisen over the pace and leadership of the Reformation, it soon spread to encompass the ritual at the heart of Christianity, the Eucharist. This was much more than a matter of doctrine: the Eucharist shaped a Christian community's deepest understanding of itself and the world, encompassing every-thing from politics and morals to its conception of reality.

Luther's position on the sacrament was complex. On the one hand, he rejected the Catholic idea of transubstantiation in the miracle of the Mass, whereby the 'accidents' of the bread and wine – taste, smell, appearance – remained the same while their 'essence' was transformed into the body and blood of Christ.[54] For Luther, this was not biblical but a human doctrine based on the philosophy of Aristotle, a tradition which he rejected. As someone trained in Ockhamist philosophy, the doctrine of 'essences' and 'accidents' was anathema to him as an abstraction that turned faith into reason.

Luther did not make the sharp distinction between flesh and spirit as did Karlstadt. Rather, his attitude to the material world was much more positive, and that made him less likely to want to distinguish between an object and its qualities, or to think that there was a radical disjuncture between spiritual and material matters. For Luther the Real Presence of Christ in the Mass was not something that could be explained. It was not that Christ was 'under' or 'below' the elements of bread and wine, although he was willing to countenance that view as long as people continued to believe that Christ was really there. As the sacramentarian controversy continued, it became clear that insisting on the Real Presence was a fundamental part of Luther's theology. This was not just a matter of doctrine: defending his position engaged Luther's deepest psychological drives.

The arguments about Communion dated back to the time of the Wittenberg disturbances in 1521–2 when first the radical monk Gabriel Zwilling and then Karlstadt introduced a new service in German.

Karlstadt had tried to encourage people to take the sacrament in their own hands, rather than just receive it from a priest, because he wanted his congregation to experience for themselves what it meant to say that every Christian is a priest. Dressed in ordinary clothes, not ecclesiastical vestments, Karlstadt had also abolished the elevation, where the sacrament was raised up for all to see at the moment of consecration, as the bread miraculously became the body of Christ. Everyone took communion in both kinds, bread and wine. As we have seen, Luther undid all these reforms on his return to Wittenberg, and when he introduced a new Mass in 1523 it was in Latin, and the elevation was retained. Karlstadt had scorned this apparent sensitivity to 'weak consciences', people not yet prepared for the Reformation, which he regarded as nothing but a fig leaf for political compromise, designed to protect the Reformation in the light of the imperial mandate. At Orlamünde he picked up where he had left off in Wittenberg, introducing Communion in both kinds, singing Psalms in German, removing images, and emphasising the priesthood of all believers, just as he encouraged his parishioners to interpret the Bible for themselves.[55]

But if the Eucharistic dispute began life as a set of practical issues, it soon became much more far-reaching and fundamental. While Karlstadt had at first angrily rejected complaints from Nuremberg that the Wittenbergers were denying the Real Presence in the sacrament, he gradually developed a theology that saw Communion as a 'heartfelt remembrance', a memorial act only. By 1524 he was clearly arguing that 'This is my body' could not be used to prove that Christ was corporeally present, because 'this' did not refer to the bread but to Christ's body. The point of Communion was to reawaken the believer's emotional connection to Christ's sacrifice on the Cross.[56] At about the same time, the leading Swiss reformer Huldrych Zwingli in Zurich, who would become extremely influential in the southern cities of the empire, was developing a similar view from slightly different arguments. Whereas Karlstadt argued that when Christ said 'This is my body' he referred only to his physical body, Zwingli concentrated on what was meant by 'is', arguing that it meant 'signifies'.

Karlstadt's road to this position was directly connected to his totemic emphasis on suffering – by which one gave up all 'lusts', emptied oneself for God and arrived at *Gelassenheit*.[57] As a Christian, he wrote in *On the Manifold, Singular Will of God*, you 'must feel a cross in your life, work, labour and resting if you intend to be in Christ. And you must die to self-will.' Although he was now married, his writings continued to display awkwardness about sexuality, defensively arguing that it was all right to be with a woman, if there were no 'lust' involved. He wrote of how 'the flesh gnaws at us with its desires', warning that 'If we develop pleasure and love of our own flesh and desires and establish friendship with our nature, our hostile flesh is like a beam in our eyes.' This convoluted position sprang from his radical separation of flesh and spirit, a dualism that marked his entire theological output, and determined his mature Eucharistic theology. He distinguished between the 'inner' reception of the sacrament and its 'outer' material form, the bread; and because he was emphatic that only the spiritual dimension mattered, he was drawn to argue that the divine could not be inherent in material objects.[58]

Karlstadt's Eucharistic theology also informed his views on morals, gender and politics. Committed to the communal Reformation, he rejected everything that smacked of priestly tyranny – the elevation of the Host, Communion in one kind, confession before Communion, the priest placing the wafer in the communicant's mouth – while his admiration of mysticism, prophecy and the power of the spirit enabled him to be more open to women's role in the Church.[59] Aiming to escape his intellectual formation, and to reach for a purer emotional mysticism, he found his outlook difficult to express within the constraints of a traditionally written and argued pamphlet, the form at which Luther excelled. He tried several other genres, including dialogues, in which he put words into the mouths of his opponents so that he could refute them, but as he rejected images, and was neither a poet nor musician, he had no other practical outlet. Whilst Luther's rhetorical style was becoming ever clearer and more rebarbative, Karlstadt pushed the pamphlet format to its limit, eschewing intellectual, linear thinking. The result was a manner of writing which seems unfinished and obscure. So, for example, he could write in *The Meaning of the Term 'Gelassen'*: 'However, we must be on guard constantly that this same yielded egoism or self-absorption is seriously judged and surrendered, for the Devil sits in wait of unsurrendered yieldedness as a fox looks out for chickens which he plans to devour.'[60] He is clearly striving for emotional honesty as well as memorable imagery, but achieves this at the cost of clarity.

The suffering and rejection Karlstadt experienced – Luther had made him feel 'anxiety, envy, hatred, and disgrace' – enabled him to reach *Gelassenheit*.[61] As he wrote in a dialogue which dealt line by line with Luther's *Against the Heavenly Prophets*: 'Through such suffering we must subdue, break, and subordinate to the spirit our untamed flesh in order to assist hope, strengthen faith, and firm up the word. For tribulation brings about patience and patience leads to a certain knowledge and experience.' This, he insisted, had nothing to do with the 'works of love', the self-mortification and asceticism practised by the monks, with which Luther identified his ideas.[62] What both men had in common, however, is that they invoked experience. For Luther, the story of his heroic stance at Worms was proof that he alone was the touchstone of truth, while Karlstadt regarded his own persecution and suffering as unique: it was something which Luther, living in his secure professorship in Wittenberg, could never understand. Thus the dispute between Luther and Karlstadt was personal as well as intellectual, reflecting both men's understanding of their individual history and destiny.[63]

Luther's sacramental theology did not determine his moral theology, but the two were of a piece. His differences with Karlstadt over the sacrament were paralleled by divergent theologies of marriage and morals, and would soon become a major fissure within the Reformation more broadly. Luther's evangelical opponents, who drew a sharp distinction between flesh and spirit, subscribed largely to two broad views. Some, like Karlstadt, could never entirely reconcile wedded life with *Gelassenheit* and remained ambivalent about marriage, not only because it involved physical pleasure, but also because it brought emotional attachments to spouse and children.[64] Müntzer too sometimes hinted that it would be better to remain chaste. (Indeed, according to the Lutheran Johann Agricola's mischievous story, Müntzer was so 'spiritual' that he showed no joy when told of the birth of his son on Easter Day 1524.)[65] This unease about the 'flesh' would be shared by a variety of spiritualist and Anabaptist thinkers – Anabaptists rejected infant baptism – many of whom were influenced directly by Karlstadt or Müntzer. Formed by their Catholic pasts, with its disgust for sex as polluting, many found it impossible to imagine that any sexual liaison could be pleasing to God. Some, however, building on the idea of marriage as a sacrament in which physical union was an integral part, tried to sacralise sex, believing that God had called them to leave their spouse and take a new 'marital sister'. One group of Anabaptists who became known as the Thuringian 'blood friends' even held that sexual union was the 'Christ-ising', the true sacrament which should replace the Eucharist. For them, the sacrament had to be experienced in the flesh, and sex itself, the epitome of 'fleshly' expression, had to be spiritualised.[66]

The other approach taken by those who made a radical separation between body and spirit was to regulate marriage and sexuality in order to create a godly community. Many of the evangelical communities influenced by the teaching of Zwingli set up consistory courts to police marriage and morals, sometimes involving laypeople only, sometimes under the control of the local church, with the participation of the clergy or 'Elders' of the congregation. In Zurich itself, a discipline ordinance was issued and a new court set up that would punish those who drank to excess, played games of chance, lived in adultery or committed fornication.[67] These courts drew on models that pre-dated the Reformation: guilds-folk had long policed the moral behaviour of their members, and town councils had punished bigamists and freelance prostitutes, who worked outside the civic brothels. But the vigour with which marital offences were now prosecuted was new, and so was the religious value that was placed upon creating a godly community. It would find its fullest expression in Calvin's Geneva.

By contrast, Luther, who believed in Christ's Real Presence in the Eucharist, and rejected drawing a sharp distinction between flesh and spirit, did not devote his energies to such things; indeed, the Anabaptists in the territory of Hesse accused him of not caring enough about them.[68] In a sense, they were right. Luther certainly preached against sin, but he continued to advocate individual confession and the importance of dealing with transgression in private, rather than collective confession and purification of the whole parish.

Luther's theology of marriage consequently also differed from Karlstadt's. His first sermon on the subject in 1519 argued along conventional lines, praising those who had the gift of chastity and presenting marriage as a remedy for sin. But his second major contribution, a sermon of 1522, started instead from the Old Testament and from Creation. Humans are created male and female, Luther argued:

'Hence, as it is not within my power not to be a man, so it is not my prerogative to be without a woman. Again, as it is not in your power not to be a woman, so it is not your prerogative to be without a man. For it is not a matter of free choice or decision but a natural and necessary thing, that whatever is a man must have a woman and whatever is a woman must have a man.' People must therefore marry, he concluded. Moreover, '"Be fruitful and multiply" is more than a command: it is a divine ordinance which it is not our prerogative to hinder or ignore. Rather, it is just as necessary as the fact that I am a man, and more necessary than sleeping and waking, eating and drinking, and emptying the bowels and bladder. It is a nature and disposition just as innate as the organs involved in it.'[69] Sex is, Luther argued, a natural function, and by naturalising it he rejected centuries of tradition which had condemned the sexual act. And by comparing it with defecation, he does not devalue sex as dirty – rather, for him, defecation was a source of pleasure, humour and play. No grandson of a peasant could see excrement as anything but positive because it was a source of fertility.

Although fundamental to society, marriage was surprisingly unregulated by secular authority. As a sacrament, it had fallen under the purview of the Church, which decided which marriages were permitted and what counted as incestuous and required dispensations; it all was made more complex because god-parenthood created an additional spiritual network of kinship and so a host of potentially incestuous unions. The Church also adjudicated annulments and divorces 'from table and bed', which did not permit remarriage. At the same time, secular authorities were disciplining people for sexual misbehaviour – adultery, violence within marriage, bigamy and sodomy.

Most time-consuming for the Church courts were the secret marriages. As a sacrament which consisted solely in the couple's promise of marriage to each other and their physical union, marriage did not require a priest to perform it: the cleric was just a witness to the couple's vows. This meant that it was possible for binding marriage promises to be made in bedchambers, or even barns and fields, immediately before a couple had sex. Once consummated, these were fully legal marriages, even though they were outside the knowledge of any institution. As a result, if a couple had had a sexual relationship, they might be genuinely unsure whether they were free to marry elsewhere. By the same token, if a woman had been made pregnant, and sued her partner through the Church courts for compensation for loss of virginity and child support, she was likely to claim that he had promised her marriage, to save her honour. But her chances of winning were slim. If her partner denied it, two witnesses were required to testify in her support. Given the circumstances in which such marriage promises were often made, and the likely disruption of social hierarchies if imprudent marriages were contracted, the two witnesses could not normally be found. Therefore it became routine for Church courts to hear both sides and, 'in the absence of proof', simply declare the two parties free to marry elsewhere. This solution compensated the woman financially, but confirmed that her honour was 'lost' and left her unable to force her seducer into wedlock.

Luther is often credited with having created the modern, companionate marriage after centuries in which monastic writings had presented married life as the spiritually lesser option. But what he understood by marriage is often very surprising and very alien. In 1520, when he argued in *On the Babylonian Captivity of the Church* that marriage was not a sacrament, he set in train a huge transformation of the institution around which economic, political and social relations in society were organised. It meant above all that Church courts and the Curia had no authority over marriage, and that canon law should not provide its legal framework. In his attempt to wipe the slate clean, Luther went even further and redefined the laws of incest. Instead of the laborious calculations of degrees of kinship and the complex system of dispensations that the Pope had administered, Luther demanded that biblical law be applied: anything, apart from the unions that were explicitly forbidden in Leviticus, should be permitted. Your marriage is perfectly valid, Luther wrote to the pastor Marquard Schuldorp in Magdeburg who had married his niece, for what is not forbidden by God is permitted. Just ignore the cries of 'it's not right, it's not right' of those who are like 'mad dogs in the woods tearing their prey', Luther advised, for no one can deny that 'God has not forbidden but left it free for sisters' children to marry each other or for someone to marry their brother's or sister's daughter.'[70] But such unions were contrary to imperial law and lawyers soon made short work of Luther's reasoning, refusing to sanction marriages of uncles and nieces; Luther would himself eventually take a much more conservative line.[71]

Having offspring, he believed, was a human need, and in his 1520 tract he had gone so far as to suggest that if a woman could not have children with her husband, then she should 'have intercourse with another, say her husband's brother, but to keep this marriage secret and to ascribe the children to the so-called putative father' – a position which even contemporaries found shocking.[72] Asked whether bigamy was permissible, Luther replied that heathens could do as they wished, but Christian freedom should be governed by love and concern for one's neighbour, 'where this can happen without injury and harm to faith and conscience'; and though it had been permitted in the Old Testament, now it would just cause offence and unrest, hardly a ringing endorsement of monogamy.[73] As a physical function, Luther believed, sex was closely related to health – he even mentioned the case of a woman he knew who had died for lack of sexual intercourse.[74] Little more than a month after Justus Jonas's wife died in December 1542, Luther wrote that now his friend's initial grief had passed, he would soon be feeling sexual desire for a good woman, adding that God would 'cure his wound'; and indeed, just five months after his wife's death Jonas remarried.[75] So important was sex to human well-being, Luther believed, that if someone committed adultery, the marriage should not only be dissolved, but the innocent party allowed to remarry. He was a realist about sexual desire, writing: 'There are two kinds of adultery. The first is spiritual, before God, where someone desires the wife or husband of another, Matthew 5. No one escapes being guilty of that.'[76] Luther retained a strong ethical ideal of marriage, yet his often contradictory and incompatible convictions led him to give some rather unorthodox advice in the many marriage cases with which he was now forced to deal.

With marriage denied the status of sacrament, and the principles of secular jurisdiction still being worked out, people now invoked Luther himself as the ultimate authority in marriage disputes – just as they had previously appealed to the Pope. With the old papist Church courts destroyed, he was increasingly asked for advice. His responses could be arbitrary and at times seemed to have been made up on the spot. So, for example, he told Josef Levin Metzsch of Wittenberg that it was fine to marry a woman related to him in the

third degree without the approval of a bishop or the Pope, but when
Metzsch followed Luther's advice, he found that lawyers were counting
the children as illegitimate.[77] He also often found it easier to sympathise with the husband's point of view. On one occasion, he and his
colleague Johannes Bugenhagen admonished Stefan Roth to exert his
husbandly authority, and force his ill wife to leave Wittenberg and
follow him to Zwickau, for her reluctance sprang not from her sickness but her wickedness. Roth should 'see to it, that you be a man'
and not permit 'marital authority, which is the glory of God . . . to
be held in contempt by her'. He ought to realise that 'The fodder was
making the ass frisky'; that is, he was just making her more self-willed
by giving in to her, a form of words which insinuated that she was
sexually out of control as well.[78]

The case of Wolf Hornung, a minor nobleman, became a particular
obsession. Hornung's wife, Katharina Blankenfeld, had caught the eye of
none other than the Elector Joachim of Brandenburg, the brother of
Luther's old antagonist Albrecht of Mainz. Joachim forced her to
become his mistress, and when Hornung discovered his wife's adultery,
he assaulted and stabbed her. The Elector had then imprisoned
Hornung, and humiliated him. Luther took up his cause, writing
repeatedly to the errant wife, her mother, and the Elector; he probably also composed Hornung's letter of defence. When all this achieved
nothing, he adopted the tactics that he had used since the beginning
of the Reformation: he went public. Luther wrote and published stern
letters not only to Katharina Blankenfeld and to the Elector, but also
to the bishops of the region and the knights of Brandenburg, telling
them to admonish their lord. Though he was careful to say in his
letter to the Elector that he was neither initiating a feud nor writing
a letter of insult, it is hard to imagine any campaign more uncom-
promisingly aimed at destroying someone's reputation. To Luther,
this was a matter of male honour. As he put it, a 'robbery' had been
committed, and a woman stolen from her rightful husband by an
unjust and overmighty ruler.[79]

Luther undoubtedly saw the case through the lens of the Old
Testament story of David's theft of Bathsheba, the wife of Uriah the
Hittite. Of course, he had to admit that Hornung had chastised his
wife by 'stabbing her a bit with a blunt knife', although he argued
that this was 'out of marital zeal'.[80] Katharina Blankenfeld – or perhaps

her seducer Joachim – replied, giving as good as she got and telling 'Bishop Luther' to look in the mirror: he was fornicating with a nun, and he should ponder his own conduct when he went strolling with his lute in the Wittenberg streets of an evening, an insult which insinuated he was a serenading womaniser. Luther promptly published her letter, with a line-by-line commentary of his own which mocked her as an uppity woman. 'And may God protect everyone from this Mrs Katharina Blankenfeld,' he wrote, 'unless a good pig-handler can get hold of her first with a sharp knife and castrate her.'[81] The affair rumbled on, and if Luther had at first been convinced that Katharina had been abducted against her will, he soon demonised her as the ultimate shrew. His passionate involvement was further coloured by the fact that Joachim's wife, a Lutheran, had fled Brandenburg for Wittenberg in 1528. Not for the first time, it seemed that Luther had stolen a woman from a Catholic grandee and was thumbing his nose at him.

His view of marriage could occasionally seem cavalier. His partisan upholding of Hornung's marriage, for example, contrasts with his equally passionate insistence, in other cases, on allowing husbands like the pastors whose wives had deserted them to remarry. Ursula Topler, who married the preacher and ex-Dominican Jodokus Kern, had left her convent because she was persuaded of the truth of Luther's teachings, but she was determined to lead a non-sexual marriage with her husband, who, unfortunately for her, did not share her ideal. When he treated her roughly she fled to the Catholic Count Ernst II of Mansfeld, while her husband went to law to get her back. Kern was minister at Allstedt, where he had been sent by Luther in late 1524 to counter the influence of Müntzer. Luther advised that she should be removed from the clutches of Ernst and his wife, who were filling her 'ears, eyes and all her senses and heart' with the wrong ideas. Moreover, she was a woman, 'who had in addition to natural weakness, also temptation both from the Devil and from humans, so that it would be a miracle if she could resist'. She should be sent to her relatives in Nuremberg to persuade her to come to her senses. But if that did not work, then, Luther opined, 'let her go and do what she wants, and the pastor should be free as if she had died'; significantly, he did not advise that she be compelled to return to him. This was too much for the Elector, however, whose counsellors worried about the scandal this would cause at Allstedt. When Kern went ahead and remarried, he was therefore accused of bigamy in the Church Visitation of 1533.[82]

Many of the newly married evangelical pastors found marriage hard after having been socialised from their youth in all-male environments, raised to view women as temptresses, dirtied receptacles for male lust. Luther, for one, rarely even saw a woman in the confessional when he was a monk; so far as we know, he had no female friends until he began to know the Wittenberg elite a little better, especially the Cranach and Krapp families. Luther could employ a misogynistic humour with women as well as men: when Justus Jonas's wife was pregnant, he wrote to her suggesting it would be a daughter because girls take up so much room in the womb, 'just like their mothers, who make the world too tight for a poor man'.[83] When Johannes Lang's wife died, Luther wrote, 'I do not know whether to congratulate or pity you.'[84] She had been a rich widow, and when Lang first married her, Thomas Müntzer had remarked acidly: 'the so-called pious people, the princes' parsons who preach the gospel to them, marry old women with great wealth, for they are worried that they might finally have to look for their own bread.'[85]

But there was nothing unusual in contracting an economically advantageous marriage. Most craft workshops were run by a married couple, and it was common for a widow to marry the workshop's journeyman, so as to keep the business going. In peasant households too the labour of husband and wife was essential to run a farm, and marriage naturalised the economic relationships of subordination and obedience. Through marriage, property and social status were transmitted, relationships solidified, political dynasties established and inheritance safe-guarded. This applied to the new profession of married clergy too. Ever practical, in 1528 Luther advised that Michael Stifel take over the parish of Lochau, vacant after the death of Luther's former student Franz Günter – and he should marry Günter's widow and look after their two children into the bargain. Stifel duly did, acquiring a house and family all in one, while Luther now knew that the widow was cared for and the succession of another Lutheran pastor assured.[86]

Luther's own household was a great concern as he and Katharina lived, of all places, in the former monastery at Wittenberg, and it

IN SILENTIO
FORTITVDO

ET SPE ERIT
VESTRA.

48. Lucas Cranach the Elder, *Martin Luther*, 1532.

rapidly filled up with dependants. He and the last prior, Eberhard Brisger, had formally handed over the keys of the by now almost deserted building to the Elector a few months before Luther's wedding, conferring ownership on Saxony although the newly-weds continued to live there. Seven years later, Elector Johann, Friedrich's brother and successor, formally gifted the entire place to Luther and his descendants.[87] It was one of the largest buildings in the town at that time, and Katharina put her stamp on it by adding the 'Luther-portal' as a birthday present in 1540 – a Renaissance-style entry door with a stone carving of Luther's face on one side, and his trademark rose on the other.[88]

Here Luther created a bridge between monastic community and secular household. It was not only huge – certainly bigger than the home in Mansfeld where he grew up – it also soon housed an assortment of guests and lodgers. By a strange irony, the Karlstadt family had been amongst the first to arrive; and like many of the other professors at Wittenberg, Luther took in students, earning extra money by feeding and housing them. There was always an audience at his table, where the reformer would hold forth, and regale his listeners with jokes and stories.[89] Hospitality was offered to visitors of all kinds, just as in the monastery. Luther valued sociability as an antidote to the melancholy he had suffered when he was a monk, and devoted considerable time to companionship. If you want any peace and quiet, Prince Georg of Anhalt was warned in 1542, don't stay with Luther.[90] Apart from the students,[91] there were also servants, including Luther's long-standing manservant Wolf Sieberger, to whom the reformer wrote an epic on his penchant for bird-catching, and a series of women servants such as the exotic Rosina von Truchsess, who first claimed to be a noble nun but then admitted she was the daughter of a peasant executed in the Peasants' War. When she became pregnant she asked one of the other maids to 'jump on her body' so as to abort the child, after which Luther condemned her as an 'arch-whore, desperate tart and sack of lies'. He also suspected her of being a papist spy and she was dismissed from her post – as unmarried servants who fell pregnant usually were – and had to leave town: the household's famed generosity did not extend that far.[92]

Luther's openness to others was legendary, however. Whole families moved into the former monastery. Simon Haferitz, a former follower of Müntzer and embroiled in disputes in Magdeburg, arrived in 1531 with his large family. 'I don't know in what nest I can put this bird . . .' Luther sighed. 'But Luther has a broad back, and will be able to bear this burden too.'[93] Johann Agricola and his family of nine children came to Wittenberg in 1536, when Agricola expected to gain a position at the university, and Luther put up his wife and daughters again in 1545.[94] In 1539 he took in the four orphaned children of Dr Sebald Münsterer, who had died of plague along with his wife – much to the fury of the Wittenbergers, who accused Luther of plague-spreading.[95] Then there was a motley collection of relatives and friends, including Katharina's aunt Mume Lena and the fourteen-year-old son of a Bohemian count.[96] The living arrangements could give rise to tension. In 1542 Luther wrote to the schoolmaster at Torgau, telling him to beat his nephew Florian every day for three days until the blood ran: the boy had taken the knife from Luther's son Paul as the two lads travelled to school. He was to be beaten the first day for taking the knife,

Warhafftige Contrafcet des Ehrwirdigen
Herren D. Mart. Luth. Die sonderm stich abgeriffen
zu Wittemberg. Anno. D. Xlvi.

1546

49. Lucas Cranach the Elder, *True Portrait of Luther*, 1546. By the early 1530s, Luther
had filled out, and the memorial images of the reformer produced the year he died
show a bulky figure, a substantial man of authority very different from the lean,
ascetic-looking young monk.

on the second for lying that Luther had given it to him, and on the
third for stealing it from Luther, whose knife it was. 'If the [arse]-licker
were still here, I'd teach him to lie and steal!' the furious Luther
wrote.[97]

\*

The thin, intense monk who had been mocked as sniffing his posy on
the Leipzig marketplace had become the solid, settled patriarch,
dispensing hospitality to others. By 1530, visitors noticed that Luther

50. Lucas Cranach the Elder, *Luther and the Saxon Elector in front of a Crucifix*. This image and variations on it became extremely influential. It was used in the 1546 edition of Luther's New Testament, published by Hans Lufft, and in several volumes of Luther's collected works on the title pages. The image also underlines the importance of the crucifix in Lutheran devotion, which Karlstadt had repudiated.

had filled out. Now he became portly, and as he would wryly remark shortly before his death, soon the 'worms would have a stout doctor to feed on'. This physical transformation created a representational problem for the evangelical movement, however: holy men were usually bony ascetics, and immune to the pleasures of the flesh. Just how difficult Luther's followers found his appearance is revealed in Melanchthon's biography of Luther, when he insisted that he had fasted a great deal, going for days without eating.[98] But Luther hardly resembled the haggard hermit and dedicated scholar Melanchthon wanted to present. Indeed, by that time a new iconography had developed, showing a monumental Luther with giant boots and tiny hands, his stance powerful, rooted to the ground and clutching a Bible. Some images showed a bulky Luther on one side, and a solid Saxon Elector on the other, both kneeling with a crucifix between them, like two giant weights on a pair of scales: there could hardly have been a clearer demonstration of the closeness of Luther's Reformation to the Saxon ruling house. This image prefaced editions of Luther's Bible and of his collected works and became an almost official representation of the Reformation.[99]

By the early 1530s, with his parents now both dead, Luther had become 'the oldest in my family', as well as father to a brood of children of his own. He had also become less mobile, intellectually as well as physically, as he ensconced himself in his study and held court at the table. Now a man of substance, his married life had transformed his theology. He had shed asceticism for a remarkably positive conception of human physicality, and a flexible, pastoral attitude towards the marital dilemmas of his parishioners. This vision would separate him not only from the old Church, but also from the rule-bound communitarian moralism of those influenced by the Swiss reformers and their heirs, the Calvinists.

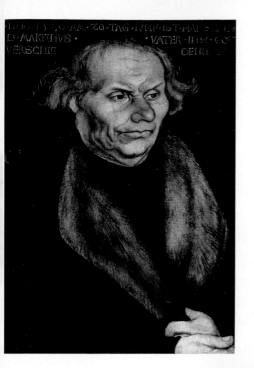

Lucas Cranach the Elder,
Hans and Anna Luder, 1527.

View of Wittenberg, 1536.
On the far left the Elector's castle is clearly visible.
The twin towers in the centre are those of the
city church, and the Augustinian monastery
can be made out on the right.

Lucas Cranach the Younger, *The Conversion of Saul*, 1547. The three castles at Mansfield can be seen in the background of this painting, each picked out in a different colour.

Johann von Staupitz. Painted in 1522, this portrait shows a large, round-faced man with real physical presence, natural authority and a warm paternal manner. Luther's later antagonist Cochlaeus described Staupitz as 'remarkable for the beauty and stature of his body'.

Lucas Cranach the Elder, *Georg Spalatin*, 1509.

*Pilgrimage of Friedrich the Wise to Jerusalem*, painted shortly after the journey in 1493. The relics the Elector obtained on that journey formed the foundation of his collection.

Lucas Cranach the Elder, *Martin Luther and Katharina von Bora*, c. 1529.

Opposite page: This detail from the epitaph of Michael Meienburg, after Lucas Cranach the Younger, shows the reformers grouped with Martin Luther: (*left to right, inner circle*) Johannes Forster, Georg Spalatin, Martin Luther, Johannes Bugenhagen, Desiderius Erasmus, Justus Jonas, Caspar Cruciger and Philipp Melanchthon. Interestingly the image includes Erasmus as a reformation hero.

NATVS ES ISLEBII DIVINE PROPHETA LVTHERE, IAPETI DE GENTE    PRIOR MAIORVE LVTHE
RELLIGIO FVLGET, TE DVCE PAPA IACET.    NEMO FVIT, TV PAR DOCTE MELANTHON ERA

Lucas Cranach the Elder, *Martin Luther and Philipp Melanchthon*, 1543.

Albrecht Dürer, All Saints altarpiece, 1511.

# 14

# *Breakdown*

The first sign of disunity between Luther and Karlstadt had been their differences over the role of images. While Karlstadt urged that images must be removed as unscriptural, Luther did not think it was necessary to ban them all; he also insisted that only the established authorities should be allowed to remove them. This disagreement became a major cleavage in the Reformation, for while Lutherans would make rich use of images both in their propaganda and their churches, Zwinglians – and later, Calvinists – with their simple whitewashed churches, could hardly have been more different.

By late 1524 the tensions centred on different attitudes to the Eucharist. It was not just a matter of personal animosity: many evangelicals were unconvinced by Luther's doctrine of the Real Presence. In Zurich, the Swiss theologian Huldrych Zwingli too had agonised about the issue, until his revelation that the word 'is' in the phrase 'This is my body' means 'signifies', which he said came to him in a dream. Zwingli was the preacher at the main church in Zurich, and he had the backing of the town council in introducing a thoroughgoing Reformation that owed little to Luther; it would become inspirational to many southern German and Swiss towns, and in due course influence the French reformer John Calvin, based in Geneva.[1] Johannes Oecolampadius, a highly respected humanist in Basle, reached a similar position (he too argued that the 'body' in 'This is my body' was the sign of Christ's body, the bread, not Christ's body itself), and his reputation meant that the Wittenbergers had to take his views seriously. For him and others the rejection of the Real Presence was also linked to their understanding of the role of the clergy, for they repudiated the idea that a priest could perform the miracle of turning bread and wine into the body and blood of Christ. This tapped into a rich vein of popular anticlericalism, especially as it concerned what many viewed as the hypocrisy of the immoral clergy. How, laypeople asked, could men who lived in sin with concubines exercise tyranny over the consciences of the laity through confession? Would the sacrament be valid, some wondered, if the priest who consecrated the bread and wine was a known sinner?

Like Karlstadt, Zwingli wanted to overturn the division between clergy and laypeople. The Swiss and southern German evangelicals were deeply concerned about the Catholic abuse of the power of confession and absolution, and they targeted individual confession, replacing it with a general confession of the whole congregation. Zwingli prized communal values. He became a citizen of Zurich and accepted the burden of military service because citizenship demanded that a man should defend his city with his life. Zwingli saw the Eucharist as a collective event; salvation involved the whole town and it was vital that it be morally pure, otherwise God's judgement would descend on the whole community. As a result, the Zurich authorities set about punishing all those guilty of fornication, adultery and gaming, and even paid spies to inform on the sins of their neighbours.[2] Civic communalism, it seemed, could bring its own unforeseen tyrannies.

*

By now Karlstadt himself was under surveillance, living at times in Segrehna with his wife's family, at times in Kemberg where the local preacher and the electoral official reported on his movements. In 1526 he asked the Wittenbergers – Justus Jonas, Johannes Bugenhagen and Luther's wife – to be godparents to his son, and a delegation of Wittenberg dignitaries including Luther descended on Segrehna for the occasion. Named Andreas after his father, the two-year-old boy was unusually old for a baptism. He had been born when Karlstadt was banished from Saxony, and his mother, who had stayed behind, had not had him baptised – perhaps because Karlstadt was questioning infant baptism at this time, perhaps because she herself was sympathetic to Anabaptist ideas, which had spread after the Peasants' War, that only adult believers should be baptised. Luther relished the irony of Karlstadt's change of heart, remarking: 'Who would have thought a year ago that those who called baptism a "dog's bath" would ask for baptism from their enemies?'[3]

The celebration at Segrehna was an attempt at reconciliation between the two men, now tied to each other anew by the bonds of godparenthood. And it seems that Karlstadt's family exploited the occasion to the full. A few days later, Luther interceded with the Elector on behalf of Karlstadt's wife's uncle, the miller at Segrehna, while another of her relatives lodged in Luther's house for several months while she recovered from the plague. In November, Karlstadt himself wrote from Berkwitz, to say that he had lost seven horses, had little livestock left and would have to sell up: could Luther ask the Elector to let him move to Kemberg? Luther frequently interceded for others with the Elector, but there is something odd in his punctilious insistence on doing everything Karlstadt requested – asking the Elector repeatedly to allow him to live in Kemberg, and mediating for his relatives – as if he was proving his devotion despite a hidden antipathy.[4]

Luther was able to keep an eye on Karlstadt, but could not control those beyond the orbit of Wittenberg. One by one, many of his former supporters went over to the sacramentarian position of denying that Christ was physically present in the Eucharist. The loss of Oecolampadius had been bad enough; but then Nikolaus Gerbel, who had been Luther's loyal lieutenant in Strasbourg, wrote that Martin Bucer had also adopted a version of the Swiss position. Bucer and the Strasbourg preachers tried to maintain unity with Luther and, realising that discussions by letter were unlikely to succeed, they instead sent an envoy to hold long discussions with him. There was no agreement, however, and even Gerbel concluded that the sacramentarians, not the papists, were now the main enemy.[5] As he had no stomach for such a fight, Gerbel wished to dedicate himself to academic work.[6]

In Augsburg, the leading preacher Urbanus Rhegius, once a Lutheran loyalist, also seemed to be open to some of Karlstadt's arguments.[7] Augsburg was one of the foremost cities in the empire with a strong populist evangelical movement, so its theological orientation mattered. But by the summer of 1526, only Stefan Agricola, Caspar Huber and Luther's old friend Johannes Frosch, in whose monastery Luther had stayed during the discussions with Cajetan in Augsburg, were still persuaded by Luther's position. Leadership of the evangelical movement in Augsburg had passed to men like Michael Keller, Johann Landsperger and Urbanus Rhegius, who preached a more communalist model for the Reformation. Luther knew how dangerous this shift was. In the autumn, in what seems to be the first letter to his friend in many years, he wrote exhorting Frosch to 'remain firm'.[8]

In Nördlingen, Luther had relied on his solid ally Theobald Billican, but now Billican too was leaning towards the Swiss in some respects;[9] while in Ulm, Conrad Sam switched to the sacramentarian position. At least in Schwäbisch Hall, Johannes Brenz remained loyal, while the Nurembergers also still held the Lutheran line. However, with the loss of the imperial cities of Augsburg, Ulm, Basle, Zurich and Strasbourg – all major centres of printing – Luther was becoming increasingly detached from developments in the south. In Strasbourg, Otto Brunfels, the humanist and friend of the knight Ulrich von Hutten, spoke for many when he published a letter to Luther in which he expressed his sorrow at the rift with Karlstadt: he admired both, he wrote, and could not love Luther without also embracing Karlstadt.[10]

Nor was dissent confined to the south. In Liegnitz, Conrad Cordatus had to be peremptorily ordered to leave the 'opponents of Christ';[11] and in other parts of Silesia the noblemen Caspar Schwenckfeld and Valentin Crautwald were persuaded that there was no bodily presence in the Eucharist. Schwenckfeld travelled to Wittenberg in December 1525 to discuss the matter with Luther in person, but despite three days of argument, neither side convinced the other.[12] In the spring of 1526 Luther sent Schwenckfeld a bitter letter ordering him to desist from his errors. If he would not, 'then God's will be done. Although I am heartily sorry, yet I am not responsible for your blood, nor for the blood of all those whom you lead astray with [your teachings]. May God convert you. Amen.'[13]

Non-theologians were inspired by sacramentarian ideas too, because they chimed with a deep-rooted, common-sense anticlericalism. Rare surviving testimony of their beliefs came from Hans Mohr, captain of the foot soldiers at Coburg Castle in electoral Saxony, who thought that it 'was wrong, that out of the created things, the bread and wine of the Lord, they want to make the Creator himself'. The common people were being piteously misled, he believed, and although he was happy to keep quiet about this, he would give his opinion if people asked him what he thought over meals or at the inn. Interrogated about his beliefs several times, Mohr was eventually sacked from his post.[14]

The group of preachers who rallied to Luther's position all said the same thing, whereas the sacramentarians arrived at their conclusions by different routes. To Luther, this merely showed that there was not one, but five or six different sects, and for him this was proof that 'they would soon perish'.[15] It was not obvious, however, that the Lutherans were winning. They certainly published more, and in more places. And they had censorship on their side. In Leipzig and Erfurt, almost nothing was published that deviated from the Lutheran line; in Nuremberg and Basle, Karlstadt's works on the sacrament were banned, with Nuremberg prohibiting Zwingli's works for good measure. But Luther heard from all sides that it was the sacramentarian pamphlets that were selling and setting the intellectual agenda. Those loyal to Luther – Amsdorf, Bugenhagen, his Nuremberg friend Andreas Osiander – were men with personal ties to him; he was therefore overjoyed when, without any urging, 'the very learned Swabians' took up the cause and wrote 'excellently' against Zwingli and Oecolampadius.[16] For the first time, however, Luther and his supporters were on the defensive, with Luther no longer the first to develop new and intellectually exciting positions.

As a result, his mood became increasingly apocalyptic, and his tone to correspondents more and more strident. In early January 1527 he worried that even his old friend Nikolaus Hausmann might be falling for the sacramentarians. When reassured by Hausmann, Luther replied that he had not credited the rumour, 'for I always believed this about you', going on to ask for his friend's prayer that God might guide his pen against Satan.[17] Even a rumour that the town council of Memmingen had decided to abolish Communion as a compulsory sacrament was enough to make Luther pick up his pen and hector the councillors: 'Oh dear lords, act before matters become worse! The Devil, let in this far, will not rest until he has made things yet worse. Be warned, watch out, dear friends. It is time, it is an emergency.'[18] Luther's relief when Michael Stifel in Tollet, a long-standing correspondent, turned out to have remained 'constant in faith' leaps off the page. Luther goes on to tell him that it is because of 'God's anger' that so many are persuaded by the 'absurd and childish' arguments of those who say that since Christ is at God's right hand, he cannot be in the bread.[19] In a letter to Johann Hess in Silesia in 1526, he mourned the loss of Crautwald and Schwenckfeld to 'these evils' and warned that the fight with the dragon of the Apocalypse was at hand.[20] In another letter to Thomas Neuenhagen in Eisenach, whom he hardly knew, Luther admonished him not to follow the Eisenach preacher Jacob Strauss. 'You should serve Christ, he has served Satan', he wrote.[21] Shortly afterwards, he wrote to Nikolaus Hausmann that the heresies were Satan's 'ragings', for 'the Last Days are at the door'. He felt 'sorry' for Oecolampadius, 'such a man, captured by such frivolous and worthless arguments'.[22]

The same phrases recur again and again in his letters: Satan 'rages', Luther's opponents suffer from '*furia*' and 'rage' against him, the Last Days are at hand. There are lurid warnings about backsliders, injunctions to remain firm, heartfelt requests that the recipient pray for Luther in his fight against Satan, and often a final confident proclamation that Luther is on Christ's side. 'Now I understand what it means that the world has gone to the bad and that Satan is the Prince of the World', he wrote to Michael Stifel in May 1527. 'Up until now I thought these were mere words, but now I see that it is reality, and that the Devil truly rules in the world.'[23]

Then, on 6 July 1527, Luther suffered a complete physical and spiritual collapse, experiencing an *Anfechtung* so severe that he fell and lost consciousness. It was like a 'rushing' in the ears, he later described it, but outside, not inside the head. He felt that Satan was beating him with his fists, a sensation that reminded him of what Paul described in Corinthians. He was utterly without colour and lay as if dead. When he came to, he worried that he had been too bitter in his polemics – just as he had worried in Worms in 1521 – fretting that he wanted to write on baptism, and against Zwingli, but God had evidently decided he should not. Then he turned to Jonas and Bugenhagen, sobbing bitterly and speaking 'gravely' against the 'sacramentarians' and about the many sects which had arisen to pervert God's Word.

Bugenhagen and Jonas wrote a full account of what had occurred, based on notes at the time.[24] It is a remarkable document, not least because it was written at all. As both men would have known, it was highly likely that Luther's enemies would interpret such an incident as possession by the Devil; indeed, Luther's opponent Cochlaeus would later allege that Luther had been possessed by the Devil all his life.

Yet their response to the event was not to suppress what took place, but to record it in the fullest detail possible. The account was published in German in the very first editions of Luther's works, in confident disregard of what opponents of the Reformation might do with it.[25]

Luther himself knew that the event was significant. 'I must note the day', he observed, adding, 'yesterday I was sent to school': it was an experience from which he had to learn his lesson.[26] Luther located the collapse in his 'heart'. It resulted in an extreme coldness and ringing in the ears, which the doctors treated by giving him plenty of warmed cushions. Luther distinguished between the bodily illness, which his friends thought very severe, and the attacks of the Devil, which continued for a long time afterwards. He certainly expected to die, and summoned his wife and young son. He told them that he had no money except the coins they had been given at their wedding, and commended them both to God, 'the judge of the widow'. He had already made his confession to Bugenhagen earlier that day, because he had planned to receive Communion the next day. In line with his beliefs, he did not ask for extreme unction.

It is hard to know exactly what these 'attacks of the Devil' were. Luther spoke of fearing that he would lose his faith, and yet all his letters radiate certainty, alongside the conviction that those who took a different line from him were led by the Devil. He prayed the seven Penitential Psalms. Always aware of his own sinfulness, this time he worried only that he had been too harsh in his polemic and that he had sometimes used 'careless' words – neither very severe sins.[27] He knew he was bitter in polemic, and although he had apologised for this fault at Worms in 1521, he had not really modified his tone.

Equally striking was what Luther did not regret. He did not worry about his attack on the papacy, feel guilt about his marriage, or show concern about his conflict with Karlstadt. Rather, he seemed gripped by the fear that he might lose his faith. Thus these *Anfechtungen* were as serious as anything he had suffered when he was a monk and when he had needed Staupitz's reassurance; indeed, he would later claim that they were the worst he had ever experienced. He had thought that, once he had passed the first years of marriage unmolested, the temptations had disappeared forever. They clearly had not.

Writing to Spalatin a few days later, on 10 July, Luther made light of the attack. Spalatin too had been ill, so Luther began by comforting him before turning to his own illness. He had thought he would die, Luther wrote, but God had quickly made him recover.[28] In fact, it took months before he was well again; as late as November he was still complaining that he could not write or work as he usually did because of his illness and Satan's attacks (although he was actually steadily translating the Old Testament).[29] The attack of 1527 was a major collapse and was followed by periods of extreme exhaustion. What caused it?

Perhaps it was not coincidental that the biblical text for preaching on the day of his breakdown was Luke 15, the parable of the prodigal son.[30] Luther, who had disobeyed his own father, had also been welcomed back twice: when he said his first Mass as a monk, and then when he married; so this passage may have had particular personal resonance.[31] Perhaps he also unconsciously feared that the kind of attacks he had unleashed on paternal figures might now be in store for him.[32] He frequently referred to the biblical story of David and his son Absalom to express both his anger, and his love and grief over those who had once been his followers, and whom he had now lost.[33] The parable may have precipitated a powerful reaction in the man who seemed to have lost all his dearly beloved Absaloms for ever. Luther had once been the prodigal son: now he was the father whose wayward sons showed no signs of returning to him.

In place of the excitement of the early years of the Reformation, Luther had become an increasingly immobile figure, no longer just the accuser but now attacked and besieged himself. Profoundly tired, he was exhausted from the years of struggle when he had attacked first the Pope, then the Catholic polemicists, followed by the peasants, Erasmus and his own former followers.[34] Anger had driven Luther's attacks, pushing him to formulate his deepest theological insights. Just a few months before, in May 1527, he had published *That these words of Christ 'This is my body' still stand firm against the Fanatics*, the fulmination against the arguments of the sacramentarians which his followers had been urging him to write for so long.[35] Luther neatly encapsulated the views of his opponents in the phrase 'the flesh avails nothing', and counterposed it repeatedly with the Gospel's clear statement 'This is my body'. He concluded in blood-curdling tones, addressing the councillors of Basle, Strasbourg, 'and all those who have such sacrament-mobs amongst you', warning them not to 'put a bag over your head, but be well aware of the game they are playing.

Müntzer is dead but his spirit has not been rooted out . . . The Devil does not sleep . . . I warn, I advise: Protect yourself, watch out, Satan has come amongst the children of God.'[36]

Anger seems always to have energised Luther, enabling him to sweep away tradition and open himself to new religious truth. It also gave him the psychological strength not to yield in the face of huge pressure – and never to recant. Yet these same qualities also made it difficult for him to appreciate the views of others, or to see that not every theological battle was a fight for Christ. If someone deviated from what he regarded as the correct theological position, they were at once called to account – Luther demanded complete intellectual and spiritual submission. As a result, he was surrounded by yes-men. Indeed, the man who had done so much to fight for conscience and freedom and against spiritual tyranny was in danger of creating a church that was in some respects less tolerant than the one he had attacked.

Other matters also troubled him. At the height of his collapse, and ready to die, Luther had prayed repeatedly to 'Christ who shed his blood for us', addressing God: 'You know that there are many, whom you have allowed now to shed their blood for the gospel, and I believed that I would be one who would shed my blood for your name, but I am not worthy of it. Let your will be done.'[37] These remarks reveal that Luther was again preoccupied with martyrdoms, recent and ongoing.[38] Just a few months before, on 23 April, Georg Winkler of Halle – an evangelical who had formerly been a close advisor of Albrecht of Mainz – was murdered on his way back from an interrogation by the archbishop's officials.[39] Luther had heard of his death the week before his collapse, and suspected that Albrecht might have had Winkler assassinated. And another case was worrying him as well. Leonhard Kaiser, a former Catholic cleric who had started to preach Lutheran doctrine in Bavaria, had been arrested, and on his release in 1525 he had gone to study in Wittenberg, where he became well known to Luther and Melanchthon. But then, after eighteen months in Wittenberg, his father fell seriously ill and he had returned home to Bavaria, only to see his father die just a few hours after he arrived. Unwise enough to preach again, Kaiser was soon arrested by the Bavarian duke's officials as a recidivist heretic, and on 7 March 1527, he was imprisoned once more. Luther and Melanchthon both wrote him letters of spiritual comfort, as did the Saxon Elector.

The news of Kaiser's imprisonment and impending martyrdom weighed heavily on Luther. In December 1524 'Brother Henry' – a Dutch Lutheran who had also been a student at Wittenberg and a follower of Karlstadt – had been murdered by hostile peasants. Luther had written a pamphlet about his martyrdom, one of the first of many martyrologies of the Reformation.[40] His reaction to the Kaiser case, however, was much more emotional and was pervaded by a strong sense of foreboding. On 20 May, a month and a half before his breakdown, he wrote to Kaiser, and was in no doubt about what fate awaited him.[41] In October, still under the impact of his collapse, Luther continued to write about how he felt 'unequal' to Kaiser; he was nothing but a 'wordy preacher', whereas 'Leo' was a powerful man of action, a 'lion' and 'emperor' true to his name.[42] It is not surprising that Luther should have identified with Kaiser. There would be even more surprising parallels as the case unfolded. Weak and debilitated from his time in prison, on 17 July Kaiser was forced to participate in a disputation with none other than Johannes Eck, Luther's antagonist at Leipzig, who had even gone to Rome to procure the bull against him. It is unclear whether Luther knew before his collapse that Eck had taken an interest in Kaiser's case. Luther had been the butt of Eck's coarse humour at Leipzig, and now Eck mocked Kaiser to his face as a man 'whose wares are even worse than his salesmanship'.[43] Unable to burn Luther, Eck meant to burn Kaiser.

Protected by the Elector Friedrich and his successor Johann, Luther was safe. In fact it was now he who was on the side of the authorities, as he had wryly noted after his encounter with Karlstadt in the Black Bear Inn: 'I who ought to have become a martyr have reached the point where I am now making martyrs of others.'[44] Karlstadt was very much on his mind too, and shortly before the breakdown, Luther had become convinced that he would never win him back to the fold. At the climax of his collapse he worried that his death or the Devil's attacks would prevent him writing against the sacramentarians, and he felt the weight and isolation of leading the movement: 'Oh what dreadful misery the *Schwärmer* [i.e. enthusiasts] will cause after my death!'[45]

The events of Kaiser's martyrdom followed closely upon Luther's breakdown. On 18 July he was taken to Passau and again given an opportunity to recant. When he refused, he was ritually defrocked in a ceremony carried out in front of a large crowd which included Eck. Piece by piece, his priest's robes were stripped from his body by the bishop of Passau, and he was shaved. Then he was dressed in nothing but a smock, or *Kittel*, a black slashed beret was put on his head, and, now an ordinary layman, he was handed over to the city judge. This ritual was not the end of his humiliation, however. Kaiser was kept in the castle dungeon for yet another month, and then paraded in chains around the town, before being taken to his home town of Schärding, where he was executed on 16 August.

Kaiser died true to his Lutheran faith. The original anonymous pamphlet account of his death insisted that his body miraculously refused to burn, but Luther rejected this spurious miracle.[46] Instead, in December he composed a pamphlet including a full account of the trial, several letters, Kaiser's will, and a precise account of the execution sent to him by his friend Michael Stifel: 'Thereupon the fire was lit, and several times he shouted loudly: "Jesus, I am thine, save me!" After which his hands, feet and head burnt off and the fire died down. The executioner took a pole and turned the body, then put more wood on the fire, and afterwards he hewed a hole in the body, stabbed it with a sword, stuck a pole in it and put it back on the scaffold and so burnt it.' All this Luther republished in detail, as if determined not to shrink from the full horror of martyrdom.[47] And he concluded the pamphlet with a very personal meditation: 'Oh Lord God, I wish that I were worthy or might yet be worthy of such a confession and death. What am I? What am I doing? How ashamed I am, when I read this story that I have not long since . . . been worthy to suffer the same. But my God, if it should be so, let it be so, your will be done.'

In August, the plague had struck Wittenberg, and Jonas and Melanchthon both left with their families. But instead of departing with the rest of the university to Jena as the Elector had ordered Luther to do, and despite suffering from what we would call depression (which lasted for many months), he determined to stay and nurse the sick. The monastery became a kind of hospital. Initially Luther made light of it, insisting that the plague was not as bad as people said. The first death was that of the wife of the town councillor Tilo Dhen: Luther was holding her in his arms shortly before she died. Then the pregnant wife of Georg Rörer, Luther's secretary, gave birth in dreadful pain and the baby was still-born. Exhausted by the birth

51. Title page of Luther's pamphlet on Leonhard Kaiser's martyrdom, *Von herr Lenhard Keiser in Beyern vmb des Euangelij willen verbrant, ein selige geschicht*, Nuremberg, 1528.

and 'more poisoned by the plague', as Luther put it, she too died.[48] Months went past and the plague continued to claim its victims. Only Bugenhagen and he had remained behind, Luther wrote to Hausmann; in fact, two chaplains, Johannes Mantel and Georg Rörer, and Luther's wife and son remained by his side as well.[49] Luther's decision to remain in Wittenberg was bold, but also revealed a reckless disregard for his own safety and that of his family. It may have been a residue of his wish for martyrdom, or, perhaps, another example of the remarkable courage that enabled him not to shirk what he felt to be his pastoral responsibility to his flock.

We cannot be certain of the full reasons for Luther's collapse, but the years of argument over the Eucharist had tested his most fundamental beliefs and put his relationship with Christ on the line. Resolutely setting his face against Karlstadt and the sacramentarians had brought him to the brink.[50] His position on the Real Presence, after all, was not rational: Christ's presence in the sacrament could not be explained, but must simply be believed; it was a matter where argument ceased. Such a position allowed him to make short work of all his opponents' arguments, because there was no need to engage in any depth with what they were saying theologically. Instead, he retreated to a defensive stance where he could be certain that he was 'with Christ', facing the enemy. Yet this also exposed him to the worst kind of *Anfechtung*, the fear that he would lose faith altogether, and the terror that his assurance that Christ was with him might dissolve. If he had been deserted by Christ, then the position he had taken on the Eucharist was wrong. And if he was wrong, then it was he, and not his enemies, who was on Satan's side. Luther had only the stark alternatives of having faith or losing it, and doubt – from which he suffered repeatedly – plunged him into despair. The rift with Karlstadt was now beyond repair, and worse, Karlstadt was accusing him of becoming like the Catholics and making martyrs himself. Around him, people were dying for the gospel and yet he was 'not worthy' of martyrdom. Two themes stand out in Luther's agonised prayer at the time: the blood of martyrs, and the need to attack the sacramentarians. Secure in Wittenberg, Luther would not be a martyr; but over the coming months he could fight the plague for his parishioners.

*

The plague receded; Luther recovered from his collapse, and his doubts faded: he became ever more certain of the correctness of his view of the Eucharist. He began to set up a new Church, and the Saxon Visitation of all the parishes in the territory began, with the instructions for the visitors of parish pastors in electoral Saxony finally agreed and printed in March 1528.[51] Luther began to see for himself just how ignorant of Christianity many Saxons were, and how many problems the fledgling ministry faced. Over the next years, Luther's energies would be devoted to creating a new catechism, institutionalising a new Church in partnership with the Elector and his officials, and continuing his battle against the sacramentarians.[52]

The last came to a climax in 1529 when he encountered the Swiss at the colloquy of Marburg, arranged by Philip of Hesse, but there was no meeting of minds.[53] Luther wrote 'This is my body' in chalk on the table where the debaters sat, and covered it over with the velvet tablecloth – as if protecting a relic – only to reveal it dramatically during the debate, to underline the importance of the biblical words. Insisting that the words 'This is my body' meant exactly what they said, he added 'here is our text. You haven't yet managed to wring it from us, as you said you would, and we need no other.'[54] Where Oecolampadius and Zwingli insisted on the importance of John 6 and 'spiritual eating', repeating their stock phrase that the 'flesh availeth nothing',[55] Luther replied that physical eating was essential too. 'My dearest gentlemen, because the text of my lord Jesus Christ clearly states: *"Hoc est corpus meum"*, truly I cannot get around it, but must confess and believe that the body of Christ is present therein', he expostulated to Zwingli, breaking out of the Latin of debate into German (although still using Latin for the words of consecration).[56] When Zwingli, who to Luther's great irritation frequently used Greek in the debate, accused him of restoring the sacrifice of the Mass yet again, Luther insisted, as at Worms, that he was 'bound and held captive by the words of the Lord'.[57] As it became clear that the two sides could not agree, Luther washed his hands of them, consigning them to the judgement of God 'who will certainly decide who is right', at which Zwingli burst into tears.[58] At the end of the meeting, Oecolampadius and Zwingli, pleased that at least they had all now met in person, wanted to embrace their opponents as brothers and allow all of them to take Communion with each other; but Luther bitterly refused.[59] He was, however, shattered by the debate, and the 'angel of Satan, or whoever the angel of Death is' was attacking him so severely that he worried he might not reach home alive.[60] Luther's intransigence in dealing with his opponents, and the toll it took on him, had settled into a pattern both grim and unrelenting. Although the energies of the early evangelical awakening were now directed towards building an institutional Church, what had once been a broad evangelical movement was threatening to split as its leaders each defended their theological territory.

# 15

# *Augsburg*

While Luther was convinced that he would never convert the sacramentarians, it also became clear that the different wings of the Reformation would have to develop a united political strategy for dealing with the implacable hostility of the emperor, Charles V. Both had to find a means of engaging with the nature of political power and the question of when it could be resisted. Charles was the ruler of an enormous empire, stretching from its heartlands in Spain through Italy to the New World, of which the Holy Roman Empire was just one part. Having ended the Italian Wars, he was now free to return to the situation in Germany – and to defeating the Reformation.

Luther's political theory, formed in 1523 when he wrote *Temporal Authority: To What Extent it Should be Obeyed*, propounded that there were two realms: that of God, and that of the world. In the world, Christians must obey secular authorities set over them; they must not resist them, even if they acted unjustly.[1] In the realm of God, in contrast, the spiritual reigns, and consciences cannot be coerced.[2] This distinction had served Luther well throughout the Peasants' War: revolt against established authorities could never be sanctioned despite the justice of the peasants' grievances. It had freed him to adopt a prophetic stance, admonishing the rulers for their treatment of the peasants whilst condemning the peasants for rebellion. His position had lasting consequences for the nature of Lutheranism, because his willingness to make compromises with political authorities, even when they were acting in an unchristian manner, provided the theological underpinnings of the accommodation many Lutherans would reach centuries later with the Nazi regime. But now Luther's Reformation needed protection, and this raised the question of when, if ever, a Christian might resist legitimate authority in defence of religious truth.

For Philip of Hesse – a shrewd political player with an imaginative grasp of the possible, who was becoming an increasingly important leader amongst the evangelicals – it was obvious that the supporters of Zwingli and Luther should unite, and that they should prepare to defend themselves. In trying to bring the two sides together at Marburg in 1529, Philip rightly saw that unless they acted together and were prepared to resist the emperor, they stood no chance of protecting their religious independence.[3] Failing to get the doctrinal unity he wanted at Marburg, Philip then proposed that the evangelicals should at least unite in refusing to support the emperor's plans for war against the Turks – who were expanding into Eastern Europe and in the autumn of 1529 would lay siege to Vienna – unless he accepted the Reformation. This had the great merit of being a bargaining tool which did not entail armed resistance to the empire. But for Luther, such cynicism was anathema. As the Turks were murderers, liars, and desecrated marriage, it stood to reason that they must be fought. Luther was careful to argue against any kind of crusade, however: the Turks were not to be attacked on the grounds of what they believed.

Many sacramentarians in southern Germany were prepared to contemplate armed resistance in the face of religious persecution. Here the powerful urban communes had long traditions of defending their independence: every male citizen paid guard-duty tax and had to own weapons, presenting their arms for inspection in military musters at regular intervals. At an annual ceremony, the whole male citizenry would bind itself by oath to obey the mayor and officials. Citizenship meant backing political responsibility with arms and was one of the reasons why women were excluded from full political citizenship.[4]

For Luther, by contrast, political responsibility meant obedience first of all; 'Render unto Caesar what is Caesar's.'[5] The emperor was set in authority over the princes, and like all authority, he must be respected. But by 1530 Luther was beginning to reconsider, a process that would go through many twists and turns over the coming years. Luther's Saxon ruler and his advisors had realised that if they were to continue passively obeying the emperor, the evangelical movement would not survive. In late December 1529 Luther told Elector Johann it was too soon to be thinking of resisting Charles – a formulation that seemed to allow that eventually, and in the right circumstances, the time might come. But, Luther insisted, they must not prepare for such an eventuality by taking to the field or arming themselves – a position which might seem to put principle above practicality. Yet Luther was probably correct in thinking that if Charles got to know of any such preparations, he would at once move against Saxony.[6] Saxon politics continued to be overshadowed by the struggle between ducal and electoral Saxony, and Johann's anxiety that the emperor might simply hand everything – land and the electoral title – to his Catholic rival Georg. This was a fear that the much more secure Philip of Hesse did not face.

Luther's unwillingness to countenance resistance was made clear in a letter of advice he wrote to the Elector on 6 March 1530.[7] Resisting the emperor, he wrote, taking a much firmer line than the previous year, was inconceivable. It would be as if the mayor of the Saxon town of Torgau were to decide to protect his citizens against the rightful authority of the Elector himself.[8] The comparison was unlikely to persuade any proud urban citizen, long used to the adage that 'city air makes you free', and to defending their rights against rapacious princes and nobles.[9] But loyalty to the emperor, who so often protected those rights, ran in the bloodstream of towns: Nuremberg housed the jewels of the Reich, Augsburg had close financial ties to the empire, and imperial cities gloried in hosting the splendid Diets.

*

A Diet at Augsburg had been called for 1530, which the emperor would himself attend. Here Charles was going to allow the evangelicals to set out their position in a confession of faith, in a final attempt to restore religious concord in the empire and create a united front against the Turkish threat. Meetings were held at Torgau to devise a Saxon strategy, and Melanchthon, ever the systematiser, was entrusted with the task of finalising the confession.[10] It was decided that Luther himself should travel only so far as Coburg, still within Saxon territory, and not attend the Diet itself, to avoid provocation. There could hardly have been a greater contrast with his heroic appearance at the Diet of Worms nine years earlier, and he chafed at the prospect of being sidelined. How he would have liked to be there, Luther now wrote, alongside Melanchthon, Spalatin, Jonas and Johann Agricola, who made up the Saxon delegation. But he would only be told, like the poor chorister, 'Be quiet! You have a bad voice!'[11]

Once the band of Wittenbergers arrived in Augsburg, they initially wrote regularly to Luther, who was marooned in the castle at Coburg, some 200 kilometres to the north. Here, Luther joked, he had his own Diet, a parliament of birds: 'You people, of course, go to Augsburg, [but] you are uncertain when you will see the beginning [of your Diet]; we came here right into the midst of a Diet . . . All are equally black, all have dark blue eyes, all make the same music in unison. I have not yet seen nor heard their emperor.' He regularly signed his letters as from 'the kingdom of the winged jackdaws'.[12] Nor was Luther the only one to talk about birds. Soon Agricola wrote from Augsburg, describing a dream of Melanchthon's. An eagle had appeared, which was magically transformed into a cat. Immediately the cat had been stuffed into a sack. But then Luther arrived, and had called for the screaming cat to be let out; it was freed. The evangelicals were agog with possible interpretations. One of their number was called Caspar Aquila, or 'eagle', so perhaps the dream foretold disaster for his house. Others were convinced the eagle represented the emperor, and the practice of sorcery meant the evil machinations of the godless sophists and cardinals, who were preventing the emperor from understanding the truth. Only Luther 's arrival could 'let the cat out of the bag' and allow Charles V to hear the true gospel.[13]

Luther used the enforced solitude to work on translating the Old Testament prophets and to write. First he penned his *Exhortation to all Clergy*, of which 500 copies were printed in Wittenberg and sent to Augsburg, where they sold out. This hard-hitting pamphlet began with Luther's devastating false modesty – people would be asking, he pretended, 'Who needs you? Who ever demanded your exhortation or writing? There are so many learned and pious people here who can give better advice than a fool like you', but he went on to list all the accomplishments of the evangelical movement, the abuses that had been swept away, the indulgence traffic, the ridiculous saints' cults, pilgrimages, monkdom itself – these were feats the bishops hadn't managed in years, but Luther had done it. If he was not allowed to be there in person, he would be there in spirit and 'in writing with this mute and weak message of mine'.[14]

Although his hiding place was meant to be a secret, a steady stream of visitors arrived, including Hans Reinicke, his old childhood friend from Mansfeld. His visit must have brought back many memories, but then, just a few days later at the end of May, Reinecke wrote to Luther to tell him that Luther's father Hans had died; Reinecke had heard the news even before reaching Mansfeld.[15] When Luther had first been informed in February that his father had fallen ill, he had written that he could not visit him because 'you know in what favour I stand with lords and peasants'. It was not safe for him to travel, and the older man was too weak to undertake the journey to Wittenberg. It was a letter of farewell: it seems that Luther knew that he would not see his father again. In an effort to comfort his father, he apologised for the travails his father had endured on his account, but gave them spiritual significance: God has 'sealed' true doctrine and teaching in you and given you a 'sign' or 'mark', 'for my name's sake'.[16] It was not the first time Luther had compared himself to Christ, but the identification was now deeper and more abstract than when he had gone to Worms in 1521. It had been strengthened by his recovery from the crisis he had undergone in 1527, for he had suffered many attacks from the Devil, proving that he was doing God's work. This conviction now underpinned all his thinking.

The Diet was overshadowed by his inner turmoil and his grief. When he heard the news of his father's death, he seized a copy of the Psalms and rushed to his room, where he wept all day; the next day he suffered from a crippling headache. He had had a dream in which a big tooth fell out, and he now decided that it had signified his father's death.[17] 'Such a father, from whom the Father of [all] mercies has brought me forth,' he wrote to Melanchthon on 5 June, 'and through whose sweat [the Creator] has fed and raised me to whatever I am [now].'[18] As he had earlier written to comfort his seriously ill father, 'God gave you a strong and hard body up till now.'[19] Yet just a few years before his death he had gone bankrupt, and had been employed as a manager in someone else's firm for a mere fifty guilders a year – half his son's basic salary.[20] Despite the earlier years of struggle with Hans, now Luther remembered his love and was well aware how alike they were. He owed much of his temperament to his father, through whom God had '*finxit*' – 'formed' or 'shaped' might capture the meaning better than 'raised' – 'whatever I am'. He also knew that the loss of his father was a coming of age for him: he was now, he remarked, 'the oldest Luther in my family'.

*

Meanwhile the movement he had inspired seemed detached from its founder. In Augsburg, the Lutherans faced a long wait for the emperor's appearance. The Saxon Elector had been the first prince to arrive in early May, and rumours circulated that the emperor might not get to the Diet before June. Philip of Hesse was one of the next princes to appear. He still seemed to be wavering between the Lutherans and Zwingli, and the potential loss of such a major, dynamic politician was a serious threat.[21] Luther insisted that his followers must remain firm against the Zwinglians and sacramentarians who had 'trodden the sacrament underfoot'; he advised the Elector to attend Catholic Mass publicly so that the sacramentarians would not be able to boast that he was on their side.[22] This move only isolated the Lutherans further from the local population, and in turn contributed to their sense of embattlement as they waited and saw the sacramentarians exercising a powerful influence over the Augsburg population. The local Lutheran Urbanus Rhegius preached to barely 200 listeners, but Michael Keller, the Zwinglian who Jonas thought both uneducated and a gossip, regularly attracted crowds of 6,000 to his rousing sermons in the huge Church of St Ulrich. When Agricola dared to preach vigorously against the Zwinglians, he stirred up a 'wasps' nest' of criticism in return.[23]

When Charles finally did arrive on 15 June, the Feast of the Ascension, he entered Augsburg in a stunning pageant, which heightened expectations after all the weeks of waiting. The procession lasted until eight in the evening and Jonas described it in loving detail to Luther, even though he knew how little store 'you set by such things'. The emperor, who had been crowned by the Pope in Bologna just a few months before, was dressed in gold, carried a golden sword, and sat astride a bejewelled white horse under a golden canopy. The Elector of Saxony rode close by, followed by Charles's brother, King Ferdinand. The papal legate Cardinal Campeggio, Jonas noted gleefully, at least did not precede the emperor, entering the city by his side.[24] For the Lutherans, the extravaganza would have driven home the sheer power of the forces lined up against them. For many years Charles had been preoccupied with affairs in Italy, so it had been possible almost to forget just how strong imperial might was: now it was on show, for all to see.

And yet this spectacle, designed to parade the magnificence of the empire, also displayed its divisions. On his arrival, Charles spoke to the Catholic and Lutheran princes separately, and lost no time in warning the evangelicals that he would not tolerate their preaching.[25] The day after his formal entry, he celebrated the feast of Corpus Christi, during which a procession ceremonially circled the boundaries of the city, with the Host held high. Charles had deliberately timed his arrival for the feast, and the ritual honouring of Christ's body was intended to celebrate the unity of the empire as the princes, cardinals and bishops all processed as one, showing secular and religious authorities in harmony. But the evangelical princes and most of the townsfolk ostentatiously declined to take part; what had been planned as a display of unity and reconciliation in fact highlighted the existence of separate factions, as the Catholics paraded through sullen crowds of Augsburgers and the evangelicals went straight to their lodgings.[26]

Yet it also demonstrated to the evangelicals how weak and outnumbered they were. Melanchthon wrote in panic that 'everyone else hates us most cruelly'; Jonas worried that 'The emperor is surrounded by cardinals . . . they are in his palace every day, and there is a swarm of priests like bees around him, who burn with hatred against us.'[27] The squabble with the Zwinglians temporarily forgotten, the evangelicals now thought only of the papists and what lay in store for them. And indeed, no sooner had the emperor arrived than the struggles over religion began. The very next day, trumpeters processed through the streets of Augsburg to announce a ban on preaching, except by licensed priests; only through negotiation did the Lutherans manage to get preaching by radical Catholics suppressed as well. The blanket ban on preaching did have its upside for the Lutherans, however, as it meant that the Zwinglians too lost their platform. Jonas might have mocked the official preachers, who did little more than read the lessons and give 'childish' homilies, not interpreting Scripture; but at least they did not incite the populace.[28]

Luther had no trouble agreeing with the Catholics on one subject: the sacramentarians were heretics, and could be punished as such.

Because they have separated themselves from us, he wrote, we can have no compunction about cutting them off. Although he did not say so, he seems to have been willing to expose them to the risk of being sent to Rome and burned for their beliefs. Melanchthon now also argued that as public blasphemers, Anabaptists merited the death penalty.[29] In the printed version of the Augsburg confession, no fewer than five clauses condemned them for their refusal to accept the baptism of infants.[30] Melanchthon believed that the sacramentarians should neither be tolerated nor be negotiated with at the Diet. In line with this policy, he at first refused to meet with either Wolfgang Capito or Martin Bucer when they came to the Diet. While Zwingli produced a printed pamphlet stating his beliefs, the *Fidei ratio*, which he wanted to present to the emperor independently, Bucer now wished to make common cause with the Lutherans. He met several when he arrived on 27 June, including Johannes Brenz, and in mid-July, under pressure from Philip of Hesse, Melanchthon also met him and agreed to review a letter of compromise Bucer planned to send to Luther. Here Bucer explained that since they too held that the true body of Christ was present and eaten in Communion there really was no difference between their positions.[31]

It was such an extraordinary concession that Melanchthon thought he was insincere, and Luther was outraged: 'I won't answer Martin Bucer's letter. You know how I hate their games of dice and their slyness; they don't please me. This is not what they have taught up to now, but they will neither recognise it nor do penance, rather they just continue to insist that there was no disagreement between us, so that we would have to admit that they taught truly but we had wrongly fought against them, or rather, that we were crazy.'[32] His response squandered the chance of a compromise that might have greatly strengthened the evangelical position.

\*

Luther, alone in an isolated castle, complained bitterly that nobody wrote to him. He was exaggerating, but communication did thin when important negotiations were going on. To make things worse, ever since his father's death he endured headaches which were like an uprising or tumult in his head, as if it were full of thunder, making him nearly faint. These were so severe that he was unable to write or read for days at a time, and he also developed toothache.[33] Stranded in Coburg – or Grobuk, as Luther, always a lover of anagrams, took to calling it – he had plenty of time to contemplate his physical ailments. Barely a letter went by without a mention of them, and discussion of illness became part of the currency of exchange between Melanchthon and Luther, as Luther worried about Melanchthon's insomnia and Melanchthon scolded Luther for working too hard and not paying attention to his health.

Luther saw a spiritual significance in these maladies, referring again to the 'colaphizings' of the Devil, using St Paul's term for the beatings or buffetings around the head inflicted by the Devil that Luther had started to use in 1527. At that time, he had suffered from piles, and in 1528, in a letter to a fellow sufferer he gave an extraordinary description of the illness: 'When emptying bowels the flesh around the border of the anal area was pushed out, swelling to about the size of a walnut, in which there was a mustard-seed-sized wounded spot. This spot was sorer the looser the bowels, and less painful the harder the poo. If it was mixed with blood, then there was a relief and almost pleasure in pooing, so that I was often inclined to defecate. And if it was touched with the finger, it itched pleasurably and the blood flowed.' He therefore advised his correspondent not to 'stop the flow, let the blood out, because they say it is the "golden artery", and it is indeed golden. It's said that everything evil to do with illness flows out; it's a dung gate for all illnesses, and those people live the longest.'[34]

Although perhaps unpleasant to modern readers, the words reflect contemporary beliefs; humoral medicine assumed that the world and the body were interrelated. 'Flows' were always good for the body, and should never be stopped: menstrual blood, pus and urine expelled bad substances from the body and thus were healthy. Luther saw illness as a disruption of the essential exchange between the body and the world, and considered his physical ills to be connected to his emotional state. How indeed could this have been otherwise at a time when the emotions and character were thought to depend on the mixture of humours in the body? What was unusual about Luther, however, was that he also sought to derive spiritual certainty from his bodily experiences, and this became increasingly so the older and sicker he became. During his time in the castle, his troubles focused mostly on his head, and he readily provided a natural explanation based on drinking bad wine. But he simultaneously provided a spiritual interpretation: since the headaches prevented him from translating the Old Testament, and thus were obstructing God's work, they consequently had to be diabolic. Thus Luther's own body became a battleground in the cosmic struggle between God and the Devil. As he wrote to Melanchthon, the Devil had now turned away from tempting him spiritually and had switched to physical assaults. 'All right,' he declared, 'if he devours me, he shall devour a laxative, God willing, which will make his bowels and anus too tight for him.'[35]

*

For about a month, from 22 May to mid-June, Luther had no news from the Wittenberg delegation in Augsburg. He knew that this was a crucial time, for Melanchthon was finalising the confession of faith which would be presented to the emperor.[36] Were they keeping secrets from him?[37] Only half-jokingly, he described the anxious wait for post to Spalatin: the first messenger arrived, and was asked: 'Haven't you brought letters? No. How are the gentlemen? Fine. The second came, and then the third and fourth: always the same, no letters. How are the gentlemen? Fine.'[38]

On 25 June, ten days after Charles's arrival, the confession was formally handed to him. The evangelicals had wanted it read in full session of the Diet, but then news arrived of yet another planned attack by the Turks on Vienna from where they had been driven away in 1529, and Ferdinand, the emperor's brother, succeeded in getting the issue of religion shelved while this important matter was discussed. Instead it was presented to the Catholic princes and the emperor in the chapel of the bishop's palace. For Spalatin, the confession's comprehensive and systematic presentation of the Lutheran faith – setting out 'all articles of faith, next to what is taught, preached and thought' – was one of 'the greatest achievements that had ever happened on earth'.[39]

The plan had been to read out the confession in both Latin and German, but in the event it was presented only in German, and even that took a full two hours.[40] Jonas reported that the emperor looked attentive as he listened, although he could not understand a word of

German, as Jonas well knew. Forcing Charles to listen to the Saxon chancellor Christian Beyer read aloud a complex theological text in a language he could not understand was hardly politically wise, but for Luther, it was the high point of the Diet. He praised the reading through which the princes themselves 'preach unhindered before [His] Imperial Majesty and the whole empire, right under our opponents' noses, so that they have to listen to it and are unable to say anything against it'.[41] It was finally a positive contrast to his appearance at Worms, where Luther had not been able to give a full and comprehensive statement of his theology.

Luther was only sent the confession after it had been presented to the emperor, however, and he complained that if he had written it, he would not have made so many concessions. He dashed off a letter which started by congratulating Melanchthon but then objected that he was going against Holy Scripture because Christ is the stone which the builders cast aside, that is, he should expect to be despised and cast aside.[42] There was little else he could now do. He saw himself as an unrecognised war hero, like the commanders at Vienna the year before, who got 'no credit' for driving off the Turks. 'Yet I am pleased and comforted that in the meantime this, my Vienna, has been defended by others.'[43]

Presenting the confession was just the beginning, however, as Charles immediately commissioned a refutation from Catholic theologians. Chief amongst them was Johannes Eck, Luther's old adversary at Leipzig and the man responsible for the martyrdom of Leonhard Kaiser. The 'confutatio' was read in the full session of the Diet on 3 August but only to the secular estates, and the evangelicals were not given a copy. The imperial side sought to prevent at all costs a theological dispute which Luther might win, so they offered the evangelicals sight of the text only on condition that they promised neither to print it nor copy it, an offer they wisely refused. Judging by what they heard, it did not seem too threatening: Jonas was scornful of the 'farrago', and the Wittenberg party were convinced they had not been bested in argument.[44]

When negotiations between the Lutherans and the Catholics began to explore the possibility of some kind of religious settlement, Luther received letters from Melanchthon pleading for advice, for the Wittenbergers needed urgently to know where they might compromise.

Everything had been discussed in advance at the meeting of Luther and his companions at Torgau, Melanchthon conceded, but real-life encounters were always unpredictable. What was essential, and what could be negotiated? Luther, incensed by feeling that he had been ignored for several weeks, now took the opportunity to sulk. He sent word that he was furious with the Wittenberg delegation, but otherwise refused to respond.[45] Melanchthon, seriously alarmed, fired off letter after letter.[46] How could Luther desert them at such a crucial time? They needed his advice. Melanchthon portrayed the dire situation the evangelicals faced, outnumbered by the Catholics. 'Sophists and monks are constantly running to the emperor and inciting him against us . . . Those who were on our side before are not there now, and we hang in great danger and in contempt . . . Read our letters and help', he pleaded. 'We spend most of the time weeping, therefore I beg you for the glory of the gospel or for the public good to reply to us, because it seems that unless you are in charge [the ship] will go under in these terrible storms.'[47] Letters from Jonas told the same story: Melanchthon was doing well, but was suffering from 'sadness'.[48]

Luther never responded well to attempts to make him feel guilty: being a martyr was his role. When, after an earlier gap in communication, post had finally arrived on 29 June, he dashed off a letter while the messenger waited, pouring out his bile: 'In these letters you remind me of your work, danger, and tears in such a way that it appears that I, in an unfair way, add insult to injury by my silence, as if I did not know of these things, or sat here among roses and cared nothing. I wish my cause were such as to permit the flow of tears!'[49] Melanchthon, he wrote, should trust in the Lord and should not worry. Nor did he like the way the younger man insisted on following his 'authority' all the time: the cause was common and shared.[50] Yet the very next day Luther was already contradicting himself, writing that 'it's my cause and mine even more than yours'.[51] The reliance on the younger man was both frustrating and infuriating: 'I don't know what to say, I'm so attacked by the thoughts about your extremely evil and completely vacuous worries, since I know I'm talking to a deaf person.' He accused him of trusting in himself alone, and failing to trust others. 'I have been in greater trouble than I hope you ever will be', he admonished him. 'So why don't you believe us, who speak to you not out of flesh or the world but out of Holy Spirit?'[52] Whereas he had previously refused to reply, Luther now undertook a virtual letter-writing campaign. He told Jonas that Melanchthon's problem was that he trusted in philosophy too much, and Johannes Brenz that Melanchthon should stop playing the martyr.[53] He even accused him of lacking manly courage: 'At least if I were being killed by papists I would protect our successors bravely and I would take revenge.'[54] Brenz replied that Melanchthon was no coward; his tears were just spurring him on to pray, and how could one pray properly if the matter did not touch one's conscience and feeling?[55]

It is clear that Luther was trying to reassert control over a movement that he feared was slipping from his grasp. By first withholding advice and then attacking Melanchthon at his most vulnerable, Luther made him reliant on his pastoral direction. In reality, Melanchthon had been working around the clock, revising the *Apology*, the elaboration of the confession which was published in 1531, and simultaneously negotiating with all sides. It was he, not Luther, who had been responsible not only for the final draft of the major and lasting confessional document summarising the Lutheran faith, but for its defence as well. Luther's tiresome wrangling with Melanchthon confronted Luther with his own mortality, no doubt the result of the death of his father. 'As I presume through weariness of old age and [bad] health and more truly of life that I think I won't have to see and endure this accursed life for long', he wrote.[56] He knew that his own death would raise the issue of succession. We cannot let Bugenhagen go, he mused to Melanchthon, as he contemplated his secondment to Lübeck; we need him in so many areas, in the schools, at Wittenberg; we will need others to take over after me.[57] Yet Bugenhagen was about the same age as Luther; Melanchthon, nearly fifteen years younger, would be his obvious successor. But could he be trusted?

For the next ten weeks the feverish negotiations continued.[58] We have the Nuremberg Lutheran Hieronymus Baumgartner's jaundiced account of what took place and, as far as he was concerned, the whole process was a sham from the start. The Catholic princes would make an offer; Melanchthon would immediately scurry to write new articles with new glosses based on the proposals, and get agreement from the evangelicals. But when this was done, the papists would reject it, offer different terms and the whole process would start again. He saw no intention on the Catholic side to reach a deal.[59]

Melanchthon, though, was desperate to secure peace, and continued to pester Luther for advice. What could be conceded? Had he gone too far? He also wrote to Luther's secretary at Coburg, Veit Dietrich, asking him to make sure that Luther replied. For his part Luther preferred to write to Jonas, evidently trusting him more: 'Be strong and remain manly and firm.'[60] His letters to Melanchthon continued to reveal his irritation. He had answered that question yesterday, he would thunder. Just stick to the gospel. Don't let your beautiful confession be taken apart. 'I ask you, isn't everything there just tricks and deceit?' he wrote. 'You've got Campeggio [Cardinal Lorenzo Campeggio, the papal legate, a hated Italian], you've got the Salzburger [Archbishop Matthaeus Lang of Salzburg, Staupitz's final patron], and you've clearly got the monkish ghosts of Speyer.'[61] With this last point, Luther was alluding to a story circulating at the Diet. Apparently a boatman at Speyer had agreed to ferry a monk over the Rhine one evening so he could journey on to Augsburg. But when he came to take him on board he found a whole group of monks on the shore. He ferried them over then returned to find another crowd of them. The shocked fisherman fell to the ground and was struck lame in all his limbs. The next night another boatman was greeted by a similar crowd of monks, wearing the habits of all the monastic orders – white, grey, black and brown. Knowing what had happened to his comrade, the fisherman demanded payment as he neared the end of the journey. In response one monk struck him hard in the ribs with a stick telling him that 'these days no one does anything for monks for free'. The boatman was somehow compelled to continue the journey, but by the end his face was covered in scratches. Both fishermen had been interrogated by the town council at Speyer and they stuck to their story. Pamphlets relating the tale were soon on sale.

Evangelical writers took it to mean that the monks were descending on Augsburg and that they were evil spirits; certainly it attests to the popular hatred of monks. Papists could have read it for the opposite message, as God's judgement on those who did not respect monasticism. There were other portents too. Melanchthon told of the birth of a deformed creature in Rome, a mule's foal with feet of different kinds, betokening division in the papacy, which recalled the early years of the Reformation when he and others had made the Monk Calf and the Papal Ass the subjects of anti-papal broadsheets.[62] Luther

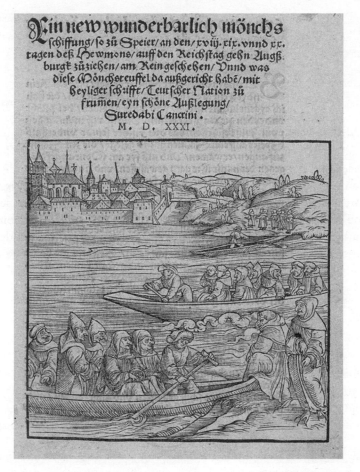

Ein new wunderbarlich mönchs
schiffung/ so zü Speier/ an den/ xviij. xix. vnnd xx.
tagen deß Hewmons/ auff den Reichstag gehn Augß-
burgk zü ziehen/ am Rein geschehen/ Vnnd was
diese Mönchsteuffel da außgericht habē/ mit
heyliger schrifft/ Teutscher Nation zü
frūmen/ eyn schöne Außlegung/
Suredabi Cancrini.
M. D. XXXI.

52. Suredabus Cancrinus' pamphlet *Ein new wunderbarlich mönchs schiffung* from 1531
provides an evangelical interpretation of the Speyer story. The monk on the right has
clawed feet, and many of the others have large or hooked noses, suggesting they are
diabolic, sexually debauched or Jewish.

could afford to laugh at the 'monkish ghosts of Speyer', but those in
Augsburg who felt the weight of the responsibility of protecting the
gospel, scanned the portents and worried about what they signified.

At the Diet, in search of an agreement one committee was set up
after another with new personnel, and it seemed that, contrary to
Baumgartner's belief, the emperor truly wanted an agreement.

53. and 54. The Papal Ass and the Monk Calf.

Sometimes, indeed, it seems that the evangelicals put up as many obstacles as did their opponents. At first the debates focused on external ceremonies, such as fasting and feast days. Here Melanchthon could argue that many of these things were not commanded by Scripture but if they were not essential for salvation, they were not detrimental to it either; it was a position with which Luther seemed to concur, up to a point, although he insisted that these things could not be imposed on others.[63] He was contemptuous, however, of regulations on fasting, 'which the clergy never stuck to', but his stance that such matters could be left to secular authority might have permitted a kind of confessional coexistence.[64] Indeed, his intransigence was often not on points of detail, but on the underlying tone.[65] It seems that his defeat at Eck's hands at Leipzig still rankled, and he had not forgiven his old opponent for the death of Leonhard Kaiser, repeatedly reminding Melanchthon that this was not just a matter of words but of life and death: these Catholic theologians had already killed people for their staunch support of the Reformation. The Catholics were devils, he had written to Johannes Agricola in June: 'They cannot live unless they drink blood.'[66] Now he admonished Melanchthon, slight of figure and physically weak, to 'remain firm', 'be a man' and 'act in a manly way'.[67]

When debate turned to the sacrament, it appeared that the Catholic side was surprisingly willing to allow the Lutherans to give the chalice to the laity, if they also taught that receiving the sacrament in one kind – the Catholic practice of offering only the bread to the laity – was sufficient for salvation. Again it seemed agreement was possible, at least until a full Church council was held, as the offer was in line with Luther's own position when, on his return from the Wartburg, he had attempted to moderate Karlstadt's reforms. Nor was the issue of clerical marriage as problematic as it had first seemed: the Catholics were again willing to tolerate those marriages that had already taken place 'until a council is held'. Moreover, on the fundamental issue of the Reformation, the Catholics were even apparently ready to agree that salvation is by faith and grace, not by works alone – an extraordinary concession, and an apparent victory for Augustinian theology.[68]

Luther, however, accused the Catholics of paying lip service to the importance of faith while continuing to preach indulgences and works, and insisted Communion *must* be offered in both kinds. While the Catholics offered to let the Lutherans continue with their practices whilst they would continue with theirs – holding Masses for the dead, for example – Luther objected to this on the grounds that it would reintroduce the idea of the Mass as a sacrifice, which could earn the individual merits. He was happy to reintroduce compulsory confession before Mass, as long as people should not be compelled to confess absolutely every sin, as it would only burden their consciences.[69] This was a sore point for the Zwinglians and south Germans, who objected to the burdens of confession; but as confession had given Luther such spiritual comfort throughout his life, he wanted to retain it. When it came to the question of bishops, Luther showed a surprising willingness to compromise. Their offices and jurisdiction could certainly be reinstituted, he agreed, after Melanchthon set out the scriptural precedents for giving some priests senior roles within the Church.[70] This troubled not only the sacramentarians, whose anti-Catholicism was animated by their hatred of the old clerical hierarchy, but also many of Luther's own supporters, especially the Nurembergers.[71] As many evangelicals saw it, giving the bishops back their power would allow them to rule over the Lutherans once more, and before long burn them as heretics. Though Luther soon back-pedalled – saying he had meant a different thing by bishops, and their jurisdiction was limited – the damage had been done.[72]

For Melanchthon, it was imperative to consider every option, for he was convinced that, if no agreement could be reached, the ultimate result would be war. By September he was worrying constantly about impending catastrophe, aware of how few princes and cities supported them, although he underestimated how much the Catholic princes were fearful of giving too much power to an already overmighty emperor.[73] On the evangelical side were only a handful of rulers: the dukes of Lüneburg and Brandenburg, the prince of Anhalt, the Saxon Elector, Philip of Hesse, and only Nuremberg and Reutlingen had signed the confession; the sacramentarians did not sign.[74] Moreover, Philip might turn to the Zwinglians at any time, and Nuremberg was unlikely to risk opposing the emperor. Melanchthon understood, in ways that the isolated Luther could not, just how desperate the evangelical position would be, politically and militarily, if there was no deal.

For Luther, however, compromise was now out of the question. Letters he wrote just before the end of the Diet reveal just how far relations with Melanchthon had deteriorated.[75] On 20 September Luther told Melanchthon that people had been complaining about his conduct of the negotiations, and asked for more detail 'so that I can stop the mouths of your detractors'.[76] On the same day he wrote to Jonas without beating about the bush: he and Melanchthon had been entrusted with defending the gospel, 'but now from some of our people, important and many of them, thunder and lightning has reached me, that you betrayed the matter and for the sake of peace would concede more . . . So that I'm driven to say, if this is how things stand, then the Devil himself has made a pretty division amongst us.'[77] Luther knew that Melanchthon and the other Wittenbergers would most likely read this letter. Both were given to the Nuremberger Lazarus Spengler, but the Diet ended before he could deliver them. Spengler sent them back to Luther as soon as he realised there was no more opportunity for Melanchthon to make the damaging concessions Luther feared.[78]

Luther was, in any case, reconsidering his position about the Diet; the alarm of Baumgartner and the Nurembergers that negotiations with the Catholics risked losing 'God's favour, without winning the emperor's', made him think that he had let Melanchthon go too far.[79] Towards the end, he suddenly started to argue that negotiations had been a complete mistake all along and, in the months after they collapsed, he began to position Melanchthon as the man who wanted to make peace with the Catholics, conveniently ignoring how far he had gone along with it.[80] Melanchthon's role at Augsburg cemented the double leadership of the Reformation, but it also underlined the differences between the two men. In subsequent years double portraits of the pair went on sale, designed to scotch rumours of divisions, yet they created a strange visual impression. Rather than radiating concord and harmony, the bulky Luther steals most of the picture space; and the double portrait was oddly reminiscent of the marriage portrait with Katharina von Bora, Melanchthon now taking her place on the distaff side.

*

After months of hectic bargaining, the negotiations collapsed; on 23 September the emperor closed the Diet. Both sides had shown willingness to compromise and in the end the differences between them scarcely seemed big enough to justify the schism that resulted from the failure. But what finally kept the two sides apart was the absence of trust – on marriage, the sacraments and other issues, the evangelicals simply did not believe that the Catholics meant what they said, or that they would keep their word. They feared that concessions would lead to their being crushed at a Church council that would be held outside Germany and set up to defeat them.[81] The result was not inevitable, but rather a narrowly missed opportunity to prevent the splitting of the Catholic Church. This was why negotiations continued for so long, with one committee succeeding another, and why Charles had been willing to countenance ever more attempts to reach agreement. Had it been left to Melanchthon – who was an irenicist, not a conservative like Luther – a deal might have been done.

55. Lucas Cranach the Elder, *Martin Luther and Philipp Melanchthon*, 1543.

In early October 1530, Luther finally arrived back in Wittenberg, having spent half a year in the 'desert' of Coburg, surrounded by the cawing of the jackdaws. He longed to see his companions: 'Just come home!', he had written to the Augsburg delegation in mid-July.[82] He brushed off rumours of illness, and to prove his point he upbraided Katharina: 'you can see for yourself the books that I'm writing'.[83]

Luther had indeed been remarkably creative during his exile amongst the birds; he had finished the translation of the Old Testament, on which he had worked for twelve long years. But much of his creativity was powered by anger and hate. As Melanchthon sought to pacify, Luther poured out *A Revocation of Purgatory* – ironic, of course – the *Letter to the Cardinal Archbishop of Mainz*, and the *Propositions Against the Whole School of Satan and All the Gates of Hell* – all attacking Catholic theology and, when sold in Augsburg, giving him

a voice at the Diet.[84] In *Warning to his Dear Germans* (written in October but not printed until 1531), he laid into 'the shameless mouth and bloodthirsty sophist', his old enemy Dr Eck, and excoriated the extravagance and splendour of the Diet 'that would have shamed even Lord Envy and Mr Liar'.[85] But the very fluency of Luther's pen sprang from the ease with which he articulated familiar rhetoric. He repeated arguments he had first developed ten years before, now clothed in bitter polemic. He was increasingly speaking to the converted, not to those wrestling with doubt.

Indeed, he now risked becoming a parochial thinker. From the outset he had focused on his 'dear Germans' in contrast to the hated '*welsch*,' or Latins, and this always limited his ability to think about the Church as a whole.[86] This had been a strength, of course, for the Elector's manoeuvring had comprehensively excluded Zwingli and the sacramentarians from the Diet and allowed Luther's supporters to negotiate without the need to take their opinions into account. But in the longer term it showed a fateful lack of vision, for as the sacramentarian cause was taken up and spread further by John Calvin, their exclusion from the Peace of Augsburg in 1555, just as they had been excluded in 1530, made that treaty utterly unworkable, contributing eventually to the Thirty Years War.

# 16

# Consolidation

The Diet of Augsburg appeared to have resulted in a complete political impasse. But in the years that followed, efforts to defend Protestantism, avoid war and find a way forward continued. In February 1531, the Lutherans, under the leadership of electoral Saxony and Hesse, formed a defensive league, which became known as the League of Schmalkalden. It grew rapidly over the following years as more areas joined, and it soon became a major political force. Negotiations with the Catholics continued as well, now from a much stronger position; and in July 1532 the Peace of Nuremberg, signed by nine princes and twenty-four cities, secured a kind of informal toleration. The possessions of each side would be protected and the matter resolved at a future Church council, effectively lifting the Edict of Worms and its threatening provisions – and in practice recognising that neither side could gain a complete victory, at least for the moment. Politics began to drive religion, and the process by which the empire would eventually become a chessboard of different denominations was under way.

Over the next few years, and through a series of polemics, pamphlets, letters, disputes and negotiations with his rivals, Luther tacitly abandoned the project of reforming *the* Church. Instead he began to create a church of his own. Acting on the idea that the princes could be emergency bishops, which he had suggested in *To the Christian Nobility of the German Nation* in 1520, he set about reforming the Church in Saxony with the support of the Elector in 1527. Every parish was to be inspected, a process that would take several years, and which was now under the direction of the Elector and the Church acting together, not the bishops. In place of the liturgical experiment that had been such a feature of the early years of the Reformation, Luther gradually devised reformed liturgies for Wittenberg that were influential beyond it. And, as he received a steady stream of requests for advice, he had to hammer out the practical theology – on baptism, marriage, divorce and death – which was essential to forming a new Church. The man who had been convinced, in 1520, that all believers were equally priests, now had to decide questions about authority and structure within the Church. Should there be bishops, as he seemed to concede in 1530? Ferocious arguments with sacramentarians, supposedly to find common ground, in fact established clear and unbreachable distance with them in matters of both belief and practice, as Luther tried to convert them to his point of view rather than listen to them. Equally, he moved away from an early commitment that matters of belief should never be settled by force, though he would always remain queasy about punishing heretics. At the same time, he slowly approached the idea that it might be justifiable to resist the emperor in certain circumstances.

Shortly after the Diet ended, Luther had written in his *Warning to his Dear Germans* that if the emperor ordered them to take up arms against their fellow Lutherans, they should not obey; and that a persecuted Lutheran who resisted death rather than enduring suffering in a Christian manner should not be accounted rebellious.[1] This was not yet resistance to the emperor, but it went further than his position of 6 March 1530. The same October, he took the view that legal experts, not theologians, should decide if resistance to the emperor was ever justifiable. This position allowed him to support the Schmalkaldic League and its military objectives without developing a political theology that sanctioned resistance.[2]

Despite the political necessity for the evangelicals to make common cause, it continued to prove difficult to get their theologians to make peace with each other. From the Swiss and southern German perspective, it was imperative to reach an accord. If the Lutherans had seemed weak and isolated in Augsburg, this was even more true of the sacramentarians. Zwingli had composed his own articles of belief, but had been unable to present them; the Upper Germans had formulated a separate confession of faith as a compromise with Lutheranism, but this had been accepted by only four towns;[3] and as the Swiss refused to sign the document, which became known as the Tetrapolitana, they would not be admitted to the Schmalkaldic League.

Zwingli and the Swiss had always been aware of the looming danger of political isolation and had looked for allies ever since the Catholic Swiss cantons had formed an alliance against the evangelicals in 1524. Zwingli had hoped to join with Philip of Hesse, and even toyed with an alliance with France. In 1529 the Catholic cantons joined forces with Austria under the emperor's brother, Ferdinand, thereby creating a much more powerful coalition, and in 1531 war broke out.

Back in 1527, Luther's Nuremberg friend Andreas Osiander had predicted that 'Zwingli would come to ignominy within three years'.[4] He was a year out. In October 1531, barely four years later, the Zurichers, with their cannon, magnificent supplies and proud arms, were defeated at Kappel by the forces of the Catholic cantons. 'You told us they would run away, that their bullets would rebound on them . . . You cooked up this gruel and put the carrots in too – now you must help us eat it', a furious citizen-soldier shouted at Zwingli at the height of the battle.[5]

Zwingli himself was wounded, and then casually finished off by an ordinary halberdier. His body was quartered and burned by the executioner of Lucerne, and his ashes were mixed with dung.[6] He had been worse than a heretic: here was a cleric who had taken up arms, disgracing his cassock. The manner of his death was deeply shocking and it could not have better encapsulated the difference between Lutherans and south Germans. Zwingli died as a citizen of Zurich, fighting alongside the members of his community and fulfilling the oath that he, like all citizens, had sworn to defend their freedoms; twenty more clergy died alongside him at Kappel.[7] Luther still regarded the clergy as a separate group, set apart by their calling, whose role was never to fight. The son of a man who knew how to defend his honour with his fists, Luther remained a theologian and pastor, while Zwingli died a citizen and a man of action. Luther wrote his epitaph on the Zwinglian party in a letter to his friend Amsdorf: 'This is the result of the fame that they sought through blasphemies against the Communion of Christ.' Luther now claimed Osiander's prophecy as his own: 'I was a prophet, when I said that God would not allow these rabid . . . blasphemies.' He quoted Jesus to his table companions: 'He who takes the sword will die by the sword.'[8] Yet for all that he might rejoice at Zwingli's downfall, the Lutherans' own cause looked bleak.

*

Luther felt surrounded by enemies of the gospel and now the Anabaptists were added to their number. He had always treated the Anabaptists as if they were simply new followers of Müntzer and Karlstadt: they too were *Schwärmer*, enthusiasts like those he had repudiated in 1524, in *Against the Heavenly Prophets*. 'Anabaptists' was a term of abuse given to them by their opponents, and meant 'rebaptisers', but they did not in fact believe in repeating the sacrament. Most considered infant baptism to be invalid and advocated the baptism of adult believers in line with gospel teaching; some suspended baptism altogether. Some had earlier taken part in the Peasants' War and had been inspired by Müntzer's ideas of millenarian violence; others were pacifists who refused to swear oaths. For the most part, they were small, isolated knots of believers, good at communicating with each other over long distances, on the margins of their communities and used to avoiding conflict with the authorities.[9]

For reformers like Luther, who insisted that the Word of God must be the sole religious authority, it was not easy to counter beliefs which derived so firmly from the letter of Scripture. Luther's argument that godparents could make profession of faith on behalf of the infant had no basis in the Gospels, and instead rested on Church tradition – this from the man who at Worms rejected any argument derived from a non-scriptural source. On the whole, though, he did not spill much ink refuting Anabaptism itself, perhaps because he felt uncomfortable about his argument, perhaps because the prime concern was fighting the sacramentarians. In 1528 he wrote a pamphlet in the form of a letter to two pastors who had asked for help refuting Anabaptism: written at speed, its argument is contradictory, mainly claiming that the Anabaptists took a spiritualist approach to baptism. The authoritative Lutheran tract was written by Justus Menius in 1530, with Luther merely supplying an approving preface.[10]

But the encounter with Anabaptism was important because it highlights Luther's thought about the role of baptism and the nature of the Church, as he set about establishing the Church in Saxony. Baptism raised the fundamental question of who was a member: everyone in the community, or a minority, those who had been saved. Luther wanted an inclusive Church, with universal infant baptism, yet in his gloomier moments, he also thought that the true Church of genuine Christians was invisible and comprised only a handful of souls. Infant baptism cemented that universal membership of the Church and it aligned the community with the congregation: everyone who was baptised automatically belonged to it. Baptism and the Eucharist were the only two of the seven Catholic sacraments that Luther regarded as scriptural; he remained unsure about the status of confession. A conservative, he made few changes to the rite because he shared much of the Catholic view of it. He believed deeply that baptism initiated the struggle against the Devil, and it is striking how often he referred to baptism when writing about Satan. Baptism is the promise made to us by God, and faith is not required to merit it: this was the deeper reason why he rejected Anabaptism. Luther's theology shared nothing of the later Protestant emphasis on the experience of 'being saved', with which his insistence on 'faith alone' is so often confused. This also gave secular authority a role in regulating the external parameters of the Church and underpinned the alliance of ecclesiastical and political authority. Rejecting infant baptism would have meant disestablishing the Church and removing the partnership with the state; it was something that Luther would never contemplate giving up.

Not only did Luther insist on infant baptism, he also retained the powerful exorcisms which had been part of the ritual, even at first including the practice whereby the priest literally 'blew' the Devil out of the infant – another element of 'papist magic' which other reformers were keen to abolish.[11] Indeed, he told the story of the medical doctor who was very taken with the words spoken at a child's baptism, exclaiming 'If I knew that I had been baptised with the same words as this child, I would no longer fear the Devil!' The godparents reassured him that these were exactly the words that were said at his own baptism; and when, shortly after, the Devil appeared in the form of a goat, the doctor grasped him by the horns and he disappeared, leaving him with the horns as a trophy.[12]

Luther proved a traditionalist too when it came to godparenthood, an institution of which he made good use, choosing the godparents of each of his children carefully to cement his ties of kinship with the Saxon nobility, other reformers and friends such as Cranach. For their part, the Lutheran reformers regularly chose each other as godparents, underlining the intimate ties between them.[13] The practice contributed to the increasing tendency for the evangelical pastorate to become set apart from the rest of society, a close-knit group that intermarried and recruited its successors from amongst its own descendants. The Catholic clergy had never constituted a caste in this sense, because its members were supposed to be celibate.

Yet despite the centrality of baptism to his theology, and his conservative attitude to the rite, Luther was less certain how to treat Anabaptists. He had been happy to agree during the Augsburg negotiations that Anabaptists, like sacramentarians, should be treated as heretics, but until then he had also consistently maintained that no one should be executed for their faith; heretics would suffer in hell, and only if they were guilty of insurrection and rejecting secular authority were they to be punished.[14] But Melanchthon, in line with the imperial mandate against Anabaptists of 1528, began to take the view that all Anabaptists were guilty of the crime of sedition, and that secular authorities ought to punish Anabaptists 'on body', rather than just with fines. While Luther still argued in 1528 that Anabaptists should not be executed, because 'It is not right, and it pains me greatly, that people kill, murder and burn these poor folk so horribly', by February Melanchthon had begun to advocate their execution, and the following year Luther was agreeing that 'although it seems cruel to punish them with the sword, they themselves are being even more cruel in damning the ministry of the Word'.[15]

Even if Luther felt queasy about it, he did not object to harsh punishment. When Fritz Erbe in the village of Herda near Eisenach refused to baptise his son in 1531, he was gaoled. Imprisoned a second time in 1533, his fame spread and he became something of a celebrity in the town, so he was moved to the Wartburg, where Luther had stayed after the Diet of Worms. Here he was held in isolation from 1540 until his death in 1548, in a prison cell underground. Luther would have known about Erbe and his miserable fate.[16]

Then, in 1534, a group of Anabaptists actually gained power in Münster, with consequences that would appal contemporaries. Reform had started there in a fairly conventional manner. As in so many towns across the empire, Lutherans had grown in numbers and been successful in council elections. But what had begun as a politically conservative Lutheran reformation suddenly changed as the leading preacher Bernhard Rothmann fell under the influence of sacramentarianism, and began to espouse a radical populism. Münster now became the focus of millenarian hopes, and Anabaptists started to flood into the town from all over northern Germany and the Low Countries, inspired by the prophecies of the Strasbourg preacher Melchior Hoffman to turn the city into the New Jerusalem, soon forming a sizeable group within the original population of around 9,000 townspeople.[17] Up to this point, Münster's Reformation was rather like the radical phase of the Reformation in Wittenberg, with city council and preachers working together to introduce a godly society, but in September 1534, the charismatic Jan van Leiden took over, establishing a theocracy with him as its head and the old mayor Bernhard Knipperdolling his 'swordbearer'.[18]

The bishop of Münster besieged the city with a coalition that included not only the archbishop of Cologne and the Catholic duke of Cleve but also the Lutheran Philip of Hesse, who all promised financial aid. Jan van Leiden tried to send out 'apostles' to other Anabaptist communities to recruit reinforcements, but Münster was isolated and in a state of military emergency, and few could get through. It mustered its menfolk to defend the town and try to repel the forces of the bishop but many of them were killed in the fighting. The apocalyptic rhetoric of Leiden now became reality, and he took on the role of judge and executioner, going so far as to behead an accused spy himself and introducing polygamy so that the Anabaptists would be able to recreate the twelve tribes of Israel.[19]

In June 1535, after a siege that lasted a little over a year, the city fell. Jan van Leiden and two other leaders were brutally tortured and executed in January 1536, their remains put in iron cages which were hung from the tower of St Lambert's Church, where the cages can still be seen. It is difficult to know exactly what happened in Münster as all the reports we have were composed by the victors and are hostile, and the town records were largely destroyed. The episode is usually viewed as an aberration in the history of the Reformation, and this is certainly how Luther regarded it. Most shocking to contemporaries was its introduction of polygamy. Yet although Luther himself

56. Heinrich Aldegrever, *Jan of Leyden, 'A King of the Anabaptists'*, 1536. Leading artists
soon produced engravings of Leiden and his wife, Queen Divara: common folk who
had made themselves into royalty, they epitomised the dangers of Anabaptism.
Contemporaries wrote of Leiden's two golden crowns; of the orb and sceptre he
carried as he sat on a horse, his retinue dressed in blue and green; and of the two
youths who rode behind him, one carrying a Bible and crown, the other a naked
sword bearing the legend 'God's power is my strength'.

condemned the Anabaptists for their theological arrogance and their
contempt for true doctrine, and though he condemned them as
'Epicureans',[20] he had consistently pointed out that the Old Testament

patriarchs had practised polygamy, an attitude that would later have important consequences.

*

In the meantime Martin Bucer had not given up trying to come to an agreement with the Wittenbergers. He had visited a grumpy Luther in Coburg Castle in late September 1530 on his way back from the Diet of Augsburg, and he finally persuaded him to begin negotiations with the sacramentarians.[21] As Luther put it in early 1531, he had begun to see 'how necessary your fellowship is for us . . . I have become so much aware of this that I am convinced that all the gates of hell, the whole papacy, all of Turkey, the whole world, all the flesh, and whatever evils there are could not harm the gospel at all, if only we were of one mind.'[22] This struck a different tone from his usual conviction that his very isolation in his struggle against the forces of Satan proved Christ was on his side, and was not one he sustained for long.[23] He continued to be wary of Bucer, who travelled tirelessly in Switzerland and amongst the cities of Upper Germany to try to produce a formula all parties could approve. The effort took him nearly four years, but when he did finally arrive at a formula Luther would accept, the Swiss then rejected it out of hand.

In 1536 a meeting was at last arranged between the Lutherans and the Upper German sacramentarians, to be held at Eisenach.[24] In the event it had to be held in Wittenberg, for Luther was too ill to travel and so the discussions took place in his house. At first only Bucer and Wolfgang Capito, the two Strasbourgers, were permitted to join in the discussions, in which they were massively outnumbered by the Wittenbergers. From Luther's point of view, the talks were not so much to reach a compromise as to signal an acceptance of the Lutheran line, with Bucer and Capito there to agree that the body of Christ truly was present in the sacrament. Even then, Luther nearly scuppered the agreement, delivering a rambling diatribe in which he accused Zwingli and Oecolampadius of having published 'godless, dreadful false teaching', of misleading the people, and of supporting revolt. It would be better 'if one left things as they were, than that one made a fictional, coloured concord which would make the matter, which is bad now, a hundred times worse'. Bucer was visibly shocked by Luther's apparent rejection of a concord he had worked so hard to broker. Luther insisted 'with great earnestness, that either there should be a true unity, or none at all'.

When the two sides met again the next day, on 23 May, Luther asked whether each of the visitors 'would recant what he taught and spread about against the Lord Christ, Scripture and the teaching and view of the Church', and whether they would henceforth 'constantly and in one spirit teach the true presence of the body of Christ in or with the bread of the Communion of the Lord'. Bucer and Capito were compelled to make this humiliating admission of error, after which Luther and his followers left the room to discuss what to do next. They then demanded that the sacramentarians concede that the unworthy, not just the believers, received the true body and blood of Christ in Communion; that is, the Lutherans wanted them to admit that Christ was really present in the sacrament, not just 'present' depending on the faith and worthiness of the believer.[25]

Luther had got the recantation he had longed for. He then heaped a further humiliation on the visitors, asking each of them to repeat their confession individually, including that the sacrament was present to the unworthy. Finally the longed-for agreement had been reached and Bucer and Capito were weeping when the theologians all shook hands. Luther advised them to introduce the new teaching to their congregations gradually, so they would not notice – a rather cynical counsel and a gross underestimation of ordinary people's investments in theological issues. The next day – Ascension Day – he preached on Mark 16:15: 'Go out into all the world and preach the gospel to all creatures.' The chronicler Myconius, who heard the sermon, wrote, 'I have heard Luther preach often, but at that time it seemed to me as if it was not just him speaking, but that he thundered out of the heavens themselves in the name of Christ.'[26]

Luther seemed to have won a complete victory, but it was a hollow triumph. Bucer had got the Upper German cities to agree to the Augsburg confession, a major diplomatic coup which would strengthen and protect the Reformation within the empire. He then tried to persuade the Swiss to accept the concord, even letting it be known that Karlstadt wanted to agree with the Wittenbergers, for he was sick of the whole dissension. Luther, however, was implacable; when at last the Swiss wrote him a conciliatory letter in January 1537, he waited until December before replying and was decidedly off-hand when he did. His sickness, he explained, had held him up, and the fact 'that there is so much business in my head, not to speak of thoughts, that I can't speak and deal with each individual as though I had nothing but one or two things to do'.[27] He went on to insist on a clear acceptance of his position, the result being that by autumn 1538, the clergy of Zurich, Basle and Bern had all concluded that the project of gaining union with the Wittenbergers had failed. Other cities fell away as well: in Augsburg, whose adherence to the concord was crucial, Johann Forster was appointed on Luther's recommendation, but overplayed his hand by vehemently accusing the former Zwinglian preacher Michael Keller and others of deviating from the concord, to such an extent that he alienated the council and was eventually forced to leave; the council then appointed Ambrosius Blaurer, a sacramentarian.[28] Even in his own Strasbourg, Bucer was not able to hold the line. Matthäus Zell, one of the most important of the Strasbourg reformers, continued to preach the sacramentarian doctrine, and there were deep divisions amongst the city clergy.

For Luther, since the Wittenberg concord was not a reconciliation or a compromise, but rather to establish that the beliefs of the sacramentarians were heretical, it was imperative to assert the truth against the forces of Satan. Although both sides had undertaken not to attack one another in print, in 1539 he issued his *On the Councils and the Churches*, a long tract which argued that any future Church council must be bound by the Word of God and finally marked the founding of his own church. In it, he also accused Zwingli of being guilty of the Nestorian heresy.[29] This was a caricature of Zwingli's actual beliefs, and not surprisingly, the Swiss were furious. The Zurich pastors wrote emphatically rejecting the slur.[30]

The Nestorians insisted on the absolute separation of divine and human nature in the person of Jesus Christ. The sacramentarians' starting point was that there was a fundamental division between things of the flesh and things of the spirit, hence their view that Christ's body could not be both in heaven and in the Host; but insisting that the sacrament was a spiritual event was not to deny the humanity of Christ. Luther was prepared to make the accusation because by this stage too sharp a distinction between flesh and spirit seemed to him to undermine the Real Presence, a doctrine which was starting to take on the status of a totemic truth. He went still further in his *Admonition to Prayer Against the Turks* in 1541, where he listed the followers of Müntzer and Zwingli and the Anabaptists in the same breath as 'cursedly evil sects and heresies'.[31] Then, in 1544, he lost all restraint in *A Brief Confession of Dr Martin Luther on the Holy Sacrament*, in which he called Zwingli a 'heathen' who held beliefs about the sacrament which meant that 'the salvation of his soul must be doubted'.[32] The work began with Luther invoking his own impending death – 'I, who am now going towards my grave' – and it enshrined his insulting treatment of Zwingli within a major doctrinal writing, as his testament. The Zwinglians then published Luther's confession alongside their own statement of faith concerning the sacrament, and so began another unseemly pamphlet war between the sacramentarians and the Lutherans.[33] By the time Luther died in 1546, it looked as if the Protestants were hopelessly divided, their antagonisms more bitter than ever.[34]

*

Luther kept on attacking the sacramentarian position despite the political need for their support because it struck at the heart of a theology that was slowly coalescing into a Church; he was no longer, it seemed, interested in reforming the whole of Christianity, but rather saw it in local terms only. As a result, he was less and less interested in compromise, and more determined to protect doctrinal purity in accordance with his own beliefs. He and Melanchthon had been closely involved with setting up the evangelical Church in electoral Saxony with the Elector's support, and Luther was now more focused on protecting the purity of this creation.[35]

The emphasis on the Incarnation and on the materiality of religion which was so central to this developing vision meant that he found it in some ways easier to make common cause with Catholic traditions than to ally with those who were part of the evangelical movement. He retained the elevation of the sacrament, abolishing it only when Karlstadt died in 1541;[36] and in Wittenberg in 1543, when some Communion wine was spilled on a woman's jacket and the back of her pew, he and Bugenhagen not only licked it off her coat but went so far as to cut out the bits of the jacket they had been unable to clean, plane away the sections of her pew where the wine had splashed, and burn the lot. The body and blood of Christ had to be treated with utmost respect.[37] Indeed, it was this insistence on the literal enactment of the sacrament which made Luther so adamant that it be given in two kinds in the first place.

When the discussions with Bucer were just beginning, Luther wrote to him demanding that he admit that in the sacrament, Christ really was received in the mouth and eaten with the teeth – or as he put it in January 1531, they should agree 'that Christ's body is also present to the mouth, or to the body, or in the bread and given to the mouth'.[38] At Wittenberg in 1536, Luther emphasised that it was no use going on about the 'spiritual reception' of Christ and the spiritual eating, since they all agreed on that. Rather, he wanted to get rid of the idea that there was nothing to the ceremony *beyond* commemoration, that one just 'remembered' the Lord 'and has him present only in empty imagination'. An abstract statement that Christ was present in the flesh was not enough; it had to be fully understood as a physical reality. His insistence that the impious as well as the pious truly received the sacrament and Christ's body, sprang from the same belief: if Christ's presence in the sacrament was a physical reality, he was present regardless of the faith or the attitude of the recipient.

The sacramentarians mocked the Lutherans as 'cannibals' who ate Christ's flesh and worshipped a 'baked' God. To his opponents, Luther appeared to be clinging to 'papist magic' – to the idea that through the words of the consecration, the priest performs a miracle. Certainly, he seems ridiculously obsessed by teeth and chewing: a grisly literalism that even Melanchthon reputedly found hard to take.[39] He was not disturbed that this might lead ordinary folk to think that the body of Christ could be digested. As he saw it, the reality of the comfort offered by the receipt of the body of Christ was far more important than worrying about whether digestion dishonoured Christ.

Although at one level he seemed unable to break with medieval tradition, at another his thought was more radical than that of the sacramentarians, as by refusing to separate the physical and the spiritual, he also rejected the powerful ascetic strain in Christian tradition. By this point in his life, as we have noted, Luther was no longer the thin, intense-looking monk, and his fabled love of German beer and wine, his enjoyment of food and his sedentary life had all taken their toll. Moreover, his marriage had opened him to the joys of sexuality and of seeing his children grow. And here too he took pleasure in the physical aspects of life. He wrote to Jonas of his delight when his son 'Little Hans' learnt to defecate with bent knees: he learnt so well, Luther said, that he 'crapped in every corner of the room'.[40]

Unlike most Christian thinkers, Luther's theology was profoundly *embodied*. He did not take what would in the next century become the Cartesian path: the insistence that mind and body are separate, and that our physical existence is inferior. He did of course distinguish between flesh and spirit – every theologian at the time did – but his emphasis was always on integration, not on splitting the two. He was well aware that by rejecting the Aristotelian explanation of transubstantiation in terms of 'accidents' and 'essences' he had put no philosophical or rational alternative in its place; instead, it was a matter of faith, exceeding reason.

The logic of Luther's denial of free will and his insistence on grace meant that God must have decided who is saved. But to those who worried about whether they were amongst the elect or not, Luther – unlike the more systematic John Calvin – responded that we should just not think about something which is beyond our grasp. A similar approach coloured his views of the afterlife, and inflected the way the Church he established dealt with death. Rejecting the sacrament of extreme unction, he developed a more pastoral approach that derived from his own honesty; when comforting the dying, he preferred to emphasise Christ's saving love.[41] Heaven should not be thought about; it certainly had no geographical location. When he light-heartedly talked about it at dinner with friends, he imagined that 'There will be such joy that we will completely forget eating and drinking, sleeping and so forth. It will be a completely different life. There we will spit at pounds and pence!'[42]

In May 1531, Luther wrote a last letter to his mother Margarethe as she lay dying. He said little about the afterlife and nothing about her seeing her dead husband or lost children again; rather, he reminded her that her present suffering was nothing compared to that suffered by the godless 'when one person is beheaded, another burned, a third drowned'. Her illness was sent by God's grace and bore no comparison with what Christ had suffered for us. For modern readers, who often find it difficult to confront death, Luther's frank refusal to pretend that all will be well, and willingness to refer to gruesome executions at such a moment, is astonishing. Yet he prided himself on his ability to comfort the dying.[43]

Luther was both wise and practical about death and mourning. When Cranach's artistically gifted and beloved son Hans died in Italy, Luther tried to ease his parents' feelings of guilt, telling them that 'I would be as much to blame as you, because I also advised him to go [to Italy].' He told his old friend to be calm: 'God wants to break your will, because he attacks where it hurts most, for our mortification.' Hans, he went on, was a good lad who died before the evil of the world overcame him. Here too his advice follows a careful progression, first recognising the parents' feelings of responsibility, next confronting their agony directly and then turning towards God. He ended by admonishing Cranach and his wife not to mourn and weep excessively, but to 'eat and drink', and take care of themselves so that they may serve others: 'Grief and care only crush your bones.'[44] And when his beloved daughter Magdalena fell mortally ill, he sent a cart to his son Hans's school to bring him home at once, because 'they loved each other very much'. Luther was distraught on her death, yet two months later he was ordering Hans to 'overcome his tears in a manly way', and refusing to allow him to return home, perhaps because he feared that if Hans gave way to grief he would suffer melancholy.[45]

*

When Luther famously burned the papal bull and the books of canon law outside the Elster Gate in Wittenberg in December 1520, he overturned all the rules that governed marriage and sexuality; and so from the start, the new Church was confronted with all the personal dilemmas that flowed from allowing divorce, rethinking incest and redefining marriage as a secular matter, not a sacrament. He put Scripture in the place of Church law but, as his attitude to the Anabaptists revealed, he was not prepared to rely on that absolutely either. Instead he relied on faith, a great wellspring for a preacher, but a shaky foundation for a Church.

Abidingly suspicious of rules, Luther always advised princes not to follow the letter of the law but to reach a judgement 'from free reason', citing the story of a magnate who had slept with the wife of a man

he had imprisoned, promising to give her husband back in return, and
the next day sent her the executed husband's head. The judge in the
case condemned the magnate to marry the widow, so making her
heir to all his goods, and the next day, he ordered the magnate's execution. No law could have prescribed such a penalty but 'everyone',
Luther opined, 'must agree and find written in their heart that thus
it must be'.[46]

Like the prince who determined issues of justice, the pastor who
dealt with marital issues had to see the issues in the round and arrive
at a judgement that fitted the circumstances, using biblical principles.
This could be a charter for moral chaos, and the new Church made
some hair-raising mistakes, most notably approving Philip of Hesse's
bigamy, an error which seriously harmed the evangelical cause and
weakened their political position. But its deeper, and abiding, legacy
was to ally the pastor's authority to marital guidance, so that helping
people find their way through conjugal turmoil became one of the
chief duties of the clergy.

When Henry VIII wanted a divorce, Luther had always insisted that
the king's marriage to Catherine of Aragon was valid, because Old
Testament law commended marriage to a brother's widow: only papal
law condemned it on grounds of consanguinity. Here Luther argued
that Scripture, not human invention, must be followed, and in any
case, he sympathised with Catherine of Aragon, who was the emper-
or's aunt.[47] This was not a politically expedient line to take, and it
poisoned English relations with Saxony. Luther's mistrust of Henry
VIII later damaged discussions about England joining the Schmalkaldic
League, which would have strengthened both the league and the
evangelical party in England. Melanchthon, more pliant, but unable
to agree to a royal divorce because of Luther's stalwart opposition,
seems to have entertained the idea that Henry might commit bigamy,
marrying Anne Boleyn without repudiating Catherine, a solution that
had the additional merit of not disinheriting Catherine's daughter
Mary.[48]

Henry, however, was in distant England; Philip of Hesse, the leading
Lutheran prince, could not be evaded when he asked for advice about
his own unhappy marriage in 1539. Rather than continue in a life of
'evil and whoredom', the syphilitic landgrave had set his eye on the
seventeen-year-old Margarethe von der Saale, whose mother would

only agree to a union if they married.[49] As the case was presented to Luther, Philip, tortured by his conscience, and racked by sexual desire, was unable to receive Communion and wanted to know how to make his situation acceptable to God. As he explained: 'Since I am of such a temperament, as the doctors know, and it often happens, that I have to be away at League and Imperial meetings, where people live it up, take physical pleasures and so forth. How I can manage there without a wife, since I can't always take numbers of court women with me, is terrible to think.'[50] His wife, however, had been faithful to him, so divorce was not an option. Even had she sued for divorce – and a Lutheran marriage court would certainly have granted her one given the patent adultery – Philip, as the guilty party, would (like Henry VIII) have been prohibited from remarrying.

The landgrave's position in the sacramentarian dispute had always been that of mediator, and although he had officially taken Luther's side he had never repudiated the Zwinglians. Indeed, he had been careful to distance himself from Luther's line at Augsburg, never accusing the south Germans of heresy and insisting on their protection; and when he drew up a new Church ordinance in 1538 it had been to Bucer, not Luther, that he turned first of all.[51] This meant that the Wittenbergers could not afford to alienate him; and Philip knew this full well; in the letter asking for advice, he cannily pointed out that he might even be forced to seek a papal dispensation if the reformers would not help him.[52] After considering the case in detail, and with Bucer acting as mediator, Melanchthon and Luther signed a memorial on 10 December 1539, in which they agreed that the landgrave could marry his concubine in secret, while remaining publicly married to his wife. This solution followed the example of the polygamous patriarchs of the Old Testament; and Luther himself had been rather willing to dissolve marital partnerships completely in circumstances where the old Church courts would certainly not even have granted separations 'from bed and board' (that is, separations without the right to remarry). Much of Luther's concern in marriage cases was pastoral, and as a result he tended to take the side of those whose dilemmas he could identify with, trying to find a solution which would help conscience.

Philip went ahead and held a wedding on 4 March 1540 to which several dignitaries were invited. Melanchthon, who was with the landgrave at the time, was inveigled into attending, as was Bucer; and the delighted landgrave sent Luther a cartload of wine, writing to him of his joy that, because his new wife was a relation of Katharina von Bora, he and Luther were now related.[53] The scandalous news soon got out, tarnishing the reformers' reputations by association. Luther's reaction was to deny everything. Unluckily for Luther, however, the duke of Saxony kidnapped the girl's mother and forced her to surrender a copy of the marriage contract; and the landgrave, of course, possessed a signed copy of the memorial of advice, and he was not slow to remind Luther of this fact.[54]

Luther now argued that he had only countenanced the bigamy on condition that it was kept strictly secret, but this hardly looked like a principled stand. Meanwhile the landgrave's preachers not only approved the bigamy, but one of them, Johannes Lening of Melsung, published a pamphlet defending it, to the great embarrassment of the evangelical movement, especially when Philip sent eighty copies for distribution to influential people.[55] For the Catholics, the affair was a propaganda gift, and it seriously compromised the evangelicals' political position, as the scandal created the possibility of imperial proceedings that might lead to his deposition.

Luther's advice in the bigamy affair looks like the triumph of expediency over wisdom. In fact, his advice and insistence on secrecy were not just expedients. He had always retained a strong belief in the power of confession and insisted that confessional advice should never be revealed – a line that would have been easier to maintain had the landgrave's copy of the memorial of advice not found its way into the hands of the new duke of Saxony. Unlike his brother Georg, Heinrich (who succeeded him in 1539) was a Lutheran, but was as dedicated as his brother had been to the interests of his lands, and the affair was political dynamite in the context of the long-standing uneasy relations between Hessians and Saxons. The electoral Saxons, who stood to gain if the landgrave died without an heir, were determined not to recognise any children of the bigamous marriage, hoping his two legitimate children might not reach adulthood.[56]

Yet Luther's signing of the memorial was fully consistent with his long-held views on marriage and on the body. Sexual expression was fundamental to how God created humans, Luther believed, and few could be sexually continent. This attitude was also part of a whole understanding of health in which the release of sexual fluids was vital to humoral balance. If sex outside marriage was sinful, the way to make sexual relations pure was to marry. This is what Luther had urged monks and nuns to do, and in 1519 he had advised women who could not have children with their husbands to have children with the husband's brother secretly, counsel which he repeated in his sermon on marriage in 1522 – of which the landgrave now gleefully reminded him.[58] In the end, Philip brazened it out, and bore children with both wives, while Luther admitted his mistake in private but did not waver from his determination to deny his advice in public.

★

As the preparations for the Church council which Charles V had promised finally got under way, Luther firmly rejected any hope that such a council might rectify the abuses of the Church. In 1539 the

57. and 58. Portraits of the Elector and Anna Kasper Dornle. Luther knew that the bachelor Friedrich the Wise had kept a mistress for many years, and it was rumoured that he had married her secretly.[59] In 1525, the year he died, the Elector had two nine-inch wooden boxes made. Inside were relief portraits, one box containing his own, the other an image labelled 'Anna Rasper [sic] Dornle's Stepdaughter'. The workmanship is of the highest quality. Visible only when the boxes are opened, they are monuments to a secret love. Her hair is braided under a fine hairnet, and she is dressed as a respectable woman. Modelled on the double portraits of married couples that were so popular in the early sixteenth century, they commemorated a partnership that was neither fleeting nor shameful. And as the world in that century was made anew, it was not surprising that reformers might have entertained the idea of regularising such unions.[60]

publication of *On the Councils and the Churches* marked his final break with the medieval tradition of conciliarism, the idea that a Church council was superior to the Pope and was the chief hope of reform. He was excluded from the talks with Cardinal Contarini at the Diet of Regensburg in 1541, when the emperor attempted once more to reach unity between the Catholics and the Lutherans. Melanchthon took part and the two sides reached agreement on justification, but not on papal primacy or on the Eucharist. Luther thundered from the sidelines, warning that 'man is justified by faith apart from works of law . . . Let the Devil, Eck, Mainz, Heinz and anyone else rage against this. We shall see what they win.'[60] His lack of interest in the proceedings at Regensburg reflected his increasingly parochial understanding of the Church.

At the meetings which resulted in the Wittenberg concord, Luther had acted out his role as 'the father' of the movement, the title even the sacramentarians accorded him.[61] In reality, however, much of the leadership of the Reformation had long since been ceded to Melanchthon. When the English representatives of Henry VIII wanted to reach an accord with the Saxons, and when the French envoys of Francis I embarked on negotiations, it was to Melanchthon they wanted to speak, not Luther.[62] His ill health held the movement to ransom, as negotiations had to be broken off or rescheduled because of his infirmities. Anger had always been allied to his greatest spurts of creativity, but now his irascibility made him a liability as a leader.

# 17

# Friends and Enemies

Within Wittenberg, Luther had no direct institutional power; he held no positions other than that of town preacher and professor in the theology faculty. But he did have direct access to the Elector and other members of the ruling family,[1] and he had his loyal inner circle – Justus Jonas, Johannes Bugenhagen, Philipp Melanchthon, Veit Dietrich, Georg Rörer, the young theologian Caspar Cruciger – whom he called the 'Wittenbergers'.[2] Spalatin in Altenburg and Johann Agricola in Eisleben were close enough to be part of this group. Wenzeslaus Linck in Nuremberg was a friend from the very first days, whom Luther described as 'one of my dearest friends on earth'.[3] Jonas, who had once worshipped Erasmus, transferred his affection wholesale to Luther, whom he always respectfully addressed as 'father'; part of the strength of their bond derived from their shared experience of melancholy.[4] No stranger to grief, seven of Jonas's thirteen children by his first marriage had died, his thirteen-year-old son drowning in the River Saale in 1541 and his wife dying in childbirth the following year, together with the baby.

Luther, who scarcely left Wittenberg in his last years, lived inside these protective circles of friends and allies just as his Saxon Church existed within the safety of the Elector's lands. The friendships mixed private interaction with an overriding sense of duty to the new Church, in Wittenberg and beyond. In Wittenberg, surrounded by students and people from all over the empire eager to study with Luther and Melanchthon, it was easy to forget just how precarious the Reformation outside the town still was, and how chaotic the situation created by Luther's assault upon the time-honoured customs, beliefs and practices of Catholicism. Men who had once been Catholic priests or monks did not always succeed in becoming

59. This image, which prefaced the Frankfurt pirate edition of Luther's *Table Talk* in 1569, shows the inner circle seated around a table with Luther on the right; Johann Forster and Paul Eber are shown in addition to the original 'team'.

exemplary evangelical pastors. The pastor of Sausedlitz went around with a rifle, which he delighted in firing in the village. He hung out in the tavern and maltreated his wife, starting a suspicious liaison with a local widow.[5] Those who copied Luther and excoriated the failings of the elite from the pulpit could soon find themselves isolated: no fewer than fifteen individuals, including the mayor, were happy to testify against the preacher of Werdau, who had insulted the councillors as 'Herods' and 'Caiaphases'.[6] Johannes Heine, the pastor at Elssnig near Torgau, had a sideline in herbal and magical healing, claiming that his cures were not magical but accomplished 'through God's grace, which was given to him'. His unworthy conduct was reported during a Church Visitation and he was thrown into prison.[7] Even Lutheran loyalists were not immune to the attractions of such quasi-magical practice. Luther had to write a long letter to Jonas's wife telling her that while it might seem like a good idea to read a gospel passage aloud as a cure, the fact that it had to be done at a certain place and time suggested that it was not pious but superstitious. One pastor refused to allow warm water for baptism because, he argued, it was a mixture of the elements of fire and water and therefore was not pure water – Luther made short shrift of this, telling him he should consult those who knew their philosophy.[8] The new pastors were meant to be theologically trained, but there were not enough of them, and in rural Saxony, local tradition and magical belief would not simply melt away in the face of university knowledge.

Luther's influence spread through his personal connections and was limited by them as well. They are thus highly important for understanding his achievements; not only friendships but also the many, bitter fights with allies and enemies alike were integral to the nature and development of the Reform movement. Georg Witzel is a good example – a former acolyte, he turned on Luther and published a stinging attack in 1532, which tried to outdo his former mentor's style. Luther, he wrote, 'maintains, furthers and drives it all alone, and according to his brain, makes and unmakes, turns and reverses, says and lies, appoints and sacks everything according to his inclination and pleasure'. He was driven by his 'raging, stormy, inconstant proud head, [and] bloodthirsty heart'.[9]

Luther's world was primarily focused on the university. He was at once part of Wittenberg society and yet he did not think of himself as an ordinary citizen, in the way that Zwingli, for example, had done in Zurich. His exemption from the Türkensteuer in 1542, a levy on every inhabitant of the Reich to finance the campaign against the Turks, was an evident demonstration of this.[10] Every other Wittenberg clergyman paid up without demur, but Luther was permitted to estimate the value of his properties himself, and the Elector paid the tax he owed. It is significant that in his letters from Coburg, Luther envisaged his son playing with Melanchthon's and Jonas's sons, or with the other children in the monastery – but not with those of the Wittenberg citizens.[11] His milieu consisted of those lodging with him, his acolytes and dependants, and the guests he invited to dinner. He called the members of the household – who would have numbered between forty and fifty people at any given time, including servants, lodgers and visitors – his 'Quirites', a classical Latin term for Roman citizens.[12] A dig at the 'Roman' Pope, it suggested that, unlike the papal court, his was a community of equals, despite the patriarchal structure he had in fact created.[13]

Even so, he knew some townsfolk well. His close friendship with Lucas Cranach stretched back to his early days in Wittenberg. Hans Lufft the printer did business for him and occasionally acted as his business agent at the city court, although Luther sharply criticised him over his daughter's wedding in 1538, famed for its extravagance when Lufft was in financial straits.[14] Peter Beskendorf, a barber and surgeon, was another long-standing friend, and Luther acted as godparent to his grandchild. He also dedicated a brief treatise on prayer to him: 'Just as a good barber has to concentrate his thoughts, mind and eyes exactly on the razor and the hair . . . for if he is wanting to chat a lot at the same time, or think or look at something else, he'll probably cut someone's mouth and nose or even slit their throat.'[15] When Beskendorf stabbed and killed his son-in-law at the dinner table in a fit of drunken stupidity only a few months later, Luther loyally interceded for him; Beskendorf was convicted only of manslaughter and exiled.[16] Amongst the town councillors, Luther was acquainted with the Krapp family, and he befriended Tilo Dhen, whose wife died in his arms; Ambrosius Reuter married the niece of Luther's best friend, Hans Reinicke, thus providing a link between Wittenberg and Mansfeld.[17] As the university grew in size and as the town became more prosperous, more of the academics became town councillors, entwining the academic and political elites ever more tightly. The university, which had prospered so greatly through Luther's fame, now dominated the town.

Luther, who suffered from spiritual struggles all his life, seems to have been particularly adept at drawing to him those who were in

60. Lucas Cranach the Elder, *Johannes Bugenhagen*, 1532.

mourning, or suffering from what we would today call depression, a staple topic of conversation at table.[18] He was, for example, very close to the Weller brothers, Peter and Hieronymus, both former students at Wittenberg, who visited often and stayed in Luther's house when he was at Coburg Castle during the Augsburg Diet in 1530. Hieronymus and his sister Barbara suffered from melancholy and from *Anfechtungen*, and some of Luther's most moving letters of spiritual comfort were written to them: 'I know the sickness well and have lain in that hospital until I nearly suffered eternal death', he wrote to Barbara. If she started to worry about whether she was elected or not, he told her to spit those thoughts out, 'just as someone immediately spits it out if dung falls into his mouth'.[19] But he thought sufferers had a duty to repulse melancholic thoughts – 'you can't stop the birds flying over your head, but you don't have to let them nest in your hair'.[20]

Melancholy also played a part in his friendship with Bugenhagen, or as Luther liked to call him, 'Dr Pommer', a former teacher and priest who was pastor of Wittenberg from 1523 (with interruptions) and acted as Luther's confessor until the reformer's death. The son of a town councillor in Pomerania, he was one of the few of Luther's followers to come from a region where Low German was spoken, and he was therefore sent to implement the Reformation in Pomerania as well as in Braunschweig, Hamburg, Lübeck, and even Denmark.[21] Crucially important in comforting Luther during his breakdown in 1527, he repeatedly provided the pastoral care Luther craved during his periods of melancholy, just as Staupitz had done.[22]

Amsdorf was another close friend on whom Luther relied, and whose intellectual formation was similar to his own. He was of noble birth, the nephew of Staupitz, and his father was a courtier of Friedrich the Wise. At Wittenberg, in a job Staupitz had secured for him, he had taught the philosophy of Duns Scotus, Staupitz's favoured philosopher.[23] He and Luther had first met in 1508 but Amsdorf was particularly drawn by Luther's theses which his student Bartholomäus Bernhardi defended in 1516; from then on, he became a doughty and determined supporter of the Reformation, devoting his entire energies to spreading Luther's message.[24] He apparently remained a bachelor, though Katharina von Bora reputedly insisted she would marry only Luther or him.[25]

Neither Amsdorf nor Bugenhagen, around Luther's age, could be considered his intellectual peers, and otherwise he seems to have found it easier to sustain close friendships with younger men who could not even pretend to be on equal terms with him. Johann Agricola, Jonas and Melanchthon for example were all a good decade younger. Luther knew how to attract the young: from his time in the monastery, he was used to employing assistants to whom he could delegate. His secretaries Veit Dietrich (who became his confidant during his time in Coburg Castle) and Georg Rörer were both central to transmitting the cult of Luther's memory after his death. Of the rising generation he trusted Caspar Cruciger as an excellent theologian, and in 1539 nominated him to be his successor: he is 'absolutely outstanding', he declared, a model 'on whom I'm relying after my death'.[26]

*

Such praise and support, however, could be withdrawn the moment Luther was displeased, and opponents mocked the bitter divisions caused by his willingness to turn on friends and allies. A long series of public and painful ruptures punctuated the 1530s and 40s and the centrality of Luther to the movement made these enmities existential for the Reformation.[27]

In 1537, for example, it was the turn of Johannes Agricola, one of Luther's closest and most long-standing followers. Agricola came from the Harz region and had close ties with Luther's friends and relatives in Mansfeld. Luther dubbed him 'Mr Eisleben' after his parish, the town where both men were born. They had fought the early battles of the Reformation shoulder to shoulder, Agricola acting as Luther's secretary in the Leipzig Debate. He may even have lit the famous fire in 1520 at the Elster Gate where the bull was burnt. Though Luther was a decade older, Agricola had married in 1520, five years before him, and he was among the first Luther told about the birth of his son Hans.[28] Their children overlapped in age, and for many years the letters between them discussed their wives' pregnancies and childcare.[29] When Agricola's wife fell ill, she came to Wittenberg to stay with Katharina, Agricola confiding to Luther that she was sick 'in spirit, not body, and no apothecary can help'.[30]

Yet in 1528, at the height of the dispute with Karlstadt, Luther heard that Agricola was preaching the erroneous idea that faith could exist without good works, and wrote him a stern warning about dressing up such nonsense in fine rhetoric and Greek words: 'watch out for Satan and your flesh'.[31] A year later, however, when Agricola got into trouble with a collection of German proverbs, a book to which he would continue to add for the rest of his life, Luther was supportive once more. Concealed in this apparently harmless work were some disparaging remarks about Duke Ulrich of Württemberg, who had been ejected by the Swabian League and the Habsburgs, and had become a follower of the Reformation. Ludwig von Passavant, a nobleman in Ulrich's entourage, noticed the remarks, and attacked

Agricola very publicly.[32] The hapless Agricola discovered he had alienated not only Ulrich, but Albrecht of Mansfeld and Philip of Hesse
to boot, major evangelical princes. Luther's response was robust: he
counselled the younger man to stick to his guns, and upbraided him
for cravenly apologising to Philip of Hesse: 'I hear you just caved in
to Philip of Hesse, gave him too humble an answer, which I was sorry
about. You should now publish an Introduction where you answer
the *Graf* [i.e. Passavant], and include that you earlier humbly sought
peace, but because they rage and do not want peace you are forced
not to be humble but to fight for the matter according to justice, and
you are sorry about your humility.'[33] Still, the misjudgement dogged
Agricola for years, and he had to be excluded from the 1537 Schmalkalden negotiations to try to reach a common front amongst evangelical theologians, because his presence might irritate Duke Ulrich,
who by then had regained his duchy.

At the Diet of Augsburg in 1530, Agricola had been one of the few
chosen to attend as part of the Wittenberg delegation. He had preached
before the Diet opened, castigating the sacramentarians for four days
in front of hostile Augsburg congregations. But he also chafed at being
stuck in a 'mining town' like Eisleben, and hankered after a wider
stage for his theological gifts.[34] When Luther suggested in 1536 there
might be an opening at Wittenberg for him in the theology faculty,
Agricola jumped at the chance, setting off for Wittenberg before a
position had even been arranged, and soon moved into Luther's house
with his wife and nine children.[35] So close were the two men that
when Luther went to Schmalkalden for the negotiations, he entrusted
his doctrine, pulpit, church, wife, children and house – his '*Heimlich-
keit*', or most intimate matters – to Agricola, licensing him to preach
and lecture in Wittenberg in his place.[36]

Ambition and proximity produced tensions. Free at last of provincial Eisleben, Agricola wanted to find his own theological voice, and
in March 1537 he preached a sermon in front of some dignitaries at
Zeitz in which he gave an unusual interpretation of Romans 1:18 where
Paul described God's retribution for the wickedness and godlessness
of man. He argued that we come to knowledge of the law through
the gospel, and that the law of the Old Testament, which had formerly
revealed the wrath of God, had been replaced by the Cross of Christ.
This conviction was rooted in Agricola's own experience, because

'from my youth on I had an evil, timid and shocked heart and conscience, so that when I was young and went to school I ran to the monasteries and hermitages seeking comfort'.[37] The experience of overwhelming guilt and his liberation through the evangelical gospel was his touchstone, and he therefore described the Christian as under-going an emotional journey of faith: 'the preaching of the death of Christ shocks and depresses the understanding and conscience of man; that is, it teaches repentance. Whereas, the preaching of the resurrec-tion of Christ raises up the conscience, shocked by the death of Christ, and restores the understanding and conscience; that is: it teaches the forgiveness of sins.'[38]

This might appear like conventional Lutheranism, but references to 'shocked consciences' were new and emotional terms, deviations from what had now become the established Wittenberg terminology. Moreover, Agricola was putting the Crucifixion in place of the Law, that is, God's law through which we come to recognise our sin. As Luther saw it, he was too quick to set aside the law of the Old Testa-ment, the 'law of anger', as if Christians did not first have to come to a realisation of their own sin as they failed to fulfil God's command-ments. Only then would they come to recognise and appreciate Christ's saving death. Having spent so much energy over the last decade in developing definitive statements of the evangelical faith, he was increasingly defensive, unwilling to tolerate the slightest devi-ation or innovation. Agricola put the subjective feelings of the believer at the heart of salvation – something that Luther refused to do – and his theology, with its concern for troubled consciences, moved too quickly to focus on the forgiveness of sin and to relieve the indi-vidual's misery.

The reaction was harsh: when Agricola published three sermons with Luther's own printer Hans Lufft in July 1537, they were seized, and the hapless printer was imprisoned.[39] Next Luther published Agri-cola's theses on the law (which had been circulating secretly and were rumoured to be critical of Melanchthon) in a broadsheet, much to Agricola's alarm. Pointedly, Luther dedicated his refutation to Caspar Güttel, the preacher at Eisleben; and it was to Güttel, too, that Luther dedicated *Against the Antinomians*, which he published in 1539, and which attacked Agricola, and denounced those who rejected the Law as binding on Christians.[40]

The dispute dragged on for several years, with passionate reconciliations followed by equally passionate denunciations. At one point, Agricola even sought Luther out in the church, begging for forgiveness. To his friends at table, Luther confided how he felt: 'As God is my witness, I loved you and still loved you', while Agricola insisted that he 'had always considered [Luther] as my father in God's place, through whom I too became a Christian and a child of God'. But for the past three years, Luther had walked all over him, 'and I crawled after him like a poor little dog'.[41]

Agricola's difficulty was that he continued to depend on Luther – without his goodwill, he stood no chance of an ongoing job or even of getting his salary paid by the Elector.[42] In 1538, Luther revoked Agricola's permission to lecture at the university, telling him that he had only been allowed to lecture to make him stop wasting time and annoying people.[43] Then Luther reversed direction and made peace with him, persuaded the Elector to permit him to preach again, and publicly declared his honour to the university.

That reconciliation only lasted a short while, however, and Agricola then formally appealed to the university and to Bugenhagen, next to the clergy of Mansfeld, the town of Eisleben and all its inhabitants, and finally to the Elector himself, threatening to publicise how unfairly he had been treated. In return, by 1540 Luther was denouncing Agricola to the university chancellor, Gregor Brück, as someone who had sought to found a new sect: 'In sum, Eisleben is our enemy, and he has insulted our teaching and shamed our theologians.' Even worse, he was personally disloyal: 'he pretended we were friends, he laughed, ate with us, and hid his enmity against us so dishonestly and shamefully' – this was a rerun of the anger and hurt he had felt when Eck had first sought his friendship and then turned against him.[44]

Whether Agricola was ever really an 'antinomian', someone who believed that saved Christians were 'perfect' and were freed from the law, is unclear, but he certainly did not found a new 'sect', and remained faithfully Lutheran all his life. Finally in 1540 Agricola fled to Berlin where he took a position as court preacher.[45] There he remained a powerful and respected evangelical theologian, but later that year, in a compromise mediated by Melanchthon, he was compelled to withdraw his complaint and write a humiliating apology.[46]

\*

Such disputes were widely known to friend and foe. One of the most vicious pieces of propaganda against Luther was a farce Cochlaeus wrote in 1538 and in which he satirised a play by Agricola about the martyrdom of Jan Hus, which had been performed at the electoral Saxon court. Agricola's ingratiating preface had lauded Luther as the 'snow-white snow', the reincarnation of Hus.[47] This was grist to Cochlaeus's mill, and in his satire, Agricola appears on stage, distraught that his play has somehow offended the reformer. Desperate to regain Luther's favour, he persuades his wife to intercede with Katharina von Bora, the only person who can get Luther to change his mind. Cochlaeus paints Agricola as a drunkard and bully, whose wife seeks in vain to control him. There was probably more than a grain of truth in this: there were complaints at Eisleben that Agricola drank too much.

Simon Lemnius, one of Melanchthon's most gifted students, was next to attract Luther's wrath, putting the friendship between Luther and Melanchthon under serious strain as a result. Taking a student prank too far, he published a volume of Latin epigrams which mocked many of the prominent citizens of Wittenberg.[48] Everything published in the town was subject to censorship but the printer, Nikolaus Schirlentz, had thought that he was dealing with a harmless volume of poetry; he either believed Lemnius's assurance that Melanchthon had given his approval or else his Latin did not stretch to understanding the contents. Melanchthon, as rector of the university at the time, was responsible for censorship, and when Lemnius left town, it was rumoured Melanchthon or his family had helped his star pupil to escape.[49]

Some argued that the verses were relatively innocuous; after all, penning gently mocking poems in Latin and Greek was a hobby in which Luther and Melanchthon had often indulged. Luther, however, was enraged; he had a poster printed and attached to the church doors, a format used to offer bounties for criminals. It roundly condemned the young man, saying he deserved the death penalty.[50] This was not quite the same thing as advocating his execution, although according to Lemnius himself, Luther had said in public that he would not preach in the town until Lemnius had been executed. Lemnius was tried by the university in his absence, was banished in perpetuity and his book was burnt.

By any measure this was an overreaction, and perhaps what excited Luther's rage was that Lemnius had also penned a poem of praise to the archbishop of Mainz, and this accolade to 'that shit bishop', as Luther called him, gained the young poet protection and patronage. 'I won't stand anyone in Wittenberg praising that damned, accursed monk, who would like to see us all dead', Luther thundered. Once safe in Halle, Lemnius began publishing much more scurrilous work that portrayed Luther as a lecher, a man who had married a nun; an authoritarian who made himself pope and bishop and had seized power in Wittenberg, and a boor with no respect for poetry and the arts.[51] Like Cochlaeus before him, he castigated Luther for fomenting rebellion, and in a long response to Luther's broadsheet, accused the reformer of conniving at murder, because Beskendorf, thanks to Luther's intervention, had not been punished severely enough for murdering his son-in-law. By contrast, Lemnius consistently praised Melanchthon as the only serious scholar in Wittenberg, the light of all Germany – an encomium which was unlikely to heal the rift between the two men. One poem about Luther spilled out pure bile:

> You suffer yourself from dysentery and you scream when you shit, and that which you wished on others you now suffer yourself. You called others shitters, now you have become a shitter and are richly blessed with shit. Earlier anger opened your crooked mouth, now your arse opens the load of your stomach. Your anger didn't just come out of your mouth – now it flows from your backside.

This is hardly great poetry, but Lemnius was not wrong about how anger was darkening Luther's final years. Luther responded by penning his own Latin verse, 'Luther's Dysentery Against the Shit Poet Little Lemmie', which pitied Albrecht of Magdeburg as the recipient of Lemnius's execrable poetic offerings, and mocked the poet as constipated: 'with your stomach you press out the shit, and you would like to poo a huge heap, but, shit poet, you manage nothing!'[52]

Lemnius kept his promise to dish the dirt on Wittenberg. In 1539 he produced the *Monachopornomachia* (*The War of the Monk's Whores*), a play which owes much to Cochlaeus's *Tragedy of Johann Hus* but is far cruder and less psychologically shrewd.[53] Its schoolboy humour derides Luther for being forced into marriage with Katharina von Bora, whom everyone knows is a whore. But Luther, suffering from gout and the stone, cannot travel, so she is permanently under his watchful eye and does not get enough time with her young lover. Her friends, the wives of Spalatin and Jonas, recount the wonderful sex they enjoyed while their husbands were away at Augsburg at the Diet. At times, Luther is presented as virile, foolishly enslaved to his lusts; but in another scene he begs Katharina to stroke his member and help it stand. Spalatin's wife explains how she manages to satisfy both her husband and her lover without having two vaginas: she 'raises her bottom' for her beau.

Lemnius and Cochlaeus let their imaginations run riot about the private lives of Luther and the reformers, and their obsession sprang from what was still so shocking in Luther's theology: his marriage to a nun and his surprisingly positive attitude towards sexuality. Lemnius could not bear it. In his eyes a cabal of old, ill and impotent men dominated Wittenberg with their sex-obsessed wives and did not appreciate his talent. But in his writings, the Wittenberg of university students also emerges, a town crammed with girls only too eager to find a student lover, and once again with its own brothels even though they had been closed in 1522 as part of Karlstadt's moral reformation.[54] Lemnius described his aristocratic friends spending their time in clubs like the Cyclops, all too easily getting into fights and duels. Their worth was measured by their ability to socialise within the right circles, bear weapons, flaunt lovers and display wit. This was a new generation, and its values were very different from those of the reformers. Gone forever was the world of German humanism, and Lemnius mourned its loss.

The generational change that Lemnius represented also meant that Luther was no longer universally revered, even in Wittenberg. For much of the 1530s he had had to deal with fawning adulation; in 1536 the mayor of Basle told him that he treated the letter he had sent him as a 'costly jewel'.[55] People treasured his signature and he had to sign and dedicate copies of his Bible translation. His image was everywhere in paintings and prints. In 1542, however, he was even attacked by an angry crowd, who invaded his house and swore and blasphemed; it is not clear what had enraged them, but their actions reveal diminishing

61. In 1539, a new edition of Fabian von Auerswald's classic wrestling treatise, *Ringer kunst*, was published in Wittenberg, illustrated by Cranach. In the woodcuts, the wily old instructor, dressed in simple clothes, throws the smartly dressed pupil with his noble airs and graces. It was printed for a student market perhaps more eager to learn martial arts than study theology.[56]

respect.[57] Within Wittenberg and beyond, Luther had made enemies who alleged that he had too much power. He is 'Pope of the Elbe', complained Lemnius. It was an insult that stuck.[58]

\*

By 1543, three years before his death, Luther's mood began to worsen along with his health. He now complained of constant headaches, which kept him from working. The headaches had begun during his stay at Coburg Castle in 1530 but now he was no longer able to work without having had a drink; he was unsure whether this was a natural infirmity or yet more buffetings of Satan.[59] His letters betray his impatience: to ease the headaches he now kept a vein in his leg perpetually open in another effort to rebalance the humours – much to the concern of the countess of Mansfeld, who advised him that this would only create a further weak point in his body.[60] The sore on his leg made it so difficult for him to walk that he had to use a little cart to get him to the university and church so he could lecture and preach, even though the buildings were just around the corner. 'I am too tired to write', became a frequent refrain in his letters. He was sixty years old, and also suffering from the stone, gout, constipation, urine retention and coldness. It was believed that the body grew colder as it aged, and Luther frequently dealt with illness by having himself rubbed and warmed. He was convinced that he was going to die. 'I am completely sluggish, tired, cold, that is, old and useless', he wrote. 'I have run my course; it is time for me to meet my fathers and for corruption and the worms to have their share.'[61]

There were even further strains, too, in the critical friendship with Melanchthon that underpinned the Reformation, although on the face of it, the personal bonds between the two men were stronger than ever.[62] In fact, each considered the other had saved his life. When Luther was suffering from urine retention at Schmalkalden in 1537, Melanchthon had insisted that he wait a day before travelling on to Gotha because the astrological signs were not auspicious. Luther had laughed at his credulousness, but the jolting cart dislodged his stone and enabled him to pass large quantities of urine, saving his life.[63] When in 1540 Melanchthon had fallen into a feverish melancholy and refused to eat after the debacle of Philip of Hesse's bigamy, Luther had travelled straight to Weimar to see him, threatening, 'You must eat, or else I'll excommunicate you.' He was convinced that Melanchthon's illness was a variety of melancholic *Anfechtung*, and that his prayer had saved his friend.[64]

Luther rarely had anything but praise for the younger man, and freely admitted that his intellect was more systematic and his knowledge of Greek and Hebrew better than his own. Increasingly, however, Melanchthon worked around Luther, as he started to delegate more of the difficult correspondence and issues on which he was asked to take a view. He and Chancellor Brück increasingly controlled the flow of letters, deciding, for example, whether to show the irascible reformer letters from Bucer which might further darken his mood. Where once it had been Luther who had encouraged Melanchthon, and given him direction and support, now it was the younger man who was managing the older, trying to prevent the worst excesses of Luther's temper.[65]

Luther, however, was not easily managed, and the attempt had its cost in that it aroused his suspicions even about Melanchthon. In 1544, when Hermann von der Wied instituted a programme of reformation in Cologne, which had been a Catholic stronghold, Luther did not at first read the draft, leaving it to Melanchthon. Amsdorf alerted Luther to an apparent lack of backbone on the issue of the Real Presence, and Luther was outraged, convinced that Melanchthon was trying to sneak a dilution of his central conviction past him.[66]

In the same year, the clergy in Eperies, Hungary, wrote that they had heard that the Wittenbergers were about to moderate their stance on the Real Presence because they had abolished the elevation of the Host. Luther had retained the practice because it emphasised the reality of Christ's presence in the Eucharist, but abolished it as a 'papist practice' when Karlstadt died in 1541. He sent the Hungarians a stinging reply, insisting that in Wittenberg there was no relaxation, for 'we fight constantly against it here, publicly and in private, and there is no suspicion or even the least trace of this abomination, unless the Devil is lurking in some hidden corner'.

He then made dark remarks about his lieutenant, saying that he certainly had no suspicion of 'Master Philip', or any of the other Wittenbergers, 'because, in public, Satan did not even dare to grumble'.[67] Just what he meant by these ominous words became all too plain a few weeks later, when Luther began to preach vigorously against the sacramentarians in their midst, and seemed to have Melanchthon in mind.[68] Shaken, Melanchthon began to think of leaving Wittenberg. Luther, he said, was utterly 'outraged and inflamed' and was preaching against both him and Bucer.[69]

In the summer of 1545, Luther set out to see his old friend Amsdorf, a journey he had long planned but had been forced countless times to postpone. No sooner had he arrived in Zeitz than he wrote to Katharina, telling her to sell everything and give the monastery back to the Elector. Let's leave Wittenberg and move to Zülsdorf where you have your farm, he wrote: 'better to do it now while I'm alive, for it will have to happen then [that is, when he died]' . What made the old, ill man suddenly want to leave Wittenberg? He told Katharina that he had heard bad things about Wittenberg now he was out of town, castigating in particular the Wittenbergers' love of indecent dancing, where women's skirts flew up, revealing their private parts 'back and front'. 'My heart has grown cold', Luther wrote.[70]

Melanchthon immediately set off to find Luther, while the Elector arranged for Luther's personal physician, Matthäus Ratzeberger, to plead with him.[71] The university also became involved, and the Elector wrote personally to both Luther and Amsdorf, pressing the latter to persuade the old man to come back. In the end, Melanchthon thought better of confronting Luther and returned home. Luther's old sparring partner the Saxon chancellor Gregor Brück had the measure of the two men: if Luther just wants to 'sit on his head', that is, turn his life's work upside down, then he was sure that Philip would leave Wittenberg too. He predicted that Luther would stay because he would not find it easy to sell all that property: there was the huge monastery in Wittenberg, several gardens, and other houses too.[72]

What worried the Elector and the university was that Melanchthon would leave with Luther, and that would be the end of the university. Whatever it was that made Luther decide so late in life to throw everything over, risking not only the future of the university but the entire Reformation, probably had something to do with tensions in his relationship with Melanchthon. It seems that despite all their achievements, and everything the two men had gone through together, Luther was prepared to jeopardise it all in a moment of melancholic bitterness. It is part of the appeal of the old Luther that he grouchily refused to play the tame patriarch, meekly handing on power to the next generation – and it was the tragedy of the Reformation that Luther had destroyed relations with so many of those who might have stepped into his shoes.

# 18

# Hatreds

Although Luther spent much time in his last years attacking friends and allies, he never forgot his true enemies, the first and greatest of whom remained the Pope. In 1538 he published a leaked memorial of advice from some cardinals about what should be discussed at the future Church council, with a biting commentary. The woodcut on the cover showed two cardinals cleaning out a church with fox tails, while the altarpiece was an image of the Pope. Fox tails stood for flattery and deceit, so the message was clear: the proposed council was nothing but a trick, and the Church really worshipped not Christ but the Pope.[1] Next, Luther personally commissioned a mock coat of arms of the papacy, remarking that the Pope 'banned me and burnt me and stuck me in the behind of the Devil, so I will hang him on his own keys'.[2]

As preparations began for another attempt to reconcile Catholics and Protestants at the Diet of Regensburg, Luther abandoned any residual willingness to compromise, and his polemic lost all restraint. In 1545 he produced the virulent, rambling *Against the Roman Papacy an Institution of the Devil*.[4] The treatise lambasts Pope Paul III as a sodomite and transvestite, 'the holy virgin, Madame Pope, St Paula III' and accuses all the popes through history of being 'full of all the worst devils in hell – full, full, and so full that they can do nothing but vomit, throw, and blow out devils'. Using the rhetoric of oppositions that had characterised Melanchthon's and Cranach's *Passional Christi und Anti-christi* in 1521, Luther contrasts Jesus's refusal of the Devil's offer of all the kingdoms of the world with the Pope's lust for power: 'Come here, Satan!' he has the Pope say. 'And if you had more worlds than this, I would accept them all, and not only worship you, but also lick your behind.' Luther concluded that 'All of this is sealed with the Devil's own dirt, and written with the ass-pope's farts.' A few extracts can

62. Martin Luther, *Ratschlag von der Kirchen, eins ausschus etlicher Cardinel, Bapst Paulo des namens dem dritten, auff seinen Befelh geschrieben vnd vberantwortet. Mit einer vorrede D. Mart. Luth.*, Wittenberg, 1538.

barely give a flavour of the whole work: even more extreme was the set of ten images intended to accompany this antipapal extravaganza, produced by the Cranach workshop, and designed by Luther himself.[5]

Such works preached only to the converted – no Catholic would have been persuaded by these words and imagery of such violence – and Luther used every weapon at his disposal: scatology, images of demons and witches, sexual denigration, and animal imagery. Text and image were designed to create a sense of identity amongst the evangelical audience, united through hatred of the enemy. But it was also intended to provoke laughter, as Luther used coarse humour to destroy the papal aura of holiness.

63. The Papal Coat of Arms, 1538. This shows the shattered crossed keys of the
Church, representing the Church's power over souls, the issue which had first sparked
Luther's Ninety-Five Theses. On the left hangs Judas; on the right the Pope. Bags
bulging with money decorate the papal shield, indicating that, like Judas, the Pope had
sold Christ for money.[3]

He even went so far as to describe this work as his 'testament', and
after his death the catchphrase 'Living I was your plague, dying I will
be your death O Pope', so often attached to images of the reformer,
gave expression to this implacable hatred.[6] Luther's prophecy was
fulfilled, for the scurrilous images became an important part of his
legacy. They were adapted and reprinted for the next hundred years
and beyond, and the mutual hatred and incomprehension turned into
images soured denominational relations for centuries to come, and
made religious peace far harder to broker.

\*

Luther was a grand hater, but not all of his enmities were of the same
kind. His attitude to the Turks, for example, was surprisingly nuanced
even though the threat from the Ottoman Empire became ever greater
as it conquered parts of Hungary and besieged Vienna. Throughout his
life he consistently rejected the idea of a crusade, insisting that the Turks
should not be attacked because of their faith.[7] During the early years of

64. *The Birth of the Pope and Cardinals.* These prints could be bought singly or as a set,
and they could then be coloured. Decorated with verses in Latin, and full of classical
allusions, they were intended for an educated audience. Here the Pope is shown being
suckled by a hag and surrounded by Furies with snake-like hair.

the Reformation, he does not seem to have been particularly exercised
by the issue: Christians, he argued, should improve their own lives and
fight the Pope rather than attack the Turks. Indeed, by refusing to identify the Antichrist as the Turk, as was usual – he reserved that title for
the Pope – he also downplayed the threat. This did not pass unnoticed:
as Luther later reminisced, the bull of 1520 also condemned him for the
stance he took on the Turks. There may have been a simple reason for
his position: like many of his contemporaries, Luther seems to have
regarded calls for a crusade as attempts by the papacy to manipulate the
emperor and the princes; the Saxon Elector also resisted such calls.

By 1529, however, the Turks had seized large parts of Hungary, and
Luther, like his contemporaries, was forced to confront the question

of Islam intellectually. As Europeans came to terms with an expansive Ottoman Empire, 'Turk books' became a vogue, informing readers about the Ottomans and their customs.[8] Luther contributed one, *On War Against the Turk* (1529) in which he applied his political theory of the two kingdoms and three estates, the secular order, the clergy, and the household, to the Turkish case.[9] True to his earlier insistence that there should be no religious crusade, he carefully justified war on the grounds that the Turks overturned the three estates: they were 'murderers', who threatened secular authority by attacking Christians militarily; they were 'liars' who interpreted Scripture wrongly; and they attacked the estate of the household by taking ten or twenty women. These were standard anti-Islamic chestnuts, intended to justify killing Turks – and yet Luther adduced them in order to present a reasoned platform for fighting a war that was not a war of faith.

Apocalyptic rhetoric did make an appearance in the second tract Luther wrote in 1529, produced when the Turks were at the gates of Vienna, the *Muster Sermon against the Turks*.[10] Now he identified them as the 'fourth horn' of the apocalypse. But although language about the impending end of the world heightened the sense of urgency, Luther still continued to reserve the role of Antichrist for the Pope and saw the Turks as a scourge sent to punish Christians for their sins, rather than as the main enemy.[11] This position led him to take a surprisingly severe view of the obligations of the conquered. Christians should fight the Turk out of obedience to their secular rulers, Luther argued, but those who had been captured and even enslaved under Ottoman rule should not rebel, or even flee, but rather obey the authorities, 'because then you would be robbing and stealing your body from your master, which he bought or acquired by some other means, which is no longer your property but his, like an animal or other of his goods'. However, if – and only if – your master forces you to take up arms against Christians, 'then you should not be obedient, but rather suffer anything [your master] does to you, yes, rather die'.[12] This respect for established authority and for property rights, even over slaves, was consistent with the line he had taken in 1523, in *On Secular Authority*; and again, Luther could not imagine resistance except in relation to the dilemmas of individuals, who were advised to suffer martyrdom passively; revolt was not envisaged. The writing also betrays considerable admiration for the excellence

65. Lucas Cranach the Elder's *The Origins of the Monks* shows a devil sitting atop a
gallows defecating tonsured friars whilst a she-devil looks on.

of Turkish government, and Luther incorporated details about Turkish
customs from Gregory of Hungary's treatise on the Ottomans, which
he edited and published to complement his tract.[13]

His description of Turkish character provided an opportunity to
ponder that of Germans as well. Whereas 'we Germans' eat and
drink to excess, the Turks show moderation; where the Germans are
given to luxuriousness of dress, the Turks practise modesty; they do
not swear and do not build such extravagant buildings. In these
respects their mores were better than those of the Germans. Luther

66. Lucas Cranach the Elder, *The Origins of the Antichrist*. This image presents the Pope
as a fat corpse whom devils are trying to resuscitate. Naked except for his tiara, even
Luther thought that the very visible genitals might offend women and, calling Cranach
a 'coarse painter', ordered them to be made less distinct.

admired how the Turkish patriarchs kept their women on a tight
leash: 'they keep their wives in such discipline and beautiful behaviour, that there is no such mischief, excess, immodesty and other
excessive ornamentation, splendour amongst their women, as there
is amongst ours'.[14] However, they did not respect marriage, because
they allowed divorce too readily; they practised polygamy, and their
marriages had all the chastity of a soldier's relation with a prostitute.
Worse, they 'practise such Latin and sodomitical unchastity that it

is not to be mentioned in front of respectable people', although he also levelled this charge against the Pope and his court. All Luther's old obsessions, with sex, sodomy and extravagance, shaped his portrait of the Turks; but he was also genuinely interested in the customs and social structure of an alien world. When the Turkish threat became imminent again in 1541, he published his *Admonition to Prayer Against the Turks*, but even then he called for repentance rather than for aggressive prayer.[15]

Luther remained genuinely curious about the Turks, and when he came across a Latin translation of the Quran in 1542, he immediately set about reading it. He strongly believed that the Quran should be published, and when the Basle city council banned publication by the leading printer Oporinus, Luther, along with many of the Strasbourg preachers, objected.[16] It was important, Luther argued, that Christians should know what was written in the Quran. Otherwise, how could they refute it? The controversy brought out Luther at his best: curious about other religions, and confident that his faith could withstand exposure to them. This did not mean, however, that he respected the Quran itself: it was, he wrote, an 'accursed, shameful, desperate book', but it was better to have such 'secret poison' out in the open, for 'you must open the injury and the wound if you want to heal it'.[17] Both he and Melanchthon wrote brief and surprisingly mild introductions to the work when it finally appeared in 1543; one contemporary noted defensively that the prefaces 'rather warned the reader about the book than encouraging them to read it', while Bucer considered asking Luther to write 'another longer and more forceful warning with thorough indication of the dreadful abominations in the Quran'.[18]

Despite his rejection of the Quran, and although Luther could be excoriating about Turkish morals and customs, he never deployed a rhetoric of incendiary hostility towards Muslims that he was so willing to let loose on others. This allowed him to develop a model of coexistence in a divided world, where the Christians had the truth, and must fight to protect themselves, but where Islam was recognised as a separate, if wrong, faith. Moreover, once the immediate danger of the Ottoman threat had receded, Luther lost interest. Instead, he directed the full arsenal of his hatred at the papacy and the Jews.

*

Luther's vicious anti-Semitism has been one of the most fraught subjects in the history of Lutheranism, because it has been difficult for scholars after the Holocaust to recognise and accept its nature and extent. Luther was not always so hostile. In 1523 he had published *That Jesus Christ was Born a Jew*, a remarkable pamphlet which recognised that Christians 'have dealt with the Jews as if they were dogs rather than human beings; they have done little else than deride them and seize their property'.[19] A remarkably tolerant piece by the standards of the time, it has often been regarded as proof that the young Luther was not anti-Semitic: his anti-Semitism, so goes the argument, was a product of his later, embittered years when he realised that the Jews would never convert to Christianity – although there is little evidence that Luther actively tried to convert Jews.[20] However, the last passages of the tract of 1523 made it clear that toleration of the Jews was dependent ultimately on the dissolution of Jewry: 'If the Jews should take offence because we confess our Jesus to be a man, and yet true God, we will deal forcefully with that from Scripture in due time. But this is too harsh for a beginning. Let them first be suckled with milk, and begin by recognising this man Jesus as the true Messiah; after that they may drink wine, and learn also that he is true God.'[21]

Anti-Semitism was not just a product of his later years, but in fact appears time and again. All three editions of the 1519 *Sermon on Usury* had images of Jews on the title page and Luther must have tacitly approved this; the 1513–15 lectures do not treat the Psalms as King David calling on God and condemning his persecutors, but rather prophecies referring to Jesus, and to his persecution by the Jews. Reading the Old Testament in the light of the New was an accepted exegetical technique, but in this case it turns a work concerned with the persecution of the Jews into one about persecution by them.[22]

Such an approach was even implicit in the tract of 1523, which begins somewhat abstrusely with a discussion of the status of Mary because Luther, like the Jews, had been accused of denying the virgin birth and the special status of the Mother of God. Throughout Christian history, Marianism and anti-Semitism have frequently gone hand in hand (chapels to Mary were often built on the site of destroyed synagogues), because denying that Christ is the Messiah meant denying the special status of Mary. Often it seems that, in the late medieval period, it was not so much the Jews' refusal to recognise Jesus that

67. This edition of Luther's *Sermon on Usury* published in 1520, included an image of a Jew, implying that usurers were Jews. The Jew says, 'Pay up, or give interest, because I desire profit'.

Christians found troubling, but rather their denigration of Mary. Stating at the outset that Mary was indeed a virgin, and the Mother of God, was therefore to insist on the issue which had ignited some of the worst treatment of the Jews.

Throughout the 1530s casual anti-Semitic stories and remarks were a staple of Luther's table conversation, with his guests complaining, for example, that there were more than thirty Jews at Torgau, or that Frankfurt was full of them; and in 1531 Luther could write to Amsdorf that it was vain to baptise Jews because they are rascals.[23] There was discussion, too, of the scandalous case of a noblewoman living in Wittenberg who married a Jew who was already married with four children. With the permission of the Elector, her relatives carried out vigilante justice, and stabbed the man to death. Luther acted as godparent to the child she had conceived with her Jewish husband and believed her to be a good woman who had been deceived; and seems not to have expressed any scruples about how the matter had been settled.[24]

When Josel of Rosheim, the first national leader of the Jews in the Holy Roman Empire, asked Luther in 1537 to intervene with the Elector to allow the free movement of Jews in Saxony, Luther refused to see him. Instead he wrote a letter insisting that he had advocated good treatment of the Jews only so that they could be brought to the Messiah, and not 'so that they should be strengthened and made worse in their error through my favour and advancement'.[25] He ordered them to 'read how you treated your King David and all pious kings, yes, the holy prophets and people, and don't treat us heathens as dogs', positioning the Jews as the enemies of the Old Testament heroes and repeatedly invoking Jesus as the Messiah who had been crucified by the Jews.

He followed that the next year with a short tract entitled *Against the Sabbatarians: Letter to a Good Friend* that, as he put it, simply 'poured out of the quill' in response to the rumours that the Jews in Moravia were starting to win converts.[26] A place where political division made it possible for many different religions to be tolerated, Moravia was one of the few areas where even Anabaptists found refuge. Luther argued that the Jews were a people who had been punished by God for 1,500 years, since the destruction of the temple in Jerusalem, because they did not recognise Jesus as the Messiah.

In the 1530s Luther's tone was relatively sober, but by 1543, it had changed markedly. In response to a request from a certain Count Wolf Schlick of Falkenau who had read a Jewish response to *Against the Sabbatarians*, Luther produced *On the Jews and their Lies*.[27] Three 'Learned Jews', he wrote, had come to him in the hope 'that they would find a new Jew in me' because he had introduced Hebrew studies at the university, but from then on the tract is a diatribe against rabbinic interpretation of Scripture and against the Jews themselves.[28] Much of it is devoted to accusations of arrogant pride in their race; Luther evokes revulsion for circumcision, describing how the rabbi rips the foreskin with his fingernails, and imagines a father's distress at the baby's scream.[29] Luther insults Jews as soiled brides and the worst kind of whores, who ignored God's prophets.

As he moves to attacking rabbinic interpretation, he blames the Jews for splitting word and sign, so that they get drawn into 'works righteousness', trusting in their obedience to the law. Luther likened those who trusted in works, like the Jews, to the sow that 'is washed only to wallow in the mire'.[30] The Jews, he alleges, look for biblical truth 'under the sow's tail', that is, their interpretation of the Bible comes from looking in a pig's anus; they accuse Christians of stupidity which could not even be assigned to a sow, which 'covers itself with mire from head to foot and does not eat anything much cleaner'; they defame Christian belief, 'impelled by the Devil, to fall into this like filthy sows fall into the trough'. If they see a Jew, Christians should 'throw sow dung at him . . . and chase him away'.[31]

Luther calls for the secular authorities to burn down all the synagogues and schools, and 'what won't burn should be covered over with earth, so that not a stone or piece of slag of it should be seen for all eternity'. The Jews' houses should be destroyed and they should be put under one roof, like the gypsies. The Talmud and prayer books should be destroyed and Jewish teachers banned. They should be prevented from using the roads, usury banned, and the Jews forced to undertake physical labour instead. Assets from moneylending should be confiscated and used to support Jews who converted. This was a programme of complete cultural eradication.[32] And Luther meant it. When Melanchthon sent Philip of Hesse a copy of the text, he told him that it 'truly' contained 'much useful teaching'. An electoral Saxon mandate of 1543 referred to Luther's 'recent book' as it ordered that anyone who encountered Jews should seize them and all their goods and report them to the authorities; they would be entitled to receive half of the confiscated goods as their reward.[33]

Indeed, Luther's violence was sometimes too much even for his contemporaries. Just a few weeks later, in early 1543 he produced *Vom Schem Hamphoras und vom Geschlecht Christi* (*On the Ineffable Name and the Generations of Christ*),[34] which the Swiss theologian Heinrich Bullinger condemned, while Andreas Osiander in Nuremberg wrote privately to a Jewish friend of his in Venice to express his revulsion. But it was not repudiated by Lutherans and was reprinted in 1577, with Nikolaus Selnecker, an early biographer of Luther's, adding a preface that included scurrilous stories such as one about the Jews in

Magdeburg who refused to come to the aid of a Jew who had fallen into a privy because it was the Sabbath. *Vom Schem Hamphoras* appeared again in 1617, the centenary year of the Reformation, alongside *On the Jews and their Lies*, as the headline work in this vicious potpourri.[35]

This was Luther off the leash, and the text reads like a revelation of his inner fantasies. Luther again assaulted the rabbinic tradition of interpreting Scripture, arguing that the Jews were led by the Devil who is behind any invocation of magic. This might seem like an abstruse accusation, but it concerned issues that were very close to home. In 1514, Luther had taken the side of the Hebraist Johannes Reuchlin – a relative of Melanchthon – as he resisted an attempt by Catholic conservatives to get all Jewish books destroyed. Yet Reuchlin's interest in Hebrew had in part concerned the mysterious powers of the Kabbalah; this was why Christians ought to learn it. Luther may have been unaware of Reuchlin's writings on the wonder-working word, but he was determined to distinguish the evangelicals' use of words from the magical use of words by the Jews.[36] Perhaps realising how close they are to each other, he is driven to explain what it is that Lutherans do when they administer the sacrament of baptism or speak the words of consecration over the bread and wine. His energies were passionately engaged in this because the background was the accusation which the sacramentarians brought against the Lutherans: that they pretended to produce God's flesh magically by means of words. Luther then suddenly breaks off to describe the '*Schem Hamphoras*' sculpture high up on the parish church of Wittenberg itself, which shows a sow suckling several Jews, while a rabbi lifts its tail and looks into its rear. Next Luther engages in his habitual wordplay, turning the wonder-working word into the 'shame here', using mock Hebrew word derivations. The rabbi, he says, is looking into the 'shame here' and it denotes not God but the Devil; the Jews are therefore sorcerers who dig around in excrement and worship only the Devil. The point of attacking the Jews for turning Hebrew into a magical code is that it allows Luther to replace the rabbis as biblical interpreter, and claim for the Lutherans the status of being the chosen people.[37]

Luther's anti-Semitism then reached a crescendo of physical revulsion. He imagined Jews kissing and praying to the Devil's excrement: 'the Devil has . . . emptied his stomach again and again, that is a true relic, which the Jews, and those who want to be a Jew, kiss, eat, drink and worship.' In a kind of inverted baptismal exorcism, the Devil fills the mouth, nose and ears of the Jews with filth: 'He stuffs and squirts them so full, that it overflows and swims out of every place, pure Devil's filth, yes, it tastes so good to their hearts, and they guzzle it like sows.' Whipping himself into a frenzy, Luther invokes Judas, the ultimate Jew: 'When Judas Schariot hanged himself, so that his guts ripped, and as happens to those who are hanged, his bladder burst, then the Jews had their golden cans and silver bowls ready, to catch the Judas piss (as one calls it) with the other relics, and afterwards together they ate the shit and drank, from which they got such sharp sight that they are able to see such complex glosses in Scripture.'[38]

Whenever Luther starts talking in this fashion, his deepest impulses are on display. This is no longer rational argument – he did not seriously believe that Jews had sharp sight because they ate ordure. Rather, he puns, condenses ideas into a single figure, leaps from one idea to another, as if caught in fantastical nightmare. Rhetoric like this stops thought; it overwhelms through the torrent of violent imagery. Luther knew how to turn this kind of anxiety into humour, and he had used it to devastating effect against the papacy. Yet here its effect is not to make the reader laugh, but to induce physical revulsion.

*Vom Schem Hamphoras* is the crazed fantasy that underpinned the apparently rational *On the Jews and their Lies*. In that work, Luther had written: 'if God would give me no Messiah but the one the Jews hope for', he would rather be a pig than a human because the Jewish Messiah does not overcome death.[39] The sow rolls about in muck, has no worries, and does not fear death: when the butcher comes, she is dead in a moment. The folksy humour cannot hide the barb: Jews, who have no Messiah, are no better than pigs. Yet despite his hatred, there were several aspects of Luther's theology which were akin to Judaism, and it is perhaps this proximity which triggered the violence of his assault: he had comparatively little to say about an afterlife; his religiosity put the importance of Scripture and exegesis of the Hebrew and Greek texts centre stage; he downgraded the position of Mary so that Christianity no longer contained a female divine figure; and his remarkably positive attitude towards the body placed him very close to the Jewish emphasis on fertility rather than virginity. He could remain fairly serene about the Turks, as they were so different and so far away. The Jews were similar and lived within the society he wished to reform. They, not the far more dangerous Ottomans, attracted the full force of his hatred.

His anti-Semitism was propagated by his many of his supporters but still went much further than most were prepared to go. In his immediate circle, Justus Jonas translated the tracts into Latin, ensuring that they could be read throughout Christendom. Even Martin Bucer, who thought that Jews should be loved above other non-believers, suggested that they should be made to clean privies to teach them humility when he drafted a 'Jewish Ordinance' for Philip of Hesse in 1539.⁴⁰ But while Bucer wanted to ban the building of new synagogues, Luther wanted existing ones razed to the ground. At the Frankfurt Imperial Diet of 1539, Melanchthon had advocated readmitting the Jews to Brandenburg, from where they had been expelled in 1530. The Lutheran Urbanus Rhegius, whose wife had also learnt Hebrew, consistently took a more tolerant line towards the Jews, interceding for a rabbi and asking the clergy of Braunschweig to oppose the expulsion of the Jewish community in 1540; while Andreas Osiander of Nuremberg bravely published a pamphlet (albeit anonymously) in which he rejected the blood libel after a ritual murder allegation surfaced in nearby Sappenfeld.⁴¹ Luther's old opponent Johannes Eck responded with a nearly 200-page reply in which, like Luther, he repeated all the old allegations of poisoning and ritual murder. Yet even Eck argued that Jews should be tolerated, that they should be allowed to renovate existing synagogues, and that they should not be harmed, killed or exiled.⁴² Unpleasant as Eck's diatribe was, it neither advocated the cultural annihilation contained in Luther's *On the Jews and their Lies*, nor displayed the phantasmagoric physicality of his *Vom Schem Hamphoras*.

Nor was Luther's virulence repeating earlier clichés. Medieval anti-Semitism had also often insisted on some toleration for Jews; Luther's views were not a medieval relic but a development of it. Even more disturbingly, it was not incidental to his theology, a lamentable prejudice taken over from contemporary attitudes. Rather, it was integral to his thought; his insistence that the true Christians – that is, the evangelicals – had become the chosen people and had displaced the Jews would become fundamental to Protestant identity. It was the central plank of his understanding of the Lutherans' providential role in history, and to secure it the Jews had to be pushed aside, discredited and, if necessary, eliminated. They are the better Jews. As he had argued in *On the Jews and their Lies*, 'We foolish Gentiles, who were not God's people, are now God's people. That drives the Jews to distraction and stupidity, and over this they became Not-God's-people, who were once his people and really should still be.'[43] The Lutherans understand the Old Testament better and their exegesis is superior, Luther claims. Having lost their status as the chosen people and therefore no longer truly 'Jews', the Jews are 'even changed into another people altogether, with nothing [of the original] left but a lazy remnant' of foreign rascals or gypsies.[44]

# 19

# The Charioteer of Israel

In January 1546, in the depths of winter, Luther set out on his final journey, to Eisleben, the town of his birth. He was sixty-two years old. Ill and weak, he knew that travel was putting his life at risk but he was determined to go because the counts of Mansfeld wanted him to settle a dispute between them: Albrecht was at loggerheads with his brother Gebhard, whilst counts Ernst and Johann Georg had fallen out with him over the administration of the mines. Although Luther had rejected his father's plans for him, he had never relinquished his obligations to protect the family business.[1]

The copper and silver mining, 'given by God, so that there is nothing like it in all Germany', and once so thriving, were in chaotic decline.[2] Mansfeld had been a boom town, its fabulous riches paying for the three Renaissance castles towering up on the hill. The five counts had divided responsibilities for the territory, and not surprisingly this had led to bitter disputes. Albrecht and Gebhard were doughty supporters of Luther, as were the new counts, Philip and Johann Georg, but the old counts Hoyer, Günter and Ernst had been Catholics, so the chapel had two entrances, one for the Lutherans, the other for the Catholic counts. The old Count Ernst had used his patronage rights over St Andreas Church in Eisleben to appoint Luther's bitter enemy Georg Witzel as pastor, whilst Albrecht had appointed Caspar Güttel, one of Luther's early associates, as preacher; one can only wonder what the congregation made of this.[3]

The counts had run the mines collectively until 1536, when Albrecht persuaded the others to divide them up as well. For years they had puzzled over how to increase their revenue as their own incomes were declining, while the mine owners and the capitalists of Nuremberg appeared to be amassing huge wealth. In 1542 – seized by 'miserliness', as Luther's physician and later biographer Matthäus Ratzeberger put it – they had revoked all the temporary leases, one of which Luther's father had held; now they wanted to run the mines themselves and turn the smelters into their employees.[4] The Lutheran Albrecht had come up with the policy, but Luther was determined to protect the rights of the smelters, even attempting to get the count's overlord, Duke Moritz of Saxony, to intervene. It was all caused by jealousy, Luther argued, 'because whoever has something, has many people who envy them'. Once again, he took things personally: the Devil was behind the plan, as Luther's enemies wanted to see the whole country reduced to poverty, 'so that they could boast: look how God curses all those who support the gospel and lets them fall into ruin, and as a sign, [Luther's] own fatherland has been utterly ruined'.[5] Despite serious illness, therefore, Luther had travelled to Mansfeld in October 1545, to stop the scheme going ahead.[6] He failed, and in the end he was proved right: the counts' experiment in running the mines was a disaster. By the 1560s they were bankrupt and the fabled wealth from the Mansfeld mines was gone, turning the town into a backwater.

In early 1546, therefore, Luther saw it as his duty to try to reconcile the counts. Perhaps intuiting that this would be no ordinary journey, Luther took with him his three sons – Hans, aged nearly twenty, Martin nearing fifteen, and Paul, just thirteen. The weather was dreadful, and the river so swollen at Halle that the party did not dare to cross. As Luther joked in a letter to his wife, 'a huge female Anabaptist met us with waves of water and great floating pieces of ice; she threatened to baptise us again, and has covered the [whole] countryside'. We followed what I know would have been your advice, Luther told Katharina, and we did not 'tempt God' by crossing. After all, he added, 'the Devil is angry at us, and he lives in the water'.[7] When they finally travelled on, he suffered from dizziness: 'Had you been here, however, you would have said that it was the fault of the Jews or their god. For shortly before Eisleben we had to travel through a village in which many Jews are living, [and] perhaps they have attacked me so painfully.'[8] Apologising for no longer being able to make love to her – 'comfort yourself with the knowledge that I would love you if I could, as you know' – Luther addressed Katharina as 'Mrs Sow Market' and 'Lady of Zülsdorf', teasing her affectionately about her farming business.[9] Luther's letters were remarkable for their warmth, frankness and the depth of shared memories.

But these final letters also displayed his propensity for hatred and gloom. At the same time as he wrote about his fears of the 'breath' of the Jews, Luther mentioned that he had one major task to which he would turn next – the Jewish question. 'After the main issues have been settled [in Mansfeld],' he wrote, 'I have to start expelling the Jews.'[10] Count Albrecht does not like the Jews either, he wrote, but he does nothing about them. During his four last sermons which he would preach at Eisleben in January and February 1546, therefore, he set about 'helping' Albrecht, as he put it, from the pulpit, by adding an admonition against the Jews to the end of his last sermon. Like the 'Italians', Luther declared, the Jews knew the art of poisoning someone so that they die instantly, or a month, a year, ten or even twenty years later. They were evil people who would never stop blaspheming against Christ, and those who protected them shared in their sin. As he neared death, Luther's conviction that the Jews had to be dealt with became stronger.[11]

Shortly before the party reached Eisleben, Luther became very ill, collapsing in the wagon. He remarked that this was again the work of the Devil, who always attacked him 'whenever I have something important that I have to do'. His body was rubbed with hot cloths and he revived. In Eisleben, Luther stayed in the house of Dr Drachstedt, a major figure in the mining business with long standing links to Luther's family.[12] Meetings had to be organised around the old man's illness, but even his precarious physical state was not enough to get the counts to agree. Negotiations dragged on for three weeks, with Luther desperate to get home.

Meanwhile, he devised a daily routine. Just as mealtimes with the whole household were central to his life in Wittenberg, so in Eisleben he kept a common table, with guests. Mealtimes were devotional occasions, as they had been in the monastery. Then, every evening around eight o'clock, he rose from the table and left the big parlour to go to his room where he would stand by the window, praying – 'so earnestly and intently that we . . . keeping silent, often heard some words and were amazed', according to his companions. Afterwards, he would turn from the window, happy, 'as if he had put down a burden', and talk to his associates for another quarter of an hour before going to bed. Luther knew that he was facing death, and he talked about how 'we old ones have to live so long that we see into the backside of the Devil, and experience so much evil, faithlessness and misery'. There was also talk at dinner about whether the dead would recognise one another, one of the very few occasions on which Luther speculated about the afterlife. He was sure that they would – just as, when Adam first met Eve, he knew at once that she was flesh of his flesh.[13]

On the evening of 17 February, when he went to his room with his two younger sons to pray, he was suddenly taken ill once more, with chest pains and coldness. Jonas and the Mansfeld preacher Michael Coelius immediately rushed to his room, and he was again rubbed with hot cloths. Countess Anna of Mansfeld was summoned to provide unicorn horn – actually the tusk of a narwhal – believed to be a powerful restorative, and Count Albrecht himself grated some of it into a glass of wine. Conrad von Wolfframsdorf, one of Albrecht's councillors, took a spoonful of it first – perhaps because Luther feared that he would be poisoned, perhaps because he mistrusted such medicine.[14] At about 9 p.m., Luther lay down to nap, and slept peacefully for an hour. When he awoke, he asked those who had kept watch 'Are you still sitting up?', wondering if they wanted to go to bed themselves. He then walked into the next room, presumably the privy, and as he crossed the threshold, he spoke the words 'Into your hand I commend my spirit, You have redeemed me, God of truth.' Returning to bed, he shook each person's hand and wished them goodnight, telling them to pray for God and his gospel, 'because the Council of Trent' – the meeting of the council of the Catholic Church which initiated the Counter Reformation had finally begun in December 1545 – 'and the evil Pope fights bitterly with him'.[15]

Jonas, Luther's two sons Martin and Paul, his servant Ambrosius and other servants kept watch by the bed. Around one in the morning he awoke, complaining again of cold and pain in the chest. 'I think I will stay here at Eisleben where I was born and baptised', he told Jonas with his usual wry humour. Again he walked into the privy unaided, repeating the same the words as before.[16] Johann Aurifaber, Coelius, two doctors, the owner of the house, and a clutch of local dignitaries and their wives had joined those looking after him, and he was again rubbed and given warmed cushions.[17] He did not receive the last rites, in line with his conviction that extreme unction was not a sacrament: he trusted instead in his baptism. Luther spoke his final prayer, thanking God 'that you revealed to me your dear Son Jesus Christ, in whom I believe, whom I have preached and proclaimed [and] whom the accursed Pope and all the godless shame, persecute and blaspheme against'. Even at the last, Luther balanced his love with his anger.[18]

Another valuable medicine was tried, but Luther said 'I am travelling hence, I will relinquish my spirit.' Again he repeated three times very quickly, in Latin, 'Father, into your hands I commend my spirit, You have redeemed me, God of Truth', after which he fell silent. Jonas and Coelius now asked him: 'Reverend Father, will you die faithful to Christ and to the doctrine you have preached?' 'Yes', Luther replied clearly, so that all those around could hear him. He fell asleep again and, after quarter of an hour, he gave up his spirit 'in stillness and great patience'. Jonas and Coelius, who wrote the account, noted that 'no one could discern (to this we bear witnesses before God on our consciences) any unrest or discomfort of his body, or pains of death'.[19]

Luther died, as he had lived, in public. The reason why his last moments were watched and chronicled in such detail was that, according to medieval belief, a good death, especially one without pain, was a sure sign that the person had lived well and would go to heaven; a bad death would have suggested that he was a heretic. Luther's last moments therefore became a final proof, for if he had died in agony, or despaired in his final hour, the Protestant movement itself would have been put into question. Everyone dreaded a sudden, unexpected end which left the individual unable to receive the last rites. In Lutheranism there was no such sacrament and no ritual framework for dying and so the death itself became its own testament.

Lutherans themselves had made much capital out of the unhappy deaths of their enemies in the past.[20] Zwingli's death on the battlefield at Kappel had been deeply shocking, and for Luther it proved God's judgement, not just on Zwingli but on the sacramentarian movement as a whole. In 1536 it was the turn of his old enemy Erasmus, who died in Basle without the presence of a priest and without having made confession. He had gone straight to hell, Luther believed, adding acidly that although it was said that he called on Christ to have mercy on his soul, this was probably an invention. For himself, Luther hoped that he would have a minister of the Word with him when he died.[21]

68. Workshop of Lucas Cranach the Elder, *Luther on his Deathbed*. Many copies were made of this image.

In 1542 Luther's old enemy Eck had been one of those fortunate (or unfortunate) individuals able to read their own obituaries. Believing that their antagonist was dead, Bucer had written a tract against him, and Eck responded with a counterblast, boldly affirming on the title page that he was very much alive. But just days after his riposte had appeared, Eck fell into a fever, soon becoming delirious. Insisting that it was too early to call a priest, he grew increasingly incoherent, and when the priest was finally summoned Eck could no longer follow the words of the rite. Finally, he died of apoplexy – 'the penalty of those who are given to lust and drink', 'vomiting out his life in blood', as the Lutherans noted. The dreadful manner of his passing was the final proof that Eck had been wrong in attacking the Reformation.[22]

The Lutherans made most capital out of Karlstadt's death, circulating a malicious tale that shortly before he died, he had been preaching in Basle when he had seen a tall man standing in an empty choir stall. The man had then gone to Karlstadt' house, where he found the preacher's young son at home alone. Picking up the boy, he made as if to dash the lad to the ground, but then let him down unharmed. He told the child to tell his father that in three days he would return. Three days later Karlstadt died. It was rumoured that the stranger had been the Devil, and that Karlstadt had died not of plague, as was claimed, but of fear. Even after the burial, the evil spirit could be heard making noises in Karlstadt's house. This story flew around the Lutheran camp, and it seemed that Luther had finally won the argument.[23] As Luther wrote to a friend, 'Karlstadt always was miserably afraid of death', referring to his fear of martyrdom in the 1520s when Luther had courageously faced the prospect of his own death.[24] It was partly because the Lutherans had played the card of the 'evil death' in Karlstadt's case, and had exploited it to the full, that they now knew they had to present Luther's own death in the most careful manner.

What made it difficult, however, was that the cause of death was obscure. Luther had been away from home, and without the advice of his usual doctors: the two local physicians who attended him did not know his medical history. They also disagreed on the diagnosis, one blaming apoplexy, the other, more senior, ascribing it to weakness of the heart. But his doctor in Wittenberg, Matthäus Ratzeberger, surmised it was the result of the closing over of the 'fontanelle' in his leg, which had driven the moist humours, unable to escape, up to his chest and so constricted his heart; Luther had forgotten to take his corrosive with him to keep the wound open while he stayed in Eisleben.[25] Melanchthon was adamant that Luther had died of neither and instead insisted that Luther had been fully conscious throughout his final hours, and had therefore died well.[26]

Luther's Catholic opponents, however, did their utmost to exploit rumours that one side of his body had gone black and his mouth was distorted, all indicative of a stroke. Cochlaeus's biography, completed in 1549, included a long account of his last days, alleging that Luther had 'lolled' about on a sofa, eating and drinking to excess. He claimed to have got the details from a pharmacist at Eisleben who had sent a report to the anti-Lutheran pastor Georg Witzel.[27] Just before he died, the apothecary had been asked to apply a clyster to his rectum. The balloon had expanded because of all the rich food and drink he had consumed. He had died of apoplexy, the Catholics insisted, the sudden death that was God's judgement on the wicked.[28] For Catholics and Lutherans alike, Luther's body itself held the truth of his message.[29]

From 4 a.m. to 9 a.m. on 18 February, Luther's body was viewed by many 'honourable citizens', sobbing 'hot tears'. Then he was laid out in a tin coffin, dressed in a white shirt. Hundreds came to view the body, among them 'many nobles, most of whom knew him personally', but also a great number of ordinary folk. The next day the body was taken to the Church of St Andreas in Eisleben, where it was placed in the choir and Justus Jonas preached a sermon. The body was left in the church overnight, guarded by 'ten citizens', a reformed version of the customary Catholic vigil where the body would be watched over by 'soul women', lay sisters paid to pray for the dead.[30]

The Saxon Elector insisted that Luther's body be brought back to Wittenberg, and so a long funeral procession began. In death, Luther was treated like an emperor, the rituals mirroring the honours paid a major prince. Another sermon was preached, and the coffin was carried out through the town gate and on to Halle, with bells tolling in every village through which they passed. As they neared Halle, they were welcomed by the pastors and the town council, and the crowd of citizens thronging the streets was so big that it took some hours for the procession to reach the church. The next day the coffin continued to Bitterfeld and on to Kemberg until it finally reached Wittenberg on 22 February. Here a procession formed to take the coffin from one end of the town to the other, past the university and the old monastery to the Castle Church. It was led by officials of the Elector, accompanied by two of the Mansfeld counts and forty-five horsemen. The coffin was followed by Katharina von Bora and a group of women in another cart; then came Luther's three sons, his brother, nephews and other relations. They were followed by the rector of the university, the young princes studying there, the most senior professors, the doctors and the town councillors. Finally there came the students and citizens, including women and girls. It was a procession 'such as had never been seen at Wittenberg'.[31]

69. This portrait of Luther appears on the reverse title page of the full account of his death, published by Justus Jonas in 1546. It shows him with his doctor's cap, famous curl, and the academic gown and collar which was now his distinctive clothing.

The sermons in Wittenberg provided the final celebration of Luther's life. Bugenhagen preached and Melanchthon delivered a Latin oration which was immediately printed, followed by a brief *Life*. A masterpiece of sober, emotional control, Melanchthon reminded the audience of Luther's faults, admitting the old charge that he was too biting in polemic, and in his brief *Life*, presented him as a man of learning, who rarely ate.[32] The chariot and the charioteer of Israel is gone, he concluded, a biblical phrase which echoed Elisha's distress as the prophet Elijah was taken up to heaven: Luther had been a prophet, a second Elijah who had led his people.

Luther's image itself became a vital part of his memorial. After his death two artists had been summoned to paint his corpse, one of them Lucas Furtennagel from Augsburg. Plaster casts were made of his hands and his face – the hands, as Johann Albrecht put it, that wrote so many marvellous books – which today are kept in the church at Halle where, by a fine irony, Albrecht of Mainz had once housed one of the largest and most splendid collections of saints' relics.[33] The

70. Martin Luther's death mask, which is still on display in the Marktkirche in Halle. By having the plaster casts made, the city had staked its claim to become a Lutheran pilgrimage site.

funeral itself became a media event. Broadsheets and pamphlets with his image, made familiar by years of Cranach workshop portraits, were published en masse, poignantly invoking Luther's presence once more. Physicality, so central to Luther's religiosity, was reflected in the way Lutherans mourned: the ceremonies focused on his body. The memorial pamphlet did not shrink from giving all the details of Luther's death, even down to his visits to the privy.

\*

Shortly after Luther died, some of the evangelical princes and towns took up arms in the war of the Schmalkaldic League. The Protestants were defeated by the Emperor, who was in alliance with Duke Moritz of Saxony, Duke Georg's nephew who, although a Lutheran, was canny enough not to resist imperial power. At the decisive battle of

71. Bust of Luther in the same church. In the middle of its side balcony Luther's face stands in sculpted relief against the mannerist background of leaves, fruit and patterns. Around the roundel is written *Pestis eram vivus moriens ero mors tua papa* – Living I was your plague, dying I will be your death, O Pope.

Mühlberg in 1547, both Philip of Hesse and Luther's ruler, Elector Johann Friedrich, were captured and imprisoned, and in the humiliating terms that ended the war, the Elector ceded his title to Moritz. The Albertine branch now took over most of the electoral territories, including Wittenberg and its university, whilst the other line had to content itself with a court at Weimar.

The legacy of the Protestant defeat was long-lasting throughout German lands, for Charles V punished their disobedience severely. The governments of proud imperial cities like Augsburg were reformed, and a new political system was established in which small groups of mainly Catholic patricians could now dominate local politics, while all political power was removed from the guilds. This made it much more difficult for a populist movement based around religious conviction to gain traction there again. It marked the end of Augsburg's, Ulm's, Strasbourg's and a host of other cities' distinctive versions of evangelicalism, though it would not mean the permanent obliteration of alternatives to the Lutheran model. In Geneva, Calvin would develop his theocratic vision of a reformed community, an inspiration for a new generation.

72. Lucas Cranach the Elder, *Martin Luther*, 1548. This woodcut portrait produced after Luther's death shows his bulky frame as authoritative and comforting.

In the German lands, Charles V imposed the 'Interim' on 15 May 1548, a settlement which required Lutheran preachers to accept many traditional Catholic practices, including the existence of seven sacraments, although it did permit married clergy and Communion in both kinds. It split the Lutheran movement between those who were willing to compromise and those who were not: many preachers went into exile. Long-standing divisions among the Lutheran leadership also became evident, as Melanchthon was prepared to reach an accord while Amsdorf angrily rejected any deviation from what he saw as

73. Lucas Cranach the Younger, *Martin Luther*, 1553.

Luther's legacy. The tensions which had long underlain the alliance between Luther and Melanchthon began to play themselves out in public; Luther was no longer there to arbitrate and balance the opposing factions, and Melanchthon lacked both the authority and the personal charisma to lead. The movement started to splinter.

This was also part of Luther's legacy, because, as he opposed the hierarchy of the papal Church he had not created an institutional structure to replace it. While his 1539 tract *On the Councils and the Churches* had grandly rejected conciliarism, it failed to detail how his new Church should function, or what the relationship should be between the individual congregation and the Church as a whole. No overall organisation constrained the haphazardly created 'superintendents', who were, as Luther recognised, bishops in all but name. Lutheran preachers, subordinate to the secular authorities who paid their salaries, now had to plot their own course through the doctrinal wars and wishes of the local political powers; if they modelled their behaviour on Luther's prophetic

mode, they often found that charisma availed little against local authorities. Adulating Luther, the movement also saddled itself with a model
of preacherly authority that encouraged each local pastor to counter
anything he considered a deviation in doctrine as though it would open
the door to the Devil – a recipe for acerbic, public argument.

Luther's personal network had enabled him to place 'his' men in
parishes all over north and central Germany, and even as far as
Denmark, Bohemia and Poland, and had given him the ear of many
rulers and princes; but this network died with the personal authority
which had generated it. The next generation saw a church that was
riven with factions, as Gnesio-Lutherans (so-called 'genuine' Lutherans,
also known as Flacians after the prominent theologian Matthias
Flacius), and Philippists (followers of Melanchthon and supporters of
a more moderate Lutheranism), all claimed Luther's mantle. Yet these
divisions, life-and-death matters as they were to those involved in
them, did not destroy Lutheranism. The heated polemical rhetoric
could not drown out the common adherence which they all shared.
In any case, the intricacies of doctrinal dispute would have meant
little to those outside the ministry.

Despite the catastrophic defeat of the Schmalkaldic League, Lutheranism survived, albeit in disarray. Moritz eventually fell out with the
emperor when he attempted to reintroduce Catholicism into Lutheran
areas; allying himself with France, Moritz campaigned with great
success. The Peace of Passau, signed in 1552, accorded recognition to
the Lutherans, and the former Elector Johann Friedrich and Philip of
Hesse were both released from captivity. At the Peace of Augsburg in
1555, the emperor formally accepted that there were two denominations
in his empire and allowed the ruler of a territory to determine the
official religion of his subjects. It did not, however, include the sacramentarians in its provisions, and the exclusion of the new movement
that would become Calvinism meant that the Peace of Augsburg would
eventually prove unable to contain religious diversity; and in 1618, the
Thirty Years War broke out, that would leave German lands devastated.

*

The old world of Wittenberg died with Luther. In the midst of the
Schmalkaldic War, Katharina von Bora herself had to flee Wittenberg,

the fate her husband had always feared for her. She returned and started to rebuild her properties, damaged by war, and to take in student lodgers. But times were hard and she died in 1552, from injuries she sustained after falling from a wagon which was taking her away yet again from the plague-stricken town. She was fifty-three years old. Some of the toll that Luther's overwhelming personality must have taken on his family can be glimpsed in the fates of his children. Hans, the eldest son, named after Luther's father, was destined for theology and had been enrolled at the University of Wittenberg at the age of seven, gaining the degree of bachelor six years later in 1539. The lad could not live up to expectations, and the pressure on him must have been unbearable. Reversing his father's trajectory, Hans ended up trying his hand at law, eventually becoming an advisor in the Weimar chancellery, a position he achieved more out of respect to his father than because of his own merits. By contrast, Martin, the second son, had been intended for the law and switched to theology, but never managed to win a post as a preacher.[34] Paul, the youngest, aged thirteen when his father died, enjoyed a full and successful career as a court physician, settling finally in Leipzig, and fathering six children. Luther's youngest daughter Margarethe made a good match, marrying a Prussian nobleman who was a student at Wittenberg; she gave birth to several children but died in 1570, aged only thirty-six.[35] By 1564 the vast monastery that had been left to the family in perpetuity had been sold.

Bucer – the sly 'fox', as his Lutheran opponents had dubbed him – went into exile in England after the Interim and worked with Thomas Cranmer on revising the Book of Common Prayer. He lived out the rest of his life in the damp cold of Cambridge, hankering after his warm German stove back in Strasbourg.[36] If he had failed to accomplish the union between Lutherans and sacramentarians for which he had worked so hard, he left a lasting legacy in shaping the Anglican Church.

As for Karlstadt, Luther's old opponent, no church commemorated him as its founder, and only one crude woodcut image of him has survived. But his influence lived on, both in the Swiss sacramentarian tradition and within Anabaptism, where his adoption and development of the old mystical stance of *Gelassenheit* inspired a sceptical attitude to secular power, and a separatist tradition of devotion as well as commitment to martyrdom. Indeed, in the first half of the seventeenth century, the new religious stirrings that would eventually give rise to Pietism began to recover elements of religion that had been lost within Luther's mature theology. There was a new vogue for the *Theologia deutsch* and the mystical works of Johannes Tauler, and in 1605, Staupitz's treatises on the love of God were republished by Johann Arndt, one of the leading Pietists.[37] The spiritual tradition that Luther had shared with his mother, and that had been so important to Karlstadt, was rediscovered and became part of Lutheran devotional life once again, even if Karlstadt himself would never be rehabilitated.

*

In the years after Luther's death, a Lutheran culture began to take shape. As he came to be remembered in sermon and print, images of the reformer remained as important as they had been in his life. Lutheran hymns were printed with a full-length portrait on the title page, standing four-square for truth. Life-size (and larger than life-size) paintings of Luther were produced by the Cranach workshop, creating the new iconography of an individual who was not a saint, but whose physical presence was evoked by these realistic images. They were also available as woodcuts that could be assembled from eleven sheets to make a cheap life-size pin-up, complete with printed 'frame'. Every Lutheran church now had to have its Luther portrait: some were twinned with a portrait of the area's local evangelical reformer, showing his conformity to the Lutheran 'brand'. The volumes of Luther's works that now rolled off the presses featured a title page with an image of the Elector on one side, Luther on the other, and a crucifix in the middle, deliberately setting the reformer apart from Karlstadt and the Zwinglian iconophobes. It also yoked the truth of Lutheranism to the political identity of Saxony: the man who had called for a reformation of all Christendom inspired a cult of local patriotism.

More of a designer than an artist, Cranach created a lasting visual style for Lutheran church art, changing the environment forever. His altarpieces popularised new iconographies in place of images of saints, like Jesus blessing the children, or visual representations of theological doctrines like law and the gospel, and he developed a didactic style that combined words and images. A whole culture of Lutheran objects

74. Lucas Cranach the Elder, *Christ Blessing the Children*, 1538.

developed, from Luther medals to earthenware beer jugs featuring the Pope as Antichrist or mocking stout monks. Luther's apocalyptic rhetoric had become part of the new material consumption of a wealthy Lutheran middle class.[38]

Luther was a brilliant hymn writer, and his introduction of sung hymns into the liturgy, with its engagement of the whole congregation – men, women and children – transformed the place of music in religion. Hymn melodies became part of German musical culture, and would be intrinsic to the music of Bach. Bach's Chorales, however, evened out their dance-like rhythms, creating a measured and sombre style; Luther's hymns were anything but dirge-like.[39] In his *St John Passion* and *St Matthew Passion*, which drew heavily on the tradition of Lutheran music, Bach dramatised Christ's death in a highly emotional manner. In the *St Matthew Passion* the angular melodic line spares the listener nothing of the viciousness of the Jews' shouts of '*Lass ihn kreuzigen*' ('Let him be crucified'), and follows this with heartfelt individual meditations on Christ's suffering; the implicit anti-Semitism of the glorious music can be hard to take. Yet Bach's legacy shaped German music for centuries, as composers like Mozart,

75. Lucas Cranach the Elder, *Law and Grace*, 1529.

Beethoven and Mendelssohn also turned to this profoundly Lutheran musician for inspiration.

Lutheranism was also part of the background to the greatest literary work of the sixteenth century: the story of Dr Faustus, the scholar

who sold his soul to the Devil. This had circulated as a folk tale, but the printed version of 1587 situated the doctor firmly in Wittenberg – and there were real life parallels. In 1538 when Valerius Glockner, a wayward Wittenberg student, had confessed to making a pact with the Devil, Luther persuaded him to forswear Satan, saving him from a secular trial that might well have ended in his death.[40] The fictional Faust, however, did not escape the Devil, and the work included swipes at the Pope and at Catholic clergy, illustrating the combination of anti-papal aggression and devotional intensity that was becoming the trademark of Luther's legacy. In England, Marlowe took the tale and transformed it into a searing tragedy within five years of the *Faustbuch* being printed. In the hands of Goethe, it would become the classic of German literature, a metaphor for the Enlightenment struggle that altogether transcended its confessional origins. It is impossible to conceive of German culture apart from Lutheranism, and its echoes have pervaded artistic production of all kinds up to the present day.

\*

People from every walk of life were touched by Luther's message, and it changed their lives forever. Just three examples give a flavour of how he inspired very different individuals. Although Germany's leading artist Albrecht Dürer never met Luther, he longed to paint 'the pious man'. When Luther disappeared from public view after the Diet of Worms, Dürer anxiously followed every rumour, convinced that he had been murdered by the Pope's minions.[41] But how did Luther transform Dürer's faith?

In 1500, he painted an extraordinary self-portrait. Dürer looked directly at the viewer, his beautiful locks filling the visual space. Twenty-eight years old, the age believed to be most perfect, he adopted a Christlike pose, his fur coat the only hint that this was a sixteenth-century person. This picture was redolent of a religiosity that owed everything to the ideals of the imitation of Christ, the spirituality that permeated the sermons of Staupitz and the sodality of his supporters in Nuremberg.

Eleven years later, Dürer included himself in another landmark picture, the All Saints Altar for Nuremberg's Landauer chapel. It is a painting that has eluded definitive interpretation. It shows the saints, led by St Augustine, while beneath them hovers another celestial group of representatives of all the different social orders, from emperors to peasants. Dürer included himself in the picture as a small figure on a grassy sward on the earth below, holding a cartouche to proclaim that he was the painter. He stands alone, observing the New Jerusalem and the heavenly hosts, to whom the Christian community is joined through prayer. The altarpiece epitomised the devotional life of the old Church – the Church of indulgences, mutual prayer and works – and it was painted for a chapel where perpetual Masses were said for the dead. This was the piety that Luther's Reformation would sweep away.

Dürer's painting of the four apostles, finished in 1528, the year he died, exuded a completely different spirituality. John and Mark are blocks of colour, their solidity conveying the authority of Scripture. Dürer incorporated into the painting quotations from Luther's German Bible of 1522. He also chose not to depict the customary four evangelists, replacing Matthew and Luke with Peter, who embodies the Church, and Paul, whose writings were key to Luther's thought. This was the religion of the Lutheran Bible. The painting was not displayed in church but Dürer donated it to Nuremberg's town council, in homage to one of the first cities to have introduced the Reformation, in 1524.

Like the peasants, Dürer used the word 'freedom' to encapsulate Luther's message. He hoped for a future where all, 'Turks, heathens and Calicutts [Indians], may turn to us'. He saw Luther as a man who preached 'clear and transparent doctrine', and who helped people become 'free Christians'. But Dürer does not seem to have made much of the corresponding concept of the absolute sinfulness of man; and where Luther looked inwards, praising his fellow Germans over the hated Italians, Dürer was a citizen of Nuremberg, open to global commerce and exchange, who knew how much he had learnt from his journeyman years in Italy. He also collected objects from around the world – feathers, weapons, 'Indian cocoanuts and a very fine piece of coral', curiosities of all kinds that found their way into his art.[42] Luther, by contrast, barely ever mentioned Africa, India or the New World, either in his writings or his conversations. While he envisaged the Reformation as the struggle of the true Christians against the Pope and the Devil, for Dürer it meant the future coming together of all the religions and people of the world in peaceful unity.

For Johann Eberlin von Günzburg, a Franciscan monk in southern Germany, Luther's central message was his attack on monasticism. His three heroes were Erasmus, Luther and Karlstadt, the trio who battled the monks and priests. Convinced that evangelical freedom must mean social liberation, he imagined a fictional land, Wolfaria, where there would be social justice and support for those in need. He wrote a series of pamphlets in support of the Reformation, the most famous of which was *The Fifteen Confederates*, where fifteen characters from various social estates explained why they supported Luther. When it came to monasticism, Günzburg wrote with extraordinary insight: it is probable that he had acted as confessor to a convent. His work went far beyond Luther's simple insistence that nuns were sexual beings subject to lust, and he diagnosed what he saw as their miserable lives and twisted spirituality. It was the insecurity of the monks, Günzburg argued, that shackled the nuns' intellectual and devotional capacities, 'for coarse, unlearned, foolish monks are assigned to the convents; for them it would be painful if the nuns know more than they do, and so they don't tolerate those who are more knowledgeable than they are. This they justify under the cover of claiming that studying is not appropriate for nuns, that it places obstacles in the way of humility, piety, and so on.' Like Luther, he thought that convents would only deform a young woman's desires and development. He understood, too, the bitterness of relationships in a closed institution: 'If she has a vindictive abbess or prioress or if she angers a sister especially beloved by her superiors, she will never have rest or peace.'[43]

For a time, excited by the radical potential of the Reformation, Günzburg became a supporter of Karlstadt, but without losing his original admiration for Luther. This drew him to Wittenberg where he spent 1522-3, and in the end he returned to the Lutheran fold. He eventually found a position with the duke of Wertheim, at first preaching in the small village of Remlingen, and then in Wertheim itself. He lost his post when the duke died in 1530 and his later years were tough. His health broken, he spent his remaining years ministering in the small parish of Leutershausen, mired in controversy; he died in 1533.

A man who would have expected to spend his life in a monastery, all his physical needs catered for, Günzburg ended up an author, traveller, father and convinced evangelical. For him, the Reformation meant the liberation of the monks, the freeing of nuns from a tyranny and perverted sexuality, and the possibility of a new world of social justice. Luther was a hero whose life had inspired and transformed his own.

Argula von Grumbach, a lay noblewoman in Ingolstadt married to a knight, and mother of four children, also had her life turned upside down by Luther's message. In the early 1520s, she devoured his writings and read his translation of the New Testament. When in 1523 the university in Ingolstadt started proceedings against a Lutheran student, she was outraged and determined to take up his cause. She wrote a letter in his support and had it published.[44] It was a runaway success, published in fourteen editions in just two months, and it made her famous. Her convictions gave her the courage to override all the contemporary expectations of what a woman could and could not do. She corresponded with Luther himself and in 1530 she even met him in the castle at Coburg.

It was doubtless her social status as a member of the noble Staufen family that enabled her to become Luther's friend – she belonged to the social group Luther had always cultivated. The world of intellectual equality between men and women which she had dared to imagine did not come to pass. She was derided by the university and mocked by men who thought her actions and behaviour inappropriate to a woman. Pressure was put on her husband to control her. Grumbach stopped publishing in 1524, and her last offering was a poem which defended her standing as a wife and mother against a slanderous poem by one of her antagonists, who alleged that she 'forgot all female modesty'. 'Paul himself', her critic proclaimed, had said 'you should not dispute, but govern the house at home and keep quiet in church. Look here, my dear Sibyl, you are like an impudent wild animal, and you think yourself so smart that you want to interpret Holy Scripture yourself.'[45] Although she was not easily cowed, the increasingly conservative environment after the defeat of the peasants in 1525 was inimical to women like her. She remained a pious Lutheran wife and mother, but in the new religion there was no role open to her as pastor, author or religious authority.

Albrecht Dürer, Johann Eberlin von Günzburg and Argula von Grumbach stand for the many thousands of men and women whose lives were transformed by Luther's ideas. What each of them understood by his message was different. For Dürer, it was a vision of a global union of religions; for Günzburg, it was about a new social order; for Grumbach, it was an issue of justice and fairness. It was Luther's genius that he could appeal to them all, and that each could take different things from his words. All of them were so deeply moved by evangelical ideas, and by Luther as a person, that they did things which they would not otherwise have dreamed of, and overturned the expectations of their upbringing.

*

By the time Luther died, he had definitively accomplished a split in the Church. He had established a new Church, closely aligned with secular authorities, where monasticism was abolished. A new married clergy were creating dynasties of Protestant clerics who would dominate the intellectual culture of Germany for centuries to come. The shy monk had stood up to the forces of the Pope, Church and empire, and had inspired others with a message of 'freedom', including peasants who risked all to rise against their feudal overlords.

Luther's political legacy was double-edged. The political theory he had developed in 1523 in his tract *On Secular Authority* had distinguished between the kingdom of this world and the kingdom of God, which enabled him to argue that the Pope should not enjoy any temporal power. Because the power of princes belonged to this world, however, Christians should obey them, while it was the ruler's duty to prevent the godless from attacking their fellow men. Luther clung to this neat apposition throughout his life. But it also left him without a positive account of what the state can do and how it might help its citizens, and it did not allow for a situation where a Christian or a Christian ruler would have to resist a superior authority. When the formation of the Schmalkaldic League finally forced him to consider that the emperor might have to be resisted, he abdicated responsibility, and left the matter for jurists to decide, eventually moving to a position that tacitly accepted the arguments for resistance.[46] At the same time, however, he was consistently disrespectful to princes himself, listing them in the same breath as beadles and hangmen, and mocking those he did not like at every opportunity, with brilliant insults. The man who railed against sedition and insisted on obedience to princes believed in his own authority as a prophet, and he thundered against the rulers from the sidelines.

Perhaps Luther's most lasting achievement was the German Bible. After the fevered translation of the New Testament in 1522, he worked with colleagues to produce the full Bible of 1534, illustrated with memorable images by Cranach.[47] It was not just that his prose shaped the German language, creating the modern vernacular as we know it.[48] Each book of the Bible was prefaced with a short and brilliantly clear introductory exegesis, so that the reader encountered the text through Luther's understanding of it. And because his authorship was not clearly indicated, his explanation appeared indistinguishable from Scripture itself. Luther always maintained that the Word of God was absolutely plain and did not need interpretation, thus avoiding the question his very first opponents had raised: how do you decide between rival interpretations of biblical passages, and should not Church tradition therefore be the guide? His conviction that the Word of God was clear prompted ordinary people for centuries to come to read the Bible for themselves – even if Luther would not have always agreed with what they took from it. At the same time, his insistence on aligning his own authority with God's Word helped give rise to a church of pastors who were theologically trained, academics whose authority rested on their intellectual command of religion, demonstrated in their sermons.

At the heart of Luther's theology lay his insistence that Christ was truly present in the bread and wine of the Eucharist. This is one aspect of his thinking which is difficult for many Protestants and non-believers to understand today, and where the gulf that separates our world from his seems at its greatest. In this book I have tried to show why it mattered.

Luther's theological legacy was a view of human nature that escaped the split between flesh and spirit that has dogged so much of the history of Christianity, and has given rise to a profound suspicion of sexuality and an unbending moralism. Not so with Luther: whatever else he was, he was no killjoy. He saw sexuality as sinful but only in the way that all our actions are sinful, and this perspective freed him to be remarkably positive about the body and physical experience.

His religiosity had nothing saccharine about it. His relationship with God was not that of a believer cheerfully confident of having been 'saved': it was wrested from his *Anfechtungen* and it engaged all his intellectual and emotional capacities. He would pray for hours a day, conversing with God, but this never gave him happy assurance: for Luther, doubt always accompanied faith. Melanchthon described how, in one debate, Luther suddenly became unsure that he was right, and he left the room, falling on his bed and praying.[49] This was not how one would expect a university professor to behave: he was utterly engaged in the subject under discussion, and shaken to the core by the thought that he might have been mistaken. Luther's extraordinary openness, his honest willingness to put everything on the line, and his capacity to accept God's grace as a gift he did not merit, are his most attractive characteristics.

Luther is a difficult hero, nonetheless. His writings can be full of hatred, and his predilection for scatological rhetoric and humour is not to modern taste. He could be authoritarian, bullying, over-confident; his domineering ways overshadowed his children's lives and alienated many of his followers. His intransigent capacity to demonise his opponents was more than a psychological flaw because it meant that Protestantism split very early, weakening it permanently and leading to centuries of war. His anti-Semitism was more visceral than that of many of his contemporaries, and it was also intrinsic to his religiosity and his understanding of the relation between the Old and the New Testament: it cannot just be excused as the prejudice of his day. His greatest intellectual gift was his ability to simplify, to cut to the heart of an issue – but this also made it difficult for him to compromise or see nuance. And yet only someone with an utter inability to see anyone else's point of view could have had the courage to take on the papacy, to act like a 'blinkered horse' looking neither to right nor left, but treading relentlessly onwards regardless of the consequences. And only someone with a sense of humour, a stubborn realism, and a remarkable ability to engage the deepest loyalties of others, could have avoided the martyrdom that threatened.

The Reformation is often lauded as heralding the arrival of moder-nity, the freedom of the individual or, alternatively, the growth of a confessional world that yoked religious to political identity. I hope to have shown that none of these views do justice to Luther or to the movement he started. Luther was not 'modern', and unless we appre-ciate his thought in its own, unfamiliar and often uncomfortable terms, we will not see what it might have to offer us today. What Luther meant by 'freedom' and by 'conscience' were not what we mean by these words now. It had nothing to do with allowing people to follow their conscience; it meant our capacity to know *with* God, a knowledge he believed to be objective truth. Luther split the Church and ushered in the denominational era, but he was always a maverick thinker who did not believe in following rules or in devising courts to impose morality. He was a man who retained a healthy mistrust of Reason, 'the whore'.

# Acknowledgements

Any book that takes over a decade to write incurs a great many debts to other scholars, institutions and friends. This book is certainly not just my work, and my first debt is to those students who have taken the Luther Special Subject at Oxford over the years, and who have commented on Luther's writings so acutely. The informal Early Modern Workshop at Oxford too has provided intellectual support and helped me repeatedly to formulate my argument.

Many institutions have provided me with support during the research and writing. An extension of an Alexander von Humboldt Fellowship in 2006–7 enabled me to undertake archival and library research, and thanks to the support of Gisela Bock, Jürgen Kocka and Claudia Ulbrich, I was a Visiting Fellow at the Freie Universität Berlin. Leave from the University of Oxford enabled me to undertake the research and finish the writing, and I am grateful to my colleagues at Balliol College, Lesley Abrams, Martin Conway and Simon Skinner, who made it possible for me to have time away. A Research Development Award from the British Academy gave me concentrated time for the book, without which I could not have written it. Grants from the Fell Fund Oxford enabled me to gain research assistance. Oriel College and the History Faculty have provided a welcoming and stimulating environment in which to complete the book. An invitation to give the Wiles Lectures at the University of Belfast in 2014 gave me a rare opportunity to try out ideas with a group of quite remarkable scholars over three intense days: I am grateful to the Wiles Trustees, and in particular to Gadi Algazi, Scott Dixon, Renate Dürr, Peter Gray, Joel Harrington, Bridget Heal, Kat Hill, Colin Kidd, Charlotte Methuen, Steve Smith, Jenny Spinks, Ulrike Strasser, and Alex Walsham, as well as to the audience in Belfast.

The staff at many archives, museums, art galleries and libraries have been unfailingly helpful and kind. First I would like to thank the staff of the Bodleian Library Oxford and the History Librarian, Isabel Holowaty; the British Library; the Wittenberg Stadtarchiv and its researchers, especially Hans-Jochen Seidel who showed me Wittenberg; the Lutherhalle Wittenberg, in particular Jutta Strehle, who took me through the Bildersammlung, Gabi Protzmann and Petra Wittig; the Evangelisches Predigerseminar Wittenberg Bibliothek; the Thüringisches Hauptstaatsarchiv Weimar; the Staatsbibliothek zu Berlin-Preussischer Kulturbesitz; the Landesdenkmalamt Halle; the Marienbibliothek Halle; the Stadtarchiv Eisleben; the Stadtarchiv Eisenach; Frau Günzel and Frau Kaiser of Schloss Mansfeld; the Landesarchiv Sachsen-Anhalt, Abteilung Magdeburg, Standort Magdeburg; the Landesarchiv Sachsen-Anhalt, Standort Wernigerode, in particular Susan Schulze; the Landesbibliothek Coburg; the Forschungsbibliothek Gotha; and the Herzog August Bibliothek Wolfenbüttel. No scholar can work on sixteenth-century German material without the extraordinary 'VD 16' and the help of the Bayerische Staatsbibliothek Munich.

Juliane Kerkhecker generously worked with me on Luther's Latin and many of her insights are in this book. Christian Preusse, Melinda Letts, Floris Verhaart, Edmund Wareham, Martin Christ, Mikey Pears and Raquel Candelas all gave invaluable research assistance; Candice Saunders made sure everything happened and provided flair. Nadja Pentzlin proved a phenomenal picture sleuth and organiser.

Many audiences have helped me shape my ideas, and I'm grateful to them, as have many individuals, including Mette Ahlefeldt-Laurvig, Sarah Apetrei, Charlotte Appel, Wolfgang Behringer, Paul Betts, Sue Bottigheimer, Patrick Cane, Charles Colville, Natalie Zemon Davis, Martin Donnelly, Michael Drolet, Liz Fidlon, Etienne François, Laura Gowing, Rebekka Habermas, Adalbert Hepp, Michael Hunter, Susan Karant-Nunn, Thomas Kaufmann, Simone Laqua, Volker Leppin, Peter Macardle, Jan Machielsen, Hans Medick, Erik Midelfort, Hannah Murphy, Johannes Paulmann, Glyn Redworth, Tom Robisheaux, Ailsa Roper, Cath Roper, Miri Rubin, Alex Shepard, Philip Soergel, Hubert Stadler, Andreas Stahl, Willibald Steinmetz, Naomi Tadmor, Barbara Taylor, Bernd Weisbrod, Chris Wickham, Merry Wiesner, Tim Wilson, Sylvie Zannier and Charles Zika whose insights have all found their way into this book.

Many friends read entire drafts, some even when the book was at a very early stage, generously discussed the ideas and made countless suggestions. I would like to thank in particular Alison Light, who has spent so many hours discussing Luther with me, and whose insights – and friendship – did much to shape the book; Daniel Pick, who helped me think psychoanalytically about Luther's character; Kat Hill, who has thought through this book with me from the start; Alex Walsham, who kept me going when I lost confidence in the project; Barbara Taylor, who helped sort out the introduction, and Gadi Algazi, from whom I have learnt so much. All of all them read and commented extensively on the book, as did Simon Ponsonby who made me rethink many of my interpretations; Rosi Bartlett, who inspired me to think differently about *where* things took place; my brother Mike Roper who saw what the book needed to do and kept me going, my Dad Stan Roper to whom it is dedicated; and Ulinka Rublack, whose work has so influenced my own for so many years. I have incorporated most of their suggestions but of course they are not to blame for my mistakes.

Jörg Hensgen has been an amazing editor, tirelessly spotting every weak point in the book, 'smoothing out the bumps', as he puts it, and arguing with my interpretations: I could not have been more fortunate in having an editor trained in Lutheran theology. David Milner has been an eagle-eyed copy-editor, saving me from many howlers, and Anthony Hippisley an excellent proofreader. Clare Alexander is far more than an agent: she supported me, protected me and made sure the book got finished. I am grateful also to Sally Riley who deals with foreign rights but so much more.

Nick Stargardt first suggested I write the book and gave me the courage to do so; he read an early version and discussed many of the ideas which gave it shape. Iain Pears generously undertook a line edit of the entire manuscript, not once but twice, and provided help and support when I needed it. Ruth Harris read the very first draft and gave me faith in the project from the start; she has read draft after draft and supported me through the difficult task of finishing it. I am lucky to have such a friend and I could not have done it without her. My stepson Anand Narsey has made me realise why it is important to understand religious traditions and my son Sam has taught me what matters in life.

Oxford
10 January 2016

# Notes

## Abbreviations

| | |
|---|---|
| CA | Confessio Augustana, in *Die Bekenntnisschriften der evangelisch-lutherischen Kirche*, 7th edition, Göttingen 1976 |
| HSA Weimar EGA | Thüringisches Hauptstaatsarchiv Weimar, Ernestinisches Gesamtarchiv |
| LHASA | Landeshauptarchiv Sachsen-Anhalt |
| LW | *Luther's Works*, Philadelphia 1957– |
| RTA | *Reichstagsakten, Jüngere Reihe – Deutsche Reichstagsakten unter Kaiser Karl V.*, 23 vols, Gotha 1893– |
| StadtA Witt | Stadtarchiv Wittenberg |
| VD 16 | Verzeichnis der im deutschen Sprachbereich erschienenen Drucke des 16. und 17. Jahrhunderts |
| Walch | Johann Georg Walch, *Dr. Martin Luthers Sämmtliche Schriften*, St. Louis, 1880–1910 (revised version of the Halle Edition, 1740–1753) |
| WB | *D. Martin Luthers Werke: Kritische Gesamtausgabe, Briefe*, 18 vols |
| WDB | *D. Martin Luthers Werke: Kritische Gesamtausgabe, Deutsche Bibel*, 15 vols |
| WS | *D. Martin Luthers Werke: Kritische Gesamtausgabe, Schriften*, 72 vols, Weimar, 1903 |
| WT | *D. Martin Luthers Werke: Kritische Gesamtausgabe, Tischreden*, 6 vols |

## Introduction

1.   He drank to it in 1527 on 1 November, a fact which has led at least one scholar to argue that the Theses were posted on All Saints' Day itself,

not the day before. Volz, *Thesenanschlag*, 38–9; WB 4, 1164, 1 Nov. 1527; Vandiver, Keen and Frazel (eds and trs), *Luther's Lives*, 22.

2.  Iserloh, *Thesenanschlag*. Martin Treu renewed the debate by discovering in 2007 a note in the hand of Georg Rörer, Luther's secretary, in the margins of a Bible used by Luther, and kept in the university library of Jena. This stated that on the eve of the feast of All Saints, Dr Martin Luther nailed up theses about indulgences on the doors of the Wittenberg churches. The finding was important because otherwise the only contemporary note of the nailing of the theses was by Melanchthon, and he was not yet in Wittenberg, so could not have witnessed the event. For an excellent summary of the debate, see Ott and Treu, *Luthers Thesenanschlag*.

3.  Rörer's mention, though it does corroborate Melanchthon's statement, does not conclusively prove the theses were posted since he was not in Wittenberg either and his note was written years after the event. However, there is every reason to believe that the theses were indeed posted on the church doors as well as sent. Melanchthon not only mentioned this in his preface to the second volume of Luther's *Works* but also described the event in detail in a sermon given in 1557. Johannes Mathesius, in his biography of Luther published in 1565, also wrote that the theses were posted on the Castle Church on 31 October, adding that they were printed: Mathesius, *Historien*, 28. In many ways the debate is an interesting example of radical scepticism about events we simply assume to have been true.

4.  Juette, 'Schwang Luther 1517 tatsächlich den Hammer?', 3; wax might have been used in place of glue.

5.  LW Letters, I, 43–9; WB 1, 48, 31 Oct. 1517, 112:57–8.

6.  Scheel, *Martin Luther*, II, 155 (Johannes Cochlaeus); WT 2, 2800b.

7.  Luther's usual printer Rhau-Grunenberg was situated just around the corner in Wittenberg, though it is possible that the workshop was in trouble at that point and so another printer, perhaps in Leipzig, was used. See also Volz, *Thesenanschlag*.

8.  See Volz, *Thesenanschlag* on the three extant editions, from Leipzig, Nuremberg and Basle. One misnumbered them, ending with eighty-seven, and another simply numbered in batches of twenty. Only the edition from Basle takes pamphlet form, an octavo booklet, and it uses Roman numerals to number the theses. If these surviving editions were therefore the only ones printed, it is hard to explain why Luther's text would have achieved fame as the 'Ninety-Five' Theses.

9.  WS 1, 233:10–11. The American edition of Luther's Works has 'When our Lord and Master Jesus Christ said, "Repent", he willed the entire life of believers to be one of repentance', LW 31, 25, but this does not quite convey the emphasis of the words.

10. Myconius, *Geschichte*, 20–I; Volz, *Thesenanschlag*, 72, n.33. This story probably has a touch of Reformation myth-making, however: a monk like Luther would not have had primary responsibility for the care of souls in Wittenberg.

11. Myconius, *Geschichte*, 15.

12. Peter Claus Hartmann, 'Albrecht von Brandenburg. Erzbischof und Kurfürst von Mainz, Erzbischof von Magdeburg und Administrator des Bistums Halberstadt' in Tacke (ed.), *Der Kardinal Albrecht von Brandenburg*, 10–13; Friedhelm Jürgensmeier, 'Kardinal Albrecht von Brandenburg (1490–1545). Kurfürst, Erzbischof von Mainz und Magdeburg, Administrator von Halberstadt' in Tacke (ed.), *Albrecht von Brandenburg*, 22–41.

13. WB 3, 860, 4(?5) May 1525, 482:81–2.

14. Erikson, *Young Man Luther*; Fromm, *The Fear of Freedom*.

15. No less a figure than the French *annaliste* Lucien Febvre himself wrote a marvellous passage mocking the undertaking: 'A Freudian Luther: we can imagine in advance what he will look like, and if an unshockable Luther-researcher were actually to produce such a depiction, one wouldn't be curious to make its closer acquaintance.' Febvre, *Martin Luther*, 46.

16. He deliberately quoted 'the ancient Greeks' here; Vandiver, Keen and Frazel (eds and trs), *Luther's Lives*, 18; Melanchthon, *Vita Lutheri*, fo. c 17r–v.

17. Schilling, *Martin Luther*.

18. The interesting exception is Lutheran Nuremberg, on which there was a very lively American literature.

19. Eschenhagen, 'Beiträge zur Sozial- und Wirtschaftsgeschichte'.

20. Thomas Kaufmann, 'Theologisch-philosophische Rationalität: Die Ehre der Hure. Zum vernünftigen Gottesgedanken in der Reformation' in Kaufmann (ed.), *Der Anfang der Reformation*.

## 1. Mansfeld and Mining

1. WT 5, 6250, 'Ego sum rustici filius; proavus, avus meus, pater sein rechte pauren gewest.' He adds 'Darnach ist mein vater gegen Mansfelt gezogen vnd doselbes ein bergkheuer worden' (afterwards my father went to Mansfeld and became a miner there).

2. The chronicler Cyriacus Spangenberg provided a detailed description of the environment, noting that many fields around Mansfeld had been destroyed by mining. He mentioned the vast quantities of wood and coal used in the mines: Spangenberg, *Mansfeldische Chronica*, Part 4, Book 1, 25, 27. Dieter Stievermann, 'Sozialer Aufstieg um 1500: Hütten-meister Hans Luther und sein Sohn Dr Martin Luther' in Knape (ed.), *Martin Luther und der Bergbau*, 49; WB 11, 4157, 7 Oct. 1545, 189: in this

letter to counts Philipp and Johann Georg of Mansfeld, Luther signs himself as 'E.G. williges Landkind Martinus Luder D'.

3.     For example, though Luther's biographer Johannes Mathesius mentions Mansfeld and mining, and has a concluding chapter that was originally a 'mining sermon' celebrating Luther's links to mining, Nikolaus Selnecker's influential sixteenth-century biographical writings do not even mention Mansfeld or mining: Günther Wartenberg, 'Martin Luthers Kindheit, Jugend und erste Schulzeit in frühen biografischen Darstellungen des Reformators' in Knape (ed.), *Martin Luther und Eisleben*, 152–3; Mathesius, *Historien*.

4.     On mining and Luther's background, see Michael Fessner, 'Die Familie Luder und das Bergwerks- und Hüttenwesen in der Grafschaft Mansfeld und im Herzogtum Braunschweig-Wolfenbüttel' and Andreas Stahl, 'Baugeschichtliche Erkenntnisse zu Luthers Elternhaus in Mansfeld' in Knape (ed.), *Martin Luther und Eisleben*; Knape (ed.), *Martin Luther und der Bergbau*; Treu, '. . . von daher bin ich'; Jankowski (ed.), *Zur Geschichte*; Kramm, *Oberschichten*, I, 109–33; Hanns Freydank, 'Vater Luther der Hüttenmeister' in Etzrodt and Kronenberg (eds), *Das Eisleber Lutherbuch 1933*; Freydank, *Martin Luther und der Bergbau*; Westermann, *Das Eislebener Garkupfer*; Mück, *Der Mansfelder Kupferschieferbergbau*; Möllenberg, *Urkundenbuch*.

5.     Kramm, *Oberschichten*, I, on copper, III; Günther Wartenberg, 'Martin Luthers Kindheit, Jugend und erste Schulzeit in frühen biografischen Darstellungen des Reformators' in Knape (ed.), *Martin Luther und Eisleben*, 36–7; Michael Fessner, 'Das Montanwesen in der Grafschaft Mansfeld vom ausgehenden 15. bis zur zweiten Hälfte des 16. Jahrhunderts' in Westermann (ed.), *Montanregion als Sozialregion*, 293: Schwaz in the Tirol, Neusohl in lower Hungary and Mansfeld together produced 80 to 90 per cent of European copper at the end of the fifteenth century.

6.     WT 5, 5362, 95:4. Although, as Andreas Stahl points out, biographer Johannes Mathesius was one of the few who got it right, describing him in his *Sarepta* of 1558 as raised as a mine owner's son; Mathesius, *Sarepta*; Andreas Stahl, 'Baugeschichtliche Erkenntnisse zu Luthers Elternhaus in Mansfeld' in Knape (ed.), *Martin Luther und Eisleben*, 356; his biography of the reformer describes him as the son of a labouring miner who made good, *Historien*, 5–6. Melanchthon also played down their wealth, emphasising their piety and character; Melanchthon, *Vita Lutheri*, 9–10; while Luther himself offered some support for the myth, remembering that his mother carried wood on her back and describing his father as a miner. Günther Wartenberg, 'Martin Luthers Kindheit, Jugend und erste Schulzeit in frühen biografischen Darstellungen des Reformators' in Knape (ed.), *Martin Luther und Eisleben*.

7.     Rainer Slotta and Siegfried Müller, 'Zum Bergbau auf Kupferschiefer im Mansfelder Land' in Knape (ed.), *Martin Luther und der Bergbau*, 13.

8.  Michael Fessner, 'Die Familie Luder in Möhra und Mansfeld' in Meller (ed.), *Fundsache Luther*.

9.  Michael Fessner, 'Die Familie Luder und das Bergwerks und Hütten-wesen in der Grafschaft Mansfeld und im Herzogtum Braunschweig-Wolfenbüttel' in Knape (ed.), *Martin Luther und Eisleben*: this, together with Andreas Stahl in the same volume, and Michael Fessner, 'Die Familie Luder in Möhra und Mansfeld' in Meller (ed.), *Fundsache Luther*, offer the best accounts of Luther's background.

10. Michael Fessner, 'Die Familie Luder und das Bergwerks- und Hütten-wesen in der Grafschaft Mansfeld und im Herzogtum Braunschweig-Wolfenbüttel' in Knape (ed.), *Martin Luther und Eisleben*, 20: he appears as such on a chance Urkunde from 1491 and he is listed for 1502; but the records are incomplete. He had probably held the post on a regular basis for some time before.

11. Spangenberg, *Mansfeldische Chronik*, 4, 1, 68–71.

12. Stahl, 'Die Grafschaft', 14; Spangenberg, *Mansfeldische Chronica*, 4, 1, 94: the fire occurred in 1496 or 1498.

13. Biering, *Historische Beschreibung*, 147; 150–1.

14. Spangenberg, *Mansfeldische Chronik*, 4, 1, 68–71; Historische Commission für die Provinz Sachsen und das Herzogtum Anhalt, *Bau- und Kunst-Denkmäler der Provinz Sachsen*, vol. 18, *Der Mansfelder Gebirgskreis*, 147–64; Andreas Stahl, 'Baugeschichtliche Erkenntnisse zu Luthers Elternhaus in Mansfeld' in Knape (ed.), *Martin Luther und Eisleben*, 368; Siegfried Bräuer, 'Die Stadt Mansfeld in der Chronik des Cyriakus Spangenberg' in Knape (ed.), *Martin Luther und Eisleben*; Scheel, *Martin Luther*, I, 4–5.

15. Spangenberg, *Mansfeldische Chronik*, 4, 1, 68–71. The original includes a sketch map of Mansfeld from around 1560 with numbers indicating the owners of many of the houses; see Andreas Stahl, 'Historische Bauforschung an Luthers Elternhaus. Archivalische Voruntersuchungen und erste Baubeobachtungen' in Meller (ed.), *Luther in Mansfeld*, 123; Andreas Stahl, 'Baugeschichtliche Erkenntnisse zu Luthers Elternhaus in Mansfeld' in Knape (ed.), *Martin Luther und Eisleben*, 369–70.

16. Our knowledge of the house has been transformed by recent archaeo-logical work on the property. See in particular Meller (ed.), *Luther in Mansfeld* and *Fundsache Luther*, and the exhibition held in Halle in 2008–9.

17. Günther Wartenberg, 'Die Mansfelder Grafen und der Bergbau' in Knape (ed.), *Martin Luther und der Bergbau*, 34; Jankowski, *Mansfeld Gebiet-Geschlecht-Geschichte*. In the sixteenth century four of the counts made their homes in the Mansfeld castle, while Graf Ernst resided in the castle at Heldrungen; Krumhaar, *Versuch einer Geschichte*, 6; Günther Wartenberg, 'Martin Luthers Kindheit, Jugend und erste Schulzeit in frühen biografischen Darstellungen des Reformators' in Knape (ed.), *Martin Luther und Eisleben*.

18. Spangenberg, *Mansfeldische Chronica*, fo. 394 (r): this was the only volume of the four-volume work which was printed in the sixteenth century; Spangenberg, *Mansfeldische Chronik*, 4, 1, 35. See also, Krumhaar, *Versuch*, 5–6.

19. Treu, '. . . *von daher bin ich*', 33; Historische Commission für die Provinz Sachsen und das Herzogtum Anhalt, *Beschreibende Darstellung der älteren Bau- und Kunstdenkmäler*, vol. 18, *Der Mansfelder Gebirgskreis*, 116–47, 141. Counts Albrecht IV and Gebhard VII became early supporters of Luther's Reformation, and the altar was probably a product of the Cranach milieu, perhaps of Christian Döring; the thief on Christ's right is the one who was saved.

20. Hans-Jürgen Döhle, 'Schwein, Geflügel und Fisch – bei Luthers zu Tisch' in Meller (ed.), *Luther in Mansfeld*. Sixty per cent of the bones found in the Luther house were from pigs, while only 10 per cent of finds related to cattle, an unusually high dominance which as Döhle points out indicates that the family chose to eat what was then becoming the meat of the better-off; beef products dominated amongst the poorer classes. The family may have kept pigs from time to time. There are also domestic geese and poultry bones; and about a third of the bones come from young birds, indicating that the family was eating good, tender poultry. See also Michael Fessner, 'Luthers Speisezettel. Die Versorgung der Grafschaft Mansfeld mit Lebensmitteln, Gütern und Waren' in Meller (ed.), *Fundsache Luther*.

21. Hans-Georg Stephan, 'Keramische Funde aus Luthers Elternhaus' in Meller (ed.), *Luther in Mansfeld*: the ceramics probably came in the main from Eisleben, where there was at least one large pottery, and date from around 1500. The surviving fragments came from at least 250, perhaps as many as over 300 ceramic objects, including a variety of kitchen equipment. They are simple objects, with little decoration, that do not yet show Renaissance style and colours. But nor do the grey earthwares typical of the mid-fifteenth century dominate, suggesting that this was a family that bought new. Hans-Georg Stephan, 'Keramische Funde aus Luthers Elternhaus' and Bjoern Schlenker, 'Archäologie am Elternhaus Martin Luthers' in Meller (ed.), *Luther in Mansfeld*.

22. LW 54, p. 8; WT 1, 55.

23. LHASA, MD, Rep. F4, Ch. 19, Lambrecht Kegel und Hans Reinicke, 1516–18: see e.g. fos. 11–15.

24. These are not the only pictures including women. See Agricola, *De re metallica Libri XII*.

25. LHASA MD Rep F4 Ak. No. 1 Berg und Handelsbuch, 1507–9, fo. 54 (v) lists forty *Hüttenmeister* including Hans Luder; Günter Vogler, 'Eisleben und Nürnberg zur Zeit Martin Luthers. Beziehungen zwischen zwei

Wirtschaftspartnern' in Knape (ed.), *Martin Luther und Eisleben*, 61: by 1536 their numbers had halved, to twenty-one.

26. LHASA MD Rep F4 Ak. No. 1 Berg und Handelsbuch, 1507–9, fos. 18 (r)–19 (v); 20 (v); 21 (r); 39 (v)–40 (r); 58 (r). See also LHASA, MD, Rep F4 Bc No. 1, Beschwerden der Berg- und Hüttenleute wegen des Lohns, 1536, addressed to the counts.

27. Mück, *Der Mansfelder Kupferschieferbergbau*, II (*Beilage*, 37); and that year there were complaints from the *Hüttenmeister* that miners would be taken on and paid but would abscond, switching to a new master, II, 41, 115, 117–18, 120, 128, 130.

28. See, for example, LHASA, MD, Rep F4, Db No. 1, Gerichtsbuch Hettstedt, *Beilage*, 1, fo. 63 (r) (1514).

29. LHASA MD Rep F4 Ak. No. 1 Berg und Handelsbuch, 1507–9, fos. 8 (v); 25 (v); 64 (v).

30. Ibid., fo. 57 (r–v): it was decreed that no one guilty of murder should be employed.

31. Spangenberg, *Mansfeldische Chronik*, 4, part 1, 74–5.

32. Biering, *Historische Beschreibung*, 10.

33. In 1517, the district of Eisleben and Mansfeld together with Seeburg and Bornstedt got through 2,196 barrels of beer: Spangenberg, *Mansfeldische Chronica*, 1, fo. 409 (v). From the court books a pattern of fights emerges, as Mansfelders slashed each other with knives, one man pulling his wife's two knives out of their scabbards to get at his opponents, another resorting to his breadknife, while the bathkeeper tried to stab one luckless client with his scissors: LHASA MD, Rep. Cop., No. 427e, Gerichtsbuch Thalmansfeld 1498–1513, fos. 132 (v), 129 (v), 40 (v).

34. Michael Fessner, 'Die Familie Luder in Möhra und Mansfeld' in Meller (ed.), *Fundsache Luther*, 21; Clein Hans Luther was involved in at least twelve brawls between 1505 and 1512. See LHASA, MD, Rep. Cop., No. 427e (Gerichtsbuch Thalmansfeld 1498–1513).

35. LHASA, MD, Rep. Cop., No. 427e (Gerichtsbuch Thalmansfeld 1498–1513) fo. 126 (r).

36. See ibid., fos. 125 (v); 65 (v): the remark is illustrated with a doodle that looks like a penis in front of a gallows; fos. 127 (v)–128 (v).

37. See LHASA, MD, Rep. Cop., No. 427e (Gerichtsbuch Thalmansfeld 1498–1513), fo. 135 (v) (1513). He is referred to as Hans Luder. It is conceivable that this entry refers to Little Hans, who regularly appears in the courtbook. But our Hans Luder also appears in the book, and 'Little Hans' is designated as such. The entry is crossed through, which probably indicates that the dispute had been settled.

38. LHASA MD Rep F4 Ak. No. 1 Berg und Handelsbuch, 1507–9, fos. 83 (r)–85 (v); 87 (r).

39.  See, for example, ibid., *passim*.

40.  So, for example, Hans Luder's first and long-term partner was Hans Lüttich, who came from an established mining family, but in 1507 he also joined forces with Dr Drachstedt to buy three 'fires'. He also operated shafts with Wilhelm Reinicke; Freydank, 'Vater Luther', 67–70: there is one account book that has survived from their partnership that covers a period of about three months in 1519 and is summarised by Freydank, but it appears now to be lost, though shown in an exhibition in 1936; LHASA Rep F4 Ch No. 19, Rechnungen Lamprecht Kegel und Hans Reinicke, 1516–18. One 'smelter' (to which various mines were assigned) formed part of Margarethe's dowry when she married Hentze Kaufmann in late 1511 or early 1512; WB 11, 192, n.28; and the two men worked together.

41.  Ekkehard Westermann, 'Der wirtschaftliche Konzentrationsprozess im Mansfelder Revier' in Knape (ed.), *Martin Luther und der Bergbau*, 70: he estimates thirty workers per 'fire', a total which excludes smiths, carpenters, charcoalers, drivers and others; Fessner estimates a workforce of around 3,000 in earlier times and well over that number by 1525; Michael Fessner, 'Das Montanwesen in der Grafschaft Mansfeld vom ausgehenden 15. bis zur zweiten Hälfte des 16. Jahrhunderts' in Westermann (ed.), *Montanregion als Sozialregion*, 301.

42.  Andreas Stahl, 'Historische Bauforschung an Luthers Elternhaus. Archivalische Voruntersuchungen und erste Baubeobachtungen' in Meller (ed.), *Luther in Mansfeld*, 368: Luder had worked with Drachstedt. See also Günter Vogler, 'Eisleben und Nürnberg zur Zeit Martin Luthers. Beziehungen zwischen zwei Wirtschaftspartnern' in Knape (ed.), *Martin Luther und Eisleben*; even Drachstedt got into financial difficulties at the end of the 1520s. On Drachstedt, see Kramm, *Oberschichten*, I, 113. He was not the only one with legal training: Johann Rühel, another *Hüttenmeister*, also had a law doctorate.

43.  Andreas Stahl, 'Baugeschichtliche Erkenntnisse zu Luthers Elternhaus in Mansfeld' in Knape (ed.), *Martin Luther und Eisleben*, 372.

44.  LHASA, MD, Rep F4 Ch No. 16 (Wernigerode), Rechnung Hüttenzins 1506–31. The number of 'fires' Luder had varied: in 1515 he had three and a half on his own and the same number in partnership, while in 1519 he had all seven. These were divided in 1522 so that he ran two with his son-in-law and his son Jacuff ran the others, also in partnership. Perhaps this marked a broader generational shift: the scribe takes a new page and heads the year 1523 with unusual flourish, and notes the date in mirror writing: fo. 117 (r).

45.  Ekkehard Westermann, 'Der wirtschaftliche Konzentrationsprozess im Mansfelder Revier' in Knape (ed.), *Martin Luther und der Bergbau*, 67.

46. Mück, *Kupferschieferbergbau*, I, 62–4; vol. 2, 88–93, esp. 91 for passage in course of negotiations between the counts in which Luder's difficulties are alluded to; Michael Fessner, 'Die Familie Luder in Möhra und Mansfeld' in Meller (ed.), *Fundsache Luther*, 23.

47. The total was valued at 1,250 fl, split between each of the five surviving children or their offspring. The division was notional, because Jacob received the property and had to pay off each of the other heirs. To make this financially possible, he was to settle accounts with one claimant first and then slowly settle with the others, Luther waiting for his share last. WB 7, 88–9, 10 July 1534, for the contract written by Luther. See also Michael Fessner, 'Die Familie Luder in Möhra und Mansfeld' in Meller (ed.), *Fundsache Luther*, 24, who points out that Luder was able to keep his private property, including some land, separate from his mining debts.

48. This was a process of concentration of economic power amongst a smaller number of men, but it also signified decline: Ekkehard Westermann, 'Rechtliche und soziale Folgen wirtschaftlicher Konzentrationsprozesse im Mansfelder Revier in der ersten Hälfte des 16. Jahrhunderts' in Jankowski (ed.), *Zur Geschichte*; Ekkehard Westermann, 'Der wirtschaftliche Konzentrationsprozess im Mansfelder Revier' in Knape (ed.), *Martin Luther und der Bergbau*, 65.

49. Michael Fessner, 'Die Familie Luder und das Bergwerks- und Hüttenwesen in der Grafschaft Mansfeld und im Herzogtum Braunschweig-Wolfenbüttel' in Knape (ed.), *Martin Luther und Eisleben*, 28.

50. WT 1, 705, 25–7; WT 4, 4617, 404:11–13; 7–9; Luther early on condemned the use of 'dowsing rods' to look for hidden treasure, though such rods (sometimes dedicated with magical formulae) were frequently used in mining. See Dym, *Divining Science*, 62; Luther condemned it in 1518 in his *Decem Praecepta Wittenbergensi praedicata populo*, 1521. Mines could, however, reveal God's truth: Luther was impressed by the discovery in 1538 in the Mansfeld mines of an image on a fossil in the shape of a pope in cassock and wearing the triple tiara. For Luther, it was further proof that the Pope was the Antichrist: Freydank, *Martin Luther und der Bergbau*, 64–6; Biering, *Historische Beschreibung*, 128–34; WT 4, 4961.

51. See in particular *(Kleiner) Sermon von dem Wucher* (1519), WS 6, 1–8; *(Grosser) Sermon von dem Wucher* (1520) WS 6, 33–60; *Von Kaufshandlung und Wucher* (1524) WS 15, 293–322; *An die Pfarrherrn wider den Wucher zu predigen, Vermahnung* (1540), WS 51, 331–424: by 1540 his rhetoric was more extreme and he linked usurers more directly with the Devil, comparing a usurer to a *Beer wolff* (werewolf): WS 51, 399. See, on the 1524 tract and its economic context, Rössner, *Martin Luther. On Commerce and Usury*.

52. Ulrich Wenner, 'Fundgrubner, Berckhauer und Schlacktreiber: Montan-
    wortschatz bei Martin Luther' in Knape (ed.), *Martin Luther und der
    Bergbau*, 214, n.18, 19; WT 5, 6374, 630:3–4; and see WT 3, 3471, from
    autumn 1536; and WT 5, 5675, 'Ich will kein kucks haben! Es ist spielgelt,
    vnd es will nicht wudelln, dasselbig gelt.' He presents shares as fraudu-
    lent.

53. Myconius, *Geschichte*, 14–15. On the popularity of St Anna amongst
    miners in Mansfeld, see Andreas Hornemann, 'Zeugnisse der spätmittel-
    alterlichen Annenverehrung im Mansfelder Land' in Knape (ed.), *Martin
    Luther und der Bergbau*, and on the cult of St Anna, which Luther regarded
    as a novelty introduced during his childhood, see Welsh, *Anna Mater
    Matronarum*, ch. 4 forthcoming; I am grateful to the author for
    permission to cite.

54. Spangenberg, *Mansfeldische Chronik*, 4, 1, 94; Andreas Stahl, 'Bauge-
    schichtliche Erkenntnisse zu Luthers Elternhaus in Mansfeld' in Knape
    (ed.), *Martin Luther und Eisleben*, 366–7; Schlenker, 'Archäologie am
    Elternhaus Martin Luthers', in Meller (ed.), *Luther in Mansfeld*, 96–9.

55. Indeed, in 1520 when writing indignantly to Spalatin that his parents
    were not Bohemians, as was being alleged, Luther referred only to his
    mother's relatives at Eisenach, not to his father's at Möhra. He may
    not have met his father's extended kin until 1521, when, after the Diet
    of Worms, he made a visit there. WB 1, 238, 10 Jan. 1520; 239, 14 Jan.
    1520.

56. Some accounts say that two of Hans and Margarethe's children died in
    an outbreak of plague around 1506 or 1507, and it is conceivable that
    these were older siblings. Barbara, a younger sister of Luther's, died in
    1520: Siggins, *Luther and His Mother*, 14. WT 1, 1108 contains a rather
    obscure comment by Luther that his parents left for Mansfeld with a
    son, and after this remark he mentions his own birth. But Luther was
    born in Eisleben, not Mansfeld, so it would be possible to read the
    account as a garbled version with himself as the child with whom they
    left Eisleben: the evidence for the existence of an older brother is not
    compelling.

57. Johannes Schneidewein (rector of the University of Wittenberg), in
    *Scriptorum publice propositorum a gvbernatoribus studiorum in Academia
    Wittenbergensi* 3, Wittenberg 1559 [VD 16 W 3761] fos. 190 (v)–191 (v):
    Siggins, *Luther and His Mother*, 14.

58. WT 1, 1016. She was apparently feeding the young Martin while pregnant
    with Paul.

59. WT 3, 2963a, 2963b. Luther had one older son Hans; but at this time
    Paul, the newborn, was displacing Martin, his elder brother who bore
    Luther's name, at the breast.

60. Andreas Stahl, 'Baugeschichtliche Erkenntnisse zu Luthers Elternhaus in Mansfeld' in Knape (ed.), *Martin Luther und Eisleben*, 366; Mathesius, *Historien*, 537. On Luther's use of mining metaphors, see Ulrich Wenner, 'Fundgrubner, Berckhauer und Schlacktreiber: Montanwortschatz bei Martin Luther' in Knape (ed.), *Martin Luther und der Bergbau*. It is surprising how rarely Luther uses metaphors drawn from mining, given that some use was unavoidable because they occur in the Bible. He certainly understood the metaphors he used. His earlier translations of the Bible until the mid-1520s used the word *durchfewern* (through-firing), while later he preferred *durchleutern*, or *leutern* (purifying), perhaps a move away from an earlier rootedness in the technical knowledge of smelting processes.

61. For instance, his father, brother, brother's wife and his sister's husband were visiting Luther in 1529; his brother Jacob visited him in Coburg shortly after their father's death, and we know he visited again in 1538 and 1540; in 1536, Luther complained that Jacob had not been writing to him, suggesting there was otherwise a correspondence, WB 5, 1410, 19 April 1529; and see n.4; WB 7, 2287, 19 Jan. 1536. As Luther lay dying, his three young sons, who had come with him, were taken to Mansfeld where Jacob looked after them, WB 11, 4207, 300:16–17.

62. WB 7, 88–9, July 1534.

63. WT 5, 6424; Luther betrayed his social circle's contempt for them in a casual conversational remark when discussing the possible marriage of a female relative: if she didn't behave he would marry her not to an academic, but 'a black miner' and 'no pious, educated man' would be deceived with her.

64. No fewer than eighteen Mansfelders enrolled at Wittenberg between 1530 and 1538: Scheel, *Martin Luther*, I, 53.

## 2. The Scholar

1. WB 2, 510, 15 June 1522; Moshauer was one of those who achieved social advancement through education: Dieter Stievermann, 'Sozialer Aufstieg um 1500: Hüttenmeister Hans Luther und sein Sohn Dr Martin Luther' in Knape (ed.), *Martin Luther und der Bergbau*, 48.

2. He appears in the list of smelter-masters as 'the younger' Hans with two fires 'on the meadow', LHASA, MD, Rep. Cop., No. 425b, fo. 121 (r), 1516; the next year he bought the house by the Silberhütte at Tal Mansfeld, fo. 126 (r), 1517; and in 1519 when his father died he took over the family house, in Tal Mansfeld, situated between the churchyard and Nickell Lebestock's house, fo. 174 (r); he bought another property in 1519 at Eissberg, and took over a set of properties formerly owned by

Steffan Schmid, in 1526: fo. 175 (v). He and Jacob Luder are listed as *Hüttenmeister* in 1534: LHASA MD Rep F4 Ak No. 8; Reinicke is listed with other mining financiers from Leipzig and Stolberg in a contract with the counts, 1536, Möllenberg, *Urkundenbuch*, 194.

3.  Ekkehard Westermann, 'Der wirtschaftliche Konzentrationsprozess im Mansfelder Revier' in Knape (ed.), *Martin Luther und der Bergbau*, 67.

4.  Kramm, *Oberschichten*, I, 114.

5.  WB 5, 1595, *Beilage*, 19 June 1530, letter of Veit Dietrich to Katharina von Bora, 379:16–17; Melanchthon's biography of Luther recorded that Reinicke's 'virtue was later so outstanding that he had great authority in these Regions', Vandiver, Keen and Frazel (eds and trs), *Luther's Lives*, 15; Melanchthon, *Vita Lutheri*, fo. 10 (v); WB 8, 3255, 1 Sept. 1538, 280:4–5; Mathesius mentions him briefly, *Historien*, 6; Adam, *Life and death*, 2.

6.  LW 45, 375; WS 15, 51:13–16.

7.  WT 3, 3566A and 3566B. – the latter comment was actually from 1543, the earlier from 1537, but Aurifaber, the editor of the first printed Table Talk, merged them.

8.  Kramm, *Oberschichten*, I, 36, figures from 1557, for 748 citizens. Eisenach suffered a devastating fire in 1636 and as a result, little is known about the earlier history of the town and we are reliant on chroniclers. The 'big' landowners according to Eisenach's regulations were those with 'two *Hufen* of land and meadows, six milking cows and four commercial animals' – which suggests that agriculture remained very significant for most of its inhabitants. By the sixteenth century, nearly half the citizens owned gardens, agricultural land, vineyards or hopfields. In 1466 the civic notary Johannes Biermast warned that 'if authority becomes weak, then craftspeople rule', suggestive of social and political tension in the town, Kramm, *Oberschichten*, I, 187, 2, 683, n.4; 1, 253, Strenge and Devrient, *Die Stadtrechte*, No. 34, 70–1; No. 43, 85. The town counted only five big traders in the mid-sixteenth century – as many as Weimar, whose population was smaller, Kramm, *Oberschichten*, 1, 166, 2, 670, n.112: on the basis of the tax register of 1542 a population of 3,030 has been estimated. See also Bergmann, *Kommunalbewegung*. Contemporaries were well aware of the decline. By the second half of the fifteenth century there were complaints about economic stagnation, and criticisms were repeated in a council investigation of 1509. See also Staatsarchiv Weimar, 389 Eisenach, 14, fo. 102 for a 1509 list of reasons why the town was experiencing decline, including that the town wall enclosed too great an area, that the citizens feasted and gourmandised too much, that they lacked a monopoly on beer brewing.

9.  Siggins, *Luther and His Mother*, 46. Even his mother's maiden name was uncertain for some time, older literature identifying it as 'Ziegler' and

confusing it with the name of her grandfather. Wolfgang Liebehenschel argues that she was originally born in Bad Neustadt about 80 km distant from Eisenach, and that her father was a 'Ziegler', that is, that he owned a brick-making oven; Wolfgang Liebehenschel, 'CURRICULUM VITAE der Mutter Martin Luthers. Die Herkunft der Mutter Martin Luthers' in Knape (ed.), *Martin Luther und der Bergbau*; see also Kurt Löcher, 'Martin Luthers Eltern – Ein Bildnispaar Lucas Cranachs von 1527 auf der Wartburg' in Knape (ed.), *Martin Luther und der Bergbau*. Melanchthon said that Luther was sent to Eisenach 'because his mother had been born of an honest and old family in those parts', and also because the teaching in Eisenach was better; Vandiver, Keen and Frazel (eds and trs), *Luther's Lives*, 15; Melanchthon, *Vita Lutheri*, 10–11, a claim repeated by Melchior Adam's 1620 biography who explains that Luther was moved 'because his Mother was born there of a worthy and ancient family' (Adam, *Life and death*, 3); Mathesius also says in his first sermon that Luther moved to Eisenach 'da er seiner Mutter Freundschafft hatte': Mathesius, *Historien*, 7; and Luther's doctor Ratzeberger also states that he was sent 'kegen Eisenach zu seinen gefreundten', Ratzeberger, *Die handschriftliche Geschichte*, 43. See also Richter, *Genealogia Lutherorum*, 13–23 who correctly identifies her as a Lindemann.

10. WT 3, 2888 51:9–10. See Siggins, *Luther and His Mother* for a brilliant portrait of their relationship.

11. Posset, *Front-Runner*, xx: *Ein seligs newes Jar*. The dedication is to 'Meyner Lieben Mutter Margarethen lutherin'.

12. Mathesius, *Historien*, 8.

13. Siggins, *Luther and His Mother*, 52; on Luther as prophet see Ingrid Kasten, '"Was ist Luther? Ist doch die lere nitt meyn": Die Anfänge des Luther-Mythos im 16. Jahrhundert' in Bok and Shaw, *Magister et amicus*, 899–931; Kolb, *Martin Luther as Prophet, Teacher, and Hero*, 75–101.

14. It is unclear where precisely this took place; some scholars argue that it occurred in Eisenach, others, at Erfurt either before or after he entered the monastery: WT 5, Ernst Kroker, 'Einleitungen', xv–xvii. See WT 1, 116, and WT 5, 5346 where the story of Samuel is the one he reads when he first encounters the Bible; WT 3, 3767 does not make the connection to Samuel. Like Samuel, Luther's own prophetic mission was different from the path on which he had set out.

15. Johannes Cochlaeus ('Georg Sachsen'), *Hertzog Georgens zu Sachssen Ehrlich vnd grundtliche entschuldigung, wider Martin Luthers Auffruerisch vn[d] verlogenne brieff vnd Verantwortung*, Dresden 1533 [VD 16 C 4323], fo. B iii (v). This pasquil went out under the name of Duke Georg of Saxony but was actually written by Luther's long-standing enemy Cochlaeus. He repeated it in his prefatory letter to his biography of

Luther, which was more widely read and appeared in 1549. The same accusation had also been made by Georg Witzel, and by Petrus Sylvius, *Die Letzten zwey beschlisslich und aller krefftigest büchleyn M. Petri Sylvii, so das Lutherisch thun an seiner person...* Leipzig 1534, Ian Siggins, 'Luther's Mother Margarethe', *Harvard Theological Review* 71, 1978, 125–50, 132.

16. Siggins, 'Luther's Mother', 133: he referred to it again in 1543 in *On the Jews and their Lies*; and see WT 3, 3838: in 1538 Luther recalled how Duke Georg called his mother a bath maid and him a *wechselbalck*, referring to the pamphlet written by Cochlaeus under the name of Duke Georg in 1533.

17. LW Letters, I, 145; WB 1, 239, 14 Jan. 1520, 610:20–3.

18. Topp, *Historia*, 8: there were of course other versions of this story.

19. Ibid., 6–32; Bergmann, *Kommunalbewegung*, 11–15; 33–7.

20. Topp, *Historia*, 10–13; see also Stadtarchiv Eisenach, *Bestand Chroniken*, 40.1/9.1 *Chronik Joh. Michael Koch*.

21. *Chronik Eisenachs bis 1409* (ed. H. Helmbold), 27–40; Kremer, *Beiträge*.

22. WB 1, 157, 24(?), Feb. 1519, 353:29–30; WT 3, 3626; 3653.

23. Topp, *Historia*, 15.

24. Topp recounts the story of a statue of the Madonna and child in St Paul's monastery in the town, where, if one prayed before the image, Jesus would turn his back as if rejecting the sinner. But if one promised a donation to the monastery, Jesus would turn his face, and if one offered more money, he would bless the worshipper: Topp, *Historia*, 15.

25. LW 44, 172; WS 6, 438:18–22; WB 2, 262, 29 Feb. 1520. The discomfort about begging was long-standing: Luther later reminisced how, back at Mansfeld, with a fellow pupil, he went begging for sausage at carnival as was customary, but when a burgher teased them they scarpered, and the householder had to run after them with the sausages: WT 1, 137: Luther uses this story as a parable of the believer's relationship to God; and he couples it, interestingly, with the story of his terror of the sacrament when Staupitz carried it in procession at Eisleben.

26. Brecht, *Luther*, I, 18.

27. The family gave so many donations to the monastery that it was locally known as the 'Collegium Schalbense'. See Kremer, *Beiträge*, esp. 69 and 89.

28. Scherf, *Bau- und Kunstdenkmale*, 9.

29. Ratzeberger, *Die handschriftliche Geschichte*, 43–4: Ratzeberger, not a reliable source, attributes this to Joannes Trebonius, but it is unclear whether such a man existed, or whether the anecdote refers to the Eisenach humanist Trebelius, not a teacher of Luther's, or whether this anecdote is about another teacher at the school, Brecht, *Luther*, I, 19. The story is repeated in Paullini, *Historia Isenacensis*, 125–6.

30. WT 1, 256.

31. WB 1, 3, 22 April 1507; 4, 28 April 1507.

32. The letter reveals that while Braun had continued to write to young Martin, he had not replied. There are three paragraphs of rather extravagant reassurance of his affection before Luther gets to the point of the letter, which is to explain that he has gone to Wittenberg, and apologise for neither having visited him nor told him of the move. WB 1, 5, 17 March 1509, 16:10–11; 17:38. He did however send him a copy of his 1515 Gotha sermon (see below) but did not invite him to his doctoral celebration.

33. Paullini, *Historia Isenacensis*, 122–4, which includes a record of his tombstone renewed in 1669, 'non cultus, sed memoriae causa', and which is a powerful anti-Catholic monument – the 'wrong' date 1516 has been corrected to 1517. See Engel, *Kurzer / Jedoch gewisser*: Engel recalled translating Hilten's prophecies from German to Latin in his schooldays) at Strausberg, fo. A 11 (r)–(v). Mathesius brings the story about Hilten as the third prophecy about Luther: an old priest told Luther, ill as a student, that God would make 'a great man' out of him; the second was that of Jan Hus who prophesied that after the 'goose' (Hus) would come a 'swan'. The prophecies follow straight on from his account of Luther's first discovery of the Bible: Mathesius, *Historien*, 8–9. See also Topp, *Historia*, 16–18; and for Luther's conviction the prophecy referred to him, WT 3, 3795. Myconius does not refer to Hilten in his history of the Reformation but refers to him indirectly in an account (at second hand) of one of his own dreams: Lehmann, *Historischer Schauplatz*, 799, where Myconius's own fate amongst the cruel monks is described as resembling Hilten's.

34. WB 5, 1480, 17 Oct. 1529; and 1491, 7 Nov. 1529; Myconius's full reply, 1501, 2 Dec. 1529. See also WB 5, 1501, 194: Luther knew from an eyewitness, through inquiries made by Myconius, that Hilten died having received the sacrament in the customary way; this account did not say that he had been starved to death. Luther also knew through Myconius that the year prophesied was 1514: WB 5, 191.

35. *Die Bekenntnisschriften der evangelisch-lutherischen Kirche* (*Confessio Augustana*), 378. Hilten predicted that the assault on the papacy would last thirty years – and so Lutheran hagiographers could link it precisely with Luther's death in 1546. Hilten thus took his place as an important forerunner of Luther, a St John the Baptist figure predicting the coming of the new prophet. The seventeenth-century Lutheran theologian and Superintendent of Eisenach Nikolaus Rebhan's account even had Hilten perish in his cell refusing to receive the sacrament in one kind only, as if he were an adherent of Hus, WB 5, 1501, *Beilage* II, 195.

36. See WS 30, 3, 491, Luther's marginal annotations to the CA, 1531.

37. Interestingly, in a letter to Braun written after he had entered the monastery, he assumed that the older man would share his preference for studying theology over philosophy, suggesting that these religious interests went back to his school days.

38. Paullini, *Historia Isenacensis*, 125–6; Mathesius, *Historien*, 7; Cotta was apparently part of the Schalbe family so the tale explains how he came to live with them; Drescher, *De festis diebus . . .*, [190–1] (Narratio I) [VD 16 D 2723], stressing the pity a 'mother' showed him when he failed to get bread by begging; Ratzeberger, *Die handschriftliche Geschichte*, 41–2; Luther claimed the water healed the fever.

39. WT 2, 2719a, 613:28–9; WT 2, 2719b. See Brecht, *Luther*, I, 30; and WT 2, 2788b; 2894 b.

40. Scheel, *Dokumente*, 15, 16. On the University of Erfurt and Luther, see Brecht, *Luther*, I, 40, 163; and Bob Scribner, 'Die Eigentümlichkeit der Erfurter Reformation' in Weiß (ed.), *Erfurt 742–1992*, 241–74.

41. Brecht, *Luther*, I, 33.

42. WB 1, 5, 17 March 1509: Luther says he would rather study theology than philosophy.

43. WT 5, 6419, 653:24–8.

44. See Oberman, *Masters of the Reformation*.

45. WT 2, 2788b, 660:24–6.

46. WS 49, 322:12–13 (sermon, 20 Jan. 1544).

47. Vandiver, Keen and Frazel (eds and trs), *Luther's Lives*, 16; Melanchthon, *Vita Lutheri*, 13; WT 1, 119, 46:23–4, 'O Maria, hilff! Da wer ich, inquit, auff Mariam dahin gestorben!'

48. WT 4, 4707, 16 July 1539; interestingly he told the story on what he said was the anniversary of entering the monastery, so it was a date that remained important to him.

49. Or, as Luther later said, he returned the textbooks to the bookseller, keeping only Virgil and Plautus: WT 1, 116.

50. WT 4, 4707, 440:14–15. See also the version Justus Jonas told in 1538, which has Luther playing the lute at the party: Scheel, *Dokumente*, 151, no. 412.

51. The story provided a model for others – Myconius, for one, described a similar farewell as he left for the monastery, Lehmann, *Historischer Schauplatz*, 799.

52. WT 2, 1558, May 1532; WT 4, 4174; WT 5, 5357, summer 1540 – in both cases, Luther concludes the story by saying that he was uncomfortable with the Mass even at this point, and praises God for having saved him from it. See also WT 4, 4574.

53. WT 4, 4574, 384:24–5 WS 49, 322:32–4 (sermon, 20 Jan. 1544); and see 1549 account of Valentin Bavarus, *Rapsodiae et Dicta quedam ex ore Doctoris Martini Lutheri*, II, 752–4, in Scheel, *Dokumente*, 184–5; WS 44, 711ff; WT 1, 623; WT 1, 881; WT 2, 1558; WT 3, 3556 A. See also Ratzeberger, *Luther*, 48–9: this account has his father upbraid Luther for not supporting his parents in their old age and becoming a monk instead. It also represents Hans Luder as consistently hostile to monks and monasticism, reading back Luther's later attitudes into the story; and it omits his father's question of whether the apparition was a diabolic illusion.

54. LW Letters, I, 301; WB 2, 428, 9 Sept. 1521, 385:3–4; and he made a similar comment in the Dedication to his Father of *De Votis monasticis*, 21 Nov. 1521, WS 8, 573; see also WT 1 872, first half 1530s.

55. Nas, *Quinta Centvria*, fos. 70 v–71 r; as he mischievously and correctly points out, Melanchthon carefully did not present the thunderstorm as a prophetic sign. Nas then goes on, fo. 73 (r) ff, to mock the Lutheran prophecies, including that of Hilten. Fo. 490 (v) has an 'irrequiem' Mass for Luther, and includes a mock creed (fo. 493 (r)): I believe in Luther, born of a bath maid virgin, conceived of a '*heyllosen Geist*'.

56. Erikson, *Young Man Luther*, 94–5; 164–6; 232–3.

## 3. The Monastery

1. Andreas Lindner, 'Martin Luther im Erfurter Augustinerkloster 1505–1511' in Schmelz and Ludscheidt (eds), *Luthers Erfurter Kloster*, 62. See also Scheel, *Martin Luther*, II, 1–28, 61. Some of Luther's seniors and teachers seem to have believed however that Hus had been unjustly condemned, so Luther may in fact have been less astonished than he appeared to be.

2. Heinrich Schleiff and Michael Sussmann, 'Baugeschichte des Erfurter Augustinerklosters – aus der Vergangenheit in die Zukunft' in Schmelz and Ludscheidt (eds), *Luthers Erfurter Kloster*, 28: it was built between 1502 and 1516; Josef Pilvousek and Klaus-Bernward Springer, 'Die Erfurter Augustiner-Eremiten: eine evangelische "Brüdergemeinde" vor und mit Luther (1266–1560)' in Schmelz and Ludscheidt (eds), *Luthers Erfurter Kloster*, 53; there were sixy-seven brothers in 1488 and fifty-two in 1508.

3. Scheel, *Martin Luther*, II, 249.

4. *Constitutiones Fratrum Heremitarum sancti Augustini ad apostolicorum privilegiorum forman p[ro] Reformatione Alemanie*, Nuremberg 1504 [VD 16 A 4142] (unpublished translation by Melinda Letts).

5. WT 3, 3517; see also WT 3, 2494a and b which estimates 18,000 or 16,000.

6. WT 2, 2494 b.

7. WB 3, 427, n.1.

8. Stefan Oehmig, 'Zur Getreide- und Brotversorgung der Stadt Erfurt in den Teuerungen des 15. und 16. Jahrhunderts' in Weiß (ed.), *Erfurt 742–1992*, 203–23.

9. Peter Willicks, 'Die Konflikte zwischen Erfurt und dem Erzbischof von Mainz am Ende des 15. Jahrhunderts' in Weiß (ed.), *Erfurt 742–1992*, 225–40; R. W. Scribner, 'Civic Unity and the Reformation in Erfurt' in Scribner (ed.), *Popular Culture*, 185–216.

10. Weiß, *Die frommen Bürger*, 95.

11. It succeeded in 1512, but there were no practical consequences: Ludolphy, *Friedrich der Weise*, 255.

12. Weiß, *Die frommen Bürger*.

13. Erfurt was not an imperial city though it longed to be one; see R. W. Scribner, 'Civic Unity and the Reformation in Erfurt' in Scribner (ed.), *Popular Culture*, 185–216.

14. Certainly the 'shameful' death of Kelner seems to have made an impression on him, and he recalled it several times: WT 1, 487; 2, 2494a and b, 2709b. He blamed Erfurt for being too proud and holding both Mainz and Saxony in contempt.

15. Interestingly the Wittenberg professor Henning Göde was centrally involved for Saxony in the negotiations that led eventually to Saxony's resumption of its dominant position in Erfurt, so Luther probably knew about these developments from Saxony's point of view; Ludolphy, *Friedrich der Weise*, 252–6.

16. WT 5, 5375. Mathesius, *Historien*, 11–2, says that the monks confiscated the Bible they had given him; Ratzeberger, *Luther*, 46–8, that he had to do the work of a '*Hausknecht*', sweeping and cleaning instead of study.

17. WT 5, 5375.

18. WS 41, 447:16 (sermon, 1535), WS 17, 1, 309. Luther was particularly opposed to the Carthusians' vegetarianism, which he considered unhealthy: WS 42, 504 (lectures on Moses, 1535–45).

19. WS 10, 1, pt. 2, 436.

20. Brecht, *Luther*, I, 64; WS 11, 202, 11ff; WS 46 24:34; WT 1, 708; WT 5, 5428.

21. WS 17, 1, 309:31–4.

22. WS 32, 327:21–2.

23. WS 11, 60:20–2.

24. WS 33, 83:31–6; 84:1–5.

25. WT 2, 1746, 203:43–5: he continued that Aristotle and Bonaventure were the figures he held in high regard.

26. WS 38, 148:6–8; the Latin term he uses is *tentatio*.

27. WT 1, 518.

28. WS 45, 152:8, 36–7;  WT 1, 137, 59: 27–32;  WT 2, 2318a.

29. WT 1, 122, 50:28; see also for example WT 2, 1492; WS 21, 358:17; WS 31, 1, 148b: 3; WS 40, 2, 91–2.

30. WT 1, 141, 14 Dec. 1531, 65:13–14.

31. WB 5, 1377, 31 Jan. 1529, 14:14–15.

32. WB 5, 1671, 1 [Aug.] 1530, 521:6.

33. WB 5, 1670, July(?) 1530, 518–20; he even suggested committing a small sin.

34. LW Letters, I, 27–8; WB 1, 28, 26 Oct. 1516, 72:6–10; 10–11; 12–13.

35. WB 1, 18, 30 June 1516; 13, 1 May 1516; he also complained about another monk who would bring shame on the convent at Eisleben.

36. Brecht, *Luther*, I, 98–105.

37. WT 5, 5344, 75:2; summer 1540.

38. Though his later self, recalling this, immediately added 'And the Devil shat his thanks on the Pope', as if the city's reputation for holiness still needed a bit of prophylactic mud-slinging: WT 5, 6059.

39. WT 3, 3781.

40. WT 3, 3479 a.

41. WT 4, 4104, 136:6. He did however remember the Pantheon, which he said was painted with pictures of all the gods, WT 1, 507; 5, 5515; and he noticed that there were no windows but that light came in through a round hole in the top of the building.

42. WS 41, 198:12–14 (sermons, 1535).

43. WT 3, 3428, 313:5; Mathesius, *Historien*, 14, which also includes this quotation. See also WT 5, 5484; and WT 5, 5347: here Luther in a very brief handwritten list of key dates of his life includes the trip to Rome, 'ubi est sedes Diaboli': it ranks with his marriage, the indulgences dispute and the Leipzig Debate.

44. Scheel, *Dokumente*, 210 for Paul Luther's account; WS 51, 89 (1545); see also WS 17, 1, 353.

45. WS 31, 226. He also recalled going to the Church of St John Lateran, where a pious pilgrim could gain indulgence for their mother by saying Mass – but he could not get through the crowds, WS 31, 1, 226.

46. WT 4, 4925, 582:3; 6, 7005; Friedrich Roth, 'Die geistliche Betrügerin Anna Laminit von Augsburg (c.1480–1518)', *Zeitschrift für Kirchengeschichte* 43/2, 1924, 335–417; *Chroniken der deutschen Städte* 23, 116–17; 25, 11–20; 85–6; Roper, *Holy Household*, 262–3.

47. The date of Staupitz's birth is not known. Zumkeller believes 1468 is likely; others 1465 or earlier; Zumkeller, *Staupitz*, 1. On Staupitz, see Wriedt, *Gnade und Erwählung*.

48. Posset, *Front-runner*, 33–5; 79–89 (he succeeded Andreas Proles as head of the Saxon reform congregation); 128: in 1509–12 he was both vicar

general of the German reformed Augustinians and provincial of the conventual Augustinians in Saxony.

49. Zumkeller, *Staupitz*, 7. Zumkeller shrewdly observes that this could be a description of Staupitz himself.

50. WT 5, 5989, 417:11–2. Staupitz apparently continued that even so, he would not stop promoting young men; Luther, who probably told the story in 1544, drew parallels with his own experiences with Veit Amerbach and Georg Agricola, whom he considered ungrateful.

51. WB 1, 6, 22 Sept. 1512, 18:10–12.

52. WT 2, 2255a, 379:10; 2255b, 1531: Luther himself interpreted this as a reference to his future interest in the questions of penance and indulgences. Luther formally began his doctoral studies early in 1512, completing them later that year.

53. WB 1, 8, 16 June 1514, 25:8 and *passim*. Yet by 1518, they had apparently made up, for he asked Lang to pass on his greetings to Nathin, WB 1, 64, 21 March 1518.

54. Posset, *Front-runner*, 280: Nathin was one of the six Augustinian friars who, when the remaining members of the reformed Augustinians failed to elect a new vicar, signed a declaration in 1523 that they were not followers of the alien 'Martinian' teaching.

55. WT 1, 173, 1532, 80:6–7.

56. WS 1, 525–7; Härle, Schilling and Wartenberg (eds), *Martin Luther*, II, 17–23 for a German translation; WB 11, 4088, 27 March 1545, 67:7–8; 6–7. Luther noted this in support of a petition from the widow Margarethe von Staupitz, who had turned to Luther for support because 'you were so close to Dr Staupitz at one time and to my husband' (4087, 61:26–7). She had married a former Augustinian.

57. Interestingly the 1523 edition of *Ein buchlein von der nachfolgung* pointed up the scriptural references and concealed many of those to the doctors of the Church, Posset, *Front-runner*, 157. On Staupitz's intellectual development and particular version of Augustinianism, see Oberman, *Masters of the Reformation*, 75–91.

58. Staupitz, *Ein nutzbarliches büchlein*, fos D iv (v), Eii (v); Posset, *Front-Runner*, 169–71.

59. Schneide-Lastin (ed.), *Johann von Staupitz*, 69. 'Siech, wie speiben die *hundt* in in mit all dem unflat, den si gehaben muegen': the 'dog' is a reference to the term in Psalms; but whether the audience would have got the reference or would just have heard the insult is less clear. Posset, however, argues that Staupitz is not anti-Semitic; *Front-Runner*.

60. Schneide-Lastin (ed.), *Johann von Staupitz*, 79, 85, 86: 'Die juden haben vil herter gesuent dann Pilatus: die juden tetens aus poshait', 'Die herten juden, die verfluecht creatur, die verwirft den herren . . .. Alle welt zaigt

an den *neid* der juden.' 'O du poser jud! Pilatus gibt dir zu erkennen, das dein natur ist herter dann ain swein; das hat erparmung mit seiner natur.' These quotations are taken from sermons 6, 7, 8 and 9.

61. See Steinmetz, *Luther and Staupitz*, who argues that Luther's debt to Staupitz was primarily pastoral, not theological.

62. Dohna and Wetzel (eds), Johann von Staupitz, *Sämtliche Schriften*, II, 193, 197. See also Kolb, *Martin Luther. Confessor of the Faith*, 27–30; Hamm, *Frömmigkeitstheologie*, 234–47; Wriedt, *Gnade und Erwählung*.

63. Staupitz, *Ein nutzbarlichs büchlein*, fo. D ii (r–v); Schneide-Lastin, 108.

64. Ibid., fo. D I (r); Wriedt, *Gnade und Erwählung*, 63–7; Posset, *Front-Runner*, 171.

65. Posset, *Front-runner*, 135 on the nuns of St Peter's. Staupitz's works were republished by the Spiritualist Caspar Schwenckfeld and rediscovered and reprinted in the seventeenth century by Pietists such as Johann Arndt and Gottfried Arnold who described him as a representative of 'antischolastic mysticism' in 1699. See Wriedt, *Gnade und Erwählung*, 15.

66. Staupitz, *Ein seligs newes Jar*, fo. D ii (r).

67. *Constitutiones fratrum Eremitarum sancti Augustini ad apostolicorum privilegiorum formam pro reformation Alemaniae*, Nuremberg 1504–6 [VD 16 A 4142], fo. A iv (v), Ch. 21 (tr. Melinda Letts); and see Scheel, *Martin Luther*, II, 121 – if a meeting with a woman could not be averted, and if conversation could not be avoided, the brother should say little. There must always be a witness, and permission sought from the prior, excepting only if the brother spoke with his own sister or mother. If a monk heard a woman's confession, another brother must be present, or if secrecy were essential, a brother must stand behind the door.

68. *Ein buchlein von der nachfolgung des willigen sterbens Christi* was dedicated to Countess Agnes of Mansfeld, and published in 1515 in Leipzig [VD 16 S 8697], 2nd edn 1523. *Von der liebe Gottes* was dedicated to the duke of Bavaria's widow: Posset, *Front-runner*, 167. On Luther's distrust of erotic mysticism, Steinmetz, *Luther and Staupitz*, 127; Posset, *Front-Runner*, 157. Interestingly the Augsburg edition of Staupitz's *Von der liebe Gottes* of 1520 was *'bewert and approbiert'* by Luther, as the title page announced [VD 16 8707].

69. The humanist Conrad Mutian, who heard it, asked Lang who the 'sharp' preacher had been: WB 1, 14, 29 May 1516, n.2, letter between Lang and Mutian the previous year.

70. WS 1, 44–52 for the text. Interestingly, Luther made some profound comments on envy in a letter of 1514 to Spalatin, suggesting that he was preoccupied with it: 'how absolutely right are those who condemn envy . . . that envy which is the most senseless of all: it is so utterly

eager to harm, yet unable to do so. Its licentiousness is without fear; its inability to damage is full of pain and disturbance'; LW Letters, I, 10; WB 1, 5 Aug. 1514, 28:1–16.

71. WS 1, 45:7–11. Luther was not unusual in elaborating a particular metaphor. A surviving sermon of Luther's friend and fellow Augustinian Wenzeslaus Linck from 1518, the 'Asses' Sermon', drove the metaphor of the ass to its limits and possibly beyond. Reindell (ed.), *Wenzel Lincks Wercke*, 1, 4–10.

72. WS 1, 46:12.

73. WS 1, 50:19; 24–5. It is interesting that Luther breaks into German here, yet further increasing the shock and vulgarity of his words.

74. WS 1, 51:15–16.

75. WS 1, 50:34–8.

## 4. Wittenberg

1. Bellmann, Harksen and Werner, *Denkmale*, 107–17; see also StadtA Witt, 9 [Bb6], fos. 16–43; StadtA Witt 345, 'Bau des Rathauses'.

2. Junghans, *Wittenberg als Lutherstadt*; see Manfred Straube, 'Soziale Struktur und Besitzverhältnisse in Wittenberg zur Lutherzeit', *Jahrbuch für Geschichte des Feudalismus* 9, 1985, 145–88; by 1530, he estimates the population at 4,500.

3. Myconius, *Geschichte*, 25.

4. It also offered pleasure cruises for the locals; and on one of these, Georg Neesen, a promising student, was drowned as Melanchthon and others looked on powerless to help: WB 3, 757, 6 July 1524; 760, 10 July 1524.

5. Scheel, *Martin Luther*, II, 159.

6. WT 4, 4997, 606:14–16.

7. Shachar, *Judensau*, 30. See also Bellmann, Harksen and Werner, *Denkmale*, 160, who date the sculpture to an earlier period than Shachar, based on the date of the construction of the Ostgiebel, of which it is an integral part. On examples of Jewish sows, see Shachar: such images were used in churches right up to the sixteenth century and were popular in sixteenth- and seventeenth-century woodcuts; a seventeenth-century broadsheet featured the Wittenberg sow.

8. Shachar, *Judensau*, 31. After the expulsion of 1304, the Jews were allowed to re-enter, but were expelled again.

9. WB 11, 4195, 1 Feb. 1546.

10. Allyson F. Creasman, 'The Virgin Mary against the Jews: Anti-Jewish Polemic in the Pilgrimage to the Schöne Maria of Regensburg, 1519–25', *Sixteenth Century Journal* 33, No. 4 (Winter 2002), 963–80; see also Hsia, *Myth of Ritual Murder*; Rubin, *Mother of God* and *Gentile Tales*.

11. On Wittenberg, see Junghans, *Wittenberg als Lutherstadt*; Edith Eschen-hagen, 'Beiträge zur Sozial- und Wirtschaftsgeschichte der Stadt Witten-berg'; Straube, 'Soziale Struktur'.

12. Kalkoff, *Ablass*, 6–7.

13. This was a massive increase on the 5,005 mentioned in Meinhardi's description in 1509; Laube, *Von der Reliquie zum Ding*, 141–96; Meinhardi, *Über die Lage*, 12.

14. See for example WB 1, 30, 14 Dec. 1516 for the involvement of Spalatin and Luther in trying to secure relics for Friedrich.

15. Kalkoff, *Ablass*, 24–36.

16. Ibid., 9.

17. Walch XV, 58–63.

18. Cranach, *Dye Zaigung*; Cardenas, *Friedrich der Weise*; Nickel (ed.), *Das Hallesche Heiltumbuch*; Ozment, *The Serpent and the Lamb*; and on relics, see Laube, *Von der Reliquie zum Ding*.

19. Junghans, *Wittenberg als Lutherstadt*; Straube, 'Soziale Struktur'.

20. Meinhardi, *Über die Lage*, 226.

21. The workshop was a big operation, employing journeymen (*Gesellen*), apprentices (*Lehrjungen*), hired hands (*Lohnknaben*) and helpers (*Knechte*). Only about two dozen are known by name, but there must have been many more: apprenticeships generally lasted about three years and there were at least two or three at any one time; Heyden-reich, *Lucas Cranach the Elder*, 267–322. He sold the original pair of houses on the square to purchase the complex in 1518, retaining the apothecary as a business. For the complex history of the buildings see Cranach-Stiftung (ed.), *Lucas Cranach d. Ä.* Cranach gained the apothecary privilege in 1520 and this also enabled him to extend the trade in fine wines, though he had already been conducting a wine business for many years.

22. WB 1, 41, 18 May 1517: in the letter to Lang, Luther passes on greetings from Döring, who happened to be with him. On the relationship between Cranach and Luther, Ozment, *The Serpent and the Lamb*.

23. WB 1, 22, 25 Sept. 1516, 22:23–6; 24, 5 Oct. 1516; 26, mid-Oct. 1516; 28, 26 Oct. 1516; 29, 29 Oct. 1516; 40, 17 May 1517: in this letter, Luther advises punishing an errant monk with the full force of the relevant monastery's statutes, so long as these do not include lifelong imprisonment or the death penalty. It is striking how seriously Luther took his duties, travel-ling frequently.

24. WB 1, 14, 29 May 1516, n.6.

25. WB 1, 15, 29 May 1516, 42:26; 22–3.

26. WB 1, 7, [Feb. 1514]; Helmar Junghans, 'Luthers Einfluss auf die Witten-berger Universitätsreform' in Dingel and Wartenberg, *Die Theologische*

*Fakultät Wittenberg*; Kohnle, Meckelnborg and Schirmer (eds), *Georg Spalatin*.

27. He did have some Latin, unusually for a ruler of this region in this period, and in his chronicle of Friedrich's life, Spalatin explicitly notes that 'Vnd wiewol sein Ch.F. Gnaden nicht gern Lateyn geredt, so haben doch seine Ch F Gnad gut latein fast wol verstanden, Zuweiln auch latein geredt'; and he also learnt French, Staatsarchiv Weimar, EGA Reg O, 25, fo. 3. Ludolphy, *Friedrich der Weise*, 45–7.

28. On the history of the founding of the university, which involved academic rifts in Leipzig, see Grohmann, *Annalen*, I, 7–8; Rummel, *Confessionalisation of Humanism*, 18–22.

29. Meinhardi, *Wittenberg*, 165–97; 187: 'Hans ist ein Beanus. Wer, wie beschaffen und von welchem Umfang ist sein Anus?' Meinhardi was probably borrowing from a comic version of this rite written around 1480 and published many times in the early sixteenth century: see Best (ed.), *Eccius dedolatus*, Introduction, 21.

30. Kruse, *Universitätstheologie*, 42–52; Kusukawa, *Transformation*, 27–74.

31. WB I, 52, 11 Nov. 1517.

32. Ulrich Köpf, 'Martin Luthers Beitrag zur Universitätsreform', *Lutherjahrbuch* 80, 2013, 31–59.

33. Brecht, *Luther*, I, 129–31; and see WS 57 for the print and manuscript notations of students for the Lectures on Romans of 1515–16; on Galatians (1516–17); and Hebrews (1517–18); WS 59 for another set of student notes on Galatians, 359–84. The original manuscript of Luther's Lectures on Romans was passed down through the family, but was then sold and eventually lost, recovered only in the nineteenth century; ironically a copy of it by Johann Aurifaber ended up in the Vatican Library. The lectures are divided into 'glosses' which were to be noted on the text itself, and 'Scholien', which were commentaries on particular passages.

34. Euling (ed.), *Chronik des Johan Oldecop*, 45–6, 47–8; and see 40; Oldecop's chronicle is written in Low German, and he was at first a supporter of Luther, who was his confessor.

35. LW 34, 336–7; WS 54, 179–87; 185:14–20.

36. WS 56, 171–2; 172:3–5; WS 57, 133–4: the student notes are similar to Luther's manuscript, and there is no indication that he might have used German at this point, or drawn particular attention to this passage. The interpretation is presented as that of Augustine.

37. WS 54, 185–6.

38. Luther had published an introduction to an incomplete edition of the *Theologia deutsch* in 1516, which included marginal notes probably by Luther, WS 59, 1–21; and a brief work, *Tractatulus de his, qui ad ecclesias confugiunt*, earlier in 1517; Benzing, *Lutherbibliographie*, I, 14.

39. WB 1, 35, 1 March 1517; LW Letters 1, 40; WB 1, 38, 6 May 1517, 93:7.

40. WB 1, 26, mid-Oct. 1516; 28, 26 Oct. 1516: 22 'sacerdotes' and 12 'iuvenes'; forty-one residents in all; Brecht, Luther, I, 121.

41. Grohmann, Annalen, 1, 114–16; Martin Treu, 'Die Leucorea zwischen Tradition und Erneuerung – Erwägungen zur frühen Geschichte der Universität Wittenberg' in Lück (ed.), Martin Luther und seine Universität; Oehmig (ed.), 700 Jahre Wittenberg; Treu, Speler and Schellenberger (eds), Leucorea.

42. Barge, Karlstadt, I, 70–5: Karlstadt gave an account of this episode in a preface to Augustine's De spiritu ct litcra, which he dedicated to none other than Johann von Staupitz; Ulrich Bubenheimer, 'Gelassenheit und Ablösung. Eine psychohistorische Studie über Andreas Bodenstein von Karlstadt und seinen Konflikt mit Martin Luther', Zeitschrift für Kirchengeschichte 92, 1981, 250–68, 264.

43. Kruse, Universitätstheologie, 2, 50–2; Kenneth Hagen, 'An Addition to the Letters of John Lang. Introduction and Translation', ARG 60, 1969, 27–32.

44. WB 1, 7 [Feb. 1514], 23:31–2. Spalatin did not ask Luther directly but via Johannes Lang. He also asked Karlstadt for his view. Luther made another strong defence of Reuchlin in a subsequent letter to Spalatin too, blaming envy as key to the attacks on Reuchlin: WB 1, 9, 5 Aug. 1514.

45. Brecht, Luther, I, 173; WB 1, 45, 4 Sept. 1517.

46. Thanks to a chance discovery in 1983 in the library at Wolfenbüttel of a broadsheet copy, we now know that a number of copies were printed by Rhau-Grunenberg; Bagchi, Luther's Earliest Opponents, 33. See also Brecht, Luther, I, 172–4; and for the text, WS 1, 224–8; LW 31, 9–18; for a critical edition and translation into German of the theses, see Härlc, Schilling and Wartenberg (eds), Martin Luther, I, 19–34. They were also included in a later collection of disputation theses from Wittenberg by Karlstadt, Melanchthon and others which appeared in around 1521; a sole copy of this, printed in Paris, survives: Insignium theologorum domini Martini Lutheri, domini Andree Barolostaadij [sic], Philippi melanthonis & aliorum conclusiones variae, Paris [1521].

47. Or 'in opposition to Gabriel' – by whom he meant Gabriel Biel, one of the foremost theologians. See Heiko A. Oberman, '"Iustitia Christi" and "iustitia Dei": Luther and the Scholastic Doctrines of Justification', Harvard Theological Review, 59, no. 1, 1966, 1–26.

48. LW 31, 12; WS 1, 44, 226:16.

49. LW 31, 10; WS 1, 17, 225:1–2. As Heiko Oberman explains it, 'The characteristic of Luther's doctrine of justification can therefore be designated as the reunification of the righteousness of Christ and the justice of God by which the sinner is justified 'coram deo', which forms the stable

*basis* and not the uncertain *goal* of the life of sanctification, of true Christian life.' That is, Christ's righteousness and God's justice are the same thing, and so Luther rejects the idea that by receiving the grace of Christ, we then become able to do good deeds which set us on the path to in the end satisfying the justice of God. Oberman, '"Iustitia Christi"', 25.

50. WB 1, 19, 225:5: Luther is rejecting Scotus's counter-example to the view that because humans are corrupt, they can only love things and not God, viz., that a brave man can love his country above all things.

51. LW 31, 14; WS 1, 65, 227:19; 38, 226. Interestingly, Luther's letters of spiritual comfort from about this period show him to be concerned with the justice of God and with recognising human evil, though he deals with this in a rather conventional and formulaic manner, writing of how *prudentia sensus nostri* [WB 1, 12, 37:12] is the root of all our unrest, and of how the eye is a great rascal, and of the great trouble it has plagued him with, and still does: WB 1, 11, 8 April 1516; 12, 15 April 1516.

52. WB 1, 5, 17 March 1509; Adam, *Life and death*. See also Melanchthon, *Vita Lutheri*, fos. 13 (v)–16 (r).

53. Johann Agricola, a student there at the time, said there was a printing 'on a half-sheet [*Bogen*] of paper': Volz, *Thesenanschlag*, 100, n.135, that is, about A3 size. Given that the Disputation against Scholastic Theology had been printed by Rhau-Grunenberg, and that this was common practice at Wittenberg, it seems likely that the Theses were printed at Wittenberg, unless (as is possible) there were particular problems with the Rhau-Grunenberg printshop at the time. See Ott and Treu, *Luthers Thesenanschlag*. The two surviving placards are the Nuremberg edition of Hieronymus Höltzel which numbered them in batches, and the edition of Jakob Thanner ending with '87', see *Martin Luther 1483–1546. Dokumente seines Lebens und Wirkens*, Weimar 1983, 38. Only the Basle edition which was done as a booklet, not a placard, had the right number.

54. WB 1, 62, 5 March 1518; by 5 January, Christoph Scheurl had got his copy from Ulrich von Dinstet; Soden and Knaake (eds), *Scheurls Briefbuch*, 2, 42.

55. Treu convincingly argues that the theses had to be posted on all the church doors, which also suggests that print copies were essential. Martin Treu, 'Urkunde und Reflexion. Wiederentdeckung eines Belegs von Luthers Thesenanschlag', in Joachim Ott and Martin Treu (eds), *Luthers Thesenanschlag*, 59-67. See also Pettegree, *Brand Luther*, 71–4.

56. WB 1, 52, 11 Nov. 1517.

57. Volz, *Thesenanschlag*, 140–1; Soden and Knaake (eds), *Scheurls Briefbuch*, 2, no. 158, 42; WS 51, 540, 26–7, *Wider Hans Worst*, 1541; Myconius, *Geschichte*, 22, embroidered Luther's remark, adding 'and in four weeks

just about the whole of Christendom, as if the angels themselves had been the messengers'.

58. WB 1, 58, [13 Feb. 1518]. He said the same to Scheurl, see Volz, *Thesenanschlag*, 82–3, n.64; WB 1, 63, 11 March 1518. See also the preface to Luther's collected Latin Writings where Luther explains that he wrote to both Albrecht of Mainz and the bishop of Brandenburg, WS 54, 179–87.

59. WT 1, 1206, 601:18–19.

60. WT 3, 3722, 564:16–17.

61. Soden and Knaake (eds), *Scheurls Brief buch*, letter 176, 2 Nov. 1518, Scheurl to Ulrich von Dinstedt, Otto Beckmann and Georg Spalatin (tr. Melinda Letts). Scheurl acted as leader, and Albrecht Dürer was one of the members. Scheurl also sent a copy to the important civic secretary Conrad Peutinger in Augsburg: König, *Peutingers Briefwechsel*, 299, 5 Jan. 1518.

62. WB 1, 33, 86:4; 11–15.

63. WB 1, 64, 21 March 1518, 155:40–1. As Luther correctly guessed, the theses were in fact composed by Conrad Wimpina to be defended by Tetzel.

64. See Leppin, *Luther*, 117–26. There are a number of interesting variations on Luther's name: a letter from 1507 has him as Luder, but in another from the same year he styles himself as Lutherus (WB 1, 4 and 5, but these are not originals; the oldest original letter of Luther's (9) has no surname. A letter of 1514 has Luder and one of 1516, Luter; but Luther/ Lutherus alternates with Luder until Nov. 1517 (17, 19, 21, 22, 27, 30, 33, 37, 38, 46, 51 Luder), and Scheurl addressed him as Luder, writing in early 1517 (32). As Leppin has shown, about the time of the composition of the Ninety-Five Theses, Luther began to refer to himself as Eleutherius, the freed one, when writing to close friends  Lang, Spalatin, Staupitz. After Autumn 1517, he hardly ever used 'Luder' again, even when writing to his parents. He also played with the signature, sometimes styling himself Martinus Lutherus, sometimes Martinus Luther, usually including 'F' or 'Frater'. Sometimes he included 'Doctor' or 'D' when he signed off, sometimes not; and throughout his life, he also frequently (but not always) wrote the concluding 'R' as an emphatic capital. Interestingly, towards the very end of his life, he employed 'Luder' on two unusual occasions, once, when writing to the counts of Mansfeld (WB 11, 4157, 7 Oct. 1545) and once in one of his final letters to his wife, he addressed her jokingly as 'Katherin Ludherin, Doctorin, Sewmarckterin' (WB 11, 4201, 7 Feb. 1546). He referred to members of his original family, however, as 'Luder'.

65. WT 2, 1681; and see Oberman, *Luther*, 154–6 for a brilliant interpretation. Recently the cloaca tower has been identified: Stefan Laube, 'Klosett oder Klosterzelle?', *FAZ*, 4 April 2015, Feuilleton, 13.

66. LW 34, 337; 1545; WS 54, 179–87; 186:3–16.

67. The material about Romans follows his discussion of the encounter with the papal emissary Miltitz in 1519, and is presented as contemporaneous with his second series of lectures on the Psalms, and as preceding the convening of the Diet of Worms by a year. This would place it in about 1519, two years after the Ninety-Five Theses. It is clear therefore that Luther himself either misremembered, or else that the process of the 'Reformation discovery' was completed over several years.

68. Interestingly, Melanchthon himself places Luther's discovery that we are justified through faith alone long before the writing of the Ninety-Five Theses, during the period in Erfurt; Melanchthon, *Vita Lutheri*, fos. 13 (v)–15 (r), attributing this to a comforting discussion he had with one of the older monks.

69. Luther, *Eyn geystlich edles Buchleynn* and *Eyn deutsch Theologia*.

70. He may also have engaged with it again in 1520, if the German annotations in the edition of that year are indeed by Luther: WS 59, 1–21.

## 5. Journeys and Disputations

1. WB 1, 72, 15 April 1518.

2. WB 1, 72, 15 April 1518, 166:21, 23.

3. WB 1, 73, 19 April 1518.

4. By August 1518, his 'Resolutions' or explanations of the Ninety-Five Theses were printed, prefaced with a letter to Staupitz and a missive of dedication to the Pope – which only inflamed the situation further: WS 1, 522–628; LW 31.

5. Bucer, who was there, wrote an important account of them. See Thomas Kaufmann, 'Argumentative Impressionen: Bucers Bericht von der Heidelberger Disputation' in Kaufmann (ed.), *Der Anfang der Reformation*, who argues that Bucer's report is reliable and that he did not simply omit the material on the Cross and suffering, but that the debate at Heidelberg seems to have centred on grace and works. A text of the elaboration of theses 1–12 is in WS 59, 409–26; for a full modern critical edition and translation into German, see Härle, Schilling and Wartenberg (eds), *Martin Luther*, I, 35–70. The 'elaborations' of the positions for the philosophical theses were printed in the first edition of Luther's Works, but not for the first twelve; and it is unclear whether the theses were printed; or whether their elaborations were formulated after the disputation or before.

6. Thomas Kaufmann, 'Theologisch-philosophische Rationalität: Die Ehre der Hure. Zum vernünftigen Gottesgedanken in der Reformation' in Kaufmann (ed.), *Der Anfang der Reformation*.

7.  LW 31, 40, 53, explanation of thesis 21; WS 1, 354:21; 362:27, 28–9, 31–2; 354; on *Deus absconditus* see Lohse, *Luther's Theology*, 215–17; see also Vitor Westhelle, 'Luther's *Theologia Crucis*' in Kolb and Dingel (eds), *Oxford Handbook*, 156–64. The concept of God 'hidden in suffering' was being developed by Karlstadt too and found a visual representation by Cranach in his broadsheet of early 1519, *Karlstadt's Wagon*, top row, far left, where Christ is depicted as hidden behind the Cross (see Chapter 6).

8.  WB 1, 75, 18 May 1518, 173:28–9; 174:45–6.

9.  WB 1, 34, 8 Feb. 1517: he had enclosed a letter for Trutfetter in his letter to Lang, which suggested that he and Usingen give up the study of Aristotle, Porphyry and the commentaries on Peter Lombard.

10.  WB 1, 75, 18 May 1518, 173, n.12: Luther must have seen Trutfetter after all, probably on 10 May.

11.  WB 1, 74, 9 May 1518, 169:13–14; 33–8; the earlier letter to Lang, WB 1, 64, 21 March 1518.

12.  Egranus had also raised doubts about the legends of the three Marys and was involved in disputes with Wimpina and Düngersheim. Luther's letter prefacing Egranus's pamphlet appeared in print in late March or early April 1518, WS 1, 315–16; and WB 1 55, 20 Dec. 1517 (to Spalatin).

13.  WB 1, 74, 9 May 1518, 170:44–5; 171:78–80; 81; 87; 85.

14.  Indeed, a year later, Trutfetter was dead: WB 1, 184, to Lang, 6 June 1519. Luther noted laconically that Trutfetter had departed this life. May God receive his soul and forgive him all his sins, and ours, he commented.

15.  WB 1, 75, 18 May 1518.

16.  Vandiver, Keen and Frazel (eds and trs), *Luther's Lives*, 155.

17.  WB 1, 74, 9 May 1518: in the whole university, Luther insisted, only one scholar did not support him, and that person did not yet have his doctorate.

18.  Thomas Kaufmann, 'Argumentative Impressionen. Bucers Bericht von der Heidelberger Disputation' in Kaufmann (ed.), *Der Anfang der Reformation*; Brecht, *Luther*, I, 216.

19.  Greschat, *Bucer*, 21–35. As well as Frecht, Billican, and Brenz, Eberhard Schnepf had also possibly been at Heidelberg. All would become important reformers in south Germany.

20.  WB 1, 83, 10 July 151, 186:51.

21.  Luther had sent his manuscript reply via Wenzeslaus Linck in Nuremberg from whom he had received Eck's text. No one else, he insisted, had seen it.

22.  WB 1, 77, 19 May 1518, 178:28–30.

23.  Originally Karlstadt had written 380 theses but, always one for overkill, added more at proof stage; WB 1, 82, 15 June 1518.

24.  Bagchi, *Luther's Earliest Opponents*, 20–2.

25.  Wicks, *Cajetan*.

26.  WB 1, 83, 10 July 1518: Luther made light of it, saying that he would be either strangled or baptised to death.

27.  LW Letters, I, 74; WB 1, 87, 28 Aug. 1518, 190:10–16.

28.  WB 1, 87, 28 Aug. 1518; WB 1, 92, 5 Sept. 1518 (Spalatin to Luther). Luther had asked Spalatin directly to secure the support of the Elector, because it concerned the honour of the university as well as Luther, WB 1, 85, 8 Aug. 1518; while Staupitz wrote pressing Spalatin to advise the Elector to remain firm, for it was not just a matter of the order: Walch, XV, 551, Staupitz to Spalatin, 7 Sept. 1518.

29.  See WS 54, 181:13 for the account he gave in the preface to the Latin Works; WT 2, 2668a and b (1532); Mathesius, *Historien*, 33; on nettling, Myconius, *Geschichte*, 28: he may also have meant that it would not come to burning straight away.

30.  Cochlaeus, *Brevis Germaniae Descriptio* (ed. Buchner), 77.

31.  WB 1, 97, 10 Oct. 1518.

32.  Zorn, *Geschichte*, 161–9; Haeberlein, *Fuggers*; Trauchburg, *Häuser*, 32–9. The frescoes were finished by 1517.

33.  At St George and Holy Cross there were foundations of Augustinian canons, but these were priests, not monks. See on St Anna and the social structure of Augsburg's religious institutions, Kiessling, *Bürgerliche Gesellschaft*, 251–87.

34.  I am indebted to Johannes Wilhelm who first showed me the Fronleichnamsaltar, and to the late Bruno Bushart's lectures on the Fuggerkapelle, Augsburg *c.*1978. See, on the history of the chapel, Bushart, *Die Fuggerkapelle*, 15–31; and on the altar, 199–230. The original setting of the altar was destroyed in 1581 and the sculpture moved to St Mark's Church in the Fuggerei. Ironically, the 400-year celebration of the posting of the Ninety-Five Theses saw an 'updating' of the Fuggerkapelle that destroyed much of its original ensemble, 49. It is unclear whether Hans Daucher was the artist, but he may have been; Thomas Eser argues convincingly that the piece comes from the Ulm-Augsburg region and that it expresses the spirit of late medieval mysticism; Eser, *Hans Daucher*, 251–62.

35.  WB 1, 97, 10 Oct. 1518; WB 1, 100, 14 Oct. 1518; Bild had initiated contact with Luther via Spalatin shortly before he arrived in Augsburg: WB 1, 95, 21 Sept. 1518.

36.  WB 1, 97, 10 Oct. 1518, 209:31–2; 37–8. See also WT 5, 5349: Luther remembered that his friends told him he would have to prostrate himself before the cardinal, then come to his knees and only then, stand.

37.  W 31, 274–5; WS 2, 16:11–12, 19. It appears amongst the 'Extravagantes communes', LW Letters, I, 84, n.6.

38. LW Letters, I, 83–7; WB I, 99, 14 Oct. 1518, 214:13–14; 25–7; 30–3. Luther is here using techniques of argument honed in his philosophical training and in years of disputation, the exact opposite of what Cajetan wanted. As Luther points out at the beginning of the letter, Cajetan expressly did not want to have a public disputation and did not wish to argue with him in private either.

39. WT 2, 2250.

40. WT 2, 2250, 376:10 (Aug.–Sept. 1531); WT I, 509, 233:9 (spring1533).

41. WB I, 104, 18 Oct. 1518, 222:4–7; 223:12; 14–16; 35; 38; 39–42; 46.

42. WB I, 104, 18 Oct. 1518 (to Cajetan), 223:20; *Appellatio M. Lutheri a Caietano ad Papam*, 1518 WS 2, 27–33, 33:5, 'melius informati'; WB I, 104, 18 Oct. 1518, 223:20; and see letter to Spalatin, where he uses the same phrase, LW Letters, I, 90–3; WB I, 105, 31 Oct. 1518, 224:3–4.

43. Froben published it along with Luther's chief publications and Prierias's reply, so that intellectuals had a handy volume that allowed them to make up their minds about the 'Luther matter': *'Ad Leonem X. Pontif. Maxim. Resolutiones disputationum de virtute indulgentiarum . . .'* [Basle] [1518] [VD 16 L 3407].

44. WB I, 100, 14 Oct. 1518, which is similar to the one addressed to Spalatin of the same date. Many of the letters to Karlstadt have been lost: this one survives in German translation only, and since a letter to Melanchthon a few days earlier tells him that Karlstadt has the details of the discussions so far, there must have been at least one earlier letter as well.

45. WB I, 99, 14 Oct. 1518; 102, shortly after 14 Oct. 1518; 104, 18 Oct. 1518. There is an undercurrent of anti-Italian feeling which Luther uses to reinforce a sense of common cause with the Elector. He remarked of Serralonga, Cajetan's intermediary, that 'He is an Italian and an Italian he will remain', making fun of his beautiful prose that hid little of substance.

46. WB I, 110, 25 Oct. 1518, Cajetan to the Elector, which reached him on 19 Nov. 1518; 110, 21 Nov. 1518, Luther's reply, is written in Latin although he usually wrote to the Elector in German, so that the Elector could simply send it on to Cajetan.

47. WS 2, 1–5 (introduction); 6–26; 25 for the blacked-out text; Brecht, *Luther*, I, 208–9; on the *Sermon on Indulgences and Grace*, WB I, 67, second half of March 1518: even a supporter of Luther like Capito thought this sermon went a bit far, so Spalatin's caution was not exaggerated.

48. *Acta Augustana*, LW 31, 259–292; WS 2, 6–26. WB I, 124, 20 Dec. 1518 to Spalatin: Luther explains that he had intended the copies of the Appellation to be distributed when the ban arrived. However, he had not actually paid the printer. This would have been more persuasive if the

same letter had not also included his explanation for his failure to follow Spalatin's advice not to print the *Acta*, which he says reached him too late, a slightly different story from what he had told Langenmantel the previous month: WB 1, 113, 25 Nov. 1518 to Christoph Langenmantel.

49.  LW Letters, I, 72; WB 1, 85, 8 Aug. 1518, 188:12–13; LW Letters, I, 75; WB 1, 87, 28 Aug. 1518, 190:30–1.

50.  Härle, Schilling and Wartenberg (eds), *Martin Luther*, II, 17–23; this was not the only time that Luther mentioned his weakened body to Staupitz, who for his part worried about Luther's health; and he referred repeatedly and vividly to the likelihood of his martyrdom too.

51.  WB 1, 98, 11 Oct. 1518, 213:8–10; 11–14.

52.  WB 1, 102, soon after 14 Oct. 1518.

53.  WB 1, 96, 3 or 4 Oct. 1518, 208:2–3; 4–5.

54.  *Acta Augustana*, LW 31, 260; WS 2, 7:10–11 (he also imagined himself as Athanasius, alone against the Arian heresy).

55.  WB 1, 90, 2 Sept. 1518, 195:8–196:15.

56.  LW Letters, I, 74; WB 1, 87, 28 Aug. 1518, 190:10–11.

57.  WB 1 140, 2 Feb. 1519 (to Egranus); the kiss became famous, and was mentioned by Scheurl in his letter to Eck a fortnight later; Soden and Knaake (eds), *Scheurls Briefbuch*, 18 Feb. 1519, and to Staupitz, WB 1, 152, 20 Feb. 1519. Interestingly, the discussions took place in Spalatin's own house in Altenburg.

## 6. The Leipzig Debate

1.  Iserloh, *Eck*, 7, 19.

2.  Iserloh, *Eck*, 12–13. Eck also taught the humanist and Anabaptist Balthasar Hubmaier; Urbanus Rhegius later became a prominent Lutheran.

3.  Eck, *Epistola*, fo. B (r).

4.  Vandiver, Keen and Frazel (eds and trs), *Luther's Lives*, 67.

5.  Karlstadt, *Auszlegung*; and see Kruse, *Universitätstheologie*, 195–200; Jenny Spinks and Lyndal Roper, 'Karlstadt's Wagon', forthcoming.

6.  Barge, *Karlstadt*, I, 133.

7.  The venue remained a bone of contention, Eck insisting that it was Luther who had first demanded they meet at Leipzig, and had later changed his mind. Years later, Eck still claimed to have a handwritten note from the 'mendacious' Luther confirming the choice: Eck, *Epistola*, fo. A 4 (r).

8.  Iserloh, *Eck*, 20.

9.  Kawerau (ed.), *Justus Jonas*, I, 24, 24 June 1519 (Jonas to Aachen); for Jonas's outrage over Eck's attacks on Erasmus, see his letters to Lang and Mosellanus of July and August 1519, 27–9.

10. Iserloh, *Eck*, 19–20; Luther had made the same criticism of Erasmus in a letter to Spalatin, WB 1, 27, 19 Oct. 1516, telling Salatin to tell Erasmus so; he did, but Erasmus did not apparently reply.

11. WB 2, 490, 15 May 1522, 527:25.

12. Oberman, *Masters of the Reformation*, 128–38.

13. Iserloh, *Eck*, 11; Mathis Miechowa, *Tractat von baiden Sarmatien vnd andern anstossenden landen, in Asia vnd Europa, von sitten vnd gepraeuchen der voelcker so darinnen wonen*, Augsburg 1518: the author was Polish. The work shows considerable interest in their attitude to horses (fo. B iii (v)); and interestingly explains that the Tartars became Islamic through the Saracens who condemned Christianity because of its idolatrous attitude to images, a comment which suggests how live the issue of images was even at this early date (fo. B iii (r)).

14. There is a good account of the course of the negotiations in Brecht, *Luther*, I, 299–309.

15. Iserloh, *Eck*, 71–4.

16. Myconius, *Geschichte*, 31. Armin Kohnle, 'Die Leipziger Disputation und ihre Bedeutung für die Reformation' in Hein and Kohnle (eds), *Die Leipziger Disputation*, 10.

17. Walch, XV, 1204–5 (Sebastian Fröschel); his account was not written until 1566; 1208 (Saxon Kanzler Pfeiffer) is also a later account. Both were written after the rift between Luther and Karlstadt which might suggest this was an invention; but Rubius mentions the incident in his contemporary poem.

18. Lotter had printed some of Luther's works; eventually his son opened a branch in Wittenberg to Luther's delight. But by 1525, following a dispute with Cranach, Lotter gave up the business. His brother who had also joined him in Wittenberg moved to Magdeburg three years later: Pettegree, *Brand Luther*, 110–14, 185–92, 195–6.

19. Walch, XV, 1184–7 (account of Amsdorf to Spalatin); 1189–91 (Aurifaber to Spalatin); 1191–4 (Mosellanus to Pirckheimer); 1194–1204 (Mosellanus to Pflug); 1204–8 (Fröschel); 1208–17 (Pfeiffer), 1217–24 (Melanchthon); 1224–32 (Eck's letters); 1232 (Cellarius); 1239–59 (Rubius); Barge, *Karlstadt*, I, 133–80; Hein and Kohnle (eds), *Die Leipziger Disputation*; Rummel, *Confessionalisation of Humanism*, 19–22.

20. Reinhold Weier, 'Die Rede des Mosellanus "Über die rechte Weise, theologisch zu disputieren"', *Trierer Theologische Zeitschrift* 83, 1974, 232–45: the speech was printed during the disputation, but it was not well delivered and failed to make a good impression; on the sung Mass, Walch, XV, 1206.

21. WS 2, 241; and for the text of the sermon, 241–9.

22. Walch, XV, 1194, Mosellanus to Pflug, 6 Dec. 1519 (soldier, butcher); 3 Aug. 1519 (Mosellanus to Pirckheimer); 1192–3 (soldier); 1241, account of Rubius 13 Aug. 1519 (lion).

23. Rubius, *Eyn neu buchlein*: (fo. A iii (v)), on Eck (fo. A ii (v)); Mosellanus in Walch, XV, 1200–1; Sider, *Karlstadt*, 13. Mosellanus described Eck's powerful body and voice, supported by a 'very strong chest' so that he could have been a tragedy actor or a herald.

24. Walch, XV, 1207. For the protocol of the debate, see WS 2, and for the protocol based on the official notarial record, printed in Paris, and rediscovered by Otto Seitz, see WS 59, 427–605, which omits the discussions between Eck and Karlstadt; see Seitz (ed.), *Der authentische Text der Leipziger Disputation*. On the history of the record of the debate, see Christian Winter, 'Die Protokolle der Leipziger Disputation' in Hein and Kohnle (eds), *Die Leipziger Disputation*. There were sideshows too. For the entertainment of the audience, Luther and Eck held a mock disputation over whether the duke's one-eyed court fool should be allowed to take a wife, Eck arguing that he should not. When the offended jester glowered at him, the theologian mimicked him by putting one hand over his eye, to the fool's fury and the onlookers' delight. This was standard court humour, but it was cruel as well: two men sworn to celibacy, laughing at the desire of a disfigured fool.

25. WS 59, 467: Platina had argued like Hus, so Luther averred, that the popes had been given power by the emperors.

26. Kaufmann (ed.), *Der Anfang der Reformation*, 37–50.

27. Walch, XV, 1221–2, 21 July 1519 (Melanchthon to Oecolampadius).

28. Ibid., 1207.

29. Ibid., 1224–32.

30. Ibid., 1122, 1123, 15 July.

31. WB 1, 196, 3 Sept. 1519.

32. Walch, XV, 1200, 6 Dec. 1519 (Mosellanus to Pflug); 1186–7, 1 Aug. 1519 (Amsdorf to Spalatin).

33. Rummel, *Confessionalisation of Humanism*, 20; Walch, XV, 1226, 24 July 1519 (Eck to Hoogstraten): one of the assistants, he noted, was the famed Reuchlin's nephew (referring to Melanchthon).

34. WB 1, 187, 20 July 1519, 423:107; though Luther apparently cared nothing for clothing, cloth and its procurement recurs in the correspondence. So for example Luther thanked the Elector's confessor for procuring cloth for him from the Elector, WB 1, 30, 14 Dec. 1516; and thanked the Elector again for cloth, WB 1, 55, 20 Dec. 1517. He noticed the arrival of cloth at Cranach's establishment, WB 2, 287, 13 May 1520. But he also liked to reminisce that his old cassock was so full of holes that Dr Hieronymus Schurf used to offer him money for a new one. He

found it difficult to finally give up his monastic habit. When Frederick read his *On Monastic Vows*, Luther recalled, he sent him fine cloth on condition he used it for a new cowl or gown, and joked that he should have it made in Spanish style, that is, in the latest fashion. WT 5, 6430; WT 4, 4414; WT 4, 5034.

35. Eck wanted, he wrote in 1545, to gain glory and favour with the Pope, and 'to ruin me with hate and envy.' LW 34, 333; WS 54, 179–87, 183:16.

36. Eck, *Epistola*.

37. Vandiver, Keen and Frazel (eds and trs), *Luther's Lives*, 68–9.

38. Rubius also wrote a longer pamphlet, the *Solutiones*, intended as a report on the debate for the bishop of Würzburg: Rummel, *Confessionalisation of Humanism*, 20.

39. WS 59, 429; Brecht, *Luther*, I, 337–8: Luther wrote a threatening letter to Erfurt when he heard a rumour that the decision would go against him; and Lang apparently also worked to get the university to refuse to judge.

40. WS 2, 241–9; 246:17–18; 244:29–30.

41. WS 2, 253; 388–435: 'Resolutiones Lutherianae super propositionibus suis Lipsiae disputatis'.

42. Rummel, *Confessionalisation of Humanism*, 19–22 for an account of this part of the debate.

43. Eck, *Doctor Martin ludders*.

44. Best (ed.), *Eccius dedolatus*, 40–50: the scene of Candida the witch riding to Leipzig on her goat is reminiscent of Dürer's *Witch riding backwards on a goat* of 1500.

45. Eck is shaved, like a witch about to undergo torture, to remove the 'sophisms, syllogisms, major and minor propositions, corollaries, porisms and so on', that is, all the techniques of scholastic argument that swarm like lice in his hair, and he 'vomits up' the commentaries on Aristotle's works that he had written. Next he is made to defecate – and coins appear, an allusion to his employment by Jakob Fugger, 'the one you hired out your tongue to' to defend usury. When that tongue turns out to be black and forked (like the Devil's) the surgeon chops it in half, before removing Eck's 'carbuncle of Vainglory' and his 'carcinoma of slander': Best (ed.), *Eccius dedolatus*, 63–71.

46. Pirckheimer certainly knew about the satire and had a hand in its authorship; and there is a sequel in his hand (though it is nothing like as good as the original). Whoever wrote it certainly knew Nuremberg well, because the author makes fun of Eck's dancing at Christoph Scheurl's wedding, and mentions a pamphlet by Lazarus Spengler, which Eck wants to 'consecrate publicly to Vulcan' – that is, to burn it in public: Best (ed.), *Eccius dedolatus*, Introduction, 22–5.

47.  WS 2, 739ff, 'Eyn Sermon von dem Hochwirdigen Sacrament, des heyligen waren Leychnamß Christi, Vnd von den Bruderschafften Für die Leyen', Wittenberg, 1519 [VD 16 L 6387]. It was the third of a trilogy of sermons on the sacraments, on penance, baptism and Communion.

48.  LW 35, 50; WS 2, 742:24–6.

49.  WS 2,738–9.

50.  LW 35, 50; WS 2, 742:26.

51.  LW 35, 68; WS 2, 754:35–755:1.

52.  Edwards, *Printing*, 1–2. Between 1518 and 1530 his vernacular works outnumbered those of his Catholic opponents five to one. Mark U. Edwards, Jr., 'Luther as Media Virtuoso and Media Persona' in Medick and Schmidt (eds), *Luther zwischen den Kulturen*.

53.  The scale of the transformation becomes apparent in the numbers of surviving works of print that were published there (this can only be an incomplete statistic because many printed works have been lost). In 1517, only five works are known to have rolled off Wittenberg's presses. By 1518, at least twenty-nine works were published in Wittenberg, with forty-eight appearing the following year. In 1520, the step change took place: no fewer than 109 books and pamphlets appeared. By comparison, in the same year, Augsburg published 199 surviving works; Basle, 107; and Nuremberg, 109. Figures taken from VD 16. On the growth of Wittenberg as a print centre, see Pettegree, *Book in the Renaissance*, 91–106; and his *Brand Luther*.

54.  He was not wrong: Reuchlin had to prevent Eck getting Oecolampadius's and Spengler's pamphlets burnt in public at Ingolstadt; Best (ed.), *Eccius dedolatus*, Introduction, 18.

55.  Spengler, *Schützred*, fo. B iii (v).

56.  Ibid., fos. A iv (v), B ii (r), B iii (r), B iii (r).

## 7. The Freedom of a Christian

1.  Luther used to count them off on the fingers of each hand. WT 5, 5428. Those who were studying were freed in part and those teaching freed fully from three of the seven 'hours' of prayer. See also WT 5, 5375.

2.  WT 2, 1253, before 14 Dec. 1531.

3.  WT 5, 5428 between 11 April and 14 June 1542. This came in the course of a discussion where those around the table competed with stories about saying hours. See also WT 3, 3651; WT 4, 4082; WS 17, 1, 112ff (sermons, 1525); WT 4, 4919, 5094; WT 5, 6077.

4.  Junghans, *Die Reformation*, 87.

5.  WB 2, 278, 16 April 1520.

6. See WS 59, xv–21: there are manuscript annotations of the Latin version of 1516 and German printed annotations of the 1520 edition which may have been supplied by Luther himself, which would suggest that he was still engaged with the text in 1520.

7. WS 38, 372:26–7; 373:10; 372:30–1. See also his prayer book *Betbüchlein* of 1522, and *Spalatins Betbüchlein*, WS 10.II, 331–501; LW 43, 5–47 which is a compilation for private devotion, including the Lord's Prayer and interestingly a Hail Mary. It also includes a Passion which by 1529 had fifty woodcuts illustrating the Bible story.

8. WB 1, 16, 8 June 1516, 45:25; 41–3. The letter is surprisingly long. Luther also indicates he knew that Staupitz's sister, abbess at Frauenwörth in Chiemsee, wanted Staupitz to take the position, so this was clearly a carefully laid plan, which would have accorded with Staupitz's noble status and would doubtless have benefited the Elector as well.

9. WB 1, 202, 3 Oct. 1519, 514:49–50; 51–3; 75–7. Interestingly in the psalm, it is the other way around: the child weans itself from the mother and is content, whereas Luther is 'tristissimus'.

10. WB 1, 202, 3 Oct. 1519, 152, 20 Feb. 1519, 344:9.

11. WB 1, 515, n.1.

12. LW Letters, I, 191; WB 2, 366, 14 Jan. 1521, 245:3–4.

13. WB 2, 376, 9 Feb. 1521, 263:23; 25–6; 264:47–50.

14. WB 2, 512, 27 June 1522, 566, reference to letter of Staupitz to Linck.

15. WB 1, 119, early or mid-Dec. 1518(?).

16. Posset, *Front-Runner*, 210; Soden and Knaake (eds), *Scheurls Briefbuch*, I, 139–40, 22 April 1514.

17. WT 5, 5989, 417:11–12: Luther recalled his confessor's words around 1544.

18. LW Letters II, 11–13; WB 2, 512, 27 June 1522, 567:13–14; 11 12; 19–20. The letter then goes on to mention the likely martyrdom of the Antwerp Augustinian prior, who (in contrast to Staupitz) had recanted and had then resumed evangelical preaching; and to ponder whether he himself might face the flames.

19. LW Letters, II, 48, 49, 50; WB 3, 659, 17 Sept. 1523, 156:23; 26–7; 155:5–8; 156:12; 36–8. Others picked up on what Staupitz's move meant, and Thomas Müntzer mocked that Luther had been safe at Augsburg because 'he could lean on Staupitz', 'though he has now deserted you and has become an abbot'; Matheson (ed. and tr.), *Collected Works*, 347; n.233; Müntzer, *Hoch verursachte Schutzrede*, fo. E (r–v); see Posset, *Front-Runner*, 296–7.

20. WB 3, 821, 23 Jan. 1525, 428:5.

21. WB 3, 827, 7 Feb. 1525, 437:8–10.

22. WT 1, 173, 1532, 80:6–7.

23. Evangelische Predigerseminar Wittenberg (ed.), '*Vom Christlichen abschied*'; fo. A iii (r–v).

24. Bagchi, *Luther's Earliest Opponents*.

25. WB 2, 284, 5 May 1520; 287, 13 May 1520; 291, 31 May 1520; on Alveld, who was writing to defend papal authority on behalf of the bishop of Merseburg, see Bagchi, *Luther's Earliest Opponents*, 50–2.

26. WB 2, 276, [7 April 1520], 79:6–7.

27. LW Letters, I, 145, WB 1, 239, 610:25–6.

28. WS 6, 135–6; 137–41; 138:20–1; 140:7; 17–19.

29. WB 2, 255, [*c*.16 Feb. 1520], 43:3–6; 35–7; 45:91. In the next letter Luther was moderating his tone with Spalatin, promising to be less biting in his Latin reply to the bishop of Meissen and to show it to Spalatin first. But he adds that if his enemy spreads the shit around more, the more widely and strongly it will stink: WB 2, 256, 18 Feb. 1520.

30. He was not alone: Capito wrote on 17 March 1520 (WB 2, 267) comparing them to Midases, that is, judges with asses' ears, who clearly made the wrong decision.

31. Martin Luther, 'Resolutio Lutheriana super propositione decima tertia de potestate Papae. Per autorem locupletata' in Härle, Schilling, Wartenberg and Beyer (eds), *Martin Luther*, 3, 17–171; 171.

32. LW 31, 354; WS 7, 27:19–21.

33. LW 44, 169, 130, 131; WS 6, 436:13–4; 409:11–15; 22–5.

34. See, on this image, Warnke, *Cranachs Luther*.

35. Zumkeller, *Staupitz*, 7, 15 March 1520.

36. WB 2, 327, 18 Aug. 1520, 167:5.

37. LW 44, 154; WS 6, 426:1–2.

38. Hans-Christoph Rublack, 'Gravamina und Reformation' in Batori (ed.), *Städtische Gesellschaft und Reformation*.

39. LW 44, 177, *To the Christian Nobility of the German Nation*; WS 6, 442:10–15.

40. LW 44, 178; WS 6, 442:33; 422:35–6.

41. Brady, *German Histories*, 152.

42. Ibid., 151–2, 260–4.

43. So, for example, Luther began to ask Spalatin, at first hesitantly, whether he might write to the Elector and tell him about the problems of inflation; interestingly he explained his involvement as '*pro re publica iuuanda*', WB 2, 291, 31 May 1520; 297, [7? June 1520]. Then he became involved in preaching and mediating in the armed disturbances between the students and Cranach's journeymen – to Spalatin's dismay; WB 2, 312, 14 July 1520; 315, 22 July 1520.

44. WS 6, 497–573; LW 36; Härle, Schilling, Wartenberg and Beyer (eds), *Martin Luther*, 3, 173–376, with parallel modern German translation and Latin text.

45. RTA 2, 478. He thought *On the Freedom of a Christian* was, however, a good book.

46. LW 36, 12; WS 6, 498:9. Luther, *De captivitate babylonica ecclesiae praeludium*, fo. A ii (r). Above it on the page is another capitalised sentence,

'INDVLGENTIAE SVNT ADVLATORVM ROMANORVM NEQVI-CIAE', that is, 'Indulgences are Wicked Devices of the Flatterers of Rome', so that the visual effect of the page is to remind the reader of the message of the Ninety-Five Theses, and then radicalise it, placing it in the context of a much wider assault on the papacy, fo. A ii (r), LW 36, 12. Luther explicitly uses the word Antichrist (as opposed to Nimrod), LW 36, 72; WS 6, 537:25. At about the same time he condemned the papal bull as the Bull of the Antichrist in *Wider die Bulle des Endchrists* of October 1520, WS 6, 614:29.

47. LW 36, 16, 17; WS 6, 500:19; 501:12; 500:33.

48. LW 36, 66, 68; WS 6, 527–36; 533:12–13; 534:11. Mortifying the flesh, Luther argues, belongs to baptism and not to works, and so he links martyrdom to baptism and faith.

49. LW 36, 32; WS 6, 510:9–13.

50. WS 6, 510:4–8.

51. See, on reason as a whore, Thomas Kaufmann, 'Theologisch-philoso-phische Rationalität: Die Ehre der Hure. Zum vernünftigen Gottes-gedanken in der Reformation' in Kaufmann (ed.), *Der Anfang der Reformation*.

52. Luther, *Von der freyheyt eynes Christenmenschen*; WS 7, 20–38; LW 31.

53. LW 31, 344; WS 7, 21:1–3.

54. LW 31, 350; WS 6, 25:7–8; 24:1 (*boeße begirde* translated in LW as 'coveting').

55. LW 31, 370; WS 7, 37:16–18. It is striking how often the word *alle* appears throughout the text, adding to its authoritative, unqualified tone.

56. For an account which downplays Luther's agency and emphasises the role of Melanchthon and Agricola, see Krentz, *Ritualwandel*, 131–6; however, the event was about Luther, and had already been discussed with Spalatin, and much of the organisation will have been done orally without leaving a trace in the written record. The Catholic side under-stood the burning of the bull in December as Luther's retaliation for the burning of his works; see letter of Andrea Rosso, secretary of Venetian ambassador Cornaro, Worms, 30 Dec. 1520; and see letter of Cuthbert Tunstal to Wolsey, 29 Jan. 1521, where it is linked to Luther's conviction he would not get a fair hearing, in Kalkoff, *Briefe*, 26, 32.

57. WB 2, 361, 10 Dec. 1520, 235, n.1.

58. LW Letters, I, 192; WB 2, 366, 14 Jan. 1520, 245:17–19.

59. Latin versions of the anonymous description were printed, and there is a single-sheet broadside of a German translation, perfectly designed for pasting up on walls. See also Kaufmann (ed.), *Der Anfang der Refor-mation*, 185–200.

60. WB 2, 269, nn.18 and 19. On New Year's Day 1521, noble youths put up a Latin mock letter of feud against Emser on the pulpit of the

Thomaskirche in Leipzig; 1,500 copies were printed. The printer and his journeymen were clapped into prison, but Emser interceded for them and their punishment was reduced.

61. Walch, XV, 1792; *Bulla coena Domini: das ist: die bulla vom Abent-fressen des allerheyligsten hern des Bapsts: vordeutscht durch Martin Luth*, Wittenberg 1522 [VD 16 K 267].

62. See David Paisey and Giulia Bartrum, 'Hans Holbein and Miles Coverdale: A New Woodcut', *Print Quarterly* 26, 2009, 3, 227–53 for an image of Luther fighting the Pope building on the Hercules woodcut which the authors convincingly attribute to Holbein, published in an English version in 1539.

63. WB 3, 382, 6 March 1521.

64. Report of Karl von Miltitz in Junghans, *Die Reformation*, 91–2.

65. Brecht, *Luther*, 1, 426–9: Aleander did not in fact publish the final Bull against Luther until October 1521.

66. WB 2, 384, 7 March 1521, 282:14; and see WB 2, 377, 17 Feb. 1521; 385, 7 March 1521.

67. Junghans, *Die Reformation*, 94; see also on book burnings WB 2, 378, 27 Feb. 1521; 382, 6 March 1521.

## 8. The Diet of Worms

1. RTA 3, 466, 8 Nov. 1520; 468–70, 17 Dec. 1520; Friedrich was to bring him only if he recanted.

2. RTA 3, 471.

3. WB 2, 383, 6 March 1521; Luther received it on 26 March.

4. Gerrit Deutschländer, 'Spalatin als Prinzenerzieher' in Kohnle, Meckelnborg and Schirmer (eds), *Georg Spalatin*.

5. Friedrich's attitude to the Reformation remained much more ambiguous. He was reluctant to give up his relics collection, though eventually he did. See Ludolphy, *Friedrich der Weise*; Höss, *Georg Spalatin*. Spalatin acted as an educational mentor to the young dukes of Branschweig-Lüneburg while they studied at Wittenberg, and may have been involved in the education of Johann Friedrich's younger brother as well.

6. For example, WB 2, 347, 30 Oct. 1520 (in response to a letter of support from Johann Friedrich to the Elector after receipt of the bull); WB 2, 393, 31 March 1521 (see below); WB 2, 461, 18 March 1522; WB 3, 753, 18 June 1524. He dedicated his Magnificat (1521) to him (WS 7, 538–604; LW 21), and his German translation of Daniel (1529–30), WDB 11, II, Daniel to Malachai, *Anhang*, 376–87.

7. WB 2, 330, 24 Aug. 1520.

8. Walch, XV, 1891.

9. Alcohol certainly played a part in the friendship: Luther's antagonist Aleander would later describe Luther as a drunkard.

10. Five of his letters to Luther up to the end of 1525 (one addressed jointly to Melanchthon) have survived in comparison to the hundreds of letters Luther wrote him. Weide, *Spalatins Briefwechsel*.

11. He had first mooted this in a letter to Linck (WB 1, 121, 18 Dec. 1518); and then developed it in letters to Spalatin (WB 1, 161, 13 March 1519, 359:29–30); and became more convinced when he had received Lorenzo Valla's proof that the Donation of Constantine was a forgery (WB 2, 257, 24 Feb. 1520, 48:26–8), promising to say more to Spalatin when they met. By August 1520, when Luther wrote to Johannes Lang (who had been shocked by the tone of *To the Christian Nobility of the German Nation*), he could state that 'we' were now certain that the papacy was the seat of the Antichrist and the Pope was owed no obedience (WB 2, 327, 18 Aug. 1520, 167:13–14); by 11 October, when he knew the contents of the bull, he wrote to Spalatin that he was finally certain the Pope was Antichrist (WB 2, 341, 11 Oct. 1520) and by the end of October, he wrote *Wider die Bulle des Endchrists* (*Against the bull of the Antichrist*), WS 6, 614:29.

12. RTA 2, 494–507 for the Saxon chancellor Brück's report of the speech: according to him, Aleander concluded by alleging that Luther and others had insulted him as a born Jew (*geborner Jude*). He countered that he had been born of poor parents, but he would not have been accepted as a canon at Lüttich if he were Jewish. However, even if he were a baptised Jew he should not be held in contempt for Christ himself was born a Jew.

13. WB 2, 389, 19 March 1521, 289:12. He wanted the papists alone to be responsible for his blood.

14. WB 2, 391, 24 March 1521, 292:7–8; 9–11, Luther to an unknown correspondent, possibly in Basle.

15. WB 2, 393, 31 March 1521, 295:7–9.

16. RTA 2, 526–7, 6 March 1521, Citation of Luther to Worms by Emperor Charles V; RTA 2, 529–33: on 10 March an imperial edict was issued ordering Luther to recant, and in the meantime all his books were to be handed over to the authorities, and were no longer to be printed, bought or sold. WB 2, 383, 280:4–6.

17. RTA 2, 526.

18. WB 2, 383, 6 March 1521; Introduction: the citation and letter of safe conduct were in the possession of Luther's son-in-law Georg von Kunheim. After Luther's death his sons were left the library, and his daughter Margarethe, permitted to take what she wanted from the household goods, probably chose the chest which happened to contain

the documents. We know that in 1532, when Luther showed them to his table companions, he took them out of the chest where they were kept with some other important letters, WT 2, 2783c, 658:11–2. Cranach also kept a facsimile copy in his *Stammbuch*.

19. WB 2, 395, 7 April 1521; and see n.9; WB 2, 392, 29 March 1521 (to Lang).

20. Myconius, *Geschichte*, 34. Justus Jonas also joined the party.

21. Walch, XV, 1836: Veit Warbeck's description to Herzog Johann of Saxony, 16 April 1521.

22. WS 7, 803–18, 803: the later superintendent of Dresden, Daniel Greser, described the event. Luther himself had been forbidden to preach so he was deliberately placing God's authority above the emperor's; he did not, however, break the ban by publishing the sermon himself; but there were soon many editions, in Erfurt, Wittenberg and Augsburg.

23. Myconius, *Geschichte*, 34; as Myconius noted, the monastery had since been turned into a parish church and school so the Devil had indeed been defeated.

24. WB 2, 395, 7 April 1521, 296 (to Melanchthon). For Luther's reminiscence, WT 5, 65; 3, 282.

25. WB 2, 396, 14 April 1521 (to Spalatin).

26. Walch, XV, 1824–5; RTA 2, 537.

27. RTA 2, 534–7: on 6 March the emperor had summoned Luther to Worms, but on 10 March he had ordered sequestration of his books, so it seemed unlikely that he would have a fair hearing; Spalatin was advised that some were arguing the safe conduct applied only if Luther were travelling to Worms to recant. If he did not, he was a heretic and therefore excluded from a safe conduct. The signs were not good; on the other hand, others argued that the safe conduct would have to be honoured because of the loss to reputation if it were disregarded; and it would also be playing into the hands of the papists not to come.

28. WB 2, 396, [14 April] 1521, 298:9–10; WB 2, 455, 5 March 1522; Walch, XV, 1828 (*Spalatins Annales*).

29. This unusual phrase was what Myconius reports Luther as saying in his version of the trip to Worms; *Geschichte*, 34–5. As the editor points out, he may have taken it from a much later letter of Luther's to Lang of 1540, which he could easily have seen, and which referred to forthcoming negotiations; so this may either be accurate oral history or else part of Reformation myth-making: WB 9, 3510, 2 July 1540.

30. *Litaneia Germanorvm*, Augsburg, c.1521, VD 16 ZV 25246, fos. A iii (v); B i. Walch, XV, 1832.

31. WB 2, 395, 7 April 1521.

32. WT 5342a; see also WT 3, 3357, from 1533, 5342b, from 1540.

33. Kalkoff, *Depeschen des Nuntius Aleander*, 133; Aleander, who commented on Luther's 'demonic eyes', was convinced people would soon be saying he performed miracles.

34. Walch, XV, 39 (*Spalatins Annales*); and see also the report of Veit Warbeck, Walch, XV, 1836–7, RTA 2, 859.

35. Kalkoff, *Depeschen des Nuntius Aleander*, 23–4. Aleander complained of constant attacks and insults from Lutheran supporters, and he again mentioned the slurs that he was of Jewish origin; Kalkoff, *Briefe*, 40–5, letter of 17 Feb. 1521. Everyone was supporting Luther, and not just all the people, 'even wood and stones proclaim the name of Luther', 42.

36. LW 32, 106; WS 7, 827:11–2. It is not clear who wrote this report, but it evidently came from Luther's side. It was translated into German by Spalatin.

37. Kalkoff, *Briefe*, 49–50.

38. LW 32, 106; WS 7, 828:8. It had another purpose, for some of the writings published under Luther's name were not his. For instance, in 1518, a pointed summary of a sermon on excommunication he had held in Wittenberg was circulated in manuscript, and this eventually reached Emperor Maximilian, convincing him that Luther was a heretic who must be stopped: WS 1, 635.

39. LW 32, 107; WS 7, 829:8–10; 11–12.

40. This is also how he explained things in a letter to Johannes Cuspinianus, written on the evening of the first day: he complained he had been given neither time nor space to put his side, WB 2, 397, 17 April 1521. Aleander certainly thought his performance unimpressive: he had come in smiling, moving his head animatedly in the presence of the emperor, but had left in a more sombre mood; and Aleander thought he had damaged his earlier reputation: Kalkoff, *Depeschen des Nuntius Aleander*, 138.

41. WB 2, 400, 28 April 1521, 305:13–14.

42. LW 32, 108; WS 7, 830:8–13.

43. Kalkoff, *Depeschen des Nuntius Aleander*, 70–1.

44. LW 32, 109–10; WS 7, 832:8; 834:3; RTA 2, 569–86; 575.

45. LW 32, 109–10; WS 7, 833:1–4; 18–20; 833:23–834:1; 6; 6–7.

46. WS 7, 834:20–1, 25; 835:1–5.

47. Remarkably, Luther's own side retained this passage in their contemporary account of events at Worms. Forty years later, however, when the Lutheran Johannes Mathesius came to write his biographical sermons about Luther, he edited it out, leaving Luther to conclude in prophetic tones with a warning lest God be angry with the Roman Reich and

German nation. Mathesius, *Historien*, 59–64; See, for Cochlaeus's reaction, Vandiver, Keen and Frazel (eds and trs), *Luther's Lives*, 105.

48. Even the Catholic Girolamo de' Medici had heard it was a very learned speech: Kalkoff, *Briefe*, 48.

49. LW 32, 112; WS 7, 835:20–836:1; 837:1–2.

50. So, for example, it appears in large type in Melanchthon's biography of Luther, *Vita Lutheri*, fo. 58 (v); and in the Latin text of 1521, it is given in German. LW 32, 112–13; WS 7, 838:3; 4–9.

51. LW 32, 114; Kalkoff, *Briefe*, 55. According to Aleander, when he left the room, Luther raised his arm in the air in a kind of victory salute like a Landsknecht; Kalkoff, *Depeschen des Nuntius Aleander*, 143.

52. *Gewissen* and its Latin equivalents *conscientz* and *conscientia* are terms which Luther used a good deal throughout his life, but especially in 1521. In that single year, *Gewissen* appears more frequently in his writings than in his entire written work up to that point; while he used *conscientia* regularly in his writings right up to the time of the Diet.

53. Staupitz was especially insightful about confession and the problems of those who made complete lists of all their sins, hoping to make a perfect confession and so perform a work. He was forthright against those who exploited nuns, and ordered them to go on pilgrimage or do extra prayers because their consciences were burdened: such 'advisors', he wrote, pile 'rubbish' on 'rubbish'; Knaake, *Johann von Staupitzens*, 41.

54. Walch, XV, 1880 (*Spalatins Annales*, 41); Kolde (ed.), *Analecta Lutherana*, 31, report of Peutinger on Luther's appearance at Worms; Walch, XV, 1891 (*Spalatins Annales*, 48).

55. He made the point in his later letter to the emperor in Latin and in German to the electoral princes and estates of the Diet, rapidly printed in many editions, WB 2, 401, 402, 28 April 1521, 'no one was willing to refute on the basis of Holy Scripture any erroneous articles [of faith] which are supposed to be in my little books. No one gave me any hope or promise that an examination or investigation of my little books would be conducted in the light of God's Word at some time in the future'; LW Letters, I, 208; WB 2, 402, 28 April 1521, 316:95–317:99.

56. WB 2, 398, 399, 17 and 20 April 1521; see, for example, Hutten, *Ulrichs von Hutten verteütscht clag/an Hertzog Friderich zu Sachsen. Des hayligen Rœmischen Reichs Ertzmarschalck vñ Churfürsten Landgrauen in Türingen vnd Marckgrauen zu Meissen*, Augsburg 1521 [VD 16 H 6251].

57. Lutz, *Conrad Peutinger*, 171–2; Augsburg merchants were amongst those attacked.

58. RTA 2, 594; 869; it was read in French and German; Kalkoff, *Briefe*, 49: Girolamo de' Medici's report; he claimed to have seen the original in the emperor's own hand.

59. RTA 2, 558; [VD 16 ZV 61]. *Acta et res gestae*, Strasbourg 1521.

60. The imperial orator read out the emperor's statement. LW 32, 129: Johannes Eck's Minutes of the Trial of Luther before the Diet of Worms.

61. RTA 2, 616–24; 616: this was a report Vehus sent to the Magraf of Baden written on 6 June, some weeks after the event. Vehus gives the speech as he recalls giving it to Luther, as they were beginning negotiations.

62. Cochlaeus, *Colloqvivm*; Greving (ed.), 'Colloquium Cochlaei', vol. 4, part 3, 179–218.

63. Vandiver, Keen and Frazel (eds and trs), *Luther's Lives*, 92; Walch, XV, 1844, for an example of the pitiless rhymes, which punned on his name, which means 'snail' or 'spoon'.

64. Yet when Cochlaeus came to write his own history of Luther's life, he plagiarised large parts of the Lutherans' pamphlet about Worms, even though he believed it to be written by Luther himself: RTA 2, 542, n.1.

65. Lyndal Roper, 'The Seven-Headed Monster: Luther and Psychology' in Alexander and Taylor (eds), *History and Psyche*, 228; WT 3, 3367, 294:23–4.

66. In his speech at the Diet in February he had also complained that the Lutherans were insulting him as a Jew, and the Strasbourg edition of *On the Babylonian Captivity of the Church* depicted two dogs, a sign of the priests biting the laity. He stated that Luther denied the Real Presence of Christ in the sacrament in *On the Freedom of a Christian*. He also alleged that Luther had had the classical author Lucian printed in Wittenberg, and just as Lucian held all heathen ceremonies in contempt, so Lutherans mocked all Christian ones. Walch, XV, 1711–12.

67. It took some time for the divisions amongst the humanists to become clear and they were not fully apparent even in 1522: Rummel, *Confessionalization of Humanism*, 22–8.

68. Lutz, *Conrad Peutinger*, 164–6; Kalkoff, *Depeschen des Nuntius Aleander*, 155; 158.

69. RTA 2, 610: this was made clear informally in discussions with Luther.

70. The author here equated 'Saxo' with Peter, who denied Christ three times. Aurifaber (ed.), *Epistolae*, vol. 2, edition of 1594, fo. 12 (v) says this refers to Elector Friedrich's pusillanimity; and this would clearly have indicated that the text did not come from Saxony or Luther's immediate circle.

71. See Rebecca Sammel, 'The *Passio Lutheri*: Parody as Hagiography', *Journal of English and Germanic Philology* 95, no. 2, 1996, 157–74: the work was originally published in Latin but was soon translated into German, and there are editions from Vienna, Augsburg, Munich, Colmar; and even one from Regensburg of 1550. It must have been first published sometime before September 1521, because Cochlaeus mentioned it to Aleander on 27 September.

72. In the Strasbourg edition, the pamphlet is coupled with a rhyming dialogue between Karsthans and Kegelhans, two peasants who complain about the Church, the rapacious clergy, their fasting regulations and their lack of godliness, yet another portent of how rapidly social discontent could ally itself with Reformation adulation of Luther. The author also attacked Peutinger as Judas, betraying Luther for a few benefices. It had a strange afterlife, however, included in Aurifaber's collection of Luther's letters, published after his death, again alongside the Karsthans dialogue, which one would think the Lutheran movement would have wished to forget by 1565.

73. LW 51, 77; WS 10, III, 19:2–3 the second of the Invocavit Sermons of 1522. As Luther's German puts it even more emphatically, 'Ich hab nichts gethan, das wort hatt es alles gehandelt und außgericht.' He joked that the Word had done it all, while he, Philip and Amsdorf drank Wittenberg beer.

74. WB 2, 400, 28 April 1521, 305:17–22, quoting Jesus before his Passion: 'A little while, and ye shall not see me: and again, a little while, and ye shall see me' (John 16:16). This letter also equates his enemies with the Jews.

## 9. In the Wartburg

1. WT 5, 5353.
2. RTA 2, 654. However, the Elector also asked the Emperor to excuse him from carrying out the mandate against Luther, which he apparently did.
3. Müller, *Wittenberger Bewegung*, 159.
4. LW Letters, I, 291–6; WB 2, 427, 15 Aug. 1521, 381:75–6; 70–1.
5. LW Letters, I, 270–3. The secret was successfully kept from many in fact. Cochlaeus still got the location wrong when he wrote his biography, published in 1549: he thought he had been kept at Altenstaig; and Agricola wrote of how people tried to find out Luther's whereabouts by invoking the Devil! Kawerau, *Agricola*, 32. On the rumour from court, WB 2, 420, 15 July 1521; and for the fake letter, WB 2, 421, 422, shortly after 15 July 1521.
6. LW Letters, I, 201; WB 2, 400, 28 April 1521, 305:6–7. In fact, Luther could not have been more wrong. Georg had been amongst those who argued that he should have an imperial safe conduct, because it was a matter of honour to protect him – even though other rulers had argued that protection should not be given to heretics and therefore his safe conduct was void.
7. WB 2, 410, 14 May 1521; LW Letters, I, 225.
8. There is an interesting exchange with Wolfgang Capito and the archbishop of Mainz, for whom he was working: WB 2, 433, 442; and Egranus wrote a letter from Joachimstal.

9. *'dominus percussit me in posteriora gravi dolore'*: the American edition has 'The Lord has afflicted me with painful constipation', LW Letters, I, 217, which is accurate but misses Luther's directness: WB 2, 407, 12 May 1521, 333:34–5; LW Letters, I, 255; WB 2, 417, 10 June 1521, 354:27.

10. WB 2, 429, 9 Sept. 1521, 388:29–30.

11. See Lyndal Roper, '"To his most Learned and Dearest Friend": Reading Luther's Letters', *German History* 28, 2010, 283–95.

12. LW Letters, I, 101; WB 2, 436, 1 Nov. 1521, 399:7–8.

13. LW Letters, I, 257, WB 2, 418, 13 July 1521, 356:7–10.

14. Müller, *Wittenberger Bewegung*, 16 (letter of Sebastian Helmann to Johann Hess, 8 Oct. 1521, Wittenberg), 135, 136, and see 137–45; one of the three prophets, Stübner, was living in Melanchthon's house; and the issue of infant baptism was being raised.

15. LW Letters, I, 257; WB 2, 418, 13 July 1521, 356:1–2, 2–3; LW Letters, I, 269; WB 2, 420, 15 July 1521 (to Spalatin).

16. WB 2, 429, 9 Sept. 1521: Spalatin was to get Cranach and Döring to bring this about; WB 2, 430, 9 Sept. 1521.

17. Plummer, *From Priest's Whore*, 51–2; WB 2, 413, 26 May 1521; Luther knew of the marriage when he wrote to Melanchthon, and it was celebrated publicly later.

18. On 1 August 1521, Luther commented on Karlstadt's theses on celibacy of 20/21 June, and on 3 August, he was commenting on the first printed sheets of Karlstadt's *De coelibatv*, see WB 2, 373, 3 Aug. 1521; WB 2, 424, 1 Aug. 1521; 425, 3 Aug. 1521; 426, 6 Aug. 1521. These two longer writings of Karlstadt's were composed around the same time as his Seven Theses on celibacy, which were debated on 21 June, and again on 19 July. They proposed that priests *ought* to marry, and that even monks should be able to marry if they suffered from desire, for although they sinned in breaking a vow, it was a worse sin to give way to lust; Barge, *Karlstadt*, I, 265, 290; WB 2, p. 370. The preface of Karlstadt's Latin writing, *De Coelibatv, Monachatv et Vidvitate* is dated 29 June 1521, though it appeared before the German one. The German version, *Uon Gelubden Unterrichtung*, did not appear until October or November, but its printed preface is dated St John's Day (24 June) 1521; Barge, *Karlstadt*, I, 266–7 and 275; see also Furcha (ed. and tr.), *Carlstadt*, 51. For a discussion of the argument of both works, Barge, *Karlstadt*, I, 265–81. Interestingly, much of Karlstadt's argument depended heavily on Old Testament authority, not on the New Testament.

19. WB 2, 428, 9 Sept. 1521; the first edition of Luther's *Themata de Votis* had appeared by 8 October (WS 8, 317) and the theses elicited some strong responses, including a counter-tract from Cochlaeus, WS 8, 318–19. The early German editions contain only the first set of theses:

WS 8, 313–22; 323–9. Luther's full tract, *De votis monasticis Martini Lutheri iudicium*, was begun after 11 November yet the letter of dedication was already finished by 21 November 1521 (WS 8, 564–5). However, Spalatin held it back from printing and it did not appear until around 25 February 1522, WS 8, 566; see WB 2, 443, *c*.5 Dec. 1521, for Luther's outraged letter to Spalatin when he discovered what had happened.

20. Furcha (ed. and tr.), *Carlstadt*, 80; Karlstadt, *Uon gelubden*, fo. E iv (r). He was more explicit in the Latin version, especially on the dangers of masturbation: Furcha (ed. and tr.), *Carlstadt*, 51; Barge, *Karlstadt*, I, 276.

21. Ulrich Bubenheimer, 'Gelassenheit und Ablösung. Eine psychohistorische Studie über Andreas Bodenstein von Karlstadt und seinen Konflikt mit Martin Luther', *Zeitschrift für Kirchengeschichte* 92, 1981, 258.

22. Furcha (ed. and tr.), *Carlstadt*, 98; Karlstadt, *Uon gelubden*, fo. H iii (v). Karlstadt was a bachelor when he wrote this. It is directly addressed to the dedicatee of the treatise, Jörg Reich, a citizen and merchant of Leipzig, who was apparently having trouble with his wife; and it deals with male authority, fo. H iii (r). The first passage on women's subordination is underlined in the VD 16 B 6245 copy! Compare *De Coelibatv, Monachatv, et Vidvitate*, [Basle] 1521 [VD 16 B 6123].

23. LW Letters, I, 294; WB 2, 427, 15 Aug. 1521, 380:34; WB 2, 426, 6 Aug. 1521.

24. WB 2, 428, 9 Sept. 1521; LW Letters, I, 296–301.

25. Luther's attack on begging, whether by students or monks, became part of his theological thinking from an early date – and it also explains why the poor law came to be central to the Wittenberg Reformation. Just why the issue of begging preoccupied him so much at this time may be connected with the fact that Luther did not know for certain who was paying for his stay in the Wartburg – he hoped, he had written earlier to Spalatin, that it was not Berlepsch, who could hardly afford it. He assumed that it was the Elector, although he could not be sure; WB 2, 427, 15 Aug. 1521.

26. 'Magis fui raptus, quam tractus': the Latin has a nice opposition of *raptus* and *tractus*, underlining the miraculous nature of Luther's entry into the monastery.

27. LW Letters, I, 296–304; WB 2, 428, 9 Sept. 1521, 384:80, 80–1; 385:97–8; 98–9; 118.

28. LW Letters, I, 303; WB 2, 428, 9 Sept. 1521, 385:128; WB 2, 249, 5 Feb. 1520: Luther considered Melanchthon needed a wife; WB 2, 327, 18 Aug. 1520. Katharina was the orphaned daughter of Hans Krapp, mayor of Wittenberg, a man of some means; so it was a good match, though there was some scandal surrounding it, and the wedding had to be brought forward for an undisclosed reason.

29. Stefan Rhein, 'Philipp Melanchthon und Eobanus Hessus. Wittenberger Reformation und Erfurter "Poetenburg"', in Weiß (ed.), *Erfurt. Geschichte und Gegenwart*, 283–95. Kolde (ed.), *Analecta Lutherana*, 25, 4 Dec. 1520, Thomas Blaurer wrote to his brother Ambrosius that Philip would marry a woman with a small dowry, 'forma mediocri', but 'charam et honestam et probam'.

30. WS 8, 654–69. There was soon a translation into German by Justus Jonas, which in theory his father could have read; but this was not a letter to him in the normal sense of the word. WS 8, 573:24; 574:3–4; 574:8–9; 574:22; 574:32.

31. LW Letters, I, 329–336; WS 8, 575:35–6; 576:4–6. The references to God's calling in the letter are reminiscent of the biblical story of the calling of Samuel. Luther's mother Margarethe was known as 'Hannah', the same name as Samuel's mother; and the letter concludes with a greeting to her.

32. WS 8, 573:25; 574:5; 575:28–9. The German translation of the treatise by Luther's close associate Justus Jonas has Luther using the informal *du* in addressing his father. This is significant because Luther's father had accorded him the polite 'you' after he gained his degree, withdrawing it when he entered the monastery. In his final letter of 1530 to his father, Luther uses the formal, respectful *Ihr*.

33. It is possible that he wrote and the letters no longer survive; but Luther does not mention letters he has written to him, as he often did with letters to others; he regularly sent greetings to Cranach, Döring and others, but not Karlstadt. It is impossible to know for sure, because Karlstadt apparently either destroyed many of the other letters Luther sent him, or else was not included in the circles of those who later transcribed letters Luther sent.

34. LW Letters, I, 257; WB 2, 418, 13 July 1521, 356:4; WB 2, 407, 12 May 1521, 333:18.

35. Preface to the Complete Edition of Luther's Latin Writings, 1545: interestingly Luther presents it here as 'he who through faith is righteous shall live'. LW 34, 337; WS 54, 176–87, 185:18; 186:8–9.

36. Lucas Cranach and Martin Luther, *Das Newe Testament Deutzsch*, Wittenberg, 1522 [VD 16 B 4318], fo. CVII (r). The New Testament was also illustrated with woodcuts by Cranach, mostly initials in the manner of a manuscript at the start of each new book. Much richer, full-page illustrations were provided for Revelation; and in the 1534 edition of the whole Bible, the Whore of Babylon is shown wearing the papal tiara. The beast is shown wearing a triple crown.

37. Stiftung Luthergedenkstätten in Sachsen-Anhalt, *Passional Christi und Antichristi* (Facsimile of the German Edition of Wittenberg, 1521, Johann

Rhau-Grunenberg) with a *Begleitheft* by Volkmar Joestel, Berlin n.d., fo. C vi (v); Gabriele Wimböck, 'Setting the Scene: Pictorial Representations of Religious Pluralization', in Andreas Höfele, Stephan Laqué, Enno Ruge, and Gabriela Schmidt, eds., *Representing Religious Pluralization in Early Modern Europe*, Berlin 2007, 270–1.

38. WS 8, 398–410.

39. Müller, *Wittenberger Bewegung*, 17.

40. He may have removed it later, since the same man also noted that when he distributed Communion, he did not wear a cowl and said the words of consecration in German.

41. Seidemann, *Erläuterungen*, 36–42: this gives three different reports of the events at Eilenburg, all of which are hostile. See 37, 38.

42. Müller, *Wittenberger Bewegung*, 69.

43. Ibid., 35–41.

44. Ibid., 42–6. Friedrich was not impressed by the lack of unanimity and rejected the proposals.

45. Ibid., 20.

46. LW 44, 189; WS 6, 450:23–5; Luther's condemnation of begging had also been an issue in the Leipzig Debate.

47. LW Letters, I, 327; WB 2, 438, 11 Nov. 1521, 402:21–2; Krentz, *Ritualwandel*, 144–8; and see also Ulrich Bubenheimer, 'Scandalum et ius divinum. Theologische und rechtstheologische Probleme der ersten reformatorischen Innovationen in Wittenberg 1521/22', *Zeitschrift der Savigny-Stiftung für Rechtsgeschichte, Kanonistische Abteilung* 90, 1973, 263–342.

48. Müller, *Wittenberger Bewegung*, 73, 74, 75; Stefan Oehmig, 'Die Wittenberger Bewegung 1521/22 und ihre Folgen im Lichte alter und neuer Fragestellungen. Ein Beitrag zum Thema (Territorial-)Stadt und Reformation' in Oehmig (ed.), *700 Jahre Wittenberg*, 104–7; Krentz, *Ritualwandel*, 149–50.

49. Müller, *Wittenberger Bewegung*, 151–64 (Ambrosius Wilken, *Zeitung aus Wittenberg*, though it is possible that this became part of the mythologisation of the event); Krentz argues that the newsletter was written afterwards, *Ritualwandel*, 155–6.

50. Stefan Oehmig, 'Wittenberger Bewegung' in Oehmig (ed.), *700 Jahre Wittenberg*, 105; and see 117–23; Müller, *Wittenberger Bewegung*, 120; 118.

51. Stefan Oehmig, 'Wittenberger Bewegung' in Oehmig (ed.), *700 Jahre Wittenberg*, 105; and see Krentz, *Ritualwandel*, 148–54.

52. WB 2, 406, [*c*.8 May 1521]; and 410, 14 May 1521.

53. WB 2, 443, [*c*.5 Dec. 1521], 410:18.

54. LW 45, 53–74; WS 8, 676–684.

55. LW 45, 69; WS 8, 670–87.

56. Müller, *Wittenberger Bewegung*, 161–3; 117–19; Stefan Oehmig, 'Witten-
    berger Bewegung' in Oehmig (ed.), *700 Jahre Wittenberg*, 106–11.

57. Müller, *Wittenberger Bewegung*, 133, 134; see also Kaufmann (ed.), *Der
    Anfang der Reformation*, 218–20.

58. Müller, *Wittenberger Bewegung*, 129, 130; Krentz, *Ritualwandel*, 205–6 down-
    plays their importance.

59. The dating of this first document is disputed. See Stefan Oehmig,
    'Wittenberger Bewegung' in Oehmig (ed.), *700 Jahre Wittenberg*, 101–3
    for an earlier dating of this text or of a forerunner on the grounds of
    textual similarity to an ordinance of Jakob Scidler's for glassworks of
    spring 1521. However, it is notable that Ulcensius describes the introduc-
    tion of the begging ordinance in a letter of 30 November 1521 and states
    that it had happened at Luther's instigation; and it is difficult to see
    why there would be a need for such an ordinance if the revenues of
    the private Masses, benefices and monasteries had not yet become
    available, as they would not have been in spring 1521. It is also strange
    that there is no reference to Seidler's ordinance in Luther's correspond-
    ence. Barge, *Karlstadt*, I, 378–86, implies that the begging ordinance
    dates from the same time as the published ordinance of 24 January 1522,
    so linking it closely with Karlstadt; but this dating is probably too late.

60. Müller, *Wittenberger Bewegung*, 163, attributed to Ambrosius Wilken.

61. Ibid., 167 [8 Jan. 1522]; 163–4.

## 10. Karlstadt and the Christian City of Wittenberg

1. An exception is Lindberg, *European Reformations*, 93–6, 104–5, 135–42.

2. See, however, Ulrich Bubenheimer, 'Gelassenheit und Ablösung. Eine
   psychohistorische Studie über Andreas Bodenstein von Karlstadt und
   seinen Konflikt mit Martin Luther', *Zeitschrift für Kirchengeschichte* 92,
   1981.

3. Ulrich Bubenheimer, 'Scandalum et ius divinum. Theologische und
   rechtstheologische Probleme der ersten reformatorischen Innovationen
   in Wittenberg 1521/22', *Zeitschrift der Savigny-Stiftung für Rechtsgeschichte,
   Kanonistische Abteilung* 90, 1973, 263–342; Kruse, *Universitätstheologie*, 323–4.

4. Andreas Karlstadt, *Von anbettung und ererbietung der tzeychen des newen
   Testaments*, Wittenberg, 1521 [VD 16 B 6218]; Furcha (ed. and tr.), *Carlstadt*, 40–51. It was published in Wittenberg, Augsburg and Strasbourg.
   The opening brief letter of dedication spoke of the 'hatred and envy'
   directed against the Wittenbergers.

5. Barge, *Karlstadt*, I, 49–50; 59–64.

6. Ibid., 55; 42–66; Bubenheimer, *Consonantia* 26–33. Sider, *Karlstadt*, 8–9:
   his was the second-highest income of the sixty-four clerics in Wittenberg.

He earned 127 fl per year, Barge, *Karlstadt*, II, 530. He pressed Spalatin for one rich soon-to-be-vacant benefice; and then even tried facilitating a petition from his students; Barge, *Karlstadt*, I, 88–9. When Henning Göde died, Luther lobbied Spalatin to get Karlstadt named provost in his place, WB 2, 370, 22 Jan. 1521, only to rescind this 'foolish' suggestion the following week; WB 2, 372, 29 Jan. 1521. Karlstadt then asked Spalatin on 2 February more modestly for one of the vacant benefices of Göde, so he could employ a secretary.

7. Barge, *Karlstadt*, I, 57; Sider, *Karlstadt*, 14.

8. Sider, *Karlstadt*, 8–10; Barge, *Karlstadt*, I, 9–31; Bubenheimer, 'Gelassenheit und Ablösung', 258.

9. Barge, *Karlstadt*, I, 72–85.

10. LW 31, 9; Barge, *Karlstadt*, I, 87, n.56: Karlstadt, Thesis 60: 'Corruit hoc quod Augustinus contra hereticos loquitur excessive'; Luther, Thesis 1: 'Dicere, quot Augustinus contra haereticos excessive loquatur, est dicere, Augustinum fere ubique mentitum esse'.

11. WB 1, 18 May 1517, 99:8, 'Theologia nostra et S. Augustinus' 45, 4 Sept. 1517; in the letter to Lang of 11 November 1517, however, he reverts to 'me' and 'mine': WB 1, 52; 64, 21 March 1518, 'studium nostrum'; 'iniuria homini a nostris illata', 155:35 (in which he includes the students); WB 1 74, 9 May 1518, esp. 170:20–9; WS 1, preface to the complete edition of the *Theologia deutsch*, 1518 'uns Wittenbergischen Theologen', 378:24.

12. Barge, *Karlstadt*, I, 75; 104–7.

13. They also shared an attachment to Staupitz. In 1519, Karlstadt had dedicated his treatise on Augstine's *De spiritu et littera* to none other than Luther's mentor Staupitz [VD 16 A 4237]; while the debt Luther owed Karlstadt was clear when he dedicated his 'In epistolam Pauli ad Galatas' of early 1519 to Petrus Lupinus and Karlstadt, WS 2, 437.

14. They were Johann Dölsch of Wittenberg; Bernhard Adelmann von Adelmannsfelden from Augsburg; Willibald Pirckheimer and Lazarus Spengler of Nuremberg; and Johannes Egranus of Zwickau; Bubenheimer, *Consonantia*, 186. Eck had been permitted to add names to the Bull, and he included several he suspected of being his opponents.

15. '*Freunde*' in the German of this period can mean kin. It begins by wishing them peace, joy and a strong faith – a very personal opening from a man who usually chose his dedicatees carefully to advance his interests.

16. Furcha (ed. and tr.), *Carlstadt*, 28–30; *Missiue von der aller hochsten tugent gelassenhait*, [Augsburg] [1520], [Grimm and Wirsung] [VD 16 B 6170], fos. A i (v), A i (v), A ii (r), A ii (v); A iii (v).

17. Furcha (ed. and tr.), *Carlstadt*, 38, 139, 138; Karlstadt, *Missiue*, fo. B iii (v); Karlstadt, *Was gesagt ist*, fos. B i (r), A iv (r–v); C ii (r), D iii (r).

18. Furcha (ed. and tr.), *Carlstadt*, 138; *Was gesagt ist*, fo. A [iv] (r). Luther makes the charge in 'Against the Heavenly Prophets', 1524, LW 40, 81, and throughout; WS 18, 63:32–3. Furcha (ed. and tr.), *Carlstadt*, 155; Sider, *Karlstadt*, 216. In 1540, the year before he died, Karlstadt wrote a series of theses on *Gelassenheit*, which he termed '*abnegatio*': this was intended to be part of a greater synoptic work of theology; Bubenheimer, 'Gelassenheit und Ablösung', 256. On *Gelassenheit* as works righteousness, see Sider, *Karlstadt*, 220–3: he argues Karlstadt was not guilty of the works righteousness with which Luther charged him, but he did place emphasis on self-mortification.

19. Müller, *Wittenberger Bewegung*, 153–4 (Zeitung aus Wittenberg): Krentz, *Ritualwandel*, casts doubt on its reliability, but it does convey the evangelical mood.

20. Müller, *Wittenberger Bewegung*, 135, 163, 170; Preus, *Carlstadt's Ordinaciones*, 28 and n.62; Krentz, *Ritualwandel*, 154–69.

21. Barge, *Karlstadt*, I, 266; *Uon Gelubden Unterrichtung*, the preface is dated St John's Day (24 June) 1521.

22. Furcha (ed. and tr.), *Carlstadt*, 132; 407, n.7 for translation of the Latin. It was to be prayed by Lutherans in honour of the Resurrection.

23. Barge, *Karlstadt*, I, 364; 'gelertter, dapffer leuth': Müller, *Wittenberger Bewegung*, 155–6 (Zeitung aus Wittenberg).

24. Müller, *Wittenberger Bewegung*, 170 (Thomas von der Heyde, Neue Zeitung); Kolde (ed.), *Analecta Lutherana*, 25, 4 Dec. 1520, letter of Thomas Blaurer to Ambrosius Blaurer.

25. WB 2, 449, 13 Jan. 1522, 423:45.

26. *Die Messe. Von der Hochzeyt D. Andre Carolstadt. Vnnd der Priestern / so sich Eelich verheyratten*, Augsburg 1522 [VD 16 M 5492], fo. A ii (v), 'Er ist zu ersten worden ain fischer der eeweyber.'

27. Müller, *Wittenberger Bewegung*, 155–9 (Zeitung aus Wittenberg); Barge, *Karlstadt*, I, 366, n.125.

28. See Bubenheimer, 'Scandalum et ius divinum', 266, n.6; Johann Pfau to the mayor of Zwickau, Hermann Mühlpfort, c.15 Jan. 1522; Spalatin's report of the events says they even burnt extreme unction: Müller, *Wittenberger Bewegung*, 169; see also the account of Albert Burer, who dates it to 11 January, 212.

29. Furcha (ed. and tr.), *Carlstadt*, 107; Karlstadt, *Von abtuhung der Bylder/ Vnd das keyn Betdler vnther den Christen seyn sollen*, Wittenberg 1522, [VD 16 B 6215], fo. B i (r-v); interestingly the pamphlet features a lush title page woodcut illustration of a naked Adam and Eve holding aloft a decorative pediment and niche, with a peasant scene of harvest and sowing below, images almost certainly not produced for this pamphlet. Barge, *Wittenberger Bewegung*, I, 389.

30.    Furcha (ed. and tr.), *Carlstadt*, 115, 117,; Karlstadt, *Von abtuhung der Bylder*, fos. C iii (v), C iv (v).

31.    Furcha (ed. and tr.), *Carlstadt*, 122; Karlstadt, *Von abtuhung der Bylder*, fo. D iv (r).

32.    Barge, *Karlstadt*, I, 422.

33.    Müller, *Wittenberger Bewegung*, 173 (Ulcensius to Capito); Kaufmann (ed.), *Der Anfang der Reformation*, 221: as Kaufmann points out, numbers of matriculations did not fall between 1521 and 1522 – though they were a fraction of the peak years of 1519 and 1520; Barge, *Karlstadt*, I, 418–20.

34.    Krentz, *Ritualwandel*, 205–6, who downplays the importance of the prophets; Kruse, *Universitätstheologie*, 360–2, pointing out that they raised the issue of the legitimacy of infant baptism; Sider, *Karlstadt*, 161–6.

35.    That Melanchthon wanted Luther to come back was therefore generally known: see, for example, Ulcensius to Capito, Müller, *Wittenberger Bewegung*, 160 (Zeitung); 129, 130, 135.

36.    WB 2, 452, 17 Jan. 1522, 443:2–3; LW Letters, I, 380.

37.    It is not clear exactly when Zwilling left town. Preus, *Carlstadt's Ordinaciones*, 41, dates it to February; Barge, *Karlstadt*, I, 362, to December. His departure would have created something of a leadership vacuum.

38.    Ulrich Bubenheimer, 'Scandalum', 324, on Karlstadt's political position; on the new poor law, Krentz, *Ritualwandel*, 186–200; Stefan Oehmig, 'Wittenberger Bewegung' in Oehmig (ed.), *700 Jahre Wittenberg*; Ulrich Bubenheimer, 'Luthers Stellung zum Aufruhr in Wittenberg 1520–22 und die frühreformatorischen Wurzeln des landesherrlichen Kirchenregiments', *ZSRG KA* 102, 1985, 147–214; Edith Eschenhagen, 'Beiträge zur Sozial- und Wirtschaftsgeschichte der Stadt Wittenberg in der Reformationszeit', *Lutherjahrbuch* 9, 1927, 9–118; Barge, *Karlstadt*, I, 380–6; Kruse, *Universitätstheologie*, 362–6. The new ordinance revised an original poor law from 1520–1 drafted under Luther's influence, which survives in manuscript with an annotation in Luther's hand; Kruse, *Universitätstheologie*, 273–7, in WS 59, 63–5. The new ordinance brought together provisions over religious services, care for the poor and the removal of images; all three were part of the same project, and the common chest was to be financed not only out of donations but from the incomes of monasteries, religious foundations, brotherhoods and so on. On the Frauen or Muhmen Hauss StA Wittenberg, 9 [Bb6] fo. 89: the final mention of the brothel-keeper Frauenwirt is in 1522. The provision of loans for poor married craftsfolk may well have been designed to undercut Jewish moneylenders, and it has many of the features of the Italian *monte di pieta*, aimed at persuading laypeople not to borrow from Jews.

39. Kruse, *Universitätstheologie*, 362–6; Oehmig, 'Wittenberger Bewegung'; and see StadtA Witt, 360 [Bp5] for a surviving book of accounts from 1545: many of the recipients of money were women, including one 'woman in a blue coat' – presumably her name was unknown. Food was given to the poor, and a loan was made to the previous pastor of Dabrun, so the original plan of lending was maintained, if not on the scale envisaged to craftsfolk; see also 16 [Bc 4].

40. *Ain löbliche ordnung der fürstlichen stat Wittenberg: im Jahre 1522 auffgericht*, [Augsburg] [1522] [VD 16 W 3697], fo. iii (r); for another printing see *Newe ordnung der Stat Wittenberg, MDXXII. jar*, [Bamberg] [1522] [VD 16 W 3698]: this is printed with a dialogue between the bishops of Lochau and Meissen; Barge, *Karlstadt*, I, 378–82. By contrast, on the title page of *Von abtuhung der Bylder* Karlstadt proclaimed himself to be 'Carolstatt in der Christlichen statt Wittenberg'.

41. Krentz, *Ritualwandel*, 170ff also points to the tension between council and Elector.

42. Müller, *Wittenberger Bewegung*, 172, n.4, 173–9; 186; 190.

43. Ibid., 202–3; and see 184–206; for the first draft, 201: originally this did specifically say that Communion could be given to the laity in one kind or two, but the final version left this unclear.

44. Kruse, *Universitätstheologie*, 371–75; Preus, *Carlstadt's Ordinaciones*, 40–50; Krentz, *Ritualwandel*, 206–10, who argues that the Eilenburg discussions were not undertaken under the pressure of a popular movement.

45. Barge, *Karlstadt*, I, 408. He may also have rejected it because it seemed to allow that the council had the right to make religious policy: Preus, *Carlstadt's Ordinaciones*, 47.

46. So also by Easter 1522 the Elector was proposing that the relics should be displayed in the church but that the congregation should not be told about the indulgences they offered. This way he could continue to argue that no changes in religion had been made, in obedience to the imperial mandate. Kalkoff, *Ablass*, 84–5.

47. LW Letters, I, 387, [*c.*22 Feb. 1522]; WB 2, 454, 24 Feb. 1522, 448:7–8; 10–11; 13; 449:22–3.

48. WB 2, 454, [*c.*24 Feb. 1522].

49. WB 2, 455, Borna, 5 March 1522, 455:32–4; 61–5; LW Letters, I, 391.

50. WB 2, 443, [*c.*5 Dec. 1521], 410:18–19; LW Letters, I, 351; WB 2, 449, 13 Jan. 1522.

51. WB 2, 456, 457.

52. For accounts of the sermons from some of those who heard them, see WS 10, 3, XLVI-LV.

53. WS 10, 3, 1–64; 18:15–16; LW 51. For an excellent account of the Invocavit Sermons, see Krentz, *Ritualwandel*, 218–42. As she points out, the surviving

print edition is from Strasbourg in 1523, a year later, and it differs from the manuscript versions that also circulated. Krentz argues that the printed edition of the Invocavit Sermons is coloured retrospectively by the increasing severity of the breach between Luther and Karlstadt. Invocavit or Invocabit is the name given to Quadragesima, the First Sunday in Lent, so called because the Introit begins with the words *Invocabit me et exaudiam eum:* 'He shall call upon me and I will answer him' (Psalm 91:15).

54. WS 10, 3, 7:3–4.

55. WS 10, 3, 53:9–10; 64:14–15.

56. Nor was it just Melanchthon: Johannes Agricola also seems to have been influenced by Karlstadt during this period, and to have been interested in Anabaptist ideas too, Kawerau, *Agricola*, 33–4.

57. WS 10, 3, 42:8–9; 46:12–14.

58. Sider (ed. and tr.), *Karlstadt's Battle*, 43; WS 15, 337:16-18 [Acta Ienensia, 1524, see chapter 11 below]: he claimed he had not acted alone when he proceeded against images, 'Rather the three councils [*rethe*] and some of your companions decided it. Afterward they pulled their heads out of the noose and let me stand alone', though *rethe*, the term Karlstadt uses, is more likely to mean 'advisor' or 'Council member'. In his later history of the Reformation, Spalatin saw the Devil's hand at work, and blamed the Wittenberg prophets and Karlstadt 'and others'; Spalatin, *Annales*, 52–3. He devotes merely two paragraphs to the Wittenberg disturbances, and has little to say about Luther's sojourn in the Wartburg despite his important role.

59. Preus, *Carlstadt's Ordinaciones*, 74–7: he had attempted to publish a treatise ostensibly directed against Ochsenfahrt, who was now responsible for reimposing Catholic practice in line with Imperial decree; but it was clearly directed against Luther's changes as well, and was banned by the University Senate. On censorship in this period at Wittenberg see Hans-Peter Hasse, 'Bücherzensur an der Universität Wittenberg im 16. Jahrhundert'; Oehmig (ed.), *700 Jahre Wittenberg*.

60. WB 2, 458, 13 March 1522, 471:21.

61. See Scribner (ed.), *Popular Culture*.

62. Williams, *Radical Reformation*, 620: in Riga, two key clerics were adherents of Karlstadt; Barge, *Karlstadt*, II, 400–18; 188–90; 194–5; in Kitzingen, Karlstadt's student Christoph Hofmann preached a Karlstadtian message. Barge also less persuasively credits Karlstadt with influencing radicals in Nuremberg. Karlstadt himself went to Oldersum and East Frisia in 1529 and hoped to introduce a reformation according to his views; in a disputation with the Lutherans, the sacramentarians had the upper hand, and there were calls in the church at Emden to 'strike the flesh-eaters dead', a reference to their position on the Real Presence (409). But a Lutheran reformation was then introduced by the ruler's fiat, and Karlstadt was forced to leave.

## 11. The Black Bear Inn

1. WS 15, 323–47, [Acta Ienensia], 334; and see Sider (ed. and tr.), *Karlstadt's Battle*, for a translation of part of the pamphlet.

2. According to Reinhard, imperial messengers and many Jena citizens were also present.

3. Sider (ed. and tr.), *Karlstadt's Battle*, 40, 41, 44; WS 15, 335:22; 26–7; 337:30–338:1.

4. Sider (ed. and tr.), *Karlstadt's Battle*, 46; WS 15, 339:11–2; 19–20; 6–8.

5. Sider (ed. and tr.), *Karlstadt's Battle*, 47–8; WS 15, 340:6; 339:31–40:1; 340:7–8.

6. WB 3, 785, 27 Oct. 1524, 361:9.

7. Some of Luther's discomfort over the exchange at the inn is evident in the letter of advice he wrote Wolfgang Stein in Weimar, who was to interview Karlstadt. He should admonish him that the guilder meant nothing, because he had always done as he pleased, so why should he seek favour now? If he were to allege that he were being prevented from debating, he should be asked why he didn't engage in debating and arguing at Wittenberg, fulfilling the duties of his university office. WB 3, 774, early September 1524: Luther seems determined not to allow it to appear as if Karlstadt had been given permission to publish. Instead he stuck to his view that the exchange was a declaration of enmity, writing in *Against the Heavenly Prophets*, Part 1 of late December 1524, 'Dr Andreas Karlstadt has deserted us, and on top of that has become our worst enemy'; LW 40, 79; WS 18, 62:6–7.

8. WB 3, 785, 27 Oct. 1524: Reinhard was ordered to leave Jena; Luther told Amsdorf that he had begged in the church for money, weeping; WB 3, 811, 29 Dec. 1524; Luther, who did not trust Reinhard, wanted him expelled from Nuremberg.

9. Furcha (ed. and tr.), *Carlstadt*, 161–2; Karlstadt, *Was gesagt ist*, fo. F i (r).

10. Sider, *Karlstadt*, 174–97; the legality of Karlstadt's calling was bitterly disputed by Luther. See also Barge, *Karlstadt*, II, 95–143.

11. Furcha (ed. and tr.), *Carlstadt*, 369–70; Karlstadt, *Anzeyg*, fo. F (r). LW 40, 117; WS 18, 100:27–9.

12. Barge, *Karlstadt*, II, 97; Sider, *Karlstadt*, 183–7; he paid people to pick grapes and employed others to make hay.

13. WB 3, 818, 18 Jan. 1525.

14. WB 3, 702, 18 Jan. 1524; 720, 14 March 1524, where he repeated the joke.

15. Furcha (ed. and tr.), *Carlstadt*, 134; Karlstadt, *Was gesagt ist*, fo. A ii (r).

16. In his Latin liturgy for the Mass of 1523, however, Luther reinstituted Communion in both kinds; WS 12, 197–220; 217. This still stuck quite closely

to the format of the Mass, retained the elevation, kept the words of institution in Latin, and involved a good deal of chant, including of the gospel. The use of incense and the lighting of candles when the gospel was read was permitted. Luther did not institute a German Mass until 1526.

17. LW 40, 116; WS 18, 99:20–1.

18. Although Luther attacked Karlstadt for taking on a parish where he had no calling, Karlstadt had in fact been careful to gain the duke's approval, and the congregation had also formally called him.

19. WB 3, 818, 18 Jan. 1525 (Glatz to Luther).

20. It was even said that he had been introduced to Tauler's sermons by the pastor Conrad Glitsch's cook, a pious woman who had had a following in Leipzig. Whether true or not, the rumour indicates the reputation of the *Theologia deutsch* and German mysticism as appealing to simple folk. Bubenheimer, *Müntzer*, 181–2. The Nuremberg Lutheran pastor Martin Glaser who noted this in his copy of Tauler, given to him by Luther, in 1529, said that Müntzer and Karlstadt were misled by Tauler and spread their error in Orlamünde, an interesting attempt by a Lutheran to blame Müntzer's and Karlstadt's radicalism on their appropriation of German mysticism.

21. See Scott, *Müntzer*, 1–45; and on the Zwickau prophets, Wappler, *Müntzer*; on the similarity between Müntzer's social background and Luther's – his family was also from a wealthy bourgeois background – see Bubenheimer, *Müntzer*, 38–40.

22. Matheson (ed. and tr.), *Müntzer*, 29–30, Agricola to Müntzer, probably early Feb. 1521; Müntzer, *Briefwechsel*, 73–6, 74.

23. Scott, *Müntzer*, 31–3; and see Matheson (ed. and tr.), *Müntzer*, 354; 352–79; Müntzer, *Prager Manifest*; the Latin manuscript photographed at http://archive.thulb.uni-jena.de/ufb/rsc/viewer/ufb_derivate_00002917/Chart-A-00379a_0011.tif, accessed 6 Dec. 2015.

24. WS 15, 199–221; LW 40, 45–59.

25. Matheson (ed. and tr.), *Müntzer*, 52–3, 21 Dec. 1522; Müntzer, *Briefwechsel*, 153–4; a strangely hostile and yet conspiratorial letter.

26. LW 40, 53; WS 15, 214:20; 23–6.

27. LW 40, 54; WS 15, 215:26–8.

28. Scott, *Müntzer*, 74–5; Matheson, *Müntzer*, 248, 250; Müntzer, *Auszlegung*, fos. D ii (r), D iii (r).

29. Barge, *Karlstadt*, II, 130–2; WS 15, 343–7. The second half of Reinhard's pamphlet concerning what took place at Orlamünde is not included in Sider's translation, 'Confrontation at the Black Bear' in Sider (ed. and tr.), *Karlstadt's Battle*.

30. The text of the letter was published in Reinhard's pamphlet, see WS 15, 343.

31. WS 15, 344:16–17. The feud is only in Reinhard's account and is not included in *Against the Heavenly Prophets*.

32. LW 40, 101; WS 18, 84:3–4; 7–8; 11–2; 13–14: Luther tries to reproduce the peasant's dialect here. For Reinhard's version of this discussion, WS 15, 346; the cobbler and other members of the community continue to argue with Luther, and in particular they point out that when Luther tried to distinguish between 'superstitious' and other images, they replied that the biblical command against graven images said nothing about 'superstitious' images. Luther's reply about wine and women is not in *Against the Heavenly Prophets*, but in Reinhard's account; WS 15, 345. Interestingly, the striking phrase the peasant used about shoving the gospel under the bench echoed Luther's own words in his preface to the *Theologia deutsch* of 1518: that the Holy Word of God had not only been lying under the bench, but had just about perished from dust and moths; *Eyn deutsch Theologia*, fo. A ii (r).

33. LW 40, 110; WS 18, 93:15–16.

34. WS 15, 346:24–5.

35. WS 15, 346:9–10.

36. WS 18, 70:37.

37. WS 15, 347:21.

38. The anecdote comes from a letter of Caspar Glatz to Luther, a hostile source: Barge, *Karlstadt*, II, 134–6; WB 3, 818, 18 Jan. 1525, 424:22–5, Glatz to Luther.

39. Luther knew that Karlstadt had written to those at Orlamünde, signing off 'Andreas Bodenstein unverhort und unuberwunden, vertrieben durch Martinum Lutherum', WB 3, 785, 27 Oct. 1524, 361:12–13. See also Furcha (ed. and tr.), *Carlstadt*, 342; Karlstadt, *Anzeyg*, fo. A ii (r); and he used the phrase against Luther at the end of the Exegesis, Burnett, *Karlstadt*, 68. Karlstadt, *Auszlegung*. The phrase echoed Luther's insistence before Worms that he had not been given a hearing, and that he had not been proved wrong by Scripture.

40. WB 3, 785, 27 Oct. 1524, 361:13–14.

41. Burnett, *Karlstadt*, 68, 143–7; Martin Reinhart had Karlstadt's work published in Nuremberg but was exiled from there, getting the *Dialogue* finally finished in Bamberg.

42. Barge, *Karlstadt*, II, 18; Gerhard Westerburg, *Vom Fegefewer vnd Standt der verscheyden selen eyn Christliche Meynung*, Cologne 1523 [VD 16 W2215]. It opens with a dedication letter to the mayor and council of Cologne. Publication in Cologne was very important because it was the gateway to the Netherlands, and 3,000 copies were reportedly sent on there. It was published in Augsburg as well. On the preaching visit, Barge, *Karlstadt*, II, 20–1.

43. WB 3 887, 11 June 1525, 527:2, Paul Speratus to Luther, describing the arrival of Martin Cellarius in Königsberg. See also WB 3, 756, 4 July 1524. Cornelius Hoen in the Netherlands and Franz Kolb at Wertheim had already written to Luther arguing similar sacramental positions (WS 15, 384); Luther wrote complaining of the number of people taking Karlstadt's position in late 1524; WB 3, 793, 17 Nov. 1524 and WB 3, 802, 2 Dec. 1524; 817, 13 Jan. 1525. See Barge, *Karlstadt*, II, 144–296.

44. WB 3, 796, 22 Nov. 1524; 797, 23 Nov. 1524; and Gerbel reported that in Strasbourg Karlstadt was blaming Luther for his expulsion, complaining that he had been neither heard nor warned.

45. WB 3, 858, Strasbourg, April(?) 1525, 477:29–31.

46. Valentin Ickelsamer, *Clag ettlicher Brieder, an alle Christen, von der großen Ungerechtigkeyt und Tyranney, so Endressen Bodenstein . . . vom Luther . . . gechicht* [Augsburg] [1525] [VD 16 I 32]. Ickelsamer was a supporter of Karlstadt.

47. LW 40, 204; WS 18, 194. Luther also accuses Karlstadt of 'envy and vain ambition', and 'envious hatred' in *Against the Heavenly Prophets*, and, in an extended passage, accuses him of being subservient to 'Frau Hulda', or Reason, a capricious elfin figure of folklore. Natural reason, Luther argues, is 'the Devil's prostitute', and he condemns Karlstadt as a clever sophist who cannot see the plain meaning of Scripture, 'This is my body'. For his part, Karlstadt would accuse Luther of delighting in trying to make him feel *'gramschaft/neyd/hass/vngnad'* (anxiety, envy, hatred, and disgrace), *Anzeyg*, fo. E [iv] (v).

48. WS 15, 391–7, 14–15 Dec. 1525.

49. WS 15, 384, 31 Dec. 1524 (Capito to Zwingli).

50. WS 15, 394:12–17; 24; in typical fashion, Luther argued that the more Karlstadt *'schwermet'* (enthused) about the idea that there was no Real Presence, the stronger Luther's conviction that he was wrong.

51. WB 3, 779, 3 Oct. 1524, 354:15. A year later, writing about Duke Georg, and echoing his earlier language, Luther compared him to Karlstadt, who along with the sacramentarians were 'the sons of my womb'; WB 4, 973, 20 Jan. 1526, 18:7. This was powerful language indeed.

52. WS 18, 66:19–20.

53. Furcha (ed. and tr.), *Carlstadt*, 366, 367, 369; Karlstadt, *Anzeyg*, fos. E ii (v), E iii (r–v), F [i] (r).

54. Furcha (ed. and tr.), *Carlstadt*, 370; Karlstadt, *Anzeyg*, fo. F i (v).

## 12. The Peasants' War

1. There is a vast literature on the Peasants' War, starting with Engels, *Peasant War in Germany*. See, in particular, Blickle, *Revolution of 1525*;

Bak (ed.), *German Peasant War*; Scribner and Benecke (eds), *German Peasant War*; Sreenivasan, *Peasants of Ottobeuren*; and the collection of documents by Franz, *Der deutsche Bauernkrieg*.

2. Scott and Scribner, *German Peasants' War*, 254; www.stadtarchiv.memmingen.de/918.html.

3. LW 46, 4–45; WS 18, 279–334, *Ermahnung zum Frieden auf die zwölf Artikel der Bauerschaft in Schwaben*, 325.

4. LW 46, 20–1; WS 18, 296b:20–3.

5. WS 18, 342:28–32; 343:7–9.

6. Scott and Scribner, *German Peasants' War*, 14–19.

7. Ibid., esp. 1–64.

8. WB 3, 874, 23 May 1525; Luther knew that Friedrich had written in these terms to Duke Johann, 508:26–7, n.7, 508–9.

9. Müntzer to the people of Allstedt, *c*.26/27 April 1525, in Matheson (ed. and tr.), *Müntzer*, 140–2; Müntzer, *Briefwechsel*, 403–15; 414–5. Luther, who probably obtained a copy of the letter on 3 May when he was in Weimar, published it with several others and a commentary as *Eyn Schrecklich geschichte vnd gericht gottes vber Thomas Müntzer*, Wittenberg, 1525, and it was quickly reprinted in a series of towns. Where Müntzer admonished not to let the sword get cold or 'hang down limply', Luther clarified 'don't let your sword get cold of blood'.

10. Müntzer was drawing inspiration from the passage where, in the valley of dry bones, God creates an army and unites the Israelites under one king; while in Ezekiel 39, God promises that 'You will eat the flesh of mighty men and drink the blood of the princes of the earth as if they were rams and lambs, goats and bulls'; Matheson (ed. and tr.), *Müntzer* 154–5; 157; Müntzer, *Briefwechsel*, 465–73, 468–70; 461–5, 464; WS 18, 371–12, 12 May 1525. These letters too were published by Luther in the WS volume.

11. Scott, *Müntzer*, 164–5.

12. WB 3, 873, 21 May 1525, 505:28–9; Scott, *Müntzer*, 165–9.

13. WB 3, 875, 26 May 1525, 511:42.

14. WB 3, 875, 26 May 1525; this is the account of Johann Rühel, who worked for the counts of Mansfeld, and so was partisan; but his finely judged account also evinces considerable sympathy for the peasants.

15. Matheson (ed. and tr.), *Müntzer*, 160–1; Müntzer, *Briefwechsel*, 491–504, 496–7.

16. WB 3, 877, 30 May 1525, 515–16:29–30. See also Scott, *Müntzer*, 166–9.

17. Spangenberg, *Mansfeldische Chronica* 4, 1, 47.

18. Scott, *Müntzer*, 151–2.

19. WS 18, 281.

20. WS 18, 344.

21. WB 3, 877, 30 May 1525; this letter to Rühel also says that the peasants should be strangled like mad dogs (516:37).

22. LW 46, 49; 50; WS 18, 357:12; 13–14; 358:14–18.

23. WB 3, 877, 30 May 1525; 878, 30 May 1525, 517:2; 890, 15 June 1525 (to Rühel, Johannes Thür and Caspar Müller); 896, 20 June 1525. Interestingly, Lutheran memorial culture tried to stick to Luther's initial view that faults lay on both sides, lords and peasants. See, for example, Spangenberg, *Mansfeldische Chronica*, 419.

24. Luther probably decided to publish this letter to Müller as *Ein Sendbrief von dem harten Büchlein wider die Bauern*, WS 18, 384–401, after talking to his Mansfeld friends at his wedding on 27 June: WB 3, 902, first half of July 1525; WS 18, 392:22–5.

25. Scott, *Müntzer*, 175.

26. WB 3, 874, n.10: Luther interceded for Meinhard, and this probably saved his life. Meinhard gave him a silver *Becher* in token of his gratitude.

27. Matheson (ed. and tr.), *Müntzer*, 161; Müntzer, *Briefwechsel*, 491–506, 498.

28. Müntzer and not Luther became the great protagonist of Marxist accounts of the Reformation, from Friedrich Engels onwards. By the time of the 500th anniversary of Luther's birth in 1983, East German scholarship had moved back to interpreting the Reformation as a religious event and seeing it through the eyes of Luther, partly because it needed to seize the celebrations of Luther – whose Reformation happened on the East German soil of Saxony – from the grip of the Federal Republic of Germany.

29. Matheson (ed. and tr.), *Müntzer*, 44, 29 March 1522 (Müntzer to Melanchthon); Müntzer, *Briefwechsel*, 127–39, 133. This letter was published by Johann Agricola in 1525 as part of a polemic against Müntzer.

30. Müntzer, *Briefwechsel*, 505, n.1: She was a former nun and her name was Ottilie von Gersen, probably of the noble family von Görschen from the region around Merseburg; we do not know which convent she had left.

31. Karlstadt, *Endschuldigung*, fos. B i (v); B ii (r). Furcha (ed. and tr.), *Carlstadt*, 383. The pamphlet probably appeared in July; there was also an Augsburg printing. See Zorzin, *Karlstadt*, 104. 'I was amongst the peasants as a hare among ferocious dogs', he writes, fo. B ii (r), Furcha (ed. and tr.), *Carlstadt*, 383. He gives several examples of threats peasant bands made to him; but he also admits 'That I lodged with peasants and ate and drank with them and at times helped them extol injustice or castigated sin too often and too severely, I cannot do anything about. I had to eat and drink, and I was not prepared to endanger the life of my wife and child. I would have been a fool had I stood up to the

peasants; they would have cut me into pieces for a single word', fo. B iii (r); Furcha (ed. and tr.), *Carlstadt*, 385.

32. Karlstadt, *Endschuldigung*, fo. B [iv] (r); Furcha (ed. and tr.), *Carlstadt*, 386.

33. WB 3, 889, 12 June 1525, 529:2–3. The original was probably in Latin, translated by Spalatin.

34. Karlstadt, *Endschuldigung*. In September he wrote *Erklärung wie Karlstadt seine Lehre vom hochwürdigen Sakrament und andere geachtet haben will* (*A Declaration of How Karlstadt Regards his Teaching about the Venerable Sacrament et cetera and Wants It to Be Regarded*, in Karlstadt, *The Eucharistic Pamphlets*, tr. Nelson), which appeared in Wittenberg and was reprinted four times in Nuremberg, Erfurt and Strasbourg; while in Augsburg, Simprecht Ruff produced an edition of both of these texts of Karlstadt together. A later edition of this has a long preface dealing with both Luther's and Karlstadt's views, and was reprinted again, by Capito, as *Frohlockung eines christlichen Bruders von wegen der Vereinigung [die sich] zwischen D. M. Luther und D. Andres Carolstat begeben (hat)*, that is, *Rejoicing of a Christian brother because of the reunion which has happened between Luther and Karlstadt*, a title revealing just how much the enmity between the two men troubled their contemporaries. Zorzin, *Karlstadt*, 104; see Thomas Kaufmann, 'Zwei unerkannte Schriften Bucers und Capitos zur Abendmahlsfrage aus dem Herbst 1525' in *Archiv für Reformationsgeschichte* 81, 1990, 158–88.

35. WS 18, 431–45; 436:18–20. He also wrote a preface to Karlstadt's other tract, the *Erklärung*, 446–66.

36. WS 18, 446–66, *Erklärung*.

37. WB 3, 915, early Sept. 1525, 566:28; 565:1; 1; 10. Spalatin translated these letters for the Elector.

38. WB 3, 920, 12 Sept. 1525; and 'Nachgeschichte', 574:39; 35.

39. Furcha (ed. and tr.), *Carlstadt*, (*Several Main Points of Christian Teaching Regarding Which D. Luther Brings Andreas Carlstadt Under Suspicion Through False Accusation and Slander*); Karlstadt, *Anzeyg*.

40. WB 3, 874, 23 May 1525: Luther also commented that some stones were found in the baby's lungs and three in his gall bladder, as thick as a little finger and about the size of pennies; though he died of the stone, none were found in the bladder. According to the medical report however, there were stones found in the urethra. It is interesting that an autopsy and section was carried out. See Neudecker and Preller (eds), *Georg Spalatin's historischer Nachlass*, 68–9.

41. WB 3, 803, 12 Dec. 1524.

42. Neudecker and Preller (eds), *Georg Spalatin's historischer Nachlass*, 66–8.

43. WB 3, 860, 4 (5?) May 1525: the forces of Albrecht burned the village of Osterhausen to the ground. The burial of the Elector prompted ques-

tions about what kinds of ceremonies should be used in the reformed Church, and Luther and Melanchthon advised that the vigil should not be sung, there should be no Mass, priests and altar should not all be clothed in black; and they rejected as 'ridiculous' the drawing of stallions around the altar and the offering of a shield and breaking of a spear.

## 13. Marriage and the Flesh

1.  See, on Luther's apocalypticism, Soergel, *Miracles*, 33–66.
2.  WB 9, 3699, 6 Jan. 1542, *Beilage IV*, *Luthers Hausrechnung*, 581: Luther sets out where the monastery goods had gone, including church ornament and vestments, sold for about 50 fl, which he used to clothe monks and nuns. WB 3, 600, 10 April 1523; 609, 22 April 1523: Spalatin was to solicit contributions from the court and for the Elector himself for their support, and Luther promised to keep any electoral contributions secret.
3.  Or so the story soon had it – he may actually only have carried them in the same wagon he used to deliver the convent's fish: Treu, *Katharina von Bora*, 16. Treu makes a persuasive case that she lived with the Cranachs before marrying Luther.
4.  WS 11, 387–400, published as a pamphlet *Ursach und Antwort, dass Jungfrauen Kloester goettlich verlassen moegen*. Versions also appeared in Low German. Luther emphasises particularly the sexual dimension: young inexperienced girls are forced into convents where they have to struggle with the problems of chastity, adding 'For a woman is not created to be a virgin, but to bear children', 398:4. Luther concludes by publicly naming all the women who left, starting with Staupitz's sister – which may have been quite humiliating for Staupitz. See also Posset, *Front-runner*, 341. In 1524, Luther published the testimony of a Lutheran nun from Mansfeld, prefacing it with a letter: WS 15, 79–94 (she describes being imprisoned for writing to Luther and being forced to sit on the floor at meals wearing a humiliating straw wreath, a sign of lost virginity). In 1525, Luther was at it again, this time taking in a group of nuns from Seusslitz in Saxony; as before he turned to Koppe again to try to get other nuns out, possibly from Grimma; WB 3, 894, 17 June 1525.
5.  WB 3, 766, 6 Aug. 1524, 327:21–4.
6.  WB 2, 426, 6 Aug. 1521 (to Spalatin), 377:4–5; in 1532, he still remembered how unlikely it seemed that he would marry, saying at table that if anyone had told him back at the time of the Diet of Worms that in five years he would be a husband with a wife and child he would have laughed at them: WT 3, 3177.
7.  StadtA Witt, Kämmereirechnungen 1524, 144: the council paid for a new 'Rock, hosen vnd Wammes', for Luther, providing six ells of fustian.

8.  LW Letters, II, 105; WB 3, 857, 16 April 1525, 475:14–23. A wife on one's left hand was a morganatic wife, that is, not a full spouse but a wife of unequal social status whose children did not inherit their father's social status. Morganatic marriages could also work the other way around as in this case, since Luther was of lower status than Katharina: the joke was somewhat heavy-handed. Hieronymus Baumgartner of the prominent patrician family in Nuremberg had originally been proposed as Katharina's husband back in 1524 (Baumgartner waited until after the wedding before marrying someone else: Stjerna, *Women and the Reformation*, 55). Barely three weeks after this letter, Luther was writing to Johann Rühel of his intention to marry 'meine Käthe': WB 3, 860, 4 (5?) May 1525, 482:81.

9.  *Melanchthons Briefwechsel – Regesten online*, 408, 16 June 1525: the wedding took place in the presence of Bugenhagen, Cranach and Johannes Apel.

10. WB 3, 886, 10 June 1525, 525–6:14.

11. WB 3, 860 4 (5?) May 1525, 481:64–6.

12. Glatz's willingness to take the poisoned chalice of the post at Orlamünde had not perhaps been entirely selfless. He certainly emerges in his letters as a tittle-tattle, passing on every nasty rumour about Karlstadt to Luther, and relying on Luther to step in to sort things out.

13. LW Letters, II, 116–18; WB 3, 900, 21 June 1525, 541:14. This letter is often quoted as proof that Luther did not at first 'love' Katharina; but it is significant that it was written to Amsdorf, the other man Katharina declared herself willing to marry once the planned marriage to Hieronymus Baumgartner failed. Amsdorf remained a bachelor, so it is possible that Luther is presenting his feelings in a way that will not disconcert his friend. It is also telling that Luther had not mentioned anything about the matter in his previous letter to Amsdorf of 12 June, and that he reckoned with gossip having already reached his friend. Revealingly, when Luther nearly died in 1537, it was to Amsdorf's care he commended his wife; WT 3, 3543 A.

14. LW Letters, II, 117, WB 3, 900, 21 June 1525, 541:6; and see also WB 3, 890, 15 June 1525. We know that he invited Wenzeslaus Linck, Georg Spalatin, Amsdorf, Hans von Dolzig, the Saxon marshal, Gabriel Zwilling (who had preached so radically during Luther's absence in the Wartburg and had been forgiven), his parents, Leonhard Koppe (who had brought the nuns to Wittenberg); and Rühel, Thuer, and Müller from the Mansfeld administration. He hesitated about whether to invite the counts of Mansfeld, Gebhard and Albrecht, asking the Mansfeld bureaucrats' advice. The invitation to the Mansfelders uses the past tense for the wedding and makes it clear that the couple had already

consummated the marriage and slept together ('mit Eile beigelegen').
On masculinity in this era, see Hendrix and Karant-Nunn (eds), *Masculinity*; and Puff, *Sodomy*.

15.   Jonas married Katharina Falk, from a Wittenberg family: Kawerau,
      *Briefwechsel des Justus Jonas*, II, xvii.

16.   Reindell, *Linck aus Colditz*, 190.

17.   WB 3, 726, 1 April 1524, 263:8–9, quoting 2 Samuel 1:26.

18.   Spalatin, much as he wanted to, could not marry until the Elector died;
      and the Elector's death may have eased the situation for Luther too.
      Clerical marriage was still not really legal in Saxony.

19.   WB 2, 26 May 1521, 349:85–6. LW Letters, I, 235: the translation does
      not quite convey the joke about the two stomachs and what might be
      produced by them.

20.   Jesse, *Leben und Wirken des Philipp Melanchthon*, 47; he wrote to Camer-
      arius on 16 June 1525, in Greek; *Melanchthons Briefwechsel – Regesten online*,
      408; he also rejected the rumour that she had lost her virginity before
      the marriage; and in general he supported the view that marriage was
      the right remedy for lust and expected the marriage would calm Luther.

21.   WB 3, 883, 3 June 1525, 522:12–13; 17–18. The unusual energy and playful-
      ness of a letter of 10 June 1525 warning Spalatin that delay in a marriage
      is a very bad idea suggests that the couple may have consummated the
      marriage about this time.

22.   WB 3, 894, 17 June 1525, 534:6–7; 9–10.

23.   WB 3, 896, 20 June 1525, 537:12.

24.   Shoes were strongly connected with sex – a deflowered virgin could
      demand a pair of shoes from her seducer. Roper, *Holy Household*, 147.
      At the wedding of Cranach's daughter, Luther could not resist a little
      joke: he should be master *when the wife is not home*. He put the groom's
      shoe on top of the marital bed, so that he would have the upper hand,
      as popular wisdom had it. WT 3, 593:22: Susan Karant-Nunn, 'The
      Masculinity of Martin Luther' in Hendrix and Karant-Nunn (eds), *Masculinity*, 179.

25.   WT 1, 814.

26.   Christiane Schulz, 'Spalatin als Pfarrer und Superintendent in Altenburg'
      in Kohnle, Meckelnborg and Schirmer (eds), *Georg Spalatin*, 70–1;
      Schmalz, *Spalatin*, 17, 22–3: his wife, the daughter of an Altenburg citizen,
      was also named Katharina. The firmly Catholic Chapter at Altenburg
      tried to get the marriage dissolved.

27.   WB 3, 952, 6 Dec. 1525, 635:26–8.

28.   Spalatin planned to hold the wedding in the castle, and would have sat
      Luther and Dr Brück at the Elector's table; Staatsarchiv Weimar, EGA
      Reg O 57, fo. 11. On Spalatin's childless marriage, mocked in Cochlaeus's

*Tragedy of Johann Hus*, see Johann Vogelsang (Cochlaeus), 'Ein Heimlich Gespräch von der Tragedia Johannis Hussen, 1538' in Holstein (ed.), *Flugschriften*.

29. WB 8, 3141, Überleitung, 55. It seems to have been common amongst the clergy for wives to address their husbands as 'Herr Doctor' and to use the polite 'you' form; see, for example, WB 10, 3829, 26 Dec. 1542, introduction, Justus Jonas's wife's last words; and see also Johann Vogelsang (Cochlaeus), 'Ein Heimlich Gespräch' in Holstein (ed.), *Flugschriften*, where the wives address their husbands and each other by their husbands' positions – Mrs Provost, Mrs Bishop, and so on.

30. He certainly entered into the female sphere of knowledge and was soon showing off what he knew about pregnancy, writing to a colleague (Brisger) about why his wife's child had not yet quickened: as it turned out, it was a stillbirth. WB 4, 980, 12 Feb. 1526 (Brisger in Altenburg); 1019, 17 June 1526.

31. WB 3, 906, 22 July 1525, 548:10–2. A little later, he ordered a new bed from Torgau, sending the exact measurements for it to be specially made. WB 4, 961, 2 Jan. 1526.

32. WT 3, 3178a.

33. WT 2, 1472.

34. On the gender divisions of the academic household, see Gadi Algazi, 'Habitus, familia und forma vitae: Die Lebensweisen mittelalterlicher Gelehrten in muslimischen, jüdischen und christlichen Gemeinden – vergleichend betrachtet' in Rexroth (ed), *Beiträge*; and Ross, *Daum's Boys*.

35. Luther did not idealise marriage, speaking of how difficult it is for men to remain faithful; how often quarrels could arise, how marriage involves work: e.g. WT 3, 3508, 3509, 3510. On Katharina von Bora, see Stjerna, *Women and the Reformation*; Jeannette C. Smith, 'Katharina von Bora through five centuries: a historiography', *Sixteenth Century Journal* 30, 3, 1999, 745–74; Treu, *Katharina von Bora*; Kuen, *Lucifer Wittenbergensis*; Mayer, *Des unsterblichen*; Walch, *Wahrhaftige Geschichte*. For a helpful overview of Luther's main writings on marriage, see Jane Strohl, 'Luther's new view on marriage, sexuality and the family', *Lutherjahrbuch* 76, 2009, 159–92.

36. WB 4, 1305, and *Beilage*, 10 Aug. 1528. She should return to her convent, like a proper Magdalen, and not even the existence of children should hold her back – her marriage ties were not binding because she had been joined not in God's name, but in the Devil's.

37. WS 6, *Neue Zeitung von Leipzig*, 550:31; and see 540:16–19: Luther also includes an acrostic on '*asini*', asses, and a woodcut of a king of the donkeys. Then he provides a fable in the style of Aesop, one of his favourite authors, featuring an ass who outwits the king of the lions. The

fable turns the order of the world upside down as the ass and not the lion gets the crown, just as Christ inverts the wisdom of the wise. Coruscating as the opening is, the rest of the pamphlet has a playful manner.

38. Johann Hasenberg, *Lvdvs lvdentem lvdervm lvdens*, 1530 [VD 16 H 714].

39. It was published under the pseudonym of Johann Vogelsang: 'Ein Heimlich Gespräch von der Tragedia Johannis Hussen, 1538' in Holstein (ed.), *Flugschriften*. See, on the play, Philip Haberkern, '"After Me There Will Come Braver Men": Jan Hus and Reformation Polemics in the 1530s', *German History* 27, 2, 2009, 177–95, whose work first alerted me to the existence of the play.

40. Erasmus, sharp as ever, was aware that Karlstadt's position on the will was not the same as Luther's, but was that 'grace alone works good in us, not *through* or *in cooperation* with, but in free will': Miller (ed.), *Erasmus and Luther*, 11.

41. LW Letters, II, 6–8; WB 2, 499, 28 May 1522, 544:11–2; 545:26–8. We do not know for certain who the recipient of the letter was, but it may have been Caspar Börner, professor at Leipzig; it was certainly an academic at Leipzig. Luther had been critical of Erasmus previously in letters; see for example WB 1, 27, 19 Oct. 1516; he wrote more negatively about Erasmus to Lang (1 March 1517), but told him to keep his views secret, doing the same in a letter to Spalatin (18 Jan. 1518). By 1522, however, he was willing openly to express his antipathy not only to Erasmus's theology but to those who were 'erasmian', like Mosellanus, the target of this letter.

42. WB 4, 1028, 5 and 10 July 1526 (Gerbel to Luther).

43. WB 4, 27 March 1526 (to Spalatin), 'vipera illa', 42:28; and see WB 4, 1002, 23 April 1526 to the Elector Johann, 'die vipera', 62:8. He termed him an 'eel' in *On the Enslaved Will*, 1525: WS 18, 716; and in 1531 at table he compared Erasmus to an eel 'whom no one can grasp': WT 1, 131.

44. Miller (ed.), *Erasmus and Luther*, 47; the first German translation was provided by none other than Justus Jonas, *Das der freie wille nichts sey*, Wittenberg 1526 [VD 16 L 6674]. He dedicated it to Count Albrecht of Mansfeld, ruler of the territory where Luther had grown up, and in his introduction, Jonas insisted that Erasmus, 'our dear friend', was 'otherwise a dear, great man', but his writings on free will were 'vexatious, and contrary to the gospel'; fo. A i (v).

45. *On the Enslaved Will*, 121; WS 18, 783:17–28.

46. Ibid.

47. WB 4, 1160, 19 Oct. 1527, 269:6–7.

48. WT 4, 5069: she had done so on the urging of Camerarius, he said, and to please her, he took up his pen. Luther told this story in June 1540, taking the book out at table.

49. The modern biographer Richard Marius, for one, wrote 'the work is insulting, vehement, monstrously unfair and utterly uncompromising' in response to a man who approached him 'gently'. Marius, *Martin Luther*, 456.

50. WB 4, 989, 43, n.10. Erasmus wrote to Luther in reply to a letter, now missing, in which he apologised for the tone of his attack; WB 4, 992, 11 April 1526. The second part of Erasmus's treatise was published in 1527.

51. *On the Enslaved Will*, 39; WS 18, 648:14–15.

52. Ibid., 687:27–34.

53. WB 4, 992, 11 April 1526 (Erasmus to Luther); WB 4, 1002, 23 April 1526 (to Elector Johann), 62:7; 62:13–14.

54. Just occasionally the qualities could alter too. There were, for example, miraculous Hosts, which actually bled like real flesh; and there were many popular pilgrimages to miraculous Hosts, including one at nearby Wilsnack, where pilgrims would flock to witness the proof that the miracle of the Mass really did happen.

55. Barge, *Karlstadt*, II, 100–1; Burnett, *Karlstadt*, 58–60: we do not know exactly what the reforms were, but he probably also introduced services in German and abolished the elevation. Caspar Glatz alleged to Spalatin that Karlstadt had also abolished infant baptism.

56. On the development of Karlstadt's Eucharistic thought, see Burnett, *Karlstadt*, 54–76; *Auslegung dieser wort Christi. Das ist meyn leyb welcher für euch gegeben würt. Das ist mein bluoth welches für euch vergossen würt* (*Exegesis of This Word of Christ. 'This Is My Body, Which is Given for You. This Is My Blood, Which Is Shed for You'*), Basle 1524 [VD 16 B 6111], in Burnett (ed. and tr.), *Eucharistic Pamphlets*.

57. Furcha (ed. and tr.), *Carlstadt* (*The meaning of the term 'Gelassen'*), 139; Karlstadt, *Was gesagt ist*, fo. B (r).

58. Furcha (ed. and tr.), *Carlstadt*, 198, 201; *Uon manigfeltigkeit des eynfeltigen eynigen willen gottes. (The manifold, singular will of God)*, Cologne 1523 [VD 16 B 6251], fo. C iii (r); fos. D i (v)–D ii (r). Sometimes he uses the 'yieldedness' of married people as an example of how we should divest ourselves of our own wills, but he also says that it is easier 'to cling to a created wife than to cling to its Creator'; (*The meaning of the term 'Gelassen'*), 137; Karlstadt, *Was gesagt ist*, fo. A iii (v).

59. For example, WB 3, 787, 30 Oct. 1524: Luther had heard that Karlstadt had explicitly written not only to the men but to the women separately to inform them of his banishment.

60. Furcha (ed. and tr.), *Carlstadt* (*The meaning of the term 'Gelassen'*), 157; Karlstadt, *Was gesagt ist*, fo. E (v).

61. Furcha (ed. and tr.), *Carlstadt* (*Several Main Points of Christian Teaching*) (1525), 368; Karlstadt, *Anzeyg*, fo. E iv (v).

62. Ibid., 367, Karlstadt, *Anzeyg*, fo. E iii (r–v); fo. E iii (v).

63. It seems that Luther did not realise at first just how different Karlstadt's position on the Eucharist was from his own, believing that it primarily concerned externals. When he wrote the first part of *Against the Heavenly Prophets*, his refutation of the Sacramentalist position denying the Real Presence of Christ in the Eucharist, he had not read all Karlstadt's pamphlets; and when he was sent a set of them by the Strasbourg preachers, he concentrated his fire on the dialogue which was written in German and aimed at a wide audience. See Burnett, *Karlstadt*, 71.

64. This was not something he lived out in his life: he was one of the first to argue that monks and nuns should be able to break their vows, and he had five surviving children with Anna von Mochau.

65. Matheson (ed. and tr.), *Müntzer*, 459–60, 459 n.1.

66. See Reinholdt, *Ein Leib in Christo werden*; Roper, 'Sexual Utopianism in the German Reformation' in her *Oedipus and the Devil*.

67. See Köhler, *Zürcher Ehegericht*.

68. Oyer, *Lutheran Reformers*, 59.

69. *The Estate of Marriage*, 1522, LW 45, 18; WS 10.II, 276:14–20; 21–6; it was composed after Luther's return to Wittenberg, probably in September 1522, WS 10.II, 267, Introduction.

70. WB 4, 966, 5 Jan. 1526.

71. WB 4, 1200, 3 Jan. 1528: As the Instructions for the Visitors were being devised in January 1528, the subject of the incest rules was debated, Luther proposing not to define them in writing, and striking out the passage in Spalatin's draft reading that people should not be permitted to marry nieces or nephews; see WB 4, 327, 331–2; 336. In 1530, Luther insisted that a man who had married his father's brother's widow must separate from her, even though the couple had been together many years and had four children; Jonas, Brenz and Amsdorf thought they should be permitted to remain together; WB 5, 1531, 26 Feb. 1530. And in 1535, Jonas, Luther and Melanchthon wrote to Leonhard Beyer in Zwickau about a case where a man had slept with his dead wife's sister and wished to marry her: this was absolutely ruled out because the two were related in the first degree, and the marriage was banned according to imperial law. The example of Jacob did not provide a precedent because Moses overrode this; and the list in Moses of who one was permitted to marry did not make it clear whether or not one could marry a deceased wife's sister; WB 7, 2171, 18 Jan. 1535.

72. LW 36, 103, *On the Babylonian Captivity of the Church*; WS 6, 558:20–32, here 25–8. The fuller passage reads 'A woman, wed to an impotent man, is unable to prove her husband's impotence in court, or perhaps she is unwilling to do so with the mass of evidence and all the notoriety

which the law demands; yet she is desirous of having children or is unable to remain continent . . . Then I would further counsel her, with the consent of the man (who is not really her husband, but only a dweller under the same roof with her), to have intercourse with another, say her husband's brother, but to keep this marriage secret and to ascribe the children to the so-called putative father.' He repeated this more emphatically in his *On the Estate of Marriage* of 1522, referring back to *On the Babylonian Captivity of the Church*: 'What I said was this: if a woman who is fit for marriage has a husband who is not, and she is unable openly to take unto herself another – and unwilling, too, to do anything dishonourable – since the Pope in such a case demands without cause abundant testimony and evidence, she should say to her husband, "Look, my dear husband, you are unable to fulfil your conjugal duty towards me; you have cheated me out of my maidenhood and even imperilled my honour and my soul's salvation; in the sight of God there is no real marriage between us. Grant me the privilege of contracting a secret marriage with your brother or closest relative, and you retain the title of husband so that your property will not fall to strangers. Consent to being betrayed voluntarily by me, as you have betrayed me without my consent." I stated further that the husband is obligated to consent to such an arrangement and thus to provide for her the conjugal duty and children, and that if he refuses to do so she should secretly flee from him to some other country and there contract a marriage. I gave this advice at a time when I was still timid. However, I should like now to give sounder advice in the matter, and take a firmer grip on the wool of a man who thus makes a fool of his wife. The same principle would apply if the circumstances were reversed, although this happens less frequently in the case of wives than of husbands. It will not do to lead one's fellow man around by the nose so wantonly in matters of such great import involving his body, goods, honour, and salvation. He has to be told to make it right' (LW 45, 20–1; WS 10, II, 278:19–28; 279:1–6).

74. WB 4, 1057, 9 Dec. 1526, 141:7–8. The German has '*Not und Fehler des Glaubens und Gewissens*'. Luther was answering a direct question from Joseph Levin Metzsch about the permissibility of bigamy. On 28 November 1526 he had answered the same question, put to him by Philip of Hesse, who now carefully noted all Luther's remarks on this subject. Luther had replied that human beings and particularly Christians should not have more than one wife 'unless there were extreme necessity' ('*Es were denn die hohe not da*'). The examples of 'necessity' he gave were if the wife had leprosy or had otherwise been taken from her husband; but the exception was there, and could be used by Philip

to justify bigamy in exceptional circumstances. The letter exists in partial form in the Marburg Archives, where the opening has been removed. It formed part of the dossier of documents Philip would later use to show that Luther had sanctioned bigamy in exceptional circumstances and that his position was long-standing and consistent (WB 4, 1056, 28 Nov. 1526, 140:15–6).

75. WB 5, 1383, 28 Feb. 1529 (wife of Claus Bildenhauer or Heffner): 'Nosse te credo, ante mensem defunctam uxorem Cl. Bild, defector, uti creditor, maritalis oficii': 22:1–2. Heffner was a member of the city council, and ate at Luther's house on at least one occasion: WT 4, 4506, 4508, 18 April 1539. At that time, Heffner was complaining that he had spent all his money on establishing his children, and now they would not care for him: Luther showed no sympathy and quoted a story including the rhyme 'The father who gives up power over his own goods, should be soon clubbed to death' (WT 4, 353:8–9).

76. WB 10, 3843, 26 Jan. 1543, 252:8; she had died on 22 December 1542 and was pregnant, her thirteenth pregnancy at least. Jonas wrote to Melanchthon that her last words had been 'Mr Doctor, I would have liked so much to bring you a fruit. I know you love children' (WB 10, 3829, 26 Dec. 1542). Luther wrote again advising Jonas to wait a little before remarrying, but if he felt strongly enough to withstand gossip he should go ahead. His new wife was aged twenty-two (WB 10, 3872, 4 May 1543). The matter did indeed cause gossip (WS 10, 3886, 18 June 1543): Luther wrote congratulating him on his marriage but added that they were fighting more for him against evil tongues than perhaps he was himself. He went on to talk about sinners not judging others, making a rather tactless comparison to 'ten whores' who ruined students with the pox, but about whom everyone was silent as a 'fish', before concluding with final congratulations and apologies for sending him only a small present, because he had so many debts and there were so many weddings. Luther made his lack of enthusiasm clear but never wavered from his view that if Jonas needed to marry, he should.

77. WT 3, 3510.

78. WB 4, 1250, 9 April 1528; 1364, 6 Dec. 1528. Metzsch wanted Luther to publish on the issue.

79. WB 4, 1253, 12 April 1528, 443:12; 442:8–10; 442:7; she was the sister-in-law of the Wittenberg printer Georg Rhau. See also WB 6, 1815, 10 May 1531. See also for some local cases in which Luther was cited as advisor, StadtA Witt, 35 [Bc 24], Privat Protocoll von Hofgerichtsurtheilen . . . (Thomas Heyllinger notary).

80. See, for example, WB 4, 1179, 1205, 1304 and Beilage, 1309.

81. WB 5, 1523, 1 Feb. 1530, 226:23–5.

82. WB 5, 1526, 232:20–3. For the full text, see 1526, 1 Feb. 1530, 230–6.

83. WB 4, 972, 17 Jan. 1526; and see Luther's letter, 975, 25 Jan. 1526, 22. Topler's marriage was arranged by her relatives and celebrated in Nuremberg; and it was consummated, probably against her will. When questioned by the official (*Schösser*) at Allstedt, she explained that her sister and relatives had sent her books when she was in the convent telling her that the spiritual estate was damned and she should leave; so she got in touch with Kern to instruct her, and left the convent. See Otto Clemen, 'Die Leidensgeschichte der Ursula Toplerin', *Zeitschrift für bayerische Kirchengeschichte* 7, 1932, 161–70: 'But to have sex with him was never in her heart' (162). God had now illuminated her so that 'she had realised that she would not be saved without her previous convent vows' (163). When he had tried to force her to return to Allstedt she would not sleep with him, so her relatives (Sigmund Fürer and Leo Schürstab) made a rod for him, telling him 'Magister, she has a devil in her, if you want to drive it out, whip her till we tell you to stop' (164). This he did; he had also beaten her many times and threatened her with a knife. Topler was related to the leading Nuremberg families of the Tucher, Nützel and Pömer. It is not clear whether Topler wanted to return to the convent as her abbess wanted her to do, but she would not have been the only ex-nun to consider re-entry. Ottilie von Gersen, Müntzer's widow, wrote to Duke Georg of Saxony when she was left destitute after Müntzer's execution, noting that she had heard that Georg believed she should re-enter the convent; she was willing to do so if he thought it right. Müntzer, *Briefwechsel*, 506.

84. WB 5, 1433, 23 April 1530 (to Catharina Jonas); in fact Luther's gynaecological predictions proved wrong and Catharina gave birth to yet another son, Luther writing to congratulate Jonas on being the creator of five sons. But the child died soon after birth, and Luther did his best to console him.

85. WB 4, 1257, 1 May 1528, 447:1–2.

86. Plummer, *From Priest's Whore*, 218; Baylor (ed. and tr.), *Revelation and Revolution*, 135. Thomas Müntzer, *Außgetrückte emplössung des falschen Glaubens der vngetrewen welt*, Nuremberg 1524 [VD 16 M 6745], fo. E ii (r).

87. WB 4, 1315, 3 Sept. 1528.

88. WB 6, 1902, 4 Feb. 1532; StadtA Witt, 9 [Bb6], 2, 201–5: it would eventually be sold in 1564 to the Elector by Luther's three sons for 3,700 fl. WB 3, 911, 556, n.4: the Karlstadts stayed for eight weeks from the end of June.

89. Laube, 'Das Lutherhaus', 50–1; Neser, *Luthers Wohnhaus*, 48; Heling, *Zu Haus bei Martin Luther*, 13.

90. He was not, however, above writing letters whilst eating at table: see, for example, WB 6, 1994, 17 Jan. 1533(?) – this letter was a rambling discourse praising marriage to the former abbot Friedrich Pistorius, who was just getting married, and Luther signs off asking him to forgive the prolixity of someone who is enjoying his meal but is neither tipsy nor drunk. Katharina, who had grown up motherless and had been sent to the convent when her father remarried, was used to large households.

91. Treu, *Katharina von Bora*, 54.

92. WB 8, 3344, 4 June 1539: Johann Schneidewein lived with the Luthers paying board for nearly ten years, and had to be prised out, marrying the daughter of the goldsmith and sometime partner of Cranach, Christian Döring. WB 8, 3401, 7 Nov. 1539 mentions Wolfgang Schiefer, another *Tischgenger* (lodger). There were probably about ten servants. See Treu, *Katharina von Bora*, 45–54.

93. WB 10, 3963, 29 Jan. 1544, 520:21–2; 16–17. When Luther heard that Rosina was in Leipzig he wrote to the civic judge there warning him about her; if it was indeed Rosina, she should be banished. In an earlier letter, WB 10, 3807, 10 Nov. 1542 (to Anton Lauterbach in Pirna), he had written condemning her for almost glorying in the birth like an idiot. The solicious concern for new mothers, the baptismal gifts, presents and advice, the lying-in celebrations, were all reserved for the 'respectable' married women. For an unmarried servant-woman with a child, there were few options, and Rosina seems to have become a traveller. Luther does not speculate on who the father might have been – Rosina was to blame.

94. WB 6, 1836, June 1531; 1860, 26 Aug. 1531; 1862, 4 Sept. 1531: Luther tried to get the council to give Haferitz a pay-off, so that at least Luther wouldn't have to pay for his upkeep. Indefatigable, Luther was writing in November to press Hausmann to come to stay – he had a new vacant room, and he would not be a burden but a comfort: WB 6, 1885, 22 Nov. 1531.

95. WB 6, 3102, 13 Nov. 1536; 3103, 13 Nov. 1536; 3117, 14 Dec. 1536; WB 11, 4098, 2 May 1545; 4100, 2 May 1545; 4101, 2 May 1545: Luther refused to let Agricola himself darken his door, and complained that his daughter was more talkative and uppity 'than is fitting for a maiden'.

96. WB 8, 3398, 26 Oct. 1539. He housed the children only briefly.

97. WB 6, 1868, 20 Sept. 1531.

98. WB 10, 3785, 28 Aug. 1542, 137:15.

99. Melanchthon, *Vita Lutheri*, fo. 12 (v); Melanchthon in Vandiver, Keen and Frazel (eds and trs), *Luther's Lives*, 16.

100. See Roper, 'Martin Luther's Body: the "Stout Doctor" and his Biographers, *American Historical Review* 115, 2, 2010, 351–84; and Christensen,

*Princes and Propaganda*, 47–56: Christensen links its use to publishing privileges for the Lufft printing concern.

## 14. Breakdown

1. On Zwingli, see Potter, *Zwingli*, 287–315. On the dream, see Zwingli, *Opera*, vol. 3, part 1, 341, 'De Eucharistia, Subsidium sive coronis de Eucharistia'; and see also Wandel, *The Eucharist in the Reformation*.

2. See Köhler, *Zürcher Ehegericht*, vols 1 and 2.

3. WB 4, 984, 9 March 1526 (or shortly before), 36:9-10 'balneum caninum'. Andreas was born in early 1525, and was probably Karlstadt's second son. In a letter to Müntzer of 19 July 1524, Karlstadt asked why Müntzer would have preferred Karlstadt's son to be named Abraham rather than Andreas. It is likely therefore that Karlstadt's first son was also named Andreas, and was born between 1523 and 1524, dying in 1524 or 1525; it was not unusual to give a second child the same name as an older deceased child. *Müntzers Briefwechsel*, 291 and n.24. If the child born in 1525 were indeed Karlstadt's second son, it may be that Luther had acted as godparent for the first, which would explain why Karlstadt addresses Luther as '*Gevatter*' and why Luther's wife, not Luther himself, acted as godparent to Andreas II in 1526. See also Barge, *Karlstadt*, II, 117, n.63; 219; 518–9; Barge proposes an eldest son named 'Johannes' which however conflicts with 117, n.63.

4. WB 4, 985, 9 March 1526; 1051, 17 Nov. 1526, Karlstadt's letter; and Luther's immediate petition to the Elector, 1052, 22 Nov. 1526. See Barge, *Karlstadt*, II, 369–76.

5. WB 4, 959, early 1526; 1004, 26 April 1526.

6. WB 4, 1030, early Aug. 1526: he was then notary of the Cathedral Chapter in Strasbourg. He wrote that if he had not been married he would have liked to move to Frankfurt. See also WB 4, 1933, 2 April 1527.

7. Rhegius's exact position remains subject to debate: see Burnett, *Karlstadt*, 140. By 1528, the Lutherans believed Rhegius was returning to the fold so far as the Eucharist was concerned: Brecht, *Luther*, II, 323–4.

8. WB 4, 1044, 28 Oct. 1526.

9. WB 4, 982, 18 Feb. 1526; Billican had at first written against Zwingli, but by the summer, began to change his view: WB 4, 1044, 28 Oct. 1526.

10. WB 3, 858, (April?) 1525, 477:29-31. Indeed, back in 1522 Johann Eberlin von Günzburg had described his visit to Wittenberg and its three heroes, Luther, Melanchthon and Karlstadt, noting that Luther wore a cassock and still kept fasts; Karlstadt, he believed, did the same, for he was 'such an honourable, good-hearted man'; Günzburg, *Vo[m] misbrauch Christlicher freyheyt*, Grimma, 1522 [VD 16 E149], fo. B iii (v).

11. WB 4, 1076, 29 Jan. 1526, 163:2.

12. WB 3, 951 [2 Dec. 1525].

13. LW Letters, II, 150; WB 4, 995, 14 April 1526, 52:13–16. See Burnett, *Karlstadt*, 129–34. He wrote in Latin in the same terms to Valentin Crautwald; WB 4, 996.

14. WB 4, 1208, before 16 Jan. 1528 (Elector Johann to Luther), 347–8; 1209. He was finally dismissed in 1529; see 350.

15. WB 4, 982, 18 Feb. 1526, 33:11; and see 989, 27 March 1526.

16. WB 4, 982, 18 Feb. 1526; on the diffusion of pamphlets see Burnett, *Karlstadt*, 115–21.

17. WB 4, 1072, 10 Jan. 1527, 159:13.

18. WB 5, 1422, 21 May 1529, 74:23–6.

19. WB 4, 1043, 25 Oct. 1526, 123:1; 123:6.

20. WB 4, 1001, 22 April 1526 (to Johann Hess in Breslau), 61:9. In January, he was ordering the formerly loyal Conrad Cordatus in Liegnitz (where Crautwald was) to leave 'those opponents of Christ'.

21. WB 4, 1036, [3 Sept. 1526?] (to Thomas Neuenhagen in Eisenach); the letter was personally delivered by Neuenhagen's pastor. Neuenhagen would eventually be dismissed in the Visitation of 1533 (117, n.1), and Luther interceded for him in 1535 with Justus Menius (7 June 1535), explaining that he did not know why he had been removed (WB 7, 2196).

22. WB 4, 1037, 13 Sept. 1526, 117:8–9 117, 11–12. He repeated this almost verbatim in another letter to him, writing about how Oecolampadius was 'pushed by Satan through such empty and ridiculous arguments': LW Letters, II, 160; WB 4, 1072, 10 Jan. 1527.

23. WB 4, 1101, *c*.4 May 1527, 199:11–14.

24. Jonas presented the account to Bugenhagen six days before Luther died, when both men knew how ill he was, on 12 February 1546; so the events of 1527 were very much on both men's minds as they began to think about Luther's life and legacy. Jonas's report almost certainly formed the basis for Cordatus's notes of the Table Talk, which he inserted under January 1533. This would suggest that Jonas's original contemporary report had been circulating amongst Luther's associates for some time; WT 3, 2922, a and b; see esp. 2922 a, 80, n.3. On the difficulties of the *Tischreden* as a source, see Bärenfänger, Leppin and Michel (eds), *Luthers Tischreden*.

25. WT 3, 2922, 80–90; Walch, XXI, 986–96; it was included in the Jena edition and the Wittenberg editions, in German (*Der Neundte Teil der Buecher des Ehrnwirdigen Herrn D. Martini* Lutheri, Hans Lufft, Wittenberg, 1558, fos. 239 (v)–243 (r); and in Latin in Aurifaber's collection of letters.

26. WT 3, 2292 b, 90:22–3. See also, for example, WT 3, 369, 3511: in 1536, Luther remarked that 'ten years ago I was in death's ditch', almost certainly a reference to the events of 6 July 1527.

27. WT 3, 2922 a, 81; 2922 b, 89–90.

28. WB 4, 1121, 10 July 1527.

29. To Melanchthon he wrote that he had been near death and hell for over a week (WB 4, 1126, 2 Aug. 1527); he asked Menius to pray for him, explaining that the torment had been more spiritual than physical (1128); Agricola comforted him and Luther replied thanking him (1132, 21 Aug. 1527); to Rühel he wrote that he was not yet back to full strength (1136, 26 Aug. 1527); to Michael Stifel, he wrote that he had been physically ill for about three months (263:9–10); to Amsdorf he wrote in November that he would reply to the sacramentarians, but was too weak to do so now (1164, 1 Nov. 1527, 275:10).

30. WS 23, 665–75; see 672, n.1.

31. When Luther said his first Mass, his father paid for the feast (as Luther always remembered). Luther's wedding feast was paid for in part by Luther and in part by the Elector Johann, Friedrich the Wise's brother, who provided the gift of game for the feast, and who was in a sense a father figure.

32. WB 4, 973, 20 Jan. 1526, 19:1–3.

33. WB 3, 779, 3 Oct. 1524, 354:15; see Chapter 11.

34. WB 4, 1164, 1 Nov. 1527. In this revealing letter to Amsdorf, Luther asked his friend for comfort and begged him to join in prayer that God would not let him become an enemy of all that he had preached with such energy hitherto. He seems to have been especially reflective about the progress of the Reformation at this point, and dated his letter 'All Saints' Day, in the tenth year after Indulgences were trodden underfoot' – interestingly placing the anniversary of the posting of the 95 Theses on 1 November, not 31 October).

35. WB 4, 1101: it was available by 4 May 1527. In the interim, some of his sermons against the sacramentarians were published by his supporters in late 1526 because of the urgent need to clarify Luther's position on the Eucharist and because Luther himself still had not done so: WS 19, 482–523.

36. WS 23, 197:14, 18; 283:1–18.

37. WT 3, 2922 b, 88:15–19 (Jonas); 83:13–17 (Bugenhagen) and see also Cordatus's account, based on Jonas, WT 3, 2922 a. According to Bugenhagen he had continued, 'But even St John didn't become a martyr, though he wrote a much worse book against the papacy than I did' (83:15–17). So surprised was Bugenhagen by this statement that he confirmed parenthetically that this was what Luther had actually said.

St John's 'book' was the book of Revelation, which Luther interpreted as unmasking the Pope as the Antichrist; this had become a settled axiom of his theological outlook, finding its most vivid expression in the set of woodcuts and commentaries entitled *Passional Christi und Antichristi* which Cranach, the goldsmith Christian Döring and Melanchthon had produced together in 1521. In Luther's eyes, Revelation was an anti-papal book that prefigured his own work.

38.   In January 1527, he had written to Hausmann: 'persecution rages everywhere and many are being burned at the stake'; LW Letters, II, 160; WB 4, 1072. On 31 May 1527 (Ascension) he had preached in the Castle Church, expatiating also on Christ's death and descent into hell, and beginning with a reference to the '*Rottegeister*', the *Schwärmer* who cannot be helped: WS 23, 696–725, 700:7.

39.   WS 23, 390–434, *Tröstung an die Christen zu Halle über Herr Georgen ihres Predigers Tod*. Winkler had attended one of Luther's sermons shortly before, on 20 March; and Luther learnt of his death on 31 May. He wrote the work at some point after 17 September. He also repeatedly referred to the suicide of Krause, suspected of the murder, who worked for Albrecht of Mainz: the man had stacked up all his money and stabbed himself to death. See, for example, the lengthy description in WB 4, 1180, 10 Dec. 1527.

40.   WS 18, 224–40; LW 32, 265–86. Luther had also noted the martyrdom of two Augustinians in Brussels in 1523, adding that together with a previous third martyr they were the first in this region; WB 3, 635, 22 or 23 July 1523. He did not write much in his letters about the martyrdom of the layman Caspar Tauber, which took place on 17 September 1524 in Vienna, though he was impressed by his bravery; a pamphlet about Tauber appeared in Magdeburg (*Ein erbermlich geschicht So an dem frommen christlichen man Tauber von Wien . . . gescheen ist*, Magdeburg, 1524 [VD 16 ZV 5338]), and others in Strasbourg, Breslau, Nuremberg, and Augsburg [VD 16 H 5770; VD 16 W 293; VD 16 ZV 24131; VD 16 W 295; VD 16 ZV 29583; VD 16 W 294]; but Tauber was not in Luther's circle, and in the writing that originally got Tauber into trouble in Vienna, he had taken a sacramentarian line on the Real Presence.

41.   WB 4, 1107, 20 May 1527.

42.   WB 4, 1161, 22 Oct. 1527, 270:5–15; He continued, 'Who will make me worthy, that I might overcome Satan not with twice his spirit but with even half of his spirit, and might leave this life?'

43.   WS 23, 463:40.

44.   WB 3, 785, 27 Oct. 1524, 361:13–14.

45.   WT 3, 81:3–4.

46. Eck was publishing a refutation of the miracle pamphlet, so Luther needed to set the record straight.

47. Martin Luther, *Von herr Lenhard Keiser in Beyern vmb des Euangelij willen verbrant, ein selige geschicht*, [Nürnberg] [1528] [VD 16 L 7268]; WS 23, 443–76. The printing was finished in the last days of December 1527.

48. WB 4, 1130, 19 Aug. 1527; WB 4, 1165, 4 Nov. 1527, 276:6.

49. See WB 4, 1130, 1131, 1165.

50. This had also driven some of his most vigorous rhetoric against Erasmus in his treatise *Against Free Will*, as Luther argued that the tradition of scriptural interpretation and the authority of the Church counted for nothing against Scripture itself; and that Scripture was clear, whereas Erasmus had argued it was not.

51. On the visitation in Saxony, and the situation there, see Karant-Nunn, *Luther's Pastors*.

52. WS 30, 1, 123–425. In 1528 he preached a series of sermons on the catechism, and in 1529 he published the *Large Catechism* and the *Small Catechism*, which would become foundational educational works.

53. At Luther's insistence, and against Zwingli's wishes, the debate was not public but held in the presence of only Philip of Hesse, the knights and the learned; and there was no official protocol: Stumpf, *Beschreibung* (ed. Büsser), 47; WS 30, 3, 98–9. Zwingli allegedly wore a black tunic, sword and sporran, and was armed like a citizen (Brecht, *Luther*, II, 328), attire which would have been anathema to Luther, who believed that clergy should never take up arms. For various accounts of the Marburg Colloquy see WS 30, 3, 92–109; 110–159; Stumpf, *Beschreibung* (ed. Büsser), 46–50 (from the Zwinglian side), and Myconius, *Geschichte*, 74–6; LW 38, 3–89.

54. WS 30, 3, 147:17–18 (Osiander).

55. WS 30, 3, 145 (Osiander).

56. WS 30, 3, 137 b:10–13 (Anonymous); Schirrmacher, *Briefe und Akten*, 15: this anonymous account, first printed in 1575, is from a pro-Lutheran (WS 30, 3, 99).

57. WS 30, 3, 140b:18–19 (Anonymous); Schirrmacher, *Briefe und Akten*, 17.

58. WS 30, 3, 149:22 (Osiander).

59. WS 30, 3, 150–1 (Osiander). Note also in Hedio's account that Zwingli remarked, at the height of their discussion of flesh and spirit, that 'he begged them not to bear him any ill will; he desires their friendship and is not embittered. He likes to see the faces of Luther and Philip', a comment which conveys the heightened emotionality of the face-to-face meeting of men who had attacked one another in print for so long; LW 38, 21; WS 30, 3, 118 a, 13–14 (Hedio). See also Stumpf, *Beschreibung*

(ed. Büsser), 46–50: the report is concise and does not give much flavour of the event, but is acute on the relations between Luther and Zwingli. As he saw it, the two parted very amicably (though he later crossed through his statement that Luther kissed Zwingli's hands). But, he added, 'the words were good, but how the heart stood, the reader will soon see' (50). Stumpf insists that Oecolampadius and Zwingli kept their promise not to publish against Luther, but that Luther did not reciprocate.

60. WB 5, 1481, 19 Oct. 1529, 163:4; WB 5, 1487, 28 Oct. 1529.

## 15. Augsburg

1. LW 45; *Von weltlicher Oberkeit*, WS 11, 245–81.
2. WS 11, 229–81; LW 45, 77–129.
3. Philip had shown his hand in the infamous Pack Affair, when Otto von Pack had forged documents purporting to show that Archduke Ferdinand and a group of other princes planned to attack Hungary and then turn on the Protestants. Whether or not Philip had connived in the forgery, as some claimed, he had been willing to oppose the emperor, create a league and begin to arm.
4. Widows formed an exception, paying guard duty when they were heads of households, but not able to vote.
5. This was the argument he had used in *On Temporal Authority*; WS 11, 266; LW 45, 111.
6. WB 5, 1511, 24 Dec. 1529.
7. The advice of 6 March, reached in conjunction with Jonas, Melanchthon and Bugenhagen, but sent as a letter from Luther, was kept strictly secret; but in 1531, Luther's antagonist Cochlaeus, who somehow got hold of a copy, published it; WB 5, 1536, 251–2. See also WB 6, 1781, 15 Feb. 1531 (to Spengler); Spengler had asked whether the electoral representatives had been correct in telling the Nurembergers back on 22 December 1530 that Melanchthon and Luther had agreed that resistance to the emperor was admissible in the current circumstances. Luther replied that they had not revoked their previous advice, but that the lawyers were insisting that imperial law allowed resistance to notorious unjust use of force.
8. Ironically, the Torgau model would later be exactly the position Calvinists would take as they worked out a theory of political resistance that would justify a legitimate political authority – a town council, for example – disobeying a prince set over them, if that prince were to act against the gospel. WB 5, 1536, 6 March 1530 in reply to the request of 27 Jan. 1530; 259:52–4.

9. The imperial free cities' freedom was guaranteed by the emperor, and this made it difficult for some of them to be persuaded to resist him and join the Schmalkaldic League; in the event, Nuremberg remained loyal, whilst Augsburg took up arms.

10. On 3 April Luther, Bugenhagen and Melanchthon met with the Saxon officials at Torgau to approve a first draft of the confession, the Torgau Articles.

11. WB 5, 1550, 23 April 1530, 283:6. In the same letter he wrote that there was no difference between his views and Melanchthon's, but the fact that he needed to say so suggested there were underlying tensions. There was already gossip that the two did not always see eye to eye; indeed, just a few weeks before, Luther had received a letter from Nikolaus Gerbel, his garrulous, ill-tempered correspondent in Strasbourg, reporting a rumour that Melanchthon had died and had left behind writings which diverged from Luther's position: WB 5, 1533, end Feb. 1530.

12. WB 5, 1552, 24 April 1530 (to Melanchthon); 1553, 24 April 1530 (to Jonas); 1554 24 April 1530 (to Spalatin: this has the most developed discussion of the parliament of the birds; LW Letters, II, 293). Later Luther investigated their nests and wrote an entire letter to Peter Weller comparing them to the pomposities of the Diet: WB 5, 1594.

13. WB 5, 1559, [4 May 1530] (Agricola to Luther); others related it to the Elector and the threats he would face at the Diet, from which Luther might free him. Agricola was an avid collector of proverbs and published collections; in fact, the reference was probably to the idea of finding that what you buy in a bag is 'a pig in a poke', that is, not a pig but a cat. On the Coburg correspondence, see Volker Leppin, 'Text, Kontext und Subtext. Eine Lektüre von Luthers Coburgbriefen' in Korsch and Leppin (eds), Luther.

14. LW 34, 10, 9; WS 30, 2, 237–356; 270a:5–7; 268a:11; Pettegree, Brand Luther, 271–2.

15. WB 5, 1584, 5 June 1530.

16. LW Letters, II, 267–71; The American edition has 'since you know how lords and peasants feel toward me', which misses Luther's ironic tone; and instead of 'for my name's sake', has 'because of me', missing the gospel reference; WB 5, 1529, 15 Feb. 1530, 239:12–13; 240:30, 31.

17. Dietrich wrote to Luther's wife, WB 5, 379, 19 June 1530; Coburg, Beilage to 1595. The source of the letter is a late seventeenth-century work on Catharina Luther, Mayer, De Catharina Lutheri, 52–3, in which it is said to have been found amongst similar manuscripts; but the editors of the Weimar edition do not cast doubt on its authenticity, and it was included in the Erlangen and St Louis editions.

18. LW Letters, II, 319; WB 5, 1584, 5 June 1530, 315:34–6; Luther's formulation has God shaping him through his father's sweat, so that he owes a debt not directly to his father, but to God the Father through his father.

19. WB 5, 1529, 15 Feb. 1530, 239:6–7.

20. In March 1530 he had written emphatically that children were responsible for their parents' debts – a matter doubtless on his mind given his father's financial difficulties. WB 5, 1537, 12 March 1530 (to Joseph Levin Metzsch): they were a cross sent from God.

21. WB 5, 1587, 12 June 1530: the Lutherans carefully tried to work out Philip's attitude. Jonas reported that Philip of Hesse was refusing to attend Agricola's sermons on the grounds that he had sinned against Christian love by publishing his collection of proverbs (which contained a veiled attack on Duke Ulrich of Württemberg), but he also thought this might be a pretext. The Lutherans did all they could to sway Philip as they worried about his attitude: see also WB 5, 1574, 20 May 1530; Luther – who knew from the conversation of Philip of Hesse's preacher Schnepf to Melanchthon that the landgrave wanted to get the Zwinglians on board – used Schnepf to deliver a letter to the landgrave.

22. WB 5, 1564, May 1530, *Beilage*, 313:22–3.

23. WB 5, 1587, 12 June 1530 (Jonas to Luther).

24. Description by Jonas, 18 June 1530; see also *Kayserlicher maiestat Einreyttung zu Augspurg, den X. tag Junij. Im M.CCCCC.vnd XXX Jar*, [Nuremberg, 1530]. The Saxon Elector Johann carried the bared imperial sword; Brady, *German Histories*, 217–19.

25. WB 5, 1598, 21 June 1530, the Nuremberg preacher Andreas Osiander wrote how, when the emperor banned evangelical preaching, one margrave had insisted he would rather have his head chopped off than be robbed of God's Word: the emperor had replied: 'no chopping off head, no chopping off head', 383:16–17.

26. WB 5, 1590, 18 June 1530 (Jonas); *Kayserlicher maiestat Einreyttung*. On ritual at the Diet, see Stollberg-Rilinger, *Des Kaisers*, 93–136.

27. WB 5, 1600, 25 June 1530, 386:9; 1602, 25 June 1530 (p.m.), 392:37–40; 1601, 25 June 1530 (a.m.); Jonas was deliberately echoing Psalm 118 here, comparing the priests with the unbelievers. I am grateful to Floris Verhaart for pointing this out.

28. For the next three months, Augsburg was to be without its evangelical preachers, who were all sent away, although princes were allowed to hear services in private with their clerics.

29. WB 5, 1618, *Beilage*, 433, article 9. Earlier in 1530, Luther, who had previously argued that people should never be punished for errant belief, now wrote to Menius and Myconius conceding that '*quando sunt*

*non solum blasphemi, sed seditioisissimi, sinite gladium in eos iure suo uti'* –
'since they are not only blasphemers, but most rebellious, so let the
sword be used in justice against them': WB 5, 1532, end Feb. 1530,
244:4–5.

30. CA, p. 63, Article IX *Von der Taufe*; 64, Article X *Vom Heiligen Abendmahl*
condemns the teaching of those who deny that *'wahrer Leib und Blut
Christi wahrhaftiglich unter der Gestalt des Brots und Weins im Abendmahl
gegenwaertig sei'* (the true body and blood of Christ was truly present
in the form of the bread and wine in communion), a direct attack on
the sacramentarians; 66–7, Article XII condemns those who teach, like
Denck, that the justified man cannot sin; 70, Article XVI condemns the
Anabaptists who teach pacifism, etc., and condemns those who leave
wife and child, etc., to follow Anabaptist teaching; 72, Article XVII
condemns those who deny that the Devil and the damned souls will
endure eternal pain. See also Mullet, *Luther*, 204.

31. WB 5, 1696, 25 Aug. 1530 (Bucer to Luther); and see 566–8, *Vorgeschichte*.
Chancellor Brück of Saxony, pressured by Philip of Hesse, persuaded
Melanchthon to see Bucer.

32. WB 5, 1716, 11 Sept. 1530, 617:15–18.

33. WB 5, 1566, 12 May 1530, 316:13–14; 19; phlegm and sore throat, 1693, 24
Aug. 1530; and toothache, 1686, [20 Aug. 1530]; 1688, 20 Aug. 1530.

34. WB 4, 1202, 6 Jan. 1528 (to Justus Jonas).

35. LW Letters, II, 329; WB 5, 1609, 29 June 1530, 406:35–7; Luther breaks
into German here as he does at several points in this letter.

36. Melanchthon wrote on 22 May to Luther (WB 5, 1576) but not again
until three weeks later, 13 June (WB 5, 1589). He and Jonas wrote several
times in the weeks following (19 and 25 June, WB 5, 1596, 1600; Jonas
on 12, 13, and 18 June, and twice on 25 June, WB 5, 1587, 1588, 1590, 1601,
1602).

37. WB 5, 1597, 19 June 1530: Luther complained to Gabriel Zwilling that
no one had written for a month. However, some of the letters had
simply been delayed, 1610, 29 June 1530; 1612; 1605, 27 June 1530 (Bugenhagen was writing).

38. WB 5, 1612, 30 June 1530.

39. Spalatin, *Annales*, 134–5.

40. WB 5, 1602, 25 June 1530 (Jonas); 1603, 25 June 1530 (Elector Johann);
1618, 30 June? 1530 (Jonas): 'Caesar was very attentive'; but according to
other reports, he fell asleep.

41. LW Letters, I, 362; WB 5, 1633, 9 July 1530, 453:15–454:17. He relished the
irony that it was the princes and not the preachers who had preached.

42. WB 5, 1621, 3 July 1530.

43. WB 5, 1635, 9 July 1530, 15–18.

44. WB 5, 1676, 6 Aug. 1530.

45. WB 5, 1604, 26 June 1530; and letter to Dietrich. More letters finally reached Luther from Melanchthon and the others on or around 29 June (1610, 29(?) June 1530). The tensions between the two men may not, however, just have concerned Melanchthon and the other Wittenbergers' failure to tell him of the progress of the work on the confession. Luther wrote to Melanchthon on 5 June 1530 and in the final paragraph, he told him of his father's death (WB 5, 1584). Two days later, he wrote again, enclosing a letter about his father from Michael Coelius, preacher at Mansfeld (WB 5, 1586); but Melanchthon did not write between 22 May and 13 June 1530 (WB 5, 1589), and said nothing about Luther's father either in that letter or in letters of 19 and 25 June (WB 5, 1596, 1600), though Jonas did allude to it (WB 5, 1588, 13 June 1530). Luther did not mention Melanchthon's failure to refer to his father's death, so it may be that he considered it to be a private matter (in which case, why send Coelius's letter?), or they may have communicated in some other way (some letters are missing), or the omission may have rankled with Luther, and may explain some of his irritation.

46. On 26 June, Melanchthon wrote begging Luther to write to them again: Veit Dietrich had told him Luther had determined not to write any more. There were certainly problems in getting messengers to take the letters, and it was expensive: WB 5, 1601 25 June 1530: Jonas had been forced to pay 4 guilders. Now rattled, Melanchthon even resorted to sending his own messengers; 1604, 26 June 1530, 397:19–20; and he wrote an extra letter for Wolf Hornung, a friend, to take with him, not missing the chance to be sure of getting another letter there; 1607, 27 June 1530.

47. WB 5, 1604, 26 June 1530, 397:8–13; 1607, 27 June 1530, 403:16–17; 9–12.

48. WB 5, 1602, 25 June 1530, 392:44.

49. LW Letters, II, 327–8; WB 5, 1609, 29 June 1530, 405:3–9.

50. WB 5, 1609, 29 June 1530.

51. WB 5, 1611, 30 June 1530, 412:30–1.

52. WB 5, 1611, 30 June 1530, 411:1–8.

53. WB 5, 1610, 29? June 1530; 1614, 30 June 1530; and see also 1613, 30 June 1530 (to Agricola).

54. WB 5, 1614, 30 June 1530, 418:16–18.

55. WB 5, 1631, 8 July 1530 (Brenz to Luther).

56. WB 5, 1716, 11 Sept. 1530, 618:25–7. He also began to cite Staupitz, and some of his sayings, such as 'When God wants to blind someone, he shuts their eyes first' (WB 5, 1659, 27 July 1530, 498:3–4); and he used the same expression, which he owed to 'meus Staupitz' in a letter to Agricola, 1662, 27 July 1530; and WB 5, 1670, (?) July 1530. He recalled how Staupitz

had said that Luther's attacks of melancholy were necessary trials sent by God, destining him for service to the Church: Luther now understood this in prophetic terms.

57. WB 5, 1716, 11 Sept. 1530.

58. Unluckily for the Lutherans, one of the Catholic negotiators fell ill and was replaced by Duke Georg of Saxony, Luther's old bête noir; 1695, p. 565.

59. Walch, XVI, cols. 1482–4, Hieronymus Baumgartner to Lazarus Spengler, 13 Sept. 1530.

60. WB 5, 1653, 16 (15?) July 1530, 486:16.

61. LW Letters, II, 390: 'Also, you are wearing me out with your vain worries, so that I am almost tired of writing to you, since I see that I accomplish nothing with my words.' WB 5, 1656, 21 July 1530; 1699, 26 Aug. 1530, 577:3–4.

62. WB 5, 1600, 25 June 1530: mules were of course famed for their sterility. The Papal Ass had been been found on the banks of the Tiber in 1496 while the Monk Calf, discovered in Saxony, had first been used by the Catholics to smear Luther; and then, with the help of Cranach, the Lutherans had turned the story around, arguing that this monster represented the monks and the Pope.

63. See the letters of 1, 3 and 4 August, where Luther goes into the problem of human ordinances, strongly rejecting Melanchthon's arguments, only to leave open the possibility that a saintly work, like that of St Bernhard, *might* be acceptable if no one else were pressed to do it, and if other works, such as marriage and so on, were presented as *more* pleasing to God (WB 5, 1671, 1 Aug. 1530; 1673, 3 Aug. 1530; 1674; 4 Aug. 1530). He also argued in a letter to the Elector that because fasting, feast days, clothes and all kinds of external ceremonies were matters of secular order, secular authority could make commands about this but the Church could not (WB 5, 1697, 26 Aug. 1530), a formulation which left it open to secular authority to do just this so long as consciences were not ensared (see 1707, *Beilage*, 595). He insisted that Communion could only be given in two kinds and that no compromise could be reached on this, but also admitted that the Visitation in Saxony had allowed Communion to be given in one kind only for the sake of the weak consciences, 'but this should not be approved as right' (1707, *Beilage*, 591).

64. WB 5, 1618, *Beilage*: 8th article: Luther's authorship is almost certain; dating may be early July; and 1707, *Beilage*, 595. WB 5, 1691, 22 Aug. 1530 (Melanchthon to Luther); Eck had complained about the Lutheran's addition of the word 'alone' but had conceded the centrality of faith; he still insisted that works played a role in salvation, but only a small one; see also Spalatin's less optimistic report of Eck's position, 16 Aug. 1530, Förstemann, *Urkundenbuch*, II, 225–7.

65. At the same time, Luther's slowness in replying also gave the negotiators in Augsburg more room for manoeuvre. So, for example, Spalatin
wrote desperately asking for Luther to write with clear advice in
response to the Catholic proposals, because he feared that Melanchthon
might concede too much, WB 5, 1692, [23 Aug. 1530], and see *Beilage*.
Then, having heard nothing from Melanchthon, probably between his
letters of 8 and 22 August, Luther was annoyed to discover that
Melanchthon had become part of a new commission with none other
than the hated Eck as his opposite number: he wrote with consum-
mate irony to tell Melanchthon this 'news from Augsburg'! (WB 5,
1693, 24 Aug. 1530.) By late August, Luther was becoming ever more
mistrustful. Even so, on 11 September 1530 he told Melanchthon not
to be worried about those who thought he had conceded too much
to the papists (1716).

66. WB 5, 1613, 30 June 1530, 416:19; 21.

67. WB 5, 1705, 28 Aug. 1530, '*viriliter*'; WB 5, 1709 29 Aug. 1530: Philip of
Hesse also believed that Melanchthon was conceding too much and
blamed his '*Kleinmutigkeit*' (lack of boldness) (600:6); and Luther replied
on 11 September 1530 to put his mind at rest, explaining that nothing
had been conceded and the negotiations had been broken off (1717).
Linck also wrote to Luther, complaining about Melanchthon's willingness to compromise (see 1720, 20 Sept. 1530).

68. Walch, XVI, 1379, 1382 (Spalatin's report of Eck's view); 1383, 1384; WB
5, 1708, 29 Aug. 1530.

69. See WB 5, 1618, 433, Article 7; Spalatin, *Annales*, 264–5.

70. This was also the line he had taken in the *Exhortation*: WS 30, 2, 340–5.

71. WB 5, 1708, 29 Aug. 1530; 1710, 1 Sept. 1530.

72. See WB 5, 1708, 29 Aug. 1530 (Melanchthon to Luther); on the Eucharist,
the Lutheran side were insisting that it could never be right to give
Communion in one kind only, and that those who did so sinned, though
those laity who *received* Communion in one kind only did not sin; that
is to say, they were not willing to accept Communion in one kind for
the rest of the Church. They would also not accept private Masses, or
the canons of the Mass which presented it as a sacrifice. However,
monks and nuns who were living in monasteries could, the Lutherans
agreed, continue to live there, and in monasteries that were empty, new
members could be taken on, but they should not follow rules or orders –
a solution that might have permitted compromise. Fasting should not
become an issue of conscience, but secular authorities might make
regulations about it. See also Philip of Hesse's understanding of what
was on offer (1709, 29 Aug. 1530). He was particularly concerned about
the concessions on fasting and the power of bishops. Schnepf, his

preacher, thought it would be very dangerous to concede to the bishops their previous power, though in other respects he agreed with Melanchthon. The model of peaceful coexistence Schnepf had in mind was like that with the Jews (Förstemann, *Urkundenbuch*, II, 311–12, late August); but this model became one the Lutherans would reject.

73. WB 5, 1711, 4 Sept. 1530: he also worried that the Lutherans' allies were starting to sympathise with the Swiss, and so it was even more important to conclude peace soon.

74. Later it gained support from Heilbronn, Kempten, Windsheim, Weissenburg and Frankfurt.

75. WB 5, 1720, 20 Sept. 1530, 624–5, Introduction to letter; and see Walch, XVI, 1482–4, first letter of Hieronymus Baumgartner to Lazarus Spengler, 13 Sept. 1530; and see also cols. 1523–5, complaining Melanchthon 'has become more childish than a child'; and second letter of Hieronymus Baumgartner to Lazarus Spengler, 15 Sept. 1530, accusing Melanchthon of cursing, shouting and insisting on his own authority. Baumgartner begged Spengler to take the matter up with Luther, and Spengler did so in person, becoming the messenger taking the letters to Jonas and Melanchthon. The complaints had gone on for three weeks: Luther had written to Spengler to defend Melanchthon on 28 August (WB 5, 1707); and then, shortly after, Melanchthon had complained to Luther that Baumgartner, furious about their concessions on bishops, had written to him that if he had been massively bribed by the Roman papacy he could have found no better way to reinstitute papal rule (WB 5, 1710, 1 Sept. 1530).

76. WB 5, 1721, 20 Sept. 1530, 628:23.

77. WB 5, 1722, 20 Sept. 1530, 628:4–5. Yet on the same day, Luther also wrote to Linck defending Melanchthon against the complaints that he had conceded too much.

78. WB 5, 1726, 28 Sept. 1530. Spengler knew that the letters would only split the movement pointlessly.

79. Walch, XVI, 1482–4, 13 Sept. 1530.

80. On how the issues were presented in Lutheran historiography at the time, see Robert Kolb, 'Augsburg 1530: German Lutheran Interpretations of the Diet of Augsburg to 1577', *Sixteenth Century Journal* 11, 1980, 47–61. Looking back, Spalatin concluded that the best deed of our Lord Christ at the Diet was that he did not allow 'such lies' (that is, what the papists offered), 'to be good or right'; *Annales*, 289.

81. See Spalatin's assessment of the negotiations for the Elector, Walch, XVI, 1516–18, 14 Sept. 1530; and Luther's pessimistic account of them, WB 5, 1723, 23 Sept. 1530.

82. WB 5, 1648, 15 July 1530, 480:21–2.

83. WB 5, 1713, 8 Sept. 1530, 608:20–1; in August he also suffered from toothache. In the same month he told Melanchthon of a new complaint he was suffering from, but said he would only talk about this with him in person; WB 5, 1690, 21 Aug. 1530.

84. He also wrote *On the Keys*, but this was not finally completed until the Diet was nearly over. *Vermahnung an die Geistlichen versammelt auf dem Reichstag zu Augsburg Anno 1530*, WS 30, 2, 238ff: this was published in many editions including in Lower German, Danish and Dutch; *Widerruf vom Fegfeuer*, 1530, WS 30, 2, 362ff; *Brief an den Kardinal Erzbischof zu Mainz*, 1530, WS 30, 2, 393ff, which purported to be a letter of conciliation but concluded with Luther fulminating, 'Don't think that you're dealing with humans when you deal with the Pope and his men, but with pure Devils' (412), and invoking the 'innocent blood' of 'Lenhard Keiser'; *Propositiones adversus totam synagogam Sathanae*, WS 30, 2, 420ff, which appeared in many German versions.

85. WS 30, 3, *Warnung an seine lieben Deutschen*, 1531, 286:23; 293:8–9.

86. So, for example, in the *Exhortation*, he had imagined letting the Catholics simply go their own way, telling the Catholic bishops that 'we wish to let you remain what you are', for if they did not act rightly, then 'it is not we, but you who will give account for that. Only keep the peace and do not persecute us!'; LW 34, 50; WS 30, 2, 314 a:8–16: he also told them (perhaps tongue in cheek) that by letting them remain bishops, and keep all their property, he was doing something which the sacramentarians (and Hussites and Müntzerites) had not been willing to do.

## 16. Consolidation

1. WS 30, 3, 249–320.

2. Cargill Thompson, *Studies in the Reformation* (ed. Dugmore), 3–41: a meeting was held at Torgau. WB 5, 1740, 28 Oct. 1528, *Beilage*, 662–4 for the tortuously worded memorial.

3. Strasbourg, Memmingen, Constance and Lindau.

4. WB 5, 1487, 28 Oct. 1529; Luther used the same words in his 1544 tract *Kurzes Bekenntnis vom Abendmahl*.

5. Junghans, *Die Reformation*, 417.

6. Potter, *Zwingli*, 413.

7. Ibid., 414; Zwingli was a combatant; we do not know whether all the others also were.

8. WB 6, 1890, 28 Dec. 1531, 236:4–5; WB 6, 1895, 3 Jan. 1532, Wenzesla as Linck, 246:17–20; WB 6, 1894, 3 Jan. [1532]; 1895, 3 Jan. 1532; WT 1, 220, 94:21; WT 2, 1451.

9. See Hill, *Baptism*. On Anabaptism see also Clasen, *Anabaptism*; Williams, *Radical Reformation*; Goetz, *Anabaptists*; Kobelt-Groch, *Aufsässige Töchter Gottes*; Stayer, *Anabaptists*; Stayer, *German Peasants' War*.

10. *Von der Wiedertaufe an zwei Pfarrherrn*, WS 26, 144–74; *Vorrede zu Menius, Der Wiedertäufer Lehre* (1530), WS 30, 2, 211–14; Oyer, *Lutheran Reformers*. Menius specialised in refuting the Anabaptists, composing four separate works against them.

11. WS 12, 42–8, 1523; it was not included in the revised baptismal liturgy of 1526 but the exorcisms were retained. WS 19, 539–41; and Luther's prefatory letter explicitly insists that the child is possessed by the Devil (537). The liturgy was not incorporated in the Book of Concord because it was thought that the exorcisms would antagonise the south Germans (532, Introduction).

12. WT 6, 6815, 208:32–4. Luther added a twist to the basic story: a bystander thought he could do the same, since he was baptised too; but when he encountered the Devil and dared to reach for the horns, the Devil wrung his neck. The point seems to be that one should not overreach oneself: not everyone has true faith and can cast out demons.

13. WS 5, 1528, 10 Feb. 1530: for example, Luther acted as godparent for Conrad Cordatus's children, Cordatus apparently sending back the customary baptismal coin Luther had sent him, reworked as an ornament; and Jakob Probst in Bremen acted as godparent for his daughter Margarethe (WB 10, 3983, [c.17 April] 1544). For his son Martin in 1531, Luther chose Johann Rühel, his old friend from the Mansfeld administration, and Johann Riedesel (WB 6, 1880, 30 Oct. 1531), a high-ranking member of the electoral Saxon administration: unfortunately, he soon lost his job when the old Elector died, and Luther wrote to console him (WB 6, 1955, 7 Sept. 1532). By 1533, Luther was choosing politically significant godparents: for his son Paul, the electoral Erbmarschall Hans Loeser, and Duke Johann Ernst, the younger brother of the Elector, as well as Jonas, Melanchthon and Caspar Lindemann's wife (WB 6, 1997, 29 Jan. 1533). The celebrations were held in the castle the day after the birth.

14. For example, in 1525 he had argued that the 'three godless painters', leading Nuremberg artists who had become interested in mystical ideas, should not be punished as heretics, but treated like 'the Turk' or apostate Christians; they could however be punished if they were guilty of sedition (WB 3, 824, 4 Feb. 1525, 432:13–14); and see Oyer, *Lutheran Reformers*, 114–39.

15. Goetz, *Anabaptists*, 124–6; WS 26, *Von der Wiedertaufe*, 145:22–23, WB 6, 1881, end Oct. 1531, 222–3: Melanchthon advised executing not just the leaders, but ordinary Anabaptists in so far as they were not just acting

out of ignorance, a much harsher stance than in Hesse at the same time. Luther agreed the memorial, adding the remarks in his own hand (223:1–3); on the development of Melanchthon's views, see Oyer, *Lutheran Reformers*, 140–78; and Kusukawa, *Transformation*, who links Melanchthon's harshness to the identity crisis he experienced during the Wittenberg unrest, 78–9.

16.  Erbe scratched his name into the wall of the tower where he was held, discovered centuries later during renovations of the castle. See Hill, *Baptism*, 81–2. Luther also knew the case of Georg Karg, imprisoned for his Anabaptist views in the Wittenberg Castle in the room where the Elector had learned to fence; WB 8, 3206, see 'Vor und Nachgeschichte' (3 Jan. 1537); Luther had at first tried to have him confined in his own house but the Saxon government refused. Karg had entered into a spiritual union with the wife of the spiritualist and radical Sebastian Franck. Luther instructed him and he accepted correction; he was released in mid-February.

17.  It numbered between 8,000–9,000 at the start of the sixteenth century; Dülmen, *Reformation als Revolution*, 238; an estimated 2,500 Anabaptists arrived in the town (275).

18.  He took over from Jan Matthys who was regarded as a prophet and had established community of goods in the town: Dülmen, *Reformation als Revolution*, 208–336; Kerssenbrock, *Anabaptist Madness* (ed. and tr. Mackay).

19.  See *Newe zeytung von den Wydertaufferen zu Münster*, Nuremberg, 1535 [VD 16 N 876], which included a preface by Luther and propositions against the Anabaptists by Melanchthon; Ronnie Po-Chia Hsia, 'Münster and the Anabaptists' in Hsia (ed.), *German People*.

20.  WT 5, 6041. Part of the reason for polygamy may also have been that with the town's menfolk decimated, the women left behind needed to be organised into households under male headship; see Hsia, 'Münster and the Anabaptists'.

21.  Greschat, *Bucer*, 96.

22.  WB 6, 22 Jan. 1531, 24–5:40–4.

23.  But soon Luther was hearing rumours that Michael Keller and his supporters in Augsburg said that the Wittenbergers had gone over to the Zwinglian view of the sacrament; WB 6, 1799, 28 March 1531. In Augsburg, there were renewed and very bitter disputes between the pro-Bucer and the Lutheran preachers, with Frosch and Johann Agricola refusing to meet their new colleagues from Strasbourg, Bonifacius Wolfart and Wolfgang Musculus. The following year, Luther was warning the Augsburgers that they faced the same fate as Müntzer and Zwingli; WB 6, 1894, 3 Jan. 1532 (Caspar Huber), 244:3–5; he also

exclaimed, 'Watch out Augsburg!' in his letter to Linck. In January 1533, he published a warning to the city of Frankfurt not to be fooled by the sacramentarians who were pretending to teach, like the Wittenbergers, that Christ was truly present in the bread and wine but actually meant spiritually and not physically. This was playing with words according to Luther: *Ein brieff an die zu Franckfort am Meyn*, Nuremberg, 1533 [VD 16 L 4164].

24. Kolde (ed.), *Analecta Lutherana*, 216–30, Musculus; and 214–16, correspondence; Friedrich Myconius, *EPISTOLA SCRIPTA AD D. Vitum Theodorum . . . DE CONCORDIA inita VVitebergae inter D. D. Martinum Lutherum, & Bucerum anno 36*, Leipzig, 1581; Walch, XVII, 2090–9. Representatives from Augsburg, Memmingen, Ulm, Reutlingen, Esslingen, Fürfeld and Frankfurt also attended but were not admitted to the key intimate discussions.

25. Walch, XVII, 2093, 2094, 2096 (Myconius). Whether Christ was present to unbelievers, or whether they received just bread and wine, was left undecided. Greschat, *Bucer*, 132–9.

26. Walch, XVII, 2098–9.

27. WB 8, 3191, 1 Dec. 1537 in response to a letter he received on 12 Jan. 1537; Bucer had written begging him to reply; WB 8, 3192, 3 Dec. 1537.

28. The man Luther recommended, Johann Forster, was impossible, according to the Augsburg council: he attacked the other pastors, drank to excess and alienated people; WB 8, 3250, 19 Aug. 1538, 3251, 29 Aug. 1538; WB 8, 616, 3418, 1 Dec. 1539. Blaurer was eventually also forced to leave, Köhler, *Zürcher Ehegericht*, II, 318–19.

29. LW 41, 5–178; WS 50, 509–653, *On the Councils and the Church*. In this work Luther also explicitly sets out his view that women are to be excluded from the ministry of the Church: LW 41, 154; WS 50, 633.

30. WB 8, 3383, 30 Aug. 1539; they also reminded Luther of the peace they had agreed.

31. LW 43, 220; WS 51, 587.

32. WS 54, 143: Luther averred that if Zwingli believed what he had written in *Christianae fidei expositio* which was published after his death, then 'one must have (and still must) despair of the salvation of his soul, if he died with such an attitude'; and he would have become a heathen (143).

33. [Heinrich Bullinger], *Warhaffte Bekanntnuss der Dieneren der Kirchen zuo Zürych, was sy uss Gottes Wort mit der heiligen allgemeinen christenlichen Kirchen gloubind und leerind, in Sonderheit aber von dem Nachtmal unsers Herren Jesu Christi: . . . mit zuogethoner kurtzer Bekenntniss D. Mart. Luthers vom heiligen Sacrament*, Zurich, 1545 [VD 16 B 9770]; Stumpf, *Beschreibung* (ed. Büsser), 137–8; 141. As the Zwinglian Johann Stumpf noted with shrewd irony, the Lutherans, who claimed to reject relics, actually treated

the *Brief Confession of Dr Martin Luther on the Holy Sacrament* as a '*Heyligthumb*', a relic (141).

34. In 1543, Luther was sent a copy of the Zurich Latin Bible by the printer Christoph Froschauer, but he asked to be sent nothing more because 'I will not participate in their damnation and blasphemous teaching, but remain innocent, I will pray and teach against them until my end', and they would meet the same judgement as Zwingli; WB 10 3908, 31 Aug. 1543.

35. See Karant-Nunn, *Luther's Pastors*.

36. WB 10, 3762, 26 June 1542: writing to Prince Georg of Anhalt, Luther explained that the elevation was a matter of choice, one of the adiaphora that were not essential religious practices. For his part, he would have kept the elevation of the sacrament but Bugenhagen had abolished it, an account that minimised his own involvement in the matter; in fact he had originally kept it to spite the Devil because Karlstadt had said that to elevate the sacrament was to crucify Christ anew; see WB 10, 3806, 1 Nov. 1542 (to Leonhard Beyer) and n.3; and see also WS 54, *Kurzes Bekenntnis vom heiligen Sakrament*, 1544, 165:25–6, where Luther explicitly explains that now the Wittenberg Church has dropped the elevation, but formerly they retained it though most other Churches had dropped it, and he would rather have omitted it.

37. WB 10, 3888, 4 July 1543. On emotions in Lutheran piety, see Karant-Nunn, *Reformation of Feeling*.

38. WB 6, 1773, [16 Jan. 1531], 21:26–8, memorial to Elector Johann; and see Introduction; WB 6, 1776, 22 Jan. 1531. Writing to Bucer, Luther gruffly insisted that he admit that an unbelieving soul also receives the true body of Christ, otherwise there could be no agreement; WB 6, 1779, 9? Feb. 1531. But he did work to create an accord nonetheless, reviving his contacts to Katharina Zell in Strasbourg whom he had long owed a letter, asking her to 'Pray, Pray, Pray' for the matter; WB 6, 1777, 24 Jan. 1531, 26:16. Zell was the wife of the Strasbourg preacher Matthäus Zell and was one of the few women to write pamphlets in support of the Reformation. She played a major role in the ministry in Strasbourg, and it is a mark of her acknowledged position that Luther thought it wise to write to her.

39. See Walch, XVII, 2017 for the report compiled by the Frankfurt preacher Bernardi, probably composed with the help of Bucer and Capito. This stated that neither side believed that the 'mouth' actually touched the 'body' of the Lord; but since 'something more coarse might always be understood by this manner of speaking than either Luther's or the Church Fathers' understanding was, we didn't use this manner of speaking, but said that with the bread and wine the body and blood of

Christ are truly given, in a divine and heavenly, but yet true and essential way'. As Ratzeberger describes Melanchthon putting it to Georg Öhmler, Luther wrote about these matters 'nimis crasse'. 'For do you think that Christ would let himself be ripped with teeth and digested through the body?', the objection the Zwinglians had made to Luther. Ratzeberger, *Die handschriftliche Geschichte*, 93–4.

40. WB 4, 1160, 19 Oct. 1527, 369:26–8.

41. This is very well explained in Kolb, *Martin Luther. Confessor of the Faith*, 114, who links it to his Ockhamist heritage.

42. WT 3, 3484. In a letter to his young son Hans written while he was at Coburg, Luther imagined a place where 'good' children will play, eat cherries and ride ponies. Hans was aged four at the time, and the fact that Luther told this story illustrates just how widespread the experience of bereavement was. But Luther clearly did not intend this as a literal view of heaven; LW Letters, II, 321–4; WB 5, 1595, c.19 June 1530.

43. LW Letters, III, 18; WB 6, 1820, 20 May 1531, 103:3–6;17. The letter was known amongst the Lutherans. Just a year later, Lazarus Spengler in Nuremberg asked for a copy, and Luther's secretary Veit Dietrich sent it to him along with Luther's last letter to his father, so both texts clearly circulated during Luther's lifetime. They were printed in 1545, the year before Luther's own death, in Caspar Cruciger's collection of *Luther's Writings of Comfort*, a selection of letters and excerpts from Luther's work on melancholy designed for pastoral use where they open the volume.

44. WT 4, 4787.

45. WB 10, 3792, 16? Sept. 1542, 147:5; 3830, 26 Dec. 1542; 3831, 27 Dec. 1542. He wrote to the school that they should not indulge this 'softness' or give way to this womanly attitude; and he wrote to his son that his mother was unable to write, but that she agreed with everything; and that when she had said he could come back home if things went badly, she meant in case of serious illness, in which case he must let them know at once.

46. LW 45, *Temporal authority: to what extent it should be obeyed*; WS 11, 'Von weltlicher Oberkeit': WS 11, 245–80, 280:14–15.

47. WB 6, 1861, a and b, 3 Sept. 1531, and 175–7; in one version of the advice he offered, which the editors argue is the contemporary memorial, Luther did consider the possibility that the queen might allow the king to take a second wife rather than repudiate her, an option which he expressly did not include in the copy of the memorial which he later sent to Philip of Hesse.

48. WB 7, 2282, 9 Jan. 1536; 2283, 11 Jan. 1536; and see 2287, 19 Jan. 1536: Luther insisted on his previous advice.

49.  As the landgrave put it in the wedding speech, 'for I desire it with God and in good conscience, because I cannot keep myself from wicked lewdness without such a remedy and medicine'; Rockwell, *Die Doppelehe*, 43.

50.  WB 8, 3423, Dec. 1539, 631:31–5. The landgrave was blaming his temperament which, according to humoral medicine of the time, was caused by the balance of humours in his body. Rich food only increased lusts. The letter is extraordinary, because it presents an elaborate argument for permission to commit bigamy, and is written in the first person singular, remarkable for rulers, who usually used the first person plural. There are annotations in Philip's own hand. Philip must have raised the possibility of bigamy with Luther years before, because there is a letter from Luther of 28 November 1526 in the Marburg archives insisting that bigamy is not permitted; WB 4, 'unless there were extreme necessity' (*'Es were denn die hohe not da'*), a formulation that may have raised Philip's hopes, even though the exceptions Luther gave as examples of what he had in mind as extreme necessity were if the wife had leprosy or had otherwise been taken from her husband, see chapter 13 above. Karlstadt, on the other hand, had advised a man to take a second wife back in 1524 (WB 3, 702, 13 Jan. 1524), and Luther had pointed out that as this was not counter to the example of the Old Testament prophets, he could not forbid it either, though he would not wish to see polygamy introduced as a general custom amongst Christians. He thought this might be a mischievous request, and could not resist adding that perhaps they would go completely 'Mosaic' in Orlamünde, and introduce circumcision!

51.  WB 5, 1709, 29 Aug. 1530; Greschat, *Martin Bucer*, 153-6: Bucer had managed to convert a group of Anabaptists in Hesse by taking their concerns about the lack of discipline in the church seriously, and had then drafted a new Discipline Ordinance, published along with a new church ordinance for Hesse in early 1539.

52.  WB 8, 3423, 635, Dec. 1539: the argumentation is interesting, for Philip explains that in order to obtain the emperor's agreement he might need to gain a papal dispensation, which although it would mean nothing to him (*'Ich nun vffs Pabsts Dispens[a]tion gar nichts achte'*), and though he was sure he could get one if he paid enough money, still the emperor might tie his hands.

53.  WB 9, 3458, 5 April 1540. Luther burnt the letter, so the surviving copy is a draft; see WB 9 3464, 12 April 1540; see also 3484, 24 May 1540.

54.  WB 9, 3491, 9 June 1540; and see 3502 (written in the landgrave's own hand) and 3503, 20 and 21 June 1540.

55. Johannes Lening, *Dialogus das ist ein freundtlich Gesprech Zweyer personen Da von Ob es Goettlichem Natürlichen Keyserlichem vnd Geystlichem Rechte gemesse oder entgegen sei mehr dann eyn Eeweib zugleich zuhaben. Vnnd wo yemant zu diser zeit solchs fürnehme ob er als eyn vnchrist zuuerwerffen vnd zuuerdammen sei oder nit*, Marburg, 1541 [VD 16 L 1174]. Some thought Bucer was the author, to his great embarrassment (Rockwell, *Die Doppelehe*, 121–30); and in 1542, Luther wrote a reply to it, arguing that though polygamy was permitted in the Old Testament, attitudes toward women were different at that time (WS 53, *Antwort auf den Dialogum Hulrichi Nebulonis*, 185–201). Luther does not mention Philip in this tract and insults Neobulus as a fool.

56. Rockwell, *Die Doppelehe*, 65.

57. Rockwell, *Die Doppelehe*, 152–3.

58. Ludolphy, *Friedrich der Weise*, 47–50, who reads it as 'Kasper' not 'Rasper': she identifies Friedrich's lover, however, as Anna Weller von Molsdorf, and points out that Luther referred to her as 'die Watzlerin' or 'die Wantzlerin', arguing that the box may not be a portrait of Friedrich's concubine after all. It is hard, however, to imagine what else it could be. See also Iris Ritschel, 'Friedrich der Weise und seine Gefährtin' in Tacke (ed.), '. . . wir wollen der Liebe Raum geben', 336–41; and Haag, Lange, Metzger and Schuetz (eds), *Dürer, Cranach, Holbein*, 207–9 for a reproduction and identification of her as Anna Rasper or Dornle. The lid has a relief of a winged siren with snake-like body and hen's feet, embodying the idea of female temptation and sensuality; his lid shows a centaur.

59. WB 9, 3515, 18 July 1540. In 1540, Luther reminisced at table about how Philip had even suggested at Worms in 1521 that he had heard that Luther taught that if a man wasn't up to it any more, then a wife could take a second husband. We don't know exactly when in 1540 Luther told this story, but it suggests he was wondering whether the landgrave's support for the evangelical cause had been just self-seeking; WT 5, 5342 b, 73:9–19.

60. WB 9, 3616, 10 or 11 May 1541, 407:36–9. The letter was drafted in Luther's hand and signed by Bugenhagen as well. By 'Heintz', Luther meant Heinrich of Braunschweig; he liked to rhyme his antagonists as Mainz and Heintz: see for example WB 9, 3670, 10 Nov. 1541.

61. Walch, XVII, 2099–100, *Synodus Witebergensis . . . von M. Johann Bernardi . . . Von den oberlaendischen Predigern gemeinsam verfasst zu Frankfurt*, 2010, 'unserm Herrn und Vater, D. Martin Luther'.

62. Brecht, *Luther*, III, 59, 60 on French overtures in 1535; the English wanted to deal with Melanchthon, WB 7, 2282, 9 Jan. 1536; 2283, 11 Jan. 1536; and see 2287, 19 Jan. 1536.

## 17. Friends and Enemies

1.  He knew the value of this privilege and was careful not to abuse it. So for example in December 1544, when his relations asked him to petition the Elector on behalf of a cousin who was facing the death penalty for counterfeiting coin, he wrote not to the Elector but to his chancellor, Gregor Brück, explaining that he believed that malefactors should be punished and so he was writing to the chancellery rather than the Elector himself. WB 10, 4058, second half Dec. 1544.

2.  On some pamphlet covers, a special design includes a Wittenberg group of 'four', like the four evangelists, represented by their monograms and initials: Luther, Melanchthon, Jonas and Bugenhagen. See for example Martin Luther, *Zwo Hochzeit Predigten*, Wittenberg, 1536, [VD 16 L 4929].

3.  But see WB 8, 3331, after 9 May 1539?: Linck had written begging Luther not to strike him from his list of friends; this may have been an attempt to guilt-trip Luther into writing him a letter, or it may have been more serious.

4.  Inge Mager, "'*Das war viel ein andrer Mann*". Justus Jonas – Ein Leben mit und für Luther' in Peter Freybe, ed., *Luther und seine Freunde*, 24, n.12.

5.  WB 8, 3248, 16 Aug. 1538 and *Beilage*.

6.  WB 8, 3334, 20 May 1539; Luther had no patience with such complaints.

7.  WB 8, 3209, 6 Jan. 1538, 187, Introduction; Luther interceded to get him out of prison.

8.  WB 10, 3752, 15 May 1542; 3767, 13 July 1542.

9.  Witzel, *Apologia*, fo. A ii (v).

10. WB 10, 3727, 26 March 1542: the salaries of university teachers were not to be taxed, but their assets were. In his letter of thanks to the Elector, Luther insisted that he had wanted very much to play his part in the war against the Turks, also because then 'the squinting eyes wouldn't be so envious, because Dr Martinus had to pay his bit as well' (20:40–2). Surprisingly Luther also said that if he were not so old and weak, he would have wished to be there among the army against the Turks in person.

11. WB 5, 1595, 19 June 1530; Philipp Melanchthon junior and Justus Jonas junior (Lippus and Jost) were born in 1525.

12. Ratzeberger, *Die handschriftliche Geschichte*, 130.

13. Luther made anti-papal jokes out of the word too, writing to Peter Weller WB 5, 1594, 19 June 1530, see n.3, about those at Augsburg now 'Quiritisantes', mixing *quiritantes* (sufferers), with the Quirites, Romans, a way of mocking the papists.

14. He acted as an advocate for Luther in 1544 when clauses were added to Luther's will, StadtA Witt, 109 [Bc 97], fo. 330 (v); Fabiny, *Luther's*

*Last Will and Testament*, 34; WT 4, 4016: he complained that people did not begin marriage in prayer and the fear of God, citing the weddings of the daughters of Lufft, Cranach and Melanchthon. We know from the mocking verses of Lemnius that Lufft held a particularly extravagant wedding, showing off in front of the whole town; Mundt, *Lemnius und Luther*, II, 39.

15. WS 38, 364:7–11.

16. WS 38, 350; Luther had known him since at least 1517. Brecht, *Luther*, III, 15–16.

17. WB 6, 1880, 30 Oct. 1531, 221, n.4.

18. When Jonas von Stockhausen, *Stadthauptmann* of Nordhausen, suffered from suicidal thoughts, he not only wrote him a letter of comfort but wrote to his wife as well, warning her not to leave him alone on any account; WB 6, 1974, 1975, 27 Nov. 1532. Though he addresses him as 'friend', there is no other mention of the man in Luther's correspondence or in the Table Talk, so this was not a man he knew well.

19. WB 6, 1811, 30 April 1530, 86:5–7; 87:55–6.

20. WB 5, 1593, 19 June 1530, 374:37–9. As with all aspects of what was now a public life, these letters were published and available as a collection, edited by one of his close associates Caspar Cruciger, *Etliche Trostschrifften vnd predigten/ fur die so in tods vnd ander not vnd anfechtung sind*, 1545. Melancholy was an important part, too, of his relationship with Joachim of Anhalt (WB 7, 2113, 23 May 1534), and Luther speculated that it ran in the family, recalling the story of Fürst Wilhelm von Anhalt-Zerbst who became a Franciscan monk and went about begging at Magdeburg. Revealingly he advised Joachim to hunt, ride and enjoy company – not like 'me who has spent my life with sorrowing and looking on the gloomy side' (*Trauren und Saursehen*, 66:20) – but now, he said, he sought happiness where he could.

21. Markert, *Menschen um Luther*, 319–29.

22. How this relationship worked emerges in a story Luther told about when he was grappling with the interpretation of a biblical passage, and the Devil disputed with him; the Devil was winning and he 'just about strangled me, as if my heart would melt in my body' (WT 1, 141, 62:32). He asked Bugenhagen to read the same text, who, not realising Luther was presenting the Devil's interpretation, apparently agreed with him. The reformer had to spend the whole night 'with a heavy heart' (WT 1, 141, 63:5-6), only to be relieved the next day when an angry Bugenhagen appeared, telling him that his abstruse interpretation of the passage had been 'ridiculous'. At one level, Luther of course knew the interpretation was wrong, but he needed Bugenhagen's pastoral authority to believe it.

23. Posset, *Front-Runner*, 101.

24. Kolb, *Amsdorf*, 16, 27–30.

25. Luther had tried to persuade him to visit in the monastery, offering him a new room, in 1531; WB 6, 1885, 22 Nov. 1531. Nikolaus Hausmann, another friend from Luther's generation, remained a lifelong bachelor and his death in 1538 from a stroke, which he suffered when he gave his first sermon as superintendent in Freiberg, was a bitter blow.

26. WB 8, 3400, 6 Nov. 1539, 586:23–4.

27. The situation was further complicated by the tensions generated in the friendship with Melanchthon and the need to show loyalty both to Luther and Melanchthon, not always on the same side. For example, Veit Amerbach was forced to leave Wittenberg in 1543 after a dispute with Melanchthon; WB 10, 3838, 13 Jan. 1543; 3943, 3 Dec. 1543; 3967, 9 Feb. 1544.

28. WB 4, 1017, 8 June 1526: he asked Johann Rühel to let Agricola know, adding 'for he must be thinking about this time of year what it means to have sons' (87:10–11). On Agricola, see Kawerau, *Agricola*.

29. See, for example, WB 4, 1009, 11 May 1526.

30. WB 4, 1111, [10 June 1527]; 1119 [early July 1527].

31. WB 4, 1322, 11 Sept. 1528, 558:10–11; 1325, second half Sept. 1528; WB 5, 1378, 1 Feb. 1529.

32. WB 5, 9 Sept. 1529 (Graf Albrecht of Mansfeld), 9 Sept. 1529 (Agricola); Kawerau, *Agricola*, 110–15: Passavant dedicated his attack to the Mansfeld counts.

33. WB 5, 1473, 9 Sept. 1529, 151:12–18.

34. Ratzeberger, *Die handschriftliche Geschichte*, 97.

35. Kawerau, *Agricola*, 168–71: he left behind a letter to Count Albrecht of Mansfeld, to whom he owed his position in Eisleben, in which he poured out his frustration at his 'low' salary. The count responded in kind, accusing him of drunkenness, failure to perform his teaching duties, and preaching more against his colleagues than against the papists.

36. Kawerau, *Agricola*, 172–3; see WT 4, 4043 (1538). He later moved to the house of Melanchthon's mother-in-law.

37. Förstemann, *Urkundenbuch*, I, 298; see also Ernst Koch, '"Deutschlands Prophet, Seher und Vater". Johann Agricola und Martin Luther. Von den Enttäuschungen einer Freundschaft' in Peter Freybe, ed., *Luther und seine Freunde*, 63.

38. WB 8, 3175, 2 Sept. 1537, 122:6–11. German translation in Koch, 'Deutschlands Prophet', 66.

39. WB 8, 3254, Aug. 1538, 279:20. The letter suggested that Luther's writings contained two different views on sin and forgiveness. Agricola later noted on his draft copy that the letter 'which I wrote out of pure simplicity' had 'set the Rhine on fire'. Next, Agricola wrote a letter of total prostration to Luther promising never to deviate in the slightest

from Luther's teaching (WB 8, 3284, 26 Dec. 1538(?), 342–3). On the attempted reconciliation in the Church, 342. Koch argues that Agricola's position was more in line with Luther's earlier views, and that Luther's emphasis on law now followed Melanchthon's position. Part of what was at stake in this dispute therefore concerned the relationship between Melanchthon and Luther.

40. See Kawerau, *Agricola*, 174–9; WS 39, 1, *Die Thesen zu den Disputationen gegen die Antinomer*, 334–58; WS 50, *Wider die Antinomer*, 1539, 461–77.

41. WT 6, 6880, 248:33–4 at the end of Jan. 1539, just before the disputation on Agricola's theses; Förstemann, *Urkundenbuch*, I, 319.

42. Humiliatingly he had to write to Georg von Dolzig to beg him not to cancel his salary, appealing on behalf of his sick wife and nine children: WB 8, 3284, 22 Dec. 1538, Introduction; letter, Kawerau, *Agricola*, 196, 342.

43. WB 8, 3208, 6 Jan. 1538.

44. WS 51, *Bericht auff die Klage M. Johannis Eissleben*, 1540, 429–43, 431 b:5–6; 436 b:6–9; and see WS 50, *Wider die Antinomer*, 1539, 461ff.

45. See WB 9, 3460, 7 April 1540; 3533, 3 Sept. 1540 (Luther reported it to Güttel).

46. Kawerau, *Agricola*, 211–15; Melanchthon had drafted a revocation in 1539; and now he warned Agricola of Luther's anger. Indeed, Luther was inexorable: at table, he said Agricola must confess 'that I [i.e. Agricola] have been a fool, and have done injustice to those of Wittenberg, for they teach rightly, and I have attacked them unfairly' (WT 5, 5311, Oct.–Nov. 1540, 54:21–2) – the verb *'genarrt'* [have been a fool] is particularly harsh. The revocation finally came in December 1540. In 1545 Agricola made a final attempt at reconciliation, but though Luther received and lodged Agricola's wife and daughter, he refused point blank to meet with Agricola himself: WB 11, 4098, 2 May 1545; 4100, 2 May 1545; 4101, 2 May 1545: he also thought Agricola's daughter was more talkative and audacious than was fitting for a maiden.

47. Kawerau, *Agricola*, 121; this was published in 1538.

48. Simon Lemnius, *M. Simonis Lemnii Epigrammaton Libri III*, [s.l], 1538 [VD 16 L 1133]; and for a modern edition and translation see Mundt, *Lemnius und Luther*.

49. Georg Sabinus, Melanchthon's son-in-law, was also involved; WB 8, 287–9.

50. WB 8, 3244, 24 July 1538; WS 50, *Erklärung gegen Simon Lemnius*, 16 June 1538, 350:9; it said that he would have justly been executed (350:20–2).

51. WS 50, 351:11; two further volumes of *Epigramme* appeared which were much more bitter about Luther and other Wittenberg characters; Mundt, *Lemnius und Luther*, II, and see the very helpful commentary, I, 205–64.

52. See Carl P. E. Springer, 'Luther's Latin Poetry and Scatology', *Lutheran Quarterly* 23/4, 2009, 373–87.

53. The title is a pun on a poem then ascribed to Homer, the *Batrachomyomachia* (*The Battle of Frogs and Mice*), a parody of the *Iliad*. I am grateful to Floris Verhaart for this information.

54. StadtA Witt, 9 [Bb6]: the *Kämmereirechnungen* (town accounts) include payments for small repairs to the civic brothel until 1522, but by 1525 it was being used for other purposes.

55. WB 7, 3088, 7 Oct. 1536, 556:3.

56. By 1546, the authorities were having to forbid students to throw rockets and use gunpowder; Staatsarchiv Weimar, Reg O 468. In 1545 the council was reporting on its ordinance against dancing and night drinking; Staatsarchiv Weimar, EGA (Witt), fo. 529.

57. One Georg Meyssner and other citizens spoke '*vnnutzen verdriesslichen bosen worten*' (useless, offensive evil words) and blasphemed in Luther's house: Meyssner was imprisoned for eight days and banished for six months; StadtA Witt, 114 [Bc 102], fo. 240.

58. Mundt, *Lemnius und Luther*, II, 143.

59. WB 10, 3846, 9 Feb. 1543. He was troubled by headaches, 'so that I can neither read nor write anything, especially sober [*jejuno*], 259:4; 3903, 18 Aug. 1543, he was writing after dinner, 'for I can't read books without danger sober [*ieiunus*]', 371:38. He may have meant 'without having eaten anything', but drink also went with meals.

60. WB 10, 3905, 26 Aug. 1543, 373; and see Rankin, *Panaceia's Daughters*, 99–100.

61. WB 10, 3983, *c*.17 April 1544, 554:2–5.

62. The disputes with Agricola and Lemnius were not the only ones in which Luther's friendship with Melanchthon was put under strain. In 1536, Conrad Cordatus had become involved in arguments first with Cruciger and then with Melanchthon over the role of works in salvation. Luther emphatically took Melanchthon's part, though his own view was closer to that of Cordatus. Luther was soon recommending him for a position at Eisleben, safely further away from Wittenberg than Niemegk where he currently was; WB 8, 3153, 21 May 1537.

63. WB 8, 3136, 3137, 3138, 3139; *Vorgeschichte*, 46–8 for a description of this very severe attack of stone: Luther was unable to pass water for ten or eleven days and experienced a state of euphoria before becoming deathly tired. He wrote to his wife that 'God has performed miracles on me this night' and that his recovery was thanks to the prayers of others; WB 8, 3140, 27 Feb. 1537, 51:20–2. However, the attacks returned and he remained very ill, making his confession to Bugenhagen and expecting to die.

64. WB 9, 3509, 2 July 1540; Brecht, *Luther*, III, 209–10; WT 5, 5407 and 5565: three people had been brought back to life through prayer: Katharina von Bora, Luther himself at Schmalkalden, and Melanchthon at Weimar. Myconius also claimed to have been saved from death by Luther's prayer; WB 9, 3566, 9 Jan. 1541.

65. WB 10, 4028, 9 Sept. 1544, and *Beilage*.

66. WB 10, 4007, 23 June 1544; 4014, early Aug. 1544; and see also WS 54, 123ff, editor's preface to *Kurzes Bekenntnis vom heiligen Sakrament*, 1544. As Luther wrote this doctrinal statement, which was directed ostensibly against the Zwinglians and not (as they feared) Bucer or Melanchthon, he had to hand his most powerful writings against the sacramentarians, *Against the Heavenly Prophets*, *Sermon on the Holy Sacrament* (*Sermon vom Sakrament, Dass diese Worte Christi 'Das ist mein Leib' noch feste stehn* ('That these words of Christ, "this is my body," still stand firm') and the *Confession concerning Christ's supper* (*Grosses Bekenntnis*, also known as *Vom Abendmahl Christi, Bekenntnis*). He was intentionally returning to these older works and to formulations that he, and not Melanchthon, had made; these were also the works (especially the *Grosses Bekenntnis*) which, after Luther's death, ultra-loyalist Lutherans would regard as non-negotiable, encapsulating their position: WS 26, 249.

67. WB 10, 3984, 21 April 1544, 556:14–16; 34.

68. WS 59, 'Sermons 1544' [3 Aug.], 529ff: this sermon condemns holy living, chastity and so on as pure fleshly thinking and argues that the sacramentarians, who seem to be spiritual, are actually fleshly.

69. WB 10, 4014, [early Aug. 1544], 616, Editor's Introduction. *Melanchthons Briefwechsel – Regesten online*, 3646, 8 Aug. [1544]; in this letter to Veit Dietrich he also mentioned Amsdorf's criticism of his draft of the Cologne Reformation, which Luther had thought mild, so he expected a new dispute to blow up; and see 3648, 8 Aug. 1544, where he praises mild sermons, and describes being himself in danger because of his measured views. In letters to Camerarius and Dietrich (3652, 3653, 11 Aug. [1544]; 3658, 12 Aug. [1544]; and see 3667, 28 Aug. [1544]; 3669 [28 Aug. 1544], Melanchthon mentioned Amsdorf's bitter critique again, repeating that Luther thought it 'mild'. Luther, he wrote, had declared war in his sermons on 1 Corinthians; and he feared a whole new dispute over the sacrament; he might have to leave Wittenberg. Luther, he worried, was writing a new work on the sacrament attacking both Melanchthon and Bucer. Bucer, to whom Melanchthon also wrote, reported all this to Landgrave Philip of Hesse, trying to get him to calm the storm by talking to the Elector.

70. WB 11, 4139, 28 July 1545, 149:15–16; 19;8. This was not the first time he had had enough of the Wittenbergers: in late 1529 he had simply stopped

preaching in the city church for several months, and did not resume until late March; WB 5, 1521, 18 Jan. 1530.

71. WB 11, 4143, 5 Aug. 1545, esp. 163ff.

72. Walch, XXI b, 3131–2, 3131, Despite suffering from very severe attacks of the stone, Luther visited his old friends Jonas and Camerarius too, travelling from Zeitz to Merseburg, Eisleben, Leipzig and Torgau; WB 11, 4143, 5 Aug. 1545, 165.

## 18. Hatreds

1. WS 50, 284–308. Luther's preface refers to the foxtails with which the bishops want to cleanse the Church, so he must have had a hand in the making of this image too. See also Brecht, *Luther*, III, 191.

2. WS 54, 346.

3. WS 54, 346; Cochlaeus described this and other woodcuts as '*obscoenas figuras*', printed at Wittenberg: Grisar and Heege, *Luthers Kampfbilder*, III, 4.

4. WS 54, 206–99; LW 41, 257–376.

5. LW 41, 273, 278, 334; WS 54, 214:30; 218:19–21; 265:11–13; 16–17.

6. WT 3, 3543A and 3543B; in 1537, when Luther nearly died at Schmalkalden, he also said that his epitaph should remain true: *Pestis eram vivens, moriens ero mors tua, papa* [Living I was your plague; dying I will be your death, O Pope.]; 3543A, 390:17. Cochlaeus also referred to it; Vandiver, Keen and Frazel (eds and trs), *Luther's Lives*, 349. On the legacy of these images in later print, see Paas, *The German Political Broadsheet*, vols. 1 and 2.

7. Francisco, *Luther and Islam*; Ehmann, *Luther, Türken und Islam*.

8. See Thomas Kaufmann, '*Türckenbüchlein*'. *Zur christlichen Wahrnehmung 'türkischer Religion' in Spätmittelalter und Reformation*.

9. WS 30, 2, 107–48, *Vom Kriege wider die Türken*, 127.

10. WS 30, 2, 160–97, *Eine Heerpredigt wider den Türken*.

11. See LW 43, *Admonition to Prayer Against the Turks*, 1541; WS 51, 374–411. As late as 1543 he called for prayer in Wittenberg because the Turks were sent as punishment for Christians' sin: StadtA Witt, 17 [Bc], *Vermanung an de Pfarrher inn der Superattendentz der Kirchen zu Wittemberg*, 1543, which went out under the names of Luther and Bugenhagen.

12. WS 30, 2, 196 a:23–4.

13. WS 30, 2, 193 a:3–5; and see 2, 198–208, *Vorrede to Libellus de ritu et moribus Turcorum*, 1530, of three pages.

14. See WS 30, 2, 189 a–190 a; 191 a: 25–6; 190 a:13–14.

15. LW 43, *Admonition to Prayer Against the Turks*, 1541; WS 51, 577–625. In 1542, he translated and republished an old medieval Dominican work

about the Turks, the refutation of the Quran by Brother Richard, which, having seen a poor Latin translation of the Quran, he now considered to be accurate. WS 53, 273–388, *Verlegung des Alcoran Bruder Richardi*.

16. WS 53, 561, Introduction; Francisco, *Luther and Islam*, 211–17.

17. WB 10, 3802, 27 Oct. 1542, 162:35–6; 163:78–9. WS 53, 561–772 for the preface Luther wrote to Bibliander's edition of Robert of Ketton's Latin translation of the Quran. See also Harry Clark, 'The Publication of the Quran in Latin: A Reformation Dilemma', *Sixteenth Century Journal* 15, No. 1 (spring 1984), 3–12; Hartmut Bobzins, 'Aber itzt . . . hab ich den Alcoran gesehen Latinisch . . . Gedanken Martin Luthers zum Islam' in Medick and Schmidt (eds), *Luther zwischen den Kulturen*.

18. WS 53, 566, Introduction. His final publication against Islam was a sermon given on 31 Jan. 1546, shortly before he died, where he inveighed against the Pope, the Jews and Islam (WS 51, 148–63). Here he argued that Islam simply would not accept a God who was also human, who was a father, and 'gave us his son', 152:18. Once again, the central issue for Luther was the incarnation, God becoming flesh.

19. LW 45, 200; WS 11, 314–36, *Daß Jesus Christus ein geborner Jude sei*, 315:3–4. See, on Luther's writings against the Jews, Kaufmann, *Luthers 'Judenschriften'*; Kaufmann, *Luthers Juden*; Nirenberg, *Anti-Judaism*, 246–68; Oberman, *Roots of Anti-Semitism*; Osten-Sacken, *Martin Luther und die Juden*.

20. On Luther's personal contacts with Jews, which were not extensive, see Kaufmann, *Luthers Juden*, 32–47. On the tract, see Prien, *Luthers Wirtschaftsethik*, 69.

21. LW 45, 229; WS 11, 336:14–19.

22. Nirenberg, *Anti-Judaism*, 252–6. Nirenberg brilliantly points out that it had been traditional to provide an allegorical reading of the Old Testament as prefiguring the New; but 'by moving it to the literal level, Luther made the engagement both sharper and more exclusive' (253). See, for example, LW 10, 'Lectures on Psalms', 93 (Psalm 9); 254 (Psalm 55); 351 (Psalm 69); WS 3, 88–91; 313–16; 441–2.

23. WT 3, 3512. So, for example, WB 6, 1998, before 9 Feb. 1531, 427:1; the letter is in Latin but this breaks into German. Or, in 1544, he complained about the power of the Jews in the Mark Brandenburg where they reigned 'because of money' (WB 10, 3967, 9 Feb. 1544).

24. She was the sister of Hartmut von Cronenberg; WB 7, 2220, 8 Aug. 1535; 2227, 24 Aug. 1535; 2228, 24 Aug. 1535; 2235, 6 Sept. 1535.

25. WB 8, 3157, 11 June 1537, 90:12–13; 42–4; he also tells the Jews not to treat Christians as 'Narren und Gänse' (fools and geese), 90:29. Capito had written to Luther asking him to hear Josel and intercede with the Elector, WB 8, 3152, 26 April 1537. In 1536, there were restrictions placed on Jews

coming to teach Hebrew, because they were attempting to proselytise: StadtA Witt, Bc 38 [49] fo. 86, 1536; in 1539, however, on the request of Josel of Rosenheim, the Jews were allowed to pass through Saxony with their goods but not to trade or live there, or convert others (fo. 85).

26. LW 47, 59–98; WS 50, 309–37.

27. See, however, Kaufmann, *Luthers Judenschriften*, 90–6.

28. LW 47 191; WS 53, 461:28–9.

29. LW 47, 152–3; WS 53, 430. This section of the tract is indebted to Anton Margaritha, *Der gantz Jüdisch glaub mit sampt eyner gründtlichenn vnd warhafftigen anzeygunge, aller satzungen, Ceremonien, gebetten, heymliche vnd öffentliche gebreüch, deren sich die Juden halten, durch das gantz Jar mit schönen vnnd gegründten Argumenten wider jren glauben*, [Augsburg] 1531, fo. J ii (r) ff, which describes this in gory detail.

30. LW 47, 162; WS 53, 438:8.

31. LW 47, 212, 261, 291, 286; WS 53, 478:32; 517:23; 541:1–3; 537:15–16.

32. LW 47, 268–72; WS 53, 523–6.

33. WB 10, 3845, 27 Jan. 1543, 258; *Melanchthons Briefwechsel Regesten online* 3147, 17 Jan. 1543; *Melanchthons Briefwechsel*, Texte 12, 17 Jan. 1543. StadtA Witt, Bc 38 [49], fo. 100. In a letter to Georg Buchholzer of 1 September 1543, Luther praised Buchholzer for preaching vigorously against the Jews, and argued that Agricola could not have made the sayings attributed to him in protection of the Jews. But if he had, then he would not be the Elector's preacher 'but a true devil, letting his sayings be so shamefully misused to the damnation of all those who associate with Jews' (WB 10, 3909, 389:24–6).

34. *Von den Jüden* appeared in January 1543, *Vom Schem Hamphoras* in March that year, and shortly after, *Von den letzten Worten Davids*, a third work against the Jews was published; Kaufmann, *Luthers Juden*, 136. Written in German, they addressed a wide lay public.

35. Luther, *Von den Jüden vnd jren Lügen. Vom Schem Hamphoras*, Leipzig 1577 [VD 16 L 7155]; Luther, *Drey Christliche/ In Gottes Wort wolgegründte Tractat Der Erste Von dem hohen vermeynten Jüdischen Geheymnuß/ dem Schem-Hamphoras . . .*, Frankfurt, 1617 [VD 17 3:306053V]

36. WB 1, 7 [Feb. 1514]; see, however, WB 1, 61, 22 Feb. 1518; Zika, *Reuchlin*; Zika, 'Reuchlin's *De Verbo Mirifico* and the Magic Debate of the late fifteenth century', *Journal of the Warburg and Courtauld Institutes* 39, 1976, 104–38.

37. See Jonathan Sheehan, 'Sacred and Profane: Idolatry, Antiquarianism and the Polemics of Distinction in the Seventeenth Century', *Past and Present* 192, 2006, 35–66. See StadtA Witt, 9 [Bb 6], 'Rabini Schemhamphoras' for a seventeenth-century crude single-leaf woodcut of the relief accompanied by a poem.

38.  WS 53, 587:2–4;21–3; 636:33–637:5.

39.  WS 53, 542:5–7.

40.  Kaufmann, *Luthers Juden*, 109–11, 119, 136. He also discussed the progress of his writings in letters to Jonas; Greschat, *Bucer*, 156–8.

41.  Scott Hendrix, 'Toleration of the Jews in the German Reformation: Urbanus Rhegius and Braunschweig 1535–1540' in Hendrix, *Tradition and Authority*, 193–201. Osiander, *Ob es war un[d] glablich sey*. Osiander, who was an outstanding Hebrew scholar, distanced himself from Luther's *Vom Schem Hamphoras* in a letter in Hebrew to Elias Levita; when this became public, Melanchthon sought to prevent Luther from hearing about it, fearing his reaction; Kaufmann, *Luthers Juden*, 138; Nirenberg, *Anti-Judaism*, 265.

42.  Johannes Eck, *Ains Juden büechlins verlegung darin ain Christ, gantzer Christenhait zu schmach, will es geschehe den Juden vnrecht in bezichtigung der Christen kinder mordt . . . ; hierin findst auch vil histori, was übels vnd bücherey die Juden in allem teütschen Land, vnd ändern Künigreichen gestift haben*, Ingolstadt, 1541 [VD 16 E 383]. Like Luther, he also drew on *Der gantz Jüdisch glaub* (*The Entire Jewish Faith*), written by the converted Jew Anton Margaritha and published at Augsburg in 1530. It was one of the chief sources for Luther's *On the Jews and their Lies*.

43.  LW 47, 219; WS 53, 483:34–5.

44.  WS 53, 614:31–2; 615:1–2.

## 19. The Charioteer of Israel

1.  So, for example, in 1538 Luther's brother Jacob and the Mansfeld preacher Michael Coelius visited Luther, complaining about Albrecht's policies toward the mineowners, WT 4, 3948, [1538]. In 1540 Luther petitioned Albrecht on behalf of his brother-in-law, Hans Mackenrod, asking he be allowed to keep the heritable leases of his mines which Albrecht was trying to convert to a lesser form of lease (WB 9, 3481, 24 May 1540); probably in 1542, he wrote a letter of spiritual counsel to Albrecht linking his problems to his greed for mining wealth (WB 9, 3716, 23 Feb. 1542) – Albrecht, enraged, trampled the letter underfoot; in 1542, Luther asked the new Lutheran ruler of ducal Saxony, Duke Moritz, to intercede with Count Albrecht on behalf of Bartholome Drachstedt, one of the old mining families with whom his father had worked, WB 10, 3723, 13 March(?) 1542; and he also wrote to counts Philip and Johann Georg of Mansfeld to get them to intercede with their co-ruler Albrecht (WB 10, 3724, 14 March 1542); see also WB 10, 3755, 23 May 1542.

2.  The words of Ratzeberger, Luther's physician and biographer; Ratzeberger, *Die handschriftliche Geschichte*, 126.

3. WB 10, 3760, 15 June 1542, see Introduction; Witzel left in 1538 and Hoyer was unable to find a Catholic to replace him. Hoyer died in 1540 and was succeeded by Philip and Johann Georg.

4. Ratzeberger, *Die handschriftliche Geschichte*, 126. Ratzeberger gives Luther's view of all this, interestingly explaining the development in moral terms, as Albrecht, seized with *Geitz* (miserliness), drives through his policy and overrides the investment and trouble the 'good people' have invested in running the mines while the counts enjoyed an '*überschwenglicher Pracht*', over-the-top splendour (127).

5. WB 10, 3724, 14 March 1542, 10:22–3; 26–9. He also wrote a letter of comfort to Hans Kegel (one of the Mansfeld region mine-owning families) at the request of his son Andreas about the '*entwanten Huettenwercks*', that is, the mine which had been taken away (WB 10, 3755, 23 May 1542).

6. WB 11, 4157, 7 Oct. 1545. He also interceded this time for his brother Jacob and his brother-in-law Henze Kaufmann.

7. LW Letters, III, 286–7; WS 11, 4191, 269:5–8; 13–14.

8. LW Letters, III, 290–1; WB 11, 4195, 1 Feb. 1546, 275:5–8; the term is '*angeblasen*' rather than 'attacked', which means that they had breathed at him, causing his illness.

9. LW Letters, III, 303–4; WB 11, 4201, 7 Feb. 1546, 34–7. He had earlier commented ironically to his wife, 'But now I am well, praise God, except that the beautiful women [=prostitutes] tempt me so severely, that I have neither concern nor fear of any unchastity' (WB 11, 4195, 1 Feb. 1546).

10. LW Letters, III, 291; WB 11, 4195, 1 Feb. 1546, 276:16–17.

11. See *Vermahnung an die Juden* 1546, which comes at the end of the four last sermons at Eisleben, printed at Wittenberg by Hans Lufft [VD 16 L 6963]; WS 51, 148–95; 195–6; and see also WB 11, 4201, 7 Feb. 1546.

12. This house was sold shortly after to Johann Albrecht, who treated the daybed on which Luther died, and the mug from which he drank as relics; Schubart, *Luthers Tod und Begräbnis*, 86–7.

13. Jonas and Coelius, *Vom Christlichen abschied* (eds Freybe and Bräuer), fos. A iii v–A [iv] v.

14. There had been several plots to assassinate Luther. See Ratzeberger, *Die handschriftliche Geschichte*, 69–72 for discussion of some of the later ones.

15. Jonas and Coelius, *Vom Christlichen abschied* (eds Freybe and Bräuer), fo. B ii (r–v).

16. Ibid., fo. B ii (v)–B iii (r).

17. The role of women in caring for Luther in his last days and advising on medicines has been remarked on by Rankin, *Panaceia's Daughters*, 8–9.

18. Jonas and Coelius, *Vom Christlichen abschied* (eds Freybe and Bräuer), fo. B [iv] (r); the prayer is in large type. Throughout his life Luther had regularly prayed against his enemies, including Duke Georg of Saxony, the Pope and Albrecht of Mainz; see Günther Wartenberg, 'Martin Luthers Beten für Freunde und gegen Feinde', *Lutherjahrbuch* 75, 2008, 113–24.

19. Jonas and Coelius, *Vom Christlichen abschied* (eds Freybe and Bräuer), fo. C (r–v). Luther's impending death had been a constant worry for his followers, and he had come close to the end several times before. For example, in 1537 at Schmalkalden, when it looked as if Luther would die, he took leave of them and made the same imprecations against the Pope that he would make when facing death in 1546; WT 3, 3543 A, 389:11–12.

20. They had also worried about the deaths of their own side. For example, when the Lutheran Nikolaus Hausmann died of the '*schlag*', the sudden end so feared by sixteenth-century people, Luther wrote to a friend that the death, though terrible, had yet been precious in the sight of God because Hausmann had been a just person; WB 8, 3286, 30 Dec. 1538; WT 4, 4084 [Nov. 1538].

21. He continued that if he could not have a pious servant of the Church, he would want a 'pious Christian' with him, who could comfort him from God's Word. In fact, Luther knew from both Bucer and Capito that Erasmus had not been alone, but was with the theologian Simon Grynaeus when he died. WB 7, 3048, 20 July 1536 (Capito to Luther); 3050, 22 July 1536 (Bucer to Luther); WT 4, 3963.

22. WB 10, 3848, 16 Feb. 1543 (Dietrich to Luther), 262:17–18; 263:21–2; 23–4; Martin Bucer, *De vera ecclesiarvm . . .*, Strasbourg . . ., 1542 [VD 16 B 8929]; Johannes Eck, *Replica Ioan. Eckii Adversvs Scripta secunda Buceri . . .*, Ingolstadt, 1543 [VD 16 E 416].

23. WB 10, 3725, 17 March 1542: it was said that he was seized by the Devil while still alive, or that he despaired of salvation because of his great errors, or that he had had himself exorcised. His friends supposedly described him as a second 'Anthony', plagued with visitations of the Devil. WB 10, 3728, 26 March 1542, Luther wrote to Jakob Propst in Bremen that Karlstadt had died of plague, 'he himself the plague of the Basle Church' as the bishops of his own Church had written to them (24:30–1), and he added the rumours concerning poltergeists in Karlstadt's house. The story about the tall stranger is given in a fragment of a letter from Veit Dietrich in Nuremberg to Luther, 3730, end of March 1542.

24. WB 10, 3732, 7 April 1542: Luther told the story Dietrich had told him to Amsdorf, adding the line about Karlstadt's fear of death. He referred

to it again in his next letter, WB 10, 3741, 13 April 1542, insisting the report had been true and that Karlstadt's death had been divine retribution for his pride and stubbornness. Writing to Jonas on 30 April 1542 (3745), he recounted the contents of a letter they had received from Karlstadt's widow, complaining of her bad treatment at his hands, their five children, debts and misery. One would say the man 'danced to Hell', Luther commented, 'no, he fairly leapt headlong to Hell', except that we cannot judge the dead. He and Melanchthon interceded with the council of Basle on her behalf (WB 10, 3756, 29 May 1542), but their petition explicitly avoided praising Karlstadt's role as a preacher, saying only that 'all the same, he was a servant of the Church amongst you'.

25. Ratzeberger, *Die handschriftliche Geschichte*, 135–41.

26. Schubart, *Luthers Tod und Begräbnis*, 24, Melanchthon to Amsdorf, 19 Feb. 1546; see also 50, 58, 82.

27. Schubart, *Luthers Tod und Begräbnis*, 74; Vandiver, Keen and Frazel (eds and trs), *Luther's Lives* (Cochlaeus), 347–9.

28. Schubart, *Luthers Tod und Begräbnis*, 77–9; 110–13. This scurrilous version was still circulating in the second half of the sixteenth century, and was reprinted by the Catholic Johannes Nas in his *Quinta Centuria*, Ingolstadt, 1570, 476 ff.

29. Coelius's funeral oration in Eisleben mentioned the gossip of people incited by the Devil who said Luther had been found dead in bed; Schubart, *Luthers Tod und Begräbnis*, 30–2.

30. Jonas and Coelius, *Vom Christlichen abschied* (eds Freybe and Bräuer), fos. C ii (v)–C iii (r).

31. Ibid., fo. D ii (r); Schubart, *Luthers Tod und Begräbnis*, 81.

32. *Oratio* (tr. Caspar Cruciger), in Jonas and Coelius, *Vom christlichen abschied* (eds Freybe and Bräuer), fo. B [iv] (r); Melanchthon freely admitted that 'his nature was ardent and irascible' and recalled that he had lacked mildness in his debate with Erasmus; Melanchthon in Vandiver, Keen and Frazel (eds and trs), *Luther's Lives*, 16; 21; 38–9; Philipp Melanchthon, *Vita Lutheri*, fo. 24 (v).

33. Ulinka Rublack, 'Grapho-Relics: Lutheranism and the Materialisation of the Word', *Past and Present*, Supplement 5, 2010, 144–66.

34. Luther may have been a little hard on Hans: on one occasion he refused to let him come into his presence for three days, insisting that he supplicate in writing and humble himself, with an apology. Katharina von Bora, Jonas Cruciger and Melanchthon all interceded to no avail, and Luther insisted he would rather have a dead son than a badly brought up one (WT 5, 6102). Luther's hatred of jurists was legendary. When young Martin was barely six months old, Luther said to him 'If you become a lawyer, I will hang you from a gallows' (WT 2, 1422).

One wonders what brother Hans, aged nearly six at the time, who eventually became a lawyer having been intended for the ministry, would have made of this. Ironically Martin was to be destined for law.

35.  Schwiebert, *Luther and his Times*, 594–602; Brecht, *Luther*, III, 235–44.

36.  Greschat, *Bucer*, 245–9. The *Kachelöfen* were tiled and very effective heating systems, the heart of every German home, and they were soon made in religious propagandist forms too, with tiles featuring anti-papal cartoons.

37.  Johann von Staupitz (and Johann Arndt), *Zwey alte geistreiche Büchlein Doctoris Johannis von Staupitz weiland Abts zu Saltzbergk zu S. Peter Das Erste. Von der holdseligen Liebe Gottes. Das Ander. Von unserm H. Christlichen Glauben; Zu erweckung der Liebe Gottes . . . in allen Gottseligen Hertzen*, Magdeburg, 1605 [VD 17 1:072800G].

38.  Reinitzer, *Gesetz und Evangelium*; Roper, 'Martin Luther's Body'; Roper, 'Luther Relics' in Jennifer Spinks and Dagmar Eichberger, eds., *Religion, the Supernatural and Visual Culture in Early Modern Europe*, Leiden, 2015.

39.  Brown, *Singing the Gospel*, 1–25; Oettinger, *Music as Propaganda*; Veit, *Das Kirchenlied*. The first hymn books were produced in 1524; Luther wrote about forty hymns himself.

40.  WT 3, 3739.

41.  The emotional passage is so out of character with the factual reportage of the rest of the journal that its authenticity has been doubted; Schauerte, *Dürer*, 235. On the self portraits, see Koerner, *Moment of Self-Portraiture*.

42.  Dürer, *Memoirs of Journeys*, 55; 62–7.

43.  Günzburg, *The Fifteen Confederates* (ed. and tr. Dipple), Third Confederate, around n.124, around n.120, three paras after n.119; Günzburg, *Ein vermanung*, fos. I iii (r); ii (v). As he writes: 'Oh mother with a heart of stone, how faithless you are to your child. Do you think she is made of wood or iron, that she will not necessarily feel the burning desires of the flesh, just as you felt them . . . ?' (Günzburg, *Ein vermanung*, fo. ii (r)).

44.  Argula von Grumbach, 'Wie eyn Christliche fraw des adels . . .' in Grumbach, *Schriften* (ed. and tr. Matheson), 36–75. The letter also circulated in manuscript.

45.  Grumbach, *Eyn Antwort*, (s.l.), 1524, fo. D ii (r); D ii (v).

46.  Skinner, *Foundations*, 2, 3–19; Brady, *German Histories*, 221; Cargill Thompson, *Studies in the Reformation* (ed. Dugmore), 3–41; see, however, Kolb, *Martin Luther. Confessor of the Faith*, 194–5. Reluctantly, Luther did eventually move to a legal position that argued that the Electors were the equal of the emperor, and so could be resisted. He also began to see the emperor as the Pope's agent.

47. These had a powerful visual legacy, inspiring, for instance, the wall paintings in the Lutheran church at Pirna, where Luther and Melanchthon are depicted on the ceiling as evangelists.

48. There was also, however, a Bible in Low German produced by Luther's co-worker Johannes Bugenhagen, first the New Testament in 1524, *Dat Nye Testament*, Wittenberg 1524 [VD 16 B 4501]; and then the complete Bible in 1533–4 [VD 16 B 2840], so Luther's Bible did not always work to unify the German language. I am grateful to Edmund Wareham for this point.

49. Melanchthon, *Vita Lutheri*, fo. 13 (r).

# Bibliography

## ARCHIVES AND LIBRARIES CONSULTED

Stadtarchiv Wittenberg
Lutherhalle Wittenberg
Evangelisches Predigerseminar Wittenberg Bibliothek
Thüringisches Hauptstaatsarchiv Weimar
Landesarchiv Sachsen-Anhalt Abteilung Magdeburg, Standort Magdeburg
Landesarchiv Sachsen-Anhalt, Standort Wernigerode
Stadtarchiv Eisenach
Stadtarchiv Eisleben
Landesdenkmalamt Halle
Marienbibliothek Halle
Landesbibliothek Coburg
Forschungsbibliothek Gotha
Staatsbibliothek zu Berlin – Preußischer Kulturbesitz
Herzog August Bibliothek Wolfenbüttel


## PRIMARY LITERATURE

*Acta et res gestae, D Martini Lvtheri* [VD 16 ZV 61]

Melchior Adam, *The life and death of Dr. Martin Luther the passages whereof have bin taken out of his owne and other Godly and most learned, mens writings, who lived in his time*, London 1643.

Georg Agricola, *De re metallica Libri XII*, Basle 1556 (repr. Wiesbaden 2006).

*Ain löbliche ordnung der fürstlichen stat Wittemberg: Jm tausent fünfhundert vnd zway vnd zwaintzigsten jar auffgericht*, Augsburg 1522 [VD 16 W 3697].

Fabian von Auerswald, *Ringer kunst*, Wittenberg 1539 [VD 16 A 4051].

Johannes Aurifaber, ed., *Epistolae: continens scriptas ab anno Millesimo quingentesimo vigesimo usq[ue] ad annum vigesimum octauum*, vol. 2, 1594.

Valentin Bavarus, 'Rapsodiae et Dicta quedam ex ore Doctoris Martini Lutheri', vol. 2, 1549, in Otto Scheel, ed., *Dokumente zu Luthers Entwicklung*, vol. 1, Tübingen 1929.

Michael Baylor, ed. and tr., *Revelation and Revolution: Basic Writings of Thomas Müntzer*, Bethlehem, PA 1993.

Thomas W. Best, ed., *Eccius dedolatus: A Reformation Satire*, Lexington, KY 1971.

Johann Biering, *Historische Beschreibung Des sehr alten und löblichen Mannßfeldischen Berg-Wercks Nach seinen Anfang, Fortgang, Fatis, Berg-Grentzen, Lehn-Briefen, Privilegiis, Zusammens*, Leipzig and Eisleben 1734.

Heinrich Bullinger, *Warhaffte Bekanntnuß der Dieneren der Kirchen zuo Zürych, was sy uss Gottes Wort mit der heiligen allgemeinen christenlichen Kirchen gloubind und leerind, in Sonderheit aber von dem Nachtmal unsers Herren Jesu Christi :. . . mit zuogethoner kurtzer Bekenntniß D. Mart. Luthers vom heiligen Sacrament*, Zurich 1545 [VD 16 B 9770].

Fritz Büsser, ed., *Beschreibung des Abendmahlsstreites von Johann Stumpf. Auf Grund einer unbekannt gebliebenen Handschrift*, Zurich 1960.

Wolfgang Capito, *Frohlockung eines christlichen Bruders von wegen der Vereinigung zwischen D.M. Luther und D. Andres Carolstat sich begeben*, Speyer 1526 [VD 16 F 3099].

Johannes Cochlaeus, *Brevis Germaniae Descriptio (1512)*, Rudolf Buchner, ed., Darmstadt 1976.

Johannes Cochlaeus, *Colloqvivm Cochlaei cvm Lvthero, Vuormatiae olim habitum, Anno Domini M.D.XXI*, Mainz 1540 [VD 16 C 4277].

Johannes Cochlaeus, *Hertzog Georgens zu Sachssen Ehrlich vnd grundtliche entschuldigung, wider Martin Luthers Auffruerisch vn[d] verlogenne brieff vnd Verantwortung*, Dresden 1533 [VD 16 C 4323].

Johann Cochlaeus (Vogelsang), 'Ein Heimlich Gespräch von der Tragedia Johannis Hussen, 1538', in Hugo Holstein, ed., *Flugschriften aus der Reformationszeit* 17, Halle, 1900.

*Constitutiones Fratrum Heremitarum sancti Augustini ad apostolicorum privilegiorum forman p[ro] Reformatione Alemanie*, Nuremberg 1504 [VD 16 A 4142].

Lucas Cranach, *Dye Zaigung des hochlobwirdigen Hailigthumbs der Stifft-Kirchen aller Hailigen zu Wittenberg*, Wittenberg 1509 [VD 16 Z 250].

Caspar Cruciger, *Etliche Trostschrifften vnd predigten / fur die so in tods vnd ander not vnd anfechtung sind*, Wittenberg 1545 [VD 16 L 3463].

*Die Bekenntnisschriften der evangelisch-lutherischen Kirche*, 7th edn, Göttingen 1976

Lothar Graf zu Dohna and Richard Wetzel, eds, *Johann von Staupitz, Sämtliche Schriften: Abhandlungen, Predigten, Zeugnisse*, 2 vols, Berlin and New York 1979, 1987.

Mathaeus Dresser, *De festis diebus Christianorum, Judaeorum et ethnicorum liber*, Leipzig 1588 [VD 16 D 2707].

Albrecht Dürer, *Memoirs of Journeys to Venice and the Low Countries*, tr. Rudolf Tombo, Auckland 1913 (repr. Hamburg 2014).

Johannes Eck, *Ains Juden büechlins verlegung darin ain Christ, gantzer Christen-hait zu schmach, will es geschehe den Juden vnrecht in bezichtigung der Christen kinder mordt . . . ; hierin findst auch vil histori, was übels vnd bücherey die Juden in allem teütschen Land, vnd ändern Künigreichen gestift haben,* Ingolstadt 1541 [VD 16 E 383].

Johannes Eck, *Doctor Martin ludders Underricht an Kurfursten von Sachssen. disputation zu Leypszig belangent : vnnd D. Eckius briue. von der selbigen Autor,* Augsburg 1520 [VD 16 L 6831].

Johannes Eck, *Epistola Iohan. Eckii Theologi, de ratione studiorum suorum,* Ingolstadt 1543 [VD 16 E 364].

*Ein erbermlich geschicht So an dem frommen christlichen man Tauber von Wien ... gescheen ist,* Magdeburg 1524 [VD 16 ZV 5338].

Andreas Engel, *Kurzer / Jedoch gewisser vnd gründtlicher Bericht / von Johan Hilten / vnd seinen Weissagungen,* Frankfurt an der Oder 1597 [VD 16 ZV 5013].

Karl Euling, ed., *Chronik des Johan Oldecop,* Stuttgart 1891.

Evangelische Predigerseminar Wittenberg, ed., *'Vom Christlichen abschied aus diesem tödlichen leben des Ehrwirdigen Herrn D Martini Lutheri'. Drei zeitgenössische Texte zum Tode D Martin Luthers,* Stuttgart 1996.

Tibor Fabiny, *Martin Luther's Last Will and Testament. A facsimile of the original document,* Dublin 1982.

Carl Eduard Förstemann, ed., *Neues Urkundenbuch zur Geschichte der evangelischen Kirchenreformation,* Hamburg 1842.

Edward J. Furcha, ed. and tr., *The Essential Carlstadt,* Waterloo, Ontario 1995.

Joseph Greving, 'Colloquium Cochlaei cum Luthero Wormatiae olim habitum', in Otto Clemen, ed., *Flugschriften aus den ersten Jahren der Reformation,* vol. 4, Halle 1911, repr. Nieuwkoop 1967.

Johann Christian August Grohmann, ed., *Annalen der Universität zu Wittenberg,* 3 vols, Meissen 1801–2 (repr. Osnabrück 1969).

Argula von Grumbach, *Eyn Antwort in gedichtsweyß, ainem aus der hohen Schul zu Ingolstadt, auff ainen spruch, newlich von jm außgangen,* Nuremberg 1524 [VD 16 G 3660].

Argula von Grumbach, 'Wie eyn Christliche fraw des adels . . .', in Peter Matheson, ed., *Argula von Grumbach, Schriften,* Gütersloh 2010.

Johann Eberlin von Günzburg, *Ein vermanung aller christen das sie sich erbarmen uber die klosterfrawen: Thuo kein Tochter in ein kloster du lassest dann diss büchlein vor: Der .III. bundtgnosz,* Basle 1521 [VD 16 E 100].

Johann Eberlin von Günzburg, *The Fifteen Confederates,* Geoffrey Dipple, ed. and tr., Cambridge 2014.

Johann Eberlin von Günzburg, *Vo[m] misbrauch Christlicher freyheyt,* Grimma 1522 [VD 16 E 149].

Kenneth Hagen, 'An addition to the Letters of John Lang. Introduction and Translation', *Archiv für Reformationsgeschichte* 60, 1969, 27–32.

Wilfried Härle, Johannes Schilling, Günther Wartenberg and Michael Beyer (eds), *Martin Luther. Lateinisch-Deutsche Studienausgabe*, Leipzig 2006–.

Johann Hasenberg, *Lvdvs lvdentem lvdervm lvdens . . .*, Landshut 1530 [VD 16 H 714].

Hermann Helmbold, ed., *Chronik Eisenachs bis 1409*, Eisenach 1914.

Ulrich Hutten, *Ulrichs von Hutten verteütscht clag / an Hertzog Friderich zu Sachsen. Des hayligen Rœmischen Reichs Ertzmarschalck vñ Churfürsten Landgrauen in Türingen / vnd Marckgrauen zu Meissen*, Augsburg 1521 [VD 16 H 6251].

Valentin Ickelsamer, *Clag ettlicher Brieder, an alle Christen, von der großen Ungerechtigkeyt und Tyranney, so Endressen Bodenstein . . . vom Luther . . . geschicht*, Augsburg 1525 [VD 16 I 32].

Justus Jonas, *Das der freie wille nichts sey*, Wittenberg 1526 [VD 16 L 6674].

Justas Jonas and Michael Coelius, *Vom Christlichen abschied . . .*, in Peter Freybe, ed., *Vom Christlichen Abschied aus diesem tödlichen Leben des Ehrwirdigen Herrn D. Martini Lutheri: Drei zeitgenössische Texte zum Tode D. Martin Luthers*, Stuttgart 1996.

Andreas Karlstadt, *Auszlegung vnnd Lewterung etzlicher heyligenn geschrifften / So dem menschen dienstlich vnd erschieszlich seint zu Christlichem lebe˜. kurtzlich berurth vnd angetzeiche˜t in den figurn vnd schrifften der wagen*, Leipzig 1519 [VD 16 B 6113].

Andreas Karlstadt, *Anzeyg etlicher Hauptartickeln Christlicher leere Jn wölchen Doct. Luther den Andresen Carolstat durch falsche zusag vnd nachred verdechtig macht*, Augsburg 1525 [VD 16 B 6099].

Andreas Karlstadt, *Auslegung dieser wort Christi. Das ist meyn leyb / welcher für euch gegeben würt. Das ist mein bluoth / welches für euch vergossen würt*, Basle 1524 [VD 16 B 6111].

Andreas Karlstadt, *De Coelibatv, Monachatv, et Vidvitate*, Basle 1521 [VD 16 B 6123].

Andreas Karlstadt, *Endschuldigung D. Andres Carlstadt des falschen namens der aufrür, so yhm ist mit vnrecht auffgelegt. Mit eyner vorrhede Doct.Martini Luthers*. Wittenberg, 1525 [VD 16 B 6152].

Andreas Karlstadt, *Erklärung wie Karlstadt seine Lehre vom hochwürdigen Sakrament und andere geachtet haben will*, Strasbourg 1525 [VD 16 B 6162].

Andreas Karlstadt, *Missiue von der aller hochsten tugent gelassenhait*, Augsburg 1520 [VD 16 B 6170].

Andreas Karlstadt, *Von abtuhung der Bylder / Vnd das keyn Betdler vnther den Christen seyn sollen*, Wittenberg 1522, [VD 16 B 6215],

Andreas Karlstadt, *Von anbettung und ererbietung der tzeychen des newen Testaments*, Wittenberg 1521 [VD 16 B 6218].

Andreas Karlstadt, *Uon gelubden vnterrichtung Andres Bo. von Carolstadt Doctor Außlegung, des xxx. capitel Numeri, wilches von gelubden redet*, Wittenberg 1521 [VD 16 B 6245].

Andras Karlstads, *Die Messe. Von der Hochzeyt D. Andre Carolstadt. Vnnd der Priestern / so sich Eelich verheyratteno* Augsburg 1522 [VD 16 M 5492].

Andreas Karlstadt, *Was gesagt ist Sich gelassen vnd was das wort gelassenhait bedeüt vnd wa es in hailiger geschrifft begriffen*, Augsburg 1523 [VD 16 B 6256].

Gustav Kawerau, ed., *Der Briefwechsel des Justus Jonas*, 2 vols, Halle 1884–5.

*Kayserlicher maiestat Einreyttung zu Augspurg, den X. tag Junij. Im M.CCCCC. vnd XXX Jar . . .*, Nuremberg 1530 [VD 16 K 37].

Hermann von Kerssenbrock, *Narrative of the Anabaptist Madness. The Overthrow of Münster, the famous Metropolis of Westphalia*, ed. and tr. Christopher Mackay, Leiden 2007.

Joachim K. F Knaake, ed., *Johann von Staupitzens sämtliche Werke*, 2 vols, Potsdam 1867.

Theodor Kolde, ed., *Analecta Lutherana. Briefe und Actenstücke zur Geschichte Luthers. Zugleich ein Suppl. zu den bisherigen Sammlungen seines Briefwechsels*, Gotha 1883.

Erich König, *Konrad Peutingers Briefwechsel*, Munich 1923.

Königliche Bayerische Akadamie der Wissenschaften, Historische Kommission (ed.), *Die Chroniken der schwäbischen Städte. Augsburg*, 9 vols, Leipzig 1865–96.

Michael Kuen, *Lucifer Wittenbergensis*, Landsberg 1747.

Christian Lehmann, *Historischer Schauplatz derer natürlichen Merckwürdigkeiten in dem Meißnischen Ober-Ertzgebirge*, Leipzig 1699 [VD 17 3:302104H].

Simon Lemnius, M. *Simonis Lemnii Epigrammaton Libri III*, [s.l.] 1538 [VD 16 L 1133].

Johannes Lening, *Dialogus das ist ein freundtlich Gesprech Zw eyer personen, davon, Ob es Göttlichem, Natürlichen, Keyserlichem, und Geystlichem Rechte gemesse oder entgegen sei, mehr denn eyn Eeweib zugleich zu haben. Vnnd wo yemant zu diser zeit solchs fürnehme ob er als eyn vnchrist zuuerwerffen vnd zuuerdammen sei oder nit*, Marburg 1541 [VD 16 L 1174].

*Litaneia Germanorvm*, Augsburg 1521 [VD 16 ZV 25246].

Anton Margaritha, *Der gantz jüdisch Glaub: mit sampt einer gründlichen vnd warhafftigen anzaygunge, aller Satzungen, Ceremonien, Gebetten . . .*, Augsburg 1530 [VD 16 M 972].

Johannes Mathesius, *Historien von dem Leben und den Schicksalen des grossen Reformators Doctor Martin Luther Im Jahre 1565 in 17 Predigten beschrieben*, 1566 (repr. Leipzig 1806).

Johannes Mathesius, *Sarepta oder Bergpostill*, Nuremberg 1562 [VD 16 M 1439].

Peter Matheson, ed., *The collected works of Thomas Münzter*, Edinburgh 1988.

Johann Friedrich Mayer, *De Catharina Lutheri coniuge dissertatio*, Hamburg 1699 [VD 17 3:019103C].

Johann Mayer, *Des unsterblichen Gottes-Gelehrten Herrn D. Johann Friedrich Mayers Unsterbliches Ehren-Gedächtnis Frauen Catharinen Lutherin einer gebohrnen von Bora,* . . . Frankfurt and Leipzig 1724.

Andreas Meinhardi, *Über die Lage, die Schönheit und den Ruhm der hochberühmten, herrlichen Stadt Albioris, gemeinhin Wittenberg genannt,* Leipzig 1508, Martin Treu, tr., Leipzig 1986.

Philipp Melanchthon, *Vita Lutheri,* Frankfurt am Main 1555 [VD 16 M 3428].

*Melanchthons Briefwechsel. Kritische und kommentierte Gesamtausgabe,* eds. Heinz Scheible und Christine Mundhenk. Stuttgart-Bad Cannstatt, 1977 ff.

*Philipp Melanchthons Briefwechsel – Regesten on line,* Heidelberger Akademie der Wissenschaften.

Mathis Miechowa, *Tractat von baiden Sarmatien vnd andern anstossenden landen, in Asia vnd Europa, von sitten vnd gepraeuchen der voelcker so darinnen wonen,* Augsburg 1518 [VD 16 M 5189].

Clarence H. Miller, ed., *Erasmus and Luther. The Battle over Free Will,* tr. Clarence H. Miller and Peter Macardle, with an Introduction by James D. Tracy, Indianapolis 2012.

Walter Möllenberg, ed., *Urkundenbuch zur Geschichte des Mansfeldischen Saigerhandels im 16. Jahrhundert,* Halle 1915.

Lothar Mundt, *Lemnius und Luther,* 2 vols, Bern and Frankfurt am Main 1983.

Thomas Müntzer, *Außgetrückte emplössung des falschen Glaubens der vngetrewen welt,* Nuremberg 1524 [VD 16 M 6745].

Thomas Müntzer, *Auszlegung des andern vnterschyds Danielis,* Allstedt 1524 [VD 16 M 6746]

Thomas Müntzer, *Briefwechsel,* ed. Siegfried Bräuer, Helmar Junghans, Manfred Kobuch, Leipzig 2010.

Thomas Müntzer, *Hoch verursachte Schutzrede und antwort wider das Gaistloße Sanfft lebende fleysch zu Wittenberg,* [Nuremberg] 1524 [VD 16 M 6747]

Thomas Müntzer, *Prager Manifest,* ed. Friedrich de Boor with introduction by Hans-Joachim Rockar, Leipzig 1975.

Thomas Müntzer, *Quellen zu Thomas Müntzer,* ed Wieland Held and Siegfried Hoyer, Leipzig 2004.

Friedrich Myconius, *Geschichte der Reformation,* ed. Otto Clemen, Leipzig 1914 repr. Gotha 1990.

Friedrich Myconius, *EPISTOLA SCRIPTA AD D. Vitum Theodorum . . . DE CONCORDIA inita VVitebergae inter D. D. Martinum Lutherum, & Bucerum anno 36,* Leipzig 1581 [VD 16 M 7350].

Johannes Nas, *Quinta Centvria, Das ist Das fuenfft Hundert der Euangelischen warheit,* Ingolstadt 1570 [VD 16 N 105].

Christian Gotthold Neudecker, ed., *Die handschriftliche Geschichte Ratzeberger's über Luther und seine Zeit,* Jena 1850.

Christian Gotthold Neudecker and Ludwig Preller, eds, *Georg Spalatin's historischer Nachlass und Briefe*, Jena 1851.

*Newe ordnung der Stat Wittenberg, MDXXII. jar*, Bamberg 1522 [VD 16 W 3698].

*Newe zeytung von den Wydertaufferen zu Münster*, Nuremberg 1535 [VD 16 N 876].

Heinirch L. Nickel, ed., *Das Hallesche Heiltumbuch von 1520*, Halle 2001.

Andreas Osiander, *Ob es war vn[d] glaublich sey, daß die Juden der Christen kinder heymlich erwürgen, vnd jr blut gebrauchen : ein treffenliche schrifft, auff eines yeden vrteyl gestelt*, Nuremberg 1530 [VD 16 O 1079].

Christian Franz Paullini, *Historia Isenacensis*, Frankfurt 1698 [VD 17 3:300044V].

Franz Posset, ed., *The Front-Runner of the Catholic Reformation: The Life and Works of Johann von Staupitz*, Aldershot 2003.

Wilhelm Reindell, ed., *Doktor Wenzeslaus Linck aus Colditz*, vol. 1, Marburg 1892.

Wilhelm Reindell, ed., *Wenzel Lincks Wercke*, vol. 1, Marburg 1894.

David Richter, *Genealogia Lutherorum; oder historische Erzehlung von D. Mart. Lutheri . . . heutigen Anverwandten; . . . Hochzeits-Tag, und seines . . . Gemahls Familie; . . . jetziger Posterität . . . also verfertiget, dass die teutschen Opera Lutheri . . . ergäntzet und . . . continuiret, auch mit . . . Kupfern gezieret worden*, Berlin and Leipzig 1733.

Johannes Rubius, *Eyn neu buchlein von d'loblichen disputation offentlich gehalten vor fursten vnd vor hern vor hochgelarten vnd vngelarten yn der warden hochgepreusten stat Leyptzick inn reymen weisz*, Leipzig 1519 [VD 16 R 3409].

Friedrich Wilhelm Schirrmacher, ed., *Briefe und Akten zum Marburger Religionsgespräch (1529) und zum Augsburger Reichstag (1530)*, Gotha, 1876 (repr. Bonn 2003).

Wolfram Schneide-Lastin, ed., *Johann von Staupitz. Salzburger Predigten 1512. Eine textkritische Edition*, Tübingen 1990.

*Scriptorum publice propositorum a gvbernatoribus studiorum in Academia Wittenbergensi*, vol. 3, Wittenberg 1559 [VD 16 W 3761].

Otto Seitz, ed., *Der authentische Text der Leipziger Disputation (1519) aus bisher unbenutzten Quellen*, Berlin 1903.

Ronald J. Sider, ed. and tr., *Karlstadt's Battle with Luther. Documents in a Liberal-Radical Debate*, Eugene, OR, 2001.

*So an dem frommen christlichen man Tauber von Wien . . . gescheen ist*, Magdeburg 1524 [VD 16 ZV 5338].

Franz von Soden and J. R. F. Knaake, eds, *Christoph Scheurls Briefbuch. Ein Beitrag zur Geschichte der Reformation und ihrer Zeit*, 2 vols, Potsdam 1867, 1872 (repr. Aalen 1962).

Georg Spalatin, *Annales Reformationis Oder Jahr-Bücher von der Reformation Lvtheri*, ed. Ernst Salomon Cyprian, Leipzig 1718.

Cyriakus Spangenberg, *Mansfeldische Chronica. Der Erste Theil*, Eisleben 1572 [VD 16 S 7635].

Cyriakus Spangenberg, *Mansfeldische Chronik*, Book 4, Part 1, Naumburg 1912, 2007.

Johann Staupitz, *Ein buchlein von der nachfolgung des willigen sterbens*, Leipzig 1515 [VD 16 S 8697].

Johann Staupitz, *Ein seligs newes Jar/ von der lieb gottes*, Leipzig 1518 [VD 16 S 8708].

Johann Staupitz, *Ein nutzbarliches büchlein von der entlichen volziehung ewiger fuersehung*, Nuremberg 1517 [VD 16 S 8703].

Johann Staupitz and Johann Arndt, *Zwey alte gestreiche Büchlein / Doctoris Johannis von Staupitz / Das Erste. Von der holdseligen Liebe Gottes. Das Ander. Von unserm H. Christlichen Glauben ; Zu erweckung der Liebe Gottes . . . in allen Gottseligen Hertzen*, Magdeburg 1605 [VD 17 1:072800G].

Stiftung Luthergedenkstätten in Sachsen-Anhalt, ed., *Passional Christi und Antichristi*, Wittenberg 1998.

Johann Stumpf, *Beschreibung des Abendmahlsstreites*, ed. Fritz Büsser, Zurich 1960.

Petrus Sylvius, *Die Letzten zwey beschilisslich und aller krefftigest büchleyn M. Petri Sylvii, so das Lutherisch thun an seiner person . . .*, Leipzig 1534 [VD 16 P 1296].

Andreas Topp, *Historia der Stadt Eisenach (1660), (= Junckers Chronik 1710 Teil 2, Historie der Stadt Eisenach)*, 1916.

Elizabeth Vandiver, Ralph Keen and Thomas D. Frazel, eds and trs, *Luther's Lives. Two Contemporary Accounts of Martin Luther*, Manchester 2002.

*Vitae Germanorum Theologorum*, Frankfurt 1620 [VD 17 1:001326M].

Christian Walch, *Wahrhaftige Geschichte der seligen Frau Catharina von Bora, D. Mart. Luthers Ehegattin*, Halle 1751–4.

Gerhard Westerburg, *Vom Fegefewer vnd Standt der verscheyden selen eyn Christliche Meynung*, Cologne 1523 [VD 16 W 2215].

Georg Witzel, *Apologia: das ist: ein vertedigs rede Georgij Wicelij widder seine auffterreder die Luteristen . . .*, Leipzig 1533 [VD 16 H 3842].

Adolf Wrede, ed., *Deutsche Reichstagsakten, Jüngere Reihe*, vol. 2, Gotha 1896.


## SECONDARY WORKS CITED

Gadi Algazi, 'Habitus, familia und forma vitae: Die Lebensweisen mittelalterlicher Gelehrten in muslimischen, jüdischen und christlichen Gemeinden – vergleichend betrachtet', in Frank Rexroth, ed., *Beiträge zur Kulturgeschichte der Gelehrten im späten Mittelalter*, Ostfildern 2010.

David Bagchi, *Luther's Earliest Opponents: Catholic Controversialists, 1518–1525*, Minneapolis 1991.

Janos Bak, ed., *The German Peasant War of 1525*, London 1976.

Katharina Bärenfänger, Volker Leppin and Stefan Michel, eds, *Martin Luthers Tischreden*, Tübingen 2013.

Hermann Barge, *Andreas Bodenstein von Karlstadt*, 2 vols, Leipzig 1980 (repr. Leipzig 2007).

Fritz Bellmann, Marie-Luise Harksen and Roland Werner, eds, *Die Denkmale der Lutherstadt Wittenberg*, Weimar 1979.

Josef Benzing, *Lutherbibliographie. Verzeichnis der gedruckten Schriften Martin Luthers bis zu dessen Tod*, 3 vols, Baden-Baden 1965–6.

Gerd Bergmann, *Kommunalbewegung und innerstädtische Kämpfe im mittelalterlichen Eisenach*, Eisenach 1987.

Peter Blickle, *The Revolution of 1525: The German Peasants' War from a New Perspective*, tr. Thomas A. Brady and H. C. Erik Midelfort, Baltimore and London 1981 (Munich and Vienna 1975).

Hartmut Bobzins, "Aber itzt . . . hab ich den Alcoran gesehen Latinisch . . ." Gedanken Martin Luthers zum Islam', in Hans Medick and Peer Schmidt, eds, *Luther zwischen den Kulturen. Zeitgenossenschaft – Weltwirkung*, Göttingen 2004.

Thomas Brady, *German Histories in the Age of Reformations, 1400–1650*, Cambridge 2009.

Siegfried Bräuer, 'Die Stadt Mansfeld in der Chronik des Cyriakus Spangenberg', in Rosemarie Knape, ed., *Martin Luther und Eisleben*, Leipzig 2007.

Martin Brecht, *Martin Luther*, 3 vols, tr. James L. Schaaf, Minneapolis 1985–93 (Stuttgart 1981–7).

Christopher Boyd Brown, *Singing the Gospel. Lutheran Hymns and the Success of the Reformation*, Cambridge, MA 2005.

Ulrich Bubenheimer, *Consonantia Theologiae et Iurisprudentiae. Andreas von Karlstadt als Theologe und Jurist zwischen Scholastik und Reformation*, Tübingen 1977.

Ulrich Bubenheimer, *Thomas Müntzer. Herkunft und Bildung*, Leiden 1989.

Ulrich Bubenheimer, 'Gelassenheit und Ablösung. Eine psychohistorische Studie über Andreas Bodenstein von Karlstadt und seinen Konflikt mit Martin Luther', *Zeitschrift für Kirchengeschichte* 92, 1981, 250–68.

Ulrich Bubenheimer, 'Luthers Stellung zum Aufruhr in Wittenberg 1520–22 und die frühreformatorischen Wurzeln des landesherrlichen Kirchenregiments', *Zeitschrift der Savigny-Stiftung für Rechtsgeschichte, Kanonistische Abteilung* 102, 1985, 147–214.

Ulrich Bubenheimer, 'Scandalum et ius divinum. Theologische und rechtstheologische Probleme der ersten reformatorischen Innovationen in

Wittenberg 1521/22', *Zeitschrift der Savigny-Stiftung für Rechtsgeschichte, Kanonistische Abteilung* 90, 1973, 263–342.

Amy Nelson Burnett, *Karlstadt and the Origins of the Eucharistic Controversy. A Study in the Circulation of Ideas*, Oxford 2011.

Bruno Bushart, *Die Fuggerkapelle bei St. Anna in Augsburg*, Munich 1994.

Livia Cardenas, *Friedrich der Weise und das Wittenberger Heiltumsbuch. Mediale Repräsentation zwischen Mittelalter und Neuzeit*, Berlin 2002.

Carl Christensen, *Princes and Propaganda: Electoral Saxon Art of the Reformation*, Kirksville 1992.

Harry Clark, 'The Publication of the Koran in Latin: A Reformation Dilemma', *The Sixteenth Century Journal*, 15/1, 1984, 3–12.

Claus Peter Clasen, *Anabaptism. A Social History, 1525–1618: Switzerland, Austria, Moravia, South and Central Germany*, Ithaca 1972.

Otto Clemen, 'Die Leidensgeschichte der Ursula Toplerin', *Zeitschrift für bayerische Kirchengeschichte* 7, 1932, 161–70.

Cranach-Stiftung, ed., *Lucas Cranach d. Ä. und die Cranachhöfe in Wittenberg*, Halle 1998.

Allyson F. Creasman, 'The Virgin Mary against the Jews: Anti-Jewish Polemic in the Pilgrimage to the Schöne Maria of Regensburg, 1519–25', *The Sixteenth Century Journal*, 33/4, 2002, 963–80.

Gerrit Deutschländer, 'Spalatin als Prinzenerzieher', in Armin Kohnle, Christina Meckelnborg and Uwe Schirmer, eds, *Georg Spalatin. Steuermann der Reformation*, Halle 2014.

Hans-Jürgen Döhle, 'Schwein, Geflügel und Fisch – bei Luthers zu Tisch', in Harald Meller, ed., *Luther in Mansfeld: Forschungen am Elternhaus des Reformators*, Halle 2007.

Richard van Dülmen, *Reformation als Revolution. Soziale Bewegung und religiöser Radikalismus in der deutschen Reformation*, Munich 1977, Frankfurt am Main 1987.

Warren Alexander Dym, *Divining Science. Treasure Hunting and Earth Science in Early Modern Germany*, Leiden and Boston 2011.

Mark U. Edwards, Jr., *Printing, Propaganda, and Martin Luther*, Los Angeles and London 1994.

Mark U. Edwards, Jr., 'Luther as Media Virtuoso and Media Persona', in Hans Medick and Peer Schmidt, eds, *Luther zwischen den Kulturen. Zeitgenossenschaft – Weltwirkung*, Göttingen 2004.

Johannes Ehmann, *Luther, Türken und Islam*, Göttingen 2008.

Friedrich Engels, *The Peasant War in Germany*, tr. M. J. Olgin, London 1927 (1850).

Erik H. Erikson, *Young Man Luther. A Study in Psychoanalysis and History*, New York 1958, 1962.

Edith Eschenhagen, 'Beiträge zur Sozial- und Wirtschaftsgeschichte der Stadt Wittenberg in der Reformationszeit', *Lutherjahrbuch* 9, 1927, 9–118.

Thomas Eser, *Hans Daucher*, Munich and Berlin 1996.

Lucien Febvre, *Martin Luther*, ed., tr., and afterword by Peter Schöttler, Frankfurt 1996 (Paris 1928).

Michael Fessner, 'Das Montanwesen in der Grafschaft Mansfeld vom ausgehenden 15. bis zur zweiten Hälfte des 16. Jahrhunderts', in Angelika Westermann, ed., *Montanregion als Sozialregion. Zur gesellschaftlichen Dimension von 'Region' in der Montanwirtschaft*, Husum 2012.

Michael Fessner, 'Die Familie Luder in Möhra und Mansfeld', in Harald Meller, ed., *Fundsache Luther: Archäologen auf den Spuren des Reformators*, Stuttgart 2008.

Michael Fessner, 'Die Familie Luder und das Bergwerks- und Hüttenwesen in der Grafschaft Mansfeld und im Herzogtum Braunschweig-Wolfenbüttel', in Rosemarie Knape, ed., *Martin Luther und Eisleben*, Leipzig 2007.

Michael Fessner, 'Luthers Speisezettel. Die Versorgung der Grafschaft Mansfeld mit Lebensmitteln, Gütern und Waren', in Harald Meller, ed., *Luther in Mansfeld, Forschungen am Elternhaus des Reformators*, Halle 2007.

Adam S. Francisco, *Martin Luther and Islam. A Study in Sixteenth-Century Polemics and Apologetics*, Leiden and Boston 2007.

Günther Franz, *Der deutsche Bauernkrieg*, Darmstadt 1956 (Berlin 1933).

Peter Freybe (ed), *Luther und seine Freunde*, Wittenberg 1998.

Hanns Freydank, *Martin Luther und der Bergbau*, Eisleben 1939.

Hanns Freydank, 'Vater Luther der Hüttenmeister', in Hermann Etzrodt and Kurt Kronenberg, eds, *Das Eisleber Lutherbuch 1933*, Eisleben 1933.

Erich Fromm, *The Fear of Freedom*, London 1942, 2001.

Hans-Jürgen Goetz, *The Anabaptists*, tr. Trever Johnson, London 1996 (Munich 1980).

Martin Greschat, *Martin Bucer. A Reformer and His Times*, tr. Stephen E. Buckwalter, Louisville 2004 (Munich 1990).

Hartmann Grisar and Franz Heege, *Luthers Kampfbilder*, 4 vols, Freiburg im Breisgau 1923.

Sabine Haag, Christiane Lange, Christof Metzger and Karl Schuetz, eds, *Dürer, Cranach, Holbein. Die Entdeckung des Menschen: Das deutsche Porträt um 1500*, Munich 2011.

Philip Haberkern, '"After Me There Will Come Braver Men": Jan Hus and Reformation Polemics in the 1530s', *German History*, 27/2, 2009, 177–95.

Mark Häberlein, *The Fuggers of Augsburg. Pursuing Wealth and Honor in Renaissance Germany*, Charlottesville 2012 (Stuttgart 2006).

Bernd Hamm, *Frömmigkeitstheologie am Anfang des 16. Jahrhunderts: Studien zu Johannes von Paltz und seinem Umkreis*, Tübingen 1982.

Peter Claus Hartmann, 'Albrecht von Brandenburg. Erzbischof und Kurfürst von Mainz, Erzbischof von Magdeburg und Administrator des Bistums Halberstadt', in Andreas Tacke, ed., *Der Kardinal Albrecht von Brandenburg. Renaissancefürst und Mäzen*, vol. 2, Regensburg 2006.

Hans-Peter Hasse, 'Bücherzensur an der Universität Wittenberg im 16. Jahrhundert', in Stefan Oehmig (ed.), *700 Jahre Wittenberg. Stadt, Universität, Reformation*, Weimar 1995.

Markus Hein and Armin Kohnle, eds, *Die Leipziger Disputation 1519*, Leipzig 2011.

Antje Heling, *Zu Haus bei Martin Luther*, Wittenberg 2003.

Scott Hendrix, 'Toleration of the Jews in the German Reformation: Urbanus Rhegius and Braunschweig 1535–1540', in Scott Hendrix, ed., *Tradition and Authority in the Reformation*, Aldershot 1996.

Scott Hendrix and Susan Karant-Nunn, eds, *Masculinity in the Reformation Era*, Kirksville, MO 2008.

Gunnar Heydenreich, *Lucas Cranach the Elder. Painting Materials, Techniques and Workshop Practice*, Amsterdam 2007.

Kat Hill, *Baptism, Brotherhood, and Belief in Reformation Germany. Anabaptism and Lutheranism, 1525–1585*, Oxford 2015.

Historische Commission für die Provinz Sachsen und das Herzogtum Anhalt, *Bau- und Kunst-Denkmäler der Provinz Sachsen*, vol. 18, *Der Mansfelder Gebirgskreis*, Halle 1893 (repr. Naumburg 2001).

Andreas Hornemann, 'Zeugnisse der spätmittelalterlichen Annenverehrung im Mansfelder Land', in Rosemarie Knape, ed., *Martin Luther und der Bergbau im Mansfelder Land*, Eisleben 2000.

Irmgard Höss, *Georg Spalatin, 1484–1545: Ein Leben in der Zeit des Humanismus und der Reformation*, Weimar 1956, 1989.

Ronnie Po-Chia Hsia, *The Myth of Ritual Murder. Jews and Magic in Reformation Germany*, New Haven and London 1988.

Ronnie Po-Chia Hsia, 'Münster and the Anabaptists', in Ronnie Po-Chia Hsia, ed., *The German People and the Reformation*, Ithaca and London 1988.

Erwin Iserloh, *Johannes Eck (1486–1543). Scholastiker, Humanist, Kontroverstheologe*, Münster 1981.

Erwin Iserloh, *Luther zwischen Reform und Reformation. Der Thesenanschlag fand nicht statt*, Münster 1966.

Erwin Iserloh, *Luthers Thesenanschlag: Tatsache oder Legende?*, Wiesbaden 1962.

Günter Jankowski, *Mansfeld Gebiet-Geschlecht-Geschichte. Zur Familiengeschichte der Grafen von Mansfeld*, Luxembourg 2005.

Günter Jankowski, ed., *Zur Geschichte des Mansfelder Kupferschieferbergbaus*, Clausthal-Zellerfeld 1995.

Horst Jesse, *Leben und Wirken des Philipp Melancthon. Dr. Martin Luthers theologischer Weggefährte*, Munich 2005.

Daniel Juette, 'Schwang Luther 1517 tatsächlich den Hammer? Die berühmtesten und folgenreichsten Thesen der neueren Weltgeschichte – handwerklich gesehen', *Frankfurter Allgemeine Zeitung*, 18 June 2014.

Helmar Junghans, *Die Reformation in Augenzeugenberichten*, Munich 1973 (Düsseldorf 1967).

Helmar Junghans, *Wittenberg als Lutherstadt*, Berlin 1979, 1982.

Helmar Junghans, 'Luthers Einfluss auf die Wittenberger Universitätsreform', in Irene Dingel and Günther Wartenberg, eds, *Die Theologische Fakultät Wittenberg 1502 bis 1602. Beiträge zur 500. Wiederkehr des Gründungsjahres der Leucorea*, Leipzig 2002.

Friedhelm Jürgensmeier, 'Kardinal Albrecht von Brandenburg (1490–1545). Kurfürst, Erzbischof von Mainz und Magdeburg, Administrator von Halberstadt', in Horst Reber, ed., *Albrecht von Brandenburg. Kurfürst – Erzkanzler – Kardinal. 1490–1545. Zum 500. Geburtstag eines deutschen Renaissencefürsten*, Mainz 1990.

Paul Kalkoff, *Ablass und Reliquienverehrung an der Schlosskirche zu Wittenberg unter Friedrich dem Weisen*, Gotha 1907.

Paul Kalkoff, *Briefe, Depeschen und Berichte über Luther vom Wormser Reichstage 1521*, Halle 1898.

Paul Kalkoff, *Die Depeschen des Nuntius Aleander vom Wormser Reichstage 1521*, Halle 1886, 1897.

Susan Karant-Nunn, *The Reformation of Feeling. Shaping the Religious Emotions in Early Modern Germany*, Oxford 2010.

Susan Karant-Nunn, *Luther's Pastors: The Reformation in the Ernestine Countryside*, Philadelphia 1979.

Susan Karant-Nunn, 'The Masculinity of Martin Luther', in Scott Hendrix and Susan Karant-Nunn, eds, *Masculinity in the Reformation Era*, Kirksville, MO 2008.

Ingrid Kasten, '"Was ist Luther? Ist doch die lere nitt meyn": Die Anfänge des Luther-Mythos im 16. Jahrhundert', in Vaclav Bok and Frank Shaw, eds, *Magister et amicus: Festschrift für Kurt Gärtner zum 65. Geburtstag*, Vienna 2003.

Thomas Kaufmann, *Luthers Juden*, Stuttgart 2014.

Thomas Kaufmann, *Luthers 'Judenschriften'*, Tübingen 2011.

Thomas Kaufmann, *'Türckenbüchlein'. Zur christlichen Wahrnehmung 'türkischer Religion' in Spätmittelalter und Reformation*, Göttingen 2008.

Thomas Kaufmann, 'Argumentative Impressionen: Bucers Bericht von der Heidelberger Disputation', in Thomas Kaufmann, ed., *Der Anfang der Reformation: Studien zur Kontextualität der Theologie, Publizistik und Inszenierung Luthers und der reformatorischen Bewegung*, Tübingen 2012.

Thomas Kaufmann, 'Theologisch-philosophische Rationalität: Die Ehre der Hure. Zum vernünftigen Gottesgedanken in der Reformation', in Thomas Kaufmann, ed., *Der Anfang der Reformation: Studien zur Kontextualität der Theologie, Publizistik und Inszenierung Luthers und der reformatorischen Bewegung*, Tübingen 2012.

Thomas Kaufmann, 'Zwei unerkannte Schriften Bucers und Capitos zur Abendmahlsfrage aus dem Herbst 1525', *Archiv für Reformationsgeschichte* 81, 1990, 158–88.

Gustav Kawerau, *Johann Agricola von Eisleben. Ein Beitrag zur Reformationsgeschichte*, Berlin 1881.

Rolf Kiessling, *Bürgerliche Gesellschaft und Kirche in Augsburg im Spätmittelalter. Ein Beitrag zur Strukturanalyse der oberdeutschen Reichsstadt*, Augsburg 1971.

Rosemarie Knape, ed., *Martin Luther und der Bergbau im Mansfelder Land*, Eisleben 2000.

Rosemarie Knape, ed., *Martin Luther und Eisleben*, Leipzig 2007.

Marion Kobelt-Groch, *Aufsässige Töchter Gottes. Frauen im Bauernkrieg und in den Täuferbewegungen*, Frankfurt am Main 1993.

Ernst Koch, '"Deutschlands Prophet, Seher und Vater". Johann Agricola und Martin Luther. Von den Enttäuschungen einer Freundschaft', in *Luther und seine Freunde*, Wittenberg 1998.

Joseph Leo Koerner, *The Moment of Self-Portraiture in German Renaissance Art*, Chicago and London 1993.

Walter Köhler, *Zürcher Ehegericht und Genfer Konsistorium*, 2 vols, Leipzig 1932, 1942.

Armin Kohnle, Christina Meckelnborg and Uwe Schirmer, eds, *Georg Spalatin. Steuermann der Reformation*, Halle 2014.

Armin Kohnle, 'Die Leipziger Disputation und ihre Bedeutung für die Reformation', in Markus Hein and Armin Kohnle, eds, *Die Leipziger Disputation 1519*, Leipzig 2011.

Robert Kolb, *Martin Luther as Prophet, Teacher, and Hero: Images of the Reformer, 1520–1620*, Grand Rapids, MI 1999.

Robert Kolb, *Martin Luther: Confessor of the Faith*, Oxford 2009.

Robert Kolb, *Nikolaus von Amsdorf (1483–1565). Popular Polemics in the Preservation of Luther's Legacy*, Nieuwkoop 1978.

Robert Kolb, 'Augsburg 1530: German Lutheran Interpretations of the Diet of Augsburg to 1577', *Sixteenth Century Journal*, 11, 1980, 47–61.

Theodor Kolde, *Analecta Lutherana*, Gotha 1883.

Ulrich Köpf, 'Martin Luthers Beitrag zur Universitätsreform', *Lutherjahrbuch* 80, 2013, 31–59.

Heinrich Kramm, *Studien über die Oberschichten der mitteldeutschen Städte im 16. Jahrhundert: Sachsen, Thüringen, Anhalt*, 2 vols, Cologne 1981.

Josef Kremer, *Beiträge zur Geschichte der klösterlichen Niederlassungen Eisenachs im Mittelalter*, Fulda 1905.

Natalie Krentz, *Ritualwandel und Deutungshoheit. Die frühe Reformation in der Residenzstadt Wittenberg (1500–1533)*, Tübingen 2014.

Karl Krumhaar, *Versuch einer Geschichte von Schloß und Stadt Mansfeld*, Mansfeld 1869.

Jens-Martin Kruse, *Universitätstheologie und Kirchenreform. Die Anfänge der Reformation in Wittenberg 1516–1522*, Mainz 2002.

Sachiko Kusukawa, *The Transformation of Natural Philosophy: The Case of Philip Melanchthon*, Cambridge 1995.

Stefan Laube, *Von der Reliquie zum Ding. Heiliger Ort – Wunderkammer – Museum*, Berlin 2011.

Stefan Laube, 'Das Lutherhaus – eine Museumsgeschichte', [http://www.stefanlaube.homepage.t-online.de/StudieTOTAL.pdf] (Accessed 1 Oct. 2015).

Stefan Laube, 'Klosett oder Klosterzelle?', *Frankfurter Allgemeiner Zeitung* 4 April 2015, Feuilleton.

Volker Leppin, *Martin Luther. Gestalten des Mittelalters und der Renaissance*, Darmstadt 2006.

Volker Leppin. 'Text, Kontext und Subtext. Eine Lektüre von Luthers Coburg-briefen', in Dietrich Korsch and Volker Leppin, eds, *Martin Luther – Biographie und Theologie*, Tübingen 2010.

Wolfgang Liebehenschel, 'CURRICULUM VITAE der Mutter Martin Luthers. Die Herkunft der Mutter Martin Luthers', in Rosemarie Knape, ed., *Martin Luther und der Bergbau im Mansfelder Land*, Eisleben 2000.

Carter Lindberg, *The European Reformations*, Oxford 1996.

Andreas Lindner, 'Martin Luther im Erfurter Augustinerkloster 1505–1511', in Lothar Schmelz and Michael Ludscheidt, eds, *Luthers Erfurter Kloster. Das Augustinerkloster im Spannungsfeld von monastischer Tradition und protestantischem Geist*, Erfurt 2005.

Kurt Löcher, 'Martin Luthers Eltern – Ein Bildnispaar Lucas Cranachs von 1527 auf der Wartburg', in Rosemarie Knape, ed., *Martin Luther und der Bergbau im Mansfelder Land*, Eisleben 2000.

Bernhard Lohse, *Martin Luther's Theology. Its Historical and Systematic Development*, tr. Roy A. Harrisville, Edinburgh 1999 (Göttingen 1995).

Ingetraut Ludolphy, *Friedrich der Weise. Kurfürst von Sachsen 1463–1525*, Göttingen 1984 (repr. Leipzig 2006).

Heinrich Lutz, *Conrad Peutinger*, Augsburg 1958.

Inge Mager, '"das war viel ein andrer Mann." Justas Jonas – Ein Leben mit und für Luther', in *Luthers Freunde*.

Richard Marius, *Martin Luther: The Christian between God and Death*, Cambridge, MA 1999, 2004.

Gerhard Markert, *Menschen um Luther. Eine Geschichte der Reformation in Lebensbildern*, Augsburg 2008.

Harald Meller, ed., *Fundsache Luther: Archäologen auf den Spuren des Reformators*, Stuttgart 2008.

Harald Meller, ed., *Luther in Mansfeld: Forschungen am Elternhaus des Reformators*, Halle 2007.

Walter Mück, *Der Mansfelder Kupferschieferbergbau in seiner rechtsgeschichtlichen Entwicklung*, 2 vols, Eisleben 1910.

Nikolaus Müller, *Die Wittenberger Bewegung 1521 und 1522. Die Vorgänge in und um Wittenberg während Luthers Wartburgaufenthalt. Briefe, Akten u. dgl. und Personalien*, Leipzig 1911.

Michael Mullett, *Luther*, London and New York 2004.

Lothar Mundt, *Lemnius und Luther. Studien und Texte zur Geschichte und Nachwirkung ihres Konflikts (1539–9)*, 2 vols, Bern, Frankfurt am Main and New York 1983.

Anne-Marie Neser, *Luthers Wohnhaus in Wittenberg. Denkmalpolitik im Spiegel der Quellen*, Leipzig 2005.

David Nirenberg, *Anti-Judaism. The History of a Way of Thinking*, London 2013.

Heiko A. Oberman, *Luther. Man between God and the Devil*, tr. Eileen Walliser-Schwarzbart, Yale 1989 (Berlin 1982).

Heiko A. Oberman, *Masters of the Reformation: The Emergence of a New Intellectual Climate in Europe*, tr. Dennis Martin, Cambridge 1981 (Tübingen 1977).

Heiko A. Oberman, *The Roots of Anti-Semitism in the Age of Renaissance and Reformation*, tr. James I. Porter, Philadelphia 1984 (Berlin 1981).

Heiko A. Oberman, '"Iustitia Christi" and "iustitia Dei". Luther and the Scholastic Doctrines of Justification', *Harvard Theological Review* 59/1, 1966, 1–26.

Stefan Oehmig, ed., *700 Jahre Wittenberg. Stadt, Universität, Reformation*, Weimar 1995.

Stefan Oehmig, 'Die Wittenberger Bewegung 1521/22 und ihre Folgen im Lichte alter und neuer Fragestellungen. Ein Beitrag zum Thema (Territorial-)Stadt und Reformation', in Stefan Oehmig, ed., *700 Jahre Wittenberg. Stadt, Universität, Reformation*, Weimar 1995.

Stefan Oehmig, 'Zur Getreide- und Brotversorgung der Stadt Erfurt in den Teuerungen des 15. und 16. Jahrhunderts', in Ulman Weiss, ed., *Erfurt 742–1992: Stadtgeschichte, Universitätsgeschichte*, Weimar 1992.

Rebecca Wagner Oettinger, *Music as Propaganda in the German Reformation*, Aldershot 2001.

Peter von der Osten-Sacken, *Martin Luther und die Juden. Neu untersucht anhand von Anton Margarithas "der gantz Jüdisch glaub" (1530/31)*, Stuttgart 2002.

Joachim Ott and Martin Treu, eds, *Luthers Thesenanschlag – Faktum oder Fiktion*, Leipzig 2008.

John S. Oyer, *Lutheran Reformers against the Anabaptists; Luther, Melanchthon and Menius, and the Anabaptists of Central Germany*, The Hague 1964.

Steven Ozment, *The Serpent and the Lamb. Cranach, Luther and the Making of the Reformation*, New Haven and London 2011.

John Roger Paas, *The German Political Broadsheet, 1600–1700*, 12 vols, Wiesbaden 1985–2014.

David Paisey and Giulia Bartrum, 'Hans Holbein and Miles Coverdale: A New Woodcut', *Print Quarterly* 26/3, 2009, 227–53.

Andrew Pettegree, *The Book in the Renaissance*, New Haven and London 2010.

Andrew Pettegree, *Brand Luther. 1517, Printing, and the Making of the Reformation*, London and New York 2015.

Josef Pilvousek and Klaus-Bernward Springer, 'Die Erfurter Augustiner-Eremiten: eine evangelische "Brüdergemeinde" vor und mit Luther (1266–1560)', in Lothar Schmelz and Michael Ludscheidt, eds, *Luthers Erfurter Kloster. Das Augustinerkloster im Spannungsfeld von monastischer Tradition und protestantischem Geist*, Erfurt 2005.

Marjorie Elizabeth Plummer, *From Priest's Whore to Pastor's Wife. Clerical Marriage and the Process of Reform in the Early German Reformation*, Farnham 2012.

Franz Posset, *The Front-Runner of the Catholic Reformation. The Life and Works of Johann von Staupitz*, Aldershot 2003.

George Richard Potter, *Zwingli*, Cambridge 1976.

Samuel Preus, *Carlstadt's Ordinaciones and Luther's Liberty: A Study of the Wittenberg Movement, 1521–22*, Cambridge, MA 1974.

Hans-Jürgen Prien, *Luthers Wirtschaftsethik*, Göttingen 1992.

Helmut Puff, *Sodomy in Reformation Germany and Switzerland 1400–1600*, Chicago 2003.

Alisha Rankin, *Panaceia's Daughters. Noblewomen as Healers in Early Modern Germany*, Chicago and London 2013.

Matthäus Ratzeberger, *Luther und seine Zeit*, Jena 1850.

Katharina Reinholdt, *Ein Leib in Christo werden. Ehe und Sexualität in Täufertum der frühen Neuzeit*, Göttingen 2012.

Heimo Reinitzer, *Gesetz und Evangelium. Über ein reformatorisches Bildthema, seine Tradition, Funktion und Wirkungsgeschichte*, 2 vols, Hamburg 2006.

Stefan Rhein, 'Philipp Melanchthon und Eobanus Hessus. Wittenberger Reformation und Erfurter "Poetenburg"', in Ulman Weiß, ed., *Erfurt. Geschichte und Gegenwart*, Weimar 1995.

Iris Ritschel, 'Friedrich der Weise und seine Gefährtin', in Andreas Tacke, '. . . wir wollen der Liebe Raum geben'. Konkubinate geistlicher und weltlicher Fürsten um 1500, Göttingen 2006.

William Walker Rockwell, *Die Doppelehe des Landgrafen Philipp von Hessen*, Marburg 1904.

Philipp Robinson Rössner, *Martin Luther. On Commerce and Usury (1524)*, ed., with intro. and trans., London 2015.

Lyndal Roper, *The Holy Household*, Oxford 1989.

Lyndal Roper, *Oedipus and the Devil. Witchcraft, Religion and Sexuality in Early Modern Europe*, London 1994.

Lyndal Roper, 'Luther Relics', in Jennifer Spinks and Dagmar Eichberger, eds., *Religion, the Supernatural and Visual Culture in Early Modern Europe*, Leiden 2015.

Lyndal Roper, 'Martin Luther's Body: the "Stout Doctor" and his Biographers', *American Historical Review* 115, no. 2, 2010, 351–84.

Lyndal Roper, 'The seven-Headed Monster: Luther and Psychology', in Sally Alexander and Barbara Taylor, eds, *History and Psyche. Culture, Psychoanalysis and the Past*, London 2012.

Lyndal Roper, '"To his most Learned and Dearest Friend": Reading Luther's Letters', *German History* 28, 2010, 283–95.

Alan Ross, *Daum's Boys: Schools and the Republic of Letters in Early Modern Germany*, Manchester 2015.

Friedrich Roth, 'Die geistliche Betrügerin Anna Laminit von Augsburg (*c.* 1480–1518)', *Zeitschrift für Kirchengeschichte* 43/2, 1924, 335–417.

Miri Rubin, *Gentile Tales. The Narrative Assault on Late Medieval Jews*, New Haven and London 1999.

Miri Rubin, *Mother of God: A History of the Virgin Mary*, London 2009.

Hans-Christoph Rublack, 'Gravamina und Reformation', in Ingrid Batori, ed., *Städtische Gesellschaft und Reformation*, Stuttgart 1980.

Ulinka Rublack, 'Grapho-Relics: Lutheranism and the Materialization of the Word', *Past and Present*, Supplement 5, 2010, 144–66.

Erika Rummel, *The Confessionalization of Humanism in Reformation Germany*, Oxford 2000.

Rebecca Sammel, 'The *Passio Lutheri*: Parody as Hagiography', *Journal of English and Germanic Philology* 95/2, 1996, 157–74.

Thomas Schauerte, *Dürer. Das ferne Genie. Eine Biographie*, Stuttgart 2012.

Otto Scheel, *Dokumente zu Luthers Entwicklung*, Tübingen 1929.

Otto Scheel, *Martin Luther. Vom Katholizismus zur Reformation*, 2 vols, Tübingen 1917.

Helmut Scherf, *Bau- und Kunstdenkmale in Stadt und Kreis Eisenach*, Eisenach 1981.

Heinz Schilling, *Martin Luther: Rebell in einer Zeit des Umbruchs*, Munich 2012.

Heinrich Schleiff and Michael Sussmann, 'Baugeschichte des Erfurter Augustinerklosters – aus der Vergangenheit in die Zukunft', in Lothar Schmelz and Michael Ludscheidt, eds, *Luthers Erfurter Kloster. Das*

*Augustinerkloster im Spannungsfeld von monastischer Tradition und protestantischem Geist*, Erfurt 2005.

Bjoern Schlenker, 'Archäologie am Elternhaus Martin Luthers', in Harald Meller, ed., *Luther in Mansfeld, Forschungen am Elternhaus des Reformators*, Halle 2007.

Bjoern Schmalz, *Georg Spalatin und seine Wirken in Altenburg (1525–1545)*, Beucha 2009.

Christoph Schubart, *Die Berichte über Luthers Tod und Begräbnis. Texte und Untersuchungen*, Weimar 1917.

Christiane Schulz, 'Spalatin als Pfarrer und Superintendent in Altenburg', in Armin Kohnle, Christina Meckelnborg and Uwe Schirmer, eds, *Georg Spalatin. Steuermann der Reformation*, Halle 2014.

Ernest Schwiebert, *Luther and His Times: The Reformation from a New Perspective*, Saint Louis 1950.

Tom Scott, *Thomas Müntzer. Theology and Revolution in the German Reformation*, Basingstoke 1989.

Tom Scott and Bob Scribner (eds and trs), *The German Peasants' War: A History in Documents*, Atlantic Highlands 1991.

Robert W. Scribner, *Popular Culture and Popular Movements in Reformation Germany*, London 1987.

Robert W. Scribner, 'Civic Unity and the Reformation in Erfurt', in Robert W. Scribner, ed., *Popular Culture and Popular Movements in Reformation Germany*, London 1987.

Robert W. Scribner, 'Die Eigentümlichkeit der Erfurter Reformation', in Ulman Weiss, ed., *Erfurt 742–1992: Stadtgeschichte, Universitätsgeschichte*, Weimar 1992.

Robert W. Scribner and Gerhard Benecke, eds, *The German Peasant War of 1525: New Viewpoints*, London 1979.

Johann Karl Seidemann, *Erläuterungen zur Reformationsgeschichte*, Dresden 1844.

Isaiah Shachar, *The Judensau. A Medieval Anti-Jewish Motif and its History*, London 1974.

Jonathan Sheehan, 'Sacred and Profane: Idolatry, Antiquarianism and the Polemics of Distinctions in the Seventeenth Century', *Past and Present* 192, 2006, 35–66.

Ronald J. Sider, *Andreas Bodenstein von Karlstadt. The Development of his Thought 1517–25*, Leiden 1974.

Ian Siggins, *Luther and His Mother*, Philadelphia 1981.

Ian Siggins, 'Luther's Mother Margarethe', *Harvard Theological Review* 71, 1978, 125–50.

Quentin Skinner, *The Foundations of Modern Political Thought*, 2 vols, Cambridge 1978.

Rainer Slotta and Siegfried Müller, 'Zum Bergbau auf Kupferschiefer im Mansfelder Land', in Rosemarie Knape, ed., *Martin Luther und der Bergbau im Mansfelder Land*, Eisleben 2000.

Jeannette C. Smith, 'Katharina von Bora through five centuries: a historiography', *Sixteenth Century Journal* 30/3, 1999, 745–74.

Philip M. Soergel, *Miracles and the Protestant Imagination: The Evangelical Wonder Book in Reformation Germany*, Oxford 2010.

Carl P. E. Springer, 'Luther's Latin Poetry and Scatology', *Lutheran Quarterly* 23/4, 2009, 373–87.

Govind P. Sreenivasan, *The Peasants of Ottobeuren, 1487–1726: A Rural Society in Early Modern Europe*, Cambridge 2004.

Andreas Stahl, 'Baugeschichtliche Erkenntnisse zu Luthers Elternhaus in Mansfeld', in Rosemarie Knape, ed., *Martin Luther und Eisleben*, Leipzig 2007.

Andreas Stahl, 'Die Grafschaft und die Stadt Mansfeld in der Lutherzeit', in Harald Melker (ed.), *Luther in Mansfeld. Forschungen am Elternhaus des Reformators*, Halle 2007.

Andreas Stahl, 'Historische Bauforschung an Luthers Elternhaus. Archivalische Voruntersuchungen und erste Baubeobachtungen', in Harald Meller, ed., *Luther in Mansfeld, Forschungen am Elternhaus des Reformators*, Halle 2007.

James Stayer, *Anabaptists and the Sword*, Lawrence 1972.

James Stayer, *The German Peasants' War and Anabaptist Community of Goods*, Montreal 1991.

David C. Steinmetz, *Luther and Staupitz: An Essay in the Intellectual Origins of the Protestant Reformation*, Durham, NC 1980.

Hans-Georg Stephan, 'Keramische Funde aus Luthers Elternhaus', in Harald Meller, ed., *Luther in Mansfeld, Forschungen am Elternhaus des Reformators*, Halle 2007.

Dieter Stievermann, 'Sozialer Aufstieg um 1500: Hüttenmeister Hans Luther und sein Sohn Dr Martin Luther', in Rosemarie Knape, ed., *Martin Luther und der Bergbau im Mansfelder Land*, Lutherstadt Eisleben 2000.

Kirsi Stjerna, *Women and the Reformation*, Oxford 2009.

Barbara Stollberg-Rilinger, *Des Kaisers alte Kleider. Verfassungsgeschichte und Symbolsprache des Alten Reiches*, Munich 2008.

Manfred Straube, 'Soziale Struktur und Besitzverhältnisse in Wittenberg zur Lutherzeit', *Jahrbuch für Geschichte des Feudalismus* 9, 1985, 145–88.

Karl Friedrich von Strenge and Ernst Devrient, eds, *Die Stadtrechte von Eisenach, Gotha und Waltershausen*, Gotha 1909.

Jane Strohl, 'Luther's new view on marriage, sexuality and the family', *Lutherjahrbuch* 76, 2009, 159–92.

W. D. J. Cargill Thompson, *Studies in the Reformation. Luther to Hooker*, ed. C. W. Dugmore, London 1980.

Gabriele von Trauchburg, *Häuser und Gärten Augsburger Patrizier*, Munich and Berlin 2001.

Martin Treu, '. . .von daher bin ich'. *Martin Luther und der Bergbau im Mansfelder Land, Rundgang durch die Ausstellung*, Eisleben 2000.

Martin Treu, 'Die Leucorea zwischen Tradition und Erneuerung – Erwägungen zur frühen Geschichte der Universität Wittenberg', in Heiner Lueck, ed., *Martin Luther und seine Universität*, Cologne 1998.

Martin Treu, *Katharina von Bora*, Wittenberg 1995.

Martin Treu, Rolf-Torsten Speler and Alfred Schellenberger, eds, *Leucorea. Bilder zur Geschichte der Universität*, Wittenberg 1999.

Martin Treu, 'Urkunde und Reflexion. Wiederentdeckung eines Belegs von Luthers Thesenanschlag', in Joachim Ott and Martin Treu (eds), *Luthers Thesenanschlag*, Leipzig 2008.

Patrice Veit, *Das Kirchenlied in der Reformation Martin Luthers: eine thematische und semantische Untersuchung*, Wiesbaden 1986.

Günter Vogler, 'Eisleben und Nürnberg zur Zeit Martin Luthers. Beziehungen zwischen zwei Wirtschaftspartnern', in Rosemarie Knape, ed., *Martin Luther und Eisleben*, Leipzig 2007.

Hans Volz, *Martin Luthers Thesenanschlag und dessen Vorgeschichte*, Weimar 1959.

Lee Palmer Wandel, *The Eucharist in the Reformation: Incarnation and Liturgy*, Cambridge and New York 2006.

Paul Wappler, *Thomas Müntzer in Zwickau und die 'Zwickauer Propheten'*, Gütersloh 1966.

Martin Warnke, *Cranachs Luther: Entwürfe für ein Image*, Frankfurt 1984.

Günther Wartenberg, 'Martin Luthers Beten für Freunde und gegen Feinde', *Lutherjahrbuch* 75, 2008, 113–24.

Günther Wartenberg, 'Die Mansfelder Grafen und der Bergbau', in Rosemarie Knape, ed., *Martin Luther und der Bergbau im Mansfelder Land*, Eisleben 2000.

Günther Wartenberg, 'Martin Luthers Kindheit, Jugend und erste Schulzeit in frühen biografischen Darstellungen des Reformators', in Rosemarie Knape, ed., *Martin Luther und Eisleben*, Leipzig 2007.

Christine Weide, *Georg Spalatins Briefwechsel. Studien zu Überlieferung und Bestand (1505–1525)*, Leipzig 2014.

Reinhold Weier, 'Die Rede des Mosellanus "Über die rechte Weise, theologisch zu disputieren"', *Trierer Theologische Zeitschrift* 83, 1974, 232–45.

Ulman Weiss, *Die frommen Bürger von Erfurt. Die Stadt und ihre Kirche im Spätmittelalter und in der Reformationszeit*, Weimar 1988.

Jennifer Welsh, *Anna Mater Matronarum: The Cult of St. Anne in Medieval and Early Modern Europe*, Farnham forthcoming 2016.

Ulrich Wenner, 'Fundgrubner, Berckhauer und Schlacktreiber: Montanwort-schatz bei Martin Luther', in Rosemarie Knape, ed., *Martin Luther und der Bergbau im Mansfelder Land*, Eisleben 2000.

Ekkehard Westermann, *Das Eislebener Garkupfer und seine Bedeutung für den europäischen Kupfermarkt 1460–1560*, Cologne and Vienna 1971.

Ekkehard Westermann, 'Der wirtschaftliche Konzentrationsprozess im Mans-felder Revier', in Rosemarie Knape, ed., *Martin Luther und der Bergbau im Mansfelder Land*, Eisleben 2000.

Ekkehard Westermann, 'Rechtliche und soziale Folgen wirtschaftlicher Konzentrationsprozesse im Mansfelder Revier in der ersten Hälfte des 16. Jahrhunderts', in Günter Jankowski, ed., *Zur Geschichte des Mansfelder Kupfer-schieferbergbaus*, Clausthal-Zellerfeld 1995.

Vitor Westhelle, 'Luther's Theologia Crucis', in Robert Kolb and Irene Dingel, eds, *The Oxford Handbook of Martin Luther's Theology*, Oxford 2014.

Jared Wicks, *Cajetan und die Anfänge der Reformation*, Münster 1983.

George Huntston Williams, *The Radical Reformation*, Kirksville, MO 1992 (London 1962).

Peter Willicks, 'Die Konflikte zwischen Erfurt und dem Erzbischof von Mainz am Ende des 15. Jahrhunderts', in Ulman Weiss, ed., *Erfurt 742–1992: Stadt-geschichte, Universitätsgeschichte*, Weimar 1992.

Gabriele Wimböck, 'Setting the Scene: Pictorial Representations of Religious Pluralization', in Andreas Höfele, Stephan Laqué, Enno Ruge, and Gabriela Schmidt, eds, *Representing Religious Pluralization in Early Modern Europe*, Berlin 2007.

Christian Winter, 'Die Protokolle der Leipziger Disputation', in Markus Hein and Armin Kohnle, eds, *Die Leipziger Disputation 1519*, Leipzig 2011.

Markus Wriedt, *Gnade und Erwählung: Eine Untersuchung zu Johann von Staupitz und Martin Luther*, Mainz 1991.

Charles Zika, *Reuchlin und die okkulte Tradition der Renaissance*, Sigmaringen 1998.

Charles Zika, 'Reuchlin's De Verbo Mirifico and the Magic Debate of the late fifteenth century', *Journal of the Warburg and Courtauld Institutes* 39, 1976, 104–38.

Wolfgang Zorn, *Augsburg. Geschichte einer deutschen Stadt*, Augsburg 1972.

Alejandro Zorzin, *Karlstadt als Flugschriftenautor*, Göttingen 1990.

Adolar Zumkeller, *Johannes von Staupitz und seine christliche Heilslehre*, Würz-burg 1994.

# Index

penguin.co.uk/vintage